OLD ENG
GRAMM

Graham A. Reid

LONDON, 28TH Feb., 1994

OLD ENGLISH GRAMMAR

BY

A. CAMPBELL

OXFORD

AT THE CLARENDON PRESS

Oxford University Press, Walton Street, Oxford OX2 6DP
Oxford New York Toronto
Delhi Bombay Calcutta Madras Karachi
Petaling Jaya Singapore Hong Kong Tokyo
Nairobi Dar es Salaam Cape Town
Melbourne Auckland
and associated companies in
Berlin Ibadan

Oxford is a trade mark of Oxford University Press

Published in the United States
by Oxford University Press, New York

First published 1959
Reprinted with corrections
1962, 1964, 1969, 1971, 1974, 1977
First published in paperback 1983
Reprinted 1987, 1991

British Library Cataloguing in Publication Data
Campbell, A.
Old English grammar
1. Anglo-Saxon language—Grammar
I. Title
429'.5 PE131
ISBN 0-19-811943-7

Printed in Hong Kong

PREFACE

THE present *Old English grammar* does not aim at superseding any existing book. It differs from the standard works in its arrangement of the phonology under the great sound-changes. Most other books have traces of a merely alphabetic arrangement, treating first *a*, and then *e*, &c., and finally reverting to the sound-changes, a method involving much repetition. Luick, however, attempted a chronological arrangement. This was difficult to achieve, especially in the sections on consonants and unaccented vowels, and led him to separate much related matter, for example, the different strata of the influence exerted upon vowels by palatal consonants are treated in widely separated places. It is hoped that the arrangement here adopted will facilitate the assimilation of the facts. The deviations from a chronological arrangement are explained in summaries at the end of the main divisions, where the uncertainty surrounding many of the familiar conclusions on the chronology of the sound-changes is emphasized.

This book differs also from most others in that a clearly limited field is taken. The main facts of early and late West-Saxon are given, and also those of the earliest Anglian remains, the great Anglian glosses, the early Kentish charters, and the late Kentish glosses. Other texts are quoted only for forms of great interest. Especially in the accidence, a more limited selection of forms is given than in Sievers–Brunner, and it is hoped that this will enable the student to acquire a groundwork of solid knowledge more easily. The Select Bibliography is intended not for mere reference, but as a list of works which every student should know and use. Accordingly, less important references are given, not in the Bibliography, but at the relevant places in the *Grammar*.

My chief obligation in writing this book has been to the standard works mentioned in the Bibliography, but I have also benefited greatly from the use of the following unpublished dissertations, to which the authors generously gave me access: *The origins of Old English orthography* by J. E. Blomfield (Mrs. G. Turville-Petre); *An edition of the Mercian portions of the Rushworth manuscript* by D. H. McAllister; *The interpretation of diphthongal spellings in Old English* by R. Quirk. I have also to thank Pamela Gradon for placing her unpublished revision of the Old English sections of the *Cambridge bibliography of English literature* at my disposal.

Of the scholars who have helped me I have particularly to thank K. Sisam, the original conceiver of the book, whose criticism of the first draft was invaluable. The first draft was also read by Bruce Dickins and Norman Davis. Advice on special problems was given by C. E. Bazell, T. Burrow, H. M. Flasdieck, A. S. C. Ross, M. L. Samuels, J. R. R. Tolkien, and C. L. Wrenn. I wish also to thank the Clarendon Press for undertaking to publish the book, and Kathleen Campbell and M. L. Samuels for efficient help with the proofs.

A. C.

September 1958

A NUMBER of corrections have been made in this reprint. Many of these were kindly suggested by friends who have used the book, especially Norman Davis, E. J. Dobson, Pamela Gradon, C. A. Ladd, Dorothy Whitelock, and C. L. Wrenn.

A. C.

June 1961

SOME further corrections have now been made, and I have to thank A. Bammesberger and C. E. Bazell for suggestions.

A. C.

July 1968

CONTENTS

ABBREVIATIONS

LANGUAGES AND DIALECTS

Angl.	Anglian	North.	Northumbrian
Gmc.	Germanic	nW-S	non-West-Saxon
Goth.	Gothic	OBrit.	Old British
I-E	Indo-European	OE	Old English
Kt.	Kentish	OFris.	Old Frisian
Lat.	Latin	OHG	Old High German
MD	Middle Dutch	OIr.	Old Irish
ME	Middle English	ON	Old Norse
Merc.	Mercian	OS	Old Saxon
NE	New (i.e. Modern) English	Vulg. Lat.	Vulgar Latin
NHG	New High German	W-S	West-Saxon

The following are often added before the names of languages and dialects:

e	Early
l	Late
Prim.	Primitive

BOOKS AND PERIODICALS

A	*Anglia*	PBB	*Beiträge zur Geschichte der deutschen Sprache und Literatur*
AB	*Beiblatt zur Anglia*	PMLA	*Publications of the Modern Language Association of America*
B–T	*An Anglo-Saxon dictionary*, J. Bosworth, T. N. Toller	S–B	*Altenglische Grammatik nach der angelsächsischen Grammatik von Eduard Sievers neubearbeitet von Karl Brunner*
ES	*Englische Studien*	ZfdA	*Zeitschrift für deutsches Altertum*
IF	*Indogermanische Forschungen*		
MLN	*Modern language notes*		
MLR	*Modern language review*		
OED	*Oxford English dictionary*		
OET	*Oldest English texts*, ed. H. Sweet		

SOURCES

And.	Andreas	BH	Bede's Historia Ecclesiastica (Latin text)
Az.	Azarias	Boeth.	Boethius (OE prose translation)
Bd. Gl.	Bede Glosses in MS. Cott. Tib. C. ii	CA	Inscription on Codex Aureus
BDS	Bede's Death-song	CH	Cædmon's Hymn
Beow.	Beowulf		
BG	Blickling Glosses		

CP	Gregory's Cura Pastoralis (OE translation)
Cp.	Corpus Glossary
Ct.	Charters selected in *OET*
Ep.	Epinal Glossary
Erf.	Erfurt Glossary
Ex.	Exodus
FC	Franks Casket
Gen.	Genesis
Gn.	Genealogies
Guth.	Guthlac
Jul.	Juliana
KG	Kentish Glosses to Proverbs
Ld.	Leiden Glossary
LG	Lorica Glosses
Li.	Lindisfarne Gospels (OE gloss)
LP	Lorica Prayer
LR	Leiden Riddle
LV	Liber Vitae Dunelmensis
Mal.	Battle of Maldon
Met.	Metres of Boethius (OE verse translation)
OEC	Old English Chronicle
Oros.	Orosius (OE translation)
PC	Parker Chronicle (*OEC*, MS. Corpus Christi College, Cambridge, 173)
Ps.	Psalms (OE metrical translation)
RC	Inscription on Ruthwell Cross
RG	Royal Glosses
Rid.	Riddles
Rit.	Rituale Ecclesiae Dunelmensis (OE gloss)
Ru.[1]	Rushworth Gospels (Mercian gloss to Matthew, and small portions of Mark and John)
Ru.[2]	Rushworth Gospels (North. gloss to most of Mark, Luke, John)
St. Chad	Life of St. Chad
VP	Vespasian Psalter (OE gloss)

N.B. *Ep.*, *Erf.*, *Cp.*, *Ld.* are quoted by gloss number in *OET*; *CP* and Oros. are quoted by page and line of Sweet's editions; *OEC* is quoted by annals.

GRAMMATICAL TERMS

a., acc.	accusative
adj.	adjective
adv.	adverb
compar.	comparative
d., dat.	dative
f., fem.	feminine
g., gen.	genitive
i., inst.	instrumental
imper.	imperative
indic., ind.	indicative
inf.	infinitive
infl.	inflected
m., masc.	masculine
n., neut.	neuter
n., nom.	nominative
opt.	optative
p., pl.	plural
part.	participle
pass.	passive
prep.	preposition
pres.	present
pret.-pres.	preterite-present
pron.	pronoun
s., sg.	singular
st.	strong
subj.	subjunctive
superl.	superlative
wk.	weak

NOTE ON SYMBOLS

THE sounds of OE are usually indicated by the symbols with which they are usually expressed in the OE spelling-system, but front and velar *c*, *g* are distinguished by a dot added when a front sound is denoted (*ċ*, *ġ*). A macron is added to long vowels and diphthongs; in falling diphthongs it is placed over the first element, in rising diphthongs over the second (*ēa*, *eā*). Phonetic symbols in square brackets are occasionally used.

In writing pre-literary forms and in discussing their sounds the following consonant symbols are used:

i̯, u̯ = y, w in NE *yet*, *wet*.
χ = ch in Scots *loch*.
ʒ = the voiced spirant corresponding to χ.
þ, ð = the voiceless (þ) and the voiced (ð) spirants in NE *thin*, *then*.
v = approximately the voiced spirant in NE *vine*, but perhaps bi-labial, not labio-dental.[1]
ŋ = the velar nasal in NE *sing*.

Pre-literary forms and forms of the literary period not recorded in manuscripts are marked *. > denotes 'changed to', < 'changed from'.

[1] This symbol is used in reconstructed forms instead of *ƀ*.

INTRODUCTION

§ 1. 'Old English' is the name applied in the present work to the vernacular Germanic language of Great Britain as it is recorded in manuscripts and inscriptions dating from before about 1100.[1] When it is necessary to quote forms more primitive than those recorded in these sources, but which may be inferred to have been spoken between the beginning of the settlement of Britain by Germanic peoples (*c.* 450) and the first records of their language (*c.* 700), these will be described as Primitive Old English (abbreviated Prim. OE), and will be marked with an asterisk (*).

§ 2. Old English is one of the Germanic branch of the Indo-European family of languages. The Germanic languages are conventionally grouped as follows:[2]

A. East Germanic. This group consists of West Gothic, known from fragments of a fourth-century version of the Bible, and a few other languages which are only very imperfectly known from names.

B. North Germanic. This is to be subdivided into East Norse (mainly Danish and Swedish), and West Norse (mainly Norwegian, Icelandic, and Faroese). North Germanic forms are usually quoted for philological comparison in the spelling system of Classical Old Icelandic (*c.* 1250).[3]

C. West Germanic. The languages of this group have certain similarities in their history, which enable us to describe each as

[1] This has been the customary term since about 1870. In 1871 Henry Sweet (ed. of OE *Cura Pastoralis*, p. v) deplored the use of the term 'Anglo-Saxon', for which he himself used 'Old English', and in 1876 (1st ed. of *Anglo-Saxon Reader*, p. xi) he wrote, 'The oldest stage of English . . . is now called "Old English", but the older name of "Anglo-Saxon" is still very generally used'. The contemporary vernacular term for OE is *Englisċ*, in Anglo-Latin of the period both *lingua Anglica* and *lingua Saxonica* occur (with obvious variants like *lingua Anglorum*). On the source of the term 'Anglo-Saxon' see *OED*, s.v., supplemented by K. Malone, *RES* v. 173–85.

[2] Of course any such grouping invites criticism, and the attempts to improve on this one are many, yet it is based on very fundamental peculiarities of the languages involved, and still holds the field. Various attempts to modify it are summarized by E. Schwarz, *Goten, Nordgermanen, Angelsachsen* (Bern and München, 1951), pp. 271 ff.

[3] This spelling as used in modern grammatical works gives a considerably regularized picture of the spelling of the manuscripts upon which it is based.

having an Old, a Middle, and a Modern period. The first of these periods ends about 1100, the second about 1500.[1] The West Germanic languages which are well recorded in the 'Old' stage are Old High German, Old Saxon, and Old English. Old High German and Old English develop into Middle High German and Middle English. Old Saxon is the language of two ninth-century poems, *Heliand* and *Genesis*, and of a few glosses and other brief texts from the North German area. Middle Dutch and Middle Low German, while they are very richly recorded in the 'Middle' period, are not exactly derived from any of the languages recorded in the 'Old' period. The language known as Old Frisian is recorded in manuscripts dating from about 1300 to 1500, and might be more properly described as Middle Frisian.[2]

§ 3. Within the West Germanic family there is a sharp distinction between Old High German and the remaining languages of the group.[3] Old Saxon, Old English, and Old Frisian agree in the following points against Old High German: (1) the Germanic consonant system is not disturbed by the group of changes known as the Old High German sound-shift; (2) the groups *mf*, *ns*, *nþ* are reduced by loss of the nasal consonant, and the preceding vowel is lengthened;[4] (3) one form is used for the three persons of the plural in all verbal tenses. On the other hand, Old English and Old Frisian are distinguished in the following points from Old Saxon as we know it from the above-mentioned Biblical poems: (1) West Germanic *ā̆* generally appear as fronted sounds; (2) before nasals, however, they appear as back sounds; (3) West

[1] This method of describing the stages of development of the West Gmc. languages was made familiar by Jacob Grimm in his *Deutsche Grammatik* (vol. i, 1819, *passim*). He bases his terms on the state of a language, not mechanically on date, and observes that the sources for *Altfriesisch* are of the same period as those for *Mittelhochdeutsch*, or even later (cf. next note). Yet he did not apply his usual terminology to English, but calls OE *Angelsächsisch*, and uses the terms *Altenglisch* and *Mittelenglisch* for respectively Early and Late ME (see especially the introduction to his section on OFris. i, 2nd ed., 1822, p. 269).

[2] Yet in the earliest Frisian MSS. the unaccented back vowels to some degree remain, and this is the chief criterion of the 'Old' stage of the West Gmc. languages. Frisian, in fact, does not quite keep step with the other languages of its group. Native Frisian scholars use the term 'Middle Frisian' of the stage of their language *c.* 1600–1800 between OFris. and the active modern Frisian literary movement, but German scholars usually distinguish only Old and New Frisian, making the line of division about 1550.

[3] E. Schwarz, op. cit., regards HG as originally a member of the Northern group, drawn into the West Gmc. orbit.

[4] Examples below, § 121.

Germanic *au* is OE *ēa*, OFris. *ā*, but Old Saxon *ō*; (4) *k* and *g* are fronted before front vowels.[1]

§ 4. It is now the opinion of many scholars that the language of the *Heliand* and the *Genesis* is a literary Old Saxon, approximated to Old High German, and that, in the 'Old' period of the West Germanic languages, all West Germanic except Old High German shared the characteristics named above as peculiar to Old English and Old Frisian. This view has emerged from the careful study of all the glosses, names, and other stray material which survive from the Low German area in the 'Old' period, as well as the *Heliand* and *Genesis*.[2] This West Germanic without Old High German is often called 'Ingvaeonic', because in Tacitus' threefold division of the Germans the Ingvaeones lie near the sea.[3]

§ 5. Writing about 730, Bede regarded the Germanic invaders of England as descended from three peoples—the Angles, Saxons, and Jutes.[4] There is no need to doubt the soundness of this tradition, which is confirmed by several of the Old English racial names. The localization of the continental areas whence these peoples came has excited much ingenuity.[5] It must, however, be remembered that they were drawn from the Ingvaeonic West Germans,[6] and that at an early date linguistic differentiation seems not to have been sharp among these, and would seem to have been practically limited to matters of vocabulary.[7] Accordingly, while there is no objection to the designation of the two main Old English dialect types as Anglian and West Saxon, the distinctions between them mostly developed in England, owing to the considerable isolation of the various parts of the country from one another in

[1] Points 1–3 are discussed and exemplified in Chapter V A; point 4 in §§ 426 ff.

[2] The main literature on this point is referred to in my article, 'West Germanic problems in the light of modern dialects', *Trans. Philological Soc.*, 1947, pp. 1–14. An important work since published is E. Rooth, *Saxonica* (Lund, 1949).

[3] *Germania* ii: *Manno tres filios assignant, e quorum nominibus proximi Oceano Ingaevones*. . . . But many of Tacitus' *Ingaevones* were not Ingvaeonic in the sense in which philologists now use the term (see Schwarz, op. cit., pp. 244 and 272). H. Kuhn, *ZfdA* lxxxvi. 23 ff., emphasizes the comparatively late origin of the Ingvaeonic linguistic unity.

[4] *Hist. Ecc.* i. 15.

[5] Clear and sufficient on this subject is Stenton, *Anglo-Saxon England*, chap. i.

[6] Procopius (*Bell. Goth.* iv. 19) states that in Britain there were Angles, Frisians, and Britons. These Frisians would, of course, also be of Ingvaeonic stock, and hence but little different from Angles and Saxons.

[7] The special problems of vocabulary lie rather outside the scope of a grammar. A considerable distinction between Angl. and W-S has been drawn by R. Jordan, *Die Eigentümlichkeiten des anglischen Wortschatzes* (Heidelberg, 1906) (*Anglistische Forschungen* 17). Some minor works are mentioned in the Bibliography.

early times. Similarly, the differentiation of Kentish from other dialects is due to the isolation of the area rather than to the descent of the inhabitants from the Jutes. In fact, the most obvious Kentish features can be observed gradually making their appearance in documents of the ninth century.

§ 6. In the extant Old English monuments four well-marked dialects are to be traced, *Northumbrian*, *Mercian*, *West-Saxon*, and *Kentish*.[1] Northumbrian and Mercian are associated as the *Anglian* dialects. The Northumbrian dialect is above all to be identified by means of the inscription in runes on the Ruthwell Cross, a bulky monument which belongs to a spot in the heart of Northumbrian territory (Ruthwell in Dumfriesshire). General linguistic agreement with this inscription enables us to regard as Northumbrian a number of short pieces of the same, or perhaps of a slightly earlier, period: the two earliest manuscripts of *Cædmon's Hymn*, the earliest manuscripts of *Bede's Death-song* and of the *Leiden Riddle*, and the runic inscriptions of the Franks Casket. The two earliest manuscripts of *Cædmon's Hymn* belong to the first half of the eighth century, and the somewhat later (ninth-century) foreign manuscripts of *Bede's Death-song* and the *Leiden Riddle* seem to preserve the linguistic features of manuscripts of the same period faithfully. The inscriptions of the Ruthwell Cross and the Franks Casket are slightly later than the other three texts in their linguistic forms.[2] A number of other Northumbrian runic in-

[1] It may be of interest to observe when each of these dialects was first distinguished. Hickes (*Thesaurus* i, 1705, pp. 87–88) already isolated North., for he distinguished the language of the Lindisfarne and Rushworth MSS. from that of the bulk of the OE texts he knew, and said that the former was used chiefly in the north during the 270 years preceding the Norman Conquest, and arose owing to the Danish invasions. The OE of the majority of texts was apparently first called W-S by R. Garnett in some unimportant work in the *Trans. Philological Soc.*, 1844, pp. 17–18. Some nineteenth-century scholars assumed that the *Parker Chronicle* differed linguistically from other manuscripts of the *OEC* because it was Merc., but no text now regarded as Merc. was recognized as such till J. A. H. Murray (*Athenaeum*, 3 Apr. 1875), who had previously seen the presence of two dialects in the *Rushworth Gospels*, decided that *Ru.*[1] was probably Merc. Sweet (*Gött. gelehrte Anzeigen*, 1882, p. 1186) followed by Sievers (first ed. of *Angelsächsische Grammatik*) suspected that *VP* was Merc. in 1882. Fr. Dietrich inferred, from the Canterbury origin of MS. Cott. Vesp. D vi, that the two OE poems which it contains were Kentish (*Marburger Vorlesungsverzeichnis*, Autumn 1854). By 1876 Sweet knew that *KG* in the same manuscript were Kentish, and that there were many charters in the same dialect (*Trans. Philological Soc.*, 1876, p. 555).

[2] The dating of these inscriptions (especially *RC*) has been much disputed: they can, however, be assigned to the eighth century without hazard.

scriptions add little to our knowledge of the dialect,[1] but general linguistic agreement with the five short texts just discussed enables us to regard as Northumbrian three extensive tenth-century texts, the glosses on the *Lindisfarne Gospels*, the *Rushworth Gospels*[2] and the *Durham Ritual*.[3]

§ 7. The names contained in the early manuscripts of Bede's *Historia Ecclesiastica* (several are of the eighth century), and in the *Liber Vitae Dunelmensis* (first half of the ninth century), are a further source for Northumbrian,[4] but in using names for linguistic purposes it should always be remembered that in them archaic and dialectal forms tend to be crystallized, so that they do not reflect the dialect of the writers of the texts in which they are preserved. For example, a number of southern names with *Eorcon-* as first element occur in Bede: they are sometimes given a Northumbrian form (*Ercon-*) in the manuscripts, but more usually the southern form is preserved, being spelt with either *ea* or *eo*, as these graphs are much confused in Northumbrian.[5] Similarly, in the *Liber Vitae* we find several names with the first elements *Beadu-* and *Heaðu-*: here we have accepted poetical forms of wide distribution in compounds, though dialectally proper only to a limited Mercian area.[6] But in the same text we also find these elements with *a* (the correct Northumbrian form), and with *eo* (again reflecting the Northumbrian graphic confusion of *ea* and *eo*).

§ 8. 'Mercian' is a term used by modern scholars to imply all the Anglian dialects excluding Northumbrian. The most obvious source for Mercian is the large collection of charters of Mercian kings, and a word must therefore now be said on the use of Old English charters for linguistic purposes. The word 'charter' (German *Urkunde*) is one used recklessly in Old English studies

[1] For a list of North. runic inscriptions see Bibliography, § F.

[2] Except the Merc. part, see below, § 11; the Merc. part is commonly referred to as *Ru.*[1], the North. as *Ru.*[2]

[3] The glosses on the *Lindisfarne Gospels* and the *Durham Ritual* were written by the same scribe at a time when the manuscripts were associated with the see situated till 995 at Chester-le-Street and afterwards at Durham.

[4] On the other hand, the text headed by Sweet, *Genealogies* (? *Northumbrian*), is a collection of lists of kings and bishops of diverse origin, and cannot be taken to represent any dialect (*OET*, pp. 167 ff.). The document was compiled *c.* 812, probably at Lichfield (Sisam, *Studies in the history of OE literature*, pp. 4–6; 'A-S Royal Genealogies', *Proc. Brit. Acad.*, xxxix. 289).

[5] See Ström, *Old English personal names in Bede's History*, pp. 105–6.

[6] See below, § 206.

to describe documents of the most varied nature: royal grants, private agreements, wills, records of proceedings of councils, &c. Many hundreds of such documents survive, but they are mostly preserved in 'cartularies', that is large manuscripts recording many documents of interest to a particular foundation. None of these cartularies is older than 1100, and therefore documents preserved only in them cannot be relied upon to preserve the practices of the period of their origin in orthography and inflexion, though they may provide evidence of value in matters of syntax and semantics. The student of phonology and inflexion must confine himself to charters preserved on single sheets which appear to be palaeographically of a date reasonably near to that of the transactions recorded in the documents. Even so, charters cease to be of great linguistic value after 900, for they tend, whatever their area of origin, to be written in the standard West-Saxon of the period,[1] and for that dialect records of other kinds are particularly rich. For the period before 900, Sweet in his *Oldest English Texts* selected fifty-nine charters as preserved in contemporary copies.[2] Sweet's work was soundly done, and few charters can be added with confidence to his selection, but nos. 1, 3, 4, and 24 are to be eliminated from it as later copies, and Birch 1334 may be added to it.

§ 9. Even the few documents left by this process of elimination are not of equal linguistic value. Many record grants of land in Kent by West-Saxon and Mercian kings, and it is not possible to be sure if the extant copies reflect the orthographical practices of the area of the grant, or those of the kingdom of the monarch concerned. The reports of the proceedings of Church councils are not of any linguistic value, for they are invariably in Latin except for names, and since ecclesiastics from all parts would be present, the lists of their names cannot be said to represent any dialect at all.

§ 10. When due regard is taken to all the methods of elimination just indicated, we are left in the period before 900 with the following Mercian charters: Sweet's nos. 9, 10, 11, 12, 13, 14, 47, 48. No. 48 and part of No. 47 are in English; the rest are in Latin and afford only English place- and personal names.

[1] See, for example, the Worcester charters collected by Sweet, *Second Anglo-Saxon Reader*, pp. 199–209, and the North. ones printed by Stevenson, *EHR* xxvii. 1 ff.

[2] He printed only the names from the Latin documents, the OE documents in full, *OET*, pp. 426–60. I am deeply indebted to Professor E. A. Lowe for advice and help in reviewing Sweet's work on the charters.

§ 11. The great phonological feature which connects Mercian and Northumbrian is the Anglian 'smoothing'. When a text exhibits this, but lacks the peculiar features of Northumbrian, we are justified in regarding it as Mercian. By this means we are able to add to the Mercian material the interlinear glosses on the *Vespasian Psalter* and the *Rushworth Gospels* (Matthew; Mark i. 1–ii. 15; John xviii. 1–3, referred to as *Ru.*^{1}), although they represent in many respects highly divergent dialects. The former belongs to the mid-ninth,[1] the latter to the tenth century. The Mercian nature of the *Vespasian Psalter* gloss emerges, furthermore, from its correspondence with the language of certain West Midland Middle English texts.[2]

§ 12. There are extant three manuscripts of a glossary containing material of very diverse origins. They are known as the *Corpus Glossary*, the *Épinal Glossary*, and the *Erfurt Glossary*. The English glosses in these are but a small part of the whole. Corpus is a more extensive copy than the others. The Erfurt MS. is the least linguistically reliable, as it is by a foreign scribe. The Corpus MS. usually has rather later forms than those of Épinal and Erfurt, but nevertheless it appears to be the oldest manuscript of the three. Professor Lowe dates it 'eighth to ninth century',[3] while the other two may be definitely placed in the ninth century.[4] These texts are to be regarded as mainly Mercian, but they are chiefly interesting for their archaic nature. The same may be said of the *Leiden Glossary*, preserved in a late eighth-century continental manuscript. Shorter texts, not rich in decisive dialect forms, but to be regarded as Mercian, are the glosses on the *Blickling Psalter* (eighth century), and the *Lorica Glosses* and the *Lorica Prayer* (ninth century).

§ 13. After 900 the use of West-Saxon as a standard language

[1] S. M. Kuhn (*Speculum* xviii. 458 ff.) dates it in the first third of the century on palaeographical grounds. But allowance must be made (1) for the charters, with which he compares the hand of the gloss, being somewhat later than the dates which they bear; (2) for the possibility that hands of this type persisted in Mercia into the second half of the century, for no contemporary copies of Merc. charters from that period are extant.

[2] The Corpus MS. of the *Ancrene Wisse*, and the lives of saints in MS. Bodley 34. The fullest treatment of the language of these texts is in the Appendix to *Þe liflade ant te passiun of Seinte Iuliene*, ed. by S. T. R. O. d'Ardenne (Liège, 1936); cf. J. R. R. Tolkien, *Essays and Studies* xiv. 104–26.

[3] *Codices Latini Antiquiores* ii. 3 (no. 122).

[4] Lowe, however, dates the *Épinal Glossary* in the first half of the eighth century, op. cit. vi. 18 (no. 760).

reduced the writing of Mercian, and only the brief *Royal Glosses* of about 1000 survive in the dialect. Some Mercian elements overlaid with West Saxon are to be observed in the *Life of St. Chad*, which is preserved in a twelfth-century copy of an Old English original.

§ 14. The Kentish dialect is known in the eighth century only from the names in Latin charters, Sweet's nos. 5, 6, 7, 8.[1] In the ninth century, however, it is used in a valuable series of vernacular charters, Sweet's nos. 34 and 37–42. To these we may add Kentish endorsements on Sweet's charters 28, 30, and 44. The *Codex Aureus* inscription and Sweet's charter 45 represent the practically identical dialect of Surrey in the same period.[2] The glosses on MS. Cott. Tib. C ii of Bede's *Historia Ecclesiastica* seem to contain Kentish elements[3] (*c.* 900), and four Latin charters, Sweet's nos. 35, 36, 43, and 44, contain Kentish names.

§ 15. After 900 the Kentish dialect is known in the Old English period only from the *Kentish Psalm*, the *Kentish Hymn*, and the glosses to *Proverbs* (*KG*), all preserved in MS. Cott. Vesp. D vi (late tenth century). The dialect of the two poems, while exhibiting many Kentish forms, is remarkably mixed.

§ 16. The West-Saxon dialect is very ill represented until the literary activity of Ælfred's later years. There survive only the names and boundaries of two charters (Sweet's nos. 3 and 20), some genealogies, and fragments of two early manuscripts of a martyrology. All these texts belong to the ninth century, for, as is noted above, the manuscript of charter 3 (dated 778) is not contemporary. In them, West-Saxon is fighting against the strong traditions of Mercian spelling (cf. § 17). Later the dialect is richly exemplified. The 'Early West-Saxon', which has come to be regarded as a grammatical norm, is based on the Parker MS. of the *Old English Chronicle* from the beginning to 924, the two oldest manuscripts of Ælfred's translation of Gregory's *Cura*

[1] While the manuscript of Sweet's charter 4 is not contemporary with the transaction (which belongs to 679), it is probably not later than 750, and preserves some important archaic spellings.

[2] Ekwall (*English studies* v. 61 ff.) regards these Surrey documents as in a Merc. literary dialect. His only weighty points are: (1) the frequence of ǣ for the *i*-mutation of *ā*, e.g. *clǣne, hǣðnum, nǣniġ, rǣrað*; (2) alleged cases of smoothing, e.g. *Berhtsiġe, ēc, -lēge*. But (1) proves only a good spelling tradition, such as is sometimes found in Kent also (§ 289), and the symbols *æ* and *e* are in any event equivalent in these texts (§ 291); concerning (2) cf. §§ 307, 314.

[3] See Campbell, *Medium Ævum* xxiv. 55.

Pastoralis, and the Lauderdale MS. of Ælfred's translation of Orosius. These manuscripts belong to the end of the ninth or the early tenth century. This 'Early West-Saxon' is in many respects contrasted with 'Late West-Saxon', which is above all exemplified in the works of Ælfric (*c.* 1000). Valuable for tracing the history of West-Saxon are the gloss on the *Junius Psalter* and the *Lǣċebōc* (both early tenth-century manuscripts, probably from Winchester), the Abingdon MSS. of the *Old English Chronicle* (late tenth and eleventh century), the West-Saxon Gospels (the early manuscripts are dated *c.* 1000), the Abingdon copy of Ælfred's Orosius (eleventh century), MS. A of the Benedictine Rule (*c.* 1000), the boundaries in the charters of West-Saxon kings, and the royal writs which are numerous in the last years of the OE kingdom.

§ 17. In a country where there had been so much vernacular literary activity as there had been in England, it is not surprising that at first texts in West-Saxon, which seems to have been late in its literary development, exhibit forms proper to the spelling systems of other dialects. Even in the manuscripts just mentioned as the main sources for Early West-Saxon, many spellings are found which reflect non-West-Saxon phonological forms rather than the forms which must have been the ancestors of those found in Late West-Saxon.[1] Even when West-Saxon had become a well-established literary dialect, and was used as something of a standard written language, many manuscripts display a considerable non-West-Saxon element in their orthography and inflexions. Such manuscripts are those of the Old English translations of Bede's *Historia Ecclesiastica*[2] (especially MS. T, late tenth century), of Gregory's *Dialogues* (all eleventh century), and of Boethius' *De Consolatione Philosophiae* (the only manuscript of any value is of the mid-tenth century); the *Blickling Homilies* (late tenth century); the D version of the *Old English Chronicle* (several hands, all after 1050).

§ 18. A lack of dialectal uniformity also characterizes the bulk of the extant Old English verse. This verse is mostly preserved in

[1] A useful survey of such forms is given by Vleeskruyer, *St. Chad*, p. 42, note 4.

[2] This work is particularly rich in Merc. forms. It is, however, controversial whether this or other W-S texts of Merc. colour (e.g. Gregory's *Dialogues*) ever existed in Merc. of a purity comparable to that of *VP*. See on this Harting, *Neophilologus* xxii. 287 ff., against S. Potter, *On the relation of the OE Bede to Werferth's Gregory and to Alfred's translations* (Prague, 1931).

copies dating from *c.* 1000, and while these are predominantly late West-Saxon, they are extremely rich in dialectal forms of various kinds. Although most of these non-West-Saxon forms can be classified as phonologically or morphologically proper to one dialect or another, it is seldom possible to declare with confidence that a given poem was originally in a particular dialect, or even that it was non-West-Saxon. For example, the two poems on the victories of Æthelstan and Eadmund in 937 and 942 can hardly be regarded as non-West-Saxon in origin, but all the extant copies are rich in non-West-Saxon forms. There seems to have been, in fact, a 'general OE poetic dialect',[1] mixed in vocabulary, phonology, and inflexion, and an originally dialectally pure poem, which achieved general popularity, would in transmission become approximated to this poetic dialect, while new poems would be written down from the beginning with considerable indifference to dialectal consistency.

§ 19. It will be apparent from the above sections that it is not possible to draw a dialect map of England in the Old English period. What our Anglian documents afford is rather a fair knowledge of the language in use at a number of centres of culture, represented by the glosses on the *Vespasian Psalter*, the *Lindisfarne Gospels*, the *Rushworth Gospels*, and the *Durham Ritual.* We should be justified in grouping *Li.*, *Ru.*², and *Rit.* together as Northumbrian, even if the history of the manuscripts was quite unknown, for they share certain features with each other and with the shorter Northumbrian texts, but this does not show us the territorial limits of the dialect, or of the distinctions which we can trace within it. Furthermore, the approximate whereabouts of only one of the points whence our major texts come is known (Durham area), for *Ru.*² is of undecided origin. Similarly, in the case of Mercian we have a bright light on the language of two unknown points, afforded by *VP* and *Ru.*¹, and just enough independent knowledge of Mercian phonology (mostly provided by charters) to place those two points in the Mercian area. We can suspect on similar grounds that there is a large Mercian element in the early glossaries. We cannot, however, set geographical limits to Mercian any more than to Northumbrian.

§ 20. Of West-Saxon we have considerable knowledge, but

[1] The phrase is K. Sisam's (*Studies in the history of OE literature*, p. 138), and his careful remarks on the poetical language are of the first importance.

again we have no means to define its limits or those of its internal inconsistencies. We can sometimes say that a given development is found at a known centre, but we cannot from this be sure of the extent of the area to which the change was proper, or even that the centre, at which the manuscript displaying the change was written, itself lay within that area. Furthermore, even evidence derived clearly from a known centre is often contradictory. For example, some Abingdon scribes have the tenth-century change *ē̆a* > *ē̆* before and after *c*, *g*, and before *h*, but others do not. In any event, no monastery would always recruit every scribe from the same area.

§ 21. The same conditions limit our knowledge of the Kentish dialect. The vernacular ninth-century charters show a steady tendency towards the development of a local *Schriftsprache*, with increasing avoidance of Anglian spellings, and care to express local sound-changes. This *Schriftsprache* we find used in the following century in the *Kentish Glosses* and two poems, but the geographical bounds of its various peculiarities (e.g. *ǣ̆* > *ē̆* ,*ȳ̆* > *ē̆*, *ēo* > *īo*) we cannot determine. When we find a similar dialect in two documents with a Surrey background, this is not evidence for the identity of the dialects of the soil of Kent and Surrey, but rather for the wide use of a south-eastern written *koinē*, which had gained prestige by use at Canterbury, for most of the documents in it make gifts or bequests to Christchurch, and Canterbury monks may well have had a hand in their shaping.

§ 22. Place-names recorded in documents of later periods are the main weapon with which attempts have been made to supplement our knowledge of the distribution of the Old English dialects. From these some light has been shed on the extent of certain dialectal peculiarities in Middle English times.[1] But while some of these peculiarities go back to Old English times, it is not possible to be sure that their geographical limits were the same then as later, or that these had not been seriously altered by linguistic expansions before we become able to trace them.

[1] Of special interest for OE studies are A. Brandl, *Zur Geographie der altenglischen Dialekte* (Berlin, 1915), and E. Ekwall, *Contributions to the history of OE dialects* (Lund, 1917). The former deals particularly with the areas of W-S *ǣ*, and of the different developments of mutated *ū̆* (*ȳ̆*, *ī̆*, *ē̆*), the latter with those of *ea* and *a* before *l*+consonant, and of *ie*, *e* and *æ* for the mutations of those sounds.

I

WRITING, ORTHOGRAPHY, AND PRONUNCIATION

§ 23. Old English is written by contemporary scribes in the Latin alphabet in insular script.[1] To this a number of additions were made for convenience in writing Old English: these will be discussed below.

§ 24. Old English manuscripts use few contractions compared with Latin ones of the same period. Very common are *⁊* = *and*, *ꝥ* = *þæt*,[2] *þoñ* = *þonne*, *hwoñ* = *hwonne*, *ƚ* (really = *uel*) = *oþþe*, and a stroke over a final vowel for *m*[3] (e.g. *cō* = *cōm*, -*ū* = -*um*). Less frequent are *ḡ*- = *ġe*-,[4] *ḡrd* = *ġeard*, *c̄* = *cwæþ*, *m̄* = *men*.[5] The group *er* can be represented by a stroke over any consonant (e.g. *æft̄* = *æfter*, *of̄* = *ofer*), *fo* by a stroke over *f* (e.g. *bef̄ran* = *beforan*).

§ 25. Occasionally a rune is used to represent the word which is its name, e.g. ᚹ = *wynn* joy; ᛟ = *ēþel* home; ᛗ = *mann* man; ᛞ = *dæġ* day. Still more rarely, a word is represented by the corresponding Latin word or its contraction, e.g. *Dn̄s* (= *Dominus*) = *Dryhten*, *prb̄* (= *presbyter*) = *prēost*, *dux* = *ealdormann*, *rex* = *cyning*.

§ 26. Vowel length is occasionally indicated, especially in early

[1] The insular script is a development of the insular half-uncial. A few charters containing English names are written in this half-uncial (*OET*, nos. 3, 5, 10), as is the fine register of names known as the *Liber Vitae*. The *Corpus Glossary* is in an early stage of transition from half-uncial to insular. There are also three charters containing English names in uncial script (*OET*, nos. 1, 4, 9). Late in the OE period the insular script is invaded by a few letter-forms from the continental script, which by then was used for writing Latin. The attribution of different phonetic values to the insular and continental forms of *g* belongs to the eME period.

[2] *⁊* and *ꝥ* are also used for the syllables *and*-, *þæt*- in compounds, e.g. *⁊lang*, *ꝥte* for *andlang*, *þætte*.

[3] In OE manuscripts this stroke very rarely stands for *n*: certain examples are limited to *ō*, *ī* = *on*, *in* (e.g. *Bd. Gl.* 89); other instances are perhaps errors, e.g. *PC*, f. 17ᵛ, l. 8, *worhtū*, past pl.

[4] Also freely used for -*ge* as a final syllable, e.g. *freoḡ* for *frēoġe*. A rare symbol for *ġe*- in the form of a Greek capital *Γ* occurs in Ct. 45.

[5] Also used for *men* as part of a word: *ḡnum̄* for *ġenumen*, Beow. 3165.

manuscripts (e.g. *Cp.*), by doubling the vowel. Some mistakes occur in the application of this device, e.g. Ep. *fraam* for *fram* bold. The acute accents, which are freely used in many manuscripts, stand most frequently on monosyllables (alone, or in compounds like *árliċe*, *Wendelsǽ*), and monosyllabic prefixes (e.g. *á-*, *úp-*, *ún-*). They are also frequent on inflected monosyllables, alone or in compounds (e.g. *módum*, *cynegóde*). The accents often stand on long vowels, but by no means always;[1] when they are over short vowels they often indicate stress, e.g. *wéġ*, *forwúrdon*, and many prefixes. The frequent use of accents on accented monosyllabic words and prefixes led to a tendency to put them on short words and prefixes even when these are unaccented. Hence we find them on the unstressed prefixes of verbs (e.g. *ágól*, El. 342; *ástah*, Ex. 468), conjunctions (e.g. *þá*, *hú*), and proclitic words, such as *ān*, *nān*, and even *sē* (e.g. *þá iġland*, Oros. ed. Bosworth, p. 26). Similarly, they may occur on pronouns where these have no special emphasis. Another use of the accent mark is as a diaeresis, e.g. Cp. *neoþoúard*, *edúaelle*, and so in foreign words, *Isáác*, *Faraónes*.[2]

§ 27. Marks indicating vowel shortness are found in some late manuscripts. On their various forms see K. Sisam, *Studies in the history of OE literature*, pp. 187–8.

§ 28. Most manuscripts are freely punctuated. The point and the comma are both used, and some manuscripts have both. Various more elaborate stops are used for the ends of paragraphs. In the late tenth and eleventh centuries a different system also appears in which the semi-colon (;) is the strongest stop, and the point the weakest, while the inverted semi-colon (⸵) is usually stronger than the point, but can be equal to it. A question mark (.~) is also used.[3] Old English verse is written out continuously, like prose, but the ends of the half-lines are indicated by some scribes by means of stops. Of the four major poetic codices, the

[1] In some manuscripts (e.g. *Beow.*) the accents are practically limited to long vowels, but this is not a general tendency.

[2] On accents see further L. Schmitt, *Die Akzente in altengl. HSS.* (Bonn, 1907) (extract from study of *Lǣċebōc*, see Bibliography, § M; unequal); W. Keller, *Über die Akzente in den ags. HSS.* (Prager deutsche Studien viii, 1907, pp. 97–120).

[3] This later punctuation is studied in detail by C. G. Harlow, *The punctuation of six of Ælfric's Catholic Homilies* (Oxford dissertation, 1955); more briefly by P. Clemoes, *Liturgical influence on punctuation in late Old English and early Middle English MSS.* (Cambridge, 1952).

Vercelli and Junius MSS. have these indications of the half-verse end.

§ 29. Word-division is inconsistent in Old English manuscripts, for the accentual group obscures the word, and proclitics (e.g. articles and prepositions) are frequently joined to the following word, or divided from it by a space less than that which normally divides words. On the other hand, compounds are frequently divided into their component parts (e.g. *ġe hwa*, *niþ wundor*, *Hroþ gar*).[1]

§ 30. The Old English vowel system was normally expressed with the following symbols, which all express both long and short sounds:

Back vowels:	a	o	u		
Front vowels:	æ	e	i	oe	y
Diphthongs:	ea	eo	io	ie	

§ 31. Before considering the phonetic value of these symbols, I wish to emphasize that our knowledge of the sounds of a dead language can never be more than approximate. The following reconstruction of the phonetic system of Old English is based on the probable value of the symbols when they are used to write Latin of the same period, and upon reasonable deductions from the history of the sounds both in Germanic and in the later periods of English.[2]

§ 32. *a* represented a back sound, which occurred chiefly before a back vowel of the following syllable, e.g. *dagas* days, *sacu* strife, *faran* go, *habban* have. It was also frequent before nasal consonants, and in this position *o* is a frequent alternative spelling, e.g. *mann*, *monn* man, *ġelamp*, *ġelomp* happened, *nama*, *noma* name (cf. § 130). It may be assumed that before nasals the *a* represents a lower or less advanced sound than elsewhere, which may even have been slightly rounded. The distinction between the vowels of *dagas* and *monn* would be approximately that between open advanced

[1] See further M. Rademacher, *Die Worttrennung in ags. HSS.* (Münster, 1921).

[2] For the meaning of the phonetic terms which I use, see Daniel Jones, *The Pronunciation of English*. I merely suggest the probable approximate positions of the OE vowels, and do not attempt to decide if they were tense or lax. It is fundamental to the history of English vowels that the long and short vowels were practically identical in quality till about 1200, and that afterwards they became distinguished by the short sounds becoming more open or more lax than the long sounds to which they had previously corresponded.

back and open full back. The long sound corresponding to the vowel of *dagas* is also represented by *a*, e.g. *stān* stone, *gāst* spirit.

§ 33. *o* (except when it is a variant of *a* before a nasal) represented a rounded back vowel, probably rather less open than that of NE *not*, more like that of NHG *Gott*, e.g. *god* god, *dohtor* daughter, *boden* offered. The corresponding long sound is also represented by *o*, e.g. *mōdor* mother, *gōs* goose, *mōna* moon. There was no long sound corresponding to the *a/o* of *monn*.

§ 34. *u* represented a rounded back close vowel, e.g. *full* full, *lufian* love, *guma* man. It also represented the corresponding long sound, e.g. *hūs* house, *cū* cow, *brūcan* use.

§ 35. *æ*, *e*, *i* represented front sounds, distinguished by their height, which would be approximately that of NE *bat*, *bet*, *bit*. They all represented both long and short sounds, e.g. *dæġ* day, *fæder* father; *dǣd* deed, *sǣd* seed, *hǣlan* heal; *etan* eat, *helpan* help, *here* army; *mēd* reward, *lēf* weak, *slēp* slept; *fisċ* fish, *þinġ* thing, *sittan* sit, *bindan* bind; *tīd* time, *fīf* five, *rīdan* ride.

§ 36. *oe*[1] and *y* represented front rounded vowels, both short and long. *ŏ̄ē* is unrounded early in the history of the language in some areas (see §§ 196–8), while *y̆̄* is unrounded in one district after another, beginning about 800 (see §§ 288, 317). It would be unwise to attempt a precise definition of these sounds, but since *y̆̄* is usually a fronting of *ŭ̄*, and *ŏ̄ē* of *ŏ̄*, and since the unrounding of *y̆̄* is usually *ĭ̄*, and that of *ŏ̄ē* is always *ĕ̄*, it is clear that *y̆̄* was close, and *ŏ̄ē* half-open. Examples of these sounds are *oele* oil, *oexen* oxen; *cwōēn* queen, *fōēdan* feed; *cyning* king, *þynċan* seem; *mӯs* mice, *ӯþ* wave.

§ 37. The symbols *ea*, *eo*, *io* represented partly the sounds developed from the West Gmc. diphthongs *au*, *eu*, *iu*. It is accordingly reasonable to assume that they represented diphthongs in these cases at least. Their use seems based on a successful attempt to analyse the diphthongs in question, and to express their components with the symbols used to express monophthongs. The West Gmc. diphthongs might be expected to develop to OE *æu*, *eu*, *iu*, and we find such spellings in early texts. Afterwards, the second element of all these diphthongs was lowered, and that of *æu* was also usually unrounded, so that the normal OE develop-

[1] In Ct. 45 (Surrey) and *CA* this symbol is reversed to *eo*, e.g. *ġefēōrum* d.p. companions.

ments are *æa* (usually written *ea*), *eo*, *io*,[1] e.g. *bēam* tree, *ċēas* chose, *þēof* thief, *ċēosan* choose, *dīore* dear, *līohtan* give light.[2]

§ 38. The symbols *ea*, *eo*, *io* were used in a great many words for sounds developed out of a monophthong. When this monophthong was long, the symbols no doubt had the same value as when they represented sounds developed out of diphthongs, e.g. *nēah* near, *ġēar* year, *nēolǣċan* (Angl.) approach, *līoht* light (in weight). But in many words the symbols *ea*, *eo*, *io* represented sounds which were derived from older short monophthongs, and which were themselves equivalent to short vowels in the metrical system. The value of the symbols in such words will be discussed below (see §§ 248–50). In this book they are written without diacritics, while diphthongs derived from old diphthongs or long monophthongs are marked long.[3] Examples of these so-called 'short diphthongs' are *ċeald* cold, *bearn* child, *ġeaf* gave, *eorþe* earth, *heofon* heaven, *siodo* custom.[4]

§ 39. The eW-S dialect had in many words the symbol *ie*. What has been said of the symbols discussed in § 38 applies to this one also. It is often derived ultimately from a West Gmc. diphthong or long vowel,[5] and in such cases can be regarded as representing a diphthong, analysed as *i*+*e* by the first W-S experimenters in writing the vernacular, e.g. *hīeran* hear, *līehtan* give light, **ċīese* cheese. It often, however, represented the W-S development of short vowels which in other dialects remain, or are otherwise

[1] But there is great dialectal variety. In North. the symbols *ea* and *eo* suffer an apparent confusion (see § 278), while *īo* should theoretically not appear in W-S, and when it does so, it early becomes *ēo* (see § 202). This also happens in Merc. (i.e. *VP* and *Ru.*[1]), but in North. *īo* is kept distinct from *ēo*, and in Kt. *ēo* and *īo* fall together in *īo* (see §§ 293–8).

[2] Diphthongs in -*u* were so completely foreign to the developed spelling-system of OE that *eo* was sometimes used in foreign names like *Deusdedit*, *Eudoxius* (OE Bede).

[3] There has been some disagreement whether the distinction in quantity of the OE diphthongs affected the first element only or the whole diphthong; and hence whether the macron on long diphthongs should be over the first element only or over both elements. See on this R. Quirk, *The interpretation of diphthongal spellings in OE* (unpublished, London dissertation, 1949). In the present work the macron is placed over the first element in normal diphthongs, which are thus distinguished from rising diphthongs (§ 44), in which the macron is over the second element.

[4] Here again there is great dialectal variation, not only for the reason indicated for the long diphthongs in the preceding note, but also owing to frequent failure of the 'diphthongizing' processes (see §§ 139 ff., 205 ff.).

[5] On W-S *īe* from contraction see § 47.

developed. In this book, *ie* is printed with no diacritic in such words, and its value will be discussed below (§ 248). Examples are *ġiest* guest, *ġiefan* give, *ieldra* older, *hierde* shepherd. *ie* was merely an archaic spelling in even the earliest extensive W-S manuscripts, for inverted spellings like *ðienga* for *ðinga*, g.p. things, show that the sound which it represented had become *i*.[1]

§ 40. The selection of the symbols *a, e, i, o, u* for the purposes indicated in §§ 32–35 offers no difficulty, apart from the hesitation between *a* and *o* in words of the type *monn*. This was no doubt due to the lack of a separate symbol for a sound which was lower, or more retracted, than the sound represented by *a* in *sacu*. It no doubt resembled the *o* of *god* acoustically. The symbols *æ*, *oe*, *y* require closer consideration. In the Latin spelling of the period, *ae*, *e*, and *oe* were equivalent graphs, and their use in different values neatly met a serious demand of Old English.[2] Early manuscripts write *ae* and *æ* indifferently, but later *æ* prevailed. There is in OE spelling no sign of a distinction, such as that made in OIr. spelling, between *ae* and *æ*.[3] The symbol *ę*, used especially in Sweet's *Oldest English Texts*, represents *æ* of the manuscripts, that is an *æ* with the loop, which represents the *a* in the insular form of that ligature, much attenuated. It is wiser to use *æ* for any ligature of *a*+*e*. The use of the symbol *y* in OE spelling to indicate a high front rounded sound will receive further consideration below (§ 42).

§ 41. The above sections have been devoted to the symbols normally and generally used for the vowel sounds of Old English. Symbols in less common use and special values sometimes given to the common symbols must now be considered.

§ 42. In early manuscripts many instances occur of the symbols *ei*, *oi*, *ui*: these are used instead of *e*, *oe*, *y* of normal OE, and practically all examples are given below, §§ 198–200. Most examples of *ei* in early texts are in words with *i*-umlaut of Prim. OE *ēa* (e.g. *nēid*-) or with theoretical *i*-umlaut of Prim. OE *ē* (e.g. *dēid*). Since *oi* and *ui* are always in positions where normally the mutations of *ō* and *ŭ* are found, it would seem that *i*-umlaut was at first a process of fronting of a vowel and epenthesis of *i* into the syllable containing it, so that *ē*, *ō*, *ŭ* became

[1] See § 300, and cf. Bülbring, *AB* ix. 96.

[2] Nevertheless, the Lat. equation of the symbols leaves its mark on some early texts in an occasional failure to distinguish the symbols *æ* and *e* correctly: see A. H. Smith, *Three Northumbrian poems*, p. 31, § 9. *c*. 2 and p. 34, § 16. *c*.

[3] See R. Thurneysen, *A grammar of Old Irish* (Dublin, 1946), § 24.

ē+i, ō+i, ŭ+i, and that these diphthongs were soon monophthongized to ē, ō̆, ŭ̆, written e, oe, y.[1] As has been pointed out above, the use of the symbol *oe* was an intelligent use of a symbol which had become useless in Latin. The substitution of the symbol *y* for *ui* probably antedates the monophthongization of the *i*-mutation of *u*, because, while there is some evidence in Latin grammatical tradition that *y* is the symbol for a diphthong *ui*,[2] there is practically none that it was ever regarded in the West as representing a rounded monophthong.

§ 43. A number of diphthongs with *-i* and *-u* as their second elements arise in OE at various times from the vocalization of final *ġ* and *w*, e.g. *wei*, *grēi*, *mēu*, *stōu*, for *weġ*, *grǣġ*, *mǣw*, *stōw*. Such forms are commonest in the early glossaries and in Kentish texts. For details see §§ 266, 272.

§ 44. In W-S and to a much lesser degree in other dialects, the graphs *ea*, *eo*, *io* are used not for the usual OE falling diphthongs, but for rising diphthongs, which were formed when palatal glides developed before back vowels, as in *ġeāra* once, *ġeoc* yoke, *ġeōmrian* be sad. A palatal glide + *u* is written *eo*, *io* or *iu* in W-S and Kt., but usually *iu* in North., e.g. *ġeong*, *ġiong*, *ġiung*, young. See details, §§ 172–5, 180–2. In Late Old English a good many ordinary diphthongs seem to have become rising by change of the position of the stress, see § 302.

§ 45. In some positions the palatal quality of *c*, *g*, and *sc* is indicated by the addition of *e*. This occurs mainly before unaccented *a*, so that a graph *ea* arises, e.g. *heriġeas*, *neriġean*, *sēċean*, *adwǣsċean*, *þenċean*, *seċġean* = *heriġas* armies, *neriġan* save, *sēċan* seek, *adwǣsċan* quench, *þenċan* think, *seċġan* say. This use of *e* as a diacritic also occurs frequently before *o*, but only rarely before *u*, e.g. *meniġeo* multitude, *strenġeo* strength, *berġeum* d.p. berries.[3] Before *u*, however, *i* is frequently inserted as a similar diacritic, and occasionally this *i* occurs before *o*,[4] e.g. *drenċium* drinks (d.p.), *ēċium* eternal (d.p.), *ġefylċio* troops.[5] An oddity is *ġebiġġiean*, Oros. 222, 29.

[1] A similar treatment of *æ* is not to be traced, for *seic* = *seċġ* sedge (*Ld.* 151) is hardly more than a slip. When *ēi* was monophthongized, the spelling persisted, and could be extended to words without *i*-umlaut, e.g. *ēil* = *ǣl* eel (*Cp.* 1331), *ġebrēicon* they enjoyed (with vowel of North. sg. *brēc*; Li., J. 6, 31).

[2] The best treatment of this subject is that of J. E. Blomfield (Mrs. G. Turville-Petre) in her unpublished thesis on *The origins of OE orthography*. The chief points are: (1) The grammarian Velius Longus (second century A.D., see *Grammatici Latini* vii. 54 and 75) considers the sound of Greek *υ* to be audible in words beginning with *ui* like *uirum*. (2) This grammatical tradition is reiterated in German, Icelandic, and French sources from the tenth century onwards. (3) It would account for the English name of the letter, which is first found in the *Orrmulum*, where *y* is transcribed as *wi* (col. 109, l. 4320).

[3] Eleventh-century glossary in MS. Cott. Cleop. A iii (Wright–Wülcker's *Vocabularies* 505, 5).

[4] I have not observed it before *a*.

[5] In this use of *e* and *i* as diacritics to indicate a palatal consonant before an unaccented vowel, we probably have the influence of Irish orthography. Irish

§ 46. It has been emphasized above that *ea* is normally a diphthong of which the first element is not *e*, but *æ*. A diphthong consisting of *e*+*a*, however, occurs in the phonological systems of Northumbrian and of the dialect of *VP*, e.g. North. *sēa*, VP *ġesēan*, for *sēon* see. These dialects also have a diphthong *i*+*a*, written *ia*, e.g. (*ġe*)*fīað* he hates. See § 238 for details. Kt. developed diphthongs *e*+*a*, *i*+*a*, and the corresponding short diphthongs by extensive unrounding of the second elements of *ĕo*, *ĭo* (§ 280).

§ 47. The W-S diphthong *ĭe* has been discussed above (§ 39). When accented *i* was followed by unaccented *e*, contraction produced a diphthong in W-S, which fell together with *īe* of other origin, but in nW-S dialects no contraction took place, and the graph *ie* stands for two syllables, e.g. *sīe*, pres. subj. of *bēon* be (see *BDS* 2[b], where the metre requires two syllables). See further § 237. 3. In all dialects, *ua* represents two syllables, e.g. *būan* dwell.

§ 48. Old English scribes are very consistent in their representation of accented vowel sounds,[1] but every accented syllable did not have the same vowel sound in every dialect, or even at every time within one dialect. Hence there is great diversity of spelling in Old English, arising not from inconsistency in the values of the symbols, but from diversity of sound.[2]

§ 49. The vowels of OE unaccented syllables are expressed with the same symbols which are used in accented syllables. Naturally the values of these symbols would here be only approximately the same as in accented syllables. In very early texts the common unaccented vowels are expressed with the symbols *æ*, *i*, *a*, *u*. *e* normally occurs only before *r* (e.g. *fæder*). But very soon *æ*, *e*, *i*, fall together in one sound, which was written *e*. Also *o* is written for unaccented *u* with increasing frequency, especially before a consonant (e.g. past pl. in *-on*, older *-un*), but also in final position (e.g. neut. pl. of nouns in *-o*, *-u*). In lOE unaccented *-a*, *-u*, *-o*, all fell together in one sound, and the three symbols are interchangeable in some manuscripts. This is very common in

scribes also prefer *e* before *a* and *o*, and *i* before *u*: see Thurneysen, op. cit., § 97. In very early texts similar diacritics are found before front vowels: *birċiae* = *birċe* birch (*Ep.* 792), *hrinġiae* = *hrinġe* ring (d.s., id. 410).

[1] In fact the only major hesitancy in the spelling of vowel sounds by OE scribes is that between *a* and *o* before nasals (see § 40). A curious fluctuation is that of W-S scribes between *iu*, *io*, *eo*, for *u* preceded by a palatal glide (see § 44).

[2] The use of the symbols has been mainly exemplified with eW-S forms in the present chapter. Some of the examples of *oe* in § 36, and of *io* in §§ 37–38, are found in Angl. texts only.

the plural of past tenses, where *-an* is as frequent as *-on* in lOE, but is also found in absolute finality, so that, for example, we find *-a*, *-o*, or *-u* in neuter plurals.

§ 50. The Old English consonant system was normally expressed by the following symbols:

	Labials	*Dentals*	*Palatals*	*Velars*	*Glottal*	*Sibilants*
Voiceless spirants	f, hw[1]	þ(= ð)	h	h	h	s
Voiced spirants	f, w[1]	þ(= ð)	g	g		s
Voiceless stops	p	t	c	c		
Voiced stops	b	d	g	g		
Voiced nasals	m	n	(n)	n		
Voiceless nasals		hn				
Voiced liquids		l, r				
Voiceless liquids		hl, hr				

(1) The ambiguity whereby *f*, *þ*, and *s* represent voiced and voiceless spirants is not serious, because the sound indicated is usually evident from the position in the word. Initially and finally voiceless spirants are represented, e.g. *fōt* foot, *þanc* thought, *seax* knife, *stān* stone, *sweord* sword, *ġeaf* gave, *bæþ* bath, *hūs* house. Internally between voiced sounds voiced spirants are represented, e.g. *drīfan* drive, *wulfas* wolves, *hræfn* raven, *snīþan* cut, *weorþan* become, *cȳþde* made known, *fæþm* embrace, *ċēosan* choose, *rǣsde* rushed, *bōsm* bosom. Internally before and after voiceless sounds voiceless spirants are represented, e.g. *sċeaft* shaft, *cyste* kissed, *miltsian* pity.[2]

(2) The use of *n* for a dental and a velar nasal causes no ambiguity, for the velar occurs only in the groups *ng*, *nc*, e.g. *singan* sing, *þanc* thought. On the temporary development of a palatal nasal see § 62.

(3) The use of *h* for a velar spirant and for a glottal spirant or breathing is not ambiguous, because it always represents a breathing initially, e.g. *hūs* house; but finally and internally it is a velar

[1] Following the usual practice, *w* is in this book used to represent ƿ of OE manuscripts and inscriptions.

[2] To these general rules there are two exceptions: (*a*) *s* and *þ* are voiceless between voiced sounds in a few suffixes, e.g. infl. *treowþe*, *miltse*; see § 445; (*b*) *s* between vowels is voiceless when it is a simplification of *ss*, e.g. infl. *hæġtese*; see § 457. Final *f* sometimes represents an old voiced spirant, and it is then not evident if unvoicing has yet taken place, e.g. *ġeaf* gave, *glōf* glove, *ġif* if; see § 446. This uncertainty does not arise with *s* and *þ*, which always represent voiceless sounds finally, as the voiced equivalents became *r* and *d* in West Gmc. (§§ 404, 409).

spirant, e.g. *seah* saw, *siehþ* sees, *brōhte* brought, and so when from final *g*, e.g. *bēah* ring (§ 446). On the palatalization of *h* in final groups *ht*, *hs* (*x*), *hþ*, see §§ 304–11; on palatal *h* after mutated vowels § 442; on *h* as a graph for *i̯* § 447.

(4) Some knowledge of the history of the language is required to distinguish whether *c* represented a palatal or a velar stop in any given word. Single *g* is a stop only in the group *ng* = [ŋg], and here again it is not immediately evident when it represents a palatal and when a velar. Examples and full discussion of the different values of *c* and *g* will be found in Chapter IX. B. The palatal stops *c* and *g* passed into [tʃ] and [dž] as in NE *church*, *judge* in the course of OE.[1] Initial velar *g* became a stop in lOE.[2]

(5) At first *sc* represented *s*+*c* or *ċ* according to the nature of the surrounding sounds. In the course of OE every initial *sc* and *sċ* became [ʃ] as in NE *ship*, but internally and finally this change affected only *sċ*, while *sc* remained or became *x*: see §§ 440–1.

(6) No difficulty arises in the case of *p*, *t*, *b*, *d*, *m*, *l*, *r*, *w* which can all occur initially, medially, and finally, e.g. *plega* play, *spere* spear, *wēpan* weep, *helpan* help, *rāp* rope; *tunge* tongue, *twelf* twelve, *metan* measure, *meltan* melt, *fōt* foot; *bēam* tree, *blind* blind, *climban* climb, *lamb* lamb; *dūn* hill, *bindan* bind, *land* land; *mōna* moon, *niman* take, *besma* besom, *ġelimpan* happen, *hām* home; *lǣdan* lead, *helpan* help, *eall* all; *rodor* sky, *grēne* green, *weorc* work, *wer* man; *wēpan* weep, *sweord* sword, *cnāwan* know, *snāw* snow.

(7) The voiceless sounds *hl*, *hr*, *hn*, *hw* occur initially only, e.g. *hlāf* loaf, *hrēosan* fall, *hnutu* nut, *hwēol* wheel.

§ 51. The following geminate consonants occur in OE: *ff*, *þþ*, *ss*, *hh*, *pp*, *bb*, *tt*, *dd*, *cc*, *cg* (= *gg*, § 64), *mm*, *nn*, *ll*, *rr*. Since OE had no voiced spirantal geminates the symbols *ff*, *þþ*, *ss* are unambiguous. The geminate stops *cc* and *cg* are ambiguously palatal or velar, e.g. *bucca* buck, *frocga* frog, but *streċċan* stretch, *eċġ* edge. The palatal geminates *ċċ* and *ċġ* passed in the course of OE into [tʃ] and [dž]: see §§ 433–4. Examples of the other geminates are

[1] But cf. § 486, footnote.

[2] In this book a dot is printed over palatal *ċ* and *ġ*, which entirely removes ambiguity in the case of *c* and *ċ*, and practically does so in that of *g* and *ġ*, because they are spirants except in the groups *cg*, *cġ*, *ng*, *nġ*, where they are stops. On attempts to distinguish *c* and *ċ* in the runic alphabet and some manuscripts see § 427, footnote.

pyffan puff, *sċeppan* injure, *cyssan* kiss, *hliehhan* laugh, *clyppan* embrace, *habban* have, *settan* set, *biddan* ask, *swimman* swim, *spinnan* spin, *tellan* tell, *afierran* remove. In final position geminates are frequently subject to graphic shortening, see § 66.

§ 52. One of the conditions under which palatal *c* and *g* developed was after a mutated vowel,[1] in which position they originally stood before *ĭ* or *i̯*, e.g. *bēċ* books, *streċċan* stretch, *drenċan* cause to drink, *fēġan* join, *leċġan* lay, *menġan* mix. It is disputed if other consonants and groups were palatalized in similar positions. It is reasonably assumed that χ would be palatalized under the same conditions as *ʒ* (§ 442). Owing to the absence of breaking before *ll* due to West Gmc. doubling of consonants (e.g. *tellan* tell, see § 139, footnote 3), a palatal pronunciation of the geminate may be assumed. There is reasonable evidence that *l* and *n*+consonant and single *n* had a palatal pronunciation after a mutated vowel, e.g. *ieldra* older, *cennan* beget, *ened* duck (cf. § 192). *m* both singly and followed by another consonant seems to have like *n* a capacity to cause raising of *æ* to *e*, and hence would seem to share its palatal nature, e.g. *cemban* comb, *gremman* irritate, *ġefremed* made. 'Palatalization' of these labial consonants would consist in the development of a palatal off-glide, *-mbi̯-*, &c.[2]

§ 53. The group [ks] is usually expressed by the symbol *x* (for examples, see § 416); rarer variants (*cs*, *cx*, *hx*, *xs*, *hs*) are exemplified by Cosijn, *Altwestsächs. Gramm.* i. 171, 180, 191. The symbol *z* is used in Biblical names (e.g. *Azarias*, *Baldazar*) with the value [ts], and hence it is sometimes used for *ts* in English words, e.g. *bezt*, *milze*, *draconze*, *bæzere* = *betst* best, *miltse* mercy (inflected), *dracontse* dragon-wort, **bæpsere* baptist. *Balzam* also occurs beside *balsam* (see § 478). In late manuscripts the French use of *c* = [ts] is found (e.g. *milce*, OEC, MS. E), and seems to appear already in *plæce* place (*Li.*, *Rit.*), *bæcere* baptist (*Rit.*). Rare graphs for [ts] are *dz* (e.g. *bædzere*, Ru.[1]) and *ds* (e.g. *palendse* palace, Oros.). Early texts have occasional initial *qu* for [kw], e.g. Cp. *quedol* talkative, Ct. 57 *Quōenðryðae*.

§ 54. The Old English consonant system described above was

[1] Or a theoretically mutated vowel, i.e. a vowel originally followed by *ĭ* or *i̯*, but incapable of mutation, e.g. *ǣ*, *ī* of *lǣċe* physician, *rīċe* kingdom.

[2] Or the distinction from the normal form of the consonant may be one of tone (J. R. R. Tolkien, private communication).

developed from an earlier one. The following are the consonant symbols in common use in the earliest texts:

Labials:	p	f	b	u	hu	m	
Dentals:	t	th	d	s		n	hn
Palatals:	c	ch	g, i			(n)	
Velars:	c	ch	g			n	
Glottal:		h					
Liquids:[1]	l	hl	r	hr			

§ 55. The model for this system was clearly the Latin one as preserved in grammatical tradition. The use of *th* and *ch* to represent voiceless spirants, respectively dental and velar (or palatal), appears, however, to have been suggested by OIr. spelling.[2] On the other hand, the ambiguity of the OIr. system, whereby *p, t, c* can represent both voiced and voiceless stops, was avoided, although *b, d, g* represented both voiced stops and spirants. This was not a great disadvantage, because Old English had initially neither voiced labial or dental spirants, nor velar or palatal stops. Hence initially *b* and *d* always represented stops, but *g* always spirants. Internally and finally there were no single voiced labial, palatal, and velar stops. Again there were no double voiced spirants, or voiced spirants after nasals: hence *bb, dd, gg, mb, nd, ng* are unambiguous symbols.

§ 56. While the broad scheme of the original Old English spelling of stops and spirants is outlined above, there are a good many inconsistencies in its application, and furthermore the system was much changed by later developments, so it will be necessary to consider the various symbols separately.

§ 57. The representation of voiceless spirants by *f, th, ch*[3] was disturbed in various ways:

(1) *f* was used in medial positions to indicate voiced spirants, and the

[1] I use a familiar but vague term, for the precise nature of OE *l* and *r* is unknown, and some argue that there were several varieties of each.

[2] In Latin, words with *th, ch* seem normally to have been pronounced with *t* and *c*; *ph*, however, was equated with *f*. Examples, § 538.

[3] The assumption that *th* at first represented a voiceless spirant is based on Irish usage, and the parallel with *ch*. No OE manuscript preserves this usage: some use *th* only initially, and have *d* medially for both the voiced and voiceless sound (e.g. English names in the Moore Bede), others extend *th* to the internal and final position for both the voiced and voiceless sounds (e.g. *Ep.*). The original value of *f* in OE spelling is uncertain, since it is not known whether the voicing of [f] between voiced sounds is later than the first spelling experiments. If it is so, then *f* originally represented a voiceless spirant, while *b* was used for the voiced one, and *Ep.* preserves this position well. Then when [f] > [v] between voiced sounds, *f* began to be used for both new and old [v]. But if the voicing of [f] between voiced sounds is very old, then [v] from Gmc. [f] must have still resembled [f] in articulation, rather than [v] from Gmc. [v], and the symbols

spelling system of *Ep.* indicates that at first *f* represented only the voiced labial spirant which arose in OE from Gmc. [f] between voiced sounds, while *b* stood for Gmc. [v] when this remained spirantal. *f* soon extended itself as the symbol for every labial spirant; *b* is less common as a symbol for a spirant in *Cp.* than in *Ep.* and *Erf.*, but it is still frequent in the early manuscripts of Bede.[1] For examples see § 444. After 800, *b* survives only as an archaism, chiefly in the Kt. charters of about 830–40, e.g. *hlābard, ġib, ob, hiabenliċe, aġiaban*, and occasionally in *LV*.[2]

(2) In early texts *pt* is often written for *ft*: this is frequent in *Ep.*, *Erf.*, and *Cp.* in compounds of *sċaept*, for *sċeaft* shaft; note also *ġidopta*, for *ġeþofta* companion, *Ep.* 189.

(3) When [χ] was lost between vowels (see § 461), the symbol *h* rapidly became the normal one for [χ]. While *ch* is used finally in the Moore Bede, it yields to *h* increasingly in the glossaries. In LV *ch* reappears extensively, both finally and as the final symbol of first elements (e.g. *Alchfrith*, *Ualchstod*). Before *t*, however, the normal symbol of a velar or palatal spirant was *c* in early OE, though *cht* is also found. Already in Irish spelling *ct* had tended to replace *cht*.[3] But here also *h* gradually replaces *c*: while *ct* is universal in the Moore Bede, it gives way rapidly to *ht* in the glossaries, though it returns in *LV*, where both *ct* and *cht* are more frequent than *ht*.[4] Later the survival of *ch* is very sporadic, e.g. *PC* 845 *Ealchstan*, Ru.[1] *ġesech* imper. see.

(4) A few instances of the use of the symbol *g* for [χ] are found in early texts, and occasionally compromise symbols like *gh, gch, hg* occur, e.g. *slāg* Cp. 289, *slāgh-* id. 1380, *misthāgch* id. 667, *-lēg* Ct. 5, for *slāh* sloe, *misþāh* (past of *misþēon*), *lēah* open country. Cf. also *fegtaþ, unnēg* in runes on *FC*.

(5) Early manuscripts (especially the Moore Bede) use *th* initially, and *d* medially and finally, for a dental spirant. The distinction seems to be one of position in the word, not of voiced and unvoiced sounds, for *d* often represents a voiceless spirant, as in the numerous names in the Moore Bede in *-frid, -thrȳd, -suīd, -hāed*, and in the first element of *Gūdfrid*. *th*, however, has already invaded the internal and final positions in *Ep.*[5] *th* is still often used in *LV*, where it is especially common finally.[6]

f and *b* must have expressed, not the contrast voiceless against voiced, but some difference in articulation, perhaps labio-dental against bi-labial.

[1] Substitution of *b* for *f* is rare, e.g. *cnēoribt* Cp. 21.

[2] For a few other survivals see S–B, § 192.*a*.4; note poetical *tiber* for *tifer*.

[3] See Thurneysen, *A grammar of Old Irish*, p. 21.

[4] Initial *ch* is hardly found: *Erf.* 364 has *achlocadum*, pass. part. d.p. from *ahlocian* pull out.

[5] Note also *mōdġithanc* CH, Leningrad MS., for *mōdġidanc*, Moore MS.

[6] Often in the Moore Bede, *th* is a graph for a spirant + *h*, e.g. *Fortheri*,

(6) In *Cp.* the symbol ꝺ̄ (i.e. *d* with a diacritic stroke) is very freely used for dental spirants, without regard to position or quality. But already in *Ep.* and *Cp.* a rival to ꝺ̄ appears in the rune *þ*. At first it appears to have been used mainly initially: *Ep.* has ten initial instances, and seven others, *Cp.* has forty-four initial instances and eight others. These two symbols, ꝺ̄ and *þ*, remain the usual ones for the dental spirants in OE: the distinction between them is purely a palaeographical question.[1]

(7) *t* rarely represents a spirant: instances are *earbet-* (Ep. 619, Cp. 1320), *hāet-* (Cp. 570), *flītat* (Cp. 680), *Sūtangli* (Ct. 9), *Cuutfert* (Ct. 11), for *earfoþ-*, *hǣþ-*, *flītaþ*, *Sūþ-*, *Cūþferþ*.[2]

§ 58. The disappearance of *b* and *d* as symbols for voiced spirants has been incidentally covered in § 57. *g* remained a symbol for both a velar and a palatal spirant, e.g. *gōd* good, *ġeoc* yoke (see § 427 for examples). In early texts *i* is also written for the palatal spirant, e.g. *hiniongae* BDS, *iēces-sūrae*[3] Cp. 380, *Iaruman* Moore Bede, *Aethiliaeardi* Ct. 6, *Æðelieard* Ct. 34; sporadic spellings of this type, especially *iū*, *iung*, *iugoþ* for *ġeō*, *ġeong*, *ġeogoþ* (cf. § 172), are always to be found, e.g. *ioc*, *iēmung* for *ġeoc* yoke, *ġīemung* marriage, Glosses in MS. Cott. Cleop. A iii (eleventh century).[4] In lOE the velar spirant became a stop initially, and so in words like *god* the *g* became a symbol for a stop (see § 430).[5] This may account for occasional use of *gh* and *hg* for medial and final spirantal *g* and *ġ* in lW-S, lNorth. and *Ru.*[1] (examples S–B, § 214.*a*.6). After [ŋ] the *g* of the graph *ng* was a symbol for a velar stop, or a palatal stop, according to the surrounding sounds (§§ 428, 429), and in later OE the palatal stop became [dž] as in NE *judge*; for examples, see § 433.

§ 59. Of the graphs *p*, *t*, *c*, only *c* offers any difficulty. It represented

Nōthelmus, *Hlōtheri* beside *Fordheri*, *Suīdhelm*. *LV* usually has *-ðh-* or *-thh-* in such words, but also *Cūthelm*, *Cūthere*, *Cūtheard*. Cf. also *Hlōtharius* Ct. 4, *Nōtheard* Ct. 33. On *Baldhild*, *Balthild* see § 414. Similarly, *-ch-* probably indicates at times *ch*+*h*, for there is much variation between these graphs in names like *Alhheard* and *Alhhere*.

[1] The first instances of the three new symbols *þ*, *ð*, and *p* (see § 60) in dated charters are: *þ* in a report of a Clofeshoas council dated 803 (Ct. 33); *ð* in a second and altered copy of a charter dating in its original form from 700 or 715 (Ct. 5); *p* in a charter of 692–3, but the copy is not less than fifty years later (Ct. 1).

[2] MS. Cott. Tib. C ii of Bede has a few instances of *t* for the final consonant of the name elements *Swīþ-*, *-swīþ*, *-þrȳþ*. Not here belongs 3rd sg. pres. ind. in *-t*, which is an alternative phonological form (see § 735.b).

[3] i.e. *ġēaces-sūre* cuckoo's sorrel.

[4] Note also *Liminiaee* Lyminge, Ct. 7. Not here belongs internal and final *i* for *ġ* (e.g. *streide*, *wei*), where a sound-change is involved (see § 266).

[5] An alternative view of the sound of initial *g* and *ġ* will be mentioned in § 398.3, footnote.

a velar or palatal stop according to circumstances (see §§ 426 ff.), and in later OE the palatal stop became [tʃ] as in NE *church*.

§ 60. In the early Northumbrian poems and the Moore Bede, *u* and *uu* are the symbols used for *u̯*, e.g. *uard*, *uueorthae*, *uyrmas*, *suē*, *Uīġhard*, *Ċaedualla*. *Ep.*, however, has the rune *ƿ* about ten times, and it is frequent in *Cp.* The older spelling, however, remains in all Northumbrian texts, and is universal in *LV* and *Rit.*[1] After consonants *u* prevails longer than initially and after vowels, and forms like *suā*, *huæt*, *cuōm*, *cuēn*, are frequent in *Li.*, *Ru.*[1], and eW-S manuscripts.[2] In late manuscripts *f* sometimes represents *u*, e.g. *glēof* for *glēow* glowed; and *u* often occurs for the labial voiced spirant, e.g. *yuel*, *selua*.[3]

§ 61. The use of *h* as a symbol for [χ] has been discussed above, § 50.3. Representing the breathing [h], it is found only initially in normal OE: its preservation in other positions is limited to a few archaic forms in the early glossaries (see § 461). It is also used as a diacritic to indicate a voiceless consonant in *hl*, *hr*, *hn*, *hw*: these four sounds are also found initially only. Sporadic forms with omission of the symbol *h* are found in texts of all periods, e.g. *aesil* Ep. 50, *lāfardsċipes* Rit. 182, 10 for *hæsel* hazel, *hlāford-* lord. Occasional incorrect addition of the symbol *h* also occurs, e.g. *haam* Ep. 177, *hāgen* Li., J. 19, 27, *ahebbad* PC 897, *herian* KG 730, for *ām* weaver's reed, *āgen* own, *aebbad* ebbed, *erian* plow.

§ 62. When in the combinations *nc* and *ng* the *g* and *c* were palatalized (see § 50.4), the velar nasal doubtless became a palatal, and subsequently, when *g* and *c* became [dž] and [tʃ], the nasal would become articulated as a dental.[4]

§ 63. Of the OE double consonants, the only ones requiring comment are *hh*, *þþ*, and *cg*. Before *h* and *þ* (*ð*) became established as the graphs for the velar and dental spirants, replacing *ch*, *th*, and *d*, various spellings are found for the clumsy doublets *chch* and *thth*. For *chch* we find in early texts *ch*, *hch*, and *chh*: for the names *Eahha*, *Eahhe*, the Moore Bede has *Acha* (dat.), *LV* frequently *Echha*, and Ct. 5 *Aehcha*. All these spellings survive to a limited degree beside the normal *hh* in Early West-Saxon, chiefly in forms of the verb *teohhian* and *hliehhan*,

[1] In *Rit.* the printed text often has *v* for *u* as both vowel and consonant.

[2] On minor (chiefly North.) variations, see S–B § 171.*a*.1; note especially *o* = *w*, e.g. Li. *ġeðoā* for *ġeðwā*, W-S *þwēan* wash; Rit. *soesternum* collective d.p. sisters.

[3] There are one or two such spellings in early manuscripts: Cott. Tib. C ii of *BH* has *Peanuahel* for *Peanfahel* of other manuscripts; *Ep.*, *Erf.* 428 *siuida* siftings, cp. *sifiðan*. There are scattered instances in the poetical manuscripts (see Klaeber's *Beowulf*[3], p. lxxxv).

[4] The occasional use of *nc*, *ng* for *cn*, *gn* may be noted, e.g. *tānc*, *ðeng*, *fræng* for *tācn*, *ðeġn*, *fræġn*. On the distribution of such spellings see Förster, *Flussname Themse*, p. 327; cf. below, § 400, footnote.

and the noun *þohha* (Cosijn, *Altwestsächsische Grammatik* i. 181). The full graph *thth* occurs in *aeththa* (i.e. *eþþa*, BDS) and a reduction of this to *tht* in *othte* (for *oþþe*, quoted S–B § 199 without reference).

§ 64. In the Moore Bede *cg* is already established as the symbol for the geminate of the palatal stop, which is frequent in the element *Ecġ-* in names.[1] The older symbol was, however, *gg* which is used in *Ep.* for both the palatal and velar geminate stops, e.g. *seġġ* sedge, 463, *sugga* a kind of bird, 422. *Cp.* introduces *cg* into most of these words, and *Erf.* is derived from a source which had both graphs. An occasional variant is *cgg*, e.g. *hyċġġanne* think, *BDS*. Rarer are *gcg*, e.g. *ġebyġċġean* buy, *CP* 327, 16, and *gc*, e.g. *Eġċberht* Ct. 29, *gārseġċ* ocean, Oros. 22, 28. Although *cg* became well established early as the geminate of *g*, the older graph *gg* always recurs sporadically. There is no ground for the traditional statement that *gg* became associated with the velar, *cg* with the palatal: *gg* is frequent for the palatal, while all the words quoted to prove the association of *gg* with the velar are also found spelled with *cg*; they are *docga* dog, *frocga* frog, *sucga* a kind of bird, *clucge* bell.[2]

§ 65. Illogical doubling of consonant symbols is a well-known feature of Northumbrian texts: e.g. *æþþilæ*, *ġistōddun*, *almeʒttiġ* RC; and many forms in *Li.* and *Ru.*[2] like *sċipp*, *ġebedd*, *eatta*, *brecca* = *sċip*, *ġebed*, *etan*, *brecan*.[3]

§ 66. Double consonant symbols are very frequently simplified at the ends of words or ėlements of compound words, e.g. *eal*, *mon*, *bed*, *ealgylden*, and forms of the contracted 3rd sg. pres. ind. like *hǣt*, *slīt*, *tosċēat*. This is only a graphic simplification,[4] and is therefore mentioned here: on phonological simplifications of geminates, see §§ 457 ff. The graph *cg* is not usually simplified, though instances of both *c* and *g* occur: a few instances of *Eġ-*, *Eċ-*, for *Ecġ-* are scattered through *BH*, *OEC*, and other texts (e.g. *Beow.* 957, 980). Graphic simplification of geminates in other positions is sporadic: it is most frequent in the case of *hh*, e.g. eW-S *hliehað* we laugh, and North. practically always *eher* ear of corn, *teher* tear.

§ 67. The special problems of runic epigraphy are not in place in a grammar, but a word must be said upon the possible influence of the runic upon the form of the Latin alphabet used for writing Old English. Clear and obvious influence is to be observed in the adoption of the runes *þ* and *ƿ* (see §§ 57.6 and 60), but beyond this it is hazardous to go,

[1] This geminate shows the only considerable trace in OE spelling of the Celtic use of *p*, *t*, *c*, for voiced stops.

[2] *Docga* is not recorded with *gg* at all, nor are *sċeacga* hair, *ēarwicga* earwig, where also the geminate is velar.

[3] Note also *Cyniberhtte*, Ct. 9 (Merc.). On the North. doubling cf. Luick, *Hist. Gramm.*, §§ 670–1.

[4] In *Li.* final double consonants are written with remarkable regularity.

because there are few OE runic inscriptions which can be shown to ante-date the first writing in the vernacular. The symbols *ae*, *oe*, and *y* represent, in the OE form of the Latin alphabet, front vowels which had become very frequent in OE, but in writing Latin *ae* and *oe* had become mere variants of *e*, and *y* was used in Greek words only. The OE form of the runic alphabet, similarly, has added three new symbols to represent the same sounds, and the question arises whether this development first took place in runes or in the Latin alphabet. It has been remarked above (§ 42), that *ui* is the earlier spelling for *y*, while the runic symbol is ᚤ, that is *i* added inside the symbol for *u*.[1] That *ui* and ᚤ are independent developments is unlikely, but it is difficult to assign priority to either the one or the other. The two alphabets express the sound which arose from the mutation of *o* in different ways. The Latin alphabet utilized a symbol *oe* which had become useless, the runic one used the old *o*- rune, ᛟ. This it was able to do, because [a] had become practically [o] before nasals (e.g. *monn, mōna*), and a variant of the old *a*-rune could therefore be used for [o]. The *a*-rune was now split into three, for Gmc. *a* gave in OE from an early date three sounds seen in *dæġ, dagas, monn*. Accordingly, from the *a*-rune ᚨ were developed three runes, ᚨ for *æ*, ᚪ for *a*, ᚩ for *o*. This system would seem to have been developed independently of the Latin alphabet. If the Latin alphabet had been the model, one would have expected the rune for *æ* to have been marked with a diacritic, and either *a* or *o* to have been given the basic symbol ᚨ. So perhaps the rune-smiths preceded the scribes in the search for ways to express the front vowels and provided them with a model.[2]

§ 68. The major innovation to be observed, when the normal OE spelling-system is compared with that of the earliest manuscripts, is the use of *f*, *þ* (*ð*) as symbols for both voiced and voiceless spirants, and *h* as a symbol for both [h] and [χ]. In the former case there is little ambiguity, in the latter none, owing to the phonetic structure of the language. The double use of *h* was probably suggested by the runic

[1] This is at least the probable origin of the symbol; yet it may be observed that in some Italic alphabets a similar symbol apparently developed directly from Gr. υ (see Conway, Whatmough, and Johnson, *Præ-Italic dialects* ii. 528).

[2] The Frisian (i.e. continental Ingvaeonic) inscriptions are too uncertain in date for their evidence to be used to decide the question of priority between scribe and rune-smith in the use of special symbols for *æ* and *œ*. Concerning these inscriptions see especially W. Krogmann, *Zur Frage der friesischen Runeninschriften* (Frisian Institute of Groningen University, 1953); P. C. J. A. Boeles, *De inheemse runen-inscripties uit Friesland en Groningen* (*Oudheidkundige mededelingen uit het Rijksmuseum van oudheden te Leiden* xxxv. 18–32). The standard texts are in H. Arntz and H. Zeiss, *Die einheimischen Runendenkmäler des Festlandes* (Leipzig, 1939).

alphabet, where ᚻ had continued in use initially, after the sound it represented changed from [χ] to [h], although it remained the symbol for [χ] in other positions. The use of *h* for [χ] would not be suggested by the spelling of either Latin or Irish.

§ 69. To judge from the Scandinavian runic inscriptions, in the earliest period the *b* and *d* runes represented the voiced spirants, and also the stops which had arisen from them initially and after nasals, while the *f* and *þ* runes represented voiceless sounds. When spirants became unvoiced finally, *f* and *þ* were extended to the new voiceless sounds: early examples are *gaf* gave, Eggjum, *bariutiþ* he breaks, Stentofta. When the voiceless spirants became voiced between vowels, *f* and *þ* remained the symbols used for them, and were extended to the old voiced spirants. Hence in the later runic inscriptions, any labial spirant may be written with the *f* rune, and any dental spirant with the *þ* rune.

§ 70. In a West Gmc. language, every *þ* represents an old voiceless sound, for every voiced dental spirant had become [d]. *þ* would therefore be the rune normally representing the dental spirant in all positions.[1] The opposition of initial *þ*, medial *d*, found in early manuscripts, is not likely to have originated in the runic alphabet, where *d* represented a stop. On the other hand, the change to a common symbol (ð) for the spirants may well have been helped by the runic system. This common symbol was soon frequently replaced by the rune *þ*. In the case of the labial spirants, the OE development seems to have been different from the Scandinavian in that, when [f] became voiced between vowels, it remained related in articulation to initial and final [f], rather than to old [v]. This may have prevented the spread of the *b* rune to the new [v], and hence have helped towards the final triumph of the *f* rune, which is complete in our earliest extant inscriptions. If this was the course of events, it no doubt helped the triumph of the symbol *f* in manuscripts, but the lack of inscriptions old enough to be regarded as certainly free from the influence of manuscript spelling makes it impossible to be sure that the steps of development were as is here suggested.

1 The use of the *d* symbol for *þ* in runes (e.g. *ġebidæd der* for *ġebiddaþ þer*, Falstone runes) is due to the influence of the Latin alphabet.

II

ACCENT

A. Word Accent

§ 71. The primitive Germanic language developed a stress accent which fell upon the first syllable of all words, and this is in essentials preserved in all the Germanic languages. Thus in Old English we find the stress on the first syllable in all simple words, and in most compound words: *wórd* word, *stā́nas* stones, *lúfiende* loving, *sī́þfæt* journey, *ándġiet* sense, *ándwyrde* answer, *únnytt* useless, *ónsǣġe* assailing.

§ 72. The main exception to this rule is due to the fact that in Germanic a syntactic combination of prepositional adverb[1] with verb was not yet a single word at the time when the main stress of words was fixed on the first syllable, and such combinations ultimately developed into compound words stressed on the second element. These remain in the West Germanic languages: OE *aþénċan* devise, *oþflḗon* flee, *wiþsácan* deny.

§ 73. A natural consequence of the different stress of compound nouns and verbs is that the prepositional adverbs have two forms in compound words, the accented form appearing in nouns and adjectives, the unaccented in verbs. The principal doublets are:

ǣ-:	*ǣ́wielm* fountain	a-:	*awéallan* well up
æf-:	*ǽfþunca* source of offence	of-:	*ofþýnċan* displease (impers.)
æt-:	*ǽtspyrning* offence	ot-:	*otspúrnan* stumble.[2]

[1] This term denotes words which can be readily used in both a prepositional and an adverbial function. As verbal prefixes, they have an adverbial function when combined with intransitive verbs; in combination with transitive verbs, they have a function approximating to that of prepositions, the object being under their government.

[2] A regular interchange of *æt-* and *ot-* is hardly to be traced in OE, for *æt-* has become the prevailing form, both accented and unaccented. *ot-* survives in a few forms in *VP* and *KG* (*otēawan* show, *VP* frequently, *otēċtun* they added, *otspurne* pres. subj., stumble, id., *otspernince* d.s., offence, *KG*), but it is mostly replaced by *æt-* (properly the accented form), or by *oþ-* (the unaccented form of *ūþ-*). Hence *oþ-* has both its original sense 'away', and that of *æt-*, 'towards'. This in turn has caused *æt-* to acquire the sense 'away'. Thus there are doublets like *ætfēolan*, *oþfēolan*, adhere, *ætberstan*, *oþberstan*, escape, while *ætberan*, *oþberan* can both mean 'bear away' or 'bear towards'.

and-:	*ándsaca* apostate	on-:	*onsácan* deny[1]
bī-:	*bī́ġenġa* inhabitant	be-:	*begā́n* occupy
or-:	*órþanc* mind	a-:	*aþénċan* devise[2]
ūþ-:	*ū́þgenġe* evanescent	oþ-:	*oþgā́n* escape
wiþer-:	*wíþersaca* adversary	wiþ-:	*wiþsácan* refuse.[3]

The accented and unaccented forms of *for-*, *ofer-*, *to-*, *þurh-*, *under-*, *ymb-*, are identical:[4] *fórwyrd* ruin, *forwrécan* banish, *ófermāþum* rich treasure, *ofergā́n* traverse, *tóhyht* hope, *tohwéorfan* disperse, *þúrhbeorht* very bright, *þurhfṓn* penetrate, *úndercyning* dependent king, *underġietan* understand, *ýmbryne* course, *ymbhwéorfan* go round. Although it is often not shown by the spelling, the prefix *inn-* is distinguished from its unaccented form by the double consonant: *ínnorf* furniture, *inǣ́lan* kindle.

§ 74. The prefix *ġe-* is always unaccented in OE,[5] e.g. *ġeféoht* fight. Unaccented *for-* and *be-* (for *bī-*) have penetrated extensively into nouns, e.g. *forbód* prohibition, *bebód* command; but there are a few words which preserve the regular accent:[6] *fórwyrd* ruin (beside *forwýrd*), *bī́leofa* food, *bī́spell* proverb, *béhat*, *bḗot* vow. The prefix *ġeond-* seems to occur only in verbs, and hence is always unaccented, e.g. *ġeondhwéorfan* traverse.

§ 75. The negative prefix *un-* was not originally used with finite verbs (though freely added to participles: *unlifiġende* dead, *un-*

[1] Historically *on-*, *an-* represents both a stressed and an unstressed prefix (Goth. *ana-*, as in *ánabusns* command, noun, *anabiudan* command, verb), and it survives extensively in OE. Stressed and unstressed *on-* can interchange regularly: *óngin* enterprise, *onġinnan* undertake. But the prefix *and-* has in OE lost its unstressed form (OS *ant-*), and unstressed *on-* has supplied the loss, so that pairs like that above quoted are fairly common (e.g. *andġiet* sense, *onġietan* understand). Stressed *and-* and *on-* are only occasionally confused, e.g. *onwlite* face, *LG* 17, *andmitta* measure, *Cp.* 793.

[2] The unaccented prefix *a-* answers to accented *ǣ-* and *or-*. The true unaccented form of *or-* is seen in OE only in *aræfnan*, perform, falsely divided to alliterate on *r*, and hence giving rise to a simplex *ræfnan*.

[3] The correct use of *wiþer-* beside *wiþ-* in participles (see § 81) leads to its occasional extension to finite verbs and nouns derived from them: *wiþercweþan* resist, *wiþercweþness* contradiction.

[4] There are alternative forms of several of these prefixes (*fer-*, *te-*, *þerh-*, *þorh-*, *ymbe-*), but they are used sporadically, not by a systematic interchange of accented and unaccented forms.

[5] An accented form of it, *ga-*, is contained in the word *ġéatwe* armour, cf. *-ġetawe* (Beow. 368, 2636, and perhaps 395).

[6] The true accented form of *for-* occurs in *frǽtwe* armour, *frácoþ* wicked. The latter word shows the original accentuation of participles (see § 81) being from **fra-cūþ*.

wrecen unavenged), and so should always be accented.[1] Occasional unaccented uses, however, occur, e.g. *unclǣne* impure, beside *únclǣne*. But already in OE the unaccented prefix *on-*, *an-* in its reversive function before verbs (e.g. *onlūcan* unlock) is sometimes replaced by *un-* (e.g. *unbíndan* unbind).

§ 76. There is in OE a tendency, which is at its strongest in lW-S, for the prep. *on* to usurp the functions of *in*. This occurs also with the unaccented prefixes, and we find e.g. *onbrȳ́rdan* inspire, *onǣ́lan* kindle, beside forms with *in-*.

§ 77. Verbs formed from compound nouns naturally retain the initial stress: *ándwyrdan*, *ándswarian* answer, *ṓrettan* fight.[2] Conversely, nouns derived from compound verbs have unaccented prefixes: *forġifness* forgiveness, *alȳ́sing* redemption.

§ 78. In OE any prepositional adverb may stand before a verb in loose syntactic combination.[3] The verse shows that such a quasi-prefix is more strongly stressed than the verb which follows it: *het ða ín beran* he ordered to carry in (*Beow.* 2152), *þe þe míd wuniað* who dwell with thee (*And.* 101). Such a prefix may be removed from before the verb,[4] and hence these quasi-compounds are syntactically equivalent to combinations consisting of verbs preceded by non-prepositional adverbs such as *eft*, *forþ*, *onweġ*, *up*, *ūt*. It is not usual to print combinations of quasi-prefix and verb as one word in editions of OE texts, yet we have in fact a system of separable verbs like those of Dutch and German.

§ 79. Prepositional adverbs which are used with verbs to form quasi-compounds, and which do not occur in an unaccented form, are: *æfter*, *fore*, *from*, *mid*, (*on*)*ġēan*. Quasi-compounds may also be formed by verbs preceded by prepositional adverbs identical in form with the stressed forms of prefixes discussed in §§ 73–74: *æt*, *bī*, *inn*, *ofer*, *to*, *þurh*, *under*, *ymbe*. The prepositional adverb used in quasi-compounds is sometimes identical in form with an unstressed prefix, because the unstressed form has been generalized in use for the independent word: *of*, *on*, *wiþ*.[5]

[1] With participles *un-* is accented, unless the participle has already an unaccented prefix; *únwrecen*, *únbunden*, but *unbefóhten* (Mal. 57), *unaþrḗotend* (Crist 388).

[2] Here belong *ándettan* confess (cf. OHG *antheiz* vow), and *ṓnettan* hasten (< **an-haitian*), which were in OE no longer of obvious nominal derivation.

[3] See the material collected by T. P. Harrison, *The separable prefixes in Anglo-Saxon* (Baltimore, 1892).

[4] Compare, for example, *niht æfter cymeð* (Order of the World 72) with *þa com æfter niht* (Gen. 2450).

[5] But note *wiþre healdaþ* resist (*Gn. Ex.* 53).

§ 80. Examples of quasi-compounds of the type defined in §§ 78–79 are: *æfter-spyrian* inquire, *fore-ġesċrīfan* pre-ordain, *from-hweorfan* turn away, *mid-wesan* be with, *onġēan-þingian* speak against, *æt-wunian* dwell with, *bī-standan* stand by, *inn-gangan* enter, *to-liċġan* lie near, *of-adrīfan* drive away, *on-lōcian* look at, *wiþ-sprecan* speak against. These accented quasi-prefixes may be used before a verb which itself has an unaccented prefix (*fore-ġesċrīfan*, *of-adrīfan*).

§ 81. Participles are properly adjectives, yet they have adopted the normal stress of verbs in most compounds. The participle *wíþerhyċġende* hostile, has, however, a stressed prefix, as has the participial noun *wiþerfeohtend* enemy, while *únderþēoded* subjected, occurs beside *underþḗoded*. The same preservation of the original stress may explain occasional *wiþer-* for *wiþ-* in participial compounds: *wiþercoren* reprobate, *wiþerwinnende* fighting against, Ep. *uuidirhliniendae* leaning against.

§ 82. Compound adverbs of which the first element is a preposition are stressed on the second, whether it be a noun or an adverb: *todǽġ*, *onwéġ*, *onbǽċ*, *beǽftan*, *befóran*, *beġéondan*, *behíndan*, *beínnan*, *benéoþan*,[1] *onúfan*, *onúppan*, *wiþǽftan*, *wiþfóran*, *wiþinnan*, *wiþnéoþan*, *wiþū́tan*, *undernéoþan*, *tofóran*, *togǽdere*, *ætfóran*, *ætgǽdere*.

§ 83. Evidence is insufficient to decide the relative stress of the two elements of conjunctions compounded of preposition and pronoun (e.g. *oþþæt* until, *forþon* because).[2]

§ 84. Of common adverbs formed from two simple adverbs, *nū́-þa* is stressed on the first element, but the majority are stressed on the second: *þā-ġḗn*, *þā-ġíet*, *swā-þḗah*.

§ 85. Compounds of *þǣr-* with a preposition (*þǣr-ínne*, *þǣr-ón*, &c.) are stressed on the prepositional element.

§ 86. The intensive prefix *full-* is subordinated in stress to the following element: *full-óft*, *full-nḗah*, *full-mániġ*. Similarly, it is an unaccented prefix in many verbs: *full-gā́n* perform, *full-trū́wian* confide.[3] On the other hand *eall-* is stressed: *éalswā* so, *éalneġ* always.

[1] Here may be added *bǽftan*, *bū́tan*, *bufan*, *binnan*, with elision of the vowel of the prefix.

[2] See H. Kuhn in *PBB* lvii. 11, note 2.

[3] The prefix is accented in the nouns *fullæst* help, *fulteam* (Erf. 360, usually *fultum*) help, and the verbs derived from them, *fullæstan*, *fultumian*. Note also *fulwian*, *fullian* baptize.

B. Half-stress

§ 87. The Old English metrical system shows that many words had both a stressed and a half-stressed syllable.[1] A half-stress always fell on the second element of a compound when both the elements retained full semantic force: *góldwlànc* proud with gold, *wǽldrèor* blood of slaughter, *gámolfèax* grey-haired, *fýrhèard* hardened by fire, *fýrġenstrèam* mountain-stream.

§ 88. The half-stress of second elements which did not retain their original semantic force fully, and that of the second elements of proper names, tended to be much reduced: their vowels were shortened, and they can undergo considerable phonological changes owing to their reduced stress.[2] The verse shows that the general rule is that they retain a half-stress only when they are either themselves disyllabic (e.g. *-bǣre*, *-rǣden*, *-sċipe*, *-wende*) or have an inflexional syllable added. So we find as a rule a half-stress in *ínwìdda*, *hlā́fòrdes*, *ónsǣ̀ġe*, *Hrṓþgàres*, *éorlsċìpe*, but not in *ínwit*, *hlā́ford*, *Hrṓþgar*. The principal monosyllabic suffixes which are thus reduced to low stress in the uninflected form, but which recover half-stress when followed by an inflexion, are: *-dōm*, *-cund*, *-fæst*, *-feald*, *-full*, *-hād*, *-lāc*, *-lēas*, *-līċ*, *-sum*, *-weard*, *-wist*.

§ 89. Similarly, heavy derivative suffixes have a half-stress after a long syllable (–́) or its equivalent (⏑́ ×), when followed by an unaccented syllable. This applies to *-els*, *-en*, *-end*, *-ere*, *-erne*, *-estre*, *-iġ*,[3] *-ing*, *-ung*, *-isċ*, *-ness*, *-oþ*; the endings *-ende* (participle), *-enne* (inflected inf.), *-est*, *-ost* (superlative); the medial *-i-* and *-od-* of weak verbs of the second class.

§ 90. As well as these suffixes, any long final syllable,[4] after

[1] The types of word which can have a half-stress are classified by J. Huguenin, *Secondary stress in Anglo-Saxon* (Baltimore, 1901).

[2] e.g. *fultum* < *full-tēam*, *fulluht* < *fulwiht*, *hlāford* < *hlāfweard*, and lW-S forms of names like *Ōswold*, *Ēadword* (earlier *-wald*, *-ward*). See below §§ 336, 338, 356–7.

[3] When from older *-īġ*, e.g. *éaldwérìġe* Ex. 50, *módcwánìġe* El. 377; but *-iġ* is mainly from *-æġ*, and its vowel is then syncopated metrically, though often written (§ 358).

[4] Such a syllable can only be long by virtue of having two consonants after the vowel. Vowel length in OE is present only under full stress, and in the second elements of compounds which either are of fully retained meaning (e.g. *hete-sprǣċ* angry speech) or have half-stress as defined in §§ 88–89. The practice of adding marks of length to the vowels of final syllables of reduced meaning (e.g. *Hrōþgar*, *heteliċ*) has nothing to recommend it. Such syllables are clearly shown to be short by the prosody of the OE Latin poets who scan them short finally

another long syllable or its equivalent, acquires half-stress when it becomes internal by the addition of an inflexion: *Héngèstes*, *ǽġhwèlċne*. Short final syllables which become long in inflexion are similarly treated: *óþèrne*.[1]

§ 91. The half-stresses described in §§ 89–90 all require to be preceded by a long syllable or its equivalent: thus *ǽþelìnges*, *séalfòde*, *síngènde*, *húntòþe* have a half-stress, but *cýninges*, *wúnode*, *wésende*, *fároþe*, do not do so. Such words, however, acquire a half-stress when they are the second element of compounds with accented first elements: *þḗodcýninga*, *cníhtwésènde*.[2]

§ 92. The half-stresses described in § 89 were clearly very light when they fell on a syllable which was itself short (i.e. did not end in two consonants). Such half-stresses are often neglected in verse,[3] and in late Old English syllables bearing them are frequently subject to change and loss, like fully unaccented syllables.

c. Sentence Accent

§ 93. Old English prosody reveals that the verb was more lightly stressed in a sentence than the noun and the adjective, especially when it was in an early place in its clause. If a verb occurs before the first metrical stress of its clause, or between the first and the second one, it need not itself bear a metrical stress. Hence we find many principal sentences in poetry like *ne wiston hie Drihten Gód* (Beow. 181), *wéorod wæs on wýnne* (id. 2014), and in a subordinate clause a metrically unstressed verb must be drawn to the beginning, after the introducing conjunction or relative: *ac þæt wæs gód cýning* (id. 863).[4] If, however, a verb is delayed till after the second

but long when an inflexion is added, e.g. *Ælfstan*, *Ælfheah* but *Ælfstānus*, *Ælfhēgus*.

[1] Such a system leaves scope for analogy, and especially in late poems (e.g. *Metres*) syllables of the type discussed in §§ 88–90 can discard their half-stress when internal if metre so demands: cf. *wæs him Beowulfes sið* (Beow. 501) with *sið Beowulfes* (id. 1971). Similarly, such syllables in final position can acquire some degree of stress when this is metrically convenient: *Hrunting nama* (id. 1457), *æþeling maniġ* (id. 1112).

[2] So the virtual compounds *feorh cyninges*, *fyll cyninges*, Beow. 1210, 2912.

[3] In the metrical system of OS, which reflects a rather later stage of linguistic development than that of OE, short derivative syllables (e.g. the medial *-od-* of the second class of weak verbs) are practically never given half-stress.

[4] We can observe this law, and the similar ones discussed below, in the language of verse only, for we have no means to determine the stress of prose. In verse, the position of unaccented verbs, adverbs, and pronouns is actually

stress of its clause, it must receive a metrical stress, although this must not throw it into more prominence than any noun or adjective in the same half-line. It may join with these in alliteration, but it must not alliterate, if they do not do so. Exceptions are few, and occur chiefly in recurrent conventional formulae, such as *swa seċġaþ beċ*; *swa bebead Metod*; *þonne hniton feþan*; *hreoþon friċċan*.

§ 94. Adverbs are stressed like verbs: while lower in stress than nouns and adjectives, they can have fully weak stress only when placed early in the sentence, before or after the first metrical stress: *oft Sċyld Sċefing* (Beow. 4); *ġewat þa ofer wæġholm* (id. 217).[1]

§ 95. Pronouns are all of weak stress (except *self* and the *ǣġ*-compounds, which are fully stressed words, equal to nouns and adjectives), but they also are allowed full weak stress only early in the sentence: *hine fyren onwod* (Beow. 915); *ne frin þu æfter sælum* (id. 1322). But like verbs and adverbs they bear a metrical stress when they occur after the second metrical stress of their clause.

§ 96. Fully unstressed words are conjunctions and relatives introducing subordinate clauses, and all proclitic words (demonstratives, possessives, prepositions). Proclitics also are the adjectives of indefinite quantity *fela*, *fēa*, *ǣniġ*, *nǣniġ*, *maniġ*, *sum*, *nān*, as may be seen by the manner in which they often stand before their noun in a metrical dip, or bearing a non-alliterating lift: *ealles moncynnes* (Beow. 1955); *þær him næniġ wæter* (id. 1514). The numerals, on the contrary, are fully stressed adjectives.

§ 97. Proclitic words receive a full stress if they are removed from their natural position immediately before the governed word: *Sċedelandum ín* (Beow. 19); *ic mínne can glædne Hroþulf* (id. 1180–1); *guðbeorna súm* (id. 314). An intervening line-end is sufficient to cause a proclitic to be stressed, even if it immediately pre-

more narrowly limited than I indicate above, but this is due to special conventions of poetic word-order, rather than to general tendencies of the language. The fundamental study of the subject is H. Kuhn, *Zur Wortstellung und -Betonung im Altgermanischen*, *PBB* lvii. 1–109.

[1] An adverb and a verb immediately following it form a quasi-compound in which the adverb carries the main stress: *swīþe ondrǣdan*, *on sēon* (cf. § 78). An intensifying adverb is more weakly stressed than a following adjective, e.g. *miċle lēofre* (Beow. 2651), but a defining adverb draws the main stress away from a following adjective, e.g. *wīde ġesȳne* (id. 1403). Expressions like *ufan grǣġ*, *æftan hwīt* are quasi-compounds with the main stress on the first elements. Similar quasi-compounds are formed by the prep. *innan*+dat. (*innan landum*, *innan burgum*, *innan brēostum*): these combinations always have a stressed first element, and the alliteration falls on the *i*. *innan* is once used as a proclitic prep., *Edward's Death* 28.

cedes the governed word: *þonne weorðeð hís | hus onhæted* (Phoen. 211–12); *þanon woc féla | ġeosceaftgasta* (Beow. 1265–6).

§ 98. The adjectives of indefinite quantity,[1] while normally proclitic, form in certain fixed formulae loose compounds with the governed noun, and they are then stressed. This applies especially to *fela* and *eall* with words of time (e.g. *fela missera, ealle hwīle*), and to *ǣniġ mon*, while in *nǣniġ mon* the adjective is proclitic. Other phrases in which the adjective of indefinite quantity is usually stressed are *fela worda, fēa worda, ǣniġ þinga, monġum reordum*.

§ 99. Any rule for sentence stress may be broken owing to special rhetorical emphasis. This explains occasional high-stressing not only of verbs, so that they are elevated even over nouns (e.g. *ða ġebeah cyning*, Beow. 2980), but even of purely proclitic words (e.g. *on þæm dæġe þysses lifes*, id. 197).

[1] D. Slay thoroughly studies the adjectives of indefinite quantity in OE verse in *Trans. Philological Soc.*, 1952, pp. 2 ff.

III

THE ACCENTED VOWELS IN PRIMITIVE GERMANIC

§ 99. If we use the letters of the Latin alphabet to represent approximately the sounds which they represent in the Old English spelling system, we may say that Primitive Germanic had at first the following vowels:

Short Vowels:	a		e	i		u
Long Vowels:		ǣ	ē	ī	ō	ū
Diphthongs:	ai	au	eu			

§ 100. It lies outside the scope of a grammar of an individual Germanic language to trace the above vowel system in detail to its Indo-European origin, but the following points may be noted:

(1) Prim. Gmc. *a* was derived from I-E *a*, *o*, and *ə*,[1] both as a monophthong and as the first element of the diphthongs *ai* and *au*.

(2) Prim. Gmc. *e* and *u* represent not only I-E *e* and *u*, but I-E ь.[2] A further source of Prim. Gmc. *u* is the development of the I-E syllabic liquids and nasals *l̥*, *r̥*, *m̥*, *n̥*,[3] to *ul*, *ur*, *um*, *un*.

(3) Prim. Gmc. *ǣ* corresponds to I-E *ē*, while Prim. Gmc. *ē* is of composite origin, representing as a rule I-E *ēi*, but also sometimes I-E *iz* (cf. OE *mēd* reward, Gr. μισθός, and see § 404). Prim. Gmc. *ē* is found in OE mainly in the past tenses of strong verbs of Class VII, but it occurs also in the words *mēd* reward, *ċēn* torch, *lēf* weak, *hēr* here, *Wēland* Wayland.[4]

(4) Prim. Gmc. *ī* represents I-E *ī* and *ei*.

(5) Prim. Gmc. *ō* represents I-E *ō* and *ā*.

[1] The vowel known as *schwa*, a term of Hebrew grammar for a vowel reduced by lack of stress; see further § 106.

[2] Known as *schwa secundum*, because discovered later than *schwa*. The symbol ь is the 'soft sign' of Slavonic grammar.

[3] They had both a short and a long form; but while this is clearly reflected in many languages, in Gmc. the short and long sounds were developed identically. Cf. OE *þorn* thorn, with IE *r̥*, and *corn* corn, with *r̥̄*. For the long sounds many use the formula *ьlə* &c., instead of *l̥* &c.

[4] The adv. *wēl(l)* well, is assumed from ME evidence to have had OE *ē* at least sometimes, but this was due to a special OE lengthening; see for possible parallels S–B, § 137.*a*.6.

(6) Most Prim. Gmc. diphthongs represent both I-E short and long diphthongs: e.g. *au* may be derived not only from *au*, *ou*, *əu*, but also from *āu* and *ōu*.[1]

§ 101. From what has been said in § 100 it will be evident that the Prim. Gmc. vowel system set out in § 99 is to be derived from the following I-E system:

Vowels:	ā̆	ē̆	ī̆	ō̆	ū̆	ə	ъ
Diphthongs:	ā̆i	ē̆i	ō̆i	ā̆u	ē̆u	ō̆u	
Vocalized Consonants:	l̥̄̆	r̥̄̆	m̥̄̆	n̥̄̆			

§ 102. I-E had had centuries of development before Prim. Gmc. developed from it, and the above vowel system is not to be regarded as particularly ancient. It owed its origin largely to changes of quantity and quality induced by the degree of stress which a syllable received in different forms and functions of any word. Short vowels which had the main stress could be lengthened in certain functions; as, for example, the nominative singular of many consonant-stem nouns: e.g. Gr. *πούς*[2] foot, OE *fōt*,[3] contrasted with the stem *ποδ-*.[4] Lack of stress frequently caused the entire loss of short vowels or their reduction to ъ. For example, in the passive participles of strong verbs of Classes I–III we have in Gmc. forms in which the *e* seen in the root syllable in the infinitive has been lost entirely. Contrast pass. parts. OE ***riden***, ***coren***, ***bunden***, where the I-E root vowels were respectively ***i***, ***u***, ***n̥***, with infs. ***rīdan***, ***ċēosan***, ***bindan***, where they were ***ei***, ***eu***, ***en***.[5] On the other hand, in the passive participles of Classes IV–V we have, not entire loss of the *e* seen in the infinitive, but reduction of it to ъ: contrast pass. parts. OE ***stolen***, ***meten***,[6] with infs. ***stelan***, ***metan***.

§ 103. The usual source of the I-E short vowels ***i*** and ***u*** and of the short vocalized consonants *l̥*, *r̥*, *m̥*, *n̥* was the loss of the vowel *a*, *e*, or *o* in the short diphthongs, and in combinations of short vowel+*l*, *r*, *m*, *n*, so that, for example, *ei*, *el* > *i*, *l̥*. This process has been illustrated above from the OE strong passive participle.

§ 104. Not only did short, long, and reduced vowels come to alternate in I-E for the reasons described in § 102, but for less clear reasons

[1] *āu* and *ōu* both became *au* in being reduced to short diphthongs, because every *o* > *a* in Gmc. It has already been noted that *ēi* > *ē*, not *ei*.

[2] Gr. *ου* = *ō*, a monophthong closer than that written *ω*.

[3] Here the *ō* is levelled through all cases.

[4] A probable instance of lengthening is the past pl. of Gmc. strong verbs of Classes IV and V. OE ***bǣron***, ***mǣton***, inf. ***beran***, ***metan*** (OE, Gmc. *ǣ* = I-E *ē*; cf. § 736.g).

[5] See further § 736.

[6] ъ normally develops to *e* in Gmc., but to *u* in a nasal or liquid neighbourhood. This *u* can become *o* by a later change (see § 115).

we can trace I-E alternations of vowel quality, especially a variation between *e* and *o*. For example, the past tense of Gmc. strong verbs of Classes I-V shows in the 1st and 3rd sg. ind. the root vowel *a* from I-E *o*: e.g. OE *rād*, *ċēas*, *band*, *stæl*, *mæt*, where the first two had the I-E root vowels *oi*, *ou*, against *ei*, *eu* of the infinitives, and the last three had *o* against *e* in the infinitives. The alternating sounds *e*, *o* could be lengthened to *ē* and *ō* for the reasons discussed in § 101, so that *e*, *ē*, *o*, *ō* may all occur in alternations: e.g. Lat. *pedem*, *pēs*, Gr. *πόδα*, *πούς*.

§ 105. The alternations of quality and quantity described in §§ 101–4 are known as ABLAUT OR GRADATION. They have been illustrated only from the *e*-series, in which all the grades (*e*, *ē*, *o*, *ō*, *ь*, loss) have been exemplified.

§ 106. I-E possessed original long vowels as well as those produced by lengthening in the *e*-series. It was long agreed that weak accent could cause the reduction of any of the original long vowels *ā*, *ē*, *ō* to *ə*, a vowel which became *i* in Indo-Iranian, but *a* elsewhere. This view was based on correspondences of the type Sanskrit *pitā*, Lat. *pater*. It cannot be regarded as certain today. It is possible that reduction of the long vowels normally led to their complete loss, and that *ə* should be excluded from the I-E vowels.[1]

§ 107. In Gmc. strong verbs of Classes VI and VII the vowel of the past tense is in most verbs the reflex of a long vowel or diphthong, e.g. OE *fōr*, *hēt*, with I-E *ō*, *ēi*. Such verbs have Gmc. *a* alone or as first element of a diphthong[2] in infinitive and passive participle, e.g. OE *faran*, *-en*, *hātan*, *-en* (OE *ā* < *ai*).[3] This *a* could be conveniently regarded as in origin the reduction of the long vowel seen in the past tense, i.e. I-E *ə*. But until the reality of *ə* has been established, the I-E form of the ablaut seen in these verbs must be regarded as uncertain.

§ 108. Much speculation has been devoted to tracing the Indo-European vocalic system to an even more primitive form than that reached by envisaging the stage before the operation of ablaut. The long vowels *ā*, *ē*, *ō* have been regarded as contractions of diphthongs *aə*, *eə*, *oə*. Some have regarded *a*, *o* as always secondary and derived from *e*. These views are all highly uncertain. Much

[1] T. Burrow, *Trans. Philological Soc.* 1949, pp. 22 ff., has argued strongly that Indo-Iranian *i* is always from I-E *i*; this view, if accepted, would render *ə* difficult to trace, for it is only recognizable from the equation Indo-Iranian *i*= other I-E languages *a*.

[2] 'Diphthong' denotes vowel+*i*, *u*, *l*, *m*, *n*, *r*.

[3] Cf. § 736.h.

modification of the traditional formulae for I-E sounds has been recently attempted on the basis of the 'laryngeal theory'. This theory offers convenient solutions of at least two major problems of Gmc. grammar, the origin of *ē* (§ 100.3), and that of the long diphthongs in the past tense of strong verbs of Class VII (§ 107), but its implications for Gmc. have not yet reached a sufficiently settled state for formulation in a general textbook.[1]

§ 109. It is evident from §§ 102–3 that Indo-European passed through a period in which the accent had a marked effect on the vowel system. During this period it is probable that the accented syllable of a word received its prominence from the *stress* with which it was pronounced. This period was followed by one in which the accent had less influence on vowels. In this period vowels were freely levelled into forms in which they could not have stood originally, so that the full vowels *ĕ*, *ŏ*, *ă* could appear outside the accented syllable of a word, and the vowels *ə*, *ĭ*, *ŭ*, *ъ*, though they could arise only in unaccented syllables, could be transferred into syllables with the accent. An example is the declension of consonant stem nouns, which usually have one root vowel throughout (except in forms with lengthening, § 102), though the accent may vary between root syllable and ending, e.g. Gr. acc. *πόδα*, dat. *ποδί*. Also, in this period many new formations appeared which could not have survived the period of strong influence by the word-accent on vowels, e.g. the present tense of verbs with stems in *e* (in ablaut with *o*). These verbs, which appear in Gmc. as the strong verbs of Classes I–V, had in I-E the vowel *e* in some forms of the present in two successive syllables, which would be manifestly impossible in the period when *e* was reduced outside the accent, e.g. **bhereti*, he bears. This period of I-E was still continuing when Gmc. began to emerge, and the Gmc. changes of vowels set out in § 100 accordingly affect vowels of all syllables, whether they bear the accent or not. During this period, in which vowels were little affected by the accent, it is probable that accented syllables were given prominence by means of *pitch*.

§ 110. Prim. Gmc, however, developed a stress accent (cf. § 71). The result is that the vowel system received from Indo-European is quite differently developed in accented and unaccented syllables. From now on, it will accordingly be necessary for accented and

[1] See further W. P. Lehmann, *Proto-Indo-European phonology* (University of Texas Press, 1952).

unaccented vowels to be separately discussed. Accented ones will be dealt with first.

§ 111. The chief modifications which the vowel system set out in § 99 underwent in accented syllables in the course of the Prim. Gmc. period were due to the development of a tendency to harmonize *e*, *i*, and *u* to the vowel which followed in the next syllable. In principle, the results of this tendency should be:

(*a*) When a high vowel (*ĭ*, *ŭ*) follows in the next syllable, *i* and *u* remain, but *e* becomes *i*.

(*b*) When a mid or low vowel (*ă*, *ĕ*, *ŏ*)[1] follows in the next syllable, *e* remains, but *i* becomes *e*, and *u* becomes *o*. This tendency to vowel harmony was, however, more vigorous in some parts of the Gmc. area than in others. Its results cannot be traced in Goth., as *e* and *i* fall together in that language, as do *o* and *u*. The harmonizing processes have been very fully carried through in OHG, but less so in the other West Gmc. languages and in ON. The individual changes must now be considered with regard to their operation in OE.[2]

§ 112. *e* > *i* before *i*.[3] This change is carried out with practically perfect regularity in all the Germanic languages. OE examples are *midd* middle, Lat. *medius*; *riġnan* to rain, cf. *reġn* rain; 2nd and 3rd pers. sg. pres. ind. of strong verbs of Classes III–V, e.g. *hilpst*, *hilpþ*, *birst*, *birþ*, *cwist*, *cwiþ*, beside inf. *helpan*, *beran*, *cweþan* (but cf. § 195); the whole present system of verbs with root vowel *e* and stem vowel *i*, e.g. *biddan*, *friċġan*, *þiċġan*, *liċġan*, *sittan*.[4] Under the same circumstances, *eu* > *iu*, as appears from 2nd and 3rd pers. sg. pres. ind. of strong verbs of Class II, e.g. *ċīest*,[5] inf. *ċēosan*.

§ 113 *e* > *i* before *u*. This change is unknown in OE and OFris,[6] but it is frequently found in OS and OHG,[7] though alternative

[1] All these sounds are not theoretically possible: *o* had become *a*, *ā* had become *ō*, and *e* had become *i* practically always in unaccented syllables.

[2] Further discussion of these changes and examples in *Trans. Philological Soc.*, 1939, pp. 79 ff.

[3] Consonantal *i* had the same effect. It generally occurred after short syllables before another vowel. In West Gmc. it also doubled the consonant which preceded it. For example OE *sittan* < West Gmc. **sittįan* < Prim. Gmc. **sitįan-* < **setįan-*.

[4] See § 331.3 for the development of *e* before *i* of the next syllable but one.

[5] *īe* is from older *īu* (see § 201).

[6] Unless in OE **cwidu* > *cwudu* cud (§ 218); see *Trans. Phil. Soc.*, 1954, p. 96.

[7] The change is relatively late in OS and OHG, for it can be caused by *-u* < *-ō*, as in the 1st sg. pres. ind. of strong verbs.

forms in which the *e* is preserved are found in those languages also, e.g. OHG, OS *fihu* money, beside *fehu*, *filu* many; OHG *mitu* mead, beside *metu*. Cf. OE *feoh*, *fela*, *medu*, and note that the *eo* of the first form is derived from *e* (see § 146).

§ 114. *i* > *e* before mid and low vowels. In OE this change is shown only by the common Gmc. words *nest* nest, and *wer* man (Lat. *nīdus*, *vir*), and by *speċ*, bacon, beside *spiċ*.[1] Instances are rather more frequent in the other West Gmc. languages, e.g. OFris. *leth* limb, *quec* cattle, *bevia* shake, *frethia* make peace, *levath* he lives, beside *lith*, &c.

§ 115. *u* > *o* before mid and low vowels. In OE forms this change occurs with considerable regularity,[2] e.g. *dohtor* daughter, *god* god, *gold* gold, *ġeoc* yoke (cf. § 172), and passive participles of strong verbs of Classes II, III, and IV, e.g. *coren*, *boren*, *holpen*. There are, however, many exceptions in OE, which have preserved *u*, very often where other West Gmc. languages, especially OHG, have *o*, e.g. *full* full, *fugol* bird, *bucca* buck, *wulf* wolf, *ufan* from above, OHG *foll*, *fogal*, *boch*, *wolf*, *obana*. Even within OE itself, there is variation in some words, e.g. *cnocian* knock, *spora* spur, *spornan* spurn, beside *cnucian*, *spura*, *spurnan*. The second element of the diphthong *eu* seems not to have been subject to this change in the form of West Gmc. from which OE was derived. In some parts of the West Gmc. area, *eu* became normally *eo* when no *i* followed, but remained before *u̯*, so that we find distinctions like e.g. OS *breost* breast, *treuwa* troth. In OE, however, the oldest texts have *eu* for Gmc. *eu* before *u̯* and before all other consonants, e.g. *trēulesnis* faithlessness, *stēup*- step-, *Ep.* 726, 1070.

§ 116. The redistribution of *e*, *i*, *o*, *u* described in §§ 111–15 does not take place before a nasal consonant followed by another consonant.[3] Before such groups *u* is retained, and *e* > *i* irrespective of what vowel follows in the next syllable.[4] OE forms exemplifying this are *hund* hundred (Prim. Gmc. **hund*-, I-E **k̥m̥tom*), *wind* wind (cf. Lat. *ventus*), and the passive participles and infinitives of strong verbs of Class III like *swummen*, *bunden*, *sprungen*, *swimman*, *bindan*, *springan*.[5]

[1] For more dubious OE instances see Ritter, *Vermischte Beiträge*, pp. 173–6.

[2] We find *o* before Prim. Gmc. -*ō*, which has become -*u* in OE, e.g. OE *nosu* < **nusō*.

[3] It should be remembered that *ng* in OE spelling implies *ŋ*+*g*.

[4] *i* would, of course, be retained also, but it is hardly theoretically possible in such a position.

[5] Contrast *holpen*, *helpan*.

§ 117. OE was clearly derived from a type of Gmc. in which a single *m* had the same effect on preceding *u* and *e* as a nasal consonant followed by another consonant. Thus we find in Class IV the strong verb *niman* take, with past part. *numen*, having the same vowels as *bindan*, *bunden*. Other examples of OE retention of *u* before a single *m* are *cuman* come, *fruma* beginning, *guma* man, *sumor* summer. The other West Gmc. languages vary between *e* and *i* in *niman*, and between *o* and *u* in the other words.

§ 118. Before a single *n* no tendency to change *e* to *i* appears in the forms of any Gmc. language (e.g. OE *cwene* woman), unless the following vowel made such a change normal (e.g. OE *wine* friend < **u̯iniz*, cf. Lat. *venia*). But before single *n* OE has a tendency to have *u* where *o* might be expected from the following vowel, e.g. *þunor* thunder, *wunaþ* he dwells, *huniġ* (older -*æġ*) honey. In such words again the other West Gmc. languages vary between *u* and *o*.

§ 119. In Prim. Gmc. the combinations *aŋχ*, *iŋχ*, *uŋχ*[1] became *ą̄χ*, *į̄χ*, *ų̄χ* by loss of the nasal consonant, and compensatory lengthening and nasalization of the vowel. *į̄* and *ų̄* were subsequently developed like original *ī* and *ū*, but while *ą̄* became *ā* in Goth., North Gmc., OHG, and OS, it retained its nasalization, and ultimately became *ō* in OE and OFris. For example OE *þēon* thrive < **þiŋχan*- (cf. OS *thīhan*, and OE past part. *ġeþungen*), *fūht* moisture, *ūhte* dawn, *þūhte* it seemed (cf. inf. *þynċan*), *fōn* take < **faŋχan*- (cf. OS *fāhan*), *þōhte* he thought (cf. OS *thāhta* and OE inf. *þenċan*), *ōht* persecution (cf. OHG *āhta*).

[1] *e* and *o* are not possible in such a position (see § 116).

IV

WEST GERMANIC INNOVATIONS IN THE VOWELS OF ACCENTED SYLLABLES

§ 120. The West Germanic languages are all distinguished by a free development of diphthongs, and accordingly the origin of these is to be placed in Primitive West Germanic. These West Germanic diphthongs have three main sources:

(1) The Prim. Gmc. double consonants *i̯i̯* and *u̯u̯* (on their origin see § 402) developed in West Gmc. to *ii̯* and *uu̯*, the vocalic elements *i* and *u* combining with the preceding vowel to form a diphthong. Hence, from Prim. Gmc. *ai̯i̯*, *ii̯i̯*, *au̯u̯*, *eu̯u̯*, *iu̯u̯* arose *ai̯*, *ī̯*, *au̯*, *eu̯*, *iu̯*. In OE *ai̯* > *āi* (cf. § 134) > *ǣi*[1] (cf. § 197), while *au̯* > *ēaw* (cf. § 135). Since Prim. Gmc. *i̯i̯* and *u̯u̯* became in Goth. respectively *ddj* and *ggw*, and in ON *ggj* and *ggv*, we get the following correspondences:

Prim. Gmc.	*OE*
ai̯i̯-	ǣġ *egg* (cf. ON g.p. *eggja*)
χnai̯i̯an-	hnǣġan *neigh* (cf. ON *gneggja*)
klai̯i̯ō	clǣġ *clay*
u̯ai̯i̯a-	wǣġ[2] *wall* (cf. Goth. *waddjus*)
frii̯i̯ō	Frīġ(e)-dæġ *Friday* (cf. ON g.s. *Friggjar*)
dau̯u̯a-	dēaw *dew* (cf. ON g.s. *döggvar*)
glau̯u̯a-	glēaw *wise* (cf. Goth. adv. *glaggwo*, ON a.s.m. *glöggvan*)
χau̯u̯an-	hēawan *cut* (cf. ON *höggva*)
χnau̯u̯a-	hnēaw *mean* (cf. ON a.s.m. *hnöggvan*)
skau̯u̯ōjan-	sċēawian *observe*
beu̯u̯a-	bēow[3] *barley* (cf. ON d.s. *byggvi*)
breu̯u̯an-	brēowan[4] *brew* (cf. OSwed. *bryggja*, older **bryggva*)

[1] Generally spelled *ǣġ*.

[2] The form is widely given in grammars, but it rests on the cpd. *grundwǣġ*, which occurs only *And.* 582, and may be for *grundweġ* (see Krapp's note *ad loc.*). The form *wǣġe* in B-T's citation of *CP* 153, 23 is a misprint for *wāge*.

[3] *eu* > OE *ēo* (see § 275).

[4] This verb forms in West Gmc. a pass. part. OE *browen*, as if originally a strong verb of Class II with root vowel *eu*+*u̯*.

χreu̯u̯an-	hrēowan[1] *grieve* (cf. ON *hryggva*)
treu̯u̯ō	trēow *faith* (cf. Goth. *triggwa*)
triu̯u̯i-	trīewe *true* (cf. Goth. *triggws*)
triu̯u̯ian-	trīewan *trust* (cf. ON *tryggva*)

(2) A similar development took place when *u̯* was doubled before *i̯* by the West Gmc. gemination of consonants (see § 407): *au̯i̯* > *au̯u̯i̯* > *auu̯i̯*, and *iu̯i̯* > *iu̯u̯i̯* > *iuu̯i̯*. In OE the diphthongs are developed normally: *au-* > *ēa-* (cf. § 135), which was then mutated to *ē-* in nW-S, *īe-* in W-S by the following *i̯*; *iu-* appears as *īo-* in nW-S,[2] *īe-* in W-S.[3] Generally, the *u̯* of *auu̯i̯* is lost, so that the final result is *ēġ* or *īeġ*, but the *i̯* of *iuu̯i̯* is lost, so that the result is *īow* or *īew*. Examples are: Prim. Gmc.**χau̯ia-* > West Gmc. **hau̯u̯i̯-* > OE *hēġ*, *hīġ*, hay, and similarly OE *hēġan* exalt, *ēġ*, *īeġ* island, *ċēġan*, *ċīeġan* call, *strēġan*[4] strew, *frīġea* lord, *trēġ*, *trīġ* tray, and with a different development of the consonants, *ēwan*, *īewan* show; Prim. Gmc. **niu̯ia-* > *West Gmc. **niuu̯i̯a* > OE *nīowe*, *nīewe* new, and similarly OE *hīow*, *hīew* form, *glīow*, *glīw*[5] mirth, *hlēowan*, *hlȳwan* warm.[6]

(3) Contraction was already in West Gmc. a fertile source of diphthongs. (*a*) *u̯* was lost before *u* (generally from older *ō*, see §§ 331.5, 405), and hence *au̯u* > *au*, and *eu̯u* > *eu*, which develop normally in OE to respectively *ēa* and *ēo*. Thus, in the nom. sg. of the *u̯ō*-declension, Prim. Gmc. **klau̯ō* > **klau̯u* > **klau* > OE **clēa*, claw (see § 598), and similarly OE *þrēa* affliction; OE *fēa* few, has its diphthong from the neut. pl. Prim. Gmc. **fau̯ō*, and so *frēa* lord, from inflected forms with **frau̯un-*; in the neuter plural of the *a-* declension **treu̯ō* and **kneu̯ō* > OE *trēo* trees, *cnēo* knees. (*b*) Diphthongs also arose when *u̯* became final, owing to the loss of the unaccented vowel of a final syllable. Thus **strau̯a-* > **strau* > OE **strēa* straw, and so **hrēa* raw;[7] **treu̯a-*

[1] This verb also follows the strong Class II in West Gmc., e.g. OE past *hrēaw* and *hrēow*.

[2] This nW-S *īo* > *ēo* in Merc. texts (see § 294).

[3] Spellings with *īe* are not actually recorded for some of the words, but only its developments to *ī* or *ȳ* (cf. § 300).

[4] *Seafarer* 97. Not recorded in W-S form.

[5] Also *glīġ*, cf. § 411.

[6] The poetical past tenses *spēowde*, *spīowde* (beside *spiowede*) would appear to be from inf. **spīowan* spit, and to belong here. The usual assumption of an inf. **sīowan* sew, from 1st sg. pres. indic. *siouu*, Cp. 1773, and the pass. part. *-siuwid*, *-siowid*, *seowed*, is less certain, as the quantity of the diphthong is uncertain in these forms. See further § 753.6.

[7] Usually found with addition of *w* from inflected forms, *strēaw*, *hrēaw*; but cf. *strēaberiġe*.

> **treu* > OE *trēo* tree, and so *cnēo* knee, *þēo* servant. (*c*) *iu*[1] arose by contraction when the ending *ō* became *u* (§ 331.5) in the neut. pl. **thriu*, OE *þrīo* three, and similarly in the analogical nom. sg. fem. forms of the pronouns, OE *hē*, *sē*, *þes*, which appear in OE as *hīo*, *sīo*, *þīos*, from **hiu*, &c., where the feminine ending *ū* (< *ō*) was added to stems in *-i*. *iu* from contraction also occurred in the prehistoric forms of OE *frīond* friend, *fīond* enemy, *frīo* free, *blīo* colour.[2]

§ 121. In OS, OFris., and OE, the so-called Ingvaeonic languages, we find evidence for a West Gmc. sound-change similar to the Gmc. one described in § 119. By this later change the groups *mf*, *ns*, *nþ* also reject the nasal consonant with compensatory lengthening and nasalization of the preceding vowel to *ą̄*, *į̄*, *ų̄*. As in the cases before Gmc. *ŋχ*, West Gmc. *į̄* and *ų̄* subsequently develop like original *ī* and *ū*, but West Gmc. *ą̄* > *ā* in OS only,[3] while in OFris. and OE it remained nasalized, and was ultimately developed to *ō*. OE examples of the change are *sōfte* soft, *gōs* goose, *hōs* company, *ōsle* ousel, *ōþer* other, *sōþ* true, truth, *tōþ* tooth, *fīf* five, *fīfel* monster, *hrīþer* head of cattle, *līþe* gentle, *mīþl* horse's bit, *sīþ* journey, *swīþ* strong, *dūst* dust, *fūs* ready, *hūsl* Eucharist, *ūs* us, *cūþ* known, *cūþe* he knew, *gūþ* war, *mūþ* mouth, *sūþ* south, *ūþe* he granted. To these should be added the prefixes *Ōs-* (in proper names),[4] and *ūþ-* (cf. Gothic *unþa-*).[5]

§ 122. A change of final accented *ō* to *ū* appears to have taken place in the form of West Gmc. from which OE was derived: OE *cū* cow, *hū* how, *tū* two, *bū* both. It is, however, possible that *cū*, which has *ū* in ON and OFris. also, is an I-E variant, and that the West Gmc. change of *ō* > *ū* only occurred after *u̯*, which was then lost. OS, OFris. *hū* (in both languages beside *huō*) suggests that the change could occur after *u̯* in all the 'Ingvaeonic' area. Similarly,

[1] On its subsequent history in OE see § 275, 293.

[2] See Ritter, *Archiv* cxxii. 98; below, § 331.6, footnote. But final *u̯* dropped after *ī* (see § 400). In North. *hīorod* family, LV *Tīouald*, we seem to have evidence that the *u̯* was not dropped in composition but contracted with *ī* to *iu* (later *īo*). W-S *hīred* would seem influenced by a simple **hī*, cf. *Tīw* (i.e. **Tī* plus *u̯* from inflected forms).

[3] Some forms with *ō* appear in OS texts.

[4] OHG *Ans-*, undoubtedly identical with ON *áss*, god; recorded as a rune-name in OE, *Runic Poem* 4, and in gen. pl. *ēsa* (§ 622).

[5] OHG is derived from a form of West Gmc. free from the sound-change under discussion, and hence it exhibits forms of the above words with preservation of the nasal consonant, e.g. *samfto* softly, *gans* goose, *zand* tooth, *fimf* five, *lindi* gentle, *funs* ready, *mund* mouth.

OE *tū* is from **tu̯ō*, and may well have influenced the vowel of *bū*. In no language is the prep.-adv. *tō* affected by this change.[1]

§ 123. OE is derived from a form of West Gmc. which shared with North Gmc. a lowering of *i* and *u* to *e* and *o* before the voiced spirant *z*, which arose from I-E *s* by Verner's law, and is later lost or changed to *r* (see §§ 398.2, 404). The OE forms exhibiting these changes are *meord* reward (cf. Gr. *μισθός*, Goth. *mizdo*), *leornian*[2] learn, the pron. *wē*, *ġē*, *hē*, *mē*, *þē* (cf. Goth. *weis*, *jus*, *is*, *mis*, *þus*; OHG *wir*, *ir*, *mir*, *dir*), and the prefixes *or-*, *tor-* (cf. Goth. *uz-*, *tuz-*; OHG *ur-*, *zur-*).[3]

§ 124. A special early development occurs in the OE words *reord* voice, *ġereord*(*e*) voice, *reord* food, *ġereord*(*e*) food, *heordan* hards of flax. All these words appear to have had in Gmc. the sound-succession *-azd-* (cf. ON *rödd*, Goth. *razda* voice; ON *greddir* feeder; *haddr* hair). The normal OE development would be *-eard-*, and the ME reflex of this appears in *rearde* voice, *Aȝenbyte of Inwyt*. The usual OE *-eord-* is shown by frequent North. spellings with *io* to have had Prim. OE *io*, not *eo* (see § 293).[4] It is therefore probable that *reord* (in both meanings) is a *i̯ō-* stem, *ġereorde* a *i̯a-* stem, *ġereord* an *i*-stem, and *heordan* a *i̯an-* stem, and that at an early period *a* > *e* before *-zdi-*, and that *e* later became *eo* by breaking, which became *io* by umlaut (§ 202).[5] In historical OE, the *io* remains in North., but becomes *eo* again in Merc. and W-S.

§ 125. In West Gmc., as in North Gmc., final open vowels are lengthened when under full accent, e.g. OE *þū*, *þē*, *mē*, *wē*, *ġē*, *hē*, *sē*, *nū*, *ġeō* (i.e. *iū*, cf. § 172), *swǣ*, *tō*, *bī*. Such words usually had

[1] Cf. literature given by S–B, § 69, and add *Trans. Philological Soc.*, 1939, p. 83.

[2] The *eo* of *meord, leornian* is from *e* by a later change (see § 146). Beside *leornian*, forms with *io* are found in North., where original *eo* and *io* are well distinguished, and reflect a Prim. OE variation of *e* and *i*. This variation recurs in OHG *lernen, lirnen* and OFris. *lernia, lirnia*, so the word can hardly be regarded as reliable evidence for the sound-change under discussion. Its variation of vowel is perhaps due purely to variation in stem-suffix between *-i-* and *-ǣ-*, and is to be referred to § 114 above.

[3] On the operation of these changes in North Gmc., see Noreen, *Altisländ. Gramm.*, §§ 72, 110.2, *Altschwed. Gramm.* §§ 83–84. It is uncertain whether their operation can be traced in West Gmc. outside OE: see *Trans. Philological Soc.*, 1939, pp. 82–83.

[4] *Heordan* does not occur in North.; the other words under discussion and their derivatives have *io* 58 times, *eo* only 4 times.

[5] The relationship of vowel seen in *riord*, **reard* seems to recur in North. *briord* point (the usual form, three instances), beside *breard* (Li., Mk. 13, 27). There also occur the ablaut variant *brord*, and its mutated form *brerd*.

unaccented forms without lengthening: e.g. OE *swă* is from unaccented West Gmc. **swa*, with or without later lengthening by transference to stressed position (cf. § 335). When lengthening occurred in West Gmc., **swā* > OE *swǣ*, *swē* (cf. § 128).[1] In the case of *hwă*, the form with West Gmc. lengthening (OE **hwǣ*) does not exist. *be* is the unaccented form without lengthening, corresponding to *bī*. In this book these words are usually printed in the unaccented form, with short vowel, e.g. *me*, *hwa*.

[1] Owing to the absence of a form **hwǣ*, **hwē*, direct equation of *swǣ*, *swē* with Goth. *swe* might be preferred to the above explanation. Either explanation leaves North. *swǣ* (LR, Li., Rit.) difficult, while accounting for VP, CH *swē*, W-S *swǣ*. Kt. has *swē* and *swǣ*, but *e* and *æ* are there equivalent graphs.

V

PREHISTORIC OLD ENGLISH CHANGES OF ACCENTED VOWELS

A. Germanic *a*, *ǣ*, and the Germanic and West Germanic Diphthongs

§ 126. The language of the earliest Old English texts, when compared with that of the other West Germanic languages, shows that the accented vowels underwent extensive changes in Old English after its separation from the body of West Germanic. The evidence for the dating of these changes is tenuous, though obviously they all belong to the period between the Germanic invasion of England *c.* 450, and the oldest surviving texts *c.* 730–50. Their relative chronology has long since been worked out on a basis of reasonable probability. Some modern scholars now challenge this chronology: their work has a certain value for its demonstration that only reasonable probability and not certainty has been achieved (cf. §§ 248–50).

§ 127. In OE and OFris., Prim. Gmc. *ǣ* appears before nasal consonants as *ō*.[1] Examples of OE *ō* from Prim. Gmc. *ǣ* are: ***mōna*** moon, ***mōnaþ*** month, ***ōm*** rust, ***spōn*** chip, ***sōna*** soon, ***cwōmon*** they came, ***nōmon*** they took, ***ġedōn*** done; and with a vocalic glide subsequently developed before it (cf. § 172) ***ġeōmor*** sad, ***ġeōmrian*** mourn.

§ 128. When not before nasal consonants, and when later sound-changes do not intervene, Prim. Gmc. *ǣ* appears in W-S as *ǣ*, but in other OE dialects practically always as *ē*. It also appears as *ē* in OFris.[2] Examples in W-S spelling are: ***dǣd*** deed, ***lǣċe*** physi-

[1] This *ō* is derived from a nasalized, but not rounded, vowel *ā̃*, for when it is subject to very early shortening the result is *a* (from earlier *ã*), not *o*, e.g. *samcucu* half-alive (cf. § 285). The written symbol varies between *a* and *o*, as in the case of *a* from originally short *a* (see § 130). Similarly, the early shortening of the corresponding mutated sound is *æ*, not *oe*, e.g. *bræmbel* (§ 193. d). *ā̃* from Prim. Gmc. *ǣ* became already in prehistoric OE identical with *ō* from Prim. Gmc. *ō*, and this change affected *ā̃* from Prim. Gmc. *ā̃* (§ 119) and from Ingvaeonic *ā̃* (§ 121) at the same time.

[2] The spelling *ǣ* is practically universal in the early manuscripts of the Alfredian translations and in *PC*. In Kt. the distinction of *ǣ* and *ē* was destroyed

cian, *hǣr* hair, *mǣre* famous, *mǣġ* kinsman, and past plural of strong verbs of Classes IV and V, *bǣron* they bore, *sǣton* they sat, &c. For examples in positions where further changes intervene, see §§ 151–2, 162, 185.

§ 129. It is tempting to assume, though not definitely demonstrable, that Prim. Gmc. *ǣ* > *ā* in the form of West Gmc. from which OE and OFris. were derived, just as it did in OHG, OS, and ONorse, and that this *ā* was then subject to change in two directions, becoming *ā̃* before nasal consonants, *ǣ* (or *ē*) elsewhere. Such a double development of *ā* would be parallel to the OE and OFris. treatment of *a* (see §§ 130, 131).[1]

§ 130. At the same time as the OE and OFris. development of *ā̃* from Prim. Gmc. *ǣ* before nasal consonants, a development of Prim. Gmc. *a* to *ã* occurred in the same position. But while Prim. OE *ā̃* appears as *ō* in all extant texts, there was no parallel development of *ã*, which became in OE a sound distinct from OE *o*, and at first also distinct from OE *a* (§ 32). It is spelled both with *a* and with *o*.[2] In later texts, however, the spelling with *a* prevails, and this together with the evidence of ME suggests that *a* before nasal consonants had become identical with ordinary OE *a* by the end

because *ǣ* (the *i*-mutation of *ā*, see § 197) became *ē* (see § 288); hence inverted spellings with *ǣ* for *ē* (whether from Prim. Gmc. *ē*, *ǣ*, or Prim. OE *ā* mutated) in the ninth-century charters, e.g. *hǣr*, *wǣron*, *huǣten*, Ct. 43, for W-S *hēr* here (Prim. Gmc. *ē*), *wǣron* they were (Prim. Gmc. *ǣ*), *hwǣten* wheaten (mutated *ā*). In Angl. texts the spelling *ē* greatly predominates for Prim. Gmc. *ǣ*. The few cases of *ǣ* in early texts are probably due to imperfect differentiation of the symbols, which were equivalent in the contemporary spelling of Latin (cf. § 40), e.g. *ġiwǣde* dress *LR*, *þǣr* there *FC*, *sprǣċ* speech *Cp*. 1852. In later Angl. texts, *ǣ* for Prim. Gmc. *ǣ* is not frequent except in *Ru.*[1], where *ǣ* and *ē* are in approximately the proportion 7:10.

The poetical word *mēċe* sword, is not put into W-S form with *ǣ* in the extant poetical manuscripts, though these are predominantly W-S in spelling: this is held to be due to its being an Angl. word not normally used by W-S speakers. The compound *mēċe-fisċ* sword-fish, occurs with both *ǣ* and *ē*.

[1] The view that OE *ǣ* was directly derived from Prim. Gmc. *ǣ*, with no intervening stage *ā*, is very familiar in this country from Wright's *OE grammar*, but most foreign authorities have long been against it. The question is far from decided: I have discussed it and mentioned much important literature not included in the bibliography of Sievers–Brunner, § 62, in *Trans. Philological Soc.*, 1947, pp. 1–14. See also Th. Frings, *Die Stellung der Niederlande im Aufbau des Germanischen* (Halle, 1944), p. 35, and E. Schwarz, *Goten, Nordgermanen, Angelsachsen*, pp. 189–90.

[2] *Ep.* always has *a*, *Erf.* and *Cp.* have both *a* and *o*. Both spellings occur also in the early North. texts and in *LV*, but *o* greatly predominates. In the tenth century North. texts *o* is practically universal except in the past sg. of strong verbs of Class III, where *a* is used (*band*, *dranc*, &c.). *VP* has *o* universally, *Ru.*[1] predominantly. eW-S and Kt. texts vary; later *a* heavily predominates.

of the OE period, except in an area in the West Midlands.[1] Examples of words in which there is variation between the symbols *a* and *o* are *gangan* go, *hana* cock, *hand* hand, *camb* comb, *nama* name, *ramm* ram, *mann* man, and past singular of strong verbs of Class III with nasal consonants after the root vowel, *swamm* swam, *sang* sang, *dranc* drank, &c. When owing to metathesis (§ 459. 1) the sound is no longer followed by a nasal consonant, the spelling variation between *a* and *o* is still found, e.g. *born*, *barn* he burned, *orn*, *arn* he ran.

§ 131. By a very early change Prim. Gmc. *a* > *æ* in OE and OFris. when not followed by a nasal consonant, but this development seems to have been later than that of *ā* to *ǣ*/*ē* (if we do not simply assume that OE, OFris. *ǣ*/*ē* is derived directly from Prim. Gmc. *ǣ*). The change *a* > *æ* seems, in fact, to have taken place independently in OE and OFris.[2]

§ 132. The view advanced in § 131 that the development of *æ* was later than that of *ǣ*, and that it may have taken place independently in OE and OFris., is based on a consideration of the development of Prim. Gmc. *ai* in OE and OFris. In OE its normal development is to *ā*.[3] Now clearly this *ā* cannot have been developed till West Gmc. *ā* (< Prim. Gmc. *ǣ*) had become OE *ǣ*/*ē*, or the new *ā* would have become *ǣ*/*ē* also. On the other hand, *ai* must have become *ā* before *a* > *æ*, otherwise it would have become *æi*, and such a diphthong could hardly have become *ā*. (The normal development of Prim. Gmc. *au* to OE *ǣa*, written *ēa*, shows that the change *a* > *æ* would affect the first element of a diphthong.) Accordingly the changes under discussion must have taken place in the following order:

(1) West Gmc. *ā* > OE *ǣ*/*ē*, unless the OE sounds are regarded as directly from Prim. Gmc. *ǣ*.
(2) West Gmc. *ai* > OE *ā*, by loss of the second element, accompanied by lengthening of the first.
(3) West Gmc. *a* > OE *æ*; West Gmc. *au* > OE *æu*.

On the other hand, in OFris. the normal development of *ai* is to *ǣ* (written *ē*), a sound which might well develop from *æi*. It is accordingly possible that *a* > *æ* before the monophthongization of *ai* to *ǣ* in

[1] Luick, *Hist. Gramm.*, § 367.

[2] Henceforth, the phonological developments of OFris. will not usually be alluded to in this book.

[3] *ai* has an unexplained alternative development to *ō* in frequent *ō* ever, *nō* not, beside *ā*, *nā*. So *ōwiht*, &c., and with mutation *ōēghwelċ* (§ 233, footnote), beside *āwiht*, *ǣghwelċ*. Cf. Pogatscher, *AB* xiii. 15. Other instances of *ō* for *ā* are sporadic, and without significance till after 1100, cf. Klaeber, *A* xxv. 270.

OFris. But in any case, since *ai* is so differently treated in OE and OFris., it must have been monophthongized after the separation of the two languages. Also, since *a* > *æ* later than the monophthongization of *ai* in OE, it follows that the former change also took place after the separation of the languages.[1]

§ 133. Examples of OE *æ* from Prim. Gmc. *a* are: *dæġ* day, *cræft* skill, *hwæl* whale, *hwæt* what, *æcer* field, *snæġl* snail, and past singular of strong verbs of Classes IV and V, *bær* he bore, *stæl* he stole, *sæt* he sat, &c. But in many cases later sound changes affect *æ*, so that it no longer appears in the forms actually recorded, or does so only in some dialects: see §§ 139, 157, 164, 185–6, 191.

§ 134. It has already been noted that *ai* > *ā* at an early date. Examples are *āc* oak, *bā* both, *bān* bone, *brād* broad, *gāst* spirit, *hāl* whole, *sāwol* soul, *wā* woe, and past singular of strong verbs of Class I, *bāt* he bit, *rād* he rode, &c.

§ 135. It has been noted that Prim. Gmc. *au* > OE *ǣa*, written *ēa* (see § 132 and cf. § 37). The first element is occasionally spelled out fully in early texts, e.g. the name-element *Ǣean-*, BH, Ct. 6, and the name *Ǣata*, BH: later manuscripts have occasional survivals like *ġerǣafie*, VP 9, 30; *þǣah*, CP 357, 11.[2] For the even more archaic spelling *aeo* see §§ 276, 278 below. Examples of the normal OE development of Prim. Gmc. *au* are *dēaþ* death, *ēage* eye, *ēare* ear, *ēast* east, *lēaf* leaf, *lēan* reward, *strēam* stream, and past singular of strong verbs of Class II, *ċēas* he chose, *sċēat* he shot, &c.

§ 136. In OE the earliest texts have *eu* for Prim. Gmc. *eu*, and show no sign of the West Gmc. differentiation of the sound into *eu* and *eo* which is traceable in some languages (see § 115). Accordingly, when some North. texts show a similar differentiation, it can be regarded as secondary (cf. § 279). On the development of the second element from *-u* to *-o* see §§ 275–8 below, where examples are given.

§ 137. Prim. Gmc. *iu* appears unchanged in the oldest OE texts, e.g. *ġeþīudde*, *þīustra*, Cp. 91, 152, *flīusum*, LR. Development to

[1] Similarly, since *au* > OFris. *ā*, it can be assumed that this monophthongization is earlier than *a* > *æ*. But the change *au* > *ā* belongs to a period subsequent to the separation of Frisian from English, and hence the change *a* > *æ* is considerably later than that separation.

[2] This spelling was revived as an archaism by moneyers of Æthelred and Cnut in the name-element *Ǣad-* for *Ead-*; hence analogically *æo* is used for *eo* on coins of the same period, e.g. *Læof-*.

īo soon followed (see § 275). In W-S, however, *īu* became *īe* by *i*- umlaut (see § 201). On the later history of *īo* in the various dialects, see § 293–7, where examples will be found.

§ 138. The development of Prim. Gmc. *au*, *eu*, and *iu* described in §§ 135–7 is shared by the same sounds when they arose by the special West Gmc. processes dealt with in § 120, where examples will be found.

B. The Breaking and Retraction of Front Vowels before Consonant Groups

§ 139. A group of early changes are very diverse in result, but are associated in that they are all due to the influence of consonants on the front vowels *ǣ̆*,[1] *ē̆*,[2] *ī̆*. The consonants which cause these changes are (1) *l*, *r*, *χ* when they are followed by a consonant,[3] (2) single *χ*, and (3) single *u̯*. Before these consonants and consonant groups front vowels are either retracted to whichever back vowel of the language is nearest in height (so that *æ* > *a*, and occasionally *e* > *o*, *i* > *u*), or are protected from the following consonant by the development of a vocalic glide, a process known as Breaking or Fracture.[4] The vocalic glide would no doubt at first be in all cases a rounded sound, but after *ǣ̆* it was generally unrounded when *ǣo* from Prim. Gmc. *au* became *ǣa* (see § 276). The diphthongs produced from *ē̆* and *ī̆* by the glide-development under discussion are still written in early texts *eu* and *iu*. Later they generally developed to *eo* and *io* (see § 277).

§ 140. In some early texts, forms occur in which the glide

[1] That *æ* and not *a* was the sound from which the *ea* of OE *eald*, *heard*, *eahta* developed, and that *æ* was retracted in OE *strawes*, Angl. *ald*, North. *barn* follows from the assumption in § 131 that Prim. Gmc. *a*, if not followed by a nasal consonant, always became *æ* in OE. This assumption was made to account for the phenomenon of breaking: since *eo* and *io* arose from *e* and *i*, it is practically certain that *æa* (written *ea*) arose from *æ*. That *æ* is a previous stage in the development of *a* in forms with retraction is not open to proof, but highly probable, in view of the similarity of the circumstances under which *a* and *ea* appear for Prim. Gmc. *a*.

[2] *ǣ* and *ē* are, of course, dialectal variant developments of Prim. Gmc. *ǣ*, not historically different sounds like *æ* and *e*.

[3] *ll*, *rh*, *hh*, have the same effect as *l*, *r*, *h*+cons. But *l* doubled by West Gmc. gemination of cons. (e.g. *tellan* tell, *sellan* sell, *hell* hell) does not have the effect of *l*+cons. Geminated *χχ* (e.g. *hliehhan* laugh) has, however, the effect of *χ*+cons. *r* is not subject to gemination (e.g. *nerian* save). Cf. § 407.

[4] I give provisionally a conventional description of breaking. Cf. § 248.

developed by breaking is not indicated in spelling. The instances are practically all of *e* for *eo* before *r* followed by a consonant. The name-element *Beorn-* is written *Bern-* in *BH* and in Cts. 4 and 5 (Kt.). *BH* also spells the name-element *Eorp-* as *Erp-* once (against three times *Eorp-* or *Earp-*).[1] The early glossaries have *herth* Ep., *huerb* Cp., for *heorþ* hearth, *hweorfa* whorl.[2] An instance of similar spelling of *æa* is *Aeldredi* Ct. 4 for *Ealdredi*. In the second element of a name *-haerdi* for *-heardi* g.s. occurs Ct. 5.[3]

§ 141. It will now be necessary to define the limits of retraction and breaking in the case of each vowel. Examples will be given in the spelling of *c.* 900. For more archaic spellings of the diphthongs see §§ 276 ff.

§ 142. *æ* is always retracted before *u̯*, e.g. *clawu*[4] claw, *þrawu*[5] punishment, *awel* hook, *ġesawen* seen.

§ 143. *æ* is retracted before *l* followed by a consonant in Angl. texts, including the early glossaries. The only exceptions in texts to be dated before 900 are *fealga* Ep. 713 (meaning doubtful), and *Ealduuft* Ct. 9 (proper name). In the later Angl. texts *a* remains practically universal except in *Ru.*[1], where there are a considerable number of *ea* spellings, especially in the word *eall*, beside predominating *a*. In Kt. and W-S, on the other hand, while *a* appears freely for Prim. OE *æ* in early texts, *ea* rapidly asserts itself as the prevailing spelling. Thus, in Kt. charters of before 800, *ea* appears once only, *Uuealhhunes* g.s., Ct. 8 (dated 770), but in the following century *ea* becomes increasingly more common, and appears practically always in the tenth-century *KG*. Similarly, in W-S, in earlier texts *ea* and *a* both appear, e.g. in the part of *PC* written by the first scribe *ea* occurs 29 times and *a* 104 times in accented syllables; but in late W-S *ea* becomes exclusively used. Examples in normal W-S spelling are *eall* all, *healdan* hold, *healf*

[1] The instances in Bede are all found in several early manuscripts. There are also extant two manuscripts of Ct. 5. A few forms in Bede are similar in appearance to those quoted above, but are to be otherwise explained: *Deruuentio* is a British river-name, latinized without modification of vowel; the same explanation applies to *Bernicii* (if to Celtic **bernā* mountain pass) and *Uurtigern*. Later OE texts have *Beorniċe*, *Wyrtġeorn*, substituting the normal OE succession *-eorn-* for *-ern-*.

[2] In *smeruui* Ep. 944, for d.s. *smeorwe* fat, we have analogy of n.s. **smeru*, with vocalic *u*; cf. *teru* Ep. 858, *blaeċteru* Ep. 677. The secondary accent explains the *e* of *Saluuerpae* Ct. 13, for the river-name *Saloweorpe*.

[3] I exclude a few relevant forms from *Ld.* as it is in a foreign hand.

[4] See § 598.2.

[5] More usually *þrēa*, but cf. *Ep.* 53, *Cp.* 200.

half, *sealfian* anoint, *wealh* foreigner, *weall* wall; the corresponding Angl. forms are *all*, *haldan*, &c.

§ 144. *æ* was broken, and appears as *ea* with very great regularity, before *r* followed by a consonant. Retraction to *a* is practically limited to North., where it is especially common when a labial consonant (*f*, *p*, *b*, *m*, *w*) precedes the vowel or follows the *r*.[1] Examples of the normal development of *æ* to *ea* before *r* followed by a consonant are *bearn* child, *heard* hard, *hearg* temple, *mearh* horse, *wearm* warm.

§ 145. *æ* was practically always broken to *ea* before χ, whether or not another consonant followed, although the development is very often obscured by subsequent changes, especially in the Angl. dialects (see § 222). Retraction to *a* is very rare, although sufficient instances occur in the word *meaht* might, and its derivatives and related forms, to suggest that these are due not to scribal error, but to retraction having taken place instead of breaking, owing to the preceding labial nasal.[2] Examples of the normal treatment of *ea* before χ are *eahta* eight, *weaxan* grow ($x < \chi s$), *seah* he saw,

[1] Instances from early North. texts are *warþ* he became, *FC*, *uarp* warp, *LR*, *þarf* need, *BDS*, *uard* guardian, *barnum* d.p. children, *CH*, *Baruæ* d.s. as place-name, *Iaruman* personal name, *BH*. The only instance in the earlier texts in a fully accented syllable not in the neighbourhood of a labial consonant is *Arduini*, personal name, *LV* 213. Instances from early North. texts where breaking occurs despite a labial consonant are *Bearuae BH* (MS. Cott. Tib. C ii), *Ġeorored* personal name, *LV* 282 (on *eo* for *ea* see § 276). In the later North. texts *Li.*, *Rit.*, and *Ru.*[2], examples of words found with *a* are: *arm* arm, *arm* poor, *barm* bosom, *farr* bull, *harm* harm, *naru* narrow, *ġesparriġa* bolt, *þarf* need, *warp* he threw, *warð* he became. Of these the majority are also found with *ea* (*eo*), and the following have *ea* (*eo*) spellings only: *bearu* grove, *ċearf* he cut, *hearpe* harp, *hwearf* he turned, *sċearp* sharp. In a non-labial neighbourhood, retraction is found only in *arg* cowardly, *Li.* (four times), for *arð*, thou art, is a low-stressed form, or is influenced by *aron*, they are, and the pret.-pres. verb *darr*, dare, is influenced by *þarf*. North. forms with *a* for *ea* in a labial neighbourhood have penetrated the early glossaries: *sparuua* calf of leg, *Ep.* 897, *tharme* entrails, *Cp.* 2140, *þuarm* cutting tool, *Cp.* 1795, *bisparrade* bolted, pass. part. n.p., *Cp.* 1451, *sarwo* artifice, *Cp.* 88, *waar* callosity (i.e. *wearr*), Cp. 426. There are a few similar forms in *Ru.*[1], elsewhere instances are rare, e.g. *barna* g.p., Ct. 38; on *ðarf*, CP 203, 15, see § 338; *arwe*, arrow, is used in OE texts only in the North. form, and the ME dialect of MS. Bodley 34, where OE *a* and *ea* are still distinguished, has *arewe* beside *earewe*.

[2] *VP* has *maht* might, three times, RG *almahtiġ* almighty, twice, Ct. 45 *almahtiġ* once. On the other hand, forms of the verbs *slēan* strike, and *þwēan* wash, with *a* are to be explained as due to the analogy of other strong verbs of Class VI, operating before the loss of medial χ, so that **sleaχan* was restored to **slaχan* and then contracted to **slān*: the actual occurrences are -*slānne*, KG 827, various forms of *slā* and *ðwā* in North. and *Ru.*[1], and the related nouns *thuachl* washing, *Erf.* 326, g.s. *ðuahles*, Li., J. 12, 3, *slahae* slay, *Cp.* 1576.

hleahtor laughter, *seax* knife, *meaht* might, *neaht* night; and with loss of the χ between vowels *ēa* river, *slēan* strike, *lēan* blame, *þwēan* wash, *ēar* ear of corn, *tēar* tear.

§ 146. *e* is broken to *eo* with very great regularity before *u̯* and χ, and before χ and *r* followed by a consonant. Examples are *hweowol* wheel, *cneowes* g.s., and all inflected forms of *cnēo* knee, *trēo* tree, *þēow* servant; *feoh* cattle, *eoh* horse; *feohtan* fight, *cneohtas* boys; *eorþe* earth, *weorþan* become, *weorpan* throw, *eorl* warrior, *sweord* sword, *steorra* star. Before *l*, breaking of *e* occurs regularly only when χ follows, e.g. *eolh* elk, *seolh* seal, *sċeolh* oblique; and with loss of χ, the inflected cases of these words (e.g. *sēoles*), *fēolan* press on. Before *lc*, breaking of *e* is regular only when *s* precedes: *aseolcan* become languid, but, on the other hand, *melcan* milk.[1] So before *lf*, nW-S *seolf* self, beside *self*, but always *delfan* dig.

§ 147. Retraction of *e* to *o* is found only between *u̯* and *r* followed by a consonant, and in North. only, e.g. *worpa* throw, *worða* become, *sword* sword, *worð* worth. Such forms are common in *Li.*, *Ru.*[2], and *Rit. Ru.*[2] has also a few forms with *eo* (*ea*), mostly from *weorþian* honour, also *cwearne* d.s. mill. *BDS* has *uueorthae*, pres. subj. from *weorþan*. Very doubtful is a North. development *fer-* > *feor-* > *fear-* > *far-*: of the occurrences, *farr* far, *Rit.*, *farra* from far, *Li.*, *farma* meal, *Li.*, the first two may be errors, the third exhibit a different vowel grade from W-S *feorm*. Similarly, *ymbhwarfað* Rit. 36, 2, may be an error for *ymbhworfað* they go round.

§ 148. *i* was broken, and appears as *io* (later *eo* in most dialects) with great regularity before *u̯*, and before χ followed by a consonant, e.g. *niowul* prostrate, *þreowa* three times, *aseowen* pass. part. sifted; *tiohhian* consider, *Peohtas* Picts, *meox* manure. Before *r* and χ, when a consonant follows, *i* appears to have been frequently broken, but since *i* follows in the next syllable in all instances, these forms will be considered below (§ 201). Breaking of *i* before *l* is not demonstrable.

§ 149. Retraction of *i* to *u* is found in all nW-S dialects between *u̯* and *r* followed by a consonant, e.g. *sinhwurfol* round.[2] Other instances all had *i* originally in the following syllable, and hence

[1] **The reduplicated past tense *leolc* played, would appear to have *eo* analogically from similar formations with *r* followed by a consonant (e.g. *leort*, *reord*, see § 746).**

[2] ***sinuurbul* Ep. 1047.**

they exhibit *y* (Kt. *e*) in historical OE (cf. §§ 199 and 288), e.g. *wyrþ* honour, *wyrþe* worthy, *wyrs* worse, and derivatives and related forms of these words. Such *y* spellings are found practically exclusively[1] in *Ep.*, *Cp.*, *Li.*, *Ru.*, *Rit.*, *VP*, while *KG* have correspondingly *werst*, &c.[2] *y* spellings are also frequent in W-S, but in view of many *ie* spellings in *CP*, and one or two elsewhere (*wierðe* Or. 292, 15, *ārwierþa* PC 716), the *y* may be regarded as from older *ie*, so W-S seems not to have had retraction in this position. Retraction is also absent in *BDS uuiurthit* he becomes.[3]

§ 150. The retraction of *e* described in § 147, and that of *i* described in § 149, are prevented by a *c*, *g*, or *χ* following the *r*, e.g. North. *werc* < *weorc* (§ 227) work; *wirċan* work, VP; *swīra* neck, *LG* (cf. § 154).

§ 151. *ǣ* from Prim. Gmc. *ǣ* is peculiar to W-S. It is retracted to *ā* before *u̯*, but broken to *ēa* before *χ*, e.g. *sāwon* they saw, *tāwian* prepare, *ġetāwe* armour; *nēah* near; and with loss of *χ* between voiced sounds *nēar* nearer, *nēalǣċan* approach, *nēawest* neighbourhood.

§ 152. In words where W-S has *ǣ* from Prim. Gmc. *ǣ*, other dialects had *ē* (see § 128). This sound was not liable to retraction. Before *χ* it was broken to *ēo*, but owing to a subsequent change (see § 227) this breaking can only be observed in recorded forms when the *χ* is lost, e.g. *nēor* Ct. 38, *nēolǣċan*, *nēowest* VP.

§ 153. *ī* appears broken to *īo* before *χ* and *χ* followed by a consonant; the *īo* frequently has become *ēo* in recorded forms, e.g. *betwēoh* between, *lēoht* light (in weight), **wēoh* idol (cf. pl. *wēos*), and the imperative of strong verbs in *χ* of Class I, e.g. *þēoh* thrive; with loss of *χ*, *betwēonum* between, *fēol* file, and many forms of the strong verbs in *χ* of Class I, *lēon* lend, *sēon* sieve, *tēon* accuse, *þēon* thrive, *wrēon* wrap.

[1] Almost the only exception is *ġeoruuierdid* disgraced, *Ep.* 990 (so also *Erf.*). The form is similar to others mentioned § 154.3, footnote 3; *Cp.* has *ġeoruuyrde*.

[2] *aferran* remove, may preserve a trace of a similar development after *f*: it occurs in Boeth. and *Kt. Psalm*, and may be a genuine Kt. form.

[3] This form cannot be dismissed as being intended for *uuuirthit*, where *ui* would be a continental symbol for *y*, for the same short text has the form *uueorthae* with similar failure to retract *e*. Obviously one explanation must cover both forms: either the dialect of the text has no retraction of *e* or *i*, or the verb has been reformed on the analogy of ones of the same class with no initial *w* (e.g. *steorfan*). The expected *y* appears in *Ru.*[1] *ġewyrð*, *ġewyrfeþ* demolitur. As a rule Angl. texts level the vowel of 1st sg. and pl. of pres. indic. of strong verbs through the tense, hence VP *-weorðeð*, Li. *wordes*.

§ 154. In a number of cases the normal processes of retraction and breaking are prevented by *-i-* in the following syllable.

(1) The retraction of *æ* fails in the group *-æu̯i-*, which appears in recorded forms as *-ewe-* (see § 194), e.g. *ewe* ewe, *strewede* he strewed.[1]

(2) The breaking of *i* fails in the group *-iu̯i-*, e.g. *spiwe* vomiting, *spiweþa* the same, *niwel* prostrate,[2] *ġesiwed* sewn.

(3) In Angl. dialects the breaking of *i* regularly failed before *r* followed by a consonant if *-i-* stood in the next syllable. The occurrences are[3] various forms and derivatives of *smirwan* smear, *afirran* remove, *hirtan* encourage in *VP*; various compounds of *smirwan* in *Ep.* and *Cp.*; and *ġesuirbet* polishes, *ċirn* churn (MS. *cirm*), *first* roof, *Cp.*; various forms of *smirwan* and *afirran* in tenth-century North. and *Ru.*[1] Sporadically the unbroken *i* becomes *e*,[4] e.g. *sifunsterri* the Pleiades, *Ep.*, *Cp.*, *smerennis* ointment, *Ru.*[1] Breaking of *i* is not, however, prevented by *rr* derived from Prim. Gmc. *rz* (see § 404), even when *-i-* follows in the next syllable; hence

[1] It is not possible to declare that the retraction of *ǣ* fails similarly, for *-ǣu̯i-* would appear as *-ǣw-* in historical OE, whether a stage *-āu̯i-* intervened or not, e.g. *brǣw* eye-lid, *lǣwan* betray.

[2] With suffix mixture *niwol*, and so *spiwol*, emetic.

[3] I exclude from this list the name-element *Irmin-* BH (all early manuscripts), Ct. 4, as these texts sometimes omit the second element of short diphthongs (see § 140); *LV* and *Gn.* have *Iurmin- Iurmen-*, with breaking, the only clear exception to the rule. VP *ċeorfeð*, *-weorðeð*, *-weorpeð*, are not exceptions, being formed analogically (§ 149, note 3). The diphthong of *hiorde* herdsman, is probably the mutation of that of **heordi-* (cf. § 202), an analogical formation with the vowel of *heord*, herd. *Leornian* learn, should show variation between *eo* and *i* (§ 123, footnote 2), the latter appearing when *-i-* stood in the next syllable: *eo* would appear to have been levelled through, and then mutated before *-i-*, giving rise to eW-S *liornian*, North. *liornia* (cf. § 202).

In two forms in *Ep* the unbroken *i* has become *ie*, *fierst* roof, 595, *orfiermae* squalid, 933; the same development occurs after *u̯* in *ġeoruuierdid* 990, cf. note to § 149 above (p. 58).

Further examples of unbroken *i* are perhaps Cp., Ru.[1] *ċirm* (< **kirmi-*, beside **karmi-*?) cry, *ċirnel* (< **kirnil-*, beside **kurnil-*?) kernel.

Here may also belong a number of forms where it might be argued that breaking took place, but that *i* was later restored by smoothing (see § 228), e.g. CH *fīrum* d.p. men, Ep., Cp. *birċe* birch, *firġin-* mountain-, VP *birhtu* brightness, *ġebirhtan* make bright, *wirċan* work, LG infl. *swīran* neck, North. *(ġe)birġa* taste.

[4] So also in FC *ferġen-* mountain-, a form of the type described at the end of the last note. A number of forms quoted by Bülbring, *Alteng. Elementarbuch*, § 186, from *Blick. Hom.* do not belong here, but reflect a tendency for *ie* > *e* in a dialect of W-S type. The words could not be subject to a common development in any Angl. dialect, as some of them have Angl. *y* (*wyrresta*), others Angl. *i* (*smirwan*, *wirċan*), others Angl. *io*, *eo* (*eorre*, *heorde*). All exhibit *e* in *Blick. Hom.*

iorre anger, angry, exhibits a diphthong (*io*, *eo*) in all Merc. and North. texts.

(4) In Angl. and Kt., the breaking of *ē* (< Prim. Gmc. *ǣ*) did not take place before χ when *i* stood in the next syllable; hence Prim. OE **nēhist-* appears as *nēst* nearest, in most Angl. texts,[1] and Ct. 45. But in W-S in this position *ǣ* was broken to *ēa*, which later became *īe* (§ 200), e.g. *nīehst*.

§ 155. Metathesis of *r* (§ 459) usually took place too late for secondary *r*- groups to cause breaking, e.g. *gærs* grass, *bærst* he burst, *berstan* burst, *þerscan* thresh, *fersċ* fresh. But in Angl., when the vowel is *i*, metathesis of *r* is early enough for breaking to occur,[2] e.g. North. *biorna* burn, *iorna* run, VP *beornan*, *eornan*; but W-S *birnan*, *irnan* (cf. § 459).[3]

§ 156. In a few words, for reasons not clear, Prim. Gmc. *o* is sometimes unrounded to *a* in Angl. dialects. This *a* is never subject to fronting and breaking before *l* or *r* followed by a consonant, e.g. past and pass. part. *warhte*, *ġewarht* worked, *VP*, *Cp.*, *Mortain Casket*; pret. *walde* would, *nalde* would not, *VP*, *Ru*² (beside *wolde*), North.; *margen*, d.s. *marne* morning, *VP*; *sċ(e)alde*[4] should, *Ru.*¹, North.; past part. *ġewarden* from *weorþan*, OE Bede.[5] These forms occur sporadically elsewhere, not only in texts with an Angl. element (e.g. OE Bede, *St. Chad*), but also in more purely W-S texts.

c. The Restoration of *ă̄* before Back Vowels

§ 157. One of the most obvious peculiarities of the OE phonological system is that *æ* and *a* interchange, the former standing in closed syllables, and in open syllables when a front vowel (*e*, in early texts sometimes written *i* or *æ*) follows, the latter in open syllables when a back vowel (*a*, *o*, *u*) follows. The paradigm (see § 574) *dæġ*, *dæġes*, *dæġe*, *dagas*, *daga*, *dagum* illustrates the prin-

[1] *Ru.*¹, like W-S, has forms with *-h-*: *nēhsta*, *nǣhsta*, also *nīhste* 25, 11.

[2] Other cases of breaking before metathesized *r* are rare: *bears* beside usual *bærs*, perch; Li. *ġeðearsca*.

[3] lW-S past tenses *bearn*, *earn* are due to late analogy of *wearþ*, &c. (based on the pl. *burnon*, *wurdon*); eW-S has *born*, *orn*, *barn*, where the vowel-sound of *mann*, &c., which may be spelled with *a* or *o*, is preserved, although divided from the nasal by a metathesized *r*. *VP* has *orn*, *born*, North., Ru.¹ *arn*, *barn* (cf. § 130).

[4] The *e* seen after *sċ* in this form in North. is due to the palatal nature of the *sċ* (cf. § 181).

[5] The North. past *darste* for *dorste* he dared, has the vowel of pres. *darr*, on which see § 144, footnote.

ciple. This interchange is clearly due to the restoration of *a* before a back vowel, for breaking can hardly be regarded otherwise than as a change affecting front vowels (see § 139), and from this it follows that OE *slēan* is developed from **slæχan*. Now it is hardly conceivable that when Prim. Gmc. **slaχan-* was at the stage **slæχan*, Prim. Gmc. **draʒan-* would not be at the stage **dræʒan*; from which it follows that OE *dragan* has restored *a* in its first syllable by later change.

§ 158. The restoration of *a* is common before all single consonants and geminates, e.g. *faran* go, *calan* be cold, *bacan* bake, *gnagan* gnaw, *grafan* dig, *stapol* pillar, *sadol* saddle, *latost* latest, *laþode* he invited, *cassoc* rough grass, *hassuc* the same, *mattoc* mattock, *crabba* crab, *hnappian* fall asleep, *racca* cord, *lappa* skirt.[1] *a* is commonly restored also before groups consisting of *f* or *s* followed by another consonant, e.g. **wasċan* wash, *asċe* ash, *flasċe* flask (after inflected *asċan*, *flasċan*), *brastlian* crackle, *saftriende* rheumatic. Before other groups, *a* is not restored except for a few instances before consonant plus liquid: W-S *appla, apla* apples, *watrode* he watered, Angl. (Rit., Ru.[1]) *accras, acras*[2] fields, beside *æplas*, *æcras*, *wæterode*, and always *sæġdon*, *hæfdon*, *fædras*, *næġlas*, &c. Yet it need not be doubted that *a* was originally widely restored before groups, and that it was subsequently removed by the analogy of forms in which a front vowel followed. This is reflected by some doublets, e.g. *gæfel*, *gafol* tribute, *hæġel*, *hagol* hail, *fæġen*, *fagen* glad, *wæcer*, *wacor* awake, which are at least in some cases due to an original distinction s. *hæġl*, p. *haglas*, &c.; but cf. § 193.c.

§ 159. The restoration of *a* was frequently due to a back vowel which subsequently became a front vowel or was lost, e.g. *gaderian* gather, *staþelian* found (cf. *geador*, *staþol*), and weak verbs in *-i-* (< *-ōi̯-*), *laþian*, *macian*, *hnappian*, &c.

§ 160. The principal grammatical categories in which the variation *a*–*æ* occurs are: (1) masculine and neuter *a*- nouns, e.g. *dæġ* day, *fæt* vessel, p. *dagas*, *fatu*. Before geminates and groups *æ* is usually levelled into the plural, e.g. *hættas* hats, *cræftas* powers; but *a* is levelled into the sg. in *bratt* cloak, *catt* cat, *facg* plaice, *prass* pride, *sacc* bag (beside *sæcc*). (2) Adjectives of the same declension generally level *a* into all open syllables, so n.p.m. *hrade*,

[1] Before geminates doublets with *æ* sometimes exist, e.g. *læppa*, *hnæppian*.

[2] An English rubric in the *Durham Ritual* (not part of the North. gloss) has d.p. *acrum*.

late, *ware*, *wlace*, from *hræd* quick, *læt* late, *wær* aware, *wlæc* warm. (3) The variation is rare in ō-nouns, e.g. *sacu* strife, inflected *sæce* or (anal.) *sace*, *latta* or *lætta*, pl. laths. (4) Strong verbs of Class VI have in W-S a strong tendency to extend the *a* of the inf. and pres. indic. pl. to forms where *-e* follows, and also to the monosyllabic imperative, e.g. subj. *fare*, pres. part. *farende*, past part. *faren*, imper. *far* from *faran* go.

§ 161. Sporadic analogical extension of *a* and *æ* beyond the limits indicated in § 160 occurs in most texts, e.g. g.s. *hwales*, d.p. *-hwælum*, Oros. 18, 17; 17, 36. The adj. *stræċ* severe, usually extends *æ* to all forms, so d.p. *stræcum*, &c.

§ 162. A change of *ǣ* to *ā*, parallel to that of *æ* to *a* just described, occurs frequently in W-S texts (in other dialects *ǣ* has become *ē*, and hence was not subject to the change). It is much less regular than the restoration of *a*, but forms with *ā* before a following back vowel occur before intervening single consonants of all types except dentals.[1] Examples are *slāpan* sleep, and related words, d.p. *māgum*, and other plural forms of *mǣġ* relative, d.p. *wārum* from *wǣr* agreement, *ġestāl* accusation, *swār* heavy, *tāl* slander (after forms with back vowels in inflexions), *lācnian* tend, and past of strong verbs of Class V like *lāgon* they lay.[2] But forms with *ǣ* are found also in most of these words.

§ 163. As noticed above, § 128, footnote, *Ru.*[1] has a considerable number of forms with *ǣ* instead of the usual nW-S *ē*. Correspondingly, it has a few forms in which *ā* has been restored before a back vowel, *ġesāgun* they saw, three times beside forms with *ē* and *ǣ*, *iāra* formerly. So Cp. *ġestālum*.[3]

D. The Second Fronting

§ 164. The position whereby Prim. OE *æ*, when not subject to breaking or retraction by the influence of the following consonant or consonant-group, appears as *æ* or *a* in historical forms, according to the conditions described in §§ 157–61, is modified in the dialect of *VP*. There *æ* became raised to *e*, and *a* became fronted

[1] Hence always *mǣton*, *cwǣdon*, &c.; so eW-S *unfæstrād* cannot be regarded as having its final element developed as if accented.

[2] The doublets *ācumba*, *ǣcumbe* oakum, are due to prefix mixture rather than to the sound-change under discussion.

[3] *Māgos* KG 368 is probably an error; the ending is influenced by the glossed word *propinquos*.

to *æ*, so that, for example, the normal OE paradigm *dæġ*, *dagas*, appears as *deġ*, *dægas*. Other examples are *beċ* back, *feder* father, *efter* after, *hefde* he had, *seġde* he said; past singular of strong verbs of Classes IV and V, e.g. *-ber* he bore, *sprec* he spoke, *-set* he sat; imperative singular and pass. participle of strong verbs of Class IV, e.g. *fer* go, *ġesċepen* created; *cwæcian* shake, *hræce* throat, *dræca* dragon, *wæcian* watch, *wræca* g.p. from **wræcu*, W-S *wracu* vengeance, *mægon* they may, *plægian* play. The *æ* produced by this sound-change was subject to a subsequent change (see § 206) when it stood before a consonant other than *c* or *g*, but for the time being the dialect had forms like **fætu* vessels, **fæsu* fringes, **gætu* gates, **fædur* g.s. from *feder* father, **hæfuc* hawk, which developed later to *featu*, &c.

§ 165. The second fronting does not take place before *l*. This is evident in the case of *a*: the relevant forms are *hwalas* whales, *wyrt-walan* roots, and derivatives of *galan* sing. In the case of *æ*, there is only one relevant form in VP, *hel* he concealed, 39, 11; this isolated form, however, is perhaps an error, for ME evidence suggests that the second fronting of *æ* also failed before *l*.[1] Similarly, the *a* produced by retraction before *l* followed by another consonant (§ 143) is immune from the second fronting, e.g. *ald*, *haldan*.[2]

§ 166. The change does not take place in a few words which regularly have weak stress: the present system of *habban* have (*habban*, *-að*, *hafast*, *-að*), *ah* but, and *ðæt*, *ðæs*, *æt* (prep.), *cwæð*, *wæs*, beside *ðet*, &c. There are a few further exceptions due to the imperfect transposition of the gloss into the dialect, e.g. *dæġ* 55, 5, *dagum* 89, 15.

§ 167. The *æ* produced by second fronting cannot be distinguished from *æ* of other origin. But it is reasonable to suppose that the *e* produced by second fronting was, at least at first, distinguished from *e* derived from Prim. Gmc. *e* (see § 195). This distinction cannot be shown to have remained into the ME period. ME evidence suggests that there was variety in different parts of the area in which second fronting operated, as to whether or not the first element of the diphthong *æa* (written in OE *ea*) was affected. Its monophthongization is in some texts *æ* (written *ea*, e.g. Corpus MS. of *Ancrene Wisse*, *hearm*), which later

[1] See S. T. R. O. d'Ardenne, *Seinte Iuliene*, p. 185.

[2] Examples of words with retracted *a* before *w* do not occur in *VP*, but they would probably escape second fronting also.

becomes *a* (e.g. Royal MS. of Katherine Group), but in others the monophthongization is to *e* (e.g. Nero MS. of *Ancrene Wisse*, *herm*).

§ 168. Second fronting is not a general Merc. change, for it is practically absent in *Ru.*[1], and ME sources show that it was limited to a small part of the vast Midland area. In OE the change of *æ* to *e*, in addition to its practically universal appearance in *VP*, is fairly common in *Ep.* and *Cp.*, and very frequent in *RG* and *St. Chad*. The change of *a* to *æ*, on the other hand, apart from sporadic forms, is not to be traced outside *VP* except in the early glossaries (see § 207). *Ru.*[1], *RG*, and *St. Chad* all have *dagas*, &c.

§ 169. The second fronting of *VP* and other Merc. texts is to be regarded as earlier than the Kt. change of *ǣ̆* to *ē̆*; the latter occurred later than *i*-umlaut, and hence affected *ǣ*, the mutation of *ā*; sounds produced by *i*-umlaut are unaffected by second fronting in *VP*. See further §§ 288 ff.

E. The Influence of Initial Palatal Consonants

§ 170. A number of sound-changes will now be discussed together, although they do not all belong to the same period, because they are all due to initial palatal consonants, and consist in the formation of new diphthongs. The initial palatal consonants of Old English must first be detailed. (*a*) Prim. OE at first possessed only one initial palatal consonant, the spirant *i̯*, which may be spelled *i* or *g*, e.g. VP *ġēr* year, *ġē* ye, *iung* young, *iugoð* youth. (*b*) Later, however, West Gmc. initial *ʒ* and *k* became fronted before front vowels, including *æ* and *ǣ*/*ē*, derived from Prim. Gmc. *a* and *ǣ*, and the first elements of the diphthongs *ĕa*, *ĕo*, *ĭo*, of whatever origin. *k* and *ʒ* were not fronted before *a* due to retraction (*cald*), or restoration (*galan*), as these processes were complete at the time of the fronting. In the dialect of *VP*, the fronting of consonants was earlier than the second fronting of vowels, as appears from ME forms, which prove that OE **gedeling* companion, **togedere* together, had back *g* in dialects subject to second fronting. Yet the accented syllable of the words quoted would have *æ* after the operation of second fronting: see § 203 on the full history of the vowel. *k* and *g* were never fronted before front vowels derived from back vowels by *i*-umlaut, e.g. *cennan* beget, *cœ̄ne* bold, *cyning* king, *gœ̄s* geese, *gylden* golden. So far as can be determined, fronted *ʒ* was identical with old *i̯* in sound. Examples of fronted *k* and *ʒ* are *ċēosan* choose, *ċēapian* buy, *ċeald* cold, *ċild* child, *ċierran* turn, *ġealga* gallows, *ġiefan* give, *ġiest* guest, *ġearu* ready, *ġierwan* prepare. (*c*) At first *sk* was either back or front under the same conditions as *k* and *ʒ*, e.g. *scand* disgrace, *scacan* shake, *scōh* shoe, *scūr* shower, *scyldiġ* guilty, *sċearp* sharp, *sċeal* shall, *sċip* ship, *sċieppan* create; it was of course back before consonants, e.g. *scrūd* garment. Later, perhaps about 800, every initial *sk* was palatalized as a first stage in development to [ʃ].

§ 171. It will be obvious from § 170 that in eOE there could be no palatal consonant before a back vowel except Prim. Gmc. *i̯*. After *i̯* there was a strong tendency in W-S and North., which appears less markedly in Kt. and Merc., to develop a glide front vowel to facilitate the passage from front consonant to back vowel. The main accent of the word remained on the back vowel, so that no diphthong of the typical OE kind with an accented front vowel as first element was formed. The usual subsequent history of the sounds under consideration is loss of the glide and development of the back vowel in ME. Thus OE *ġeoc* becomes ME *yok*, just as if the glide vowel had never existed. It has, therefore, sometimes been argued that the symbol (*e* or *i*), which is generally supposed to represent a glide, is merely a diacritic to indicate the palatal nature of the preceding consonant. The existence of the glide vowel is, however, proved by cases in which the accent is transferred to it. The glide is usually written *e*, but sometimes *i*. In W-S and Kt., glide+*u* is usually written *eo* or *io*, probably to avoid the multiplication of graphs: North. uses the more phonetic *iu*, e.g. *ġiung* young, and this graph is occasionally found in W-S also.

§ 172. In W-S the glide is written with considerable regularity, though forms without it are frequent, especially in early texts. So for Prim. Gmc. initial *i̯ŭ* we find *iŭ* (*gu*), *ġiŏ*, *ġeŏ*, the last being practically established in later texts,[1] e.g. *iung*, *ġiong*, *ġeong* young, *iuguþ*, *ġioguþ*, *ġeoguþ* youth, *iuc*, *ġioc*, *ġeoc* yoke, *ġiocđa* itch (*CP* 71, 11), *iū*, *ġiō*, *ġeō* formerly; less frequent spellings are *io*, *giu*, e.g. *io*, *iongum*, *ġiungan*, CP 213, 24; 385, 10; 178, 21. For Prim. Gmc. *i̯a* before nasals W-S has *ġio*, *ġeo*, e.g. *ġiond*, *ġeond* throughout, *beġiondan*, *beġeondan* beyond, *ġeon*[2] yonder. W-S *a*

[1] An interesting spelling is *Ġeoweorþa*, which apparently represents the natural W-S pronunciation of *Iugurtha* (Oros., freq.).

[2] Only d.s.f. *ġeonre*, CP 443, 25.

restored before a back vowel (§ 162) develops a glide before it in *ġeāra*, formerly; similarly *ō* from Prim. Gmc. *ǣ* in *ġeōmor* sad, and its derivatives.

§ 173. The North. forms corresponding to those quoted for W-S in § 172 are *ġiung* (but cf. § 176), *beġeonda*, *beġeande*. In Li. *ġeocc* the basis is probably *o* not *u*, cf. *ioc* Rit., Ru.[1] Other North. forms with glides are *ġeong*[1] way, *ġeonga* go (both with *i̯* transferred from past *ġēong*), *ġeōna* yet.

§ 174. In Merc., *VP* shows development of a glide only in the prefix *ġeond-*, and in *ġeāmrung* sadness; *Ru.*[1] only in *ġeond*, *be-ġeonda*. Cp. has *biġeonan* beyond, and *ġeond-*, *ġeoc-* as prefixes.

§ 175. In Kt. before 900, diphthongization occurs in *ġioc* Ct. 42, beside *iocled* Ct. 35; *ġeocled* occurs Ct. 49 (Merc.-Kt.). *KG* have *ġionne* (read *ġiongne*) 183, *ġiogeðe* 109, *ġiohðhade* 1097, *ġiond-* 201, *ġiōmras* 94; but also *iunges* 815.

§ 176. More usual in North. than the form *ġiung* quoted above is *ġing*, and the same development appears exclusively in *ġigoð*. VP also has *ġing*[2] beside *ġung*, and the form occurs sporadically in other texts containing a Merc. element (*BG*, OE Bede, *St. Chad*), and in the poetry. The explanation of these forms would seem to be that first a glide developed after the initial palatal, producing the rising diphthong *i̯u*, and that the accent was then transferred to the first element of that diphthong. Subsequently the second, now unstressed, part of the diphthong was lost, having perhaps communicated its rounding to the first element. Finally this rounding was lost by the influence of the preceding palatal. The development thus would be *i̯u* > *iu̯* > *y* > *i*. This seems confirmed by the forms actually recorded in North. corresponding to W-S *sculon* they shall. In this word, a palatal consonant seems to have been transferred from the sg. *sċeal*, at least in North., and the various manuscripts of *CH* offer forms corresponding to those just postulated for North. *ġing*, &c.: the early Moore and Leningrad MSS. have respectively *sċylun* and *sċilun*, the Dijon and Paris MSS. (late, but preserving ancient forms) *sċiulun*. *Sċilon* appears in *Li.*, so it is to be regarded as the latest form: it developed early enough for its vowel to undergo back umlaut (§ 205), hence *Li.* has also *sċiolun*, *sċiolon*, and *Ru*[2] has *sċiolun*.

§ 177. The history of the diphthongs developed from back vowels after palatal consonants when *-i-* stood in the following

[1] Cf. *hin-iong*, departure, *BDS*.

[2] Only in compar. *ġingra* 118, 9; 148, 12; but this is not a mutated form, for *y* does not become *i* in *VP*.

syllable is obscure. In eW-S, beside *ġeond*, *ġiond*, there occur also *ġiend* and *ġind*, forms which may be reasonably regarded as from **i̯andi-*. The *ie* spellings are fairly frequent, so it seems likely that the rising diphthong seen in *ġeond*, *ġiond*, could undergo umlaut to a diphthong written *ie*, of which the phonetic nature is uncertain, but which was in any event soon simplified to *i*. *ġind* occurs also in Kt. both as preposition and prefix (Ct. 45, 31; *KG* 111). *Ep.* has *biġinan* beyond, Li. *beġienda*. Accordingly *io* > *ie* > *i* can be assumed for all dialects as the development of the vowel when *i̯a* was followed by a nasal consonant and *-i-*.

§ 178. Evidence is even less extensive for the development of *i̯u* before *-i-*. The only evidence for a diphthong is *ġieċða* itch, *CP* 71, 18, beside *ġiċða*, id. 70, 19, presumably forms showing umlaut of the vowel seen in *ġiocða*. Comparative and superlative of *ġeong* have always *i* in eW-S, *ġinġra*, *ġinġest*, except once, *CP* 451, 28, *ġiongrum* without umlaut. The analogy of the treatment of *eo* (§ 177), and the one occurrence of an *ie* spelling, are perhaps enough to suggest that, before *-i-* of the following syllable, initial *i̯u-* > *i̯iu* > *i̯ie* > *i̯i*.[1]

§ 179. The development of a glide vowel after the new palatal *sċ*, when a back vowel followed, is well established already in eW-S texts in the groups *sċă* and *sċŏ* (including *sċa*/*sċo* with Prim. Gmc. *a* followed by a nasal consonant). Accordingly, we find forms, derivatives, and compounds of the following written with both *sc* and *sce* initially: *sċeacan* shake, *sċeadu* shadow, *sċeamian* be ashamed, *sċeorian* refuse, *sċeond* disgrace, *sċeonca* shank, *sċeādan* divide, *sċeolde* he should, *sċeop* poet, *ġesċeōp* he created, *sċeōġian* shoe. In the oldest manuscripts a few words and their related forms are written with *sc-* only but this is due to chance, e.g. *forsċapung* crime, *sċaru* cutting, *sċort* short, *sċot* shot, *sċōc* he shook. The glide is very rarely written *i*, e.g. *sċiolde*, CP 77, 11.

§ 180. The group *sċŭ-* does not develop a glide in eW-S except in *sċeolon* they shall, beside *sċulon*. Here we may suspect that a palatal *sċ* was early transferred from the sg. *sċeal* (cf. § 176). Otherwise we have in eW-S initial *sċŭ-*, e.g. *sċuldor* shoulder,

[1] The absence of a positive *ġing* in W-S makes it difficult to regard the *-i-* of compar. and superl. as developed without mutation from *-u-*, as in other dialects. Thus, however, R. Vleeskruyer, *St. Chad*, p. 96. On the other hand, *ġinġra*, *ġinġest*, can hardly be held to show mutation of undiphthongized *u*, because they are regularly spelled with *i*, and never with *y*, and *y* is hardly ever unrounded in eW-S (see § 316).

onsċunian shun, *sċūfan* shove, *sċūr* shower. In later texts, however, a glide is frequently developed, and glide plus *ŭ* is generally written *eo* (as after *i̯*, cf. § 172), e.g. *sċeōfan* shove, *onsċeonian* shun, *sċeōr* shower, and similarly *sċeocca* demon, *sċeorf* scurf, beside *sċucca*, *sċurf*. Less frequent is the spelling *eu*, e.g. *sċeucca* (Ps. 105, 27; W-S *Gospels* MS. A, Mt. 4, 10), *sċeūfan* (Ælfric, *Gramm.* 137, 11).

§ 181. In North., *Li.* and *Rit.* exhibit a glide written *e* practically always between initial *sċ* and *ă* or *ŏ*, as in forms and derivatives of *sċeacca* shake, *sċeaða* enemy, *sċeāda* divide, *sċeoma* shame, *sċeond* disgrace, *sċeort* short, *sċeōh* shoe, and the past tenses *sċeān* he shone, *ġesċeōp* he created.[1] Between *sċ* and *ŭ* the glide is written *y*, e.g. *ofsċyufon* they shoved, *sċyūr* shower.[2] But the more usual development of *sċŭ-* is *sċȳ̆-*, a development similar to that of *i̯u* (see § 176), e.g. *sċya* shadow (beside *sċua*), *sċyldrum* d.p. shoulders, *sċynia* shun, *-sċȳfa* shove.

§ 182. In *Ru.*², a glide is developed after *sċ* before *ă*, but not before *ŏ* and *ŭ*, hence (in various forms and compounds) *sċeaca*, *sceaða*, *sċeān*, but *sċomu*, *sċortiġa*, *sċōh*, *sċūr*.[3]

§ 183. In the Merc. texts, including *VP*, *Ru.*¹, and the early glossaries, and in Kt., there is no trace of the development of a glide between initial *sċ* and a back vowel.[4]

§ 184. In a few W-S and North. forms, a glide developed between *sċ* and a front vowel due to *i*-mutation. The instances in North. are all of *eǣ*, *eōē* appearing where we should expect the mutations of *ā* and *ō*: *tosċeǣna* break, *Li.* (beside *-sċǣna* Li. Ru.²), *sċeǣð* sheath, *Li.* (beside *sċǣð* Ru.²), *ġ(e)sċeōē* shoes *Li.* (beside *ġisċōē* Ru.²). In W-S the glide combined with the mutated vowels to form diphthongs: glide +*ĕ* gave *ĭe*, glide+*ǣ̆* gave *ĕa*, and these diphthongs were normal falling diphthongs, which had the same subsequent history (§§ 301, 313) as *ĭe* and *ĕa* of other origin. Beside the forms with these diphthongs there are usually others without any sign that a glide was ever developed (cf. § 179).

[1] A few forms with no indication of a glide occur: *sċort* Rit. twice, *sċoma* id. 190, 15, *sċōes* Li., J. 1, 27. Both early manuscripts of *CH* have *sċōp*.

[2] Past pl. *-sċriungon*, and pass. part. *-sċriuncen*, *-sċryncan*, from *sċrincan*, shrink, seems to show the same development *u* > *iu*/*y* after *sċr*.

[3] On Ru.² *sċiolun* for *sċulon*, see § 176.

[4] Apparent exceptions are due to another process (see § 207 below), e.g. *sċeadu* shadow, *Ep.*, *sċeaba* plane, *Ep.*, *Cp.*, *-sċeaðan* a.s. enemy, *Cp.* *Ru.*¹ has *-sċeādan* divide, beside *-sċādan*, but this may be due to the influence of W-S spelling.

Examples are: with *e*, the mutation of *a* before a nasal: *sċiendan* hurt, beside *sċendan*; with *ē*, the mutation of *ō*: **ġesċīe* shoes, later *ġesċȳ*; with *æ*, the mutation of *a* (cf. § 193.c): *sċeaþþiġ* hurtful, beside *sċæþþiġ*; with *ǣ*, the mutation of *ā*: *sċēaþ* sheath, beside *sċǣþ*; *-sċēat*, 3rd sg. pres. ind. of *sċeādan* divide, *CP* 453, 17, beside *-sċǣt*, Ælfric, *Hom.* ii. 232, 8. Other words show no glide, e.g. *sċenċ* cup, *sċenċan* pour, *sċǣnan* break.

§ 185. One of the most regular changes in the West Saxon dialect is the diphthongization of front vowels after palatal consonants. This change is caused not only by original palatal *i̯*, but by the new palatals which arose from Prim. Gmc. *k* and *g* in OE before all front vowels which existed after the restoration of *a* before following back vowels. These palatals are in this book written *ċ* and *ġ*: the latter was identical in sound with old *i̯*, and this is also written *ġ* in quoting OE forms. *sk* became palatal at the same time as *k* before front vowels. By the diphthongization, *ĕ* became *ĭe*, and *ǣ̆* became *ĕa*. Examples are:

e > *ie*: *sċieran* cut, *ġiefan* give (and related words), *ġieldan* pay, *-ġield* sacrifice, *-ġietan* get, *ondġiet* sense, *ġielpan* boast. (Forms of all these words are actually recorded with *ie* in eW-S.)

ē > *īe*: *ġīet* yet (eW-S frequently), *ġīeta*, *ġīena* the same (both forms poetical), *ġīe* ye (lW-S, beside *ġe*, the unaccented development.)[1]

æ > *ea*: *sċeaft* shaft, *ġesċeaft* creature, *sċeabb* scab, *sċeal* he shall, *sċear* he cut, *sċeatt* treasure, *ċeaster* city, *ċeaf* chaff, *ġeat* gate, *onġeaġn* against, *ġeaf* he gave, *-ġeat* he got.[2]

ǣ > *ēa*: *sċēap* sheep, *sċēaron* they cut, *ċēace* jaw, *ġēar* year, *ġēafon* they gave, *ġēaton* they got, *ġēa* yea.

Exceptions are not numerous in W-S texts, but examples are *sċeld*, *ġelp-*, *-ġeld*, Oros. 188, 25; 214, 1; 154, 34; *ġæġlbǣrness* CP 73, 11. These and similar forms are, no doubt, to be attributed to the influence of Merc. spelling.

§ 186. In North. the same processes are found, but less regularly

[1] But the past of *sċeādan* divide is *sċēd* in W-S, beside *sċeād*, a different formation (see § 745.a).

[2] Naturally the symbol *ea* is sometimes ambiguous, e.g. n. pl. *ġeatu*, gates, d.p. *ġearum* years, may have respectively *ea* and *ēa* transferred from forms in which no back vowel followed; but they may also have restored *ă* before a back vowel preceded by a glide, according to § 172. (This in *ġeatu* would imply the transference of an initial palatal from the sg.) The adv. *ġeāra* is usually assumed to have the phonological *eā*, as its semantic development to 'formerly' has removed it from the influence of *ġēar* year.

than in W-S. In early texts we have only *sċeal* he shall, *ġeatum*[1] ornamentally, *L.R.*, against *-ċæstri*, loc. sg., city, *FC.* In *Li.*, *Rit.*, and *Ru.*[2] there is often diphthongization of *æ* (least frequently in *Ru.*[2]) so that we find e.g. *sċeal*, *sċeatt*, *ċeaster*, *ġeaf*, *ġeat*, *-ġeat* beside (in most instances) forms with *æ*. When *æ* escaped diphthongization to *ea*, a palatal glide was frequently developed before it after palatal consonants, so the spelling *eæ* also occurs in *Li.*, e.g. *-ġeætt* Mt. 26, 7, *-ġeæf* Mk. 10, 4, *onġeæġn* L. 19, 30, &c. *e* is not affected in North., but *ē* becomes *īe* in *ġīe* ye (*Li.*, *Rit.*, *Ru.*[2]) and *ġīe* yea (*Li.*, *Rit.*), and this can be monophthongized to *ī*.[2] Undiphthongized forms of both words, with *ē* or *ee*, are also frequent, occurring in all three texts for the adverb, and in *Li.* and *Ru.*[2] for the pronoun. *Li.* has also the spelling *ġiee* (Mk. 15, 44) for the adverb, and *ġǣ*, *ġiǣ* (Mk. 14, 42; L. 11, 42) for the pronoun. The first is perhaps to be regarded as indicating a glide before undiphthongized accented *ē*, the others are hardly due to more than the recurrent uncertainty of distinction of the symbols *æ* and *e*. *Li.*, *Rit.*, *Ru.*[2] all have *sċīp* sheep, presumably from **sċīep* with palatal diphthongization of nW-S *sċēp*. Other words with *ē* are undiphthongized, e.g. *ġēr*, *ġēfon*.

§ 187. The diphthongization of front vowels after palatals is unknown to all Kt. and Merc. texts except *Ru.*[1], where a few forms occur with *ea* from *æ*, *ċeaster*, *ċeaf*, *sċeal*, *-sċeatt*, *ġeat* beside *ċæster*, *sċal* (with the vowel of *sċalde*), and once *sċīp* (18, 12), beside usual *sċēp*.

§ 188. The W-S diphthongs *ĕa* which arose from front vowels by palatal influence were identical with *ĕa* produced by breaking and the normal development of Prim. Gmc. *au*, and were distinguished from *eă*, which arose from the development of a glide between a palatal consonant and a back vowel, as their subsequent history shows (see § 313, and cf. § 44). Accordingly their mutation will be discussed together with that of *ĕa* of other origin below (§ 200). In North., since the mutation of *ea* is *e*, it is not possible to determine if *sċeþþa* hurt, *sċeppa* create, *ċefis* concubine, *ġest* guest, contain the mutation of *æ* or of *ea*. Undiphthongized *æ* is, no doubt, mutated in VP *sċeððan*,[3] *sċeppend*, *ġest*, *ċele* coldness,

[1] Adverbial d.p. of *ġeatwe*.

[2] The pron. occurs with *ī* in *Ru.*[2], the adv. in *Li.*, *Ru.*[2]

[3] This form invades W-S prose: pure W-S *sċyþþan* < **sċieþþan* is limited to poetical manuscripts.

Ep., Cp. *ċebis* concubine, KG *sċerian* divide, *sċepttenras* (245, read *sċeppendas*).[1]

§ 189. *Rit.* has *e* regularly in words of this type, but *ī* always appears in *ġīmung* marriage, and its derivatives (thirteen occurrences), a word containing the mutation of *ēa* from Prim. Gmc. *au.* In these forms, *ē* produced by umlaut seems to have become *ie*, and later *ī*, owing to palatal influence. This is parallel to the treatment of old *ē* in the text (*ġie*, *sċīp*),[2] though old *e* is unaffected by a preceding palatal.

F. *i*-Mutation

§ 190. The process known as *i*-umlaut or *i*-mutation operates on practically all the sounds which it could theoretically affect in OE. When *i* or *i̯* stood in the following syllable, all back vowels were invariably fronted, so that the following changes took place:

ă̄ > *ǣ̆* (and *æ* undergoes further change to *e* before *m* and *n* in most dialects)
ŏ̄ > *œ̄̆* (> *ē̆* in most dialects)
ū̆ > *ȳ̆* (> *ē̆* in Kt., and often *ī̆* in lW-S).

There is considerably more variety in the mutation of diphthongs. In W-S the diphthongs *ēă* and *īŏ*, whether derived from Prim. Gmc. diphthongs or arising from breaking or from palatal influence on front vowels,[3] were mutated to *īĕ*. On the other hand, in all nW-S dialects *ēă* was mutated to *ē̆*, while *īŏ* was not subject to mutation. The diphthong *ēŏ* is capable of mutation in very few words in original position, for it did not normally exist before *i* or *i̯*: it is, however, probable that in the few words where it arose before *i*, and in words where it was analogically introduced before *i* and *i̯*, its mutation was *īŏ* in all dialects.

§ 191. Just as all back vowels are subject to fronting by *i*-umlaut, so certain front vowels are subject to raising. It is certain that *æ* > *e* under the same conditions as those in which back vowels are fronted, but whether *e* > *i* is not demonstrable. The long vowels, W-S *ǣ*, nW-S *ē*, are not believed to be subject to raising

[1] These two forms are editorial errors for MS. *sċeppend*, *sċæppend*.

[2] *Li.*, J. 1, 42 *ġeċiġed* is probably an error for *ġeċēiġed*, the usual spelling in the text.

[3] The diphthongs arising from palatal influence on back vowels were different in quality: their mutations have been discussed, §§ 177–8, 184.

by *i*-umlaut: the evidence is the three words *dǣd* deed (*i*-stem), *lǣće* physician, *mǣre* famous (*i̯a*-stems), which show unaffected *ǣ* in W-S, *ē* in nW-S.[1]

§ 192. Very considerable discussion has taken place of the precise cause of *i*-umlaut.[2] Many scholars (pre-eminently Sievers and Luick among the earlier masters, Rooth among the moderns) consider that the *i* or *i̯*, standing in the syllable following the vowel to undergo umlaut, palatalizes the intervening consonant, and that the umlaut is the assimilation of the preceding vowel to this consonant. In favour of this view it is to be argued: (1) that the palatal quality of *ć* and stop *ġ* remained after a mutated vowel, and led to their ultimate assibilation (see § 433 for examples); (2) that groups consisting of *m*, *n*, or *l*, followed by another consonant, when they were preceded by a mutated vowel, remained palatal and capable of causing a second mutation of the vowel, so that e.g. *cæmpa*, *cænde*, *ældra* became *cempa*, *cende*, *eldra* (see details below, § 193); (3) that early in OE certain consonants and consonant groups were changed in nature (presumably palatalized) by a following *i* or *i̯*, so that breaking sometimes failed to take place before them (see § 154); (4) that early OE spellings suggest that *i*-umlaut was, in fact, begun by epenthesis of *i* into an accented syllable (see § 42), and such an epenthetic *i* could hardly be anything but a glide anticipating a palatal consonant. In spite of these arguments, it might be maintained that, although palatalization of some consonant groups before *i* or *i̯* is easy to demonstrate, it cannot be assumed for all groups, and *i*-umlaut can take place before any group. Therefore *i*-umlaut may be a mere vowel harmony, approximating the mode of utterance of an accented vowel to that of an *i* or *i̯* of the following syllable.[3] It would then be necessary to assume that *i*-umlaut was accompanied (or preceded or followed, for the processes need not have been simultaneous) by the palatalization of at least the consonant groups detailed in (1) and (2) above, and that such palatalized consonant groups sometimes changed preceding *æ* to *e*.

§ 193. The *i*-mutations of the various sounds will now be considered in detail.

[1] On *mēće* for *mǣće* in manuscripts of W-S colour, see § 128, footnote.

[2] A very useful selection of references is given by Samuels, *Trans. Philological Soc.*, 1952, pp. 38–39.

[3] It can hardly be other when no consonant intervenes between the vowel influenced and the *i* or *i̯* (examples §§ 237, 120.2).

a: the *i*-umlaut of this sound occurs in OE in the following positions:

(*a*) When retraction of *æ* to *a* took place before *l* followed by a consonant in Angl., and before *r* followed by a consonant in North. (see §§ 143–4), the result when *i* stood in the following syllable was *æ*. Before *l*-groups, we find *æ* practically universally in Angl. texts: examples from *VP* are *cwælman* kill, *ġemæltan* melt, *ældra* older, *-hældan* bend, *ġefællan* fell, *fæll* fall, *wælle*[1] well. But, nevertheless, ME evidence shows that in the majority of dialects this *æ* passed into *e* before the end of the OE period, a change no doubt due to the influence of the palatalized consonant group which followed it. *æ* seems to have remained (to become ME *a*) only in the West Midlands.[2] The only OE text to show undoubted traces of the beginning of this change is *Ru.*[1]: there we find various forms of *eldra*, *cwelman*, *-heldan*, *belgas* wine-skins, in all ten occurrences, beside twenty-four cases of *æ* in the same and other words.[3] Since we find in North., in the early glossaries, and in *Ru.*[1] frequently *a* for *ea* before *r* followed by a consonant, it is natural that we should sometimes find *æ* for *e* in the same position when *i* stands in the following syllable. Hence, although we find prevailingly in these sources forms like *ġerd* rod, *ferd* army, &c., there also occur Ep. *-ġaerd*, *auuaerdid* damaged; Cp. *-ġærd*, *faerd*, *ġeuaerpte* he recovered, *ġeġaerwendne* pres. part. a.s.m. preparing; *Li.* forms and derivatives of *hwærfa* turn, *wærma* warm, *wærċ*[4] pain, *ċærra* turn, also *unðærfe* useless; *Ru.*[1] forms of *wærfan* turn, *wærġan* curse, and *astærfan* kill, also *-ġærwende* pres. part. preparing, *ġeġærelum* d.p. garments.[5] It will be noticed that in most of these forms the vowel is in the neighbourhood of a labial consonant.[6]

(*b*) *a* derived from *æ* by restoration before a following back

[1] Also twice *welle*, perhaps another formation with original *e* and no following *-i-* (cf. OHG *uuella*).

[2] See Ekwall, *Contributions to the history of OE dialects*, p. 62.

[3] *e* spellings sporadically occur in other manuscripts (e.g. Blick. Hom. *cwelman*, *eldo*, *welm*), but they are to be regarded as the mutation of southern *ea*, not of Angl. *a*.

[4] In this form the word and its verb *wærċan* penetrate W-S: pure W-S *wyrċ* from **wierċ* is rare.

[5] Note also *baerċae* barking, *Cp.* 1191, with first *a* cancelled by subpunctuation.

[6] The peculiar *a* of *margen* (§ 156) seems to be mutated in Ru.[1] dat. *mærġne*. The mutation of the *o* of normal *morgen* appears in the form *merġen*, dat. *merne*, found in North., *Ru.*[1], lW-S.

vowel (§§ 157–60) can be subject to umlaut only when the back vowel is *u*, and *i* follows in the third syllable (see below, § 203).

(*c*) In many forms, *a* could be analogically placed before *i* or *i̯* of the following syllable, though phonologically *æ* should always stand in this position. Consequently, we find in the historical forms of such words *æ* (the *i*-mutation of *a*), instead of, or beside, *e* (the *i*-mutation of *æ*), and the origin of the mutated *a* can usually be readily seen in related forms, e.g. *ræċed* hall, beside *reċed*, North., Ru.[1] *gæfel* tribute (cf. *gafol*), Ep., Cp. *haeċid* pike (cf. *hacod*), Ep., Cp. *haeċilae* cloak (cf. *hacele*), *hæleþ* man, beside *heleþ*, poet. *gæst* guest, beside nW-S *ġest* (cf. g.p. *gasta*, Gen. 1346), *stæpe* step, beside *stepe* (cf. pl. *stapas*), *sæċċ* strife (cf. *sacu*), *næss* cape, beside *ness* (cf. *nasu*), *wæċċe* watch, *wæċċende* watching, North. *wæċċa* to watch (cf. *wacian*), *wræċċa* exile, beside *wreċċa* (cf. *wracu*), Rit. *sċæppend* creator, beside *sċeppend*, *ġemæċċa* companion (cf. *ġemaca*), *mæċġ* man, beside *meċġ* (cf. *magu*). To these may be added the W-S 2nd and 3rd sg. pres. indic. of strong verbs of Class VI, *dræġð*, *færð*, *sæċð*, &c. (cf. inf. *dragan*, *faran*, *sacan*), and all forms of *habban*, have, with *-æbb-*, W-S 1st sg. pres. indic. *hæbbe*, W-S, *Ru.*[1], North. pres. part. *hæbbende*, pres. subj. *hæbbe*.[1] In *VP*, since *a* had become a sound approximating to *æ* before mutation took place, its mutation was *e*, and this appears in the above forms so far as they exist in the dialect, *stepe*, *ġest-*, *wreċan* (a.s. 93, 6, read *wreċċan*), beside once *wræċċan* (a.s. 145, 9), with the vowel of **wræcu*, W-S *wracu*.[2] On the corresponding Kt. forms see § 288.

(*d*) A sound closely related to *a* was derived from Prim. Gmc. *a* before nasals. Its umlaut was at first *æ*,[3] which is extensively preserved in early texts, e.g. *cænde* he begot, *LR*, *Raendles-*, *Haenġist* BH, MS. Cott. Tib. C ii, and many forms in *Ep.*, including *aenid* duck, *-haen* hen, *lændino* loins, *ġiuuaemmid* corrupted, *ġifraemith* he performs, *caempan* warriors, *laempihalt* lame, *graennung* grinning, *faenġae* d.s. capture, and various forms and derivatives of *maenġan* mingle, *graemman* irritate. But the palatalized consonant or consonant group early caused a further change of *æ* to *e*:[4] such forms are already found in *Ep.*, and outnumber the

[1] On W-S, *Ru.*[1], North. *sæċġa(n)* say, beside *seċġan*, see § 766.

[2] So VP *wæċen* watch, has the vowel of *wæcian*, W-S *wacian*.

[3] On this mutation Förster, *Flussname Themse*, pp. 470–8, has valuable material but unreliable conclusions.

[4] Luick's attempt to place here *stemn* stem, *hremn* raven, (*Hist. Gramm.*, § 186) is to be regretted, as the forms *stefn*, *hrefn* are common and suggest that

æ- forms in *Cp*. by more than three to one. In all later texts *e* is the normal spelling, and *æ* the exception, although *Ru.*[1] has a few more instances of *æ* than is usual, with 27 instances against about 260 of *e*. ME evidence enables one to determine that in a limited south-eastern area, including Essex, but not Kent, the mutation of *a* before nasal consonants remained at the stage *æ*.[1] It is difficult to decide if the influence of this area is to be observed in any Old English texts. In eW-S *æ* spellings are of great rarity, but in some later manuscripts they are frequent:[2] they can, however, be mere inverted spellings, for in normal Angl. and W-S the sound [æ] no longer existed before *m*, *n*, or in some cases they may be due to Kt. influence, for in that dialect [æ] and [e] had fallen fully together and *æ* and *e* were hence equivalent graphs.

In W-S *bærnan*, *ærnan*, causative formations to *beornan* burn, *eornan* run, metathesis of *r* broke the contact between *æ* and the palatalized consonant group too soon for the latter to cause *æ* to become *e* (primitive forms **brannian*, **rannian*).[3] On the other hand *VP*, *Ru.*[1], North. have *bernan* (except *Ru.*[1] 3, 12, *forbærneþ*).

If *ǣ*, the mutation of *ā* (< Prim. Gmc. *ai*) or of West Gmc. *ā* before nasals, undergoes early shortening, the resulting *æ* becomes *e* before the palatalized consonant group, like the originally short

the change of *æ* to *e* preceded that of *f* to *m*. The words would seem to be in OE *i*-stems (Prim. OE **stævni*-, **hrævni*-). The form *hræfn* without umlaut is comparable to *gæst* beside *ġest* (see below, § 204.5). *ærn* house, *hærn* wave, are also not relevant; their development rather is **razn* > **ræzn* > **rænn* (before breaking was caused by *r*+cons.; this stage remains in *hraen* Ep. 400) > *ærn* by metathesis of *r*. -*ren*, -*ern* in the second element of compounds have a vowel due to reduced stress. *Erf*. 1137 *rendeġn*, *Beow*. 770 *renweardas* are forms due, if correct, to Merc. or Kt. change of *æ* to *e*: cf. *mete-ren*, Ct. 31 (Saxon–Kt.).

The mutation of *æ* to *e* by a palatalized group was limited to fully accented syllables; hence lW-S *mæniġ* many, represents the form with reduced stress (cf. § 96), North. *meniġ* the accented form. The noun *mæniġo* is influenced by *mæniġ*. *Mæniġ* could, of course, be regarded as simply W-S unstressed development of *moniġ* without mutation, cf. *þænne*, *hwænne*, *þæne*, *hwæne*, *ætsæmne*, for *þonne*, &c. (see § 380).

[1] Cf. Luick, *Hist. Gramm.*, § 363.*a*.2.

[2] e.g. MS. D of the *OEC*, the glossary in MS. Brussels 1829, Wright–Wülcker i. 284 ff. (eleventh century), and the copies of homilies in MS. Hatton 116, especially nos. 2–18 (list in Vleeskruyer, *St. Chad*, pp. 3–5). In the study of this question, the forms *mæniġ* (and hence *mæniġo* which it influences) are irrelevant (cf. § 380): hence correct Bülbring, *Alteng. Elementarbuch*, § 171*a*. *Spænð*, he entices, beside *spenð*, is due to other verbs of strong Class VI (*færð*, &c.).

[3] So *wrenna*, wren, but with metathesis *wærna*; and by contamination *wrænna*, *werna*.

sound, e.g. *endlufon* eleven, *enwintre* one year old, *endemes* together, *enne* a.s.m. one (*VP*, *Ru.*[1], North.) beside *ǣnne* (W-S, *Ru.*[1], North.), *bremblas* brambles, pl. of *brēmel* (< **brāmil*-), from **bræmblas*, whence sg. *bræmbel* and *bræmel*.

§ 194. **æ**: the *i*-umlaut of this sound is *e*, e.g. *bedd* bed, *betera* better, *hebban* raise, *eft* again, *here* army, *leċġan* lay, *nerian* save, *rest* rest. In nW-S this mutation can appear where W-S has the mutation of *ea* after a palatal consonant (see § 188). *VP* has similar forms, for the *i*-umlaut of *e* from Prim. OE *æ* by second fronting is *e* (cf. § 195). Before consonant groups and geminates, however, there is a strong tendency to eliminate the umlaut, and to restore *æ* from the analogy of related forms without umlaut, e.g. *hæftan* bind, *mæstan* feed on mast, *fæstan* make firm, *ġehlæstan* load, *fæþman* embrace, *næġlan* nail, *pæþþan* traverse, *stæþþan* stay, *stæppan* step, with which the related nouns may be compared, and *ġedæftan* arrange, *hwættan* sharpen, beside *hwettan*, *lættan* delay, beside *lettan*, with which compare the related adjectives. *Bræġden* wily, beside *breġden*, is due to interchange of *-æn-* and *-in-* in the suffix in Prim. OE (§ 381). More difficult to explain is *æfnan* perform, beside *efnan*. In *VP*, of course, *e* appears for restored *æ*, as well as for original *æ*, hence *ġeheftan*, &c.

§ 195. **e**: it would seem reasonable to assume that the analogical paradigm **farō*, **faris*, **fariþ*, which underlies W-S *fare*, *færst*, *færþ*, would be paralleled by **berō*, **beris*, **beriþ*. Since such restoration of *e* is rarely traceable, while restoration of *a* (see above) and of *o* (see below) is traceable in many forms, an *i*-umlaut of *e* to *i* must be assumed for OE, to explain the prevailing absence of analogical forms with *e* where *i* stood in the following syllable. It would follow from this that the VP *e* from *æ* by second fronting was distinguished from *e* from Prim. Gmc. *e* till at least the time of umlaut, for the umlaut of the former is not *i* but *e* (cf. above, and § 167).

§ 196. **o**: this sound could be subject to *i*-umlaut only in loan-words, and in native words in positions into which it had been analogically introduced, for it was not phonologically developed in Prim. Gmc. before a following *i* or *i̯* (see § 115). In such forms its umlaut was *oe*, and this sound had a strong tendency to become unrounded to *e*. The oldest glossaries have the following examples: Ep. *loerġe* poles, Cp. *ðroehtiġ* vigorous, *oefsung* shearing, *cellendre* coriander, and in a medium-stressed syllable

Cp. *ċerfelle* chervil (< *chaerefolium*).[1] From this it is evident that the tendency *oe* > *e* was very early. *VP* has *doehter* d.s. daughter, *oexen* oxen, forms and derivatives of *oefestan* hasten, but *ele* oil, *reċetung* eructation (cf. *rocettan*), and also, with shortening of a vowel originally long, forms and derivatives of *bledsian* bless. *Ru.*[1] has *oele*, and *ġebloetsian* beside (*ġe*)*bletsian*. *BG* have *ele*-. North. has *doehter*, *oefistiġa*, &c., *oele*, but *Li.*, *Ru.*[2], *Rit.* all have *exen*, and while *Li.*, *Rit.* have mostly (*ġe*)*bloedsiġa*, *Ru.*[2] has *ġibletsiġa*, *bletsiġa*. A number of strong pass. participles appear in *Li.* with the mutation of *o*, where normally OE has *o* (cf. § 736.m): *ġecnoeden*, *ġesuoeren*, *ġewoerden*, *awoerpen*; so Ru.[2] *ġibroeċen*. eW-S has both *oele* and *ele*, and always *efesian* shear, *bletsian*; lW-S has *e* in all forms.[2] On the Kt. development see §§ 288 ff.

§ 197. ā: the *i*-umlaut of *ā* was always *ǣ*: most instances are of *ā* from Prim. Gmc. *ai*, e.g. *hǣlan* heal, *ǣniġ* any, *dǣlan* divide, *lǣdan* lead, *sǣ* sea, *stǣnen* of stone. W-S *lǣwan* betray (and connected words), *brǣw* brow, may be regarded as having the mutation of *ā*, the retraction of Prim. OE *ǣ* before *u̯* (§ 151), but it might also be assumed that they have unchanged *ǣ* before *u̯i*: this would be parallel to the failure of *æ* to retract before *u̯i* (§ 154). North., Ru.[1] *hwǣlċ* which, *swǣlċ* such, appear to contain the mutation of *ā*, introduced into these words from *hwā*, *swā* (§ 125); so Ru.[1] *twǣlf*, twelve, perhaps contains the mutation of the *ā* of *twā*.[3] It is plain that nasalized *ā̃* had not become fully identical with *ō* at the time of mutation, for when it is subject to early shortening the product is *a*, not *o* (§ 127), and when its *i*-umlaut is shortened the product is *æ*, not *oe* (§§ 127, 193.d). We must, therefore, assume that *ā̃* was at first mutated to an *ǣ* slightly different from *ǣ* the mutation of *ā* < *ai*. The former sound became in historic OE *ōē*, while the latter remained. The future history of *ōē* was the same as that of *ōē*, the mutation of *ō*, i.e. it remained in Angl. (e.g. *cwōēn* queen, *smōēþe* smooth, *wōēn* hope), but became *ē* in W-S.[4]

[1] On *Ep.* 79 *soærġændi* for which *Erf.*, *Cp.* have *sorgendi* see § 764.

[2] On the texts with the form *merġen*, containing probably mutated *o*, but not recorded with *oe*, cf. above, § 193.a, footnote 6.

[3] But if it has *æ* it belongs to § 328; Kt. *twælf* is merely inverted spelling (*æ* = *e*).

[4] Difficult are the words *nǣm* taking, *nǣming* the same, *niednǣm* taking by force, *be*-, *ġe*- *nǣman* deprive. Holthausen (*Archiv* cxiii. 43, developing Sievers, *Angelsächs. Gramm.*, § 68.*a*.1) regards them as from **naim*-, and as not connected with *niman* take; Björkman (*AB* xxix. 338) takes them, more probably, as re-formations of *oe* words, which arose in consequence of the early re-formation

Examples are: with Prim. Gmc. *ǣ* (§ 119), *ēhtan* persecute, *fēhþ* he takes; with Ingvaeonic *ǣ* (§ 121), *gēs* geese, *tēþ* teeth, *ēst* favour, *sēfte* soft, *smēþe* smooth, *ġesēþan* testify, *nēþan* venture, *fēþe* movement (and related words); with Prim. OE *ǣ* (§ 127), *cwēn* queen, *wēn* hope, *cwēman* please.

§ 198. ō: the *i*-mutation of *ō* is *ōe*. This remains in Angl. texts, where occasional *o*- and *e*- spellings can be regarded as errors. *Ru.*[1], however, has nine forms of *hēran* hear, spelled with *ōe*, and this inversion probably implies unrounding of *ōe*. eW-S sometimes has *ōe* in *ōeþel* home, beside *ēþel*, and in names in *Cōen*- in the *Chronicle.*[1] On the Kt. development see § 288. Examples of the mutation of *ō* are *fēt* feet, *bēċ* books, *fēdan* feed, *cēlan* cool, *swēte* sweet. It has been remarked above (§ 42) that in early texts *oi* is found as a graph for the mutation of *ō*: the examples are chiefly from early manuscripts of Bede, where names in *Cōin*- and *Ōidil*- for later OE *Cēn*-, *Ēþel*- are frequent,[2] and where the same graph is used in a number of names of less clear etymology, but of which some at least probably contain the mutation of *ō*: *Oiddi*, *Oisċ*, *Boisil*, *Coifi*;[3] cf. *Cp.* 1017 *wōidiberġe* hellebore. Occasionally the graph *æ* is used to represent the mutation of *ō*: examples from W-S texts are *onhrǣran* CP 225, 5, *ġedǣmde* Oros. 258, 10, *ġefǣġð* Boeth. 54, 17, from *hrēran* stir, *dēman* judge, *ġefēġan* join. *Ru.*[1] similarly has three times *wǣsten* beside *wōesten* wilderness, and *ġedrǣfde* 24, 6, from *ġedrōefan* disturb.[4] If correct, *Cp.* 143 *laerġae* poles, for Ep., Erf. *loerġ(a)e*, is the same treatment of the mutation of short *o*. The significance of these spellings is uncertain.

§ 199. ŭ: the *i*-umlauts of the short and long sounds seem

of past pl. *nōmon* to *nāmon* (Ep. 113 already *naamun*). Either view is preferable to that of Morsbach, who assumes abnormal operation of umlaut in the group West Gmc. -*āmi*-, disregarding *ġesēman*, &c. (*AB* vii. 325, followed by Bülbring, *Alteng. Elementarbuch*, § 192.*a*.) The compar. and superl. *sǣmra*, -*ost*, worse, worst, may belong here. VP *ġemrung*, quoted by Bülbring, loc. cit., is an error for frequent *ġeāmrung* (§ 174), and *bræmbel* is to be otherwise explained (§ 193.d).

[1] W-S *dōe*, -*dōendum*, CP 8, 2; 13, 3, pres. subj. and pres. part. from *dōn* do, are to be regarded as analogical disyllabic formations for usual *dō*, -*dōndum*.

[2] So MSS. Leningrad and Cott. Tib. A xiv once *Quōinburg*, for later *Cwēn*- (with the mutation of Prim. Gmc. *ǣ* before a nasal).

[3] If Bede's *Loidis*, Leeds, has a short vowel, it is the only word in which the mutation of short *o* is spelled *oi* (see *ES* lvi. 222–4).

[4] Cf. *Beow.* 1942, *onsǣċe*. *Ru.*[1] has also a few instances of *ǣ* for the mutation of Prim. Gmc. *ǣ* before a nasal, *cwǣen* 12, 42, *cwǣmdon* 12, 10, *hwǣne* a little, 26, 39.

identical in quality and history: they are both written *y*. On subsequent unrounding see §§ 316–17, and on the special Kt. treatment see §§ 288 ff. Examples are: with Prim. Gmc. *u*, *bryċġ* bridge, *byċġan* buy, *cyme* coming, *hyġe* thought, *hyll* hill, *styrian* stir, *yfel* evil; with *u* by retraction of *i* (§ 149), Angl. *wyrþ* honour, *wyrþe* worthy, *wyrs* worse; with Prim. Gmc. *ū*, *brȳd* bride, *mȳs* mice, *lȳs* lice, *fȳr* fire, *lȳtel* little; with Ingvaeonic *ū* (§ 121), *cȳþan* make known, *dȳstiġ* dusty, *fȳsan* send forth, *wȳsċan* wish, *ȳst* storm, *ȳð* wave. The early spelling *ui* for *y̆* (§ 42) occurs in *Thrūidred* BH (Moore MS. only), *grūiit* g.s. meal, *Cp.* 1619, *buiris* chisel, *Cp.* 11, for normal *Þrȳþ-*, *grȳt*, *byres*. Similar spellings occur in *Li.*, presumably as archaisms, e.g. *drūiġe* dry, *fuilġendo* following, *ġeðuild* patience, *suindriġ* separate.[1] In a very few cases in early texts *u* is written for *y*;[2] these may be regarded as errors for *ui*, e.g. *þun* BC, *hurnitu*, *sculthēta*, *ontūdri* Cp., for *þynne* thin, *hyrnetu* hornet, *sċyldhǣta* bailiff, *ontȳdre* barren.[3]

§ 200. **ĕ̄a**: the *i*-umlaut of these sounds is with great regularity *ĭ̄e* in W-S, and *ĕ̄* in nW-S, although, in this matter as in others, spellings of Angl. type often penetrate W-S texts. Examples of the mutation of *ĕ̄a* will now be given, classified according to the origin of the mutated sound.

(1) *ea* by breaking before *l* occurred and could be subject to *i*-umlaut in W-S and Kt., while Angl. dialects had the mutation of *a* in the same position, e.g. W-S *bieldan* to make bold, *ieldra* older, *wielle* well, *fiell* fall;[4] Kt. *eldra* older, *helt* he holds, *wellan* boil, *ġeweldan* subdue.

(2) *ea* by breaking before *r* occurred and could be subject to *i*-umlaut in all dialects, though North. and Merc. sometimes have the mutation of *a* in this position (§ 193.a), e.g. W-S *ċierr* turn, *dierne* secret, *hierdan* make hard, *mierran* hinder, *fierd* army, nW-S *ċerr*, &c.

[1] Forms also occur with *uy*, *wy*, *wi*; for even rarer variants, see W. Stolz, *Der Vokalismus . . . der Lind. Ev.*, p. 55; M. Ångström, *Studies in OE MSS.*, p. 20.

[2] Cf. occasional *o* for *oe* or *oi* noted above (e.g. FC *ōplæ*).

[3] So later *Vuunhere*, *Cunehelm* (ninth-century moneyers) and a few similar names of moneyers after 900.

[4] While forms with Angl. *æ* or Kt. *e* are infrequent in W-S texts, it seems evident that the name-element *Ælf-* was not given W-S form (cf. *ielf* elf). Undoubted *æ* forms are far rarer in eW-S than the corresponding unmutated *a*; but the relatively early W-S Ct. 20 (dated 847) has only one *ie* (*ǣwielme* d.s. source), against frequent *wæll* fountain.

(3) *ea* by breaking before χ occurred and could be subject to *i*-umlaut in all dialects, e.g. W-S *hliehhan* laugh, *nieht* night, *-mieht* might, *-slieht* blow, *wiexð* he grows, *sliehð* he strikes, *ðwiehð* he washes; nW-S *hlehhan,*[1] *neht*, &c., in so far as forms with mutated vowels occur.

(4) *ea* developed by palatal influence is subject to *i*-mutation in W-S and perhaps in North., see § 188. Examples are: W-S *ċiefes* concubine, *sċieppend* creator, *besċiered* deprived, *ġiest* guest (cf. *ġiesðhūs* CP 125, 8).

(5) *ēa* the OE development of Prim. Gmc. *au* is subject to *i*-umlaut in all dialects, e.g. W-S *bīeċnan* beckon, *bīeġan* bend, *ċīeġan* call, *ġīeman* care for, *hīeran* hear, *līefan* allow, *nīed* need; nW-S *bēċnan*, &c.

(6) *ēa* by breaking is subject to *i*-umlaut only in W-S *nīehst*(*a*) nearest.

(7) *ēa* due to palatal influence is subject to *i*-umlaut only in eW-S **ċīese*, cheese, inferred from lW-S *ċȳse*.

On the later history of W-S *ĭe* see §§ 300–1. In early texts the *i*-umlaut of *ēa* is sometimes written *ǣ*, instead of *ē*: the instances are chiefly in the early manuscripts of Bede, e.g. *Āeduini*, *Āedġils*, *Āenheri*, perhaps also *Bāeda*, LV *Bāede*.[2] On the spelling *ei* in BDS *nēidfaere*, see § 42. but cf. § 270.

The mutation of the rising diphthongs *eă* has been discussed above, §§ 177, 184.

§ 201. ĭo: the *i*-umlaut of these sounds in W-S is *ĭe*, but in nW-S they were not changed; examples are:

(1) *io* by breaking before *r* is frequently subject to *i*-umlaut in W-S forms, e.g. W-S *bierhto* brightness, *fierr* farther, *afierran* drive out, *hiertan* encourage, *ierre* anger, angry, *smierewað* they anoint (*CP* 69, 11), *-wierpð* he throws, *wiers*(*a*) worse, *-wierð* he becomes, *wierðe* worth, *hierde* shepherd. Kt. examples, except *stiorċe*, d.s. calf, *iorsienne* become angry, *KG*, all show the later change *io* > *eo* (§ 297), e.g. *weorðe* Ct. 41, and 3rd sg. pres. indic. *-weorpð*, *-weorð*, *ġeornð*, KG. In this position Angl. texts practically always have unbroken *i*: see § 154.3 and footnotes. When *w* precedes,

[1] This form occurs in poetry (e.g. *Brun.* 47, *Gu.* 1331), and is inferred for Kt. from 3rd sg. pres. indic. *hlihð* KG 1150, from **hlehð* with palatal umlaut (see § 306). Angl. had **hlæhan* (pres. indic. pl. *hlæhað* VP, *-eð*, *-as* Li.) with *-æh-* from *hlæhtor* (W-S *hleahtor*, see § 222).

[2] Occasional spellings with *ǣ* elsewhere are insignificant, e.g. *atǣfred* painted, *CP* 467, 19, and thirteen forms of *ċēġan*, *lēfan*, *nēdan* in *Ru.*[1]

Angl. texts have *y* (§ 149), to which Kt. *e* corresponds in *werstum*, *werðnes*, KG, so perhaps the forms with *eo* just quoted have analogical *eo* from unmutated forms.[1]

(2) *io* by breaking before χ is subject to *i*-umlaut in W-S, e.g. *fieht* he fights, *ġesiehð* he sees, *ġesiehð* vision; Kt. *-siohð* he sees. In Angl. the diphthong is removed by a later change, e.g. *ġesīð* he sees, *VP*, from **-siχiþ*.

(3) *īo* from Prim. Gmc. *iu* is subject to *i*-umlaut in W-S only, e.g. W-S *līehtan* lucere, *bīet* he commands, *ġesīene* manifest, *onsīen* face, *ġestīeran* steer, *underðīedan* subject, *elðīediġ* foreign, *ġetrīewe* true, *ðīestra* darkness; so with *īo* by early contraction, *frīend* friends, *fīend* enemies. Corresponding forms with *īo* are found in North. and Kt., e.g. Li. *onsīon*, *ellðīodiġ*, *ðīostro*, KG *-bīot*, *underðīod*, *ðrīostrie* (21 *tenebrosas*, read *ðīostriġe*). On the development of *īo* in Merc. see §§ 294–5.[2] Very early texts have a few instances of the spelling *īu* for *īo* (see § 275).

(4) *īo* by breaking before χ is subject to *i*-umlaut in W-S **līehtan* alleviate, inferred from lW-S *lȳhtan*, and in 2nd and 3rd sg. pres. indic. of contracted strong verbs of Class I, e.g. **þīehþ* he thrives, from *þēon*, but such forms all have *ī* or *y* in the recorded instances (cf. § 300).[3]

§ 202. ĕo: a small group of words (§ 124) suggest that the mutation of *eo* was *io*, for they appear in W-S always with *eo* (from older *io*, which they still have in North.), and never have *ie*. This confirms and supplements the view of Sievers[4] that when *ēo* was analogically introduced into a position in which it was followed by *i* or *i̯* in the next syllable, the product of *i*-umlaut was *īo* even in W-S, and that this *īo* became *ēo* later (see § 296). Hence we find many forms in W-S texts with *ĭo* (*ĕo*) where we should expect

[1] The equation W-S *ĭe* = nW-S *ĭo* > *ĕo* often causes false substitution of *ĕo* for W-S *ĭe*, the mutation of *ĕa*, in Boeth., e.g. *sċeoppend*, *ġehēordon*.

[2] Unexpectedly *VP* has a few cases of *īe*: *onsīen* face (always spelled with *ie*, over 60 instances) corresponding to North. *onsīon*, W-S *onsīen*, is regarded as a re-formation of *onsīon* on the model of other nouns formed from a verbal stem + *-en*, e.g. *lyġen*, *selen* (so Björkman, *ES* xlviii. 115–23). The forms *fīenda*, *-um*, g. and d.p. of *fīond* enemy, occur 9.4, 14, 26; 26.11. Flasdieck (*AB* xli. 287) regards these forms as from West Gmc. **fiandi-*, beside **fiundi-* (cf. § 120.3 c). But since g. and d.p. should have no umlaut at all it is perhaps better to regard the forms as due to the influence of the pres. part. ending.

[3] Kt. has *oferwrīhð* with intervention of a later change (§ 310). In Angl. forms the diphthong is eliminated by smoothing, VP *ġelīhtan*, Rit. *underlīhta*.

[4] *Vokalismus*, p. 44: he termed the process *Halb-umlaut*.

ĭe, because before umlaut took place, *ĭo* had been replaced by analogical *ĕo*. In eW-S we find always with *ĭo* or *ĕo*, *leornian* learn, (cf. § 154, footnote 3), *lēode* people, *ġeþēode* language, and variants of many of the *īe*-forms quoted above to illustrate the *i*-umlaut of *īo*, e.g. *elðēodiġ*, *stīoran*, *ġeortrēowan*. It is, of course, not possible to distinguish forms of this type from ones due to the influence of Merc. spelling.

§ 203. **Double Umlaut.** When in Prim. OE an accented vowel, capable of undergoing *i*-umlaut, was followed by *u* in a medial syllable, and then by *i* in the second syllable after the stress, both the accented vowel and the *u* suffered *i*-umlaut. The mutation of the medial -*u*- generally appears reduced to an indistinct vowel, written *e*, in historical forms. The majority of the instances had Prim. Gmc. *a* in the first syllable: this would become *æ* by the Anglo-Frisian fronting, but *a* would be restored before the following -*u*-. Hence the result of the double umlaut was that the succession *a*+*u*+*i* became *æ*+*y*+*i*. The only other successions certainly exemplified are *ā*+*u*+*i*, which became *ǣ*+*y*+*i*, *o*+*u*+*i*, which became *oe*+*y*+*i*, and *ŭ*+*u*+*i*, which became *y̆*+*y*+*i*. The examples are:

a+*u*+*i*: *gædeling* companion (OS *gaduling*), *æðeling* prince (ON *öðlungr*), *ætgædere* together, *æfest* envy (< **av-unsti*-), *fæsten* fasting (OS *fastunnia*), *lætemest* last (cf. Gothic superlatives in -*umists*), *Sæterndæġ* Saturday (< Lat. *Sāturni*+OE *dæġ*), and probably *hælfter* halter, *hærfest* harvest (< **haluftri*-, **haruvist*-), *ǣċe* eternal (< **ai̯uki*-, cf. § 237.1).[1]

[1] In the dialect of *VP*, the succession *a–u–i* would become *æ-u-i* by second fronting; *i*-umlaut would then give *e–u–i*. *VP* has accordingly *festen*, *efestiġ*, and ME evidence enables us to add -*gedere*.

For less certain instances of double umlaut, see O. Ritter, *Vermischte Beiträge*, pp. 168–73.

Not here belong words with the Prim. OE succession *a-a-i*. This simply gave *æ–æ–i* by Anglo-Frisian fronting, e.g. *mæġden* maiden (OHG *magatin*), *næċed* nakedness (Goth. *naqadei*), *æþele* noble (OS *aðali*), *hæleþ* man. The accented *æ* can then become *e* by second fronting, VP *eðele*. VP *æcesum*, d.p. axes, *Cp.* 703 -*æcus*, appear to have second fronting of *a*, not umlaut: cf. *Ld.* 197 -*acus*, North. *acas*, Ru.[1] *axe*. On WS *æx*, see § 341.

In *Cp.* 958 *aeðile*, RC n.p. *æþþilæ*, the formative suffix of **æþeli* has been replaced by that of **eþili* (cf. OS *aðali*, *eðili*); so in the corresponding name-element we have in early sources (*BH*, *LV*) *Aedil*-, *Edil*-, where the former has acquired the suffix of the latter. Later *Æþel*- becomes general, owing perhaps to the influence of the adj. *æþele*, though *Eþel*- remains frequent on coins.

ā+u+i: *ǣmyrġe*, *ǣmerġe*[1] embers (OHG *eimuria*), W-S *ǣrende* errand (OS *ārundi*; *ā* would be restored in W-S and then mutated, see § 162).

o+u+i: North. *oefest* haste, VP *oefestan*, W-S *efstan*, and other related words.

ŭ̄+u+i: *yfemest* upmost, *ȳmest* (< **uχumist-*, Gothic *auhumists*) upmost, *ȳtemest* outmost.

§ 204. **Apparent failure of *i*-umlaut.** The chief cases in which *i*-umlaut seems not to function where it might be expected can be classified as follows:

(1) Some words, which normally exhibit umlaut, sometimes fail to do so as the first elements of compounds, owing to early syncopation of the *-i-*, e.g. *Cantware* men of Kent (cf. *Cent*), names in *Sā-* (beside more frequent *Sǣ-*), *hup-* beside *hype-* (simplex always *hype*, hip), *ælþēodiġ* beside *elþēodiġ*, *sam-* half- (OHG *sāmi-*), *wūscbearn* adopted child (cf. *wȳsċan*).

(2) It is essential to *i*-umlaut that the *i* or *i̯*, which causes it, should be in an unstressed syllable. Hence medium stressed second elements of compounds do not usually cause it, e.g. *nēawist* neighbourhood, and many names such as LV *Ōsriċ*, *Waldfrith*, *Cūthuini*, *Ēaduini*, *Cūthġils*; yet with reduction of the stress of the second element, umlaut could take place, and hence BH *Ēduini*, *Hǣmġils*, and with double umlaut LV *Ēdgyth* (beside *Ēadgyð*). Similarly, we have *ānliċ*, *þusliċ*, *samtinġes*, *ārliċ* early, *ārmorgenliċ*, beside *ǣnliċ*, *þysliċ*, *sǣmtinġes*,[2] *ǣrmorgen*. Umlaut always appears in *hlǣfdiġe* and the forms *endlufon* (< **ānliv-*), *enwintre* quoted above, § 193.d.[3]

(3) Second elements of compounds, which normally received a

[1] Only in this word is the mutation of the medial *-u-* recorded as *y*.

[2] The practically universal spelling of the mutated form of this word with *æ* suggests a long vowel (cf. Luick, *Hist. Gramm.*, § 186, against most authorities), cf. § 193.d.

[3] A number of compounds exhibit umlaut of the first element, when only umlaut of the second would be expected: *ǣnīġe* one-eyed, beside *ānīġe*, *ǣnlīpe* single, beside *ānlīpe*, *endēmes* similarly, *ǣrlēst* cruelty, beside *ārlēast*. *Ǽrlēst* occurs once (*Met.* 9, 1), and is probably an error, the other words are perhaps influenced by *ǣniġ*, *ǣne*, *ǣnliċ*. The suffix *-nes*, *-nis* sometimes caused umlaut, no doubt when in the form *-nis*, and the umlauted vowel could be transferred to stand before *-nes*, e.g. W-S *untrymnes* weakness, *fyrhtnes* fear, VP, North. *untrymnis*, *fylnis* fullness, North. *fyrhtnis*, *towyrpnis* casting out, *dīopnis* mystery, Ru.[1] *untrymnis*, with which cf. *trum*, *forht*, *full*, *toworpnis*, *dēop*. The element *-wiht* is reduced so as to cause umlaut in North. *ǣniht* anything, *nǣniht* nothing (cf. W-S *nānwiht*).

suffix containing *-i-*, and hence should exhibit umlaut, sometimes appear without umlaut by the influence of the simplex, so *ānēage* one-eyed (beside *ānīġe*), *metelēast* lack of food (beside *-līest*, cf. *-lēas*), *fiþerfōte* four-footed (beside *-fēte*), *twībōte* with double compensation (beside *twībēte*).

(4) The medial *-i-* of the second class of weak verbs (*lufian*) is derived from *-ōi̯-* and hence does not cause umlaut of the root syllable.

(5) It has already been pointed out (§ 193.c), that some forms of *i*-declension nouns (*gasta*, *stapas*) occur without umlaut. This is due to partial substitution of endings of the *a-* and *ō-* declensions for the original ones at a date before umlaut. Fluctuation between mutated and unmutated vowels occurs similarly in *meaht*, *mieht* (Angl. *mæht* § 223, *meht* § 200.3), *sliht*, Angl. *-slæht* blow, while only unmutated forms occur from *ġesċeaft* creature, *Seaxe* Saxons. So with consonant stems there is fluctuation between *neaht*, *niht* (§ 628.3) and similarly with many old *-es*, *-os* stems (see § 636). The adjs. *sēfte* soft, *swēte* sweet, *myrġe* merry, *enġe* narrow, *clǣne* clean, have advs. *sōfte*, *swōte*, *murge*, *ange*, *clāne* (beside *clǣne*), on which see Ross in *Trans. Philological Soc.*, 1952, pp. 131 ff.

(6) The suffixes *-ing* (patronymic), *-isċ*, *-iht*, *-en* (< *-īn*, of material), are frequently preceded by unmutated vowels, due either to the influence of the simplex, or to the word having been formed after the period of umlaut, e.g. *Bronding*, *eorlisċ* noble, *folcisċ* popular, *stāniht* stony, beside *stǣniht*, *þorniht* thorny, beside *þyrniht*, *lēaden* of lead (but *gylden* of gold, &c.). All forms in *-inċel* lack umlaut, e.g. *hūsinċel* little house, *stāninċel* little stone.[1]

(7) The suffix *-iġ* represents Prim. OE *-æġ* (> *-eġ*, e.g. CH *hāleġ*) and *-īġ*, cf. § 376. Thus there was fluctuation between mutated and unmutated vowels before *-iġ*; the influence of the simplex would no doubt often help the unmutated form to prevail. Examples are *huniġ* honey, *mōdiġ* brave, *hāliġ* holy, beside North. *hǣliġ*, *meahtiġ* mighty, beside *mihtiġ*, *moniġ* many, beside North. *meniġ* (cf. § 193.d), *stāniġ* stony, beside *stǣniġ*, *þurstiġ* thirsty, beside *þyrstiġ*.

(8) The suffixes *-el*, *-er*, *-en*, *-ing* (abstract) are partly from Prim. Gmc. *-il*, &c. (e.g. *yfel* evil), but are also due to Prim. OE formation of parasite vowels (e.g. *seġel* sail, *æcer* field, *swefen* dream), and to substitution for *-ol*, *-or*, *-on*, *-ung* (e.g. *tungel**, *wunder*

[1] On **wīlinċel*, little slave, see *ES* xxxii. 352–4.

wonder, *bēacen* beacon, *leorning* learning, *eallinga* entirely). Naturally in the latter two cases there is no umlaut. More usual, however, is the extension of suffixes which would not cause umlaut to stand after umlauted vowels, e.g. *hetol* hateful, *dīegol* secret, *eosol* ass (cf. § 211). The suffix *-en* also represents Prim. OE *-æn* (e.g. CH *hefaen-* heaven-, Ep. *ġibaen* given): this is the origin of the ending of the strong passive participle, which hence normally has no umlaut. The form *-in* also occurred as a passive participle ending, and caused umlaut when original (Ep. *-sleġinum*, North. *woerpen*, &c.), but it also occurs without causing umlaut, when it is merely substituted for *-æn* (e.g. Ep. *binumini*).

(9) The pronominal ending *-iċ* does not cause umlaut in extant forms (*ūsiċ*, *ēowiċ*).

G. Back Mutation

§ 205. At the close of the prehistoric period of OE an extensive group of changes occurred, whereby the short front vowels, *æ*, *e*, *i*, were diphthongized to *ea* (= *æa*), *eo*, *io*, when a back vowel stood in the following syllable. In W-S these changes take place only when the consonant intervening between the vowel affected, and the back vowel which causes the change, is a labial or liquid (*f*, *p*, *w*, *m*, *l*, *r*). In Anglian they take place before all consonants except perhaps the back ones (*c*, *g*),[1] which were about to cause the monophthongization of all diphthongs standing before them (see H, below). In Kentish they could take place before any consonant. Before geminates and consonant groups they are everywhere rare. The unaccented back vowels which occasion the changes are Prim. OE *u* and *a*. The former appears in historical forms as *u* or *o* (e.g. *sċipu* or *sċipo*, *ridon* from early *ridun*), and may be reduced to *e* in medial syllables (e.g. *heoretas*, *stapelian*, cf. *heorot*, *stapol*); the latter appears in historical forms as *a* (e.g. *guma*, g.s. *suna*, g.p. *stāna*, 3rd sg. pres. indic. *leofaþ*). Back Umlaut or Mutation is accordingly a general term to include *u*-umlaut and *a*-umlaut.[2] In general *u*-umlaut functions more regularly than *a*-umlaut. The affinity of these changes with breaking (whereby also *æ*, *e*, *i* become *ea*, *eo*, *io*) is obvious. Furthermore, when

[1] See, however, § 247 below.

[2] *a*-umlaut is often called *o*/*a*-umlaut because the unaccented *a* which causes it was a shortening of *ō* (cf. § 355), and may have been still in the stage *o* when it caused diphthongization of preceding vowels.

breaking was taking place, *u̯i-* and *u̯e-* in certain cases developed to *u̯u-* and *u̯o-* instead of to *u̯io-* and *u̯eo-* (§§ 147, 149), and this recurred in the operation of back umlaut. The change of *u̯i-* and *u̯e-* to *u̯u-* and *u̯o-* when a back vowel stood in the next syllable may be termed Combinative Back Umlaut.

§ 206.[1] *æ* does not normally appear before a back vowel of the following syllable, as *a* was restored in that position (see § 157). In the Merc. dialect of *VP*, however, where the second fronting affected *a*, many forms have *æ* before a back vowel of the following syllable, and this *æ* was preserved before *c* and *g* (see § 164). On the other hand, the *æ* becomes *ea* by back umlaut before all other consonants, e.g. *-wearan* inhabitants, *earun* are, *feasum* d.p. fringes, *creatum* d.p. chariots, *featu* vessels, *geatu* gates, *eadesan* d.s. adze, *fearu* I go, *heafuces* g.s. hawk, *ġehleadað* ye draw (water), *steaðul* foundation, *feadur* g.s. father (hence d.p. *feadrum*), *ceafur-tūn* hall, *ġedeafenað* is fitting, and all forms of many verbs of the second weak class,[2] such as *gleadian* make glad, *þeafian* need, *spearian* spare, *hreaþian* hasten, *leatian* be slow; and in some instances before geminates and groups, e.g. *leappan* d.s. skirt, *eappul-* apple, *hneappian* sleep, *-sċeattum* d.p. treasures (hence sg. *-sċeat*), *gneat* gnat (after pl. forms), *eascan* a.s. ashes (beside *esċan*, after n.s. **esċe*), *gongeweafran* n.p. spiders (hence n.s. *-weafre*).[3]

§ 207. Outside the dialect of *VP* the second fronting of *a* to *æ* was rare, and back mutation of the latter was hence seldom possible. The only considerable group of forms with second fronting of *a* is seen in the early glossaries, e.g. Ep. *baeso* purple, *haegu-* enclosure, *sċaedu-* shadow, *claedur* rattle, *-laeppan* skirts.[4] Ep. has back umlaut of this *æ* in *sċeadu* shadow, *-sċeada* criminal ($d = ð$) and *sċeaba* plane, and in *Cp.* forms with *ea* are much more frequent,[5] and are found even before *c* and *g*, e.g. *-ðeaca* roof, *heago-* enclosure, *reagu-* lichen, *onseacan* deny, *weagat* he wags. There are also a few such forms in ninth-century Kentish:

[1] With reference to the following sections, it should be noted that declensional forms of pronouns showing back umlaut (e.g. *hiora, ðeara, ðiossum*) are excluded from the examples, as they are given fully in Chapter XV.

[2] Such verbs have very freely *-ea-* in the forms with *-i-* (e.g. sg. pres. subj. *gleadie* 103, 15) from the many forms with *-a-* and *-o-* (e.g. *spearað* 71, 13).

[3] ME *weater* water (Katherine Group) suggests OE n.p. **weatru*. *VP*, Hy. 13, 7, *ġegadrades* is an error: cf. *Cp.* 512 *ġegaedradon*.

[4] *-hebuc* 497 is no doubt an error for *-haebuc* (so *Erf.*).

[5] In *geaduling* Cp. 914, 1496, we appear to have back umlaut of the *æ* of *gædeling* (§ 203), following formation of a mixed form **gæduling*.

many forms of *þeafian*, Cts. 41 and 42, *Reacoluensae* adj. of Reculver, Ct. 35, *teapera*, g.p. tapers, Ct. 41, *earan* are, Cts. 34 and 58, and the names *Ealawynne*, Ct. 39, *Eacca* Ct. 44. Against these, however, must be set similar forms with *a*, partly in the same words, *ġeðafie*, Ct. 40, *aloð*, Cts. 37 and 41, *Acca*, Ct. 44, and names in *Bada-*, Cts. 35 and 36. Accordingly, the *ea* forms are to be regarded as illustrating the influence of Merc. scribal practice in Kt., rather than an actual sound-change of the dialect. Kentish scribes advanced slowly towards the phonetic expression of their dialect. In other texts we may notice the name-elements *Heaðu-*, *Beadu-*, in *LV*; they are no doubt due to the use of poetical forms, ultimately derived from the Mercian area, as name-elements. *Heaðu-* occurs also in *Gn.* (a Merc. MS.) and Ct. 12 (Merc.), and *Beadu-* in MS. Cott. Tib. C ii of *BH*.[1] Ct. 48 (Merc.) has *hiobbanne*,[2] have, and Ru.[1] *ondsweorede*.[3] Before back consonants we have *lund-leogan* kidneys, *LG* 51, 62, while *haga* and its compounds often have *ea*: *Ru.*[1] 21, 33, *LG* 34, in addition to forms from *Cp.* quoted above. Of later Merc. texts, *RG* has *helwearum*, St. Chad *andswearede*, *eadusan*, *earun*. Instances of back umlaut of *æ* are practically unknown in W-S texts[4] but they are quite a feature of the W-S transcripts of OE poems: *Beow.* alone has *beadu- heaþu-*, *eafora*, *eafoð*, *eatol*, *heafo*, *ġeheaðerod*, *heafola*.

§ 208. Forms in which the syllabic succession, accented *æ*+back vowel, required to produce back umlaut of *æ*, arose without the operation of second fronting are North. *leassa* less (< *lǣssa* with early shortening), *meassa* mass (< *mæsse*, a form arising from the transference of Kt. *messe* into other dialects, where *æ* usually corresponded to Kt. *e*), *geadriġa* gather (< **gædor-*,[5] with the vowel of *-gædre*, § 203), W-S *ealu* ale (< **ælu*, with vowel of inflected **ælæþ-*), *cearu* care (< **cæru* with vowel of infl. **ċære* > *ċeare*).[6]

§ 209. On the other hand, W-S and North. forms with *ea* for *a* after a palatal (e.g. *sċeacan*) are otherwise explained (§ 179); while in all

[1] *BH* has also the names *Peada*, *Eafa*, *Eabae*, all of persons of Merc. birth, but their etymology is uncertain. Elsewhere *Eafe*, *Eafing* are found in Merc. charters, but *Eafa* is more widely spread.

[2] The form is an error due to the following *siollanne*.

[3] *teoma*, Ru.[1] 21, 5, is doubtfully from *tam* or *tēam*.

[4] e.g. *ġeleaþade* past part. pl. invited, *PC* 449; W-S *meatte*, *-a*, mat, beside Cp. *matte* (< Lat. *matta*); *geaflum* d.p. forks, Thorpe's *Ælfric* i. 430.

[5] *ġegederad*, KG 831, shows this form with the vowel *æ* changed to *e* by normal Kt. development.

[6] *ġefeastnadon* Li., *ġifeasta* Rit., appear to be from *ġifæst(niġ)a* with back umlaut of analogically restored *æ* (§ 194). *æ* forms are usual in North. texts in these and related words, except for a few instances of *-feast* in compounds: here the back umlaut no doubt arose in forms like **fæstum* with analogical *æ* from *fæst*.

dialects, forms where *ea* is followed by *l* or *r*+*u* have the diphthong from inflected forms where it developed by breaking (e.g. *bealu*, *nearu* owing to *bealw-*, *nearw-*).

§ 210. The treatment of *e* differs greatly in different areas.

(1) In W-S *u*-umlaut is general before labials and liquids, e.g. *heofon* heaven, *eofor* boar, *Eoforwiċ* York, *beofor* beaver, *heorot* hart, but also with suffix containing front vowel, *hefen*, *befer*, and hence with suffix mixture *hefon*, *befor*, *efor*, *Eforwiċ*. Analogical removal is frequent, e.g. *speru* spear, *nefum* d.p. nephews, after infl. *spere*, n.s. *nefa*. After *u̯*, combinative back umlaut generally but not always intervened, e.g. *woruld* world, *swostor*[1] sister, *swoloþ* heat, all beside forms with *eo*; but always *weorod* troop (or *werod*, after *wered*), and similarly *weorod*, *werod*, *wered* sweet, *weolor* lip (or *welor-*, after *weler*). *a*-umlaut and combinative *a*-umlaut are generally absent,[2] e.g. *fela* many, *helan* conceal, *beran* bear, *nefa* nephew, *sefa* mind, *weras* men, *wela* wealth.

(2) In Angl. both *u-* and *a*-umlaut of *e* are general before all consonants except *c* and *g*. In the earliest texts, however, the changes are not yet always indicated in spelling, e.g. CH *metudaes* g.s. creator, but RC *heafunæs* g.s. heaven, LR *ġoelu* yellow (read *ġeolu*). *BH* has always *Herut-* in compounds in early manuscripts, except Cott. Tib. C ii, which has also *Heorut-*. The latter has also *Ċeortesēi*, against *Ċerotaes-* of the other early manuscripts. *LV* has *Eofor-*, but also *Heruuald* 162.[3] *Ep.* has only one instance of back umlaut (*ġeolu* 1064), elsewhere *e* remains, e.g. *felo-* much-, *ebor-* boar-, *teru* tar, *-fetor* fetter, *helostr* concealment, but in *Cp.* the *eo* spellings prevail in these and similar words. In the chief later Angl. texts, *VP*, *Ru.*[1], *Li.*, *Rit.*, *Ru.*[2], the back umlaut of *e* is extensively developed; examples are VP *oferġeotul* forgetful, *-cweodulnisse* a.s. utterance, *feoður-* four-, *weorud* troop, *weolure* n.p. lips, *eofor-* boar, *weoruld* world (also *weruld*), *heorut* hart, *heofen* heaven, *weolan* n.p. wealth, *ġeofu* gift, *ġebeodu* prayers, *weoras* men, and many

[1] The preceding *u̯* apparently helps combinative back umlaut or, if this failed, back umlaut to take place in this word, although the consonant group *st* would not normally permit it. This, however, does not apply in the case of *ġeocsa*, *ġeocsung* sobbing, which appears to have back umlaut (*Ep.* 958 *iesca*), but can hardly be the W-S development, which is represented by *ġihsa* < **ġiehsa* (§ 185).

[2] *PC* 530 has *feala*, 830 *Feoloġid*; CP *heolað* 449, 5, and *o* is sometimes added to such forms above the line in the Hatton MS.

[3] Unless this is *Her-wald*; cf. *Herred* three times in the same text.

forms of strong verbs of Classes IV and V, as ***beorað***, ***eotað***, ***onġeotað***, ***cweoðað***, ***aġeofað***, ***treodað***, ***meotu***. A feature of the dialect of *VP* is the very extensive analogical extension of *eo* to positions before back consonants, so that we have ***spreocu***, ***wreocu***, ***-breocu***, and many other forms of these verbs, including ones where the *eo* is extended to forms where no back vowel follows, e.g. ***spreocende***. So we have frequently ***ġespreocu*** n.p. talks, but only once ***ġesprecu***. On the other hand, ***wegas***, ***wegum***, are frequent beside three times ***weagas***, once ***weogum***. Ru.[1] has frequent forms with back umlaut of *e*, e.g. ***feola***, ***heofun***, ***weoruld***, ***ġeofu*** gift, ***pleagade***,[1] ***ġebeodum***; but in the present system of strong verbs of Classes IV and V (e.g. ***beoran***, ***-ġeofan***, ***-ġeota***) both *e* and *eo* forms are used, and the former only in ***etan***, ***wesa***. Otherwise there are only a few sporadic *e* forms, e.g. ***weras***, ***hefonum***, ***setulas*** (from sg. ***sætil***). Before a back consonant *eo* appears in ***spreocaþ*** 12, 34, ***spreocan*** 6, 7, beside many forms of the verb with *e*, and in ***weogas*** frequently. The North. forms resemble the Merc. ones, apart from the greater frequence of confusion of the graphs *eo* and *ea*. Examples of forms will be found below, §278.b. As in *Ru.*[1], *e* forms are frequent in strong verbs of Classes IV and V, and they are also found in nouns, e.g. Li. ***ġefo***, ***weras***, ***hefon***.[2] Combinative *u*-umlaut intervenes in Li., Rit. ***woruld***, Li. ***worud***.[3] Combinative *a*-umlaut is limited to a few North. forms, especially ***wosa*** be (W-S ***wesan***), ***cuoða*** say (*Li.*), beside ***cweoða***, ***cweða*** (Ru.[2]), ***cuoeða*** (Li., Rit.).[4]

(3) In Kt. back umlaut is found before all consonants, and hence we find in the ninth-century charters not only ***-ġeofan*** give,

[1] Assuming, in view of the great rarity of back umlaut of *æ* in the text, that the form corresponds to W-S ***plegode***, not to VP ****plægade***; but perhaps, in view of pl. ***plagadun***, West Gmc. *a* should be assumed in all *Ru.*[1] forms of the word, and another case of back umlaut of *æ* before a back consonant recorded.

[2] *Eofolsiġa*, blaspheme, and related words have back umlaut in *Ru.*[2], but not in *Li.*, which has *ebolsiġa*, &c. *Ru.*[1] also has no back umlaut in these words.

[3] The word 'sister' does not have umlaut in North.: Li. *suoester*, *soester*, Ru.[2] *swester*. In Merc. *VP* lacks the word, *Ru.*[1] has *swæster* (§ 328), but also *swuster*, which points to combinative back umlaut of *swist-*, beside the usual *swest-*: in W-S *swiostor* occurs once, Oros. 126, 6, beside usual *sweostor*, *swostor*, and may be significant, as *swustor* is recorded in lW-S.

[4] Developments of *we-* to *wa-* and *wæ-* in positions where back umlaut might be expected occur in *Li.* and *Rit.* in *waras* men (both), *wæras* (Li.); various forms of *wala* wealth (both), *wæla* (Li.), and *wæliġ* wealthy (*Li.*, with vowel from noun); *ualerum* and *uælerum* d.p. lips (*Rit.*). *Li.* has also (in various inflexions) *wearas*, *weras*, *weala*, *wealiġ*, *weliġ*. The cause of the *wa-*, *wæ-* forms is uncertain.

beġeotan obtain, *feola* many, *weorolde* world,[1] but also *reogol-* rule (< **rĕgula*), *forespreoca* advocate. In *KG* there occur *weolan* wealth, and derivatives, *neofan* nephews, *sweostor* sister, *weogas* ways, and with Kt. *io* for *eo*, *ġiofa*, n.p. gifts, *onġiotað* imper. understand. But in *KG* a tendency to analogical removal of the umlaut is to be observed: *etað*, *ġefol*, *setol*, *forberan*; and, without clear reason, *tela*, well.

§ 211. All dialects provide instances of the back umlaut of an *e* produced by *i*-umlaut. After the latter change took place, a back vowel might be placed in the syllable after the *e* by suffix transference, and cause back umlaut. Examples are *eosol* ass (beside *esol*) for **esel* (cf. § 518), and similarly *meowle* maiden (Goth. *mawilo*), *eowu* ewe for *ewe* (< Prim. Gmc. **aui̯*), Cp. *freomo* benefit (usually *fremu*),[2] *speoru* spear, and before a geminate North. *seolla*, *sealla* give,[3] beside *sella*. Also, some verbs pass into the second weak conjugation from the first, and there acquire back umlaut of an *e* produced by the -*i*-suffix of the first conjugation, e.g. the forms recorded in lW-S *freomian* (with *eo* from forms where a back vowel followed) *underwreoðod*, *streowode* for *e*W-S *fremman* do, *underwreðed* supported, *strewede* he strewed; also KG -*wreoðað* he supports.

§ 212. The back umlaut of *i* presents a simpler picture than that of *e*, for *u*-umlaut and *a*-umlaut are equally frequent, and both are common to all dialects. They are, however, limited by the following consonant, and do not appear before back consonants in Angl. or before any consonants except liquids and labials in W-S. Analogical extension of unmutated *i* is very frequent, especially in W-S. In the earliest texts the state of development recalls that of the back umlaut of *e*: *Ep.* retains *i*, e.g. *sifun-* seven, *hnitu* nit, *unlidouuāc* inflexible, *nihol* prostrate, but while *Cp.* has *i* occasionally (e.g. *tigule* tile, *pisan-* peas, *wituma* dowry, *sibun-*, *hnitu*), it has prevailingly *io*, and some cases of *eo* (see § 294). In LV *Friðu-* and *Frioðu-* both appear.

§ 213. In considering the forms of the chief later monuments, it should be noted that *io* has become *eo*, and is usually so written

[1] Also with Kt. *ia* for *eo* (§ 297), *wiaralde*, -*ġiaban*, *hiabenliċe*.

[2] In VP *freamsum* benign, for W-S *fremsum*, we appear to have the vowel of a form **freamu*, in which the *i*-mutation of West Gmc. *a* before a nasal consonant has undergone back umlaut, while in the stage *æ* (§ 193.d; cf. Flasdieck, *AB* xli. 283).

[3] So *siollanne* Ct. 48 (Merc.).

in W-S and Merc. Forms recorded in eW-S with *io* are *siolufres*[1] g.s. silver, *mioloc* milk (§ 628.5, footnote), *tiola* well (< **tila* for *tela*, with the vowel of *til*), forms and derivatives of *tiolian* strive for, and of *cliopian* call, *liomu* limbs, *siofan* seven, *liofað* he lives; with *eo* only, *eorþbeofung* earthquake. But we find also *silofr*, *clipian*, *tilian*, *limu*, *lifað*, and in lW-S *-bifung*; and with *i* only *clifu* cliffs, *sċipu* ships, *niman* take (all forms), *hnipode* he drooped, and past plural of strong verbs of Class I, *drifon* they drove, *ripon* they reaped.

§ 214. The dialect of *VP* is particularly rich in examples, and as in the case of back umlaut of *e*, it also analogically extends the diphthongal forms to positions before back consonants. Examples are *liomu*, *sċeopu*, *ġewreotum* d.p. writings, *cleopiu* I call (and other forms and derivatives), *teolung* zeal, *leofað*, *reopað* they reap (from *ripan*, see § 739), *nioman*, *nioðerra* lower, and past plural of strong verbs of Class I, *biodun*, *-reosun*, *-smeotun*, *weotun* (pret.-pres.), and after them *-steogun*, *-sweocun*.[2] *Ru.*[1] offers similar forms, but analogical removal of the diphthong is frequent (e.g. *ġewritu* beside *ġewriotu*), and *i* appears exclusively in the past plural of Class I strong verbs (e.g. *ġegripon*), except *wriogan* once, *wreogan* twice.

§ 215. While North. forms resemble Merc. forms, it may be observed that, while in *Rit.* and *Ru.*[2] the past plural of strong verbs of Class I has *io*, in *Li.* the diphthong is very often removed. In North. the Merc. tendency to extend diphthongs to positions before gutturals is absent, e.g. *-stigun*, *wrigun*.

§ 216. In the ninth-century Kt. charters the relevant forms are *niomanne*, *ġewriota*, *bewiotiġe* pres. subj. look after, and in a medial syllable *ġeornliocar*.[3] To these *-stiogol* stile, Ct. 29 (W-S–Kt.), may be added. *KG* have many forms in which back umlaut of *i* is lacking: *ġewiton* they went, *ofsticoð* he stabs, *ficol* fickle, *ġewita*

[1] eWS spellings (not in themselves conclusive, § 296) and the lWS development (§ 299.c) point to the back umlaut of *i* in this word; cf. unmutated *silofr*, CP 368, 20. Li. *seulfres*, Rit. *seolferes*, *seolfre* point to back umlaut of *e*. VP *seolfur* is inconclusive (§ 294). *e* was perhaps proper to the noun (cf. OFris. *selover*), *i* to the adj., OE *silfren*, *seolfren* < **seluvrīna-* (§ 331.3, footnote 3), and to the verb, *VP* pass. part. pl. *besi(l)frede*. Oros. past and pass. part. pl. *ofersylefrede* appears influenced by *sylofr*, CP 368, 6 (Junius' transcript), in which the development described § 299.c was early; Ru.[1] *sylfur* is influenced by a similar W-S form.

[2] The only Class I strong past lacking back umlaut in *VP* is *edwiton* they reproached (three times).

[3] Here the *i* is due to shortening of *ī* in medium stress.

witness, *cwidas* sayings, *witodliċe* indeed; but *clepað* he calls, may be an error for *cleopað*.

§ 217. Back umlaut of *i* before geminates occurs in a scattered group of forms. To W-S *siððan* (also *sie-*, *sy-*, § 299.c), corresponds Kt. *sioððan*, *seoððan* (Ct. 41, *KG*), VP *seoðan*, Ru.[1] *seoþþan*;[1] also Li., Ru.[2] *soððа* (beside Li. *siðða*) points to **sioðða* (§ 302). *Ru.*[2] has *ionna* womb, *bionna* within, *ionnað* womb. Before groups, the back umlaut of *i* appears in *siondon*, *seondan* they are, (Cts. 37, 45) for W-S *sindon*, *siendon*; Li. *ġioster-* yesterday;[2] *Ru.*[2] and Li. *bihionda* behind (*Li.* also *bihianda*).

§ 218. Combinative back umlaut generally intervenes in the case of *u*-umlaut of *i*, and has already taken place in the oldest texts, e.g. BH *Derauuda* d.s. (after *-wudu*), Ep. *uudu-* wood, Cp. *-cudu* cud,[3] although *Ep.* has some forms without the change, e.g. *uuidu-*, *uuiloc-*, *-quidu*, and *Cp.* has also forms which show that *i* could escape combinative *u*-umlaut, and then undergo normal *u*-umlaut, e.g. *wioloc*, *seotol* evident (770, read *sweotol*). In W-S many forms have combinative *u*-umlaut of *i*, and the change seems not to be limited, like *u*-umlaut, to positions before liquids and labials, e.g. *wudu* wood, *wuduwe* widow, *wucu* week, *swutol* evident, *cwudu* cud, *swugian* be silent, (*w*)*uton* let us; but there occur also in many cases forms with *io* (*eo*) or *i*, e.g. *weoduwe*, *widuwe*, *wicu*, *cwicu*, *swiotol*, *sweotol*, *cweodu*, *swigian*, and always *swiocol*, *swicol* treacherous, *wioton*, *witon* they know, *swicon* they deserted. Practically the same applies to all the dialects, except that *i* remains unchanged before *c*, *g*, in Angl. (e.g. *cwicu*, *wicu*, *twigu* twig, *swigian*), apart from the analogical forms, mostly in *VP*, mentioned in § 214. The material offered by the chief texts is: VP *wudu*, but *sweotulliċe*, *widwe*, *weotun*; Ru.[1] *wutu* let us, *wutan* we, ye know, but *widuwana* g.p. widows; North. *wutun* let us, *wuton* they know, *uutodliċe* indeed (also with *eo*, *io*, *i*), *-uutol* wise, *uudu* (and hence *uuda*), but *widwe*, *ġiswiopornisse* a.s. cunningness (also with *i*); KG *wuton* let us, but *witodliċe*.

§ 219. Combinative *a*-umlaut of *i* is practically limited to various forms of *wuta*, know, and *wuta* wise man, in North. W-S has very rare instances, *wutan* wise men, *CP* 2, 2, *ġewuta* witness, id.

[1] Here also the *i* is due to shortening.

[2] But Ru.[2] *ġestor-*, VP *ġeostran*, W-S *ġierstan-* point to *-e-* as the original vowel.

[3] In *huītcudu* mastic.

145, 13; 449, 1. All these forms could be regarded as having the vowel of *wuton*. W-S and *VP* extend the vowel of *wudu* to infl. *wuda*, but Kt. has *wiada, weada* (Cts. 28 and 39).

§ 220. In pure W-S, where *e* became *ie* after an initial palatal, it seems that this *ie* underwent back umlaut to *io*: the only such form recorded with *io* is *ġiofol* generous, but we can infer similar eW-S forms from the later forms *ġeofu* gift (beside *ġiefu*), *ġeolu* yellow, *ġeoloca* yolk, *ġeolstr* pus,[1] *ċeorian* murmur, *ċeole* throat (after infl. *ċeolan*). *Onġiotan*, however, is not pure W-S (see § 221), as the dialect does not admit back umlaut before *t*.

§ 221. It may be observed, with general reference to the back umlaut of *e* and *i*, that many forms which are Angl. or Kt. rather than W-S appear in the extant manuscripts of W-S texts. It is evident from a number of forms quoted above, that if combinative back umlaut of *i* failed, ordinary *u*-umlaut could take place after *u̯* even before dentals and back consonants (*weoduwe, swiotol, swiocol*).[2] But there are many cases where there is no initial *u̯* to explain back umlaut before an unusual consonant, e.g. *siodo* custom, *-tiogoða* -tieth (in numerals), *nioðor* down, *nioðemest* lowest, *behionan* on this side of, and with original *e*, *onġeotan, onġiotan*.[3] In other forms, though *u̯* precedes, only the conditions of *a*-umlaut exist, e.g. *wiotan* wise men, *ġewiota* witness.

H. Smoothing

§ 222. One of the most marked characteristics of the Anglian dialects developed at the end of the prehistoric period. The back consonants *c*, *ʒ*, *χ* would no longer tolerate diphthongs of the usual OE type (accented front+unaccented back vowel) before them, and such diphthongs accordingly rejected their second elements when these consonants followed, either directly, or with an intervening *r* or *l*, so that *ĕa* (= *ǣ̆a*), *ĕo*, *ĭo* became respectively *ǣ̆*, *ĕ*, *ĭ*. This process is termed smoothing. Very soon a further change took place: *æ*, produced by smoothing, became *e* before *r* or *l* plus back consonant, but remained directly before a back consonant, while *ǣ*, produced by smoothing, became *ē* everywhere. Hence we find, for example, in *VP* the forms *mæht* might, *merg*

[1] Cp. *ġelostr*.
[2] *Wiogoraċeaster* Worcester, might be added.
[3] *hweogol* wheel, perhaps has *ēo* from *hwēol*.

marrow, *feh* money, *werc* work, *ġesihð* sight, *birhtu*[1] brightness, *hēh* high, *nēh* (< **nēoh*) near, *betwīh* between, corresponding to W-S *meaht*, *mearg*, *feoh*, *weorc*, *ġesiehþ*, *bierhtu*, *hēah*, *nēah*, *betwīoh*.

§ 223. It will now be necessary to examine the smoothing of each diphthong as reflected in the chief Anglian texts. The short diphthong *ea* produced by breaking is smoothed to *æ* before *χ* in the oldest glossaries, e.g. Cp. *aex* axle, *aehtað* he considers, *saex* knife, *waexit* he grows. Beside *naeht-* (four times) we have *neht-* (once) in *Cp.*, the former due to smoothing, the latter to *i*-umlaut (cf. § 204.5). *Ep.* has similar forms, except for one unsmoothed diphthong (*leax* salmon, 555), and *brectme* d.s. noise, 928 (Cp. *braechtme*). Before *rh*, *rc*, *rg*, these texts have as a rule *æ*, e.g. Cp. *faerh* pig, *haerg* shrine, *spærca* spark, *waerg-* criminal. Unsmoothed *ea* occurs in Cp. *mearh* horse, Ep. *mearc* mark (547, cf. 227), and *e* appears already in Cp. *merc-* mark, *merg* marrow. In VP *æ* is found practically always before *h*, e.g. *ġefaeh* he rejoiced, *ġesaeh* he saw, *maehte* he might, *-saex* knife, *wæx* wax, *hlæhað* they laugh, *-aehtatiġes*, g.s. eighty. In the past and pass. part. of *aweċċan* wake, *biðeċċan* cover, and various compounds of *reċċan* direct, we find eighteen instances of *e* against four of *æ* (e.g. prevailingly *-rehte*, not *ræhte*). Here the vowel of the infinitive has been extended to the past system, especially as these and similar verbs have frequently *e* instead of *ea* in W-S in the corresponding forms.[2] Otherwise *e* is found once only, *wex*, wax, 96.5, except in words in which *æ* and *e* interchange as respectively the smoothing and the *i*-umlaut of *ea*: *naeht*, *maeht*, *maehtig*, and *ġeðaeht* thought. Before *r* followed by *c* or *g*,[3] *VP* has always *e*, e.g. *merg-*, *werg-*, *herg*, *ġesnerc* it shrivelled. *Ru.*[1] has similar forms, e.g. *sæh*, *mæhton*, *waexaþ* they grow, *slæhþ* he strikes, *æchir* ear (of corn), *mæht*, *ġemerkade* he marked. Corresponding to the *VP* variation *næht*, *neht*, we find in Ru.[1] *næht*, *niht*, the latter being due to a later change (see § 308). *Ru.*[1] also has the forms *wehton*, *ġereht*, due to the *e* of the infinitive. In this text, however, there are many *e* spellings which cannot be so explained, e.g. *wexan* grow, *exlan* shoulders, *ġepehtunge* a.s. consultation, *ehtu* I consider, and, unless it be regarded as having mutation (against usual Anglian practice) *wexeþ* he grows.[4]

§ 224. In North., smoothing of *ea* before final *-χs* was frequently followed by a change of *æ* to *e* caused by the final consonant group, which was becoming palatalized. Hence *BH* has *Sex-* more frequently

[1] But see above, § 154.3 and footnotes, on *i* before *r*+cons. in Angl.

[2] For the forms of other texts see § 753.9b.1.

[3] There happens to be no example in the text with *rh*.

[4] *Ru.*[1] frequently has *ea* in *ġeseah*, a southern form fossilized in the spelling, beside (*ġe*)*sæh*, and once *ġeseh* (Mk. 1, 10, probably with *ē* from the pl.).

than *Sæx-* in names in most early manuscripts, Moore having *Sex-* five times, *Saex-* once. *LV* similarly has *Fexstan*. The only other examples of smoothed *ea* in early North. are *maecti* a.p. powers, *CH* (so Moore, but Leningrad *mehti* with umlaut), and *aerig-* arrow- *LV*, where the expected change of *æ* to *e* before *rχ* is prevented by the division of the consonant group by a parasite vowel. The later North. texts have similar forms to *VP* and *Ru.*[1]: before *χ* we have practically always *æ*, and before *r* followed by a back consonant *e*: e.g. Li. *æhto* eight, *mæhton* they might, *fæx* hair, *-sæh* he saw, *berg* pig, *mercung* marking, to which the forms in *Ru.*[2] and *Rit.* correspond. *Ru.*[2], however, has the further change of *æ* to *e* before *χs* which appears in *BH* and *LV*: the examples are *wex-* wax, and eight forms of *wexan* grow. In North., as in *VP* and *Ru.*[1], we find past tenses like *wehte*, due to the infinitive, and although *næht* and *mæht* have very few forms with *e*, the alternation of *æ* due to smoothing and *e* due to *i*-umlaut is found in *æhher*, *eher*, ear of corn, *tehher*, *tæher*, tear.

§ 225. The smoothing of *ēa* has still not taken place in a number of forms preserved in Ep.: *lēag* lye, *flēah* flea, *ġēacaes-* g.s. cuckoo, *tēac* tye, and in the second element of compounds, *-bēacn* beacon, *-bēag* ring, *-lēac* leek. Smoothing to *ǣ* appears in *ǣc* also, *-bǣcon* beacon, *lǣc* leek, and the further stage *ē* in *ēgan* eyes. *Cp.* has smoothing always, except *ġēac*, 965, most forms having *ǣ*, but *ē* also occurring in a few instances: *-leec*, *-bēcn* (also *-bēnc*), *ēgan*. The early North. texts have mostly the final stage *ē*: BC *-bēcn*, LR *hēh-* high, *ðēh* although. *BC* has (if correctly read) one *ea* spelling, *ēac* also. *BH* offers no material, *LV* has both *Bēg-* and *Bēag-*. In *VP* and *Ru.*[1], smoothing of *ēa* is practically universal, appearing as *ē* except in *ðæh* (both texts), *æc* (Ru.[1] only); these words were probably shortened in low sentence stress, and hence the vowel was treated like short *ea* directly before a back consonant, becoming *æ* and remaining at that stage. Similarly, in *Li.*, *Rit.*, and *Ru.*[2], *ēa* is smoothed to *ē* in practically all words except *æc* (Li., Rit., Ru.[2]) and *ðæh* (Li., Rit.) beside *ēc*, *ðēh*. It may be observed that in North. strong verbs of Class II sometimes extend the smoothed *ē* of the past singular to the forms which had historically *u* (e.g. *ġebrēcon*, past pl. from *ġebrūcan*), but, on the other hand, the past singular itself sometimes has *æ*, presumably a short vowel derived analogically from Classes IV and V, e.g. *flaeh*, *ataeh* (Li.). A few stereotyped *ēa* spellings remain in most Angl. texts, e.g. *þeah* (Ru.[1], Rit.), *ēage* (Ru.[1] three times).

§ 226. Traces of the smoothing of *ĕa* in W-S and Kt. are not to be distinguished from early instances of a later change (see § 312).

§ 227. The smoothing of *ĕo* is *ĕ*, and it is practically always carried out in Angl. texts. *Ep.* and *Cp.* have *el(c)h*, elk, and Ep. *sċeolhēġi*, squinting, has simply introduced *h* from the simplex *sċelh* (cf. Erf.

sċēolēġi). Before *r* followed by a back consonant they have a few more preserved diphthongs, e.g. Ep. 556 *-uueorc* -work, Cp. 1672 *-biorg*, 1771 *-beorg* protection. But mostly they have smoothing of *eo* before *r* followed by a back consonant and before χ, e.g. Cp. *berc* birch, *duerg* dwarf, *þuerh-* cross-, *-cneht* servant, *-ġefeht* fight. In the case of *ēo*, Cp. has smoothing in *flēge* fly, *lēht-* lumen, *thēgh* thigh, beside *þēoh-*; the only one of these words occurring in *Ep.* is *-flīogae* 817 (also with *īo* in *Erf.*), and here, in view of the mixed origins of the glossaries, we may suspect a Kt. form. *BH* and *LV* have always smoothing in the elements *Berht-* and *Peht-*,[1] and perhaps the name *Echha* LV (if connected with *eoh*) should be added. The short early North. texts offer the forms CH *uerc* work, FC *fegtaþ* they fight, *unnēg* not near, *-berig* mountain, LR *ðer(i)h* through. Practically the only point concerning the smoothing of *ĕo* in *VP*, *Ru.*[1], and the later North. texts[2] is occasional *ī* for the expected *ē* in strong verbs of Class II in *VP* and *Ru.*[1]: *līgende* mentiens (*VP*, *Ru.*[1]), *flīgu* I fly (*VP*), *smīkende* smoking (*Ru.*[1]), beside many regular forms in *VP*, although such are by chance lacking in *Ru.*[1]

§ 228. The forms illustrating the treatment of *i* before *r* followed by a back consonant have already been quoted above (§ 154), where it was shown that it cannot be proved that breaking ever took place in them in Angl. As examples of *i* before χ, we have in the earlier texts only the name-element *Wiht-*, which always has smoothing in *BH*, *LV*, and the Merc. charters (except once *Ueoht-* Ct. 47), and the following forms all with smoothing: Ep., Cp. *frihtrung* divination; Cp. *uurixlende* exchanging, *rihtebred* ruling-board; VP *stihtian* establish, *pliht* danger, *wrixendliċe* in turn, *ġesihð* sight, *ġefihð* he rejoices. Similar material is offered by the later North. texts, and by *Ru.*[1]: from them may also be added *mixen* dunghill (*Li.*, *Ru.*[2]), *ġerihta* correct (*Li.*, *Rit.*, *Ru.*[2]), *ġesihþ* he sees (*Ru.*[1]).

§ 229. The smoothing of *īo* to *ī* is carried out in all Angl. texts. West Gmc. *iu* appears as *ī* in the following forms: *ċīken* chicken, *Ru.*[1], a.p. *ċīcceno*, Li.; *līhtan*, *līxa* lucere (and related words), *Li.*, *Ru.*[2], *Ru.*[1] West Gmc. *ī* appears as *ī* instead of *īo* (§ 153) in the following forms: *þīxlum* d.p. axles, *Cp.*, *Erf.* (*Ep.* misspells *dislum*); *līh* imper. lend, *Li.*, *Ru.*[2]; *onwrīh* imper. uncover, *VP*; *wī(g)bed* altar, *VP*, *Ru.*[1],

[1] On the element *Eorcon-* in *BH* see § 7; *LV* has *Ercin-* 305.

[2] *Ru.*[1] has a fair number of *eo* forms, e.g. *feoh*, *beseoh* (imper.), *weorc*, *-sēoc*, *lēoht*, *wēox*, beside forms with smoothing, and the imperatives *flēoh*, *atēoh*.

Ru.[1] and the tenth-century North. texts have very frequently *cnæht* servant for *cneht* (which *Ru.*[1] and *Rit.* have also). The cause of this development is unknown, and it appears to have no reflection in ME or modern forms. In other words it is sporadic, *ġefæht* Ru.[1], *unafæhtendliċ* Rit., *-sæh* (imper.) *Li.*, *Ru.*[2] Ru.[1] *wærc* (twice) beside *werc* and *weorc* is perhaps due to confusion with *wærċ* pain.

Li., *Rit.*, *Ru.*[2]; *-uich*, *-uych*, as second element in names, *LV*, *Gn.* (but *Gn.* also *Alouuioh*); *Līct-* (i.e. levis) as first element, *LV*; *līht* levis, *Ru.*[1], and compar. *līhtra*, Li.; forms of *līhtan* alleviate, *VP*, *Rit.*; *betwīh* between, *VP*, *Ru.*[1], *Li.*, *Rit.*, *Ru.*[2] (cf. *bituīhn* Cp., *betwīnum* VP); *fiil* (i.e. *fīl* < **fīχl-*) file, *Cp.* Instances where the smoothed *ī* contracts with another vowel will be discussed below. The only difficulty connected with these forms is that occasionally we find *ē* instead of the expected *ī*: *lēht* levis, *Li.*, Mt. 11, 30; *betuēn* between, *Li*, *Rit.* (five times); *fēla* g.p. files, *Beow.* 1032.[1]

§ 230. In the forms *wībed*, *bitwīnum*, *fiil*, just quoted, χ standing before a consonant is lost, but not until it had caused smoothing of a diphthong preceding it. In a number of forms, however, χ before a consonant disappeared early, and a preceding diphthong was not affected: Cp. *hēalēċas* skilled physicians, *ēorod-* troop-; VP *hēanis* highness, *ēored* troop, *nēosian* visit, and words connected with *nēh* near, such as *nēowest* neighbourhood, *nēolǣċan* approach; *LV*, *Gn.*, and Charters offer many names in *Hēa-*; *LV* has also names in *Plēo-*. Similar material is found in *Ru.*[1] and the later North. texts.[2]

§ 231. When a diphthong stood before *l*χ or *r*χ, the χ was lost too early to occasion smoothing if a back vowel followed; if a front vowel followed, the χ caused smoothing before it was lost. This principle is shown by Cp. *elch* elk, *ēola*[3] the same, VP *ætfēalan* adhere, pres. subj. *fēle*; *ðuerh* crooked, infl. *ðwēoran*. BH *Sēlæsēu*, 'insula vituli marini', may be taken to follow the same principle, though diphthongs caused by breaking are not always written in this text.[4]

§ 232. There is some inconsistency, when the first element of a compound ended in *l*χ or *r*χ, whether smoothing took place before the χ was lost or not: Cp. *sċēlēġi* squinting, but Erf. *sċēolēġi* (Ep. *sċeolhēġi*, with analogical *h*, see § 227); LV *Sēoluini*.

§ 233. From the forms *līhtan* lucere, *ċīken* chicken (with Prim. Gmc. *iu*), and from *ġesihð* sight, *ġefihð* he rejoices, *ġerihta* correct, it is plain that an originally back consonant could cause smoothing, even if *-i-* followed. In such positions, *ĕa* became *ĕ* in Angl. by *i*-umlaut, and *ĕo* did not exist, so only the smoothing of *ĭo* is to be observed; yet the forms just quoted are sufficient evidence that smoothing could be

[1] Bülbring, *Alteng. Elementarbuch*, § 199, seems to regard these forms as exhibiting the smoothing of *ēu*: but this is not possible, firstly because *īu* (*īo*) did not anywhere become *ēu* (*ēo*) before it suffered smoothing (see ample evidence above), and secondly because *īu* (*īo*) never became *ēu* (*ēo*) in North. at all in the OE period (see § 293).

[2] When *h* remains or is restored by analogy of the simplex, the smoothed vowel of the simplex is usually found before it: Cp. *hǣhnisse*, *þuerhfyri*; LR *hēhcraeft*; VP *hēhnisse*, *ġenēhlǣċu*.

[3] *Cp.* D12 (not in Sweet's *OET*).

[4] See § 140.

caused by an originally back consonant, even if this were advanced towards the front position by a following *-i-* (cf. § 192). It is, however, evident that the change of *ǣ* (the smoothing of *ēa*) to *ē* took place only before full back consonants, for *ǣ* the *i*-umlaut of *ā* escapes it, e.g. *ǣht* property, *cǣġ* key, *rǣċan* reach. In such words the originally back consonant had been fronted. Fronting could, however, be prevented (or perhaps removed), if another consonant followed, and then *ǣ* (*i*-umlaut of *ā*) could be changed to *ē*. Hence the frequent forms in *ēg-* beside less frequent *ǣġ-* in North.: *ēghwelċ* each, *ēghwer* everywhere, *ēghwona* from everywhere.[1]

1. The Contraction of Vowels

§ 234. As the prehistoric period of OE drew to a close, the hiatus of an accented vowel or diphthong with a following unaccented one ceased to be permitted, except in the case of *ū̆+a* (e.g. *būan*), and in nW-S of *ī̆+e*[2] (e.g. pres. subj. *sīe* be). The number of forms with hiatus had just been immensely increased by the loss of intervocalic χ (see § 461), and it is well known that these cases of hiatus, and also older ones, have frequently to be restored in OE verse to obtain the necessary number of syllables. Hiatus was eliminated in OE by the following means; if the vowel succession to be simplified consisted of the normal elements of an OE diphthong, i.e. front vowel+back vowel, it was contracted into a long diphthong; if, however, the vowel succession to be simplified was back vowel (or diphthong ending in a back vowel) + any other vowel, or front vowel + front vowel, the first vowel or diphthong simply absorbed the second, becoming itself long, if it were originally short. These principles may be illustrated as follows: Prim. OE **slæχan* strike, **seχan* see, by breaking and subsequent loss of χ, gave W-S **sleaan*, **seoan*. With absorption of the unaccented back vowel, and compensatory lengthening of the diphthong, the recorded forms *slēan*, *sēon* were reached. In the present subjunctive of the same verbs, **slea-æ*, **seo-æ* became *slēa*, *seō*. In the same way a back monophthong absorbs following vowels: **fōχan* receive, subj. **fōχæ* become *fōn*, *fō*; and a front monophthong absorbs front vowels: **drȳæs* g.s. magician, becomes

[1] But VP *ōēġhwelċ*, a form found also in *Ep.*, *Erf.*, *Cp.*, and containing the *i*-umlaut of *ō* instead of that of *ā*: see § 132, footnote.

[2] W-S naturally contracts *ī̆+e* to *īe*, but other dialects had not such a diphthong, and hence their *īe* is disyllabic (cf., for example, the metre of *BDS* 2[b], where *sīe* fills a lift and dip).

drȳs. But a front vowel contracts with a back vowel into a diphthong: in Angl., from **sleaχan*, **seoχan*, the forms **slæχan*, **seχan* were produced by smoothing. Contraction then gives VP **slēan* (cf. pres. ind. pl. *-slēað*), *-sēan*.

§ 235. The various types of contraction may now be examined one by one.

Diphthong+vowel. (1) This succession arises by loss of *u̯* before *u* (cf. § 405) in *rēon* they rowed (< **rēowun*, Beow. 539). Analogical *rēowon* usually replaces this form.

(2) Most cases are due to the loss of *χ* between diphthong and vowel in dialects where there was no smoothing. Many examples are provided by the present systems of contracted strong verbs of Classes I, II, V, and VI. Thus **wrīoχan*, **tēoχan*, **seoχan*, **sleaχan*, give *wrīon*, *tēon*, *sēon*, *slēan*. The Class II weak verbs *twīoġan* doubt, *þrēaġan* punish, *smēaġan* consider, 3rd sg. pres. indic. *twēoþ*, *þrēaþ*, *smēaþ*, are contracted from **twioχōi̯an*, **twioχaþ*, **þrēaχōi̯an*, &c. Nominal instances are provided by *ēa* water (< **eaχu*), *twēo* doubt (< **twīo* < **twioχō*), *ġefēa* joy (< **ġifeaχō*), *sēo* pupil of eye (< **seoχæ*), *hwēol* wheel (< **hweoχul*), *swēor* father-in-law (< **sweoχur*, cf. Ep. *suehoras*), *ēar* ear of corn (< **eaχur*), *tēar* tear (< **teaχur*),[1] *ēam* maternal uncle (< **ēaχam*, cf. Ger. *Oheim*). Further instances are provided by the inflected forms of many nouns and adjectives in *χ*, e.g. *feoh* money, g.s. *fēos* (< **feoχæs*), *hēah* high, g.s.m. *hēas* (< **hēaχæs*). Such contracted inflected forms also occur from *eoh* horse, *þēoh* thigh, *pleoh* danger, *lēah* open country, *hrēoh* rough, *sċēoh* shy. Note also *flēah* flea, *flēah* albugo, of which no inflected forms occur, but cf. the weak forms, *flēa* flea, *flēa*[2] albugo. Note also the adverb W-S *nēar* nearer (< **nēaχur*), Kt. *nēor* (< **nēoχur*, Ct. 38), later *nīor* (Bd. Gl., cf. § 152).

(3) The W-S diphthong *ǐe* contracts with *i* in a few forms: with loss of *u̯*, *ætīede* he showed (< *-*īeu̯id*-, CP 43, 19), *ġehlȳde* pass. part. pl. warmed (< -**hlieu̯id*-, Job iv); with loss of *χ*, g.s., d.s. *īe* (< **ieχi*-), cf. *ēa* water. The formation of *flīe*, albugo, is uncertain.

§ 236. Back vowel+vowel. (1) Cases of contraction of original hiatus are g.s. *cū*, *cūs*, d.p. *cūm*, from *cū*, cow, past *būde*, pass. part. *ġebūn*, from *būan* dwell.[3] But *ŭ*+*a* remains: *būan*, g.p. *cūa*, *sċua* shadow.[4]

(2) Loss of *u̯* in *clawum* (itself restored for *clēam*, § 120.3) d.p. claws,

[1] Prim. OE forms with parasiting (§ 363) are assumed for *ēar* and *tēar*; this is necessary to explain Angl. *tēar* < **teaχur* (§ 238.2).

[2] Also *flīo*, *flēo*.

[3] In *flā* arrow, *dā* doe, the endings of the weak fem. declension were possibly added to the root vowel, with which they contracted to give *flān*, **dān*.

[4] Or perhaps *sċūa* < *scuwa*, with *uu̯* > *ū* as *ii̯* > *ī* (§ 267); cf. lWS *trūa*, KG *ġetrūa* for imper. *truwa* trust, lW-S *trūa* beside *truwa* faith.

leads to contraction to *clām* (Phoen. 277), but *clawum* is usually restored by analogy.

(3) Most cases are again due to the loss of χ, e.g. the present system of *fōn* take, and *hōn* hang, in all dialects (< **fōχan*, &c.); the nouns *ġefā* enemy, *tā* toe (Cp. *tāhae*), *ðō* clay (Cp. *thōae*, Ep. *thōhae*), *rā* roe (Cp. *rāha*), *slā* sloe; and many inflected forms of *hōh* heel, *sċōh* shoe, *slōh* mire, *þrūh* trough, *fāh* hostile, *flāh* treacherous, *ġemāh* shameless, *tōh* tough, *wōh* crooked. Here belong also *slā*, *þwā*, for W-S *slēan*, *þwēan* (see § 145), found in North. and *Ru.*[1]

§ 237. **Front vowel+front vowel.** (1) Front vowels produced by umlaut contract with a following vowel in many forms. (*a*) Without loss of an intervening consonant, *drȳ* magician (OIr. *drui*); *gǣst*, *gǣþ*, *dōest*, *dōeþ*, 2nd and 3rd sg. pres. indic. of *gān* go, *dōn* do (< **ʒāis*, &c.); past parts. *-dēn*, *-fēn* (And. 43, *Crist* 1265, 1157) from *dōn*, and *fōn* take. (*b*) With loss of u̯ before *i* (cf. § 406), VP *ċēð*, *ċēde*, *ġeċēd*, 3rd sg. pres. indic., past, and pass. part. of *ċēġan* call, and some similar forms in North.[1] (< **kaui-* > **kei-* > **kē-*), and similarly VP *strēn* bed, Ru.[2] *strēdun* they strewed, *Beow.* 2436 *strēd* pass. part. (cf. past *streide* Cp.), North., Ru.[1] *ēde* flock. Uncontracted *e*+*i* is still required by the metre in *Beow.* 2436, and may be indicated by the spelling in Cp. *streide*. Loss of u̯ before *i* and subsequent contraction occur also in compounds with *nī-* new (e.g. *nīcenned* newly-born < **niwi-*), and similarly in *glīman* minstrel, if this is not simply a spelling for *glīġ-*. (*c*) Loss of *i* and subsequent contraction seems to occur in *ǣċe* eternal < **ǣċi* < **æyċi* < **æi̯yki* < **ai̯uki* (cf. § 203, and Goth. *ajukdu*þ*s*); but this form, though frequent (*VP*, *Ru.*[1], North.; also Kt. charters, where, however, *æ* = *e* in spelling), is always less frequent than *ēċe*, a form not to be precisely explained (*CH* already *ēċi*). (*d*) With loss of χ, 3rd sg. pres. indic. *þȳþ*, *tȳþ*, past *þȳde*, *tȳde* (< **þūχiþ*, &c.), and hence infs. *þȳn* press, *tȳn* instruct, beside *þēon*, *tēon*;[2] *fōeþ*, 3rd sg. pres. indic. of *fōn* (< **fōχiþ*, VP, North.); Ep., Cp. *fāēdun* they painted (< **fāχidun*, cf. 3rd sg. pres. indic. *fāēhit*, Ep., Cp.); *slēs*, *slēð*, *ðwēs*, *ðwēð*, 2nd and 3rd sg. pres. indic. of *slēan* strike, *þwēan* wash (< **sleχis*, &c., with nW-S umlaut of *ea* to *e*, VP);[3] *hēra*, *hēst*, comparative and superlative of *hēah* high (< **hēχir-*, **hēχist-* with nW-S umlaut of *ēa* to *ē*, VP, North.); similarly *-hēst*, *-hēð*, 2nd and 3rd sg.

[1] But in North., *Ru.*[1], and W-S, forms with *ġ* are usual, *ċīeġþ*, *ċīeġde*, &c.

[2] Unless this is always the transferred use of *tēon* draw, strong verb of Class II. Other rare verbal forms have a similar formation: so *rȳn*, roar, 3rd sg. pres. indic. *rȳð*, from **ruχi-*, cf. OHG *rohōn*; *aþrȳn* (ES xliii. 331), 3rd sg. pres. indic. *ġiðrīð*, past *ġeþrȳde*, press, bind (a book); 3rd sg. pres. indic. *ġeweþ*, past *ġewēde*, make crooked (< **-u̯ōχi-*), 3rd sg. pres. indic. *sċȳþ*, past *sċȳde*, persuade.

[3] Other Angl. texts level out the unmutated vowel to these forms: Cp. *slāēt*, Ru.[1] *slǣþ*. North. *slǣs*, *ðwǣs*, *slǣð*, from **slæχiþ*, &c., with the smoothing of *ea*.

pres. indic. of *-*hēan* exalt (< **hēχis*, **hēχiþ*, VP); *nēsta* nearest (< **nēχist-*, VP, North.).

(2) Many Angl. forms with smoothing of a diphthong before inter-vocalic χ afterwards lost belong here. They are derived from contracted strong verbs, of which the W-S and Kt. forms belong to § 235.2. The pres. subj. forms **tēoχæ*, **seoχæ*, **sleaχæ*, and 3rd sg. pres. indic. **tīoχiþ*, **sioχiþ*, would become **tēχæ*, **seχæ*, **slæχæ*, **tīχiþ*, **siχiþ* by smoothing, and **tē*, *sē*, *slǣ*, *tīþ*, *sīþ* by contraction. The actual forms found are *ġiflee* Rit., *flēn* VP (pres. subj. from *flēon* flee), *-sē* (id. from *sēon*, VP), *ġefee* (id. from *ġefēon* rejoice, *VP*), *slǣ* (id. from *slēan* Ru.[1], Ru.[2]), *-tīð* (3rd sg. pres. indic. of *tēon* draw, *VP*), *fliið* (id. of *flēon* flee, *Li.*), *-sīð* (id. of *sēon* VP, Ru.[1], North.).[1] In Class I of the strong verbs 3rd sg. pres. indic. **wrīχið* gives regular *wrīð* (VP, Ru.[2], cf. Cp., Ep. *siid*, he sieves, from *sīon*), but present optative should be **wrīe*, uncontracted, a form not recorded, but replaced by various analogical formations. Nominal and adjectival forms which could exhibit this type of contraction are rare, and the few which occur have undergone analogical reformation, e.g. *fæes* g.s. of *feh* money, Li., *hēae* pl. of *hēh*, high (with vowel of infl. *hēan*, &c.+-*e*, VP).

(3) It has been remarked above that ĭ+*e* does not contract in nW-S. The succession occurs, as well as in the subjunctive form *sīe* there quoted, in the pron. *hīe* she (usually acc.), they, found in many texts (see § 703), in the W-S numeral *þrīe*, three, and in North. *betuīen* between (< **betwīχen*). ĭ+*e* occurs also in very many Angl. verbal forms, e.g. *VP* past *fīede* for normal *fīode*, from *fīoġan* hate, VP *-siende*, pres. part. from *sēon*, see; Li. *ġetwiedon* past from **ġetwīa* doubt; Li., Ru.[1] *dīendra*, pres. part. g.p. from **dīon*, suck; Cp. *ðīendi* thriving, 1118; Ru.[1] *fīeġæ*, *fīeġaþ*, subj. and pl. pres. indic. from *fīoġan*. Many of these are analogical formations of an obvious kind. VP *-sieð*, Li. *-fīeð*, 3rd sg. pres. indic. from *sēon* and *fīoġan* are also simple analogical formations, but VP *-sie*, *-fie*, 1st sg. pres. indic. from *-sēon* see, *-fēon* rejoice, are difficult, as the contraction should be with *-u* in the dialect.[2]

§ 238. **Front vowel+back vowel.** (1) By West Gmc. contraction, successions consisting of vowel+*u* had become diphthongs (see § 120). Now ĭ+*ō*, ĭ+*a* were also contracted. The result was *īo*,[3] *īa*, respectively, but this distinction was kept up only in North. and *VP*. Elsewhere the second element of *īa* was made identical with that of *īo* (the normal second element for an OE diphthong with a high or mid first element).

[1] For many phonologically less regular variants of the above verbal forms, see §§ 739 ff.

[2] *sliet*, 3rd sg. pres. indic. of *slēan*, BG, is hardly more than an error.

[3] By the time of contraction, unaccented *ō* was already changed to *u* (§ 331.5, 6), so contraction of *i*+*ō* was strictly to *iu*, which soon become *īo*, like *iu* of other origin (§ 275).

io became *ēo* later in W-S and Merc. (*VP*, *Ru.*[1]). Similarly, in VP, *īa* has become *ēa* (i.e. *e*+*a*, not *æ*+*a* like *ēa* of other origin). Naturally, this change of *īo*, *īa* to *ēo*, *ēa* is reflected in spelling, both directly, *ēo* and *ēa* appearing where historically *īo*, *īa* would be expected, and also by inverted spelling, the symbols *īo*, *īa* appearing for historical *ēo*, *ēa*. Contraction of *i* with a following back vowel, without the loss of any intervening consonant, occurs in the present tense of *bēon* be: *VP* has 1st sg. *bīom*, *bēom*, pl. *bīað*,[1] North. *bīom*, *bīað* from **bī-u*, **bī-aþ*; W-S Kt., *Ru.*[1] have, however, *īo*, *ēo* in 1st sg., pl., and inf. Similarly, *bēo* bee, has in W-S (forms do not occur in Kt. or *Ru.*[1]) always that form, infl. *bēon*, but in *VP* and North. it is possible to trace an original distinction between **bīon* and *bīan* as inflected forms, reflecting an original variation in formation between **bīōn-*, **bīan-*; either diphthong could be transferred to the uninflected form.[2] *VP*, *Rit.* have pl. *bīa*(*n*), and *VP* has *bīa-* once in composition; but *bīo-* is found in composition in *Ep.*, *Cp.*, *VP*, North., and the older stage *bīu-* is preserved in LV *Bīuuulf*. The same contraction may give rise to OE *Swēon* Swedes (cf. ON *Svíar*), and *Erf.*, *Cp.*, North. *scīa* shin. Many examples are provided by forms of *fīoġan* hate, *frīoġan* free, originally weak verbs of Class III, but reformed in OE according to Class II. Hence in W-S we find 2nd and 3rd sg. pres. indic., imper., and past all with *ēo*,[3] older *īo*, from **fī-as*, *-aþ*, *-odæ*, &c. But in *VP* we find a distinction between 3rd sg. pres. indic. *fīað*, past *fīode*, *fēode*, though the distinction **ġefrīað* (*ġefrēað*), *ġefrīode* is less well preserved, *īo* (*ēo*) being levelled into the former, and *īa* (*ēa*) into the latter (and the pass. part.).[4] In North. confusion has advanced even further in both verbs. VP *frēa*, free, is from older **frīa*, and reflects *frī*+*a*; VP *frēo-*, North. *frīo* reflect *frī*+*u* (see § 120.3.c; *LV* still *Frīu-*).

(2) The Anglian forms of the words discussed § 235.2 frequently exhibit contraction of a front and a back vowel into a diphthong. In Angl. the diphthongs were smoothed to front vowels before the loss of χ, and contraction of *æ*, *e*, or *i* with a following back vowel to a diphthong takes place. (On forms in which a front vowel followed the χ see § 237.2.) (*a*) The contraction of *ǣ* with a back vowel occurs in *VP* *hēa*, *hēan*, *hēam*, inflected forms of *hēh* high (< **hǣχa*, &c.); *VP*, North. *ēa* water (< **æχō*), *tēar* tear (< **tæχur*); Cp. *flēan* flay (< **flæhan*); VP *slēa*, *ðwēa*, *-slēað*, 1st sg. and pl. pres. indic. of *slēan* strike, *þwēan* wash (< **slæhō*, *-að*, &c.); *ðrēas*, *ðrēað*, *ðrēa*, *ðrēade*, 2nd and 3rd pres. indic., imper., and pret. of *ðrēaġan* punish, and similar forms from

[1] But more frequently analogical *bīoð*, and always inf. *bīon*; Li., however, has inf. *bīan* once, no occurrences in other North. texts.

[2] Which historically should, of course, be **bīe* < **bī-*+*æ*.

[3] But Ru.[1] *fiað* 6, 24, by adding the frequent ending *-að* to *fī-*.

[4] But imper. always *ġefrēa*, *ġefrīa*.

smēaġan consider, found *Cp.*, *VP*, North. (< **smǣχas*, &c.).[1] It is clear that *ǣ* contracted with any back vowel to *ēa* (= *æ*+*a*). Yet when the contraction was with *ō*(*u*), the second element of the diphthong may have been at first rounded, and this seems reflected by Ep., Cp. *ēo-* (for *ēa* water), and by the element *-ēu* in many place-names in *BH*.[2] (*b*) The contraction of *ĕ* with a back vowel, with loss of intervening *χ*, is usually *ēo* in *Ru.*[1], e.g. inf. *ġeseōn* see, pl. pres. indic. *ġeseōþ*, beside occasional analogical *ġeseāþ*. In *VP* the contrast of *eχō* > *ēo*, *eχa* > *ēa* is clear: the former gives *ēo*, the latter *ēa*, and for these as explained above *io* and *īa* respectively may appear as inverted spellings. Hence 1st sg. pres. indic. *ġesīo* I see, *ġefīo* I rejoice, pl. *ġeseāð*, *ġesīað*, *ġefēað*, *ġefīað*, inf. *ġesēan*, *ġesīan*. Analogical *ġesīoð*, *ġefīoð* occur, but are rare. The noun *ġefēa* joy, varies between *ēa* and *īa* in spelling, which points to **ġifeχō* (cf. OHG *gefeho*), infl. **ġifeχan*, rather than to an exact equivalent of W-S *ġefēa* (< **ġifeaχa* < **ġifaχō*). *Flēon* flee, levels out *ēo* to all forms: 1st sg. pres. indic. *flēom*, pl. *flēoð*. In North., *ēa* forms prevail in these contracted verbs, except in 1st sg. pres. indic. *sēom* Li., *sīom* Ru.[2] (with *si-* levelled out from 2nd and 3rd sg.), *sīum* Li., Rit. Other instances of the development of *eχ*+back vowel are VP *sēan*, *sīan* a.s. pupil of eye (< **seχan-*); North. *swēor* father-in-law (< **sweχur*, cf. Ep. *suehoras*); Ep., Cp. *huēol-*, VP *hwēol*, *hwīol* wheel (< **hweχul*). (*c*) The following forms illustrate the contraction of *ĭ* with a following back vowel, after loss of *χ*: VP *-wrēan* wrap (< **wrīan* < **wrīχan*), North. pl. pres. indic. *-wrīað*; but *Ru.*[1] pl. pres. indic. *-wrēoþ*, contracting *ī*+*a* to *īo* > *ēo*; Ru.[2] *bitwīon* between, Ru.[1] *betwīon*, *betwēon* (< **bitwīχun*); CH *tīadæ* arranged, Ep. Cp. *ġitīung* order (< **tiχadæ*, *-ung*); North. *twīas*, *-ade*, *-ode*, 3rd sg. pres. indic. and past of **twīa* doubt (< **twiχaþ*, &c.), and so *twīa* doubt (n.); W-S *bēot* boast, *frēols* freedom (< **bi-hat*, **frī-hals*).

(3) *ȳ* contracted with a following back vowel after loss of intervening *χ* to *īo*, later *ēo*. No doubt *īo* and *īa* would interchange in *VP* and North., as in the case of the contraction of *ī*+back vowel, but forms are lacking in these dialects. The chief instances are the verbs *þēon* press, *tēon* instruct, discussed above § 237.1.d (< **þūχian*, &c.), *rēo* blanket (Ep. *rȳhae*); the same explanation would fit the recorded spellings of *cēo*, *cīo*, Ep. *chȳae* (< **cȳχæ*?) crow.

[1] In the forms of these two verbs with original *i̯*, VP has *ē* for W-S *ēa*: 1st sg. pres. indic. *ðrēgu*, *smēgu*, pl. *smēġað*, &c. One would expect *ǣ*: **smēaχōi̯-* > **smǣχei̯-* > **smǣi̯-*. Forms with *ē* in W-S and Kt. are otherwise explained (§ 314). North. extends the diphthong of *smēað*, &c. to the *-i̯-* forms: *smēaġe*, *smēoġe* (cf. § 278), &c. *Ru.*[1] inf. *ðrēiga* is a form of *VP* type (*iġ* = *ġ*, see § 270).

[2] This form has been much discussed, but it can hardly be explained without assuming confusion of a form meaning 'island' with *ēa* water: cf. Förster, *Flussname Themse*, pp. 291–2; K. R. Brooks, *English and Germanic studies* v. 29–30.

§ 239. With reference to the preceding sections on vowel contraction, it may be remarked that analogical forms with the contraction eliminated quite often occur. Some have been mentioned above; others are *hēaum* d.p. of *hēah*, North. superls. *hēista*, *nēista*, from *hēh*, *nēh*, and North. infs. *dōa*, *fōa*, *hōa*, for W-S *dōn*, &c.

J. Compensatory Lengthening

§ 240. The absorption of a following unaccented vowel is not necessary to occasion the lengthening of an accented vowel. Vowels often undergo compensatory lengthening owing to the loss of following consonants only, usually the spirants χ, *ġ*, and *ʒ*. Metrical evidence, however, shows that short quantity was often replaced from related forms, e.g. *meares* (beside *mēares* with compensatory lengthening) with the short quantity of *mearh*.[1]

§ 241. **Compensatory lengthening following loss of χ.** (1) Loss of χ took place between vowel and voiced consonant with lengthening of the vowel. Instances are provided by: (*a*) a few words where loss of χ is proved by the etymology, *þwēal*[2] washing (Goth. *þwahl*), lW-S *stȳle* steel (< **stīeli*, cf. *Cp.* 55 *stēli*,[3] OS *stehli*), lW-S *ġesȳne*, Ang. *ġesēne* visible, *ȳmest* upmost (cf. Goth. *auhumists*), and probably *ġeðrȳl* crowd (cf. *ġeþrȳn* press, bind);[4] (*b*) compounds of *eoh* and *pleoh* quoted above, § 230, show the same process, e.g. *ēored*, *plēoliċ*.

(2) χ is lost after a consonant (generally *r*, *l*) with compensatory lengthening of the vowel which precedes the consonant. Examples are: (*a*) inflected forms of many words, such as g.s. *fēores*, *mēares*, *sēoles*, *Wēales*, inf. *fēolan*, cf. n.s. *feorh*, *mearh*, *seolh*, *Wealh*, past *fealh*; (*b*) some words where loss of χ is proved by etymology, e.g. *þȳrel* hole (cf. *þurh*), *swēora*[5] neck, *fīras*[6] men; (*c*) a few com-

[1] See Sievers, *Altgerm. Metrik*, § 77. In words of this type (2 (*a*) below) there is no evidence except that of metre that lengthening took place: e.g. place-name evidence points always to *Wăla* as g.p. of *Wealh*, and *hăle* as d.s. of *healh*.

[2] If from **þu̯eaχl*, not **þu̯eaχol* (cf. § 363 below). So *Cp.* 1991 *ðuǣlum*, d.p. fillets, may represent **þu̯eaχl-* or **þu̯eaχol*, while *Cp.* 2120, *Ep.* 1060 *thuēlan* represents **þu̯eχil-* (cf. OHG *duuehila*).

[3] But *Cp.* 1431 *stǣli*, hardly a correct form.

[4] North. *hwēl* wheel, *swēr* mother-in-law, are probably from **hu̯eχl*, **su̯eχr*, with smoothing, and without parasiting.

[5] Beside *swīra* (§ 154.3, footnote), and the obscure lW-S *swura*, *swyra*, which suggest earlier *sweora* without lengthening (cf. § 321 below).

[6] Cf. *feorh* life, and see § 154.3, footnote.

pounds, *ōrettan* fight, *ōnettan* hurry, *īfiġ* ivy, from **or-haitian-*, **an-haitian-*, **if-hīeġ*.[1]

§ 242. In types 1*a*, 1*b*, 2*a*, 2*b*, it is evident that the loss of χ is later than breaking, but generally earlier than smoothing (cf., however, § 231). χ is preserved in spelling in Ep. *furhum* d.p. furrows, *ebhat*, but in Erf. *thuachl*, Cp. *ðhuehl*, Li. *ðuahles*, *fihles* g.s. rag, we appear to have forms with gemination, **þwa$\chi\chi$l-*, &c. (see § 408). On the loss of χ, see further §§ 461 ff.

§ 243. Compensatory lengthening following loss of ġ. Typical of W-S is the loss of *ġ* before *þ*, *d*, and *n*, with lengthening of the preceding vowel. Instances occurring in early texts are *rēn* rain, *-wǣn* wagon, *-þēn* thane, *ðēnung* service, *mǣden* maiden, *onġēan* against, *-hȳdiġ* minded; all these, except *rēn*, also occur with *ġ* in eW-S. There is much fluctuation in W-S in the various forms of *bre(ġ)dan* brandish, *fri(ġ)nan* ask, *stre(ġ)dan* strew, past *bræ(ġ)d*, *fræ(ġ)n*, *strægd*,[2] and of the weak pasts and pass. parts. *sæ(ġ)de*, *le(ġ)de*, *sæ(ġ)d*, *le(ġ)d*, from *seċġan* say, *leċġan* lay. In eW-S we have always *ē* in *rēnian* arrange, and related forms, but later *reġnian*, &c., appear also.[3]

§ 244. Occasional instances of similar loss of *ġ* in Angl. texts are: Li., Ru.[1] *onġǣn* (beside frequent *onġæġn*, &c.), Cp. *onġēn* against, Li. *mǣden* maiden (beside *mæġden*), Li. *ġeðuǣn*, *unðuēn* pass. part. washed (for **ġeðwæġn*, *-ðweġn*). *Wēn*, wagon, occurs Ct. 28 (Saxon-Kt.), and *KG* have *ġēnet* compulit 573 (for *ġeġneþ*), *-hēdiġra* 352 (for *-hyġdiġ-*), *-brōdenum* twice.[4]

§ 245. Similar loss of *ġ* before *l* is rare and sporadic, e.g. *Ep.* 61 *snēl* snail (beside *sneġl*), Ep., Cp. *strēl* curtain (*Cp.* also *streġl*), Li., Ru.[2] *wāghrǣl* curtain (beside *-hræġl*), Ælfric's Vocabulary *sǣsnǣl* sea-snail.

K. Chronological Summary

§ 246. The developments so far discussed in the present chapter may be termed prehistoric, because they can all be exemplified to

[1] But no lengthening in *eofot*, Ep. *ebhat* crime, *eofolsian* blaspheme, from **ef-hat*, **ef-halsian*.

[2] Hence analogical forms from these three verbs arise with loss of back *g*: *frūnon*, *ġefrūnen*, *brūdon*, *brōden*, *strōden*, beside forms with *g*. Note also past sg. *frān* (for *frǣn*) formed from *frīnan* on the model of *rīdan*, *rād*.

[3] *Ru.*[2] has *ġirīnad* ornatum, *ġirīno* aedificationes, so in view of the rarity of loss of *ġ* in nW-S, and the fact that in W-S forms without *ġ* are the earlier, confusion of two roots is perhaps to be assumed in these words.

[4] Note also BH *Ġēnlādae* g.s., Yenlet, apparently from *ġæġn*+*lād*.

some degree from the oldest surviving texts, although there are also spellings in these which reflect a time previous to the later of the sound-changes under consideration (especially back umlaut, smoothing, and vowel contraction). It is accordingly not possible to date any of these sound-changes by observing their gradual appearance in texts, and we can establish their approximate dates and arrange them in chronological order by theoretical means only.

§ 247. Vowel contraction is evidently later than the Anglian smoothing (see § 238.2), and many forms are preserved in early texts in which it has not yet taken place (see §§ 236–7). Smoothing would also appear to have been a recent change when the earliest extant manuscripts were written, as some forms appear in these in which it has still not operated (see §§ 223, 225, 227). Back umlaut must for several reasons be placed in approximately the same period. Its relationship in time to smoothing has been disputed. On the face of it, it would be reasonable to assume that the complete absence in Anglian except in analogical forms of back umlaut before back consonants indicates that its effects were removed by smoothing, and that it in fact took place earlier than that change.[1] An indication that this is in fact the case is offered by occasional forms preserved in spelling with *ea* from West Gmc. *a* by back umlaut, see § 207. If the normal *VP* development *dægas* be assumed never to have had *ea*, it is inexplicable why *ea* spellings occur at all.[2] But if in fact such forms had *ea* for a time, this method of spelling might to some degree outlast its phonetic appropriateness, and even penetrate Kentish, where it had never been appropriate. The chronological relationship of *i*-umlaut to back umlaut is reasonably certain, for vowels produced by the former process can be affected by the latter (see § 211). Hence we must regard *i*-umlaut as the older change, and with this its full development in the earliest texts agrees. In these early texts there are many forms in which back umlaut has not taken place (see §§ 207, 210.2, 212).[3]

[1] This was the original view of Sievers (*Angelsächs. Gramm.*³, § 162.*a*.2) and Bülbring (*Alteng. Elementarbuch*, §§ 202, 204, 208), but Luick (*Hist. Gramm.*, § 235.*a*.3) considers that back umlaut was prevented by back consonants in Angl., just as by back and dental consonants in W-S.

[2] It is, of course, not possible to regard the *-eag-* spellings as due to Kt. influence, for West Gmc. *a* is not subject to second fronting to *æ*, and subsequent back mutation to *ea*, in Kt. at all (cf. § 207).

[3] A modification of the traditional chronology is attempted by Girvan, *Angelsaks. Handboek*, § 107, but it rests on the assumption that VP *ðwēoran*, *ætfēalan* had short diphthongs due to back umlaut, not to breaking (cf. § 231 above).

§ 248. The chronological relationship of breaking and diphthongization of front vowels by the influence of palatal consonants to *i*-umlaut is a difficult question. It was long agreed that since the diphthongs *ēa* and *īo*, from West Gmc. *au* and *iu*, appear as W-S *īe* when subject to *i*-umlaut, it follows that W-S *īe* was itself a diphthong. From this it was inferred that *ie* in words like *ieldra* older, *fieht* he fights, was also a diphthong, and was the *i*-umlaut of short diphthongs seen in *eald*, *feohtan*.[1] Hence it was assumed that short diphthongs were produced by breaking, and were subsequently subject to *i*-umlaut to *ie*, itself a short diphthong. Similarly, the diphthongs produced from front vowels by palatal influence were held to be subject to *i*-umlaut at least in W-S, and this assumption placed palatal influence earlier than *i*-umlaut.[2] Recently Miss M. Daunt attacked this view,[3] arguing that the OE short diphthongs *ea*, *eo*, *io*, produced by breaking, palatal influence, and back umlaut, and their W-S mutation *ie*, never existed, but that the spellings represent *æ*, *e*, *i*, followed by a diacritic vowel symbol to indicate the nature of the following consonant. Hence, for example, in *eald*, *eorþe*, the liquid consonants are represented by *al*, *or*, and so distinguished from the phonetically different liquids of Angl. *ældra*, *derne*.[4]

§ 249. Samuels (op. cit.) rejects Miss Daunt's views on the short diphthongs, but questions the traditional chronology of the sound-changes. He stresses that the view that breaking is older than *i*-umlaut is based on the *i*-umlaut of the diphthongs produced by breaking in W-S to *ie*. But he suggests that this *ie* might be of late origin (like those discussed below, § 299.a). If *ieldra* be derived

[1] Of course strictly *io*, not *eo*, undergoes *i*-umlaut to *ie* (see § 201).

[2] Definitely demonstrable only in the case of the long sound, since W-S *ġiest* might be developed by palatal influence from **ġesti-*, and this be by mutation from **ġæsti-*. But since *ǣ* is not subject to *i*-umlaut (see § 191), lW-S *ċȳse* must represent older **ċiese* < **ċēasi-* < **cāsi-* (Lat. *cāseum*), and *ġiest* may fairly be assumed to have the same development.

[3] *Trans. Philological Soc.*, 1939, pp. 108–37.

[4] Miss Daunt's views have been subjected to much criticism, see, for example, C. L. Wrenn, *Trans. Philological Soc.*, 1943, pp. 31–32; M. L. Samuels, id., 1952, pp. 15–47; S. M. Kuhn, R. Quirk, *Language* xxix. 143–56; R. Quirk, C. L. Wrenn, *An OE grammar* (London, 1955), pp. 146–7. K. Brunner, *English studies* xxxiv. 247–51, takes a conventional view of breaking and back umlaut, but denies the reality of the diphthongs assumed to arise from palatal influence, and holds that *e*, *i* in *ġeaf*, *ġiefan* are merely indications of the palatal nature of the consonant. He also doubts the actuality of the Angl. smoothing, holding that the second element of diphthongs was always particularly clear in Angl. before velar consonants, and hence did not require to be written.

from **eldra* we cannot postulate a stage **ealdir-*. **ælda-* and **ældi-* might have developed simultaneously to **ealda-* and **eldi-* respectively. It may even be that the occasional spellings in early manuscripts in which breaking is not indicated (see § 140) reflect a spelling system developed before breaking took place: this would make breaking relatively late.

§ 250. The present writer wishes to stress that in his opinion only a balance of probability can be claimed for the traditional view, but that this balance is sufficiently in its favour for it still to be presented as prǫbable. It is unlikely that the diphthongs of *ieldra* and *hīerra* spring from so different a succession of processes as Samuels suggests.

§ 251. If breaking and palatal influence be regarded as older than *i*-umlaut, their chronological relationship to each other is settled by words where they conflict: *ċeorl*, *ġeorn*, show that **kerl-*, **ʒern-*, had developed *e* to *eo* before the time of palatal influence, otherwise **ċierl*, **ġiern* would have developed, and (as there is no reason to think *ie* would be subject to breaking) would have been the historical forms. Hence breaking must be regarded as the earlier change.[1]

§ 252. That the fronting of West Gmc. *a* preceded breaking follows from § 139. This agrees with the fact that the long sound had already been fronted (supposing a back vowel for Prim. Gmc. *ǣ* ever developed in the Anglo-Frisian area) in the continental period, see § 129. The short sound was apparently fronted separately in English and Frisian. The development of nasal *ā̆* is shared by English and Frisian and therefore belongs to the continental period (§§ 127, 130).

§ 253. The type of Mercian which has the second fronting has no diphthongization of front vowels by palatal consonants, therefore the relative chronology of these changes cannot be decided. They are both to be placed after the restoration of *a* before back vowels. Palatal influence is shown to be later than the restoration of *a* by forms like *calan*, *galan*: here *kæ*, *ʒæ* became *ka*, *ʒa* before palatals could develop and produce *ċea*, *ġea*. Second fronting is by definition later than restoration of *a*: the paradigm *deġ*, *dægas* could not be developed from *dæġ*, *dagas* until this latter paradigm itself existed. The reasons for placing palatal influence before *i*-

[1] Girvan, *Angelsaks. Handboek*, § 64, refuses to accept this simple argument: again, the appeal against him must be to the balance of probability.

umlaut have been already indicated. Second fronting may be taken to precede *i*-umlaut because all sounds produced bv *i*-umlaut escape it: this applies to the mutations of *ā* (from *ai*), and of retracted *a* before *l* groups (types *lǣran*, *ældra*).[1] This chronology agrees well with evidence from the development of initial palatal consonants from Prim. Gmc. *k* and *ʒ*. These became palatal before front vowels due to the fronting of West Gmc. *a*, which were not liable to restoration before a following back vowel. But they were not palatalized before front vowels due to second fronting or *i*-umlaut. This suggests that when the palatalization of these consonants took place, restoration of *a* had occurred, but second fronting and *i*-umlaut lay ahead (§ 170).

§ 254. The diphthongizations of back vowels by palatal consonants took place at various times as indicated in §§ 171–6, 179–81. Their beginnings may no doubt be placed back in the period of the diphthongization of front vowels, before *i*-umlaut (§§ 177–8).

§ 255. From what has now been said, we can suggest the following chronological order as probable for the sound-changes discussed in the present chapter:

1. Anglo-Frisian development of nasal *ā̆*; and of *ǣ*/*ē* from West Gmc. *ā*.
2. West Gmc. *ai* > *ā* (§ 132).
3. Fronting of West Gmc. *a* to *æ*.
4. Breaking and the related processes of retraction.
5. Restoration of *ă* before back vowels.
6. Second fronting (mainly *VP*). Palatal diphthongization of front vowels, and early diphthongizations of back vowels (mainly W-S and North.).
7. *i*-Mutation.
8. Back Mutation.
9. Smoothing.
10. Contraction of vowels, compensatory lengthening.

[1] It is true that the types *ald*, *galan* also escape second fronting, but this is due to the *l* (see § 165). It is very doubtful if a similar influence could be exerted by the *l* of *ældra*, through which the influence of *i*-umlaut had passed, and before which a comparatively general change to *e* was to take place later (§ 193.a).

L. Dialectal Summary

§ 256. It may be useful to recapitulate the main dialectal distinctions produced by the above sound-changes. It must first be emphasized that the dialectal names are in this book used practically without claim to territorial significance. North. means the agreement of *Li.*, *Rit.*, *Ru.*[2], and the early names and fragments, or of such of all these sources as offer evidence on the point under discussion. Mercian means similarly the agreement of *VP*, *Cp.*, *Ep.*, and the majority forms of *Ru.*[1], or of such of these as afford evidence. Angl. means the agreement of North. so defined with Merc. so defined. Kt. means such forms in the charters of Kt. origin as are shown to be genuinely Kt. by their reappearance in *KG*, or the appearance of their obvious reflexes (i.e. forms descended from them) there. nW-S is the agreement of Angl. so defined with Kt. so defined. W-S means the agreement of the majority forms of the four generally accepted eW-S manuscripts (see § 16) with a large body of later W-S. lW-S means forms prevailing in a considerable body of the later W-S manuscripts, but not prevailing in the four manuscripts accepted as eW-S.

§ 257. The Germanic invaders of Britain already most probably possessed one clear dialect distinction: the dialects from which W-S was to descend had *ǣ* from Prim. Gmc. *ǣ*, but those from which are descended all other known OE dialects had *ē* (§ 128).[1]

§ 258. The early changes grouped together above as breaking and retraction caused further dialectal distinctions to arise. Before *l* groups, Angl. develops *a* from West Gmc. *a*, but W-S and Kt. have *ea*. Spellings with *a* penetrate eW-S and eKt. extensively, spellings with *ea* invade Angl. only in *Ru.*[1] This is to be attributed to the mutual influence of established orthographical systems. The development of *a* for West Gmc. *a* before *r* groups, generally in a labial neighbourhood, is mainly a North. feature, but invades some Mercian texts (§ 144). The development of *wer-* followed by a consonant to *wor-* is North., that of *wir-* followed by a consonant to *wur-* is nW-S (§§ 147, 149). The failure of *i* to undergo breaking

[1] But *ǣ* extensively penetrates the spelling system of *Ru.*[1] It is a natural consequence of the development of *ǣ* instead of *ē* in W-S that that dialect is the only one in which *ǣ* can revert to *ā* by retraction before *u̯* (§ 151), and by restoration before back vowels (§ 162). In the latter case, *Ru.*[1] has again admitted a few forms of W-S type.

before *r* groups, when *i* stands in the following syllable, is Angl. (§ 154.3).

§ 259. The second fronting whereby *æ* > *e* and *a* > *æ* is mainly a mark of *VP*, but forms of this type, especially ones with *a* > *æ*, have extensively penetrated *Ep.* and *Cp.*;[1] *RG* and *St. Chad* have frequent *æ* > *e*.

§ 260. W-S and North. are distinguished from Kt. and Merc. by much more extensive diphthongization of vowels by the influence of preceding palatal consonants. In Kt. and Merc. such influence is limited to the development of a few glides before back vowels, except for some cases of *æ* > *ea* in *Ru.*[1] This agreement of North. with W-S against the intervening Merc. is puzzling from the point of view of dialect geography.

§ 261. The chief dialect distinction arising from *i*-umlaut is the mutation of *ĕa, ĭo* to *ĭe* in W-S, instead of to *ĕ, ĭo*, as in nW-S.[2] Naturally some distinctions arise because previous changes had left different conditions for *i*-umlaut to operate upon in different dialects. One may note: (1) W-S, Kt. mutation of *ea*, Angl. mutation

[1] S. M. Kuhn (*PMLA* liv. 1–19; lx. 631–69) regards second fronting as common to *VP*, *Cp.*, and *Ru.*[1] He holds that in *Ru.*[1] (1) while *æ* generally appears for Prim. Gmc. *a*, a falling together of *æ* and *e* under the latter is indicated by the frequent spelling of Prim. Gmc. *e*, and of *e* the *i*-mutation of *æ*, with the symbol *æ*, and (2) that second fronting of *a* to *æ* is to be observed in the forms *cæfertūn*, *fæder* (g.s.), various parts of *færan*, *gæfel*, *fætu*, *ġedæfnade*, all of which occur in *VP* with *ea*. Second fronting was followed, presumably, by back umlaut of *æ* to *ea* as in *VP*, but this sound Kuhn thinks may have been early subject to monophthongization to *æ* in the *Ru.*[1] dialect. To Kuhn's view it may be objected that the bulk of the instances of *æ* for Prim. Gmc. *e* are due to a combinative change of the dialect, *we* > *wæ* (§ 328); most of the rest are due to the consistent abnormal spelling of a few words, especially *þæġn* for *þeġn*. The cause of these abnormal spellings requires investigation, but it is not a general identification of *æ* and *e*. Even less conclusive are forms with *æ* for the mutation of Prim. Gmc. *a*: most are to be explained under § 193.a, c, d, above. The forms alleged to show second fronting of *a* to *æ* are not typical of *Ru.*[1], which also has e.g. *fasu*, *naru*, *-swarade*, *ġetalu*, *dagas*, *-a*, *-um*, *þacu*, *-um*, *wacane*, *nacud*, *ġestaþulad*, *magun*, *wagende*, *plagadun*, *ġelaðadum*. Hence the *æ* forms must be otherwise explained, by analogy or *i*-umlaut: it should be noted that *færan*, *cæfertun*, *ġedæfnade*, *gæfel* are also North., and easy analogies explain *fæder*, *fætu*. (*Fæder* g.s. occurs 9 times, *fader* once; but *fætu* occurs once only, *fatu*, *fatum* 7 times.) Kuhn regards *Cp.* as too early to show second fronting in its spelling, apart from occasional *e* for *æ*, and some instances of *æ* and *ea* like *rægu*, *reagu-*. This position he is able to maintain only by making second fronting a relatively late change: on reasons for regarding it as prehistoric, see § 253.

[2] Significance can hardly be attached to one or two forms in Angl. texts of W-S type: *Cp.* 774 *alīeset* he frees, 1135 *forsliet* slaughter (read *-slieht*); Ru.[1] *ġehȳrde* heard (twice); on forms with *īe* for *īo* see § 281.

of *a*, in type *ieldra, eldra, ældra*, § 193.a; (2) occasional mutation of *a* instead of *ea* before *r* groups in North. and the early glossaries; (3) W-S mutation of *io*, Angl. unbroken *i* before *r* groups, §§ 154.3, 258; (4) W-S mutation of *io*, nW-S of *u*, in words of type *wierþe, wyrþe*, §§ 149, 199, 258; (5) better preservation of a rounded sound as mutation of *ŏ* in nW-S, § 198; (6) mutations of diphthongs due to palatal influence on front vowels are W-S, and doubtfully North., § 184; (7) preservation of *æ* as the mutation of *ă* is of doubtful provenance, appearing in scattered sources, § 193.d.

§ 262. Many more diphthongs due to back umlaut appear in nW-S than W-S, where the change is severely limited as to the conditions in which it can occur, and is frequently removed by analogy.

§ 263. Smoothing is an outstanding feature of Anglian. Apart from archaic survivals in the early glossaries, and forms with analogical diphthongs (especially in *VP*), the only noteworthy exceptions occur in *Ru.*¹, which has again been penetrated by W-S spellings.[1]

§ 264. The chief dialectal distinction arising from vowel contraction is the development of diphthongs with mid or high first elements and unrounded second elements, *e*+*a*, *i*+*a*, in North. and *VP*, § 238. Otherwise, the chief differences in the processes of contraction in different dialects arise from whether or not smoothing had previously taken effect, §§ 235, 238.

[1] It may be useful to recall how many striking non-Angl. features invade *Ru.*¹: (1) *ǣ* for West Gmc. *ā*, and hence restoration of this *ǣ* to *ā* before back vowels; (2) *ea* before *l* groups from Prim. Gmc. *a*; (3) forms lacking smoothing.

A consequence of the introduction of W-S *ǣ* for West Gmc. *ā*, beside nW-S *ē*, is that *ǣ* is freely substituted for *ē* in words where no dialect has *ǣ*: with the smoothing of *ēo*, frequently *nǣhste* beside *nēhste*; with the smoothing of *ēa*, *bǣg* 27, 29, *hǣmæhte* Mk. 1, 22; for examples with the *i*-umlaut of *ēa* see § 200, footnote 2. Here might also be placed the forms with *ǣ* for the mutation of *ō*, but they have parallels elsewhere (§ 198).

VI

CHANGES OF ACCENTED VOWELS FROM ABOUT 700 TO 1000

A. *niu̯i-* > *ny*

§ 265. In all dialects at an early date the negative adverb *ni* contracted with a following accented *u̯i-* to produce *ny-*. Examples are provided only by negated forms of *willan* will, and *witan* know, e.g. *nylle*, *nyllaþ*, *nylle*, *nyton*, *nyte*, *nyste*, and by the noun *nytenness* ignorance. Such forms are established in *VP*, eW-S, and eKt. (examples in Ct. 41 from *nyllan*). The other Angl. texts have largely adopted other formations,[1] but sufficient *ny-* forms are scattered through *Ru.*[1] and North. to suggest that this is an early, general OE development, afterwards partly eliminated. *KG* have *ne-* from *ny-* (§ 288): *netenes*. lW-S has with great frequence *ne-* instead of *ny-* in forms of *nyllan* (*nelle*, *nellaþ*, *nele*), and such forms already appear in eW-S. In view of the absence of a similar development in forms of *nytan*, these *ne-* forms from *nyllan* are best regarded as arising in low sentence stress.[2]

B. Vocalization of *i̯* and *u̯*

§ 266. In early OE a marked tendency is to be observed for *ġ* to be vocalized and to combine with a front vowel belonging to the same syllable to form a diphthong, *ǣ̆i*, *ĕi*, or *ī* (< *ĭi̯*). But there were many forms in which *ġ* did not belong to the same syllable as the preceding vowel, and hence did not become vocalized and combine with the preceding vowel, and by analogy of such forms the diphthongs were usually removed, so that, for example, *weġ* way, *wīġ* war, are more usual than *wei*, *wī*, owing to the influence of inflected *weġes*, *wīġes*.[3] Examples of such diphthongs are: Ep. *grēi*,

[1] e.g. Ru.[1] *nuton* < *ni wuton* (§ 218), *nallað* < *ni wallað* (§ 768).

[2] North. forms in *ne-* (Li., Ru.[2] *nelle* imper., Li. *nellað* imper. pl.) do not belong here, as the dialect has sometimes uncompounded forms with *e* (Li., Ru.[2] *welle* subj.).

[3] On the other hand, in ME vocalization and diphthongization took place over the following syllable boundary: not only was restored *weġ* re-changed to *wei*, but *weġes* became *wei-es*.

bodæi, Cp. *grēi*, *popei*, eKt. *mēi-* (Ct. 38), *ēihwelċ* (Ct. 40), *dei* (Ct. 42), *hēi-* (Ct. 43), LV *Mēi-* 213, 268, KG *wæi* weighed, *wei* the same, *meiden*, *meiðhades*, *-strēide* strewed, *wrēi* imper. accuse, *swǣið*[1] sounds, *ġeċēide* called, *adrēið*[2] dries, *ēihwilcum*.[3]

§ 267. There are more examples of *ī* from *ĭġ*. Many texts have *brīdel(s)* bridle (*Ep.*, *Cp.*, *VP*, *KG*, W-S; *Erf.* still *briġdels*); eW-S *frīnan* ask, *hlīsa* fame, *rīnan* rain, *-brītt*, *-līð*, 3rd sg. pres. ind. from *breġdan*, *liċġan*, *ġelīres* g.s. adultery (*CP* 143, 2), *Wī-* for *Wīġ-* in names; Cp. *sīðe* scythe (cf. Ep. *siġdi*); VP *rīneð*, *rīnde*, from *rīnan* rain; eKt. *Wī-*, *Sī-* in names; KG *wīlung* sorcery (cf. *wīġlian*), *wī-* way,[4] *hlīsa*. So in unaccented syllables in lW-S and *KG* the syllable *-iġ* interchanges freely with *-ī*, and there are already a few examples in earlier texts, e.g. *menīu* Cp. 685, *dysī* CP 267, 1, *mēðīe* Oros. 86, 28; *VP* has often *-īe* for *-iġe*, e.g. *hefīe*. In such unaccented positions, however, *ī* would doubtless soon be shortened. In eW-S *-iġ-* and *-i-* also interchange in the medial syllable of verbs of the second weak class, and there is also much fluctuation in the forms of other dialects: see § 757 for details.

§ 268. A few forms show contraction of *-īe-* from *-iġe-* to *ī*: eW-S *īl*, *iil* hedgehog, lW-S *Sīlhearwan* Ethiopians; already *Cp.* has *iil*, *sīras* (1241 for **siġeras* gluttons). In early instances the contraction would still be of *-iġi-* (§ 369).[5]

§ 269. For *ǣ̆i*, *ĕi*, from *ǣ̆ġ*, *ĕġ*, we often find the compromise spellings *ǣ̆iġ*, *ĕiġ*. Cp. already has *grēiġ* 850, *seiġn* 2093, but instances are mostly lW-S and lNorth.: e.g. in W-S manuscripts of eleventh century *weiġ*, *læiġ*, *mǣiġ*, in Li. *ðeiġn*, *hēiġ*, *ċēiġde*. In Northumbrian the spelling *iġ* is sometimes extended to intervocalic *ġ*: Li., Rit. *ċēiġa*. Similarly, *Ru.*[1] has *ċēiġde*, *ðrēiġa*. KG have several forms with *iġ* between vowels for *ġ*: *deiġe* (d.s.), *swēiġas* (a.p.), *meiġe* possis.

§ 270. It is possible that forms like those dealt with in § 269 caused an equation in spelling of *ē* and *ēi*, for if *mēiġ* = *mēġ*, it follows that *ēi* = *ē*. This would provide another explanation for BDS *nēid-* for *nēd-* and other forms quoted in § 42 above.

§ 271. The interchange of forms with *ī* and *iġ* described in § 267 leads to an equation of *iġ* and *ī* in spelling, and hence of *yġ* and *ȳ*: already in

[1] i.e. *swēið* with Kt. inverted spelling. [2] i.e. *-drȳġð*, cf. § 288.

[3] Since *eġ*, *ei* were alternative spellings, *eġ* was used for Latin and Norse *ei*, e.g. *Aquileġia*, *Sweġn*.

[4] In *wīferend* 137, from curious local form *wiġ* 207, 475, 772; *wigas* Bd. 58; cf. Bliss, *Sir Orfeo*, p. xx.

[5] But *Erf.* 138 *tuiġin* shows inverted spelling, *igi*=*ī* (cf. Cp. *tuīn*, and § 404).

eW-S such spellings are found, e.g. *biġ*, *ānwiġġe*, *astiġgende*, *swiġgende*, for *bī* by, *ānwīġe* d.s. combat, and present participles of *astīġan* ascend, **swīġan* be silent, and so *dryġġe*, *adryġġean*, for *drȳġe* dry, &c. Already the early glossaries have spellings which may be of this type, e.g. *ġiġ* vulture; see § 411 below.

§ 272. Theoretically *w* should never stand finally after a vowel in OE, for it was lost after some vowels, and combined with others into diphthongs, see §§ 120.2 and 3, 400. It was, however, often replaced by analogy, e.g. *snāw*, *stōw*, *trēow*, *strēaw*, *mǣw*, *brīw*, after inflected *snāwes*, &c. Similar are W-S 2nd and 3rd sg. pres. indic. of verbs in *-w-*, like *cnǣwð*, *sǣwð*, *flēwð*, *hīewð*, after *cnāwan*, &c. (Cf. *ġecnǣð*, CP 29, 1, the phonological development, with loss of *w*, before *-i-*, cf. § 406.) In all these forms with analogical *w* a diphthong with *u̯* as its second element is present. In early texts and Northumbrian the symbol is sometimes *u*: Ep. *mēu* mew (610, so read for manuscript *men*), Cp. *-stōu*, Li. *stōu*.

§ 273. lW-S manuscripts sometimes have *-ēow-*, *-ēaw-* where *-ēw-*, *-ǣw-* might be expected: in Thorpe's ed. of Ælfric's *Homilies* occur *flēowð* flows, *spēowþ* succeeds, *hrēaw* corpse, *ēaw-* law, other manuscripts have *brēaw* eyelid, beside more usual *flēwð*, *spēwð*, *hrǣw*, *ǣw*, *brǣw*.[1] These forms give rise to a few inverted spellings, e.g. *glǣwne* a.s.m. wise, *Gen.* 41, 33, MS. L, for *glēawne*. S–B, § 126.1.*a*.2, regard these spellings as due to the general eleventh-century monophthongization of diphthongs, and consequent inverted spelling: *ēa*, *ēo* became *ǣ*, *ē*, and hence *ēaw*, *ēow* are graphic equivalents of *ǣw*, *ēw*. Luick, *Hist. Gramm.*, § 258, considers that *hrǣw*, *flēwþ* ultimately approximated their diphthongs *ǣu*, *ēu* to the prevailing OE diphthong types *ēa*, *ēo*, and that from the forms **hrēa*, **flēoþ*, by analogical reintroduction of *w*, the lW-S *hrēaw*, *flēowþ* were produced. A phonological explanation is to be preferred to the purely graphic one of S–B, for traces of a similar process are to be observed in Cp.: *hēawi* 444, 981, *mēau* 955, 1183, and inverted *glēu* 1768, and so *Ep.* 649 *sċrēuua*, for W-S *hǣwe* blue, *mǣw* mew, *glēaw* wiŝe, *sċrēawa* shrew.[2] If Luick's explanation be true of these early forms also, *hēawi* must be regarded as graphic, due to the spelling equation of *mēau*, *mēu*.

§ 274. Diphthongs in lW-S manuscripts sometimes assimilate their second element partially or completely to following *-w-*. Thus manuscripts of Ælfric have *hrēow*, *strēow* for *hrēaw* raw, *strēaw* straw,

[1] Probably add *lēawfinger*, forefinger, *Ps.* 72, 11, not recorded as *lǣw-*.

[2] A few instances of *ēw* for *ēaw* in *Li.* and *VP* are probably errors (Li. *sċēware*, *ēwunga*, VP *sċēwað*, beside many forms with *ēaw*; so Ru.[1] *strēu*).

Lambeth Ps. *flēuwð* 57, 9, for *flēowð*, Leechdoms *strēuw* iii. 114, for *strēaw*.

c. The Second Elements of the Old English Diphthongs

§ 275. The diphthongs derived from Prim. Gmc. *au*, *eu*, *iu*, and from the corresponding West Gmc. diphthongs (§ 120) may be reasonably supposed to have passed into OE with the second element -*u*, though this stage of development is rarely recorded in the case of the diphthong derived from *au*. Recorded spellings for those derived from *eu* and *iu* are: *stēupfaeder* Ep., *Hrēutford* BH, *Strēunaeshalch* BH (MSS. Leningrad and Cott. Tib. A xiv), *Sċēutuald* LV, *glīu* Ep., Cp., *ġeþīudde*, *þīustra* Cp., *Īuti*[1] BH (in various inflexions), *flīusum* LR, *Bīuuulf*, *Frīubet*, *Frīumon*, *Līutfrith* LV. Already, however, in the earliest texts *eo*, *io* are the prevailing spellings, e.g. Ep. *ċēol*, *sprēot*, *anhrīosith*. The change of the second element from *u* to *o* is more slowly carried out when *u̯* followed, hence Ep. *trēulesnis*, Cp. *mundlēu* basin, Ep., Cp. *ġesīuwid* sewn (if the diphthong is long, see § 120.2, footnote 6), *snīuuith* it snows. Although we should no doubt be justified in assuming that *au* became OE *ǣu*, and that this became *ǣo* when *ēu*, *īu* became *ēo*, *īo*, yet the most archaic spelling in a fully reliable form is *ǣo*:[2] BH *Ǣodbald*, Cp. *ġenǣot* companion, LV *Ǣostoruini*.[3] More frequent is *ēo*, e.g. BH (MSS. Leningrad and Tib. A xiv) *Ēodbald*, North. coins *Ēotberehtus* (i.e. Eadberht 737–58), Cp. *earnġēot* vulture, *ġefrēos* froze, *ēorsċripel* ear-scraper,[4] VP *dēode* a.p. dead, *hēofud* head, and twice in forms of *otēawan* show, 90, 16; 91, 8, Ct. 35 *Ēostoreġe*, poetical *frēo* for *frēa* lord.[5] Similarly, with a diphthong due to OE contraction (§ 238.2), Ep., Cp. *ēorisċ* rush, VP *ēoland* island. However, the prevailing spelling is already *ēa* in even the earliest texts, e.g. Ep. *ēast*, *rēad*, *strēam*. On the more archaic *ǣa*, see § 135.

§ 276. The diphthong which arose from Prim. Gmc. *a* by break-

[1] Hence by direct literary borrowing g. and d. *Īutna*, *Īutum*, OEC 449, MS. E.

[2] Possible archaic spellings: *Ld.* 207 *arngeus*, *Erf.* 40 *aerngeup*, glossing *arpa* (i.e. ἅρπη) may represent an original -*ġēup* or -*ġēut*, cf. Cp. *earnġēot*, Ep. *earnġēat*: see Kraliks, *Gött. gel. Anz.*, 1914, pp. 158 ff.; manuscripts of *BH* vary between *Hēuuald* and *Hēauald*, where the first element is presumably *hēah*.

[3] Beside which LV *Ǣestor-*, *Ǣestur-*, are hardly more than slips.

[4] But Ep., Cp. *snidstrēo*, Cp. *snithstrēo*, Erf. *snidstrēu* (an unknown plant) is influenced by *trēo* tree.

[5] For examples from genealogies see K. Sisam, *Proc. Brit. Acad.* xxxix, 308.

ing, back umlaut, and the influence of palatal consonants, was no doubt at first apprehended as a short equivalent of that derived from *au*, whether this was then in the stage *ǣu* or *ǣo*. The most primitive spelling is Urswick Cross d.s. *bæurnæ*, if this is to *bearn* child, not *beorn*. *eo* is frequent in early texts, e.g. with a diphthong due to breaking, Cp. *weorras* hard skin, *seorwum* d.p. devices, LG *speorulīran* suras, VP *ġeeorningum* d.p. merits, *beorn* child (twice), *ðeorfan* a.s. poor man, LV *Georored*, Ct. 38 *beorn* children, Ct. 48 *ġeeorniġan* merit, Ct. 37 *ġeġeorwien* 3rd pl. pres. subj. prepare, to which a few cases of *-heord*, *-weord*, in the second element of names in *LV* and Kt. charters may be added; with a diphthong due to back umlaut, VP *feodrum* d.p. fathers, *ġedeofenað* is fitting,[1] LG *lundleogan* kidneys, Cp. *beosu* purple,[2] BH *Peoda* (MSS. Leningrad and Cott. Tib. A xiv), LV *Beodu-*, *Heoðu-*.

§ 277. Similarly, the diphthongs derived from Prim. Gmc. *e* and *i* by breaking and back umlaut were at first short equivalents of those derived from Prim. Gmc. *eu* and *iu*. In these short diphthongs the stage with *-u* is recorded with breaking in BDS *uuiurthit*, LV, Gn. *Iurmin-*; and with compensatory lengthening BH *Ēumer* (from *eoh* horse); with back umlaut in Bd. *eutende*,[3] LV *Friuðuulf*. But *eo*, *io* are the established spellings already in the earliest texts.

§ 278. While what has been said concerning the development of *ĭu* to *ĭo* applies to all dialects, the North. developments of *ǣ̆u* and *ĕu* require separate discussion.

(*a*) In the type of North. represented by *Ru.*[2], the *ǣo* derived from Prim. Gmc. *au* did not unround its second element, and this is reflected in the spelling, which is usually *ēo*, e.g. *ēostan* from the east, *hēofud* head, *ġilēofa* belief, and many singular past tenses of strong verbs of Class II, *ġiċēos* chose, &c. Similarly, the short diphthong arising from the breaking of Prim. Gmc. *a* is usually written *eo*, e.g. *-ċeorf* he cut, *eorm* arm.[4] This reluctance of the *Ru.*[2] dialect to unround the second element

[1] I exclude VP *ondsweorian*, which always has *eo*, to which occasional Li. *ondsweariġa* corresponds with North. *ea* for *eo* (§ 278). It would seem that these forms have back mutation of *e* transferred from *swerian*, rather than of the *a* of *andswarian*.

[2] But Cp. *meottoc* mattock, pl. *meottucas*, in view of Ep. *mettocas* 565, 586, 878, may be regarded as having basic *e*, despite Ep. 1003 *maettoc*, W-S *mattuc*. The word is of unknown origin (see § 565).

[3] Not in Sweet's *OET*; cf. *ZfdA* xxxi. 28.

[4] Back umlaut of Prim. Gmc. *a* is foreign to the dialect; *ea* from palatal influence is written *ea* so far as it occurs, e.g. *sċeattas* treasures.

of *ǣ̆o* naturally leads to graphic confusion between *ǣ̆o* and *ē̆o*, both being usually written *ē̆o*. *BDS* seems to show affinity with *Ru.*[2], having *dēoth-* death. Clear affinity is shown by *LV*, which has occasionally *ēo* from Prim. Gmc. *au* in the elements *Ēad-*, *Ēan-*, beside frequent *ēa* and once *Ēostur-*, twice *Hēouald*. This text also has a few instances of *eo* for the breaking and back umlaut of Prim. Gmc. *a*: the forms are quoted in § 276.

(*b*) In the dialect of North. represented by *Li.* and *Rit.*, *ǣ̆o* is developed to *ǣ̆a* in the normal OE manner, and practically always written *ē̆a*. On the other hand, the tendency to unround the second element of diphthongs is stronger than in other dialects, and *ē̆o* appears prevailingly as *ē̆a* except when *w* follows, or when *o* or *u* stands in the next syllable,[1] e.g. with *ēo* from *ēu* or from breaking of *ē*, *lēaf* beloved, *ðēaf* thief, *ċēasa* choose, *nēawung* nearness, *ġenēaleċa* approach; with *eo* by breaking and back umlaut of *e*, *fearra* from afar, *hearta* heart, *stearra* star, *seatul* seat, *ġeafa* gift, *eatta* eat. Very often, however, *eo* appears for the back umlaut of *e* before *o* or *u*, e.g. *seofo* seven, *heofon* heaven, *feolo* many, *feotrum* d.p. fetters.[2]

(*c*) The names in the various manuscripts of *BH* have, as has been shown, often *ēo* or *ǣo* for *ēa* (§ 275), but this might be there regarded as an archaic rather than a dialectal feature. They have practically always *ea* for the short diphthong (except only *Peoda* quoted above). They have prevailingly *ē̆o* where it would normally occur in OE: exceptions are the archaic forms with *ēu* quoted above and a few cases of *ē̆a*: *Earpuald*, *Ċearl*, *Strēanæshalch*.[3]

[1] On the other hand, the second element of *io* is rarely unrounded: *Li.* has, however, *bihianda*, frequently, against *bihionda*, once.

[2] *RC* has forms with *ē̆a* for *ē̆o* according to the usual transliteration: *fearran*, *heafunæs*, *bihealdun*; but it cannot be shown that the value of the rune ᛠ was *ē̆a* rather than *ē̆o* in this inscription (cf. Girvan, *Angelsaks. Handboek*, § 42.*a*.2).

[3] J. W. Watson, *Language* xxii. 19–26, regards the modern dialect of Lorton, Cumberland, as described by B. Brilioth, *A grammar of the dialect of Lorton* (Philological Society, 1913), as providing evidence that OE *ēa* and *ēo* fell together in North. According to Brilioth the Lorton reflex of OE *ǣ*, *ēa*, and *ēo* is *eī*, while that of *ē* is normally *ī*. If this is accurate, it may be that in this dialect *ēa* and *ēo* fell together already in OE, but this was not the case in the whole North. area because (1) the evidence of rhymes in ME shows that the usual ME distinction of the reflexes of OE *ēa* and *ēo* was generally found in the Northern dialect: see Heuser, *A* xviii. 114 ff., xix. 319 ff.; (2) other Cumberland dialects show a less clear-cut picture than that of Lorton as described by Brilioth (information supplied by Ian Catford), and other dialects belonging to the ONorth. area show a distinction of the reflexes of OE *ēa* and *ēo* (e.g. Adlington, Lancs., described by A. Hargreaves, *A grammar of the dialect of A.*, Heidelberg, 1904). It would then seem that the view taken above, that *ēa* and *ēo* remained distinguished in their first elements in ONorth., is correct. For the corresponding short diphthongs Watson accepts such a distinction (see *Studies in honor of J. S. Wilson*, pp. 167–74).

§ 279. Before *w* there is no regular unrounding of the second element of *ĕ̄o* in any Northumbrian text,[1] but it is often approximated to the *w*, so that *ĕ̄uw* results, and this is often written *ĕ̄w*, *ĕ̄u*. Similarly, *ĭ̄ow* is often developed to *ĭ̄uw*, and this can be written *ĭ̄w*, *ĭ̄u*. Spellings of this type are frequent in *Li.*, e.g. *cnewa* a.p. knees, *ðeua* d.s. servant, *ðiua* maid-servant, a.p. *ðiuwas* (but d.p. *ðiowum*), *ġiwiġa* desire (many forms), *trēu* tree, *cnēw* knee, *trēwufæst* faithful (and various related words), *ġehrēues* repents, *oncnēu* knew, *ġeblēuu* blew, *fēwer* four, *nīwe* new, *īw* you (and related forms). Similar forms are frequent in *Rit.*, but rare in *Ru.*[2], where *-ĕ̄ow-*, *-ĭ̄ow-* prevail in words of this type. Here and there, the development appears in *VP*, e.g. *trēw*, *oncnēw*, *ġetrēwliċe*, *ðiwġen.*[2] *Ru.*[1] also has a few forms of this type, e.g. *trēuw*, *cnēu*, *-þēu(w)*, *hrē(u)w-nisse*, *ġetrēuwe* (< **ġetriuwe*, cf. § 295), *þriuwa*; also in reduced stress *lāreuw* teacher, *lateuw* leader, pl. *lārewas*, *latewas*.

§ 280. Unrounding of the second element of diphthongs, similar to that of *Li.* and *Rit.*, is seen in the Kt. charters of the ninth century, but here both *ĕ̄o* and *ĭ̄o* are affected, appearing often as *ĕ̄a*, *ĭ̄a*,[3] e.g. with *eo*, *aġiaban* give, *wiaralde* g.s. world, *hiabenliċe* heavenly, *Biarn-* (in many names), *fiah* money;[4] with *io*, *wiada*, *weada* g.s. wood, *Wiaht-*; with *ēo*, *bebīade* I command, *bibēadeð* he commands, *Ċīal-* (in several names); with *īo*, *frīandum* d.p. friends, *ġeðīan* thrive, *bīan* be, *hīa* she, *sīa* the (f.s.). *KG* also have a few instances of such unrounding: with *eo* by breaking, *hearran* hinges, *awearp* imper. cast thou; with *ēo*, *atīara* imper. be exhausted; with *īo*, *ahrīasð* he falls, *forbīet* he forbids.

§ 281. In other texts the unrounding of the second element of *ĕ̄o*, *ĭ̄o* is sporadic. *VP* has a number of examples: with *eo*, *ætfēalan*[5] adhere, *earðe* earth (5 forms), *wearðiað* imper. honour ye, *afearra* imper. be far away,[6] *weagas* ways (3 times), *cweaðað* they say, *eatað* they eat, *ðeawde* he served; with *io*, *earre* anger (2 forms), *ondwleatan* d.s. face; with *ēo*, *ðēada*, *ðīada* g.p. peoples, *nēasade* he drew near (2 forms);[7] with *īo*, *astēapte* pass. part. n.p.m. deprived, *ðēastrum* d.p. darkness (87, 7,

[1] But *Li.* has occasional *ēa* for *ēo* in *hrēawnise* penitence (and related forms), and also in the past tenses *oncnēaw* knew, *ġesēaw* sowed, under the influence of other verbs of strong Class VII. There are scattered instances of *-ǣw-*, e.g. Li. *hrǣwende*, *oncnǣw*, *rǣuun* rowed, and so Rit. *ġiflǣue*, Ru.[2] *sǣwe*, past subj. and 2nd sg. indic. from *flōwan*, *sāwan*.

[2] i.e. pres. subj. pl. of *ðeowian* serve, so that here *iw* is for *euw*, a confusion promoted by the free interchange of *eo* and *io* in *VP* (cf. § 294).

[3] It will be observed that the first element of *ĕ̄o* tends to be raised in Kt., producing *ĭ̄o*, or, with unrounding of the second element, *ĭ̄a* (cf. § 297).

[4] So in the second element, Ct. 31 *Ċīalbearht*; coins of Eċġbeorht from Canterbury have *Eċġbearht*.

[5] With compensatory lengthening of the diphthong.

[6] Also in medium stress *mildheartnisse*, Hy. 1, 6.

[7] The loan-word *lēa* lion, beside once *lēo* and always inflected *lēon*, &c., may be added.

reading uncertain).[1] There are also a few instances in *VP* where the second element of these diphthongs is reduced to a more indistinct sound, written *e*: *hiefene* d.s. heaven, 32, 13, *ðīeda* g.p. peoples (3 times), *ġeðīeda* g.p. languages, 30, 21, *ġehīewade* he formed, 32, 15. With these spellings cf. *Ep.* 983 *unhīeri* fierce (MS. *hun-*), and KG *forbīet* quoted above. VP *onsīen*, *fīenda*, *-um* are discussed above (§ 201). In *Ru.*[1] unrounding of the second element of *ĕo*, *ĭo* is even more rare, e.g. *hrēad* reed (twice), *hrēanis* roughness, 16, 3, *bīatadae* threatened, 9, 30, and a few forms of *weorþan* and *weorpan*. Such spellings occur also sporadically in W-S, e.g. *ðeawas* servants, *CP* 196, 23, *feala* many *PC* 530.

D. Changes of Quantity

§ 282. The vowels of the composition forms of the numerals 'two' and 'three', *twi-* and *þri-*, are lengthened in OE, e.g. *twīfeald* double, *þrīfeald* threefold.[2]

§ 283. Although it does not occasion a change of spelling in OE, the lengthening of vowels before a liquid or nasal consonant followed by a homorganic voiced sound, thus before *ld*, *rd*, *rl*, *rn*, *mb*, *nd*, *ng*, and also before *rs*, *rþ* when a vowel follows,[3] certainly belongs to the OE period. Hence, at least for late OE, we can assume long vowels in such words as *eald*, *heard*, *eorl*, *beorn*, *lamb*, *land*, *lang*, *eorþe*, *earses*.[4] The change would probably not take place when a third consonant followed the consonant group, e.g. *lambru*, *englas*, *heardra*, *cembde*, *hundred*, and this gave the possibility of transferring the short vowel to the simple form. Hence, in the future history of the language, there is great fluctuation in the quantity of vowels in words of this type, and already certain OE sound-changes show lengthening to be absent in some words where it might be expected, e.g. lW-S *swurd*, *wurd*, *cwyrn*, for *sweord*, *word*, *cweorn*, show changes possible only in short syllables (§§ 320–4). Low stress could also cause lengthening to be absent in such words as *and*, *under*, *sċeolde*, *wolde*.

§ 284. In date this change seems later than the latest prehistoric changes: it was not early enough to prevent *æ* > *e* before

[1] It will be observed that the first elements of *ĕo*, *ĭo* are no longer distinguished in *VP* (see § 294 below).

[2] The evidence for this is the metrical value of these syllables in OE, and later phonological developments (e.g. NE *twilight*).

[3] Finally, *s* and *þ* are voiceless in OE.

[4] Following the usual convention I do not mark quantity in such words in OE.

nasals (e.g. *cemban*, *sendan*, § 193.d), or the operation of back umlaut in North. *bihionda*, Kt. *siondan* (§ 217). On the other hand, it was in time to prevent the tenth-century W-S change *sel* > *siel* (§ 325), for this does not occur in *seldan*. Other tests of date have been suggested but are unreliable: long vowels before groups of late origin (e.g. *fald* fold, older *falud*), and in loan-words (e.g. *wrang* wrong, ON *rangr*, **scarn* scorn, OF *escarn*) may be due to reforming the word to obtain a normal OE sound-pattern.

§ 285. Shortening of vowels normally occurred in OE (1) before groups of three consonants, and (2) before groups of two consonants, if at least two unaccented syllables followed in the word. This system is the forerunner of the system developed in the period of transition from OE to ME, by which vowels shorten (1) before groups of two consonants (other than the groups which cause lengthening), and (2) before a single consonant or a lengthening group, if at least two unaccented syllables follow. Examples of OE shortening before triple consonants are *godspell* gospel, **bræmblas* brambles, and probably many words with consonant gemination before liquids (cf. § 453), e.g. *nǣddre* adder, *āttres* g.s. poison.[1] Hence the geminate (and no doubt the short vowel) could be transferred to forms like *āttor*. Examples before two consonants when two more syllables follow are *bletsian* bless (cf. *blōd*), **spannīewe* very new (cf. *spōn*), *Hlammæsse*[2] Lammas, *semtinġes* immediately, compounds in *en-* (< **ǣni-*) like *enlīepiġ* individual, *enetere* one winter old, and in *sam-* (< **sōm-*) like *samcucu*[3] half-alive. In these, the phonological form of the word often suggests shortening (cf. §§ 127, 193.d).

§ 286. There seems to have been in OE sporadic shortening before geminates. Phonological developments prove short vowels in *leassa* (§ 208), *sioððan* (§ 217), *enne* (§ 193.d), lW-S *sylla*[4] (§ 325). Shorts may be suspected in the etymologically obscured *wimman* woman, *latteow* leader, *bliss* bliss, *liss* mercy, beside *wīfman*, *lād-teow*, *blīþs*, *līþs*.

§ 287. A number of forms show shortening of a vowel, and com-

[1] Again I follow the convention in marking the vowels of such words long.

[2] But in the form *Hlāfmæsse*, the obvious etymology would preserve the length.

[3] And hence *sam-* is generalized to words where only one syllable follows, e.g. *samworht*.

[4] Li. *sella* always has *e* (not *oe*) and this suggests a short vowel, which has been transferred to *sel*, beside *sōel*.

pensatory gemination of the following consonant. The causes of this development are obscure. The chief instances are: *reċċan* care[1] (for **rōēċan*, cf. *rōhte*), *lin(n)en* of linen,[2] eW-S *ġeliċ(ċ)ettan* pretend, *siċ(ċ)ettan* sigh, *sċien(n)ess* suggestion, *ġemet(t)ing*, meeting. Forms found in later texts are lW-S, North., Ru.[1] *þrittiġ* thirty, lW-S *þreottyne* thirteen, *Þrinness* Trinity, *wissian* direct, *wittiġ* wise, *orrettan* disgrace, *ġeliċċost* most like, *riċċeter* power, *hleappettan* leap.

E. Modifications, mainly Kentish, of the Front Vowels

§ 288. The spellings of *KG* make it clear that by the tenth century *ǣ̆* of whatever origin had been raised to *ē̆* in Kt., while *ōē̆* had been unrounded to *ē̆*, and *ȳ̆* unrounded and lowered to *ē̆*. These changes are proved by the glosses both by direct orthographical evidence (the symbol *e* appearing for *æ*, *oe*, *y*) and by inverted spellings, in which *æ*, *y* appear for *e* (e.g. *wær*, *byrene* for *wer* man, *berene* g.s. she-bear). Examples from *KG* of the changes under consideration are:

ǣ̆ > *ē̆*: with *æ* from Prim. Gmc. *a*, *fet* vessel, *glednes* joy; with *æ* due to double umlaut, *ġegederad* gathered, 831; with *ǣ* the *i*-umlaut of *ā*, *ġelēred* learned, *todēl* imper. divide.

ōē̆ > *ē̆*: *efst* he hurries, *bēnum* d.p. prayers.

ȳ̆ > *ē̆*: with *ȳ̆* due to mutation of *ū̆*, *gerdels* girdle, *ferht* fear, *brēċð* enjoys, *ontēnð* opens; with *y* due to umlaut in group *wur-* < *wir-* (§ 149), *werstum* d.p. worst, *werðnes* dignity; with *ny-* < *niu̯i-* (§ 265), *netenes* ignorance.

Since Kt. had *e* for the *i*-umlaut of *a* before nasal groups and *l* groups (§§ 193.d, 200.1), and *ē* for Prim. Gmc. *ǣ* (§ 128), it is plain that all front vowels except *ī̆* appeared in l.Kt. as *ē̆*.

§ 289. It is difficult to determine precisely the age of the various changes which led to the disappearance of *ǣ̆*, *ōē̆*, *ȳ̆* from the Kt. sound-system. In the ninth-century charters *ōē̆* and *ȳ̆* are still in general use. Some few cases of *ē̆* for *ōē̆*, however, occur: *bledsung*

[1] This word probably has early shortening in all dialects. *Cp.* 1646 already has *reċċileas*, Li., Ru.[2] have *reces* Mk. 4, 38, and the *e* suggests a short. There is no other nW-S evidence. W-S has always *ċċ* in the verb except once in Ælfric's *Colloquy*, *ċċ* beside *ċ* in *reċ(ċ)eleas* and derivatives.

[2] Already recorded with *nn* in *Ep.*, but *n* in *Cp.*; it fluctuates between *n* and *nn* in North. and lW-S.

[3] *Fiffalde* butterfly, beside *fīfalde* is perhaps due to false etymology; *Cp.* has already *ff*.

blessing, *ġerēfa* reeve,[1] and inverted *bōēm* for *bēm*, W-S *bǣm* dat. both, also *twǣġen* for *twōēġen* two, since *ǣ* and *ōē* were both equivalent to *ē*. The symbol *y* is even more fixed, but note *Hereġēðe* (Ct. 28), and inverted *yfter* for *efter*, W-S *æfter* after. The eighth-century charters provide no evidence for the treatment of *ŏĕ* and *ȳ̆*, except the name *Byrnham* Ct. 8, where *y* is undisturbed. *ǣ̆* is used still for West Gmc. *a* and for mutated *ā* in the Kt. will added to Ct. 34 in the first quarter of the ninth century, e.g. *æt, ðæt, ælmesliċ, arǣddan, nǣniġ, ġedǣle, ǣhte, ðǣm, bǣm*; this, however, proves a good spelling tradition rather than the existence of the sounds *ǣ̆*, and in fact several inverted spellings occur: *onċærrende, swǣ* (for nW-S *swē*, § 125). After this the symbols become increasingly confused, *e* appearing for *æ* (< Prim. Gmc. *a*), and for *ǣ* the mutation of *ā*, while *æ* appears by inverted spelling for Prim. Gmc. *e* (*ġæfe*), *ē* (*hǣr* here), *ǣ* (*mǣgas, swǣsendum, ðǣr*), and for the *i*-mutations of *æ* (*sælen*), and *ea* (*ærfe, ærðe-*). This confusion cannot be traced back to the eighth century, where we find *æ* used for Gmc. and Lat. *a* in *-paeð* and *ċaestr-*, and for its double umlaut in *Æthel-*, and not extended to the place of *e*, at least in any name of certain etymology.[2]

§ 290. If the evidence of spelling set out in § 289 be directly assessed, the Kentish modifications of the front vowels must be placed in the ninth century. It would, however, be possible to argue that the ninth-century charters preserve a spelling tradition Merc. rather than Kt., and that the process we can observe in them is not the occurrence of Kt. sound-changes, but the gradual emancipation of Kt. spelling from Merc. tradition, leading to a better expression of the phonological facts of the dialect.[3] If this be the case, the Kt. modification of *ŏĕ* and *ȳ̆* may have taken place at any time after *i*-umlaut caused these sounds to arise, and the same applies to *ǣ* the *i*-umlaut of *ā*. *æ* (< Prim. Gmc. *a*) existed before *i*-umlaut operated, but it is reasonable to assume that it was modified to *e* when *ǣ* became *ē*, otherwise two periods of raising have to be assumed for Kt. Here Kt. is sharply distinguished from the dialect of *VP*, where the older *æ* is raised before umlaut, and *ǣ̆* due to umlaut is unaffected (*ældra, clǣne*).

[1] Cf. *Cēnwald* (moneyer of Ceolnoth, 833–70) for *Cōēn-*.

[2] I refer to the evidence of Cts. 5–8, dated 700–70. I exclude the suspect Ct. 4.

[3] Angl. influence on Kt. spelling has been noted §§ 207, 258.

§ 291. The dialect of Surrey, as seen in Ct. 45 and *CA*, from the last quarter of the ninth century, shows much the same features as Kentish of the same date. The symbols *ȳ̆* and generally *ōĕ* (here written *ēŏ*) remain used in the places historically justified, but *ǣ̆* is sometimes retained, sometimes changed to *ē̆*, e.g. *deġe*, *ġemēne*; there are also inverted uses of *æ* for *e*, e.g. *ærfe*. Before nasals *æ* is so frequent for the *i*-mutation of Prim. Gmc. *a* (e.g. *mæn*, *acænned*, *Cænt*) that the influence of the type of language found in Essex in the ME period may be suspected (see § 193.d).

§ 292. In other dialects *ǣ̆* is relatively stable till after 1000, and *ȳ̆* till after 900 (see §§ 315–18, 329). The history of *ōĕ* has been given above (§§ 196, 198). In Angl., however, *ǣ*, the *i*-umlaut of *ā*, is often changed to *ē* by a following dental consonant, e.g. Cp. *ġelēstunne* accompany, *-tēnel* basket, *sċulthēta* bailiff (i.e. *sċyld-hǣta*); *VP* many examples including *lēreð* he teaches, *alēdde* he led, *ġebrēded* pass. part. dilated, *forðrēsted* crushed, *flēsċ* flesh; *Ru.*[1] many forms and derivatives of *clēne* clean, *hēlend* saviour, *ēr* before, *hwēte* wheat, and single occurrences of many other words; *Li.* single occurrences of *flēsċ*, *huuēte*, *-ġelēred*; Rit. *clēne*; Ru.[2] *ēlċ* each. Other instances of *ē* for the mutation of *ā* are sporadic and of no significance.

F. Later History of Diphthongs

ī̆o

§ 293. *ī̆o*, derived from earlier *ī̆u* according to §§ 275, 277, is retained unaltered in North. until after the period of our OE texts. Exceptions are *beorna* burn (cf. § 155), *heona* hence, *frēond* friend, beside *biorna*, *hiona*, *frīond*; on *leornia* beside *liornia*, see § 154.3, footnote. Other verbs to be explained like *leornia* are *lēora* go, *ġetrēwa* trust (§ 279), beside *līora*, *ġetrīowa*. Ru.[2] *siofu* seven, perhaps represents inflected **sifuni*, Li. *seofo* uninflected **sefun*. In a few isolated cases, probably errors, *ī̆o* is written for *ē̆o*, e.g. Li. *ġiorne* eagerly, *bebīodo* I command; and so *ē̆o* for *ī̆o*, e.g. *ueototliċe* certainly, *ġestrēonde* he gained.

§ 294. In Merc., *ē̆o* and *ī̆o* are still in great measure distinguished in the early glossaries. Nevertheless, a few forms occur with *ī̆o* for *ē̆o*, e.g. Ep., Cp. *crīopungae* d.s. creeping; Ep. *buturflīogae* butterfly; Cp. *ġestrīon* treasure, *brīost-* breast, *tīonan* injuries, *ġetrīowad* trusted, *-biorg* protection, so LP *iorðan* infl. earth. The symbol *eo* encroaches upon *io* only in the case of the back umlaut of *i* in Cp. *neoþouard* lower, *ġeonath* he yawns, *biheonan* on this side, *seotol* evident (770, read *sweotol*). In *VP*, *io* does not encroach upon *eo*, but, on the other hand, *eo* appears instead of *io* by breaking in *eorre* anger or angry, *heorde* shepherd, and frequently instead of *io* by back umlaut, e.g. *sċeopu* ships, *ġewreotum* d.p. writings. The long diphthongs *ēo* and *īo* are completely confused, both appearing in *ēo*-words like *lēof*, *tēona*, and in *īo*-words like *nīowe*, *hīow*, and their derivatives. It seems evident that *ĕo* and *ĭo* have fallen together in *VP*, and in the case of the short sounds under *eo*; in the case of the long sounds, ME evidence makes it plain that the falling together was in *ēo*.[1] The falling together of *ēo* and *īo* in *VP* was accompanied by a similar falling together of the contracted diphthongs *ēa* and *īa*: this is fully exemplified, § 238 above.

§ 295. In *Ru.*[1] the position resembles that of *VP*: *io* is practically never found for *eo* by breaking or back umlaut, but *eo* has replaced *io* in *eorre* and related words, and has often replaced *io* by back umlaut.[2] In the case of the long diphthongs, *īo* seldom replaces *ēo* (e.g. *þīof*), but *īo* is often replaced by *ēo*, e.g. *þēostre*, *ġetrēowe*, *dēorwyrþe*, *nēowe*, beside forms with *īo*.

§ 296. In W-S it is evident that the graphs *ĕo* and *ĭo* had become equivalent in force by the time of the oldest manuscripts, but it is difficult to decide if vestiges of an old distinction can still be traced. For *eo* by breaking, Oros. and *PC* have only *eo*, but a number of *io* spellings occur in *CP*, e.g. *ðiow-*, *fioh*, *plioh*, *biorht*, *ċiorl*, *cwiorn*, *fiorm*, *fior*, *hiord*, *mildhiortnes*, beside *eo* spellings. Similarly, *eo* by breaking, when subject to lengthening, appears as *īo* (beside *ēo*) in *CP* only of the eW-S texts, e.g. *fīos*, *twīon* d.s. doubt (358, 13), and various forms of *ġefīon*, *plīon*, *sīon*. *eo* by back umlaut is never certainly written *io*, though possible instances are Oros. *swiostor* (cf. § 210.2, footnote), CP *tiogoðiað*, *siofan*. *io* by breaking and half-umlaut (§ 202) is always replaced by *eo* in *leornian* and related words in Oros., but in *CP io* and *eo* both appear. *io* by back umlaut is frequently preserved in *CP*, though *eo* often replaces it (cf. § 213); in Oros. it is usually *eo* (note, however, *siolfre*, *-es*, 70, 34; 170, 27); *PC* preserves *io* in *wiotan* 755. For *īo* by breaking, *CP* has

[1] See D'Ardenne, *Seinte Juliene*, pp. 192–3. On the dating of the coalescence of *ĕo* and *ĭo* in the dialect of *VP*, see Flasdieck, *AB* xli. 37–39.

[2] e.g. *cleopaþ*, *weotudliċe*, *leoman* g.p. limbs, beside forms with *io*; see also § 214 above.

both *ēo* and *īo* in *lēoht*, and in various forms of *þēon* thrive, and *wrīon* wrap, but *ēo* only in *betwēoh*. *PC* and Oros. have no relevant material except in *betwēonum*. For Prim. OE *ēu* we find both *ēo* and *īo* in *CP* in the majority of words, but in Oros. and PC *īo* is rare except in *dīofol*: Oros. has *īo* in *dīor* 286, 12, and in *īower*, five times, all in two passages. The half-umlaut of *ēo* similarly varies between *ēo* and *īo* in *CP*, but is practically always *ēo* in *PC* and Oros. except in a few derivatives of *þēod*.[1] We may sum these facts up thus. In Oros. and *PC* the symbol *ĭo* is becoming disused. In *CP*, however, *ēo* and *īo* heavily invade each other's domains. The historical position is rather better preserved in the case of the short vowels: *eo* by breaking and by back umlaut is rarely written *io*, and *io* by breaking and half-umlaut and by back umlaut is still often written *io*, though *eo* often replaces it. In lW-S the symbol *ĭo* is little used.

§ 297. In ninth-century Kt. documents a marked tendency appears to raise the first element of *ĕo*, so that spellings occur like *siolf*, *wiorð*, *fiah*,[2] *aġiaban*, *wiaralde*, *hiabenliċe*, *bebīade*, *Ċīal-*, *līofast*, *prīost*, *īow*, *ðīow*. Occasional inverted spellings with *eo*, *ea* for historical *io* occur: *weada* g.s. wood, *awreotene* written. It is, however, evident that the tendency was less strong in the case of the short than of the long diphthong. From *KG*, it is evident that ultimately *ēo* and *īo* fell together in *īo* (*īa*), but that *eo* and *io* fell together in *eo* as in W-S and Merc. These conclusions, based on the prevailing spellings of *KG*, are confirmed by the history of the dialect in the ME period.

§ 298. There is no reason to think that the first element of *ĕa* was raised in Kt. in the OE period: *smȳaġenne*, KG 749, is simply for *smēaġenne*, as *e* and *y* were equivalent graphs in late Kt. (§ 288).

ĭe

§ 299. The main sources of this W-S diphthong were palatal diphthongization of *ĕ* (§ 185), *i*-umlaut of *ĕa*, *ĭo* (§§ 200–1), and contraction of *ĭ*+*e* (§§ 234; 237.3). A number of subordinate sources of *ie* may now be mentioned:

(*a*) When *i* was followed by *r*+another consonant, if the group had arisen too late to cause breaking, we find very often that the *i* appears as *ie* in eW-S, though *i* frequently remains, e.g. *bierð* he bears, *iernan* run, *biernan* burn, *fierst* period.

[1] *Elþiodiġness* PC 891, *elðiode* Oros. 126, 16, *elþiodiġe* 120, 13.

[2] On *-a* in the second element, see § 280.

(*b*) *ie* apparently replaces *io* from *i* by back umlaut in eW-S under circumstances not clear, e.g. *tielung* effort, and related forms, *wietað* imper. know, and various forms and derivatives of *witan*, *ġewrietum* d.p. writings, *ġeflietu* p. disputes, *ġefrieðode* he defended, *nieðemest* lowest, *cliepiað* they call, *behienan* on this side of. The significance of these spellings is uncertain: they seem too frequent to dismiss as graphic variants of *i* (cf. § 300). In the majority of the forms, there should be no back umlaut in W-S: it may be that when back umlaut of *i* failed to take place, there was later a tendency for *i* to become *ie*.

(*c*) Initial *sio-* seems to have frequently developed in eW-S to *sie-*. The only recorded instances are frequent *sient*, *siendon*, are, beside *sint*, *sindon*, but frequent lW-S *syfon* seven, *syppan* after, *sylfor* silver, with *y* from *ie* (§ 301), indicate that the change was common.

(*d*) A later change of *sel-* to *siel-* will be discussed below, § 325.

§ 300. It is clear that W-S *ĭe* had undergone monophthongization before the period of our early W-S manuscripts, for in all of them *ĭ* and *ў̆* spellings appear for *ĭe*, and by inverted spelling *ĭe* appears for *ĭ*, especially in the Hatton MS. of *CP*, e.g. *bieterness*, *wieðerweard*, *briengan*, *ondliefene*, *flīetað*, *ġīetsiað* (and related words), *ġegrīepð*, *ġīefernes*, *īedelre*, *ġelīeffæsð*, *rīeċe*, *sċīenð*, *tīema*, *unðrīestan*, *ryhtwīesnes*, *ġewīeten*, *wīese*. *ĭ* is so freely used for *ĭe* in eW-S that one example only of each of the main phonological types will be given: with *i*-mutation of *ea*, *wille* fountain, *fird* army, *hlihhað* they laugh, *sċippend* creator; with *i*-mutation of *io*, *smirewað* they anoint, *fiht* he fights; with *ie* by palatal influence *ġesċinded* pass. part. hurt, *forġitan* forget;[1] with *i*-mutation of *ēa*, *ġehīran* hear; with *i*-mutation of *īo*, *ġestīran* control.[2] The monophthongization of *ĭe* to *ў̆*, on the other hand, is less frequent in eW-S, and practically limited to the position between a labial consonant and *r*: *hwyrfan* turn, *wyrnan* refuse, *awyrġed* cursed, *wyrsa* worse, *wyrresta* worst, *wyrðe* worthy (and its compounds), *wyrð* he becomes,

[1] In *ġifan* give, pass. part. *ġifen*, beside *ie* spellings we may have, not change of *ie* to *i*, but an alternative root form *ġif-*, which may also be reflected in frequent lW-S *ġifan*, &c., beside *ġyfan*, in *Ep.* 525 *ġibaen*, pass. part., and in *Rit.* 66, 15 *forġif* imper.

[2] S–B § 107.*a*.5 are not justified in assuming a divergent W-S treatment of mutated *īo* before *w* at least in the words *hīew* shape, *nīewe* new; *īe* is recorded in these words, and there is no reason to suppose that the more usual *ī* is not its normal monophthongization.

wyrpð he throws, occur frequently with *y*. These words are also recorded with *i* and *ie*.[1] Other instances of *ie* > *y* are *fyr* further (and related forms), Oros., *byrhto* brightness, *CP* 69, 22, and with *ie* as defined under § 299.a, *byrð* he bears, *CP* 72, 13, *fyrste* d.s. period, *CP* 228, 6, Oros. 72, 1, forms of *byrnan* burn, Oros. 142, 15; 160, 24.

§ 301. The picture obtained from later West Saxon texts is different. It is plain that the type of language found in the manuscripts accepted as eW-S differed considerably from that which contributed most to the formation of lW-S. In the latter type *ĭ̄e* became *ĭ̄* before palatal consonants, but *ȳ̆* in all other positions, hence we find prevailingly in lW-S manuscripts e.g. *miht* might, *niht* night, *sihð* sees, *ġinġra* younger (§ 178), *hīġ* hay, *ċīġan* call, *līhtan* alleviate, but *yldra* older, *yrmþu* poverty, *yrre* angry, *hȳran* hear, *ċȳse* cheese, *frȳnd* friends, &c. On the subsequent treatment of *ȳ̆* from *ĭ̄e* see §§ 316–17.

TRANSFERENCE OF STRESS

§ 302. A few forms in lNorth. and lW-S point to occasional shift of stress from the first to the second element of diphthongs, with loss of the first element. The chief instances are Li., Rit. *sulfer* silver (cf. *Li.* g.s. *seulfres*), Li., Ru.[2] *soððа* afterwards (for **sioððа*, cf. § 217), *Ru.*[2] *solf* self (for *seolf*), Rit. *fōuer* four (beside *fēouer*), *ġitrōwaliċe* faithfully (for -*trēow*-). In lW-S most instances are after palatals, e.g. *sċāwian* observe, *onġān* against, for *sċēawian*, *onġēan*, but also *sufon* seven, *sufoða* seventh.

§ 303. Some late texts have spellings which suggest a tendency for initial *ġĕ̄a*-, *ġĕ̄o*- and *ĕ̄a*-, *ĕ̄o*- to become identical in sound. The process would involve a shift of stress: *ĕ̄a*, *ĕ̄o* > *i̯ă̄*, *i̯ŏ̄*; *ġĕ̄a*, *ġĕ̄o* > *i̯eă̄*, *i̯eŏ̄* > *i̯ă̄*, *i̯ŏ̄*. So we find spellings like *ēoc* (Wald. 1, 25), for *ġēoc* help; and, on the other hand, *ġealgodon* (Brun. 9, MS. D), *ġeornustliċe* (*A* xiii. 439) for *ealgodon* they defended,[2] *eornostliċe* earnestly. *aġīode* for *aēode*,

[1] In view of these *ie* spellings, there can be no doubt that the eW-S *y* spellings reflect a development of *ie*. *ȳ̆* from *ĭ̄e* not between a labial and *r* is very rare in eW-S, except in Junius' transcript of the Cotton MS. of *CP*: it is to be feared that the scribe's familiarity with lW-S has impaired his accuracy. Oros. has about eight instances in words with mutated *ea* (e.g. *yldo*, *besyrede*), and *fēowersċȳte* 74, 13, *aþrȳtton* 238, 10, *sċȳt* 10, 35, etc. (3rd sg. pres. indic. from *sċēotan*). (The vowel of *lȳþre* may be mutated *ū*, Oros. 166, 16; 292, 27.)

[2] S–B, § 212.*a*.2, quote *Ġēanberht* as an early instance of such a spelling (Ct. of 781, Cott. Ct. vi. 4). But this is an error for *Iǣnberht*, and the manuscript is a late copy (? tenth century). In *middaneard*, beside more original -*ġeard*, the elements *eard*, *ġeard*, are confused; so in *wīneard*, -*ġeard*.

happened (Ct. of 1038, Cott. Aug. ii. 90), is an attempt at a phonetic writing of *i̯ō*; *eador* for *geador* (with velar *g*) shows graphic equation of *gea-* and *ea-*.

G. Palatal Umlaut

§ 304. This change may be defined as follows: before *χt*, *χs*, *χþ*, in absolute finality, and perhaps when followed by *-e*, the diphthongs *eo*, *io*, and the monophthong *e*, all became *i*. Obviously, before *χ* groups *eo* and *io* would occur only in W-S and Kt.: smoothing would have reduced them to *e* and *i* in Angl. On the other hand, owing to breaking *e* would not be found before *χ* groups in W-S and Kt., apart from Kt. forms with the mutation of *ea*, e.g. **hlehþ* he laughs.

§ 305. In eW-S we already find *cniht* boy, *riht* right, *siex* six, *wrixl* change, *Wiht* Wight, *wiht* creature, *-bryht* (name-element).[1] It is doubtful whether occasional *ie* spellings indicate that the change *eo/io* > *i* was through a stage *ie*, or whether they are merely graphic (see § 300).[2] Since consonant groups were not palatal before back vowels, and possibly not before *-e*, they would not there cause palatal umlaut, and hence normal paradigms are *cniht*, *cneohtas*, **Piht*, **Piohtas* later *Peohtas*. Hence analogical forms like *cneoht*, *cnihtas*, *Pihtas* are freely formed; *meox* manure, rarely has palatal umlaut, and *ġefeoht*, fight, *feohtan* to fight, and related words never have palatal umlaut, the diphthongal forms with a back vowel after the *ht* having prevailed.

§ 306. In *KG* the same change has occurred, for we find *-riht*, *cniht-*, *wiht* weight, *ġewricl* (for *ġewrixl*). The dialect had a number of forms with *io* or *e* in the 2nd and 3rd sg. pres. indic., where W-S had *ie* from the mutation of *ea* or *io*. These forms should have Kt. *i* by palatal umlaut: actually we find *hlihð* laughs (and hence 1st sg. *hlihe*),[3] but *-siohð* sees (by analogy of type *sīoð*, with loss of *χ*),

[1] In lW-S *-bryht*, *-briht* is often transferred to the first element of names. *Byrht* is found in lW-S in both the first and second elements of names (e.g. *Byrhtnoð*, *Ordbirht*). It is rare except in names, e.g. *byrhtword*, *unbyrhtor*. It seems due, not to palatal umlaut, but to a special development of *beor-* seen also in *Byrn-* in names for *Beorn-* (e.g. *Byrnstan*), *Intebyrgan* for *-beorgum*, Inkberrow (Robertson, *A-S charters*, p. 162). *Bern-* for *Beorn-* in moneyers' names on ninth-century W-S coins may reflect the beginning of the change.

[2] Since *riht* is very rare, and *ryht* the normal spelling in eW-S, and since the name-element *-bryht* practically always has *y* in *PC*, it might be argued that *eo/io* became *ie* by palatal umlaut, and that this sound became *i* normally, but *y* after *r*.

[3] Perhaps add *tirhð*, he mocks, despite the intervention of *r* between the vowel and the palatal group. Cf. poetical *fyrhþ* for *ferhþ* soul.

slehst strikest, *slæhð* strikes. Special Kt. *e* < *y* (§ 288) is subjected to palatal umlaut in *ġenihtsumiað* they abound.

§ 307. In Kentish before 900, spellings seem to suggest that in this dialect at least palatal umlaut took place in two stages—first monophthongization (*eo*, *io* > *e*, *i*), then raising (*e* > *i*). Ct. 38, 14, *reohte* d.s. right, shows the original diphthong, id. 5, *rehtlicast* most right, Ct. 41, 62, *sex* six, show the first change, while the second appears in *KG*. So *io* appears as a diphthong in the Kt. form *ia* in Ct. 30 *Wiahtred*, but in *KG* we have *wiht*.

§ 308. In the earlier Mercian texts (*VP* and the early glossaries), there is no sign of palatal umlaut. In *Ru.*[1], however, we find *niht* (< *neht*, § 200.3), *riht* beside *reht*, *sihþe* behold, *syxta* sixth, beside *sex*(*ta*); and in RG *niht* beside *neht*, *cniht*, *sihþe*.

§ 309. In North. there is no certain trace of palatal umlaut in the OE period. ME forms show that it eventually reached North.

§ 310. *ēo* and *īo* seem not to be often affected by palatal umlaut in OE; yet ME *liht* from *lēoht* (*lumen* and *levis*) shows that it was a long-operative tendency, which could intervene after the shortening of vowels before groups of two consonants (§ 329). In the OE period the only traces of such a change are Ru.[1] *līht* lumen (perhaps influenced by the verb *līhtan*), *nīhste* nearest, beside *lēht*, *nēhste*; KG *-wrīhð* (hence imper. *-wrīh*), *-flīhð*, *-flīġð*, 3rd sg. pres. indic. from *wrīon* wrap, *flēon* flee, *flēġan* (W-S *flīeġan*, with *i*-umlaut of *ēa*) put to flight, beside *-tīohð* from *tēon* draw (perhaps with analogical *īo*), *-bēġð* from *būgan* bend (with Kt. *ē* < *ȳ*); so *nīh*, near, may have the vowel of **nīhst*.[1]

§ 311. It will be clear from the above sections that palatal umlaut is a change which began in the south: it can be seen operating in ninth-century Kt., and in W-S it has affected all possible short sounds by 900. In the tenth century it appears in Merc., still later in North. It was apparently due to a palatalization of the groups *χs*, *χt*, *χþ* when final, or followed by the vowel *e*, which enabled them to exert an influence on *eo*, *io*, *e*, similar to *i*-umlaut. Long sounds were rarely subject to the change.

[1] The operation of palatal umlaut, and its imperfect representation in spelling, so that *hlihð*, *flīġð* were written beside *slehst*, *bēġð*, and contained the same vowel (ī̆), leads in *KG* to the misuse of the symbol ī̆ for ē̆, e.g. 723 *sliċċ* sledge-hammer, 699 *hinrað* he is hungry (for *henġrað*, with Kt. *e* for *y*), 141 *aflīġed* apostate; and similarly of ē̆ for ī̆, e.g. 353 *lēċetere* hypocrite.

H. Late West-Saxon Smoothing

§ 312. In lW-S a change occurs by which *ĕa* > *ĕ* before *c*, *g*, *χ* and after *ċ*, *sċ* and *ġ* (not after *h*, which was initially not a palatal or velar spirant, but a breathing, or glottal spirant). Hence we find such forms as *seh* he saw, *ehta* eight, *fex* hair, *hēh* high, *bēcon* beacon, *ēge* eye, *ċerf* he cut, *ġef* he gave, *sċēp* sheep, *ċēs* he chose, *ġēr* year, beside *seah*, *eahta*, &c. The operation of these changes seems to have been limited by factors no longer recoverable, for they are not indicated with anything approaching consistency by the spelling system of any manuscript, although W-S spelling is fairly quick to allow for phonetic developments down to 1000, and the changes under discussion are relatively early, for traces are to be observed in eW-S, e.g. *þēh* though, frequently Oros., *toēcan* in addition, Oros. 130, 30, *mehte* he might, frequently, *unmeht* weakness, *CP* 465, 32. Of lW-S manuscripts the Abingdon version of *OEC* (i.e. MSS. B and C) down to 977 is very rich in forms of the type, often having *ġēr*, *Sexe*, &c.

§ 313. It should be observed that these changes affect falling diphthongs only: hence words like *ġeāra* formerly, *sċeadu* shadow, *sċeādan* divide (§§ 172, 179) are not subject to it. On the other hand, not only *ĕa* from palatal diphthongization of original front vowels (e.g. *ġef*, *sċēp*), but *ĕa* from palatal diphthongization of mutated vowels (§ 184) is subject to this change, e.g. *sċēþ* sheath, *Mal.* 162, &c.

§ 314. In Kt. of the ninth century there are a few forms which arose from a process similar to that to be observed in W-S: *Bǣgmund* Ct. 42, *Hǣgȳðe* Ct. 34, *ǣc* also (frequently). These forms are not to be attributed to the influence of Angl. spelling, for this would be to postulate influence of eighth-century Angl. on ninth-century Kt. (see § 225). *KG* have only *meht* thou mayst, *ðēh* though, beside many forms with *ĕa* unaffected.[1]

[1] Perhaps to be placed here are *CP* 152, 13 *smēġeanne*, *KG* 953 *smēġan*, although the *ġ* is palatal as the spelling of *CP* indicates (< **smauχōįan-*). Lack of material, however, makes it difficult to decide if a following palatal could have the same effect as a following back consonant.

Bliss (*English and Germanic studies* iii. 82–87) assumes that the change *ǣ̆a* > *ĕ* indicates a narrowing of the first element of the diphthong before monophthongization. It seems evident that the change was not through a stage *ǣ̆*, at least in W-S, otherwise *lǣgon* would have become **lēgon*, when the second stage of *ĕa* > *ǣ̆* > *ĕ* took place.

1. Unrounding and Rounding of Front Vowels

§ 315. In early texts *i* occasionally occurs where we should expect *y*, and should perhaps be regarded as a spelling slip for *ui* (§ 42), e.g. Ep. *cistiġian*, *smiġilas*, Cp. *risel*, from *cystiġ* generous, *smyġel* retreat, *rysel* fat. Of later Merc. texts, *VP* has *i* for *y* only in *ġetrime*, 50, 14, imper. of *ġetrymman* strengthen, *RG* only in the word *drihten* (invariably), and *Ru.*[1] only in *kining* and *drihten* frequently beside *y* forms, two forms of *ġenihtsumian* suffice, *hinġrade* hungered 21, 18, *ðinċaþ* seem, 18, 12. In early North. texts unrounding does not appear; in *Li.*, *Rit.*, *Ru.*[2] it is invariable in *drihten*, frequent in *cining*, otherwise sporadic, e.g. Rit. *ġestir* movement; Li. *ofcimes* he proceeds, *ġetri(m)að* he strengthens. *y* for *i* in these North. texts is invariable in *symle*, always, sporadic in other words, e.g. Rit. *suyppa* whip; Li. *wynn* work, *wynnes* they work. Since these *y* spellings are all in a labial neighbourhood, they represent rounding of *i*, not inverted spelling due to unrounding of *y*.

§ 316. In eW-S *ȳ̆* is hardly ever written *ī̆*: instances are a few forms of *cyning*, *ġenihtsumnisse* Oros. 182, 15, *CP* 325, 13, *disiġan* CP 279, 19, *unsċildiġ* CP 379, 14, and occasionally i.s. *þīs*, *hwī*. In many lW-S texts *ȳ̆* has a tendency to appear as *ī̆* before *h*, *ċ*, and *ġ*, and groups containing them, and in such positions *īĕ* tends to be monophthongized to *ī̆* instead of to the usual lW-S *ȳ̆*, e.g. *drihten* lord, *hiġe* mind, *biċġan* buy, *hinġran* hunger, *drīġe* dry, *wīsċan* wish, instead of *dryhten*, &c.;[1] and *miht* might, *niht* night, *hīġ* hay, *ċīġan* call, *līhtan* alleviate, for eW-S *mieht*, &c.[2] Yet *y* often remains before *r* groups, e.g. *wyrċan* work, *byrġ* d.s. city; and develops from *ie*, e.g. *awyrġan* curse.

§ 317. Some lW-S manuscripts show that in some areas *ȳ̆* (both mutated *ū̆*, and from *īĕ*) was becoming unrounded by isolative change. This appears in spellings with *ī̆* for *ȳ̆*, and inverted spellings with *ȳ̆* for *ī̆* where there is nothing to cause rounding. An example of such a manuscript is MS. Laud Misc. 509 of the OE *Heptateuch*.

§ 318. In lW-S *ī̆* often becomes *ȳ̆* in the neighbourhood of labials and before *r*, e.g. *clypian* call, *ċyriċe* church, *myċel* great,

[1] Also *cining*, *cinn*, where no *h*, *ċ*, or *ġ* is present.
[2] And so probably *ġinġra* from **ġienġra* (§ 178).

swȳþe very. A few such spellings already occur in eW-S,[1] also sporadic *y* for *i* in other positions, especially in cases of *þes* this (*þysne*, *þysses*, &c.).

§ 319. In North. there is a tendency in the tenth century to round *ĕ* to *œ̆* after *w*. With *e* this is practically always carried out in *Rit.*, very frequently in *Li.*, e.g. *woe* we, *woeġ* way, *woer* man, *woerc* work, *woes* imper. be, *cuoeða* say, *twoelf* twelve, *huoelċ* which, *suoelċ* such, *woenda* go, *awoerda* destroy. With *ē* the rounding is less frequent, e.g. *wōēron* they were, *cuōēdon* they said, *huōēr* where, *wœ̄de* garment, *wōēpen* weapon, *swōēr* mother-in-law. In *Ru.*[2] rounding is practically limited to *woeġ* way; it is sporadic in other words, and absent in the case of the long vowel.

J. Vowels between *w* and *r* in West-Saxon

§ 320. In W-S texts an increasing tendency is seen to allow groups consisting of *w*+short vowel+*r* to fall together in *wur*. Of groups of this type only *wear* is quite unaffected by the tendency, which successively affects *weor*, *wyr*, *wor*.

§ 321. The change is first to be traced in the case of *weor*: Oros. has *Ġeoweorþa* for *Jugurtha*, with assimilation of the second part of the name to the adj. *weorþ* worth, and this presupposes a form *wurþ*, which is directly recorded *CP* 200, 23 (a.s.m.). lW-S manuscripts usually have some *wur* spellings, e.g. in manuscripts of the W-S Gospels, *swurd* sword, *wurþan* become, *wurpan* throw, *wurþian* honour, beside many *eo* forms;[2] so before vowels, *þwuru*, *-e*, inflected forms of *þweorh*, crooked, *swura* neck (cf. § 241.2, footnote 5).

§ 322. The change of *wyr* to *wur* is ill represented in our texts, e.g. with *y* the *i*-mutation of *u*, W-S Gospels, *wurtruma* root, *awurtwalian* unplant, *ZfdA* ix. 453, *wurdwrītere* historian, Wulfstan 145, 10, *wurmum* d.p. worms; with eW-S *ie*, W-S Gospels, *wurþe* worthy, Ælfric's *Lives of Saints* 20, 65, *ġewurþan* recover.

§ 323. The change of *wor* to *wur* is even less well evidenced in spelling; of the forms usually quoted only *wurd* word, *ġewurden* past part. become, are etymologically certain examples for *wor*; they occur in the W-S Gospels.[3]

[1] See Cosijn, *Altwestsächs. Gramm.* i. 64–65.

[2] Rarely before *r*+back consonant: perhaps only *wurca* g.p. works, Cott. Tib. A vii, Wright–Wülcker 249, 18; 250, 20. On eW-S *worc*, see Luick, *Hist. Gramm.*, § 266.2.

[3] *Wurold* world, may be from *weorold* not *worold* (§ 210.1); *wurms* pus,

§ 324. ME evidence shows that these changes were extensive, and even in OE the meagre spelling evidence is increased by many inverted spellings with *wyr* for *weor*, and *weor* for *wyr*, showing that these groups had coalesced (in *wur*), e.g. *swyrd* sword, Ælfric's Voc., *cwyrn* mill (for *cweorn*), W-S Gospels, *weorm* worm, *And.* 769.[1]

K. The Group *sel*

§ 325. In W-S, after the period of the group of manuscripts regarded as 'early', the group *sel-* developed (presumably through *siel-*) to *syl-* or *sil-*: in lW-S *sylf* and *syllan* (and related words) usually appear for *self* self, *sellan* give, and more sporadically occur *sylra*, *syllic* for *selra* better, *sellic* wonderful. The change does not occur in *sele* hall (a poetical word of fixed form), or before *ld*, where *ē* had developed (§ 283): *seldan* seldom, *seld* seat, *selde* porch.

§ 326. Outside W-S there are few OE traces of the change, though ME forms suggest that it was widespread, and that the consonant following the vowel did not always require to be *l*.[2] In OE, however, *sile* I give, Ct. 48, is hardly more than an error in view of infl. inf. *siollanne*, also Ct. 48; *sylf*, Ct. 41, is a Kt. inverted spelling for *self*; Ru.[1] *sylle*, imper. sg., once, and *sylf*, four times, beside frequent *sel* forms, are to be attributed to the influence of W-S spelling; Li., Rit. (*ġi*)*sileð* he gives, beside more frequent (*ġi*)*seleð*, is due to the change and has influenced Li., Rit. *silo*, *-a*, 1st sg.

L. Anglian *e* > *æ*

§ 327. The many instances of *æ* for *e*, the *i*-umlaut of *æ*, in North. and *Ru.*[1] are for the most part to be explained under § 193 above.[3] The instances in North. texts of *æ* for Prim. Gmc. *e* are mostly due to a penetration of the present system of strong verbs by the vowel of the preterite (see §§ 741–3). In a few words, however, North. and *Ru.*[1] show an opening of *e* before *ht*, indicated by the spelling *æ* (see § 227, footnote); the curious forms Li. *cnaihtes*,

wurdlian speak, may have had *y*, see Gabrielson, *Influence of w*, p. 254; S–B, § 117.*a*.

[1] Already *CP* 191, 15 and 339, 18 (Hatton MS.) has *wyrðen* for *weorðen*; but *wyrð-* for *weorþ-* in compounds is influenced by *wyrðe*; and *þwyres*, crosswise, has *y* always in Oros., so it must be regarded as a form with *i*-umlaut.

[2] At least ME *suggen* points to OE **syċġan* for *seċġan* say.

[3] Bülbring, *Alteng. Elementarbuch*, p. 70; Kuhn, *PMLA* lx. 642–6.

Rit. *cnaihtas* are hardly due to more than a sporadic equation of *æ* and *ai* (but cf. *A* lxxviii. 145–6).

§ 328. On the other hand, *Ru.*[1] shows a well-marked change *we-* > *wæ-*, e.g. *cwæþ-* appears for *cweþ-* with very great frequence in the present system and pass. part. of *cweþan*, say, while other verbs of the strong Classes IV and V preserve *e* with great regularity. Other words appearing with *wæ-* for *we-* in *Ru.*[1] are *wæs* imper. be, *wæġ* way, *wær* man, *wæl-* well, *wæliġ* rich, *swælteþ* he dies, *swæġre* a.s. mother-in-law, *swæster* sister. There may be a similar change before *ġn* and *fn*, for *þæġn* is frequent for *þeġn* servant, and *ræġn* rain, *forlæġnisse* adultery, *fræġnast* thou askest, also occur, while *æfne* even (and compounds), *stæfn* voice, are frequent. Other instances of *æ* for *e* are insignificant, e.g. *aġæfeþ* gives, *forstælan* pres. subj. steal, *tægþiġaþ* ye tithe (once each), and unaccented *þæċ* for *þeċ* thee (3 times).

M. The Transition to Middle English

§ 329. The eleventh century was a period of great change in the accented vowels, but these changes did not generally receive expression in the by then fairly stable Old English spelling, and they are to be traced mainly through Middle English evidence. The great changes of the eleventh century were:

(1) The quantitative system was completely changed. Vowels were shortened before all consonant groups, other than those which cause lengthening (§ 283). Vowels were also shortened three syllables from the end of a word before any consonant or consonant group. Hence, for example, OE *brōhte*, *hēafodu* no longer had long vowels.[1]

(2) Diphthongs short and long were monophthongized, so that *ĕ̄a* > *ǣ̆* and *ĕ̄o* > *ō̆̈*. (*ĭ̄o* had by now become *ĕ̄o* in North.; *īo* still existed in Kt., see below.) Monophthongs first begin to be indicated by spelling soon after 1000.[2] *Ēd-*, *Lēf-* for the name-elements *Ēad-*, *Lēof-*, are frequent on coins of the period of Æthelred (978–

[1] Consonant doubling in closed syllables to indicate vowel shortness (the system afterwards developed by Orrm) is found in the mid-eleventh century, see Weyhe in *Germanica* (Festschrift Sievers), p. 318.

[2] Unless very occasional North. and *Ru.*[1] spelling with *æ* for *ea* before *r* groups be regarded as due to the beginnings of the process: Li. *ðærf* (noun, and some compounds and related forms), *-wærð* (pret. from *worða*, become), *Ru.*[2] *nēdðærfe* (frequently), Ru.[1] *þærf* (noun).

1016) and later. In Kt., however, the long diphthongs *ēa* and *īo* (from *ēo* and *īo*, § 297) underwent a shift of stress, to become level or even rising, and hence were not subject to monophthongization, which affects only the typical OE falling diphthongs. This shift of stress seems to have occurred, though more sporadically, in other dialects. Some spellings suggest that even short diphthongs could survive if they underwent a shift of stress, but it is unlikely that any falling diphthongs survived to 1100.[1]

(3) The sounds represented in OE by *æ* and *a* coalesced in *a*, so that OE *dæġ*, *dagas* now had the same accented vowel. This naturally had the result that dialects with *e* for Prim. Gmc. *a* were now even more sharply distinguished than before, having a distinction in the phonological types *deġ*, *dagas*, whether these represented older *deġ*, *dagas* (Kt.) or *deġ*, *dægas* (VP). *æ* derived from *ea* by (2) above shared the change to *a*, so that in the course of the century OE *hearm* > **hærm* > *harm*. Spellings of older *æ* (from *æ* or *ea*) with *a* appear about 1100,[2] but the change was not complete in all areas at that time; in the dialect of MS. Bodley 34 of the Katherine group, for example, the vowels of OE Merc. *all*, *hearm* are still distinguished about 1200 as *a* and *æ* (written *a*, *ea*).

[1] See Samuels, *Trans. Philological Soc.*, 1952, pp. 25–27; Kuhn and Quirk, *Language* xxix. 150, and other references there given.

[2] Both *a* for *æ*, and *æ* for *ea*, occur in Cott. Aug. ii. 85, to be dated on subject-matter 1035–40, but probably a copy of rather later date (see Whitelock, *Anglo-Saxon wills*, p. 182). *æ* > *a* earlier in the name-elements *Æþel-*, *Ælf-* when the second element contains a back vowel: instances are frequent after 950, e.g. *Alfwold*, *Aþelmod*, Hyde *Liber Vitae*.

VII

THE VOWELS OF UNACCENTED SYLLABLES

A. The Germanic and West Germanic Periods

§ 330. In Indo-European the accent might fall on any syllable of a word, but in Germanic it became limited to the first syllable.[1] Germanic had at first the same vowels in accented and unaccented syllables, except that Gmc. *ē* was developed in accented syllables only.[2] In final syllables, however, the Indo-European long vowels had had two intonations, the normal one, resembling that of internal syllables, and the abnormal one, which left vowels less prone to undergo shortening in Germanic.[3]

§ 331. The accent was in Germanic an expiratory stress, which threw the syllable upon which it fell into sharp relief, while the other syllables of the word became very prone to reduction.[4] The principal Germanic changes of unaccented vowels of which the effects are to be traced in Old English are:

(1) IE *a, o, e* were lost in Gmc. in absolute finality, i.e. when no consonant had followed them in IE,[5] e.g. OE *wāt* I know, he

[1] On the accentuation of compound verbs see § 72.

[2] See § 100.3.

[3] The normal intonation is variously termed in English 'acute' or 'broken', and the abnormal 'circumflex' or 'slurred'. Acute and circumflex are adopted from the terminology of English grammars of Greek, broken and slurred are derived from the terms *Stosston* and *Schleifton* used in German of the two intonations of Lithuanian. A vowel of a final syllable which had abnormal intonation in I-E appears as a long vowel in Gothic (where normal I-E long final vowels are shortened), while in Greek it has a circumflex accent, in Lithuanian a *Schleifton*; e.g. the g.s. of the *ā*- (Gmc. *ō*-) declension has Goth. *-ōs*, Gr. *-âs*, Lith. *-õs*. Further examples and discussion in *Trans. Philological Soc.*, 1936, pp. 11–13, 34–36.

[4] All consonants which had been final in I-E except *s* and *r* were dropped in Prim. Gmc.: examples below, § 399. Final *m̥* developed regularly to *um* (§ 100.2), and then the consonant dropped, leaving *u*, e.g. a.s. *fōtm̥* foot, Goth. *fōtu*. The final group *-ns* of most pl. accs. is retained in Goth., dropped in ON, e.g. Goth. *dagans*, ON *daga* days, acc. The acc. pl. seems to have adopted the form of the nom. in West Gmc. (cf., however, § 586).

[5] It is not possible to decide if *a* and *o* had fallen together before this loss; unaccented *e* had not yet become *i*, for final *i* remains in Gmc.

knows, Gr. *οἶδα*, *οἶδε*; OE *ber* imper. bear, Lat. *fer* < **fere*; probably g.s. *-æs* of *a*-declension, believed to be from *-oso*.

(2) IE *e* remained in Gmc. in unaccented syllables before *r*, e.g. OE *fæder* father, *æfter* after, *hwæþer* which of two, cf. Gr. acc. *πατέρα*, *ἀπωτέρω*, *πότερος*. Otherwise unaccented *e* > *i*,[1] e.g. OE *fēt* feet, *hilpþ* he helps, < Gmc. **fōtiz*, **χilpiþi*, cf. Gr. *πόδες*, **φέρετι*.

(3) When two or more syllables preceded, *i* (generally from IE *e*) was usually lost in Gmc. Examples are the g.s. and d.s. of weak nouns (OE *guman* < *-niz*, *-ni*), 2nd and 3rd sg., and 3rd pl. of present indic. (OE *hilpst*, *hilpþ*, *helpaþ* < *-isi*, *-iþi*, *-anþi*), and d.p. ending OE *-um*, in so far as this is from *-miz*, IE *-mis*.[2] There are a few exceptions in the g.s. and d.s. of trisyllabic consonant stems, especially **milukiz*, **miluki* > Prim. OE **milyki* > Angl. *milċ* (generalized to nom. and acc.), beside n.s. **meluk*[3] (§ 628.5) > W-S *meolc* milk; from this, retention of *-i* can be assumed in these cases of all trisyllabic consonant stems, e.g. **aluþi(z)* > *ealoþ*.

(4) In final unaccented syllables, *a* (< *a* or *o*) was lost even when a consonant followed, or had done so in IE, as in the n.s. and a.s. of the *a*-declension, **stainaz*, *-am*, OE *stān*.[4] This caused syllabic liquids and nasals to arise again, e.g. **fiŋgraz* > **fiŋgr̥z* > Goth. *fingrs*.[5] Similarly *u̯* often became *u*, e.g. **baru̯az* > **baruz* > OE *bearu*.[6] At this stage, however, unaccented *-a-* was retained as the connecting element of compounds, cf. OHG

[1] In unaccented syllables *e* was not subject to the vowel harmony which is frequent in accented syllables (§ 114), but passes into *i* even before *a*, e.g. adjs. in *-ila-*, and participial formations in *-ina-*, OE *lȳtel*, *ǣġen*, *cymen*, from **lūtilaz*, &c. Unaccented *u* similarly seems not to have been subject to vowel harmony in the type of Gmc. from which OE was derived, e.g. *eobor* beside *eobur-* boar, *Cp.* 179, 558, suggests that OE *eofor* is for earlier *eofur* by § 373 below, though derived from **evura-*.

[2] The evidence on the precise origin of this ending is conflicting.

[3] The variation in root vowel seen in **meluk*, **milukiz* is due to the harmonization of accented *e* to the following *i* (§ 112), a process which, like umlaut (§ 203), was not hindered by an intervening *u*. Similarly in Prim. OE **sefun* existed beside **sifuni* (§ 293).

[4] This loss of protected *a* was later than the losses dealt with under (1) and (3), for though lost in Goth. protected final *a* remains in the oldest Norse runic inscriptions when a nasal had followed it. It is not clear why *-as* < *-oso* in g.s. of the *a*-declension escapes syncopation.

[5] On the subsequent treatment of these new syllabic consonants in OE see §§ 363 ff.

[6] Vocalization of *i̯* due to a similar cause is rare: OE *here* army < **hariz* < **χari̯az* (§ 575).

alamahtig, *tagalīh*, but OE *ælmihtiġ* almighty, *dæġliċ* daily, owing to later syncopation (§ 341).

(5) In final unaccented syllables long vowels with the normal intonation were shortened:

ō (< I-E *ā* and *ō*) in shortening became in the East Gmc. area subject to the tendency *o* > *a*: e.g. Goth. *baira* I bear, *giba* gift, *juka* yokes. But in the North and West Gmc. areas, *ō* was closed in shortening, and, when preserved, appears as *-u*, OE *beoru* (nW-S), *ġiefu*, *ġeocu*. But in all areas *ō* > *a* when a nasal had followed, e.g. OE a.s. *ġiefe* < *-æ* < *-a* < *-ōm*, and so n.s.f. of weak nouns, *tunge* < *-ōn*.[1] This indicates that at the time of shortening the vowel was nasalized by influence of the lost nasal, and thus was prevented from closing.

ī (< I-E *ī* and *ei*) > *i*,[2] e.g. n.s. of *i̯ō-* stems (Goth. *bandi*, OE *bend*), endings of past subj. (OE *sċyle*, *-en* < *-i*, *-int*).

ǣ > *æ*, e.g. OE 3rd sg. of weak past indic., *-de*, earlier *-dæ* (e.g. CH *astelidæ*).

(6) It has been shown under (4) and (5) that I-E *o* > *a*, *ā* > *ō* in Gmc., in unaccented as in accented syllables. But in North and West Gmc., in medial unaccented syllables when *m* followed, or when *u* stood in the following syllable, I-E *o* > *u*, Gmc. *ō* (< I-E *ā* and *ō*) > *ū*; e.g. with I-E *o*, d.p. of *a*-declension, OE *stānum*, Goth. *stainam* < I-E *-omis*; a.s. and p. of disyllabic consonant stems, **brōþuru*, *-uns*, and of masc. weak nouns **ʒumunu*, *-uns* (on these forms in OE see §§ 617, 630); with Gmc. *ō*, d.p. of *ō*-declension, OE *ġiefum*, Goth. *gibōm*, and so of fem. weak nouns, OE *tungum*, Goth. *tuggōm* < I-E *-āmis*; a.s. and p. of fem. weak nouns, **tungūnu*, *-uns* (cf. OE *foldu* a.s. *CH*); nouns in I-E *-ātus* > West Gmc. *-ūþuz*, Goth. *-ōþus*: **fiskōþus* (Lat. *piscātus*) > OE *fiscoþ*[3] fishing, cf. Goth. *gaunōþus* mourning; superlatives in *-ōst-* had *-ūst-* before *u*, as d.p. *-ūstumiz*, and hence OE has *-ost* < *-ūst*, beside *-ast* < *-ōst* (§§ 355.4); the past of weak verbs of Class II varied between such forms as *-ōðō*, *-ūðunt*, either vowel might be generalized, and hence OE *-ode* beside *-ade*.[4]

[1] Other possible cases of OE *-e* from Gmc. *-ōn*, *-ōm*, are the a.p. *ġiefe* (nW-S § 586), 1st sg. pres. ind. *bere* (W-S, § 731.a).

[2] In OE, the *i* is either lost (§ 345) or becomes *e* (§ 369).

[3] On OE *o* < *u* in unaccented syllables see § 373.

[4] West Gmc. **friund*, **fiund* exhibited contraction of the succession *ī*+*ŭ* (§ 120.3), which arose owing to the development of *u* in certain cases, such as

(7) In North and West Gmc., *ai* and *au* (< *ai*, *oi*; *au*, *ou*) > *ǣ* and *ō* respectively in unaccented final syllables; e.g. OE pres. subj. *helpe*, *-en*, d.s. *stāne*, *ġiefe*, *ēste*, g.s. *ēste*, n.p.m. *gōde*, d.s.f. *gōdre*, g. and d.s. *suna*, *eahta* eight,[1] cf. Goth. *hilpai*, (*staina*), *gibai*, *anstai*, *anstais*, *gōdai*, *þizai*, *sunaus*, *sunau*, *ahtau*.

The history of *ai* and *au* in unaccented medial syllables is difficult to determine. If OHG g.s.f. *blintera*, d.s.f. *blinteru*, g.p. *blintero*, correspond exactly in formation to Goth. *blindaizos*, *-aizo*, and if the suffix seen in OE *lifen* sustenance, *lufen* joy, is identical with that of Goth. *libains*, *lubains*, it is clear that medial unaccented *ai* > *ǣ* in West Gmc. For unaccented medial *au* there is no evidence.[2]

B. The Operation of the Major Ingvaeonic and Primitive Old English Vowel Changes in Unaccented Syllables

§ 332. The Ingvaeonic loss of nasal consonants before voiceless spirants with compensatory lengthening of the vowel, and change of *ā* to *ō*, described in § 121, occurs in unaccented syllables also, e.g. pres. indic. pl. OE *-aþ* < *-ōþ* (§ 355.4) < *-anþi* (§ 331.3); *oraþ* breath < **oranþ-*; *duguþ* chivalry < **dugunþ-*, and so *ġeoguþ* youth; a.p. endings *-ans*, *-uns*, *-ins*, > *-ōs*, *-ūs*, *-īs*.[3]

§ 333. *a* is subject to the same alternative developments in unaccented as in accented syllables, becoming *æ* normally, but *a* before nasals. Before nasals in early texts the symbol is *a*, the hesitation between *a* and *o* found in accented syllables does not appear, e.g. *helpan* help, *guman* men, *ēastan* from the east.

In a group of words generally used in low sentence stress *o* appears: spellings with *a* are rare, and this points to *o*, not to the accented vowel variously spelled *a* and *o* (§ 130); they are *þone*, *hwone*, *þon*, *hwon*, *þonne*, *hwonne*, *on*. In a number of second elements, a further development to *u* takes place before *m* and *ŋ*:

a.s. and p., where *u* stood in the final syllable; hence North. *frīond*, *fīond*, other dialects usually *frēond*, *fēond* (§ 293).

[1] On OE *e* (Prim. OE *æ*) and *a* from unaccented *ǣ*, *ō*, see § 355.

[2] *Eahtatyne*, *eahtatiġ* are too obviously connected with the simplex *eahta* to provide evidence for medial *au*. On *ai*, *au* in the second element of compounds, see § 356.

[3] These endings so fell together with the corresponding n.p., except *-ūs*, which in West Gmc. is replaced by the nom. in both the *u-* and consonant declensions (OE *suna*, *fēt*).

līcuma body (beside *līchama*), *ācumba* oakum, *æfþunca* offence (beside *æfþanca*), *furlung* furlong (beside *furlang*).[1]

Except before nasals, unaccented *a* > *æ* (later *e*, § 369), e.g. n.s.f. and n. of weak nouns, OE *tunge*, *ēage*; a.s. of *ō*-declension, OE *ġiefe* (§ 331.5); g.s. of *a*-declension, OE *-es*, earlier *-æs* < *-as* < *-oso* (§ 331.1); ending OE *-æġ*, *-eġ* (later *-iġ*, § 376) < *-ag*, e.g. *hunæġ*, *haleġ*.

§ 334. Unlike the accented vowel, unaccented *a* > *æ* before a nasal consonant if this did not belong to the same syllable, and this *æ* could be transferred to forms where vowel and nasal belonged to the same syllable. Thus CH *hefaen-*, *heben*, are due to infl. **hevænæs*, &c. This is the origin of OE *-en* when absence of umlaut shows it not to be from *-in*, and when it is not due to parasiting, e.g. strong pass. parts. in *-en* (still often *-æn* in *Ep.*), *mæġen* might (OHG *magan*), *fæġen* glad (OS *fagan*), *þēoden* prince (Goth. *þiudans*).

§ 335. In a group of words frequently used in weak stress, and in the second element of some compounds, *a* is treated as if it stood before a nasal, appearing as *a* or *o*: *of* of, *of-*, *ot-* (unaccented forms of *æf-*, *æt-*, § 73), *was* was, *nas* was not (beside *wæs*, *næs*), *swa* so (§ 125), *ac* but, *ondsworu* answer, *sīþfat* journey (beside *andswaru*, *sīþfæt*), *herepaþ*, *-poþ* main road.

§ 336. A similar development occurs in the case of *ā* < *ai*. When shortened in low stress (§ 356), it appears in historical forms as *a* or *o*: *bēot* boast (< **bihāt*, § 238.2), *eofot* crime (*Ep.* 854 *ebhat*), *ēorod* troop, *earfoþ* trouble, *wulmod* distaff (OHG *uuolla-meit*); etymologically uncertain is *innoþ*, *-aþ*, inside (of body). A different development is shown by *ēored*, *earfeþ*, where the accent of the second element was reduced sufficiently early for *ai* to become *ǣ* under § 331.7, and unaccented *ǣ* was developed in OE as usual (§§ 356, 372).

§ 337. *ā* > *ǣ* in OE in unaccented as in accented syllables, e.g. nomina agentis in *-ere* < *-ǣri* (§§ 355.5, 369), as *leornere* learner (OHG *-āri*), and perhaps with shortening and syncopation, *ġeatwe* armour, *frætwe* ornaments (cf. *ġetāwe*, § 151, but see § 358, footnote).

[1] A similar development occurs in *oruþ* breath, beside *oraþ* from **oranþ-* (§§ 332, 356); on *oroþ* see § 374. *Beornaþ* is developed like *oraþ* (< *-nanþ-*), while *Beornnōþ* has stressed development of the second element. The etymology of *sūlung*, Kt. measure of land, is uncertain: not to *sulh*+*lang* because *o* is rare, *a* unknown in the second element, and medial *ll* never occurs.

§ 338. Breaking seems not to take effect in OE unaccented syllables, but instead we have retraction of *æ* (< Gmc. *a*) before *l* or *r*+consonant to *a*, and this *a*, like those dealt with in § 335–6, tends to become *o* later, e.g. *hlāfard*, *-ord* lord, *toward*, *-word* towards (beside *toweard*), North. *efolsiġa*, *ebalsiġa* blaspheme, *nalles* not at all, *weorold*, *-ald* (Ct. 40, 20) world, *onwald*, *onwold* power, and proper names with *-bald*, *-bold*, *-wald*, *-wold*, *-ward*, *-word*, *-hard* in the second element.[1] So eW-S *art* art, *þarf* need, beside *eart*, *þearf*, are forms developed in low stress. A further development to *u* appears in *hlāfurd* (lW-S, rare), *weoruld* (frequent), *eofulsiġa* (Ru.[2]).

§ 339. *i*-umlaut was fully operative in unaccented syllables, but *ŏē* and *y* became prehistorically already *ĕ* and *i*, and *æ* > *e* soon after the earliest texts (§ 369). This left *ĕ* and *i* as the only unaccented products of umlaut, and these soon fell together in *e* (§§ 355.5, 369). Examples of umlaut in unaccented syllables are:

u: all words quoted in § 203 to illustrate double umlaut have *i*-umlaut of *u* in the medial syllable.

o: suffix *-ehte* (OHG *-ohti*), as in *stānehte* stony.

ō: suffix *-ede* (OS *-ōdi*) as in *hōcede* hooked; suffix *-erne* < *-rēni* (ON *-rœnn*), as in *sūþerne* southern; medial *-ii̯-* < *-ei̯-* < *-ōi̯-* in the present system of weak verbs of Class II (written *-i-* or *-iġ-*, cf. §§ 355.5, 376, 267).

a: pres. parts. in *-ende*[2] (< *-andi*), and gerundives in *-enne* (< *ani̯-*);

æ: suffixes *-ettan*, *-estre* (< *-ati̯an*, *-astri-*) as in *hlēapettan* leap, *sēamestre* sempstress; *æþele* noble (OS *aðali*). The mutated vowel was often syncopated (§ 341), e.g. *mæġden* maiden (OHG *magatin*), *lāwriċe* lark (< **laiu̯arīkōn-*, cf. § 364), and

[1] Forms like *Ēadweard*, *Beornheard*, have the vowel of inflected *Ēadweardes*, &c., where the development proper to accented syllables takes place, since the medial syllable has a half-stress (§ 90). This *ea*, transferred into low stress, could be reduced to *e*, e.g. W-S *towerd*, *andwerd*, names in *-werd* for *-weard*, Li. *hlāferd*. (But Li. *towærd* rather to § 329.2, footnote.) Similarly *ĭo* by breaking, if transferred to low stress, was shortened (§ 356) if long, and can appear as *u* in historical forms, e.g. *nānwuht*, *wuht*, in low sentence stress, and with *īo*, *fulluht*, *betwuh*, *betwux*. So in eKt., the name-element *-beorht* can appear in low stress as *-barht* (Ct. 38 *Ċīalbarht*), no doubt over a stage *-biarht* (§§ 280, 297, cf. Ct. 31 *Ċīalbearht*). But in dialects not subject to smoothing, forms with unchanged vowels are due to absence of breaking in low stress, e.g. *CA*, Ct. 45, W-S *fulwiht*, W-S *nōwiht*, eKt. *-berht*.

[2] Ep. still *-ændi*.

with double umlaut *hæġtess* witch (< **hagatussi̯-*, OHG g.p. *hagazussun*).

§ 340. Back umlaut did not operate in unaccented syllables, but it could operate under half-stress. Its results were often much modified by subsequent loss of the half-stress, e.g. *ondwlata*, VP *ondwleata* face (< *ondwliota*); *sċiptara*, *sċipteara* pitch (< *sċipteora*); *-lucor*, *-lucost* rare for *-licor*, *-licost* (cf. Kt. *ġeornliocar*, with back umlaut of shortened *i*); *endlufon* eleven (beside *endlifan*, *-leofan*); *-togoþa* in ordinal numerals (beside *-tigoþa*, *-tiogoþa*).[1]

c. Early Old English Loss of Unaccented Vowels

§ 341. *a* of unaccented final syllables was lost in Gmc. (§ 331.1, 4). In prehistoric OE it was also lost in all internal open syllables, irrespective of whether it had been retained before a nasal, fronted to *æ*, or fronted and mutated to *e*. Examples are *-ne* < *-anōn* in a.s.m. of strong adjs., e.g. *gōdne*; inflexions and derivatives of adjs. in *-iġ*, older *-æġ* (§ 376), as *monġes*, *hālgian*; inflexions and derivatives of words in *-el*, *-er*, *-en*, older *-æl*, &c., including pass. parts. (§ 334), as *awles*, *ōþres*, *þēodnes*, *fæġnes*, *fæġnian*, *opnian*, *ġedafnian*, *ġebundne*, from *awel* hook, *ōþer* other, *þēoden* prince, *fæġen* happy, *open* open, *ġedafen* fit, *ġebunden* bound; words in *-þa* < *-aþô*, as *sċeafþa* shaving, *spiwþa* vomit; isolated words, as *sāwl* soul (< **saiu̯alō*), *hātte* is called (Goth. *haitada*), *hwæþre* however, infl. *æxe*, and hence *æx* axe,[2] and the words *mæġden*, *hæġtess*, *lāwriċe*, discussed § 339; the thematic *-a-* in compound words with *a*-declension nouns in the first element, as *dæġliċ* daily, *ælmihtiġ* almighty (OHG *tagalīh*, *alamahtig*).[3]

[1] But *ǣrendraca*, *wiðerbraca*, are different formations beside *ǣrendwreca*, *wiþerbreca*.

[2] Taking the form from **acas-* > **æcæs-* > *æx-*. There also existed **acus-* (see § 203, footnote), whence *VP* d.p. *æcesum*, Cp. *-æcus*, Ld. *-acus*; and **acasōn-*, whence Ru.[1] *axe*. Li. *acas(a)*, Ru.[2] *acase*, are abnormal; *acas* is perhaps for *acus* with confusion of the unaccented back vowels (§ 377), and this form by mixture with *axe* has produced weak *acasa*, *-e*. (Ross, *Studies in the accidence of the Lindisfarne Gospels*, p. 66, assumes a weak declension in W-S also, but the forms he quotes are strong plurals from *æx*.)

[3] It is due to the analogy of these formations that the medial syllable is lost also in compounds with nouns of the *ō*-declension and weak nouns in the first element, e.g. *ġiefstōl* gift-throne, *heortlēas* dispirited: similar forms occur in many languages, see Brugmann, *Grundriss* ii. 1, pp. 81, 84. Forms like *Beardanēu* (BH), *Francancumb*, *marmanstān*, are genitival expressions, not true compounds (cf. *Beardsǣte*, *Francumb*, *marmstān*). The thematic vowels of other declensions mostly follow the normal rules for syncope or retention (§§ 348, 359).

§ 342. Since *e*, the *i*-umlaut of *æ*, suffered the above syncope, it is reasonable to suppose that original *e* would also be subject to it. Here may belong g. and d.s.f. *-re*, and g.p. *-ra* in the strong declension of adjs., if they are from West Gmc. *-erōs*, *-erai*, *-erôm*, transferred from the pronominal declension seen in OHG *dera*, *deru*, *dero*. Cf. § 331.7.

§ 343. When syncopated and unsyncopated forms existed together, analogical replacement of the vowel in forms in which it phonologically disappeared was frequent, e.g. forms like *hāliġe*, *opene*, and especially often inflected pass. parts. like *ġecorene*, from *hāliġ*, *open*, *ġecoren*. But some apparently irregular forms are due to the existence of alternative formations, especially *-eþa*, *-oþa* (e.g. *spiweþa*, *sċeafoþa*) from *-iþô*, *-uþô*, beside *-aþô* (§ 341).

§ 344. Syncopation does not take place in closed syllables, e.g. the suffixes *-ettan*, *-estre* (§ 339). It also fails in *bedecian* beg (cf. probably Goth. *bidagwa*).

§ 345. *u* and *i*, whether originally short, or due to Gmc. reduction of older long vowels (§ 331.5), were lost in Prim. OE, in final unaccented syllables after a long accented syllable, or a short accented syllable and another syllable. They remained after a short accented syllable, or a long accented syllable followed by a short syllable. Examples are neut. pls. of the *a*-declension (*word*, *weorod*, beside *fatu*, *hēafodu*); n.s. of the *ō*-declension (*ār*, *firen*,[1] beside *ġiefu*), of the *u*-declension (*feld* beside *sunu*), of the *i*-declension (*ġiest* beside *wine*), and of *u̯a*- and *u̯ō*- stems (*beadu*-, *bearu*, beside *mǣd*, *gād*); n.p. of cons. stems (*fēt*, *cælf*; beside *hnyte*); imper. of weak verbs of Class I (*dēm* beside *nere*); isolated examples are *twǣm* dat. two (< **tu̯aimiz*), and so *þǣm* dat. them, *milc* (§ 331.3). The long syllable causing loss may itself be due to the loss of *a* just described, e.g. *sāwl* < **sāulu* < **saiu̯alō*.

§ 346. In such a system levellings are very prone to occur, e.g. nW-S 1st sg. pres. indic. of strong verbs has *-u* after both short and long syllables (e.g. VP *haldu*); n.p. lW-S *weredu* (beside *werod*), VP *hēafud* (beside *hēafudu*). Generally analogy intervenes less in disyllabic than in trisyllabic forms, and in nouns the distinctions *sċipu*, *word*, *ġiefu*, *ār*, &c., are well observed.[2]

[1] And so nouns in *-uþ* and *-ung*, e.g. *duguþ*, *monung*.

[2] Unexplained exceptions are *bet* better (Goth. *batis*), perhaps due to the analogy of *sēl*, and *ymbe* about, beside *ymb*. FC *fisċflōdu* is probably an error; read with Chadwick *fisċflōd up* (*Heroic age*, p. 69, footnote); *Erf*. 440 *aetgāru* is

§ 347. When *i* and *u* of a final syllable are followed by a consonant, there is no loss, e.g. *dōemed, middel, wǣron* (with *e, o*, for older *i, u*, see §§ 369–73).[1] Syncopation, however, passes its usual limits in the W-S and (in part) Kt. 2nd and 3rd sg. pres. indic. of strong verbs and weak verbs of Class I, where *i* is lost before consonants after both long and short syllables, e.g. *birst, birþ, dēmst, dēmþ* (see §§ 732–4 for details).

§ 348. *i* and *u* are lost after long syllables in the formation of compound words, e.g. *ġiesthūs, hȳþgyld, mǣdland, handseax, flōdblāc.*[2] In names, this loss is frequently extended to elements with short first syllables, so that *Cyn-*,[3] *Her-, Hyġ-, Siġ-, Friþ-, Haþ-, Bad-* occur as name-elements beside *Cyni-* (later *Cyne-*), &c., *Friþu-*,[4] &c. Similar syncopation in common nouns is seen in BC *siġbēcn*[5] beacon of victory, Li. *metbæliġ* meat-bag, W-S *metseax* meat-knife, *metfæt* dish, *cwidbōc* book of sayings, *herpaþ* main road, *heġstōw* enclosure. So there is variation in the prefix *el-, ele-* foreign.

§ 349. The weight of the second element seems to have had influence upon the loss of medial vowels in compounds. Loss was less prone to occur before –́ or –́ × than before ⏑́ ×, hence *hilderinċ*,

an error for Ep., Cp. *aetgǣeru*, pl. of *Cp.* 167 *aetgǣre*, neut. *ja*-stem (for an alternative view see § 591, footnote).

[1] On forms like *dēmd*, see § 643.5.d.

[2] It has been pointed out (§ 341, footnote), that *u* is lost even after short syllables in compounds with *ō*-declension nouns in the first element, as is seen in compounds of *lufu, ġiefu, caru, sċeamu* (e.g. *carlēas, sċeamfæst*). Exceptions can be regarded as late formations with the OE n.s. or g.s., e.g. *nafugār, nafegār*.

There are some exceptions to the syncopation of *-i-* in compounds both with *jō*-nouns, e.g. *cwildeflōd, restedæġ, hellehund*, and with *i*-nouns, e.g. *brȳdeliċ, ġebyrdetīd, ġewyrdeliċ, ġifteliċ, tīdeliċe, hlȳpeġet, ærðelond* (Kt., Ct. 42). The former are relatively late compounds with the g.s., the latter are perhaps due to contamination with the *ja*-declension, which regularly has a connecting vowel in composition (§ 359). All such forms are beside ones with no connecting vowel (*cwyldbǣre, brȳdguma*, &c.).

[3] Late compounds of *ja*-stems have commonly the first element in the nominatival form, e.g. *hryċġmearh, bedtīd*; so lW-S *cynliċ* for *cyneliċ* is to be explained, and not by the old fluctuation *cyn-, cyne-*.

[4] But *Selred, Selered* reflects a variation already existing in the simplex (*sel, sele*).

[5] *-siġ* is also frequent in the second element of compounds, e.g. *Ælfsiġ*, but here the element follows the *a*-declension. Similar divergence in declension between the form of a noun in independent use and as the second element of compounds appears in *riċe, -riċ, mǣre, -mer, līþe, -liþ*, e.g. *Ælfriċ, Ēumer* (BH), *Hildilid* (BH), and cf. *Rīcberct* (BH), *Rīcred*, &c. (*LV*). So in the first element we find as a rule *friþu-* (*u*-stem, Gothic *friþus*), but in the second always *-friþ, -ferþ* (*a*-stem).

hildewīsa, but *hildfruma*, *hildfreca*, and inflected *hildfrome*, *hildlata*; so LV *Hildiburg*, &c., but *Hilduini*.[1]

§ 350. On occasional early syncopation of *-i-* in compounds, so that umlaut fails to take place, see § 204.1.

§ 351. *i* and *u* are also lost in open medial syllables after a long stressed syllable. This applies to original short vowels only, as *ī* and *ū* had not yet been shortened in this position. The principle is clearly seen in past tenses of weak verbs of Class I: contrast *hīerde* (Goth. *hausida*) with *nerede* (Goth. *nasida*). Other examples are compar. adj. with *i*-mutation, *ieldra*, *grīetra*, *ġinġra*, &c. (< *-izô*); many inflected forms like *enġles*, *ēþles*, *hēafdu*;[2] probably some inflexions of adjs. originally of the *i*- and *u*-declensions, e.g. *blīþne*, *heardne* < *-inōn*, *-unōn*, and *ǣnne* a.s.m. one < **aininōn*; diminutive names in *-ca* (< *-ika*), LV *Brȳnca*, *Drēmca*, *Hȳnca*.[3]

§ 352. There is usually no syncopation before consonant groups, as the inflexions of nouns and adjs. in *-isċ*, *-iht*, *-est* (< *-ist*), *-ing*, *-ung* show, e.g. *Englisċe*, *ǣresta*, *sċēawunge*. But syncopation is extended beyond its usual limits in W-S superls. *ġinġsta*, *lǣsta*, *strenġsta*, *wiersta*, and these forms can be extended to uninflected *hīehst*, &c. In lW-S a few more similar forms occur: *yldsta*, *lenġst*.[4]

§ 353. When both a middle and an end syllable contained either *i* or *u*, and both were in conditions demanding loss of the vowel, the middle syllable was the one affected; phonological developments appear to be *hēafdu*, *rīċu*, *strenġþu* < **hǣofudu*, **rīkiu*,[5] **strangiþu*. There are many analogical forms, e.g. *hēafodu* (after n.s.), *hēafod* (after type *weorod*, § 345), *strenġþ* (extracted from oblique cases).

[1] In *And.* 1092 *hildbedd* is an error: read *hildebedd strēd* (Holthausen).

[2] While in this type analogical replacement of the vowel is found (e.g. *hēafodu*, see § 353), *ǣlċ*, each, has conversely loss of the vowel from analogy of inflected forms (**ǣlīċǣ* > *ǣlċe*, &c.), cf. § 394. Similarly many weak pass. parts. in dentals, especially in W-S, e.g. *ġesend*, *ġelǣd*, have analogical syncopation from inflected *ġesende*, *ġelǣdde* < **ġisendidǣ*, **ġilǣdidǣ*.

[3] There is usually no syncopation of the suffix *-uc* after a long syllable, e.g. *beallucas*, *bulluce*, *mattucas*. The suffix perhaps had an originally long vowel.

[4] W-S parts. of the type described in note 2 can extend analogical syncopation to forms where two consonants followed the medial vowel, e.g. *ġesċendne* < *ġesċendedne*.

[5] But *-u* drops after syllables made long by West Gmc. consonant gemination: **kunįō* > **kunnįō* > Prim. OE **kynnu* > *cynn*. The difference in development of **kunnįō* from **rīkiō* was due to the fact that in the former *į* was consonantal and hence *-ō* followed one long syllable, while in the latter *-ō* followed long+short (see § 398.4).

Unaccented *i* and *u* seem to have been lost at exactly the same time; otherwise, if *i* were lost first, **rīkiu* would have become **rīku* and then **rīk*; while, if *u* were lost first, the development would have been **rīkiu* > **rīki* > **rīk*. The syncopation of *a* (*æ*, *e*) was earlier than loss of *i* and *u*, for **saiu̯alō* had become **sāulu* by the time of loss of *u* (§ 345). Yet even this loss of *a* was later than *i*-umlaut, otherwise **maȝadīn* would have become **mæȝdin* > **meġden*, instead of *mæġden*.

§ 354. In a small group of words, unaccented *i* is lost in pretonic syllables; the examples are all with the prefixes *bi-* and *ni-*: *binnan* within, *būtan* without, *bufan* above, *blinnan* cease (< **biinnan*, &c.), *nāhte* had not (< **niāhtǣ*), *nis* is not, North., Ru.[1] *nam*, VP *neam* am not, North. *naro(n)* are not; with loss of the initial consonant of the stressed syllable, all forms of *nabban* have not, *nāt* know not, *næs* was not, *nolde* would not (< *ni*+*habban*, *wāt*, *wæs*, *wolde*).[1]

D. Early Old English Shortening of Unaccented Long Vowels

§ 355. All the unaccented long vowels which still remained were shortened in Prim. OE. These were:

(1) Vowels of final syllables which had had the abnormal IE intonation[2] (§ 330), e.g. n.p. of *ō*-declension *-ôz* > *-ô* > OE *-a* (e.g. *ġiefa*); g.p. of all declensions *-ô* > OE *-a*; g.s. of *i*-declension in *-êiz* > *-îz* > OE *-i* (LR *uyrdi*, but cf. § 605); n.s. of masc. weak nouns in *-ô* > OE *-a*.

(2) *ǣ* and *ō* from *ai* and *au* in final syllables (§ 331.7)[3] were shortened to *æ* (later *e*, § 369) and *a*; e.g. d.s. of *a*- and *ō*-declensions, n.p.m. and d.s.f. of strong adjs., pres. subj. of all verbs, OE *stāne*, *ġiefe*, *gōde*, *gōdre*, *helpe*, all with *-e* < *-æ* < Gmc. *-ai*; g. and d.s. of *u*-declension, OE *suna* < Gmc. *-auz*, *-au*; OE *eahta* eight, cf. Goth. *ahtau*.

(3) Gmc. *-ia-* of final syllables existed only after long syllables (Sievers' law, § 398.4), and might better be represented as *-i̯ia-*. With the loss of *-a-* (§ 331.4), *-i̯i-* > *ī*, but either this development

[1] For *booflīċ* Li., Matt. I. 5, 8 read *behōflīċ* (the usual form in *Li.*); on *nistiġ* hungry (perhaps from *ni*+**wistiġ*) see *PBB* ix. 212.

[2] In this book ^ is used to indicate that a sound had I-E abnormal intonation, and ~ is reserved to indicate nasalization.

[3] It is unnecessary to distinguish normal and abnormal intonation in these diphthongs in order to explain Gmc. developments.

was too late for early shortening to take place, or *ī* so developed had an intonation similar to the old IE abnormal intonation, which preserved its length. It underwent later shortening in OE, hence in the *i̯a*-declension **andiaz* > **andī* > OE *endi*, later *ende*, and so **rīkiam* > OE *rīċe*.

(4) Long vowels in syllables which had become final by the loss of original final syllables, e.g. the formative elements *-īġ*, *-īn* (diminutive), *-īn* (adjectival), *-ūþ* (§ 331.6), *-ūþ* (§ 332) > *-iġ*, *-in*, *-uþ*, e.g. OE *mihtiġ*, *ċīcen*, *stǣnen*, *fisċoþ*, *duguþ*; the inflexional endings seen in OE g. and d.s. *strenġe* (< *-iniz*, *-ini*, §§ 331.3, 483), 3rd pl. pres. indic. *beraþ* (< *-anþi*, § 332), forms of weak verbs of Class II, *lufas*, *-aþ*, *-od*, *-ad* (< *-ōsi*, *-ōþi*, *-ūd-*, *-ōd-*, § 331.6), superl. in *-ast*, *-ost* (< *-ōst-*, *-ūst-*, § 331.6).

(5) Long vowels in unaccented medial syllables, as in the inflected forms of suffixes under (4), e.g. OE *mihtiġe*, *fisċoþe*, *lēofosta*; suffixes seen in *hōcede* (§ 339), *sūþerne* (§ 339), *leornere* (§ 337): forms of weak verbs of Class II with medial *-i-* < *-ii̯-* < *-ei̯-* (§ 376) < *-ēi̯-* < *-ōi̯-* (§ 339), and past tenses in *-ade*, *-ode* (< *-ōd-*, *-ūd-*, § 331.6); g.p. of fem. weak declension *-ena* < *-ōnôm*.

With regard to all these shortenings, it will be observed that, even when shortened late, *ō* became *a*, but that this *a* was of too late origin to become *æ* by Anglo-Frisian fronting (§ 333). Thus *ō* if shortened early gives OE *æ*(*e*), but if shortened late it gives *a*. The other long vowels *ǣ*, *ī*, *ū* > *æ*, *i*, *u*, and later *æ* and *i* become usually *e*, and *u* becomes frequently *o* (§§ 369, 373).

§ 356. To the same process as this shortening is to be attributed the shortening of long vowels in the second elements of compounds of obscured meaning, e.g. *lāreow* teacher (< *lār*+*þēow*), *fulwiht* baptism (< **-wīht* consecration), *æfest* malice (< *æf*+**unsti-*, cf. Dutch *afgunst*), adjs. in *-liċ*,[1] and advs. *sōna*, *āwa*, *ġēna*, *ġīeta*,[2] all containing the element *ā*, ever.[3] In the second element of such formations, *ai* > *ǣ* as in unaccented syllables (§ 331.7), if the reduction in the semantic force of the second element was early. By the further reduction now under consideration *ǣ* > *æ* (later *e*, § 372), e.g. *ēored* troop (< *eoh*+**raid*), *earfeþ* trouble (Gothic

[1] In these adjs. the short vowel developed early and extended to the inflected forms, so that final *-u* was retained after the medial syllable, which had half-stress before the inflexion (§ 88), e.g. *heardlicu* like *wynsumu* (§ 642).

[2] Also *āwo*, *ġēno*, see § 132, footnote 3.

[3] *Ofust* haste, Erf. *obust*, probably belongs here, but the etymology of its second element is uncertain (*IF* xx. 320; *ES* liv. 97–100).

arbaiþs). If the obscuration of the meaning of the second element was later, *ai* > *ā*, and the development was as described in § 336. A development of *au* to *ō* and hence before *m* with shortening to *u*, appears in *fultum* help, beside *fultēam*. Similarly *ō* < West Gmc. *ā*, if shortened, can become *u* before *m*, e.g. *andluma* utensil, beside *andlōma*.[1]

§ 357. In the second element of compounds of obscured meaning, diphthongs are very prone to modification. Examples with diphthongs due to back umlaut are given in § 340. Examples with diphthongs due to OE shortening (§ 356) are Ru.[2] *lārow*, Li. *lāruu*, *hlatuu*,[2] VP *lādtow*, Li. *ānlap* single (cf. W-S *ānlīepe*), North. *ðah* (< *ðēah*), lW-S *racentagæ* d.s. fetter (< *-tēag*), *hēadorhund* deer-hound (< *hēahdēor-*); cf. also the instances of original and shortened *io* > *u*, § 338 footnote.[3] W-S *ĭe* seems in similar low stressed positions to shorten if long, and develop to *e*; e.g. *ānlepe*, *fulteman*, *ǣwerdla*, *cyneġerd*[4] (sceptre, beside *-ġyrd*).[5]

§ 358. Short medial vowels due to the process defined in § 355.5 had a half-stress in OE after long syllables, and were so preserved (§§ 89, 91). Loss of the half-stress, however, could lead to loss of the vowel, e.g. VP *mōnðes*, *gyldnum*, Li., Ru.[2] *mæġdne*, Li. *nētna*. Such forms may be transferred to uninflected cases, e.g. *mōnð* Menol. 164. In W-S syncopation of Prim. OE long vowels is unusual except in *mōnaþ*.[6] Adjs. in *-iġ* (< *-īġ*) have syncopation very frequently in the inflected cases in Angl. after long syllables, sometimes after shorts, e.g. *VP*, North. *hālġe*, Ru.[2] *hefġe*, and syncopation is the rule in OE metre (often against the manuscript spelling). Unsyncopated forms prevail in W-S. It is impossible to decide how far we have genuine syncopation of Prim. OE *-īġ*, and how far contamination with forms of *-æġ*, which has syncopation in any position when an open syllable (§§ 341, 376).

§ 359. The Prim. OE long vowels under discussion are not usually lost in composition after one syllable, e.g. *endeleas*, *lǣċecræft*, *rīċedom*.[7]

[1] Cf. the same treatment of originally short *o* (< *a*) in *līċuma*, &c. (§ 333).

[2] i.e. *latteow*.

[3] *Fulwiht* (§ 356) had earlier loss of half-stress and hence never developed a diphthong by breaking; but if a diphthong was developed, by later loss of stress the development of § 338, footnote, could follow.

[4] Also *cyneġeard*, ingeniously explained by Barowski, *Lautdubletten*, p. 61.

[5] Such forms may of course be dismissed as nW-S.

[6] The relationship of OE *frætwa*, *ġeatwa* to *ġetāwa* is doubtful, see Luick, *Hist. Gramm.*, § 314.*a*.2, Pope, *Rhythm of Beowulf*, p. 322.

[7] On compounds with *ō*-nouns in the first element, see § 341, footnote 3.

After two syllables, however, the connecting vowel is lost: *ǣrendwreca*, *cāserdom*. Adjs. ending in cons.+liquid or nasal+*e* drop the *e* in composition, and develop a parasite vowel, e.g. *frēcenlić*, *lȳþerlić*, *wǣfersȳn*, *ġerisenlić*, *efenlić*, from *frēcne*, &c. There is also no connecting vowel in compounds of the following adjectives: *cēne*, *clǣne*, *dīere*, *dierne*, *hnesċe*, *mǣre*, *stierne*, *swēte*, *ġetǣse*, *þiċċe*, *wierþe*, *unwēne*, and compounds ending in *-þwǣre*, *-mǣte*, *-bǣre*, *-wende*. Some adjectives are inconsistent, e.g. *ēcnes* but *ēcelić*, *mildheort*, &c. but *mildelić*, *īeþnes* but *īeþelić*, *rīclić*, but *rīcedom*, &c., *ġesċrēpnes* but *ġesċrēpeliċe*, *ġemǣnnes* but *ġemǣn(e)lić*, *ġedēfnes* but *ġedēf(e)lić*, *ġebyrd(e)lić*, *ēst(e)liċe*, *ġedæft(e)liċe*, *blīþ(e)mōd*, *wild(e)dēor*. Fluctuation with the *i*-declension may explain the forms without connecting vowel (cf. § 348). Similar inconsistency is less common with nominal first elements, but *ġemǣre*, boundary, always rejects *-e-* in composition (*ġemǣrpōl*, &c.), lW-S has *sticmǣlum*, *yrfweardnys*, beside older *styċċe-*, *yrfe-*.[1]

E. Parasite Vowels

§ 360. **Accented syllables.** Forms with a parasite vowel after the vowel of an accented syllable between *r* or *l* and a consonant are scattered through early texts. The vowel is *i* (rarely *e*) when the accented vowel is front, usually *u* (less often *a*) when it is back. Examples are FC *wylif* she-wolf, *-berig* mountain, LR *ðerih* through, *aerig-* arrow, Mortain Casket *ġewarahtæ*, BH *Tilaburug*, Ct. 47 *Hēanbyriġ*, and the name-elements LV *Aluch-*, *Eorup-*, *Berecht*, Ct. 5 (Kt.) *Bericht-*, BH *-berect*, Ct. 25 (Sax.-Kt.) *Alah-*, *Walah-*[2] (but cf. Stevenson's Asser, p. 203).

§ 361. This process may reasonably be presumed to be later than smoothing, since Angl. **beorht* > *berht* > *beriht*. (On Ct. 5 *Bercht-*, *Bericht-* see § 140.) Similar forms in lNorth. may be inherited from the early period or be due to a repetition of the process, e.g. Li. Ru.[2] *burug*, Ru.[2] *suluh*, *arog-*, Li. *worohton*, *forohtan-*

[1] The connecting element of compounds of verbs of Class I seems to have resembled that of *ja*-nouns, rather than that of *i*-nouns, being normally retained in OE, e.g. *ġīemeleas*, *ċīepemann*, *hierstepanne*, *hīeremann*, *reċċeleas*, *ġereċċelić* (clearly, beside *ġereclić* from *ġereć*). Again, forms with loss of the connecting vowel occur, e.g. lW-S *ċȳpman*, *ġīmlesliċe*, *herlić* (praiseworthy, *Metres*). Before *-nes*, these verbal elements have no connecting vowel if long, e.g. *acennes*, *alīesnes*, *cȳðnes*, *hīernes*, *inlīhtnes*, *todǣlnes*. After short syllables, however, there is a connecting vowel, e.g. *herenes*, *styrenes*, *smirenes*, *ġićenes*, *ġerećenes*, *trymenes* (beside *trymnis* from the adj. *trum*, § 204.2, footnote), *aðenenes*.

[2] But Ep., Cp. *bearug* pig, is probably an old disyllabic form, ON *bǫrgr* (with *u*-umlaut).

dum, Li., Rit., Ru.[2] d.s. *byriġ*, Li. *wyrihta*, Ru.[2] *fyliġde, berehtnað, sweriġa, aweriġdun*; also with change *-iġ-* > *i* (cf. § 267), Li. *sueria*, Rit. *heriað*.

§ 362. The only Old English text which has parasiting in accented syllables before the vowel is the Brussels Cross, *berōþor* brother (twice).

§ 363. Unaccented syllables. In OE there was considerable divergence, whether syllabic *l, r, m, n* arising owing to the loss of unaccented vowels of final syllables (§§ 331.4, 345) were retained or developed a parasite vowel. This vowel, if developed, was *i* (later *e*) after a front vowel, *u* (later *o*) after a back vowel. Already *Ep.* has, for example, *seġil-* sail, *spinil* spindle, (*h*)*aesil* hazel, *tebel-* gaming-board (W-S *tæfl*), *thōthor* ball, *-bāecon* beacon, and *BH* has *-ċaestir* in place-names, and the name-element *Eorcun-*, *Earcon-*. Accordingly, the parasiting must be regarded as prehistoric, and the frequent early forms in which it is absent (e.g. Ep. *bebr* beaver, *ātr* poison) as due to inflected cases in which the liquid consonant was not syllabic, or to scribal neglect of the parasite vowel. Normal OE forms are *fugol* bird, *tungol* star, *cumbol* banner, *sāwol* soul, *næġel* nail, *æppel* apple, *seġel* sail, *þunor* thunder, *wundor* wonder, *winter* winter, *fæġer* fair, *æcer* acre, *hræfen* raven, *ofen* oven, *bōsum* bosom, *māþum* treasure, *wæstum* fruit. Forms without parasiting are, however, frequent, e.g. *hūsl* Eucharist, *hrīþr* head of cattle, *seġl, næġl*; with *n* and *m* they are the rule after short syllables, frequent after long ones, e.g. *hræfn* raven, *fācn* crime, *tācn* token, *wǣpn* weapon, *wolcn* cloud, *botm* bottom, *māþm* treasure, *wæstm* fruit: they are also the rule with *l* after *t* and *d*, e.g. *setl* seat, *botl* building, *spātl* spit, *ādl* disease, *nǣdl* needle. Owing to the coexistence of the types *næġl* and *næġel*, the groups *el, er, em, en* became regarded as expressing syllabic consonants, and hence they frequently appear after back vowels, e.g. *fugel, wunder, wolcen, tācen, breahtem* noise, and always *ċeaster* city.[1] Less frequent is *-or* (early *-ur*), &c., after front vowels although it is to be similarly explained, e.g. *fefor* fever, *pipor* pepper, VP *bitur* bitter, *wæstum* fruit, Ru.[2] *ġestordæġ* yesterday.

Extension of a parasitic vowel to internal open syllables is frequent only with *r* after short syllables, e.g. *fæġeres, æceras*, less frequently *fugoles*.

[1] *Cp.* 1152 already *þuner*. Angl. has both *bēcon* (North.), and *bēcen*: the former is older, from **bēacun* (Cp. *-bǣcun*), with parasiting before smoothing, the latter is to be explained like *wunder* above.

§ 364. Parasiting in medial syllables occurs in North. past tenses like *hynġerde*, *dēġelde*, *ġetimberde*; cf. Cp. *afrōebirdun* (W-S *āfrēfredon*); in many adjectives before inflexions and formative syllables beginning with consonants,[1] e.g. *fæġerne*, *fæġernes*, *snotorlić*; in forms of *ġīfre*, *lȳþre*, *sȳfre*, *tīdre*, *þīestre*, *fǣćne*, *frēćne*, and also *dīeġle*, so far as the relevant forms are not regarded as from *dīegol*, before inflexions and formative syllables beginning with unlike consonants, e.g. *ġīferne*, *dīeġelnes*, but a.s.m. *fǣcne* < **fǣcnne* (§ 476);[2] in a few isolated words, e.g. *lǣwerće* lark (< **lǣu̯rćan-* < **laiu̯rikōn-*),[3] *Emerca* (< **Emr̥kan-* < **Amrikan-*, cf. Ann. Qued. *Embrica*).

§ 365. **Later parasiting.** Especially W-S, already present in Ælfred, and increasingly frequent in later texts, is a tendency to develop *i̯* and *u̯* after a short syllable to *ii̯*, *uu̯*, e.g. *heriġas* armies, *heriġan* praise, *byriġ* d.s. city, *byliġ* bag, *miriġþ* joy, *fyliġan* follow, *byriġan* bury, *ġearuwe* n.p. ready, *beaduwe* d.s. battle, *seonuwa* n.p. sinews, *swaluwe* swallow. *ii̯* can be monophthongized to *i*, like *iġ* of earlier origin (see § 267), e.g. *byriweard* (i.e. *byrġweard* town-guard), *fylian* follow, *awyridum* d.p. accursed (cf. *awierġan*). By §§ 373, 385, *u* often appears as *o* and *e*, e.g. *beadowe*, *swalewan*; less frequent is *e* for *i* (cf. § 371), e.g. g.p. *hereġa* armies, *hereġung* harrying. In nW-S these processes are very rare: e.g. *KG* 720 *ġerewe* n.p.n. ready. *Ru.*[1] has a few forms recalling the lNorth. forms quoted § 361, e.g. *heriġæs* g.s. army, *sweriġe* answer, *beliġas* bags, but these may be due to the influence of North. or W-S spelling.

§ 366. In lW-S parasiting is frequent before *-re*, *-ra* of the strong adjectival and pronominal declension, e.g. *sumere*, *þissere*, see §§ 641, 711. Some lW-S manuscripts show also a revival of the early process of parasiting in accented syllables, e.g. *ileca* < *ilca*, *wyrihta*, *burug*, *weoruc*.

§ 367. **Parasite connecting vowels.** Although many cases of inconsistency in the presence of connecting vowels may be explained by §§ 348, 359, it seems also that often a parasite connecting vowel was

[1] See § 359 on these adjs. in composition.

[2] Elsewhere *i* is not lost after *l*, *r*, *n*, if two consonants, or long vowel+consonant, precede, hence *timbrede*, *dīġlede*, etc. Other weak past tenses have vocalic consonants, e.g. *seġlde*, *æfnde*.

[3] But in *lāwerće*, *er* = *r̥*, for after a back vowel the parasite vowel would be *u* (*o*); but perhaps the form arises simply by transferring to *lǣwerće* the vowel of *lāwriće* (§ 339). Another view, Flasdieck, *A* lix. 38.

developed. In forms with *a*-stem first elements this is especially striking, for phonologically the connecting vowel should be lost (§ 341). Examples from lW-S manuscripts are: (1) Short *a*-stems, *bærefōt, dæġered, godeweb, godefyrht, hrædoliċe, ġemeteliċe, wereġild, werewulf, wereliċe.* (2) Long *a*-stems, *cūðeliċe, goldefrætwum, hālewende, holdeliċe, swiftiliċe.* (3) Weak and consonant stems, *nomecuð,*[1] *nihteliċ,*[2] *frēonderedden.* (4) Rare late forms of prefixes, *ore-, mede-, æle-, æli-*, for *or-, med-, æl-.* (5) Forms of personal and place-names in late sources, e.g. *Baldewine, Ċadewalla, Canteuuariorum, Coleman, Coloman, Cūðeredus, Ealdered, Fordewiċ, Hūnewald, Pidewælla, Plegomundus, Tūnewald, Wērefrið, Wiliġeld, Willegoda.*[3] In nW-S texts such forms are very rare: *Rit.* has *godecund, ġimetomicla, rehteliċe.*

F. Reduction in Variety of Vowels in Unaccented Syllables

§ 368. By the processes so far described in this chapter, OE had the unaccented vowels *a, æ, e, i,* and *u.* Certain changes of these must now be described.

§ 369. *æ, e,* and *i* fell together in a sound written *e* in unaccented syllables. *æ* and *i* remain undisturbed only in very early texts. They are used with considerable historical accuracy in the early North. short texts, e.g. CH *hefaen-*, BDS *uueorthae* (pres. subj.), LR *biuorhtæ* (pass. part. a.s.f.), *uundnae* (pass part. n.p.), *hafæ* (1st sg. pres. indic.), *ueflæ* (ō-stem, n.p.), *huethrae, uīdæ* (advs.), *sīæ* (pres. subj.), RC *hinæ, riičnæ, æþþilæ* (n.p.), *-wōēriġnæ*, FC *hiæ* (a.p.), and many instances of g.s. of m. nouns in *-æs*, d.s. of m. and f. nouns in *-æ*, 3rd sg. past. indic. of weak verbs in *-dæ*; CH *maecti* (a.p.), *astelidæ, ǣrist*, BDS *uuiurthit* (3rd sg. pres. indic.), *dōēmid* (part.), LR *hlimmith* (3rd sg. pres. indic.), *hælithum*, RC *æþþilæ*, the forms with parasite *i* (§ 360), and many instances of unaccented *ni, bi-, ġi-*. Occasionally, however, in these early texts *e* replaces *æ*, e.g. CH *heben, hrōfe* (d.s.), BDS *fore, sīe* (pres. subj.), *-daeġe* (d.s.), RC *walde*; more rarely *e* replaces *i*, e.g. LR

[1] But *ġewuneliċ* not to *ġewuna* noun, but to *ġewuna* adj.

[2] But *nihtegala* has an old connecting element (OS *nahtigala*, Strassburg Glosses), which appears in *Ep.* as *-i-* or *-ae-* (673, 857), and is presumably identical with the g.s. ending of *niht* (§ 628.3).

[3] But *mihteleās* (OEC 1053, MS. C), **feldefare* (miswritten *feldeware*, eleventh-century glossary) are genitival compounds; *ġesundeliċ* is for *ġesundiġliċ* (§ 371); *hym(e)liċ, bil(e)wit*, and *þolo-, þole-, þol-mod, þolo-, þole-byrde* are of uncertain formation, but the forms with connecting vowels are probably the older.

ǣrest, *ne* (neg., once for usual *ni*), RC *ġeredæ* (3rd sg. past indic.). At least in two forms, RC *rōdi*, FC *-ċæstri* (d.s.f., in sense loc.), *i* is difficult to explain. *æ* similarly is found for *e*, e.g. LR *ofaer*, RC *bismæradu*, FC *ġibrōþær*, which again points to confusion of the sounds. In the early manuscripts of BH *æ* and *i* are hardly disturbed,[1] but in LV, while *-æ* generally remains (e.g. n.s.f. of weak nouns usually *-æ*, twice *-e*), *e* is fairly often written for *i*, especially in the elements *Dene-*, *Here-* (but usually *-heri*). The early glossaries illustrate the change clearly, for in the glosses common to *Ep.*, *Erf.*, and *Cp.* the two former have practically always *i* in final syllables (56 *i*; 4 *e*), but *Cp.* has *i* and *e* almost equally (33 *i*; 27 *e*); the two former have very frequent *æ* in final syllables (*Ep.* 158 *æ*, *Erf.* 136 *æ*; *Ep.* 8 *e*, *Erf.* 30 *e*), but *Cp.* has rarely *æ* (18 *æ*; 148 *e*). So in the charters, *æ* and *i* are rare in documents dated later than Ct. 8 (*c.* 770), and this already has g.s. *-es* (*a*-declension), *-stede*, but preserves g.s. *-is* (*i*-declension, see § 601, footnote).[2] In later texts the retention of *æ* is rare,[3] that of *i* infrequent,[4] except in *Li.* and *Rit.* after *i*, *y*, *ġ* and dentals (e.g. *miċil*, *cyrtil*, *ðeġin*, *drȳġi*, *ġisēni*, *silið*), and in *Rit.* and *Ru.*[2] in the unaccented prefixes *bi-*, *ġi-*.[5]

§ 370. After the change of *æ* and *i* to *e*, normal OE forms were, e.g. with old *æ*, g.s. and d.s. of *a-* and *ō*-stems *stānes*, *stāne*, *ġiefe*, a.s. of *ō*-stems *ġiefe*, n.s. of weak fem. nouns *tunge*, n.p.m. of adjs. *gōde*, pres. subj. *helpe*, 3rd sg. past indic. of weak verbs

[1] That is, in the Moore and Leningrad MSS.; Cott. Tib. A xiv and the foreign Namur MS. preserve *i* well, *æ* > *e* very often; in Cott. Tib. C ii both *i* and *æ* > *e* frequently. Cf. Storms, *English studies* xxxvii. 104 ff.

[2] The charter evidence thus points to the reign of Offa (757–96) as the period when *e* was developed from all unaccented front vowels in the Midlands and South (cf. *AB* xli. 39), and this is confirmed by the inscriptions of Offa's coins, where *e* for *i* becomes frequent. In the early ninth century *e* for *i* is fully developed on coins of Kent (Cuthred, 798–*c.* 806), East Anglia (Æthelstan I, *c.* 828–37), and Wessex (Eċġbeorht, 802–39). Coins, however, confirm the evidence of *LV* that the change was later in Northumbria, where *Eaduine* occurs on one coin of Eanred (*c.* 807–*c.* 840), but otherwise *e* spellings are not found before the reign of Æthelred II (*c.* 840–*c.* 849), when they become frequent.

[3] In *Ru.*[1] unaccented *æ* often appears as a spelling variant for *e* (e.g. g.s., d.s. of *a*-nouns in *-æs*, *-æ*), and can be used even for *e* < *i* (e.g. 2nd sg. pres. indic. *ġeseæs*, *stǣnæst*, 3rd *sweræþ*). Such spellings are also found in lNorth., where they are fairly frequent in *Li.* and *Rit.*, not in *Ru.*[2] (see Mincoff, *Archiv* clxxiii. 32).

[4] lW-S *y* for unaccented *e* is probably of no significance, e.g. *hǣlynd*, *fædyr*, *æftemysta*, *huntiġystran*.

[5] Li. has *bi-*, *ġi-* occasionally.

dēmde, strong past part. *coren*, pres. part. *rīdende*; with old *i*, n.s. of *i*-stems *wine*, and of *i̯a*- stems *ende*, superl. with umlaut *ieldest*, 2nd and 3rd sg. pres. indic. *rīdes*, *-eþ*, past subj. *ride*, weak past tense *nerede*, forms with parasiting *æppel*, prefixes *be-*, *ġe-*,[1] unaccented words *ne*, *be*.

§ 371. The formative elements *-iġ*, *-iċ*, *-isċ*, *-ing*, *-iht*, *-liċ* (e.g. *mihtiġ*, *ēowiċ*, *Englisċ*, *pening*, *stǣniht*, *strongliċ*) are generally not subject to the change *i* > *e*, though *e* is fairly frequent before back vowels, e.g. *mihteġu*, *fīfteġum*, *weleġode*, *Denescan*, *penengas*, *eallenga*, *Basengum* (PC 871), *strongleċu*. In lOE, however, *-iġ* often > *-i* (§ 267), and could then be reduced to *e* before a heavy syllable, e.g. *dyseliċ*, *mihteliċe*.

§ 372. In the second elements of compounds, with reduction of stress, *æ* and *i* (after shortening, if long) can become *e* as in fully unaccented syllables, e.g. with *æ*, *ǣfest* lawful (beside *ǣfæst*), compounds of *ærn* house (as *bēodern*), *ēored*, *earfeð* (cf. § 336), *hancred* cock-crow (< *-crǣd*), *āwer* anywhere (beside *āhwǣr*), *hired* household (< *-rǣd*), *Ælfred* (< *-rǣd*), *Æþelmer* (< *-mǣr*), Li. *ġenēoleċa* (VP *ġenēolǣċan*), *fullestan* (beside *fullǣstan*), *ōnettan*, *ōrettan* (< **-hai̯tian*, if the suffix is not contaminated with that of *hlēapettan*, § 339); with *i*, *nēawest* neighbourhood (beside *nēawist*), *ǣrest* resurrection (beside *ǣrist*), *fyrwet* curiosity (beside *fyrwit*), *endlefan* (beside *-lifan*), *enetere* a year old (beside *enitre* < **ǣnwintri*), names in *-ferþ* (rarely *-freþ*, beside *-friþ*, § 459.4); with *i* from *y*, *cynren* generation (beside rare *cynryn*), *æfest* (§ 356), *nosterl* (§ 481.1), VP *ymbhwerft* (once for *ymbhwyrft*).[2]

§ 373. Unaccented *u* is preserved in all instances in the early North. short texts,[3] *BH*[4] and *LV*.[5] In *Ep.*, however, protected *u* > *o* very often, e.g. *uuiloc-*, *helostr*, *dēatlicostan*, *suornodun*, and occasionally in absolute finality, e.g. *seto* (neut. p.) 896, *sċeado* 902. In later sources *u* has an increasing tendency to change to *o*, but it was far more stable in absolute finality than when protected. *VP* preserves even protected *u* extensively, e.g. *hēafud*, *wuldur*,

[1] So *te-* (CP 49, 11) for older *ti-* (Ep. 195). In late OE *ġe-* > *ī-*, and is sometimes so written after prefixes, e.g. *unīliċ*; also *iġ* (= *ī*), *uniġmetes*, Beow. 1792.

[2] Cf. unaccented *embe* from *ymbe*.

[3] The instances are past pl. in *-un* (frequently), d.p. in *-um* (frequently), North. a.s. of weak declension in *-u* (3 instances, § 472), CH *metudaes*, *uuldur-*, *-fadur* (§ 331), *middun-*, LR *hrūtendu*, RC *heafunæs*. *BC* has *setton*, but the inscription is hardly clear enough to be of linguistic value.

[4] Except the parasite vowel of *Earcon-* beside less frequent *Eorcun-*.

[5] Except only *Aebbino* (st. f.), *LV* 29.

past indic. pl. *-un* (very rarely *-on*), and it remains frequent in lNorth. and *Ru.*[1] Ordinary OE forms are, however, e.g. *hēafod* head, *heofon* heaven, *tungol* star, past indic. pl. *-on*, weak past of Class II *-ode*, superl. *-ost*, but n.s. of *u̯a-*, *ō-* and *u*-stems *-u* (*bearu*, *ġiefu*, *sidu*), n.p.n. of *a*-stems *-u* (*sċipu*), nW-S 1st sg. pres. indic. *-u* (VP *fearu*). *o* for unprotected *u* is increasingly common in late texts.

u is always well preserved after accented *u*, e.g. *sunu*, *wudu*, *duguþ*; before *m*, e.g. *māþum*, d.p. *-um*, *-sum* as suffix; in the suffix *-ung*; in the suffix *-uc* of whatever origin, e.g. *beallucas*, *bulluc*, *gafeluc*, *hassuc*, *mattuc*, *munuc*.

§ 374. Similar change *u* > *o* occurs in the second element of compounds of obscured meaning, e.g. *oroþ* (§ 333, footnote), *fracoþ* bad (< *-*kunþ*-), *ofost* haste (beside *ofust*, § 356); cf. preps. *þorh*, *oþ* (beside *þurh*, *ūþ-*).

§ 375. In contrast to *æ*, *i*, *u*, unaccented *a* is fairly stable in OE till the late period; eW-S gerundive in *-onne*, beside more frequent *-anne*, may be noted.

§ 376. Contrary to the usual change *i* > *e*, there is a change *e* > *i* before *i̯*. This is seen in the suffix *-iġ* (< *-eġ* < *-æġ*), which except in the earliest texts appears as *-iġ*, and is distinguished from *-iġ* < *-īġ* (Goth. *-eigs*) only by the absence of umlaut in the preceding syllable, e.g. *hāliġ*, CH *hāleġ*, *bodiġ*, Cp. *bodeġ*.[1] The same change is seen in the formative suffix of weak verbs of Class II, *-iġ-* (< *-ei̯-* < *-ōei̯*, § 355.5).[2]

§ 377. As a result of the changes described above, OE had virtually two unaccented back vowels, *o*/*u* and *a*. The distinction of these is clearly seen to be weakening in Kt. charters of the ninth century, *-a* sometimes appearing for *-o*/*-u*, e.g. *ġeðinġa*, *fōðra* (neut. pls.), *willa* (1st sg. pres. indic., Ct. 40), *dohtar*, *alað* (g.s.), and past indic. pl. *-an* (very frequent). Conversely *-on* appears for *-an* (d.s. *ġemanon*, Ct. 37), and *-u* for *-a* (*sunu* d.s., Ct. 45, Surrey). In eW-S, while not frequent in *CP*, *-a* for *-o*/*-u* increases in Or. In lW-S and *KG* the endings *-on* (past indic. pl.) and *-an* (weak declension, infs., advs.) are very confused, though *-an* is used more freely for *-on* than *-on* for *-an*. In *KG* and some lW-S manuscripts final *-u*, *-o*, *-a* are freely interchangeable (§ 49),

[1] *Ep.*, *Erf.* have the very archaic *bodæi*.

[2] *Samtinġes* shows a similar change before *nġ*, if the second element is that seen in *ġetenġe*.

so that, for example, neut. pls. occur in *-a*, and (more rarely) gen. pls. in *-o*.

§ 378. In lW-S[1] *-um* of the d.p. of nouns and adjs., and dat. sg. masc. and neut. of adjs., appears very frequently as *-on*, *-an*. Presumably *-m* > *-n*, and when no longer followed by *m*, unaccented *u* changed to *o* (§ 373) and *a* (§ 377). Fairly frequent dat. pl. in *-un* in eW-S may show the first stage of the change.[2] Note also lW-S *furþon*, *-an* for adv. *furþum* even.

§ 379. In the eleventh century unaccented *e* (< *æ*, *e*, *i*) and the unaccented back vowel in which *a*, *o*, *u* had largely coalesced, became confused, and spellings appear like *hlēfdiġen*, *mīnas* for *hlǣfdiġan*, *mīnes* (Cott. Aug. ii. 85; cf. p. 136, note 2). It is doubtful if significance should be attached to earlier spellings of this type, e.g. *Beow.* 63 *-sċilfingas* (gen. sg.), 519 *-rǣmes* (acc. pl.).[3]

§ 380. In lW-S and *Ru.*[1], the pronominal accusatives *þone*, *hwone* (§ 333) are often affected by the change of unaccented *o* > *a* (§ 377), appearing as *þane*, *hwane*.[4] In Ru.[1] *þonne*, *hwonne* also appear with *a*. lW-S has in these words also a peculiar development to *æ*, *þæne*, *hwæne*, *þænne*, *hwænne*, and this seems to be shared by the low-stressed *moniġ* (§ 96), which appears as *mæniġ* too often to be explained by § 193.d. *Mæniġ* then influences related words like *mæniġo*. This *æ* can in Angl. appear changed to *e* in low stress (§ 369), and can then be returned to stress, and rounded after *w* (§ 319), hence North., Ru.[1] *þæne*, *þene*; Ru.[2] *hwenne*, Li. *hwoenne*. Ru.[1], Rit. *mæniġ* (rare) may belong here, though frequent North. *meniġ* is probably the umlaut form (with old *-īġ* not *-æġ*, § 376).

[1] Not in lKt. (*KG*), lMerc. (*RG*); lNorth. and *Ru.*[1] also preserve *-um* prevailingly.

[2] Occasional *-em* for *-um* in eKt. (*mīnem*, *ðisem*, Cts. 39, 40, 41) is hardly of significance, perhaps due to analogy of *þēm*.

[3] I. Williams, *Bonner Beiträge* xix. 122, 124, regards the change of unaccented *a* and *u* to *e* as already evidenced in *KG*: the instances are, however, all to be otherwise explained.

Ru.[1] and the three lNorth. glosses (*Li.*, *Rit.*, *Ru.*[2]) were probably written after the unaccented back vowels had coalesced in *e*; hence *e* often replaced *a* (as in the n.p. of *a*-stems in *-es*, and the pl. pres. indic. in *-eþ*, for *-as*, *-aþ*) and *u*/*o* (as in n.s. of *ō*-stems in *-e* for *-o* or *-u*). For this *e* the spelling *æ* is fairly frequent, as for *e* < *æ*, *i* (§ 369, footnote 3, p. 154). Conversely, *a* can be written for *e* (as in g.s. of *a*-stems in *-as* for *-es*). Yet in the main these texts preserve the unaccented back vowels in their spelling. It is difficult to decide if unaccented *a* for *o*/*u* in these texts is due to the falling together of all the back vowels with *e*, or whether, as in W-S and Kt. (§ 377), there was a previous stage when the back vowels fell together with each other but were not yet confused with *e*.

[4] Ru.[1] has only *þane*.

G. Suffix Confusion

§ 381. An important principle of Old English word-formation is that etymologically related suffixes can interchange. This has already been illustrated by the interchange of *-æġ* with *-īġ* (§§ 358, 376). Other examples are provided by *-in*/*-un*/*-an* and *-il*/*-ul*/*-al*; e.g. *dīegol* secret, *hetol* hostile, are clearly from **dīeġil*, **hetil*, with the suffix of *dēagol*, **hatol*. So *heofon* is for older *hefæn* (CH), *eosol* for **esel* < **esil* (§ 211). Cf. § 193.c on *ræċed*, *gæfel*, *hæċid*, *hæċile*, *hæleþ*, in all of which *a* was first preserved before a suffix with a back vowel, and then mutated after the suffix vowel was changed to *i*; also § 210.1 on forms like *hefon*, *werod*, which lack back umlaut.

§ 382. The interchange of *e* and *o* in *ēored*, *-od*, &c. (§ 336), leads to a similar interchange in *wēofod* altar (Li. *wīġbed*),[1] North. *hīorod* family < **hiu̯ræ̅d* (W-S *hīred*, §§ 120.3.c, footnote 2, 372).

§ 383. The suffixes *-ung*, *-ing*, in abstract fem. nouns interchange fairly systematically. In all dialects *-ing* prevails in derivatives of weak verbs of Class I (e.g. *grēting*, *ġemēting*, *ġewemming*, *ielding*, *fylġing*, *forċirring*), and *-ung* in derivatives of weak verbs of Class II (e.g. *costnung*, *leornung*).

Derivatives of strong verbs have *-ing* in lNorth. practically always (e.g. Li., Ru.[2] *flōwing*, *lesing*, *onwrīting*), lW-S sources vary, elsewhere the instances are too few for any conclusions to be drawn (details in H. Weyhe, *Zu den alteng. Verbalabstrakten auf* -nes *und* -ing, -ung). In W-S there is a tendency to prefer *-ing* to *-ung* in compounds, e.g. *leorningcniht*, *bletsingbōc*. *VP* changes *-ung-* to *-ing-* before back vowels (d.p. *-ingum*, g.p. not recorded, but cf. advs. *fēringa*, *nīowinga*, *wōeninga*).

§ 384. The suffix *-nes* is mainly W-S, while *-nis* prevails heavily in *VP*, *Ru.*[1], and North. *KG* have only *-nes*, but both forms appear in the ninth-century Kt. charters.

H. Medial Unaccented Vowels

§ 385. **Vowel harmony.** Already in *VP* and eW-S, there is a strong tendency for the first of two successive unaccented back vowels to be reduced to a sound written *e*, and hence forms are frequent like *fugelas*, *roderas*, *heoretas*, *ġedwimeru*, from *fugol*,

[1] But if the second element be regarded as *bēod*, table, the development in W-S is according to § 357.

rodor, *heorot*, *ġedwimor*; *eafera*, *adesa*, *nafela* beside *eafora*, *adosa*, *nabula* (Cp.); verbs like *swutelian*, *staþelian*, *gaderian*[1] from *swutol*, *staþol*, *geador*. To this process is due g.p. of weak nouns in *-ena* for older *-ana* (Cp. 687, and still frequent in North. and *Ru.*[1]); superl. in *-esta* beside *-osta*; *-edon* for *-odon* in past. pl. of weak verbs of Class II (and hence sg. *-ede*, especially *KG*). The back vowels are, of course, always liable to analogical restoration.

§ 386. Second elements of compounds of reduced force are subject to the same process; e.g. *fultemian* beside *fultumian* (§ 356), *fraceðu* (n.p.n. of *fracoþ*, § 374), *hlāferdas* (Li.); and with the second element following the reduced back vowel, *Badenoð* beside *Badanoð* (< *beadu*+*nōþ*, § 377).

§ 387. A phonetically related process is the reduction of back vowels of formative syllables or obscured second elements to *e* before heavy formative additions, e.g. *fraceðlecum*, *rūmedliċe* (beside *rūmodliċe*), *aredlicor*, beside *fracoþ*, *rūmmōd* (cf. § 458), *arod*.

§ 388. **Loss of medial vowels after short syllables.** Medial unaccented vowels are very freely dropped after short syllables,[2] when the loss causes a group consisting of consonant+*l* or *r* to arise. Hence forms like *yfle*, *miċle*, *betra*, *byrle*, *ætgædre*, beside *yfele*, *miċele*, *betera*, *byrele*, *ætgædere*. So *Sætresdæġ* (< *Sæteres-*, § 474.3), *Dæġlesford* beside *Deġiles-*, *dysliċ* (< *dyseliċ*, § 371). Such loss is frequent in weak verbs of Class II between consonant and nasal, e.g. *medmian*, *opnian*.[3]

§ 389. Similar loss of vowels between consonants other than those dealt with in § 388 is more sporadic. It is frequent in weak verbs of Class II, e.g. *or(e)ðian*, *ef(e)sian*. Other examples which mostly appear beside forms with preserved middle vowels are *fremde*, *eġsa*, *eġþe*, *miġþa*, **siġþe* (§ 267), *fyrsta*, *betsta*, *smælsta*, *winstre*, *heolstor* (Ep. pl. *helustras*), *culfre*, *seolfor*, *heolfor* (Napier's *OE glosses*, p. 218, *helabr*), *ġeolca*, *balca*, *pylċe*, *ċirċe*. So *Hysca* beside *Hysica* (LV).

§ 390. Disyllabic forms which can appear as monosyllables (or

[1] The medial *e* would arise first before the endings with back vowels (*-ast*, *-aþ*, *-a*, *-ode*).

[2] In open syllables, after long accented syllables, medial *i* and *u* had been previously lost (§ 351), while *a* (*æ*, *e*) had been lost after short syllables also (§ 341). Medial vowels remaining in open syllables after long syllables were derived from old longs by shortening, and carried a half-stress (§§ 89, 91).

[3] From *openian* with the second vowel (Gmc. *a*) replaced from *open*; so *ġedaf(e)nian*, but in *fæġnian* the forms without *e* heavily predominate, and probably directly represent the form with early syncopation.

when inflected as disyllables) owing to similar loss are *cyl(e)n* kiln, *myl(e)n* mill, *fir(e)n* crime, *þyr(e)l* hole, *meol(o)c* milk, *seol(o)c* silk, *weol(o)c* whelk, *cler(i)c* clerk, *mer(i)sċ* marsh, *heor(o)t* hart, *fal(o)d* fold, *ar(o)d-* swift (simplex *arod*), *war(o)þ* shore, *or(o)þ* breath, *byr(e)s* chisel. Only monosyllabic forms occur for *twelf* twelve, *dalc* clasp, *eln* ell, *hwelċ* which, *swelċ* such. It is, of course, not possible to decide how far the vowel-losses recorded in this section arose first in trisyllabic forms.

§ 391. Monosyllables arising through loss of an unaccented vowel after a short syllable before a consonant group are *æfst* (eW-S) for *æfest*, *cyng* (Ru.[1], lW-S) for *cyning*, *ofst* (frequent, and so *efstan*) for *ofost*, *world* (lNorth., lW-S) for *woruld*, *bern* (lW-S) for *berern*.

§ 392. **Syncopation after long syllables.** After long accented syllables, all fully unaccented vowels had been lost in open medial syllables in prehistoric OE (cf. § 388, footnote). In the historic period, vowels preserved in this position by a half-stress (§§ 89, 91) were sometimes dropped if the half-stress was lost (§ 358). Similarly, heavy formative suffixes after long syllables sometimes, especially in lOE, lost their half-stress and were reduced, e.g. nomina agentis in *-ere* (as lW-S *bōcre*), comparative adjs. from advs. (as lW-S *æftra*, *inra*, *ȳtra*, for *æfterra*, &c.), eW-S *bismrian*, *fultmian*, *ōþre*, *-ra* (for *bismerian*, *fultemian*, *ōþerre*, *-ra*), lW-S *dēofliċ*, *þylċ*, *hēafre* (for *dēofolliċ*, *þylliċ*, *hēahfore*), Ct. of 938 *Wīðlēagate* d.s. (beside *Wīðiġlēa*).

§ 393. Instances of loss of a vowel in a closed syllable after a long accented syllable are eW-S *ǣmtiġ* beside *ǣmettiġ* and the late forms *fulhtere*, *ġefulhtnian* for *fulluhtere*, &c., *ǣrndian* for *ǣrendian*, *hætse* for *hæġtesse*, *Henċstes* for *Henġestes*. More extensive reduction appears in *(n)āuht*,[1] *(n)āht* < *(n)āwiht*; *(n)āteshwōn* < *(n)āwihtes-*; *wǣpman* < *wǣpen-*; *ǣlpiġ* < *ǣnlīpiġ*; *heardra* < *heardhara*. The genitival *-es* is dropped after a long syllable in *Sætern(es)-dæġ*, and loses its vowel in *Ċēolsīġe* (Ct. of Ælfred in Winchester Cartulary, beside *Ċēolesīġ*), *Þursdæġ* (lW-S *Gospels*).

I. Chronological Summary

§ 394. Of the changes dealt with in this chapter, those described in Section A belong to the period before the Germanic conquest of

[1] *VP* already *nōht* beside *nōwiht*.

England, while the relative chronology of those described in Section B has been discussed in Chapter V, Section K. The Old English losses and reductions of vowels described in Sections C and D lie before the period of the oldest texts, but after *i*-umlaut, for *i* was lost neither finally nor medially till it had caused that change (e.g. *ēst*, *dēmde* < **anstiz*, **dōmiðō*). It appeared in § 353 that *i* and *u* were lost at the same time, and that the loss of *æ*, although earlier, was itself later than *i*-umlaut. It is, of course, evident that the reduction of long vowels described in Section D was not completed at the time of the vowel losses of Section C, for the new shorts would then have been lost like the old ones. Nevertheless, the reduction of the long vowels had gone sufficiently far, when the old shorts were dropping, for the new shorts to count as such in the quantitative patterns which governed loss and retention of vowels (§ 356 and footnote on *heardlicu*). In *ǣlċ* each < **ǣlīċ* a new medial short is syncopated like an old one. Accordingly, the changes of Sections C and D are closely associated, and must all belong to nearly the same period.

§ 395. The parasiting described in §§ 363–4 is older than smoothing: Angl. *bēcun* clearly developed a back parasite vowel because a back vowel preceded, and hence it presupposes a form *bēacun*. It is, however, not possible to relate this parasiting to back umlaut, for there is no certain case of a parasite vowel causing that change.[1] The parasiting in accented syllables of §§ 360–1 is present in the earliest texts, but may be assumed to be later than smoothing, for Angl. **beorht* > *berht* before the new vowel of *beriht* divided the back consonant from the *r* (and so *þerih*). The parasiting described in §§ 365–6 is mainly W-S, and as it appears in eW-S but is not yet at its height, it can be regarded as a change which began about 800, and continued to gain ground till about 1000.

§ 396. The changes of unaccented vowels described in §§ 369–76, 380 are to be dated by their appearances in texts, as is indicated in the discussion of them. The confusion of the unaccented back vowels began before 900, and was completed in Kentish and Northumbrian in the course of the tenth century, rather later in West-Saxon (§§ 377–8). It was followed in the eleventh century by confusion of all unaccented vowels (§ 379).

[1] It is uncertain if the vowel of the suffix of *beofor* is parasitic (Prim. Gmc. **bevur*- or **bevr*-). If it is parasitic, it must be explained like that of *bitur*, &c. (§ 363); **bevr*-, Ep. *bebr*, gives normally *befer* (§ 210.1).

§ 397. The vowel harmony described in §§ 385–7 is first traced in the ninth century, and remains alive into the eleventh, when the confusion of front and back unaccented vowels ended it. The syncopation of vowels described in §§ 388–91 began prehistorically,[1] but continued to occur throughout the Old English period, while the various losses of §§ 392–3 appear for the most part in late texts, a few only in Early West-Saxon.

[1] The loss of the vowel in *fald* was clearly later than breaking. Although unsyncopated forms are not recorded, a similar loss is assumed in *balca*, *dalc* to explain the absence of breaking.

VIII

THE INDO-EUROPEAN CONSONANTS IN GERMANIC AND WEST GERMANIC

§ 398. By the operation of the Germanic sound-shift (Grimm's law), and various other processes which lie outside the scope of a grammar of an individual language, Primitive Germanic received the following consonantal sounds:[1]

	Labials	_Dentals_	_Velars_	_Palatals_	_Sibilants_
Voiceless stops	p	t	k		
Voiced ,,	b	d	g		
Voiceless spirants	f	þ	χ		s
Voiced ,,	v, u̯	ð	ʒ	i̯	z
Nasals	m	n	ŋ		
Liquids		l, r			

(1) Of these, the following could appear as double consonants in medial position: _p, t, k, m, n, l, r, s_. Such geminates are preserved in OE _hoppian_ hop, _cnotta_ knot, _liccian_ lick, _swimman_ swim, _rinnan_ run, _wulle_ wool, _steorra_ star, _wisse_ knew.

(2) Medially and finally _f, þ, s, χ_ interchanged with their voiced equivalents _v, ð, z, ʒ_, according to a system by which a voiceless spirant was voiced if the preceding vowel did not bear the main stress according to the original Indo-European system of variable accent position. This is known as Verner's law. The interchange of consonants is seen most clearly in the strong verbs, where the infinitive, the present system, and the 1st and 3rd sg. indic. of the past contrast with the rest of the past system (including the 2nd sg. past indic. in West Gmc.) and pass. part. Thus in Prim. Gmc. the infs. and pass. parts. of OE _drīfan_ drive, _ċēosan_ choose, _snīþan_ cut, _tēon_ draw, _sēon_ see, would be *_dreifan-_, *_drivan-_; *_keusan-_, *_kozan-_; *_sneiþan-_, *_sniðan-_; *_teuχan-_, *_toʒan-_; *_seχu̯an-_, *_seʒu̯an-_ (but 3rd pl. past indic. *_sǣʒunt_).[2]

[1] The symbols are mostly used with the approximate value which they prevailingly have in NE, but _i̯, u̯_ = _y, w_ in _yet, wet_; _ŋ_ = _ng_ in _sing_; _þ_ and _ð_ = _th_ in _thin, then_; _χ_ and _ʒ_ = _ch_ in _loch_ and its voiced equivalent.

[2] In North. and West Gmc. medial _χu̯_ became _χ_, but medial _ʒu̯_ became _u̯_ normally, _ʒ_ under uncertain circumstances, but at least before _ŭ_.

(3) *z* existed only owing to the operation of Verner's law, and before other voiced consonants, e.g. **mizðō* reward, **χuzða-* treasure. *b*, *d* existed only initially, and in the groups *mb*, *nd*, e.g. **beran-* bear, **kamba-* comb, **daʒa-* day, **bindan-* bind. *ð*, *v* did not exist initially or after nasals, *ʒ* existed initially but not after nasals, e.g. **ʒoða-* god, **ʒaiza-* spear; *g* existed only in the group *ŋg*, e.g. **laŋga-* long. Thus in the labial and dental series, the voiced stops, *b*, *d*, and the spirants, *v*, *ð*, could not be used in the same positions: the stops occur initially and in nasal groups *mb*, *nd*, the spirants medially and finally. The back series is not symmetrical, for the spirant *ʒ* is used in the initial position, so that the stop *g* is limited to the nasal group *ŋg*.[1]

(4) There was in Prim. Gmc. an interchange between consonantal *i̯* and its syllabic equivalent. *i̯* was vocalized to a syllabic sound which may be represented by *i*, or better by *ii̯*, after a long accented syllable ending in a consonant,[2] so that, for example, n.s. **χari̯az*, imper. **biði̯e* contrasted with n.s. **andii̯az*, imper. **sōkii̯e*.[3] When the following vowel was in absolute finality, and was lost early (§ 331.1), *ii̯* contracted into final *ī*, e.g. **sōkī* > OE *sēċ* (§ 345). With later loss of the following vowel, *ii̯* > *ī*, and this was then treated as if it had the IE abnormal intonation, remaining in OE, e.g. *ende* (§§ 355.3). When the vowel following *ii̯* was not lost, *ii̯* was syncopated in OE like *i*, e.g. **sōkii̯an-* > *sēċan*, **sōkii̯iþ* > *sēċeþ*.[4] After a preceding syllable was made long by West Gmc. consonant gemination (§ 407), *i̯* appears to have remained consonantal (§ 353, footnote), and was subject to loss in OE, e.g. **frami̯an-* > **frammi̯an* > *fremman*. The interchange does not affect IE *i*, which remains vocalic, and hence causes no consonant gemination in West Gmc. before a vowel after short syllables, e.g. g.p. of *i*-declension, OE *winia*.

[1] Luick, *Hist. Gramm.*, § 618, reverting to a view supported by Henry Sweet in the *History of English sounds*, holds that Gmc. had *g* not *ʒ* in initial position, and hence that the back series was symmetrical with the labial and dental ones. This view raises many difficulties, and has little to recommend it: cf. Flasdieck, *A* lxix. 268.

[2] *ii̯* also appeared after an unaccented syllable, e.g. Goth. 2nd sg. pres. indic. *mikileis*, like *sōkeis*. After a long syllable ending in a vowel *i̯* appeared, e.g. Goth. *stōjis*, like *satjis*, OE *ċīeġan* < **kaui̯an-* (§ 120.2).

[3] This interchange of *i̯* and *ii̯* is called Sievers' law, owing to the discussion by Sievers, *PBB* v. 129 ff.; cf. Edgerton, *Language* x. 235 ff.

[4] Like *hīerde*, § 351. So OE *rīċu* is developed from **rīkii̯ō*, as *hēafdu* from **χauvudō*.

§ 399. In Prim. Gmc. final *s*(*z*) and *r* remained (e.g. Goth. *stains* < **stainaz* stone, *fadar* father) but other final consonants were dropped in unaccented syllables,[1] although a lost final nasal consonant can influence the development of a preceding vowel (see examples § 331.5). The acc. sg. of all nouns illustrates the loss of final *-m*, the 3rd sg. of the pres. and past subj. that of final *-þ*, e.g. OE *stān* < **stainam*, *bere*, *bǣre* < **beraiþ*, **bǣrīþ*. So in cons. stems there is interchange between OE *hæle* and *hæleþ*, with *þ* restored from the inflected forms.

§ 400. The loss of vowels of final syllables, described in § 331.1–4, leads to the consonants *l*, *m*, *n*, *r*, *i̯*, *u̯* becoming syllable-bearers in some words. *i̯*, *u̯* > *i*, *u*, e.g. OE *here* < **heri* < **χari̯az*, *bearu* < **baru̯az*. This process repeated itself later, after the vowel losses described §§ 341–53, e.g. OE a.s.m. *ġearone* < **ʒaruna* < **ʒaru̯anōn*. After a long syllable, *i* and *u* of this origin drop in OE like originally vocalic *i* and *u* (§ 345), e.g. *sǣ* sea < **sǣi* < **saiu̯i-* (§ 406), and so *ǣ* law, *hrǣ* corpse; *gād* want (Goth. *gaidw*); *hrā* corpse < **χraiu̯-*, and so *snā* snow,[2] *ā* always (Goth. *aiw*); and cf. § 120.3.c, footnote, on **Tī*, **hī*.[3] Syllabic *l*, *m*, *n*, *r* remain in Goth.[4] (e.g. *fugls* bird, *maiþms* treasure, *ibns* even, *fingrs* finger), and frequently do so in OE, whether due to early or late vowel loss (see §§ 363–4).

§ 401. Consonant groups not ending in consonants capable of becoming syllable-bearers,[5] and all geminates, were retained without difficulty in Prim. Gmc. when they became final, and when they immediately preceded final *-s*. They remain in OE, where, however, final geminates are frequently graphically shortened (§ 66), e.g. *wulf* wolf, *horn* horn, *word* word, *healþ* helped, *band* bound, *eal*(*l*) all, *coc*(*c*) cock, *secġ* man (§ 61).

[1] In accented syllables final consonants remained, at least after short vowels, e.g. OE *hwæt* (with the neut. pronominal suffix seen in Lat. *quod*), OE *æt* (Lat. *ad*), Goth *þan* (Lat. *tum*). But in long accented syllables they perhaps disappear, e.g. OE *cū* a.s., if this is not nom. used for acc.

[2] Usually *hrāw*, *snāw* with *w* from inflected forms.

[3] See § 120.3.b on cases where *u* stood finally after a short vowel.

[4] Luick, *Hist. Gramm.*, § 625, regards OE spellings like *tānc*, *bēnc*, for *tācn bēacn* as due to a metathesis in Gmc. aimed at eliminating the syllabic consonants. They rather indicate a development of *cn* to *ŋ*; *ng* for *gn* (e.g. *reng* for *reġn*) similarly indicates probably a change to *ŋ*. (So S–B, § 185; Förster, *Flussname Themse*, p. 327, believes in metathesis, others regard these spellings as graphic variants.)

[5] This includes *l*, *m*, *n*, *r* after *r*, and *l* after *l*, e.g. OE *eorl*, *earm*, *earn*, *feorr*, *eall*.

§ 402. *i̯* and *u̯* were frequently doubled after a short vowel in Gmc. On the development of the resulting groups *ai̯i̯*, &c., in OE see § 120.1. The doubling was not always carried out, e.g. **χau̯i̯a-* > OE *hīeġ* (§ 120.2), but cf. **χau̯u̯an-*, ON *höggva* (§ 120.1); **au̯i* > OE *eowu* sheep; **ai̯az* > OE *ār* bronze; **treu̯a-* tree; **kneua-* knee. The conditions under which this gemination took place or failed are unknown.[1]

§ 403. On Gmc. and Ingvaeonic loss of nasal consonants before the homorganic spirants, see §§ 119, 121.

§ 404. Gmc. *z*, whether due to Verner's law or of earlier origin (§ 398.2.3), became *r* in North and West Gmc. Between vowels this remains in OE, so that *s–r* is a frequent variation in related words, such as the principal parts of strong verbs, like *ċēosan*, *curon*, and causative verbs like *nerian* save, against *nesan* escape. Other examples are the comparative suffix *-ra*, *ēare* ear, *dēor* animal (Goth. *-oza*, *auso*, *dius*). Between vowel and consonant *r* usually remains, e.g. *hord*, *reord*, &c. (see § 123–4); but it is lost with compensatory lengthening in OE *hād-* hair (cf. ON *haddr*), *mēd* reward (beside *meord*), *twīn* linen (cf. Ger. *zwirn*); cf. OS *līnon* learn, MD *hede* hards of flax (beside OE *leornian*, *heordan*, § 124). *zn* is assimilated to *nn* in Prim. OE **rænn* house, **hrænn* wave, but this change is later than the Anglo-Frisian fronting (§ 193.d, footnote 4).[2] *z* is lost in West Gmc. finally in unaccented syllables, e.g. many n.s. and n.p. inflexions, e.g. OE *dæġ*, *ġiefa* (cf. Goth. *dags*, *gibōs*); the unaccented pronominal words OE *we*, *ġe*, *he*, *me*, *þe*, *hwa*.[3]

§ 405. West Gmc. paradigms show regular loss of *u̯* before *u* and of *i̯* before *i*, e.g. weak verbs of Class I, 2nd and 3rd sg. pres. indic. **neris*, **neriþ*, inf. **neri̯an*, OE *nerest*, *nereþ*, *nerian*; fem. nouns in *u̯-ō* > *-u̯u* (§ 331.5) > *-u*, as OE *beadu*-battle, infl. *beadwe*; forms like *clēa*, see §§ 120.3.a, 235.1, 236.2; see also § 122 on final *u̯ō* > *u̯ū* > *ū* (OE *tū*, &c.).

§ 406. OE forms often show loss of *u̯* before *i*,[4] although *u̯* is often analogically restored, e.g. forms of weak verbs of Class I

[1] References in Prokosch, *Comparative Germanic grammar*, p. 93.

[2] *dunn* dark < **dusna-* shows a similar development, if it is not a Celtic loan-word (Förster, *Keltisches Wortgut*, p. 137).

[3] For most of these, however, OHG exhibits accented forms with *r* retained, *wir*, *ir*, *mir*, *dir*, *wer*.

[4] This loss is probably also OFris., but its results are so prone to be obscured by analogy that its extension in West Gmc. is impossible to trace.

like *ġierest*, *-eþ*, *-ede* < **ȝaris*, &c. < **ȝaru̯is*, beside inf. *ġierwan*, and so *wyleþ*, &c., beside *wylwan*; various, mostly verbal forms with loss of u̯ cited § 237.1.b, as *ēde*, *strēn*, *ċēð*, *strēd*, *nī-*; forms in which u̯ was lost between a long vowel and *i*, and *i* was subsequently lost (§§ 345, 351) as *sǣ* sea < **sǣi* < **sāi-* < **saiu̯i-*, &c., and so *ǣ* law, *hrǣ* corpse, and sporadic verbal forms like CP *ġecnǣð*, *ætīede*, North. *bilēde*, Ru.[1] *crǣd* from Gmc. **knaiu̯i-*, **auu̯i-*, **lǣu̯i-*, **kraiu̯i-*, by phonological development beside analogical *ġecnǣwð* knows, *ætīewde* showed, *belǣwde* betrayed, *crǣwþ* crows.

§ 407. W. Gmc. consonant doubling is particularly[1] strongly developed before i̯, every consonant except *r* being affected after short syllables. The i̯ is most consistently preserved in OS., e.g. *skeppian*, OE *sċieppan* < **skapi̯an* create. The forms in which u̯ is doubled are dealt with in § 120.2. Examples with other consonants are many weak verbs of Class I, as *sellan* give, *fremman* do, *þennan* stretch, *clyppan* embrace, *settan* set, *cnyssan* knock, *weċċan* awake, *byċġan* buy; nouns and adjs. of the *i̯a-*, *i̯ō-*, and *i̯an-/i̯ōn-* declensions, as *cynn* race (cf. Goth. g.s. *kunjis*), *sibb* relationship, *wreċċa* exile, *smiþþe* smithy, *nytt* useful. But *r* was not doubled, whether original or from *z* (§ 404), and *-ri̯-* remained in OE, e.g. *nerian* save, *herias* armies (Goth. *nasjan*, *harjōs*). When doubled, *v* and *ȝ* became the corresponding stops, *bb* and *gg* (written in OE *cg*), e.g. OE *hebban* raise, *liċġan* lie < **χavi̯an*, **liȝi̯an*. So, if *ð* had not already become *d* before the doubling (§ 409), *ði̯* > *ddi̯*, e.g. OE *biddan* ask < **biði̯an*.

§ 408. There was clearly already in West. Gmc. extensive doubling of consonants before *l* and *r* after short vowels, for there is evidence in all the languages, e.g. OS *appul* apple, OHG *snottar* wise, OE *æppel*, *snottor*. After long vowels the process was rare, and was perhaps accompanied by shortening of the vowel, e.g. OS *hlūttar* pure, OE *hlūttor*. Doubling took place when consonant and liquid belonged to the same syllable, and the geminates were transferred to other forms, so **hlūttr̥* (Goth. *hlūtrs*) took *tt* from

[1] Many handbooks following Kauffmann, *PBB* xii. 508 ff., regard the double consonants in weak nouns such as OE *docga*, *sugga*, *crabba*, *lobbe*, OHG *tropfo* drop, *chnappo* boy, as due to West Gmc. gemination before *n*, in forms where the thematic suffix was *-n-*, and the consonant to be doubled was hence in contact with it. But these geminates are of earlier and diverse origin. Cf. H. Krahe, *Germanische Sprachwissenschaft* i (Berlin, 1948), pp. 113–14; and on various theories A. Martinet, *La gémination consonantique d'origine expressive dans les langues germaniques* (Copenhagen and Paris, 1937).

**hlūttrō*, &c. Examples occur of such doubling of *p*, *t*, *k*, *h* only, e.g. OE *æppel*, *snottor*, *wæccer* awake, *hweohhol* wheel. Forms with single consonants are sometimes generalized from the uninflected form, e.g. *æcer* field (OS *akkar*). Sometimes double forms occur, e.g. *wæc(c)er*, *snot(t)or*, *bit(t)er*, *wæt(t)res*. So beside *ēar* ear of corn, *tēar* tear, *hwēol* wheel, with loss of single χ (§ 235.2), we have *hweohhol* and North. *æhher*, *tæher*.[1]

§ 409. In West Gmc. *ð* whether original (i.e. from IE *dh*), or due to Verner's law (§ 398.2), became *d*: e.g. with original *ð*, OE *gōd* good, *word* word, *stōd* stood, cf ON *góðr*, *orð*, *stóð*; with *ð* due to Verner's law, OE *flōd* flood, *fæder* father, *mōdor* mother, cf. ON *flóð*, *faðir*, *móðir*; also many past pls. and pass. parts. as *snidon*, *sniden*, *wurdon*, *worden* from *snīþan* cut, *weorþan* become.[2]

§ 410. Owing to West Gmc. processes, there is in a few OE words interchange between *i̯* and *u̯*. In West Gmc. *ī* contracted with *u̯* to *iu*, OE *īo*, *ēo* (§ 120.3.c) and later OE *ī*+back vowel > *īo*, *ēo* (§ 238.1). But before a front vowel, *ī* passed into a consonantal glide in Prim. OE. Hence beside *frēo* free (< **frīa-*, **frīu-*), a.s.m. *frīġne*, g.s.m. *frīġes*, n.p. *frīġe* (< **frīi̯ænæ*, **frīi̯æs*, **frīi̯ǣ*). Then analogical forms like g.s.m. *frēos*, d.p. *frīġum* develop.

§ 411. In absolute finality *u̯* dropped in West Gmc. after *ī* and hence in a few words in *-īu̯a-* there is variation between final *ī* (which may be written *iġ*, § 271), *īo*, *ēo* (with restoration of *u̯* from inflected forms, and development of *iu̯* to *īo*, *ēo*), and *īw* (with late restoration and retention of *u̯*). Hence *ġīġ*, *ġīw* vulture, *briiġ*, *brīw* porridge, *slī*, *slīw* mullet, *Tiiġ*, *Tīwes-*, a heathen god. The forms in *ī(ġ)* are the oldest, being mainly recorded in early glossaries; *-īġ* is transferred to an inflected form in *Tīġes*. The development *ēo* with addition of *u̯* from inflected forms occurs in *slēow*; *ēo* is transferred to an inflected form in *ġēowes*. The variation of *īġ* with *īw*, *īow* in these words caused a form *glīġ*, *glīġes* to arise beside *glīw*, *glīow* mirth (§ 120.2), and southern place-names suggest that **nīġe* existed beside *nīwe*, new (*AB* xxviii. 295).

§ 412. The alternation of *w* and *ġ* described in § 411 should be carefully distinguished from that due to the development of *ʒu̯* as *ʒ* or *u̯* according to the following sound (§ 398.2). This appears

[1] *h* = *hh*, for single *h* is lost between voiced sounds (§ 66).

[2] W-S *fremde*, Angl. *fremþe*, foreign, reflect alternative forms of the suffix due to Verner's law.

in OE *hīgan* family, *mūga* heap, *hweogol* wheel, *brēġ* (Angl.) eye-lid, beside *hīwan*, *mūwa*, *hweowol*, *brǣw*. By Verner's law, beside *īw*, *ēow* yew (cf. *ġīw*, *ġēow-*) we find *ēoh* < **īoh* < **īh*. Furthermore, the interchange of *h–w*, due to Verner's law, can become one of *g–w* owing to inverted spelling of final *h* as *g*, and false introduction of internal *g* (§ 447), e.g. *holh*, *holg*, **holwes*[1] hollow, *horh*,[2] *horg*, *horu*, *horwes* rheum, *rūh*, *rūgan*, *rūwes* rough.[3]

§ 413. The group *þl* at the beginnings of words became in North and West Gmc. *fl*, e.g. OE *flēon* flee, ON *flýja*, but Goth. *þliuhan*, and probably *flāh* deceptive, cf. Goth. *gaþlaihan* comfort. This change cannot be traced with certainty in internal position.

§ 414. In West Gmc. medial *lþ* > *ld*, and final *lþ* became replaced in OE by *ld* from inflected forms, e.g. *wilde* wild, *fealdan* fold, *wuldor* glory, cf. Goth. *wilþeis*, *falþan*, *wulþus*; and after inflected forms, *beald* bold, *gold* gold, *feld* field, Goth. *balþ-*, *gulþ*. Final *þ* is preserved in a few forms in early OE: *-felth* often in *BH*, and transferred to internal position in *Cp.* 1797 *feltha*; *Balth-* Cts. 6 and 7 (Kt.), *Balð-* LV, always before second elements with initial *h*; and the existence of alternative forms with *lþ*, *ld* seems to produce some spellings of *ld* as *lth*, *lð*: Ep. Cp. *spilth*, Ep. *halði*, *ōhaelði*, for *spild* ruin, *healde* i.s. sloping, *ōhielde* sloping. *lþ* arising by syncopation in Prim. OE is not subject to this sound change, e.g. *hǣlþ* health, *hilð* he hides.

[1] Cf. ME *holwe* (adj.), Mod. E. *hollow*.
[2] And hence *horheht* for phonological *horweht*.
[3] And so *rēowe*, *rūwe*, beside *rēo*, Ep. *rȳhae* blanket.

IX

THE GERMANIC CONSONANTS IN OLD ENGLISH

A. Early Changes of Groups

§ 415. A number of consonant changes may be mentioned here, which are to be put comparatively late in the Primitive Old English period, but which are found in other Germanic languages also. This must be due to linguistic expansions, which brought groups of dialects into relationship, rather than to descent from a common type of Germanic. One can compare the loss of final *-n*, which, cutting across the old linguistic grouping, linked North Germanic to Frisian and Northumbrian (§ 472).

§ 416. *χs* > *ks* in North Gmc., OE and O.Fris. This change cannot be placed back in the Gmc. period, for *χs* remained late enough to cause breaking, e.g. OE *feax* hair, *weaxan* grow, *Seaxe* Saxons.[1] Other examples are *fox* fox, *siex* six, *meox* manure, *oxa* ox, *ōxn* arm-pit, *wēocsteall* altar-place, (i.e. **wēoh+steall*), *Wēoxtan* (PC for *Wēohstan*), *līxan* shine. *hs* in eW-S appears occasionally as a spelling (e.g. *weahsan*), and may be extended to *ks* of other origin (e.g. *āhsian* beside *ācsian*, Oros.). This sound-change is a remarkable link of OE and OFris. to each other and to North Gmc., for in OS *χs* > *s*, while in OHG *χs* remains (written *hs*), cf. OFris., ON *sex*, OS *ses*, OHG *sehs* six. On the later repetition of the change in OE, see § 481.4.

§ 417. When a consonant follows, *χs* > *s* in OE, e.g. *wæstm* fruit, *-wæsma* growth (both related to *weaxan*), North. *sesta* sixth, beside W-S, Ru.[1] *syxta*, with *ks* from *siex*), but *wrixlan* exchange (from *ġewrixl*, where *l* is vocalic), *pīxl* axle beside *pīsl* (from paradigm originally *pīxl*, *pīsle*), and weak *pīsle*.[2] This change is found in all West Gmc. languages, and in North Gmc., e.g. ON *pīsl* axle; OS *uueslon* exchange, *uuastum* fruit; ON *nýsa*, OS

[1] See § 65 on the symbol *x* = *ks*, and rarer variants.

[2] *Nēosan* visit (< **niuhsian*, cf. Goth. *niuhsjan*) is difficult to explain, as the medial element would be vocalic by Sievers' law (see § 398.4); cf. *līxan* < **liuhsian*.

niusian, OHG *niusen* visit; OS, OHG *lastar* reproach (< **laχstra-*, cf. OE *leahtor* < **laχtra-*).

§ 418. *fs* > *ps* in OE relatively late, for the original sounds are recorded in early texts: *wæps* wasp (Ep., Cp. *waefs*, but Erf. *uaeps*), *ræpsan* reprove[1] (in this and related words, *Erf.*, *Ep.*, *Cp.* all have both *fs* and *ps*, Ep. once *bs*). This sound-change seems to have had some spread in the West Gmc. area. In view of the *fs* spellings of the glossaries, it would seem that the change is late, and that regular forms like *drīfst*, thou drivest, are due to paradigm analogy.

§ 419. A group of changes arise from a tendency to develop stops from spirants before liquids and nasals. After a short vowel, *þl*, *þm* > *tl*, *tm* in W-S, e.g. *botl* building, *bytla* builder, *setl* seat,[2] *botm* bottom, *bytme* keel.[3] However, *fæþm* embrace, *mæþl* talk, preserve *þ*, and possibly the change took place only when *þl* and *þm* belonged to one syllable, and hence did not take place in uninflected forms, e.g. *fæþm*. If this is so, levelling must have taken place in individual words in favour of *þ* or *t*.

§ 420. In Angl., however, *þl*, *þm* remained after short vowels and the spirant became voiced by a normal process (§ 444): *seþel*[4] (Li., Ru.², Rit., Ru.¹, OE Bede), *boðle*[5] d.s. (OE Bede), **boþm* (cf. ME *bothem*), *bythne* (Cp.).

§ 421. An alternative development with entire loss of *þ* and compensatory lengthening of the preceding vowel appears in *mǣl*, *mǣlan* (beside *mæþl*), and *stǣl* place, *stǣlan* impute. This development seems not to be peculiar to a dialect.

§ 422. In W-S the phonological development of *þl* after a long

[1] Here, whether the OE forms are from **rafisịan* or **ravisịan*, OE *f* arose from a voiced sound (§ 444) by assimilation to *s*. (Hence the distinction drawn by Sturtevant, *Language* vii. 190 ff., is unreal.)

[2] Possibly add *wætla* bandage, see *OED*, s.v. *wattle*, sb.¹

[3] Also *bytne* with the same change before *n*.

[4] In *-sedlum* Cp. 1667 *d* = *ð* Angl., however, has, beside *seþel* < **seþla-*, also *setel* < **setla-* (Li., Ru.¹, RG); hence Ru.¹ *settlas* (§ 408). In W-S the forms fall together. But Li. *seatul*, *seatlas*, Ru.² *seotlas*, *seatlas*, Ru.¹ *setulas*, VP *-seotle* to **setula-*. Prevailingly *setel*, *seatul*=*cathedra*, but *seþel*, *sedl*=*sedes*.

[5] OE *botl*, *boðl*, **bodl*, *bold* in place-names is discussed by Ekwall, *AB* xxviii. 82 ff. He would derive *Bootle*, *-bottle* in northern place-names (forms occur from the twelfth century) from OE **bōtl*, to explain the modern vowel. He assumes that in this form *ō* could be retained and normally developed, or shortened with consonant gemination (§ 285). This assumes two abnormalities: that *þl* > *tl* in Angl., for which there is no parallel; that *þl* > *tl* after a long vowel (the only parallel is W-S *spātl*). The normal Angl. development of a form with *ō* appears in *Bothel* (Cumberland, pron. *ū*), *Budle* (Northumberland).

vowel was *dl*: *nǣdl* needle, *ādl* disease (also *Bd. Gl.*), *mīdl* horse's bit, *wīdl* impurity, *wǣdla* poor man (and related words; also *KG*).[1] *þl* due to syncopation of *i* is not subject to this sound-change, e.g. *ēþles*, &c., from *ēþel* home. Similarly *þr* > *dr* in *ǣdr* vein (also KG *ēdr*). But eW-S always *māðm* treasure, *ǣðm* breath, for the same reason as *fæþm* (§ 419). After long vowels Angl. kept the spirant, which ultimately became voiced, the development thus being the same as after shorts: Ep. *nāēðlae*, *ēthm*, Cp. *nēthle*, *āēthm*, *wēðl*, *mīðlum*,[2] VP *wēðla*, *āðle*. So before *r*, Cp. *hēðir* (renes), VP *ēðre*. Later North. has *āðl*, *wīðlia* (Li. once each; Ri. once *uīdðil* n.s.), Ru.[1] *spāðl*.

§ 423. The extent to which these sound-changes operated in other languages is difficult to decide, as medial *ð* became *d* in the later Middle Ages in Low German and Frisian, and while there are no early Frisian texts, the spelling of OS is ambiguous on this point (see Holthausen, *Altsächs. Elementarbuch*, § 201). Yet in W-S *þl* must have become *tl* after short vowels before the voicing of medial spirants (§ 444). The change *þl* > *dl* after a long vowel presupposes a voiced spirant, and if it belongs to the same time as *þl* > *tl*, a special voicing of *þl* after long vowels must be assumed. Otherwise, the change *þl* > *dl* must lie between the voicing of spirants and the syncopation of *i*.

§ 424. In lOE the distribution of *tl*, *dl*, &c., against *þl* as outlined above is disturbed by a new change *ð* > *d* before liquids and nasals. To this are due lW-S forms like *fædm*, *mādm*. lNorth. has, beside the forms quoted above with preserved *ð*, more frequently *sedl*, *ādl*, *spādl*, *nēdl*, *wīdliġa*, also *bydla* cultivator.[3] Remarkable extensions of the tendency are *ōedle* (d.s. of *ēþel*, Ru.[2] 4 times), *hǣdna* (and many other forms from *hǣþen* heathen, *Li.*) where *ðl*, *ðn* due to syncopation of *i* are affected. So with *ðl* arising in composition, lW-S *þrȳdliċe* powerfully, *ēadmod*, lNorth. (in derivatives) *ēdmod* humble. *Ru.*[1] has similar forms: *sedle*, *-um*, *nēdle*, *ādle*, *ēadmod*, but some Merc. areas may have escaped the tendency, for *ðl* forms are often preserved in the OE Bede (see § 420, also *āðl*, *wēþelnysse*).

§ 425. An alternative development of *-þl* is metathesis to *-ld*. Its basis seems to have been *ðl* with a voiced spirant, not *dl*, for

[1] But *spātl*, saliva, developed as if the vowel were short.

[2] *Cp.* 66 *nētl* is an error; *Erf.* 796 *nēdlæ* has *d* = *ð*.

[3] Add **bodm*, ME (northern) *bodome*.

dl is late in developing in Angl., and already *Cp.* 2001 has *-āld*, *LG* 73 *āld*, VP *seld* (frequently), *LV* 18 *-maeld*. To these forms poetical texts add *bold* (rarely prose), *bylda* (builder), *spāld*, and lOE has *byldan* build. Note also *-bold* as a place-name element.

B. Fronting and Assibilation

§ 426. It was an outstanding feature of Prim. OE and Prim. OFris. that the velar consonants *ʒ* and *k* developed sensitivity to the nature of vowels preceding and following them. This sensitivity began in the continental period of OE, but continued well after the conquest of England.

§ 427. In Prim. OE a distinction arose between front or palatal and velar *k* and *ʒ*. Palatal *k* probably differed from velar *k* hardly more than do the initial consonants of NE *kit*, *cat*. Palatal *ʒ* was a spirant which coincided with the sound derived from Prim. Gmc. *i̯* (i.e. *y* as in NE *young*). At the beginnings of words, these palatal sounds were developed before the front vowels of OE (*ǣ̆*, *ē̆*, *ī̆*, alone and as the first elements of diphthongs) as they existed after the restoration of *ǎ* before back vowels (§ 157). Hence palatal sounds arose not only before the front vowels of West Gmc., and the diphthongs developed from them by breaking, but also before *ǣ* (*ē*) and *ēa*, which had developed from West Gmc. *ā* and *au*, and before *ēa* (*ēo*), the breakings of *ǣ* (*ē*). On the other hand, *a* from retraction before consonant groups instead of breaking (Angl. *cald*, *galla*), and from restoration before back vowels (*caru*, *galan*) had velar consonants before it. Velars also appeared before all consonants even if a front vowel followed, e.g. *climban*, *cnēo*, *cræft*, *cweþan*, *glæd*, *gnætt*, *grimm*. Examples of initial palatal sounds are:[1] *ċiriċe* church, *ċīdan* chide, *ċeorl* churl, *ċēace* cheek, *ċeald* cold,

[1] In the OE runic alphabet the front and velar sounds were sometimes distinguished as ᚳ (*ċēn*), ᚷ (*ġyfu*) against ᛣ (*calc*), ᚸ (*gār*). *RC* has a further symbol ᛤ used for velar *c* before a front vowel, as in *cyning*. But *ċēn* and *ġyfu* are sometimes used for both the front and velar sounds. In the Latin alphabet as developed to write OE they are not systematically distinguished except in *Ru.*[1], where an attempt, better sustained initially than in other positions, is made to use *k* for *c*, and *c* for *ċ*; see Bülbring, *AB* ix. 289 ff. Elsewhere there is only sporadic use of *k*, especially in *kyning*. Occasional use of *ch* seems to be without phonetic significance, as it is found for both *c* and *ċ*; it is fairly frequent in *Ru.*[2] (e.g. *folches*, *stenċhes*), and is found also in *Li.* and lW-S. On the use of vowel symbols as diacritics to distinguish palatals, see § 45. In quoting OE forms in the present work the palatal consonants and the affricates ultimately developed from palatal stops are marked with a dot (*ċ*, *ċċ*, *ġ*, *ċġ*).

ċeariġ sorrowful, *ċēas* chose, *ċēosan* choose, *ċīecen* chicken, *ġift* gift, *ġīfre* greedy, *ġinnan* begin, *ġefan* (W-S *ġiefan*) give, *ġeorn* eager, *ġeaf* gave, *ġeard* yard, *ġēat* poured, *ġēotan* pour; see also §§ 185–7 on the development of diphthongs from front vowels after these palatal consonants. Velar consonants, however, remained before back vowels and their umlauts, e.g. *cū* cow, *cōl* cool, *camb* comb, *cāf* (*ā* < *ai*) brave, *guma* man, *gold* gold, *gōs* goose, *gūþ* war, *cyning* king, *cemban* comb, *gylden* golden, *gēs* geese.[1]

§ 428. In final position, *k* and *ʒ* were palatalized after OE front vowels, including those due to *i*-umlaut, because this umlaut implies that *i* or *i̯* had originally followed *k* or *ʒ*. Examples are *bæċ* back, *freċ* bold (see § 435), *piċ* pitch, *dīċ* ditch, *ġelīċ* like (and so *hwelċ*, *swelċ* < *-līċ*, § 390), *dæġ* day, *mǣġ* relative, *bodiġ* body; and after umlauted vowels, *bēċ* books, *swēġ* sound, *-hyġd* thought. *ʒ* in final *gd* is similarly treated, e.g. *bræġd*. The development is the same at the end of a syllable, e.g. *wæċnan* wake, *līċhoma* body, *rīċne* a.s.m. powerful, *næġled* nailed, *mæġden* maiden, *stiġrap* stirrup. Palatalization takes place in the same circumstances of *k* in the group *nk*, of *ʒ* in the groups *lʒ*, *rʒ*, and of *g* in the group *ng*,[2] e.g. *finċ* finch, *drinċ* imper. drink, *þinġ* thing, *fēnġ* received, and after umlauted vowels, *benċ* bench, *fenġ* grasp, *strenġ* string, *bielġ* bag, *byrġ* cities. Similar palatalization took place of the geminates *kk* and *gg* (the instances are all after umlauted vowels), e.g. *cryċċ* crutch, *seċġ* man, *eċġ* edge, *bryċġ* bridge. Velar consonants remain after back vowels, including *ā* < *ai*, and the second elements of diphthongs in *-a* and *-o*, e.g. *bōc* book, *ēac* also, *sēoc* sick, *plōg* plough, and in groups, *long* long, *burg* city.[3]

§ 429. Medially, the same sounds and groups of sounds are affected as finally, i.e. *k*, *ʒ*, the geminates *kk*, *gg*, and the groups *nk*, *ng*, *lk*, *lʒ*, *rk*, *rʒ*. The circumstances of palatalization are between any two front vowels, between front vowel and syllabic consonant, and always after a vowel which has suffered *i*-umlaut.[4] Examples are *blæċes* g.s.m. black, *cwiċe* n.p.m. alive, *breċe* sg. pres. subj.

[1] A front vowel due to the second fronting of *a* (mainly peculiar to *VP*, § 164) also retained a velar consonant before it: **gætu* gates, later *geatu*, and so *ceafurtūn*, **-gedere*, ME *togederes* together (§ 203).

[2] Theoretically all groups of liquid or nasal + *c*, *g*, or *ʒ* would be affected, but they do not all occur finally: *nk*, *ng*, *lk*, *lʒ*, *rk*, *rʒ*.

[3] Velar consonants remained even when a diphthong became a front vowel owing to Angl. smoothing, e.g. *ēc* also, *bēg* ring.

[4] Including vowels which have suffered theoretical *i*-umlaut, by which they are not changed, e.g. *lǣċe* physician, *mēċe* sword, *rīċe* kingdom.

break, *dæġes* g.s. day, *siġe* victory; so before syllabic consonants irrespective of whether these developed a parasite vowel or not: *æċer* field, *næġl* nail, *fæġr* fair, *wæġn* wain, *reġn* rain, *seġl* sail; with groups: *finċes* g.s. finch, *þinġes* g.s. thing,[1] *finġer* finger. Examples after mutated (or theoretically mutated) vowels are: *lǣċe* physician, *mēċe* sword, *rīċe* kingdom, *sēċan* seek, *īeċan* increase, *bīeġan* bend, *fēġan* join, *drȳġe* dry; with groups: *drenċan* cause to drink, *þenċan* think, *þynċan* seem, *senġan* singe, *menġan* mix, *birċe* birch, *wyrċan* work, *byrġan* bury, *felġ* felly, *bielġas* bags; with geminates: *streċċan* stretch, *wæċċende* watching, *styċċe* piece, *ġyċċan* itch, *liċġan* lie, *leċġan* lay. Velar consonants, however, remained when there was a back vowel (or back element of a diphthong) either before or after them, e.g. *wicu* week, *brecan* break, *āces* g.s. oak, *sēoce* n.p.m. sick, *wegas* ways, *nigon* nine, *þinga* g.p. things. It is important to note that an umlauted vowel is followed by a palatal consonant, even if a back vowel followed, e.g. *fēġan*, *drenċan*, *streċċan*, *liċġan*. But velar consonants remained between a front vowel and the umlaut of a back vowel, as is seen in verbs of the type *syngian* sin, *myngian* remind, *sċyldgian* sin, *witgian* prophesy, *wērgian* grow weary (< *-æʒōi̯an* or *-īʒōi̯an*, cf. § 430, footnote).

§ 430. The subsequent history of *i̯* (*ġ*), whether produced by the processes just described or original (< Gmc. *i̯*), is as follows: initially it remained (hence NE *yard*, *yield*, &c.), while after vowels it combined with them into diphthongs or long vowels, in OE when it was in the same syllable, in ME when a syllable boundary preceded it (§§ 266–9). Velar *ʒ* became a stop initially by the end of the OE period. This change may explain why it no longer alliterates with *i̯* in lOE verse.[2] Internally and finally *ʒ* remained till the ME period (after 1200), when it became *i̯* or *u̯* (OE *lēogan*, *dragan* > ME *leien*, *drawen*).[3]

§ 431. Palatal stops (*ċ*, *ċċ*, *nċ*, *ċġ*, *nġ*) could have one of two subsequent histories. They were either assibilated, so that *ċ* and *ċċ* > [tʃ], *ġ* and *ċġ* > [dʒ], or were retracted to be velar stops again.

[1] Note *Ep.* 410 *hringiae* d.s. ring, where *gi* = *ġ*.

[2] See Campbell, *Battle of Brunanburh*, p. 33.

[3] Development to a stop was rare internally, except in verbs of the type *syngian*; see Flasdieck, *A* lxx. 225 ff. Some lW-S manuscripts have occasional *w* as a spelling for the medial velar spirant, especially in forms of *swugian*, *adrūgian* (references in B–T; cf. S–B, § 214.8).

§ 432. Initially, palatal *ċ* was always assibilated: examples are all words with initial *ċ* given above to illustrate fronting (§ 427).[1]

§ 433. Finally and medially before vowels, palatal stops were assibilated after *ī̆*, and when umlaut had affected the preceding vowel. Examples, in most of which the assibilation is shown by the NE form, are finally *dīċ*, *piċ*, *hwelċ*, *swelċ*, *finċ*, and after umlauted vowels *benċ*, *cryċċ*, *eċġ*, *seċġ*, *bryċġ*; medially *miċel*, *ċiriċe*, inflected forms of words just quoted, as *dīċes*, *finċes*, and after mutated vowels *lǣċe*, *sēċan*, *streċċan*, *ġyċċan*, *cyċġel*, *wyrċan*, *birċe*.

§ 434. The development of the palatal stops to assibilated consonants was through the stage *ti̯*, *di̯*, and hence *ti̯* and *di̯* of other origin were caught up in the development, so that *ċ*, *ċċ*, *ċġ* are found written in such words: eW-S *ġefeċċan* fetch (< **feti̯an*, § 764), lW-S *orċeard* orchard (beside *ordċeard* for *ort-ġeard*), *miċġern* fat (for **mid-ġern*, OHG *mittigarni*).[2] So *cræftġa* (for **cræfti̯a* workman, § 267) > *cræfċa*,[3] for which *cræfta* of manuscripts is probably a scribal error.[4]

§ 435. In other positions *ċ* was not assibilated, and soon reverted to *k*, e.g. *bæc*, *bæces*, *frec*, *freces*, and all occurrences before consonants, whether the group was old or caused by OE syncopation, *exen* oxen, *fyxe* vixen, *bīcnan* signify, *ēcness* eternity, *rixian* rule. The assumption of a palatal in such forms, where assibilation did not arise, is due to the parallel with *ʒ*: since *dæġ* and *weġ* clearly developed *i̯*, *bæċ*, *freċ* must have had *ċ*. This view seems supported by some peculiar spellings in *Li*., e.g. *bæcg*, *ġebræcg*, for *bæċ*, *-bræċ*.

§ 436. The assibilation of stop *ġ* (in the groups *ġġ*, *nġ*) was limited like that of *ċ*, and hence did not occur in forms like *fingras* (and hence *finger*), *hyngran* hunger.[5]

§ 437. The distribution of velar and palatal or assibilated consonants outlined above is very prone to analogical disturbance, and

[1] It is doubtful if there are any exceptions, except those caused by sound substitution by Scandinavian settlers, as ME *kaf* (northern) for OE *ċeaf* chaff, and the northern type *-caster* in place-names (but see Ekwall, *AB* xxx. 224–5).

[2] But *CP* (Hatton) *orcġeard*, Napier's Wulfstan, p. 152, 9 *Muncġiu* (v.l. for *Muntġiu*) are copyist's errors of a common type (*c* for *t*).

[3] Ælfric, *Gramm.*, ed. Zupitza, p. 215, l. 9 (v.l.).

[4] So Sievers, *A* xiii. 328; other views, Borowski, *Lautdubletten*, pp. 17–18. On the other hand, *cræftica* is for **cræftċa*, with partial assimilation of *ġ* to *t* (*tġ* > *tċ*), and then restoration of the unaccented vowel from *cræftiġ*.

[5] It is doubtful if assibilation ever passed the limits above defined: some doubtful cases are discussed by Luick, *Hist. Gramm.*, § 685.*a*.1; of these the best known, ME *thatch* for OE *þæċ*, is clearly influenced by *þeċċan*.

ME and NE forms show that there was much variation in OE, e.g. ME *kerven*, *beginnen*, show the initial sound levelled out from *curfon*, *gunnon*; and many forms like NE *like*, *dike*, Scots *breeks*, beside *such*, *ditch*, *breeches* are explained from OE doublets like *ġelīċ-ġelīcum*, *dīċ-dicas*, *brōc-brēċ*.

§ 438. The assumption that assibilation did not follow palatalization before consonants (§§ 435–6) explains many verbal forms, e.g. beside *þenċan*, *þynċan*, *sēċan*, *senġan* with assibilation, 3rd sg. pres. indic. would be *þencþ*, *þyncþ*, *sēcþ*, *sengþ*, in which the palatal stops reverted to velars; from these velars could be transferred to the inf., hence NE *think*, *seek* (beside *beseech*), dial. *sing* (for *singe*), and so *reck*, *work* (OE *reċċan*, *wyrċan*), and various dialectal forms. It is more difficult to explain similar alternative forms in nouns, e.g. dial. *brig*, *rig*, *steek*, *eg*, *seg*, *weg*, *birk*, ME *benk*, for *bridge*, *ridge*, *stitch*, *edge*, *sedge*, *wedge*, *birch*, *bench*. Luick (*Hist. Gramm.*, § 690) would explain such forms by assuming that assibilation did not take place before a back vowel, and hence would derive them from inflected *brycgum*, *ecgas*, *sticas*, *bircan*, &c. Similarly he explains dial. *lig*, *leg* from OE *licgan*, *lecgan*. It is, however, more likely that the explanation lies in complete failure to assibilate by Scandinavian settlers.[1]

§ 439. On the other hand, *i̯* due to the palatalization of *ʒ* after an umlauted vowel (§ 429) reverted to *ʒ* before back vowels. Examples are *wrēgan* accuse, nW-S *tēgan* tie, *flēgan* put to flight, and inflected forms like *brēgas* brows, *cǣga* keys, *belgas* bags, *felga* fellies. So with Gmc. *i̯*, 3rd sg. pres. indic. *hergaþ*, and so inf. *hergian* ravage (< **χari̯ōi̯an*). The reasons for assuming this reversion of *i̯* to *ʒ* before back vowels belong to the field of ME philology.[2]

§ 440. [sk] is more prone to palatalization and assibilation than [k]. Initially it was probably originally palatalized before front vowels only, but at least before 900 it was palatalized before back vowels and their umlauts also. On the phonological consequences of this, see §§ 179–84, where many examples are given. The subsequent history of English suggests assibilation of initial *sc*, not only

[1] OE *ċiecen* chicken seems already to have had medial [k] in OE (*Ru.*[1] a.p. *ċiken*). Since the suffix contained an originally long vowel there would not normally be syncopation, and no forms actually occur in which *-c-* is before *n*, and hence would not be assibilated. Dissimilation of the initial sounds of two successive syllables may be the explanation (Ritter, *AB* xxi, 152).

[2] See Luick, *Hist. Gramm.*, § 373.*a*.5.

before vowels, but before *r*, e.g. *sċrēad* shred, *sċrēawa* shrew-mouse, *sċrīċ* shrike, *sċrīfan* decree, *sċrīn* coffer, *sċrincan* shrink, *sċrūd* dress, 'shroud'. Internally, also, *sc* was palatalized and assibilated before all front vowels, even if a back vowel preceded, e.g. *wasċe* I wash, *þersċe* I thresh, *asċe* ashes, *risċe* rush, and inflected forms like *æsċes*, *disċes*, *fisċes*, *frosċes*, &c. The assibilated consonant also followed a mutated vowel, even if a back vowel followed, e.g. *blysċan* blush, *wȳsċan* wish. Finally *sc* was palatalized and assibilated after any front vowel, original or due to umlaut, e.g. *æsċ* ash, *disċ* dish, *fisċ* fish, *risċ* rush, the suffix *-isċ*, and after an umlauted vowel *flǣsċ* flesh. But internally before back vowels (if the preceding vowel had not undergone umlaut) and finally after back vowels [sk] remained, and frequently underwent metathesis to [ks] in lW-S, e.g. *frosc* frog, *husc* insult, *tusc* tooth, *fiscas* fishes (and forms with a back vowel after *sc* from *disċ* dish, *risċ*, *risċe* rush, *æsċ* ash, *flasċe* flask, *asċe* ashes), **wascan* wash, *þerscan* thresh, *þerscold* threshold, *āscaþ* asks (and hence *āscian*), *hnescian* soften,[1] *tosca* frog. Hence lW-S *āxian*, *dixas*, *dox* dusk, *fixas*, *frox*, *flaxe*, *ġeoxa*, *-ung* sobbing, *hnexian*, *hux*, *max* neut. pl. meshes, *rixe*, *toxa*, *tux*, *þerxan*, *þerxold*, *waxan* wash (past pl. *wōxon*).[2]

§ 441. The system outlined in § 440 would be ready prey to analogy, and OE doublets like *æsċ æscas*, *frosc frosċes*, *-isċ -iscan* are much reflected in ME and NE, e.g. ME *ash*, Orrm pl. *asskess*, Orrm *-ish* beside *-issk*, NE dial. *frosh* beside *frosk*, and so ME *busk*, *bush*.[3]

§ 442. Palatalization of χ parallel to that of ȝ is to be assumed for forms with *i*-umlaut like *hlihhan* laugh; North. *tehher* tear, *eher* ear of corn; W-S *siehþ* sees.[4]

[1] The vowel of *hnesċe*, soft, is not due to umlaut (see S–B, § 303.*a*.2).

[2] Here belong the river-names *Axe* (OE *Axe*, beside once *Æsċe*) and *Exe* (OE *Exe*, beside **Esċe*, ME *Esshe*), where [sk] > [ks] in the frequent g.s. *Axan*, *Exan*. *muxle* beside *muscle*, *muscelle* mussel, has metathesis of [sk] of Lat. *musculus*. Although metathesized forms are rare outside W-S in OE, ME evidence shows them to have been more widely spread. Even in OE, *Ru.*[1] has *āxast*, *āxsade*, and many texts, eW-S, eKt. (Ct. 44), *Ru.*[1], have *betwix* between, eW-S also *betwēox(n)*, *betwuxn*, with vowel of *betwēoh*, *betwuh* (§ 338, footnote). *Betwix* has *x* (< *sk*) from forms with a following back vowel, **betwiscum*, but cf. Scots *bitwish*.

[3] Luick, *Hist. Gramm.*, § 691, notes, discusses various irregularities of development. NE *bishop*, *cushat* (OE *biscop*, *cuscute*) may owe their medial [ʃ] to a strong medium stress, so that the initial of the second syllable developed as if before a stressed syllable.

[4] Only such forms are here relevant, for a front vowel before χ was broken

§ 443. On palatalization of the groups *χt*, *χs*, *χþ*, and its consequences, see §§ 304–11.

C. Voicing and Unvoicing of Consonants (mainly Spirants)

§ 444. Of the Prim. Gmc. spirantal pairs *f–v*, *s–z*, *þ–ð*, *χ–ʒ*, the second and third had been disturbed by the changes *z* > *r*, *ð* > *d* (§§ 404, 409). By a prehistoric OE change, spirants were voiced between voiced sounds. *χ* no longer existed in such positions (§ 461), but *f*, *s*, *þ* did so extensively, so the pairs *s–z*, *þ–ð* reappeared, though OE spelling does not show the distinction, e.g. *hrēas* fell, *snāþ* cut, had voiceless spirants, but infs. *hrēosan*, *snīþan* voiced ones. In the case of *f–v* OE spelling at first distinguished old *v* (written *b*), and new *v* (written *f*). Examples from *Ep.* are, finally, *halb-* half, *hualb* convex, *salb* ointment, *-rēab* spoil, *sċāb-* splay, *staeb-* staff, *thēb-* thief, and medially *aelbitu* swan, *ċebisae* concubines, *earbet-* trouble, *gaebuli* i.s. tribute, *ġibaen* given, *anhaebd* suspensus (pass. part. of *-habban*), *hebild* thread, *-hebuc* hawk, *hraebnæs* g.s. raven, *libr* liver, *ġilēbdae* allowed, *sċeaba* plane, *sċēabas* sheaves, *sibaed* siftings (error, but cf. Cp. *sibi* sieve), *faersċribaen* decreed, *sċribun* they decreed. So *BH* has *Aelbfled*, *Ġebmund*, *Suǣbheard*, *Cnōbheri*; other early examples are CH *heben*, Erf., LR *ob.*[1] *Ep.*, however, has already *f* for old *v* in *sifun-* seven, *ofaer-* over- (beside *obaer-*), *clofae* buckle, *staefnændra* g.p. alternating (beside d.s.f. *ġistaebnændrae*); also compromise *nabfogār* auger, *efbor-* boar (beside *nabae* naves, *ebor-*). Otherwise *Ep.* uses *f* for the new voiced sound regularly, e.g. *hofr* hump, *ġirōefa* reeve, *sċofl* shovel, *uulfes* g.s. wolf. On the disappearance of *b* as a symbol for a spirant see § 57.1. The spelling distinction *f–b* of early texts can reflect only a fine phonetic distinction[2] between the old and the new voiced spirants, not the distinction of voiced and voiceless, for this had ceased to exist between vowels by the time of the loss of unaccented medial *i*

before palatalization took place, and then the *χ* remained velar because in contact with a back vowel, e.g. *ġeneahhe*, *ġetiohhian*, *feoh*, *nēah*. (For the laws of palatalization, a smoothed diphthong is equal to a back vowel, e.g. *feh*; see § 428, footnote.)

[1] Note the curious inverted spelling, FC *afitatores* for Lat. *habitatores*.

[2] It has been suggested that this may have been bi-labial against labio-dental. No doubt the distinction was short-lived.

(§ 351), as may be seen from weak past tenses of Class I such as *rǣsde* rushed, *cȳþde* made known: if the spirants had been voiced in West Gmc. they would have become *r*, *d*, yet they must have been voiced before loss of *i*, or the forms would have been **rǣste*, **cȳþte* (see § 480.1). Normal OE words, where *f*, *s*, *þ* represent sounds voiced between voiced sounds, are *fīfe* pl. five, *hrōfe* d.s. roof, *wulfas* wolves, *ċēosan* choose, *bōsm* bosom, *ēþel* home, *brōþor* brother, *fæþm* embrace.

§ 445. A number of formative elements seem to have escaped the voicing, especially the abstract suffix *-iþō*, e.g. *trēowþ* truth, *strenġþ* strength, *cȳþþ* home-land, *ofermētto* (< **-mōdiþō*) pride. So the ordinal suffix *-oþa* had a voiceless consonant, e.g. *seofoþa* seventh. The evidence for voiceless spirants in these words is partly OE sound-change (e.g. *-mētto*) partly the subsequent history of the words.[1] The suffix seen in *blīþs* bliss, *līþs* mercy (> *bliss*, *liss*, §§ 286, 481.2), *milts* mercy, clearly had voiceless *s*, but its origin is obscure.

§ 446. The voicing of medial spirants was followed by the unvoicing of final spirants. West Gmc. *v* and *ʒ* were the only sounds involved, for *ð* and *z* had become *d* and *r*, and *i̯* was not affected. The change receives no expression in spelling in the case of *v*, which is written at first *b* and then *f* both medially and finally (§§ 57.1, 444), but for final *ʒ* there is an increasing use of the symbol *h* after Ælfred's time. In the earlier period, *Ep.*, *Erf.*, *Cp.* already have *mærh* marrow,[2] but *VP* has no *h* spellings. eW-S has a few examples: *wāh* wall, *ġenōh* enough, *burh* city, *-slōh* struck, *lōh* blamed, and also in composition, *ġefōhstān* fitted stone, *burhware* citizens. In lW-S the use of *h* for West Gmc. final *ʒ* is frequent, e.g. *bēah* ring, *plōh* plough, *stāh* ascended, *sorh* sorrow, *bealh* was angry; less frequently in composition, e.g. *lahbryċe* breach of law, *bēahġifa* ring-giver, *ēahþyrl* eye-hole; and at the syllable-end, *fuhlas* birds, *āhnian* possess. *KG* have *h* often, e.g. *burh*, *ġenōh*, *orsorh*, *borhhond*. In Li. and Ru.[1] *ġenōh* is frequent, otherwise final *h* for *ʒ* is very rare in lNorth. and *Ru.*[1]

[1] Luick, *Hist. Gramm.*, § 639, attributes the voiceless spirants of these suffixes to their position between two unaccented vowels. But this leaves isolated exceptions, each of which has to be separately explained away, e.g. *clǣnsian* cleanse (contrasted with *bletsian* bless, § 480.3), *sīþe* scythe (Ep. *siġdi* < **siʒiþi*), *adesa* adze (but 'addice' supports Luick), infl. *Temese* Thames.

[2] *Ep.* has also a few cases of *c* for *ch* (as in *ct* = *cht*, § 57.3) from *ʒ* at the ends of words and syllables: *tēac* 964, *brocdaettendi* 735. So analogically *c* is written for *ġ* in *hraecli* 84.

§ 447. The interchange of *h* and *g* in forms like *burh–burge* leads in lW-S to forms like *hēage*, *blēoge*, from *hēah*, *blēoh* (where *h* is from West Gmc. *χ*, or due to analogical addition, § 466). There are also inverted spellings like *mearg*, *þurg*, Ru.¹ *betwīg*, for *mearh* horse, *þurh* through, *betwīh* between.[1] The consequent confusion of the symbols *h* and *g* enables *h* to be used for *ʒ* medially, especially in the OE Boethius, e.g. *dahum*. *h* is also extended as a symbol for *i̯* from *ʒ* (§ 428), although this was not unvoiced, e.g. *stīh* imper. ascend, 2nd and 3rd sg. pres. indic. of weak verbs, W-S *bȳhð* bends, K.G. *felhð* follows, *tirhð* mocks,[2] *byrh* d.s. city (already *CP* 164, 10).

§ 448. There was also unvoicing of final West Gmc. *v*: examples are provided by the normal forms of the words quoted from early texts with the symbol *b* in § 444.

§ 449. The result of the changes described in §§ 444–8 was an alternation of voiced medial spirants with final voiceless ones both in nominal and verbal forms, e.g. *stæf–stafas*, *fīf–fīfe*, *ċēas–ċēosan*, *smiþ–smiþas*, *snāþ–snīþan*. The basis of these alternations is always an old voiceless spirant except in the case of *f–v*, which can be based on West Gmc. *f* or *v*. These alternations, with their rich opportunities for the play of analogy, have been of profound importance in the later history of English.[3]

§ 450. Unlike the continental West Gmc. languages, English has never been prone to unvoice final stops. OE instances in accented syllables, both finally and at the end of accented elements in composition, are sporadic, e.g. LR *ðrēt* thread, Ep. *dēatlicostan* most deadly, Cp. *sċulthēta* bailiff (for *sċyld-*), Li. *heartliċe* hardly, *lāt* guidance, KG *lamp* lamb, *ðinċ*[4] thing, *Beow.* 1121 *-spranc* sprang, and many texts *sint* they are (§ 768.d). There are rather more in unstressed position: Cp. *hǣlsent* augur, *uulātunc* disgust,[5] RC *cyninc* king, BH *Lyċċitfeldensis* (beside *Lyċċid-*), Ct. Cott. Aug. ii. 82[6] *-hāt* (in names, for *-hād*), Ct. 1 (copy before 800) *-felt* (for *-feld*), W-S *elpent* elephant, *færelt* way, *weorþmynt*

[1] *CP* already *sylġ* d.s. from *sulh* plough, 403, 2.

[2] Similar forms from strong verbs are frequent, but are due to extension of *ʒ* from other forms to the 2nd and 3rd sg. pres. indic., followed by assimilation *ʒs*, *ʒþ* > *hs*, *hþ*, e.g. *abelhð*, see § 732.

[3] On the voicing of initial spirants in southern OE, which is to be traced only by ME evidence, see especially Luick, *Hist. Gramm.*, §§ 703 ff.

[4] Extended to an inflected form in *ðinċe* 446.

[5] But *wīċincsċeaðan* may have assimilation (§ 480.3).

[6] Anno 704, copy very late (? *c.* 800).

honour, Li. *hēafut* head, and so at the syllable end, North. coins *Ēotberehtus* (737–58), Li. *hēhstaltnisse* virginity, *wutotliċe* certainly.[1] *Li.* has also often weak past part. in *-et*, *-at* after dentals, e.g. *ġesetet*, *ġemōetet*, *ġeendat*, and already *Cp.* has *ġerǣedit*, and twice *raefsit*.[2] *KG* and lNorth. have many nouns in *-inc*, *-unc* for *-ing*, *-ung*,[3] and this spelling may be extended to medial position, e.g. KG *otspernince*. An equation of the graphs *ng*, *nc* due to such spellings accounts for Li. *wlonga*, *ðongung* for *wlonca*, *ðonc-*.

§ 451. The unvoicing in finality dealt with in §§ 446–50 evidently began prehistorically, for the early glossaries already have some spellings indicating the change. The changes are very open to analogical removal, and there may be purely orthographical as well as phonological removal. It is hence difficult to determine the precise phonological history of these changes.

D. Change of Final *k* to χ

§ 452. A change of final *k* to χ is expressed in spelling in most areas in *ah* but (*VP*, *Ru.*¹, W-S, North.). The change seems limited to low stress, for North. has also the pronominal forms *ih*, *meh*, *ðeh*, *ūsih*, *īowih*, and occasionally final *-lih* for *-liċ*. Final χ from *ċ* can also be spelled *g*, e.g. Li. *sæġdiġ* said I, *ūsiġ*, *hūliġ* for *hūliċ*, and hence final *-iġ* can be written *-ih*: Li. *ðrittih*, *sextih*. It seems evident that both the palatal and velar stops were affected. The forms *ih*, *-lih* are of great importance for the history of the language, NE *I*, *-ly*. In the case of the palatal stop, the change to *h* was no doubt older than the development to an affricate (§ 433).

E. Doubling of Consonants in Old English

§ 453. Consonants appear to have been doubled in OE after a short syllable when the syncopation of vowels brought them before *r* and *l*, thus re-creating conditions which caused doubling in West Gmc. (§ 408). Hence spellings like *VP*, *Ru.*¹, eW-S *bettra*, eW-S *ætgæddre*, lW-S *miccle*, *buttor-* (< **buttre*).[4] There are also frequent instances of consonant doubling before *r* after a long vowel, which was probably shortened (§ 285), e.g. eW-S

[1] Cf. the frequent inverted spelling Li. *æd-* for the prefix *æt-*.

[2] 1084, 1087; *Erf.* confirms the *-t* in both glosses, *Ep.* has *-d*; 669 *ġerǣedit* is only *Cp.*

[3] Cf. lW-S *Lyfinc* beside *Lyfing*.

[4] VP *feddras*, *feddra*, once each beside frequent forms with *-dr-*, presumably belong here, for though some cases had *-dr-* from I-E *-tr-*, there was no West Gmc. doubling of *d* before liquids (§ 408).

nǣddre adder, ***āttres*** g.s. and hence ***āttor*** poison, and so lW-S ***hlǣdder*** ladder, ***fōddor*** fodder, ***mōddor*** mother, ***tūddor*** progeny, (all after infl. forms), ***ǣddran*** veins, ***blǣddre*** bladder, ***tȳddre*** weak. Consonant doubling after an originally long vowel is practically only found before *r*: lW-S has, however, ***māþþum*** treasure, ***lȳttle*** infl. little, and lNorth. ***lȳttel***.

§ 454. Although *CP* has ***ġelīċċran*** (227, 24), doubling before ***-ra*** of the comparative, and ***-re***, ***-ra*** of the strong adjectival inflexion becomes common first in lW-S, e.g. ***wīddra***, ***swēttra***, ***dēoppre***, and hence by transference ***hāttost***, El. 579. Li. ***sellra*** probably has shortening (*oe* is more prone to unrounding in North. than *ōe*, §§ 196, 198), while lW-S ***sylra*** has a sound-change only affecting short vowels (§ 325).

§ 455. Conditions for the West Gmc. doubling before *i̯* were re-created by shortening in an unaccented syllable in ****anhaitian*** > ****anhǣtian*** (§ 336) > ****anhetian*** (§ 372) > OE ***ōnettan*** hasten, and so ***ōrettan*** fight, ***andettan*** confess.

§ 456. On North. apparent doubling see § 65.

F. Simplification of Consonants

§ 457. Double consonants generally remained in OE, though the graph is often simplified (§ 66). In the metre of late OE poems *eall*, for example, is still a long syllable, *ll* making quantity both finally and medially.[1] But already before 900 heavy medial syllables resulting from adding ***-ne***, ***-re***, ***-ra***, ***-līċ***, ***-nes***, ***-dōm*** lost stress,[2] and this led to the simplification of double consonants, e.g. ***gyldene***, ***ōþera***, ***æftera***, ***dīġeliċ***, ***reċċendom***, for ***gyldenne***, ***ōþerra***, ***æfterra***, ***dīġelliċ***, ***reċċenddom***.[3] Similarly, in formative elements with geminates, e.g. ***ǣmetiġ***, ***bliċċetung***, infl. ***hæġtese***, ***bærnetes***, ***byrþene***, ***gydene***. Here belongs also ***þises***, ***þisum***, which developed a single consonant as low-stressed demonstratives.[4]

[1] e.g. *Mal.* 304b, *ealle hwīle*. Early in ME (or in lOE, cf. § 329.1, footnote) double consonants were simplified at the ends of syllables, and hence Orrm's use of the doubled consonant symbol as a diacritic to show the preceding vowel to be short became possible.

[2] Such syllables bear a half-stress after a long syllable in early verse, e.g. *ōþerne*, but in the Ælfredian *Metres* this can be neglected.

[3] The process is the same in *Eðeriċ*, *Æðered*, for *Eðerriċ*, *-red* (§ 484). But pairs in *-n(nes)* like *drunce(n)nes* represent different formations.

[4] The interchange of double and single consonants in identical forms leads to some false use of double consonants. They are all sporadic (examples S–B, § 231.*a*.3, add *tȳdde* instructed, OE Bede), except a.s.m. *cuconne* alive (also *cwicenne*).

§ 458. After fully accented syllables such simplification is much rarer: examples are *rūmedlič*, *ġelēaful*, *lateow* for *rūmmōdlič*, *ġelēafful*, *latteow*. After another consonant, however, simplification is the phonological norm and is often expressed in writing, e.g. *ġeornes*, *eorlič* for *ġeornnes*, *eorllič*, and even in full compounds, e.g. *wildēor*, *wyrtūn*, *emniht* for *wilddēor*, &c. So with assimilation of *dt* to *tt* and subsequent simplification, *čiltrog*, *sčeltruma*, *teltrēo* for *čildtrog*, *sčyldtruma*, *teldtrēo*.

G. Metathesis of Consonants

§ 459. By full metathesis a consonant moves from immediately before a vowel to immediately after it, or the reverse.

(1) The most frequent metathesis in OE is that of *r* from before to behind a short vowel followed by *s* or *n*. In § 155 and notes, forms are quoted which show that this change was sometimes earlier, sometimes later, than breaking; see also § 193.d with footnotes on *hærn*, *ærn*, *wærna*, *ærnan*, *bærnan*. Further examples are *bærstlian* crackle, *burna* stream, *cerse* cress, *cyrps* curly,[1] *first* period, *dærstan* dregs, *forsc* frog, *forst* frost, *hors* horse. Many of these words and of those quoted in §§ 155, 193 occur without metathesis: *brastlian*, *cresse*, *crisp*, *frist-*, *dræstan*, *frosc*, *frost*, *græs*, *hraen* (Ep. 400), *ren-* (Erf. 1137, Beow. 770), *wrenna*. Beside *eornan* occurs *rinnan*, and there are scattered forms of *beornan*, *berstan*, *þerscan* without metathesis (§ 741); beside *burna*, *brunna* occurs in place-names (e.g. *Denisaesbrunna* BH, Namur and Leningrad MSS.).

(2) Metathesis is much less frequent when *d* followed the vowel: lNorth. *birdas* young birds, *ðirda* (beside rare *ðridda* Li. only). After a long vowel, *And.* 1313 *ġesčȳrded*, Psalter Gloss 92, 1 (several late manuscripts) *ġesčȳrd* for *ġesčrȳd*(*ed*) clothed.

(3) Metathesis by which *r* is moved from behind to before a vowel is much rarer, and is practically limited to before *ht*: lNorth., lW-S *wrohte* worked (beside usual *worhte*); lNorth. *breht* bright, *froht* afraid, *frohtiġa* fear, *fryhto* fright, *wrihta* maker[2] (all beside forms without metathesis); Ru.[1] *frohtiġa* (beside

[1] ME *kers* shows OE *cerse* to have had velar *c*: hence metathesis was later than assibilation; the same no doubt applies to *cyrps* (Lat. *crispus*).

[2] It is unnecessary to assume with S–B, § 166, that forms with parasiting (*worohte*), followed by transference of stress to the new vowel, were the origin of these North. forms.

forhtiġa); poet. *frið* soul (for *fyrhþ*). Examples before consonants other than *h* are *þrop* farm (beside *þorp*), lW-S *sċruf*, *wrusm* (rare beside *sċurf* scurf, *wursm* pus).

(4) Low stress promotes metathesis of *r*, e.g. *eodorcian* ruminate (cf. *edroc*), adjs. in *-erne* (see § 339), the name-elements W-S, Kt. *-ferþ* for Angl. *-friþ*,[1] lW-S *-erd* (e.g. *Ælferd*, *Ðēoderd*, Ct. of 931, original copy), *handwyrst* wrist, *cnēowwyrst* knee (beside *wrist*), *ondyrstlić* terrible (§§ 477.5, 478), *Ru.*[1], North. *tinterġ* torment; and with regressive metathesis, the name-element W-S *-bryht*, Angl. *-berht* (rarely *-breht*), Kt. *-bearht*,[2] *stīðfrihþ* stern of mind (*Gen.* 107, for *-firhþ*).[3]

(5) A curious reciprocal metathesis occurs in *welor* lip (Goth. d.p. *wairilōm*).

§ 460. More usual than full metathesis is reversal of order in consonant groups, so that e.g. *sk* > *ks*, *sp* > *ps*.

(1) The mainly lW-S metathesis *sk* > *ks* is dealt with in § 440.[4]

(2) The metathesis *ðl* > *ld* is dealt with § 425.

(3) *ps* > *sp* in *wæsp* beside *wæps* (§ 418).

(4) *sp* > *ps* in *æpse* aspen, *cops* fetter, *hæpse* hasp, *wlips* lisping, for all of which except *hæpse* forms with *sp* occur; also in *cyrps*, combined with metathesis of *r* (§ 459.1).

(5) *ts* > *st* in *þrūstfell* leprosy (Goth. *þrūtsfill*); Li. *bæstere* baptist < *bæzere* (§ 53).

(6) Miscellaneous reversals of order in consonant groups are *clǣsnian* cleanse, *worms* pus, *ġyrstandæġ* yesterday, beside *clǣnsian*, *worsm*, *ġystran-*, and rare cases mentioned S–B, § 183.a.

(7) Reversals of order in consonant groups in unaccented syllables are: the formative elements *-els* (e.g. *gyrdels*) < *-isl-*

[1] On the vowel see § 372; *-firþ* is rare (e.g. *Tīdfirþ*, Monk Wearmouth runes). Attributions of areas to name-elements are only generally true: e.g. Ct. 11 (Merc.) has *Cuutfert* (i.e. *Cūþferþ*, § 57.7) of a bishop of Lichfield, and Cynefriþ of Lichfield (*c.* 840) is *Cyneferð* in Mercian charters (Cts. 47, 48). *LV* has *-ferð* 27 times beside usual *-frið*.

[2] Cf. lW-S *frēabriht* gloriously bright; on the vowel, see § 305.

[3] The forms *mōderġe* aunt, *suhterġa* nephew, beside *mōdriġe*, *suhtriġa*, may be due to metathesis, but the Prim. Gmc. form of the suffix is uncertain.

In *īrenn* iron, beside *īsern*, metathesis of *r* was followed by assimilation and simplification of the double consonant so produced: **īsarn-* > **īsrannį-* (§ 647, footnote) > **īrrannį* > *īrenn*. On this development see Kluge and Braune, *PBB* xliii. 516–17; Hirt, *Urgermanisch* i. 122, footnote; on *-sr-* of later origin see below, § 484.

[4] The reverse, *ks* > *sk*, does not occur: once *æsc* for *æx*, axe, is an error.

(cf. OS *dōpisli* baptism); name-element *-ġīls* < *-ġīsl*;[1] *innelfe* intestine (Ep. *innifli*); *færeld* journey (if suffix is *-iþl-*, but cf. ON *farald*).

H. Loss of Consonants

§ 461. Loss of χ. In all Gmc. languages, initial χ became a breathing or glottal spirant. Before *l, n, r, u̯*, it disappeared, leaving the consonant voiceless, and *h* is written in OE as a diacritic to indicate this: OE *hlāf* loaf, *hnutu* nut, *hrēosan* fall, *hwā* who. In all West Gmc. languages, medial χ became a breathing between vowels, and between vowel and *l, m, n, r*. A few forms occur in the early glossaries in which this breathing is still written as *h*, e.g. Cp. *bituīhn, rāha, tāhae*, Ep. *furhum, rȳhae, thōhae, uulōhum*, for W-S *betwēonan* between, *rā* roe, *tā* toe, *fūrum*, d.p. furrows, *rēo* blanket, *þō* clay, **wlōm* d.p. fringes;[2] so Ct. 4 *Uelhisċi*. The medial breathing was, however, lost early in OE: examples will be found of loss between vowels §§ 234; 235.2, 3; 236.3; 237.1.d, 2, 3; 238.2, 3; between vowel and voiced consonant §§ 230, 241.1; between voiced consonant and vowel §§ 231, 241.2. On analogical restoration of χ see §§ 230 footnote, 463. Further examples of loss of χ are *flēam* flight, *hēla* heel, *lēoma* light, *lǣne* temporary, connected with **flēoχan, hōh, lēoht, *līχan*; inflexions in *-ne, -re, -ra* of adjs. in *-h*, e.g. *hēane, wōra*; so before *-nes, -liċ, hēanes, wōliċ*, &c.; owing to the phonological structure of I-E, no inherited Gmc. word had χ before voiced consonants other than those above exemplified, but this could arise in new compounds, and in these χ can disappear in OE, e.g. *Plēowald, Hēaberht, furlang, sūlong* (< *furh*+*lang, sulh*+ ?), *hēadēor* stag.[3] But not before voiceless sounds, e.g. *hēahcræft*; and usually not even before voiced ones when the compound has full meaning, e.g. *hēahburh*.

§ 462. In W-S and to some extent in Kt. (see §§ 306, 310, 733) there was very early syncopation of *i* in the 2nd and 3rd sg. pres. indic. of strong verbs, so that, if χ preceded, it was brought into contact with *s* or *þ* before it became *h*. Hence eW-S had from

[1] This can be transferred to the first element: *Ġīlsuīþ*, Thornhill Cross II, *Ġīlsheard*, Ct. 32; unmetathesized *-ġīsl* is frequent in *BH* in Leningrad and other early manuscripts, though not in Moore.

[2] But on Erf. *thuachl* and similar later forms see § 242.

[3] But not *rādēor* (as S–B, § 218.2) where the simplex is *rā*, § 236.3. In *wēofod* < **wīoχbed* or *-bēod* loss of χ was followed in W-S by substitution of *v* for *b*, owing to the lack of *b* between vowels in normal words; cf. Angl. *wībed*.

sēon see (<* *seχan*), 2nd and 3rd sg. pres. indic. *siehst*, *siehþ*,[1] and similarly 3rd sg. *þīhþ*, *flīehþ*, *sliehþ*, *fēhþ* from *þēon* thrive, *flēon* flee, *slēan* strike, *fōn* receive, from Prim. OE **þīχan*, **fleuχan*, **slaχan*, **fōχan*. But *KG* has partly similar forms, partly ones with loss of χ as in Angl., e.g. *-siohð* beside *-sīoð*. For Angl. forms (e.g. VP *sīð*) see § 237.1.d, 2. It should be noted that these forms with *h* occur only from the 2nd and 3rd sg. pres. indic. of strong verbs: contracted weak verbs show loss of χ always, e.g. *þȳþ*, *tȳþ*, *rȳþ*, see § 237.1.d.[2]

§ 463. The W-S comparative *hēahra* higher, and superlatives *hīehsta* highest, *nīehsta* nearest, and similar nW-S forms (e.g. VP *hēhsta*), occur beside forms without *h*, and are to be attributed to the analogy of *hēah*, *nēah*.[3]

§ 464. χ remained finally in OE (written *h*), e.g. *seolh* seal, *mearh* horse, *seah* he saw, *feoh* cattle. Internally, since *χs* > *ks* (§ 416), the only group in which χ was followed by a voiceless consonant in Prim. OE was *χt*, and this group remained, e.g. *feohtan* fight, *ġefeoht* fight, *sōhte* he sought, *miht* might, *niht* night, *tyht* training. On its history in later OE see §§ 304–11. The gemination of χ remains (written *hh*) in OE whether due to doubling before *i̯*, e.g. *hliehhan*,[4] before *l* and *r*, e.g. *hweohhol*, North. *æhher*, *tæher*, or to other causes, e.g. *ġeneahhe* enough, *crohha* pot, *pohha* pocket, *tiohhian* consider (§§ 407–8).

§ 465. *h* remains in OE between unaccented and accented vowel in compounds like *behindan* behind, *behealdan* hold, *ġehelpan* help, *toheald* leaning; and also in similar forms before *l*, *r*, *n*, *w* (where it is a diacritic, § 461), *tohrēosan* fall, *tohweorfan* separate.

§ 466. The interchange between loss of χ internally and preservation finally as in *feoh*, *fēos*, leads in W-S (already *CP*) to incorrect addition of the symbol *h* to words ending in vowels, e.g. *frēoh* free, *blēoh* colour. See further § 447 on this, and also on the use of the symbol *g* for *h*.

§ 467. **Loss and modification of *ġ*.** On the loss of *ġ* with compensatory lengthening see §§ 243–5.[5] On the vocalization of *ġ* see

[1] These and some forms to be quoted below are recorded only in compounds in eW-S (e.g. *ġesiehð*).

[2] *Ġesihþ*, vision, has internal χ in all dialects (W-S, North., *V.P.*, *Ru.*[1]).

[3] On the subsequent development of *χs* in pres. indic. and superl. (*siehst*, *hīehsta*), see §§ 304–11.

[4] On palatalization of this sound, see § 442.

[5] To the examples there given add in unaccented syllables *finol*, *finul*, Ep. *finugl* (Lat. *feniculum*), fennel; *holen*, Ep., Cp. *holeġn*, holly.

§§ 266–71, and note that this sound could be from both palatalized ʒ (*hefiġe* > *hefie*) and Gmc. i̯ (*clǣnsiġan* > *clǣnsian*). In late texts the prefix *ġe-* can become *ī-* especially after another prefix, e.g. *unīwemmed*, *uniġmetes* (Beow. 1792; cf. § 271.)

§ 468. **Loss of *h* and u̯ in composition.** *h* and u̯ are often lost at the beginning of the second elements of compounds of obscured meaning. OE words of which the vowels have been discussed above, and which show such loss of *h* or u̯, are *eofot* (§ 336), *eofolsian* (§ 338), *līcuma* (§ 333), *hlāford* (§ 338), *fulluht* (§ 338, footnote), *enitre* (§ 372). Others are *hwīlende* temporary, beside *hwīlwende*, *durere* folding-door, beside *durhere*, *ealneġ* always (< *ealne weġ*), and many names in *-here*, *-helm*, *-wulf*, as *Waldere*, *Ælfelm*, *Hrōþulf*.[1] Loss of u̯, or apparent loss of *h* (really voicing of a consonant) occurs in *ǣrendraca* messenger, beside *ǣrendwreca*, *ondliotum* d.p. faces (*Rit.*, usually *ondwliota*, cf. *Cri.* 1435 *ondlata*), *wælrēow* cruel, beside *wælhrēow*, *sċyldrēða* phalanx, beside *sċyldhrēoða*, *earmrēad* (i.e. < **earmhrēad* armlet, *Beow.* 1194), *ānlīepiġ* individual. On cases of such loss of *h* leading to compensatory lengthening (*īfiġ*, *ōrettan*, *ōnettan*) see § 241.2.c; on cases leading to vowel contraction (*frēols*, *bēot*) see § 238.2.c. Cases of more drastic reduction of compounds with initial *h* or u̯ of the second element are *heardra*, *ǣlpiġ*, *nāht*, *nāteshwōn* (see § 393); also *ōb*, *āb*, beside and from *ōweb*, *āweb* woof.[2]

§ 469. Although the vowels of unaccented prefixes usually remain even in hiatus (e.g. *airnan*, *beurnen*, *ġeunnan*), there are a few instances of elision of the vowels of *be-* and *ne-* (§ 354). This involves loss of *h* in all forms of *nabban* have not: this contraction is found in all dialects. u̯ is lost in all forms of *nāt* know not (all dialects), *næs* was not (W-S, North., not VP, Ru.[1]), *nalde*, *nolde* would not (all dialects). On *ne-* with the present system of *willan*, and with forms of *wāt* with root vowel *i*, see § 265.

§ 470. **Loss of u̯ before *u*.** Loss of u̯ occurs irregularly between another consonant and *u*. Examples are: (1) with combinative back umlaut (§ 218): *cucu* alive, *cudu* cud, *sugian* be silent, *sutol* clear, beside *cwucu*, *cwudu*, *swugian*, *swutol*; (2) with development of

[1] Less often with *-wine*, e.g. *Hyġine*, LV twice.

[2] *Āhwǣr*, *nāhwǣr* have unstressed forms with loss of *h*, *āwer*, *nāwer* (§ 372). So LR *ōuana* for *ōhwanan* (on *ō-* cf. § 132, footnote 3). *Āhwæþer* is more drastically reduced to *āwþer*, *āþer*; so *ǣġhwæþer* to *ǣġþer*.

diphthong to *u* (§ 338, footnote): *betuh* beside *betwuh*.[1] *Tuwa* twice < *twuwa* has retraction of *i* to *u* between *u̯* and *u̯*, similar to that between *u̯* and *r* (§ 149), followed by loss of *u̯*; retained *twiwa* (due to analogy of *twiga*) can become *tweowa* (back umlaut).

§ 471. An isolated loss of *u̯* not preceded by a consonant before *u* is *uton* beside *wuton* let us (§ 218).

§ 472. Loss of final *-n*. Already in eNorth. loss of final *-n* is frequent. Examples are: weak nouns, CH *foldu*, LR *eorðu*, RC *galgu*, all a.s., FC *sefa* g.s.; infs. CH (Leningrad) *herġa*, RC *hælda*, *ġistīga*; past indic. pl. RC *bismæradu*, *cwōmu*; adv. LR *ōuana*. In all these categories forms with *-n* are found in these texts. The g.s. of weak nouns seems to appear without *-n* in many place-names in *BH*, note especially *Degsastan id est Degsa lapis*; it is not clear if names belonging to the weak declension are indeclinable in a Latin context in Bede, or how far, for example, *Penda* in oblique functions beside *Pendan* reflects loss of *-n*. In lNorth. loss of *-n* is established in weak inflexion, in advs. in *-an* (e.g. *biġeonda*, *bihianda*, *ūta*), in numerals (*twōēge*, *tēa*, *seofo*), in infs., and in subj. pl. pres. and past. It is, however, not lost in strong pass. parts., nouns in *-en* (e.g. *drihten*, *mæġden*), and unstressed words (e.g. *on*, *in*), nor as a rule in the past indic. pl. (except in *Li.* in the pres. of pret.-pres. verbs). *Ru.*[1] has frequent loss of *-n* in weak inflexion; in the other categories it has loss frequently, but less so than North.; it does not drop *-n* in the pres. indic. pl. of pret.-pres. verbs, though it has a few cases of loss in the weak past.

§ 473. Loss of final *-n* extended further after *ī* than after other vowels. eW-S has frequent past subj. pl. in *-e* < *-īn*, though later *-en* is mostly restored from analogy of pres. subj. *-en* < *-ǣn*.[2] The same tendency explains oblique cases of abstract fem. nouns, e.g. *strenġe* a.s. strength, cf. Goth. *managein* (§ 589.7).[3] So *pyle* pillow < **pylwīn*, Lat. *puluīnus*. The retention of *-n* in nouns like *nīeten* animal < **nautīn-* is due to the influence of inflected forms.

§ 474. Loss of medial *n*. (1) The unaccented prefix *on-* can be reduced to *a-* in *aweġ* (eW-S, lNorth.) beside *on weġ*, *abūton* (Bl.H.)

[1] Hence occasional inverted spellings like *twuxan* for *tuxum* d.p. tusks, *swūlung* for *sūlung* (< *sulh*+uncertain element).

[2] Though instances of *-e* occur in later manuscripts, e.g. *Dan.* 101 *dæde*.

[3] Here may also belong uncompounded proper names in *-i*, e.g. BH *Aelli*, *Coifi*, *Betti*, from diminutives in *-īna-*. See various opinions discussed in I. Dahl, *Substantival inflexion in early OE*, p. 56.

and so in verbs, lW-S *adrǣdan*, &c. The prefix *a-* is transferred to *adūne* (Bl.H.) for *ofdūne*. (2) Loss of *-n* of the pres. subj. pl. occurs in the imper. forms *bindewe*, *bindeġe*. (3) Loss of *n* before *r* occurs in lW-S *Þures* < *Þunres* g.s. Thor, and hence *Þuresdæġ* Thursday; unaccented pronominal g. and d.s.f. and g.p. *mīre*, *mīra*, *āre*, &c., for *mīnre*, &c. (already Whitelock, *OE wills* xiv, eleventh century). (4) Loss of *n* after *r*: lW-S *Sæteresdæġ* < *Sæternesdæġ* Saturday. (5) The suffix *-ing* is reduced to *-iġ*, *-eg-* after *n* in lNorth. *cyniġ*, lW-S *cynegas*,[1] *þenegas*, *þēniġman*, *leorniġman*.[2] (5) Sporadic cases of loss of *n* are *enetere*, *enitre* < **ǣnwintri*; *reċedom* government, for *reċċendom* < *reċċenddom* (§ 457).

§ 475. **Loss of *r*.** The lOE loss of *r* in *sprecan* speak and related words first appears in *KG* (four forms without *r*, one with *r*), and then in lW-S. So lW-S *spæċ*, *pætiġ*, Li. *ġiuixla*, for *spræċ* twig, *prætiġ* sly, *ġewrixlan* exchange. Loss after a stressed vowel appears in *endian*, *-ændian* for *ǣrndian* (§ 393; cf. Klaeber, *AB* xxxii. 37). Instances in medium stress are *VP*, W-S *endebyrdnis*, *-nes* order (and related words), but Li., Ru.², Rit. *endebrednis* (related to *brord* point, cf. *onbryrdan* beside lW-S *ġeanbyrdan*); *Li.*, *Ru.*² d.s. and p. *ondesne*, *-num* fear (and derivatives in *Rit.*), cf. W-S *ondrysnu*; W-S *īsen* iron (< *īsern*), and lW-S compounds with *-ærn* house, as *cwearten* prison, *beren* barn.[3]

§ 476. **Loss in triple groups.** Groups of three or more consonants were often reduced in OE in pronunciation, though the full form generally continues to be written. Geminates were always simplified before and after other consonants: examples in composition have been given in § 458. Further examples are provided by words with metathesis of *r* before a geminate (§ 459.1, 2), e.g. *wærna*, *irnan*, *cerse* < **wærnna*, **irnnan*, **cersse*, cf. *wrenna*, *rinnan*, *cresse*. Many examples are due to syncopation of medial vowels, e.g. 2nd sg. pres. indic. of verbs in *-s-* (*ċȳst* < **ċīesist* thou choosest; KG *alēst* thou releasest), past of weak verbs in cons.+*d* (*sende* < **sændidæ* sent),[4] and inflected adjs. in *-ne*, *-re*, *-ra* (*ealne*, *þynne*,

[1] But sg. more often *cyng* (§ 391).

[2] But *huniġ* honey, Ep. *hunaeġ-* (§ 376) has a different suffix from OHG *honang*.

[3] *Li.*, *Ru.*², *Rit.* (but not *Ru.*¹) all spell the unaccented syllable *-en* as *-ern* with great frequency, e.g. *ēfern* evening, *fæstern* fast, *wōēstern* desert. This perhaps indicates by inverted spelling that *berern* was pronounced *beren* as in lW-S.

[4] Etymological writing of *dd* is rare, e.g. *begyrdde* PC 189, *hierdde* CP 213, 8 (second *d* added above the line to avoid confusion with *hīerde* heard).

dierne, ierre < *eall,- þynn-, diern-+ne, ierr-+re*). Cases involving assimilation of consonants are discussed below (§ 480).

§ 477. Groups of three unlike consonants are sporadically reduced in OE. Examples are frequent in *KG*, where, however, scribal carelessness may be a contributory factor.[1] Examples from other texts are:

(1) Loss of *t* before *s*: 2nd sg. pres. indic. of strong verbs, and weak verbs of Class I, as *ēhst* from *ēhtan* persecute, and with assimilation of *ds* > *ts*, *finst* from *findan* find; lW-S *besta* < *betesta* best (§ 389), *ynse* < *yntse* ounce (§ 533), and with *ds* > *ts*, *mils* < *milts* mercy.

(2) Loss of *t* between *s* and another consonant: l-WS *wæsm* < *wæstm* fruit, *blōsma* < *blōstma* blossom, *braslian* < *brastlian* crackle, *nosle* < *nostle* fillet (also eW-S), *belisnian* < *belistnian* castrate (rare with *t*), and compounds like *sōþfæsnes* for *-fæstnes* truth.

(3) Loss of *d* occurs after *l* before the ending *-liċ* in W-S *selliċ*[2] < *seldliċ* wonderful (rare with *d*); Li., Ru.[2] *balliċe* < *baldliċe* boldly; Li. *moniġfalliċe* manifoldly. lW-S-*enliċ* < *-endliċ*, as *un-ġefērenliċ* inaccessible, *unacumenliċ* unbearable, and so *anlang*[3] < *andlang* (Cleopatra Glossary). *ond-* > *on-* in Ru.[2] *onġett* sense.

(4) Reduction of the group *ŋċ* to *n* before a third consonant appears in eW-S *-brinþ* < *brinċþ* < *brinġþ* brings; lW-S *lenten* < *lenċten* spring, *strenþ* < *strenċþ* strength. *ŋgn* > *gn* in lW-S *agneras* beside *ongneras* corners of the eyes.

(5) Loss of *n* between consonants: lW-S *elboga*[4] < *elnboga* elbow, *fǣmhālicum* < *fǣmnhādlicum* d.s.n. virginal (cf. § 484), *emliċe* < *emnliċe* equally, *wǣpman* < *wǣpnman* man, *Sæterdæġ* < *Sæterndæġ* Saturday (§ 393), *nemst, nemþ, nemde*[5] from *nemnan* name, *aremdest* from **aremnan*[6] for *aræfnan* endure; Rit. *ondesliċ* (§ 475), lW-S *ondrysliċ* < *ondrysnliċ* terrible.

(6) Miscellaneous instances are: eW-S *awierda* < *awierġda* accursed; lW-S *cemde* < *cembde* combed, *myrþ* < *myrhþ* joy, *ferþ* < *ferhþ* spirit,[7] *selcūþ* < *seldcūþ* strange, *elcian* < *eldcian* delay (and so *elcung*), *horsliċe* < *horscliċe* readily, *musle* < *muscle*

[1] Full material in I. Williams, *Grammatical investigation of OKt. glosses*, pp. 129–30.

[2] Whence *sylliċ*, § 325.

[3] Also *ollung*, Add. Ch. 19795.

[4] Whence *eleboga* with parasiting (§ 367).

[5] *Nemde* already eW-S.

[6] Apparently influenced by *efn, emn*.

[7] And so from *fyrhþ* (i.e. *firhþ*, § 306, footnote), **firþ* and with metathesis *frið* (Gen. 1142, *And.* 174).

mussel; lNorth. *ðorleas* < *ðorfleas* useless; *VP*, *Ru.*[1], OE Bede *marne*, lNorth. *merne* d.s. from *morgen* morning (so g.p. *morna*, Beow. 2450); *Ælgar*, *Ælmær*, *Ælriċ*, *Ælsiġ*, *Wulgar*, *Wulmær*, *Wulred*, *Wulstan*, *Lēostan*, and similar forms of names in *Ælf-*, *Wulf-*, *Lēof-*, in late sources.[1]

A further extensive collection of instances of consonant loss is given by Klaeber, *MLN* xviii. 243–5; for many forms of names with loss of final *t* of *Beorht-*, *Wiht-*, *Torht-* before another consonant see O. von Feilitzen, *Pre-conquest personal names of Domesday Book*, p. 95.

I. Intrusion of Consonants

§ 478. Intrusion of consonants occurs in a few forms only.

(1) *ml* > *mbl*: W-S *simble* always (and hence *simbel*), *bræmbel* bramble,[2] *cumbl* sore place, beside *simle*, *brēmel*, *cuml*; Ep. *hymbliċae* hemlock (Cp. *hymliċe*); less certain is *cumbol* banner.

(2) *mt* > *mpt*: lW-S *ǣmptiġe* I empty, *ǣmptiġ* empty, beside *ǣmtiġ* (§ 393).

(3) *nl* > *ndl*: W-S *endleofan* eleven (beside *enlefan*).[3]

(4) *nr* > *ndr*: lW-S *gandra* gander (beside *ganra*).

(5) *sl* > *stl*: *hwistlian* whistle (and related words; ON *hvísla*); *elmestliċ* charitable (eKt., Ct. 38, but *ælmesliċ* Ct. 42); lW-S *mæstling* brass, *mistliċe* variously, *ondrystliċ* terrible, beside *mæsling*, *misliċe*, *ondrysliċ* (§ 477.5).

(6) *sn* > *stn*: OE Bede *towestnis* discord (beside *towesnis*).

(7) *ls* > *lts*: lW-S *balzam* balsam (beside *balsam*).

§ 479. The significance is uncertain of occasional initial *scl* for *sl* as in Cp. *sclāt* tore, *asclacade* loosened, KG *scleacnes* laziness, *asclacad*. Such forms recur in later texts and ME. Less frequent is *stl*, and it is uncertain if this expresses the same sound. *scm* and *scn* are very rare for initial *sm*, *sn* (VP 118, 129; *CP* 155, 17).[4]

J. Assimilation of Consonants and Kindred Changes

§ 480. The syncopations of medial vowels described in Chapter VII, Section C above often caused groups of consonants to arise

[1] *Wulf-* more rarely loses *l*, e.g. *Wufgar*, *Wufred*.

[2] So before *r* in *brember* bramble.

[3] But lW-S *andlīcnes* image (beside *an-*) is due rather to prefix mixture.

[4] See Sisam, *Archiv* cxxxi. 305; other references S–B, § 210.1.

which were subject to assimilation. If double consonants so arose in a group of three or more consonants, they were simplified under the principle laid down in § 476. Common assimilations are:

(1) *d* > *t* after voiceless sounds. This is chiefly seen in weak past tenses, e.g. *mētte* met, *cyste* kissed < *mōet-*, *cyss-*+*-idǣ*. This formation is more fully discussed in § 751.2.

(2) All consonants become voiceless before *t*, e.g. *lenċten* (§ 477.4), W-S *mettrum*, *metrum* infirm (i.e. *med-*+*trum*).

(3) Before the voiceless spirants *s* and *þ*, every consonant was unvoiced.[1] This cannot affect spelling in the case of *f*, *þ*, *s*, which stand for both voiceless and voiced sounds, e.g. 2nd and 3rd sg. pres. indic. *drīfst*, *drīfþ*, *cȳþst*, *cȳþþ*, *ċīest*, **ċīesþ* from *drīfan* drive, *cȳþan* declare, *ċēosan* choose.[2] Groups in which spelling shows the unvoicing are *ds* > *ts*, *ngs* > *ncs*, *ngþ* > *ncþ*, e.g. *milts* mercy, *bletsian* bless, *ancsum* troublesome, *strenċþ* strength (derivatives of *milde*, *blōd*, *ange*, *strang*), *Henċstes* (§ 393), Cp. *etsith* a looking again (i.e. *ed-*+*sihþ*), and 2nd and 3rd sg. pres. indic. like *rǣtst*, *brinċst*, *brinċð* from *rǣdan*, *bringan*.[3] The groups *sþ*, *þs*, *tþ* (< *dþ*), *χs*, *χþ* undergo further change and will be dealt with below.

§ 481. The following modifications of consonant groups also occurred:

(1) *sþ* > *st* whether the voiceless *s* was original or in accordance with § 480.3, e.g. 3rd sg. pres. indic. *cyst*, *wiext*, *ċīest* < *cyss-*, *wiex-*, *ċīes-*+*iþ*, *-līestu* lack (e.g. *metelīestu* < *-līes-*+*iþō*), 2nd sg. *berestu*[4] (< *beres*+*þu*), compound *nosterl* nostril (< *nosþyrl*).[5]

(2) *þs* (most instances are due to § 480.3) > *ss* by phonological development, e.g. *bliss* bliss, *liss* kindness < *blīþs*, *līþs*, 2nd sg. pres. indic. *cwist* thou sayest < **cwiþist*. Hence verbal forms like *cȳþst* are due to analogical restoration: such restored *þs* can become *ts* in lW-S, e.g. *snītst* thou cuttest.

(3) *tþ* > *tt* whether from *t*+*þ*, or *d*+*þ* due to § 480.3, e.g. 3rd

[1] Except *į*, e.g. *eġsa* terror. Hence eW-S *līehþ*, he lies, from *lēogan*, had analogical velar *ʒ* introduced from other forms, and this was unvoiced. On *h* as a mere spelling for *į*, e.g. *myrhþ* joy, see § 447.

[2] So in formations with *-iþō*, *-sįō*, in which the consonants were voiceless (§ 445), *cȳþþ*, *blīþs*.

[3] So the river-name *Wantsumo* (cf. *wendan*). Final *d* of first elements of names can be unvoiced before any voiceless consonant, e.g. LV *Altċeorl*, *Ēatðryð*, *Līutfrith*, *Tītfrith*, late sources *Ētsiġe*, *Goltsiġe*, *Gōtsunu*, *Tītstan*.

[4] Whence was extracted *st* as a personal ending.

[5] Hence, especially in *CP* (Hatton MS.), inverted *sþ*, *sð* for *st*, e.g. *dūsð* dust, *wæsðm* fruit, *ǣresð* first, beside *hilpesð* thou helpest.

sg. pres. indic. *itt* eats, *rǣtt* advises, *fint* finds, < *it-*, *rǣd-*, *find-*+*iþ*, *þætte* < *þæt þe*, *mitty* < *midþy*, *latteow* leader < *lād*+*þēow*, *ofermetto* pride, *ġesynto* health < *ofermōēd-*, *ġisynd-*+*iþō*.

(4) *ʒs*, *ʒþ* > *χs*, *χþ*, but in most instances *ʒ* was an analogical replacement for *ġ* (§ 480.3, footnote), e.g. eW-S *līehþ* lies, lW-S *adrīhð* bears, *stīhst* ascendest from *lēogan*, *adrēogan*, *stīgan*; with original *ʒ*, KG *ġiohð-* for *ġeogoþ-* youth. Neither *χs* < *ʒs* nor original *χs* usually repeats the early change *χs* > *ks* (§ 416), though lW-S has *hēxta* highest, *nēxta* next, and less frequently verbs like *syxt* seest, *ōxta* beside *ōhsta* arm-pit.[1] *χþ* > *χt* in *ġesiht* vision beside *ġesihþ*.[2]

(5) *fþ* > *ft* in lW-S *þēoft* theft; not in verbs, e.g. *drīfþ* drives.

(6) *fs* does not repeat the change to *ps*, see § 418.

(7) *þd* > *dd* in lOE, e.g. lW-S, lNorth., Ru.[1] *cȳdde* declared.

(8) *ċþ* > *ċt* in KG *ofðreċt* oppresses, *ġehyðlǣċt* repeats, cf. W-S *ofþryċċan*, *ġeedlǣċan*.

§ 482. Even the commonest of the changes described in §§ 480–1, and the simplification of geminates in triple groups described there and in § 476, are often disguised by etymological spellings, e.g. *lenġten*, *medtrum*, *milds*, *blīþs*, *angsum*, *strenġþ*, *lādtēow* (and even *lādþēow*). Verbs are less prone to such disturbance, yet forms like *findst* occur, and are especially frequent with *ng*, e.g. *singð*, *bringð*.[3] *KG* have three times *-þīod* for *-*þīot* joins, with *d* from *þīodan*; so eW-S *hȳd* from *hȳdan*, and by compromise *bidt* from *biddan*. It has been suggested above that forms with *þs* are not phonological. The later assimilations are far more disturbed, and here the resistance was phonological, e.g. lW-S, lNorth., Ru.[1] *cȳðde* beside *cȳdde*; so paradigm analogy prevents the change *fs* > *ps*, and hinders *χs* > *ks*, *fþ* > *ft*. Etymological graphic retention of geminates in triple groups is also frequent, e.g. a.s.m. *eallne*, g.p. *fullra*.

§ 483. In lW-S the final palatal groups *ċst*, *ċþ* sometimes appear as *hst*, *hþ*, e.g. 2nd sg. pres. indic. *beþǣhst*, 3rd *beþǣhð*, *asīhð*, *sēhþ*, from *beþǣċan* deceive, *asīcan* sigh, *sēċan* seek. Conversely we find

[1] So a few late names have *χs* > *ks* after loss of *t* in *Briht-*, *Wiht-* (§ 477.6), e.g. *Bricstan*, *Brixsie* for *Brihtstan*, *-siġe*, *Wixie* for *Wihtsiġe*.

[2] ME evidence suggests that the change *hþ* > *ht* was more extensive than OE spellings suggest, see Luick, *Hist. Gramm.*, § 718.2. In a few scattered forms, OE has *hþ* > *ht* in 3rd sg. pres. indic., VP *ġefiht* rejoices, *onfōēht* receives, lW-S *siht* sees, *tȳht* draws.

[3] Hence inverted *dringð* from *drincan*, &c.

cþ for final *hþ*, e.g. *afēcð*, *flīcð*, *-swylcð* from *afōn* receive, *flīeġan* put to flight, *swelgan* swallow.[1] Compromise spellings also occur, e.g. *-tǣchð*, *-tǣhcð* from *tǣċan* teach.

§ 484. In groups consisting of a consonant followed or preceded by a liquid or nasal, assimilation is not usual, e.g. adjs. with the inflexions *-ne*, *-re*, *glædne*, *glædre*, *rūmne*, *ealre*, and weak past tenses like *hiērde*, *hǣlde*, *wēnde*. Assimilation in such groups is sporadic. Examples arranged according to the second consonant of the group are:

fn > *mn*: W-S *emn* even, *hremn* raven (§ 193.d, footnote 4), and the homonyms *stemn* voice, *stemn* period, *stemn* stem (beside *efn*, *hræfn*, *stefn*); nW-S only Ru.[1] *stemn* voice (beside *stæfn*), and perhaps poetical and Angl. *nemne* unless, beside *nefne*.[2]

mn > *mm*: lW-S *hrem* raven, pl. *hremmas*.

hn > *nn*: W-S *hēanne* a.s.m. high; lW-S, lNorth. *hēannes* highness.[3]

pn > *mn*: lW-S *wǣmn* (very rare) < *wǣpn* weapon.

sn > *nn*: Li. *ðionne* a.s.m. this (beside usual *ðiosne*).

fm > *mm*: BH *Ġemmund* (MS. Cott. Tib. C ii, for *Ġefmund*); lW-S *wimman*, *Hlammæsse* < *wīfmonn* woman, *Hlāfmæsse* Lammas; *Leomman* < *Lēofman*, and so *Leommær* in late sources.

dl > *ll*: lW-S *fǣmnhālicum* < *-hādlicum* d.s.n. virginal (Napier's *OE glosses*, i. 535, 2280; on *ll* > *l*, cf. § 457).

nl > *ll*: North. *ællef* eleven.

sl > *ll*: Li. *ðulliċ*, lW-S *þylliċ* < *þusliċ*, *þysliċ* such.

hr > *rr*: W-S *hīerra* higher, *nēarra* nearer, Rit. *hērra*, Ru.[1] *nǣrra*.[4]

lr > *ll*: lW-S, Li. *sella* < *sōelra* better.

lr > *rr*: *Aeðerred* (Ct. 29), and hence *Ǣðered* (Cts., frequently) < *Æþelred*; so *Eðeriċ* (Cts. 27, 43) < *Æþelriċ*.[5]

[1] Luick, *Hist. Gramm.*, § 674.4; S–B, § 359.*a*.6.

[2] See Flasdieck, *A* lxix. 142.

[3] *hn* was due to analogical replacement: the undisturbed development was *hēane*, *hēanes* (§ 461).

[4] *hr* was similarly due to analogical replacement.

[5] The name-element *Æþel-* seems liable to reduction to *Æþe-* and *Æþ-* irrespective of what consonant follows, e.g. *Aeðeuulf*, *-wald* (Ct. 24), *Æðestan* (moneyer of Ed. II). Reduction to *Æþ-* (e.g. lOE *Æðferð*, *-red*, *-riċ*, *-ulf*; Ct. 24 already *Aeðelm*) was perhaps helped by the existence of another name-element *Æþ-* (LV *Aeðuini*); yet it occurs of persons who elsewhere have *Æþe(l)-*, e.g. *Æðred*, Birch, Ct. 469; *Æstan* < **Æþstan* beside *Æðestan* (moneyer of Cnut). The development *Æþel-* > *Æġel-* > *Aġel-* (ME *Ail-*) seems to be due to a French

nr > *rr*: *Cyrred* (Ct. 22) < *Cynred*.

sr > *ss*: *lǣssa* less, *wiersa* worse (all dialects); *þisse*, *þissa*, g. and d.s.f. and g.p. of *þes* this (W-S, Merc., Kt., analogically disturbed in North., see § 711); d.s.m. *ūssum*, g.s.m. *ūsses* < **ūsrum*, &c., from *ūser* our[1] (see § 706).

nd > *md*: eW-S *emdemes* < *endemes* together.[2]

nd > *nn*: poetical n.p. *benne* (once), d.p. *bennum* (three times) from *bend* fetter.

nb > *mb*: lW-S *elmboga*, poetical *hlimbed*, *ġimfæst* < *elnboga* elbow, **hlinbed* bed of rest, *ġinfæst* huge.

mb > *mm*: eW-S *oferclom* climbed; lW-S *ācuma* < *ācumba* oakum (with simplification).

rþ > *rr*: *lāreow* teacher < *lār*+*þēow* (with simplification).

hġ > *hh*: lW-S *nēh(h)ebūr* < *nēahġebūr* neighbour; so Li. *nēhebūr* (with simplification).

ct > *ht*: lW-S *lēahtūn* < **lēactūn* garden; cf. § 534 for this change in loan-words.

§ 485. Syncopation far passes its normal limits in hypocoristic names.[3]

K. Chronological Summary

§ 486. The dating of the changes in consonant groups dealt with in Section A is there discussed. The sensitivity of *k* and *ʒ* to the nature of following sounds described in Section B doubtless began in the continental period, for it is a major link of OE and OFris., and continued through the periods of Anglo-Frisian fronting, breaking, and retraction before consonant groups and before back vowels. Hence we find in OE *ċ*, *ġ* initially before front vowels, which existed at the completion of these processes, but *k*, *ʒ* before back vowels which then existed, e.g. *ċeaf* chaff, *ġeaf* gave; *ċeald* cold, *ġealla* gall, but Angl. *cald*, *galla*; *caru* care, *galan* sing. Soon afterwards this sensitivity ceased, for when back vowels were changed

sound-change, and its use in OE charters and on coins to be an affectation: it is frequent from the late tenth century.

[1] These syncopations must be earlier than the majority and precede the voicing of *s* between vowels, for *zr* would not produce *ss*. Hence syncopation must have intervened at the stage **lǣsir-*, **ūser-* **þiser-*.

[2] Due not to assimilation, but rather anticipation of the second *m*.

[3] See, for example, names discussed by O. S. Anderson, *OE material in the Leningrad MS. of Bede's Eccl. Hist.*, pp. 121–2.

to front ones by second fronting and *i*-umlaut, *k* and *ʒ* appear before these new front vowels: for examples see § 427 and footnote. The period at which fronted stop consonants passed into affricates is uncertain. Spellings of [tį] and [dį] as *cc*, *cg* appear from the later ninth century (§ 434), and this suggests that these symbols were then already familiar as representing sounds which had progressed towards assibilation.[1] There is no evidence to show how long the assibilation of *sċ* in positions in which it took place, though that of *ċ* was absent (§ 440), was delayed after the other assibilations.[2] The palatalization of the groups *χt*, *χs*, *χþ* when not followed by a back vowel is only to be dated by its results, which begin before 900 in the south and spread north (§§ 304–11).

§ 487. Of the processes of voicing and unvoicing described in Section C, the voicing of medial spirants is prehistoric (§ 444), the unvoicing of final spirants and the sporadic unvoicing of final stops is already to be traced in the earliest texts (§§ 446, 450).

§ 488. The change of final *k* and *ċ* to *χ* is only datable as being older, at least in the case of *ċ*, than assibilation (§ 452).

§ 489. The OE consonant doubling described in Section E was a tendency which had developed by the ninth century, though evidence for it is wanting in very early texts. *RC* has *ætgadre*, Cp. *ġegaedradon*, but this does not establish that the gemination had not begun, for *VP* has *ġegadrades*, although this text has some forms with gemination (§ 453). The tendency continued through the whole OE period. The metathesis of *r* before *s* and *n* had already begun before breaking (§ 459.1). The common assimilations of consonants are early, and would follow the syncopations of un-

[1] While the above interpretation of these spellings seems reasonable, the matter has been much disputed. For an alternative view, and references to older literature, see G. van Langenhove in the Jespersen *Miscellany* (Bibliography, § C). Assibilation in *feċċan* < **fetįan* is due to its being a weak verb of Class III (§ 764). In verbs of Class II (e.g. *hatian*) *-i-* is vocalic, and there is no assibilation. Failure to recognize this distinction invalidates much of the arguments of Kuhn, *ZfdA* lxxxvi. 30–31.

BH *Lyccidfelth* hardly proves assibilation: British *-tg-* (in **Lētgẹ̄d* < *Lētocẹ̄t-*) may have been assimilated to palatal *ċċ* in OE, and this would be assibilated later, as it stood after a vowel-sound which would be due to *i*-umlaut in a native word.

[2] In the metrical *Psalms* and the alliterative prose of Ælfric, initial *sċ* alliterates with *s*, but this is not evidence that assibilation had not yet taken place, as [ʃ] and [s] would provide a jingle sufficient for inexact poets. (Another view, Schubel, *Stud. Neophil.* xiv. 255–76; a compromise, Slettengren, *Stud. i mod. språkvetenskap* xv. 45–50; cf. also Flasdieck, *A* lxix. 269–70).

accented vowels. The loss of medial $h < \chi$ belongs to approximately the period of the earliest texts (§ 461). North. loss of final -*n* is well established in the earliest texts (§ 472). The typically W-S loss of *ġ* before dentals is well established in the oldest W-S texts, but is probably much older, for traces of similar changes occur in the earliest Anglian texts (§ 243–5). Evidence is inadequate for dating the various losses of *h* and *w* detailed in §§ 468–71, but they may with probability be regarded as belonging to the same period as the loss of medial χ.

§ 490. The remaining changes dealt with in this chapter (minor cases of metathesis and of consonant loss, the simplification of consonant groups, the intrusion of consonants, and assimilations and kindred changes of the less frequent types) were neither universally carried out nor invariably expressed in spelling when they operated. All that can be done to determine their dating is to observe when they are first expressed in spelling in manuscripts, and this has already been done in discussing them.

X

LOAN-WORDS IN OLD ENGLISH

A. Graeco-Latin Loan-words

§ 491. While many problems of vocabulary cannot be handled in a grammar, it is relevant to consider how far the operation of the sound-changes so far described can be observed in borrowed words, and to note any other sound-changes which take place in the assimilation of such words.

§ 492. In the case of a few Greek words of wide dispersion in Germanic, it may be suspected that they reached Germanic directly from Greek, and especially when they occur in Gothic, direct passage from Greek into that language and hence to West Germanic is probable. But since all such words were also borrowed into Latin, passage through Latin to Germanic cannot be regarded as impossible. The chief examples are: OE *dēofol* devil, North. *dīofol*,[1] Gr. διάβολος, where Gmc. *iu* has been used as a substitute for ια, while *v* (written *f* in OE) corresponds to the spirantal β of late Gr.; the Prim. Gmc. form would be **diuvul-*, with substitution of a common native formative element for Gr. -ολ- (cf. Goth. *diabulus*), and from this the OE form is derived. OE *Crēcas* Greeks, Goth. *Krekos*, shows substitution of *k* for *g* of Γραικοί due to the lack of a back voiced stop in Gmc. except in the combinations *gg*, *ŋg*.[2] OE *enġel* angel, is from Gmc. **angil-*, in which unaccented *-el-* (cf. Gr. ἄγγελος) > Gmc. *-il-*, which causes umlaut, and appears in OE as *-el-*, as in native words. OE *ċiriċe* church, is from Prim. Gmc. **kirikōn-*, with substitution of *i* for υ of Gr. κυριακόν.[3]

[1] North., however, has frequently *īa* in the first syllable, and *b* for the medial consonant, owing to the influence of Lat. *diabolus*. North. also has frequently *w* (*u*, *v*) for the medial consonant: the reason is unknown.

[2] The same substitution occurs in OE forms of Celtic place-names: see Förster, *Flussname Themse*, p. 325.*a*.2. But Kretschmer, *KZ* xxxiii. 472, prefers to explain the first *k* of Gmc. **Krēk-* as assimilated to the second. The relationship of the *ē* to Gr. αι or Lat. *ae* is uncertain: Gmc. *ǣ* would be expected to correspond to monophthongized development in either case. On OE *Crēacas* beside *Crēcas* see Flasdieck, *AB* xl. 342, who explains it as due to W-S derivation of the word from Angl. sources, *-ēac* being a frequent W-S equivalent of Angl. *-ēc*.

[3] If the word passed through Lat. to Gmc., the change of gender may have taken place there, and also the medial syncopation: cf. Walahfrid Strabo, *ab ipsis autem Grecis kyrica . . . accepimus* (*ZfdA* xxv. 99).

B. Early Latin Loan-words

§ 493. The Latin loan-words found in Old English can be roughly classified into (1) those in which the sound-changes operate which would effect the same sound-successions in native words, and (2) those which were introduced into Old English by scholars without modification of their sounds, or at least without the indication of such modification in spelling. Words of type (1) often exhibit sound-changes of late spoken Latin (Vulg. Lat.), showing that their classical form had been modified before they were borrowed, yet the Latin from which they were taken had still mainly the Classical not the Vulgar Latin quantities. Words of type (2) retain the Classical Latin sounds with little qualitative change, yet the monastic Latin from which they were derived appears to have adopted a quantitative system similar to that of Vulgar Latin, and further quantitative changes took place when such words were given the invariable initial stress of Old English (cf. §§ 547–8).

§ 494. The chief stress in Latin fell on the first syllable of words of two syllables. In words of three or more syllables, it fell on the last syllable but one if this was long, but on the last syllable but two if the last but one was short. Examples are *grádus*, *mấter*, *ménsa*; *Rōmấnī*, *patérnus*; *dóminus*, *clḗricus*. In all Germanic languages the chief stress fell on the first syllable in loan-words as in native words, but some vowels develop differently according to whether they were already stressed in Latin or became stressed when borrowed into Germanic.

§ 495. **Short vowels.** Lat. *a* was modified in loan-words as the ordinary sound-patterns of OE suggested, developing to *æ*, *a*, *a/o*, or *ea*, whether the syllable had the chief stress in Lat. or acquired it when the word was borrowed. In early loan-words this would arise by the operation of native sound-changes, but in later ones sound-substitution might produce similar results. Examples are: *ċæster* city, *læfel* bowl, *tæfl* gaming-board; *sacc* sack (§ 160.1), *abbod* abbot, *draca* dragon; *ancor/oncor* anchor, *candel/condel* candle; *ċealc* plaster, *sealtian* dance, *sealm* psalm; *earc* ark, *ċearcern* prison, *mearm-* marble; *leahtriċ* lettuce, **treaht* text (cf. *treahtere*) from Lat. *castrum*, *labellum*, *tabula*, *saccus*, *abbātem*, *draco*, *ancora*, *candēla*, *calcem*, *saltāre*, *psalma*, *arca*, *carcer*, *marmor*, *lactūca*, *tractus*. Further sound-changes frequently intervene. *æ* > *ea* by palatal influence in W-S, North. *ċeaster*; *a* > *æ* by second fronting in VP *dræca*; mutation of *a*/*o* is *æ* > *e* as in native words, e.g. *Embene* people of Amiens, *ċemes* shirt, *lempedu* lamprey, *mentel* cloak, from Lat. *Ambiāni*, *camisia*, *lamprēda*, *mantellum*; the mutation of *æ* is *e*, e.g. *eċed* vinegar, VP *ċelċ* cup, from Lat. *acētum*, *calicem*; mutation of *æ* to *e* and subsequent back umlaut to *eo* (§ 211) occurs in *eosol* ass, *ċeosol* hut, from Lat. *asellus*, **casellum*; mutation of *ea* < *æ* by palatal influence occurs in *ċytel* kettle, *ċyren* sweet wine, from Latin *catillus*, *carēnum*; double umlaut of *a*+*u* to *æ*+*e* (§ 203) occurs in *sælmeriġe* brine,[1] *sæþerie* savory, and with *a* due to pre-tonic shortening (§ 504) in *Sætern-dæġ*, from Lat. **salmuria*, *saturēia*, *Sāturni dies*.

§ 496. In some words borrowing took place too late for *a* to become *æ* or *ea* by the usual OE sound-changes, but it remained, and was later mutated to *æ*, e.g. *ærċe-* arch-, *cæfester* halter, *Læden* Latin, *mæġester* master, from Lat. *archi-*, *capistrum*, *Latīna*, *magister*, and so *cæren*, North. *æċed*, *cælċ* beside *ċyren*, *eċed*, *ċelċ* quoted above.

§ 497. Late Lat. loan-words are independent of the native changes, and preserve *a* in all positions; they include doublets of many words cited above, e.g. *arc*, *carcern*, *marm-*, W-S *salm*, *traht*, *satureġe*, *magister*, *calic*. Other late borrowings with Latin *a* are *castel* village, *plaster* plaster, *sanct* saint, *alter* altar, *fals* falsehood, *carte* document, *martyr* martyr, from Lat. *castellum*, *emplastrum*, *sanctus*, *altāre*, *falsum*, *charta*, *martyr*. Cf. § 545.

§ 498. Lat. *i* and *u* were originally close sounds, but became more open in Vulg. Lat. Hence in an early group of loan-words they appear as *i*, *u*, both when they had the chief stress in Lat. and when they acquired it when the words were borrowed; but in a later group of loan-words they appear as *e*, *o*. Examples of the first group are *disċ* dish, *piċ* pitch, *trifetum* d.p. tributes, *cugele* cowl, *culter* knife, *must* must, from Lat. *discus*, *picem*, *tribūtum*, *cuculla*, *culter*, *mustum*; examples of the second group are *ċest*, W-S *ċyst* box, *peru* pear, *seġn* banner, *inseġel* seal, *copor* copper, *torr* tower, from Lat. *cista*, *pirum*, *signum*, **insigillum*, *cuprum*, *turris*. Both developments occur in *piper*, **peper* pepper, Lat. *piper*. On *mæsse* mass, from Lat. *missa*, see § 208.

§ 499. Before nasal consonants, and when *i* or *i̯* followed in the

[1] Developed from **salmuri-* borrowed after the operation of breaking, but before umlaut.

next syllable, Lat. *i* and *u* were developed as *i* and *u* (with mutation *y*) in OE, e.g. *impian* graft, *pirġe* pear-tree, *-humele* hop-plant, *byden* barrel, *cymen* cumin, *cylen* kiln, *pyle* pillow, *pytt* pit, from Lat. *imputare*, **pirea*, *humulus*, **butīna* (Gr. *βυτίνη*), *cumīnum*, *culīna*, *puluīnus*, *puteus*. But since *e* may stand before single *n* in native words (§ 118), Lat. *i* may > *e* in that position: *senop* mustard, *senoþ*[1] synod, beside *sinoþ*, from Lat. *sināpi*, *synodus*.

§ 500. Lat. *e* and *o* remain in OE loan-words, both under original and acquired chief stress. Examples are: *fefer* fever,[2] *regol* rule, *sester* jar, *sċolu* school, *mortere* mortar, *port* harbour, from Lat. *febris*, *rĕgula*, *sextarius*, *schola*, *mortārium*, *portus*. The Lat. *e* was more open than OE *e* from Gmc. *e* and Lat. *i*, and its breaking is *ea* (not *eo*): *earfe* tare, Lat. *eruum*. Breaking is absent in the later borrowings *mertze* payment, *persoc* peach, from Lat. *mercem*, *persicum*. Back umlaut of *e* occurs in *eofole* danewort, *teosol* die,[3] from Lat. *ebulus*, *tessella*.

§ 501. Before nasal consonants, and when *ĭ* or *i̯* followed in the next syllable, Lat. *e* and *o* were developed as *i* and *u* (by mutation *y*) in OE, e.g. *ġimm* gem, *minte* mint, *pinsian* consider, *ċiris*-cherry, *miltestre* harlot, *pyleċe* robe, *munuc* monk, *munt* mount, *nunne* nun, *pund* pound, *cyċene* kitchen, *mydd* bushel, *mynet* coin, *mynster* monastery, *syrfe* service-tree, from Lat. *gemma*, *mentha*, *pensare*, **cerasia* (cf. § 541.6), *meretrix* (§§ 515, 541.3), *pellicia*, *monachus*, *montem*, *nonna*, *pondo*, *coquīna*, *modius*, *monēta*, *monastērium*, **sorbea*.

§ 502. In later loan-words Lat. *e*, *o* were developed as *e*, *o* (by mutation *oe*) even before nasal consonants and *ĭ*, *i̯*, e.g. *aspendan* spend, *lent* lentil, *tempel* temple, *font* font,[4] *oele* oil, from Lat. *expendere*, *lentem*, *templum*, *fontem*, *oleum*.

§ 503. **Long vowels and diphthongs.** Long vowels which had the chief stress in Latin, and retain it in OE, remain long in OE. But since pre-tonic long vowels were shortened in Vulgar Latin, they appear as short vowels in OE even when the chief stress is moved on to them.

[1] With back umlaut *sionoþ*, *seonoþ*.

[2] But cf. Förster, *Flussname Themse*, p. 574; Flasdieck, *A* lxxii. 191.

[3] The alternative form *tasul*, *-ol*, Cp., Ep., Erf., is unexplained; *Ld.* has *tesulas*.

[4] Spelling with *a* is also found, so the sound in this word was sometimes *a/o*; but *a*-spellings are not found in *domne* lord (generalized voc. of Lat. *dominus*), so a regular substitution of *a/o* for Lat. *o* before nasals is not to be assumed.

§ 504. Lat. *ā* was represented by W-S *ǣ*, nW-S *ē*. This would be a necessary substitution until the development of OE *ā* < *ai*. Examples are *nǣp* turnip, *rǣdiċ* radish, *strǣt* street, nW-S *ċēse* cheese, from Lat. *nāpus*, **rādĭca*, *strāta*, *cāseus*. Mutation of *ēa* < *ǣ* by palatal influence to *īe*, later *ȳ* occurs in lW-S *ċȳse*, and retraction of *ǣ* to *ā* before *u̯* (cf. § 151) in *pāwa* peacock,[1] Lat. *pāuo*. *a* < *ā* by pre-tonic shortening undergoes umlaut in *Sætern-dæġ* (§ 495). Later loan-words preserve Lat. *ā*, e.g. *pāl* pole, *pāpa* pope, from Latin *pālus*, *pāpa*.

§ 505. Lat. *ī* and *ū* remained in OE loan-words when they retained the chief stress, e.g. *mīl* mile, *wīn* wine, *mūr* wall, *plūme* plum, from Lat. *mīlia*, *uīnum*, *mūrus*, *prūnum*. *ū* undergoes mutation in *plȳme* plum, *strȳta* ostrich, from Lat. **prūnea*, *strūthio*. Pretonic shortening of *i* in *trifolian* grind, Lat. *trībulāre*.[2]

§ 506. Lat. *ē* (< *ē*, *oē*) and *ō* develop in OE as *ī*, *ū*, e.g. *clīroc* clergyman, *mīse* table, *pīnung* torture, *pīs* heavy, *Sīgen* Seine, *tīgle* tile, *Rūm-* Rome, from Lat. *clēricus*, **mēsa* (< *mensa*), *pēna*, **pēsus* (< *pensus*), *Sēquana*, *tēgula*, *Rōma*. But *ō* is retained in later borrowings: *mōr-* mulberry;[3] mutated in *glēsan* gloss, from *mōrus*, *glōssāre*.[4] When shortened pre-tonically *ē* and *ō* can develop as *i*, *u* or *e*, *o*, e.g. *diner* coin, *finugle* fennel, *sicor* secure, *elehtre* lupin, *Custantin* Constantine, *moraþ* sweet wine, *solor* chamber, from Lat. *dēnārius*, *fēnuculum*, *sēcūrus*, *ēlectrum*, **Cōstantinus* (< *Const-*), *mōrātum*, *sōlārium*.

§ 507. An irregular mutation of the shortening of pre-tonic Lat. *ō* occurs in *læriġ*, part of a shield, Lat. *lōrīca*. Original Lat. *o* seems to receive the same treatment in *stær* history, Lat. *historia*. It is possible that W-S scribes assumed that Angl. **leriġ*, *ster* (OE Bede) with *e* < *oe* had Angl. *ē*, and that the spelling *æ* implies *ǣ*, the W-S equivalent of *ē*, although *læriġ* has a short first syllable in verse.

§ 508. The Lat. diphthongs *au* and *ae* were identified with Gmc. *au* and *ai*, and developed to *ēa* and *ā* in early loan-words, e.g. *ċēac* jug, *ċēas* strife, *sēam* burden, *cāsere* emperor, from Lat. *caucus*, *causa*, *sauma* (< *sagma*), *Caesar*. Mutation of *ēa* < *au*

[1] Beside *pēa* from a.s. **paun* > *pēan*, in which the West Gmc. loss of *u̯* before *u* was repeated in the borrowed word (cf. § 405).

[2] But *Eotol*, *Eatal* Italy, has back umlaut of *i*: the long *ī* of *Italia* is a metrical convention, see *Archiv* cxlvi. 131.

[3] Beside *mūr-* (once).

[4] Retention of *ē* is rare: *bēte* beet, and *mēse* beside *mīse*.

occurs in *sīman* load. An alternative Lat. development *au* > *ū*[1] is reflected by *clūse* enclosure, *clūster* bolt, and mutated in *-clȳsan*, close, from Lat. *clausa*, *claustrum*. Lat. monophthongization *ae* > *ǣ*, followed by pre-tonic shortening, gives in OE loan-words a sound represented by *e* or *y*: *ċerfille*, *ċyrfille* chervil, *predician*, *prydician* preach, from Lat. *chaerefolium*, *praedicāre*. Before a following back vowel this sound was very open, and retracted to *a* in OE like native *æ*: *prafost* officer, Lat. *praepositus* (beside *profost* < *propositus*).

§ 509. Lat. *au* remained in later borrowings, e.g. *clauster* cloister, Lat. *claustrum*. Before *r* and *l* belonging to the same syllable *au* > *ā*; but before *r* and *l* not belonging to the same syllable, *au* > *ā* > *āu*,[2] hence e.g. *cāl* cabbage, Lat. *caulis*, infl. *cāules*, whence a new n.s. *cāul*, and with parasiting *cāwel*, and so *lāwer* laurel, *Pāwel* Paul, Lat. *laurus*, *Paulus*.

§ 510. Lat. *eo*, *eu* are represented by OE *ēo*, North. *ēa* in *lēo*, *lēa* lion, *lēowe* league, from Lat. *leo*, *leuca*. *Prēost* priest, has *ēo* of disputed origin.[3]

§ 511. **Vowels of unaccented syllables.** In early Latin loan-words no half-stress fell upon syllables because they were accented in Latin, if the chief stress was removed from them. But OE in conformity with its native accent system might develop a half-stress on second elements of compounds, e.g. *ċérfìlle* chervil, *cúneglæ̀sse*[4] dog's tongue, *sṓlsèċe* 'heliotrope', from Lat. *chaerefolium*, *cynoglōssum*, *sōlsequium*; and similarly on heavy formative syllables, e.g. *céllèndre* coriander, *ǽlmæ̀sse* alms, from Lat. *coliandrum*, **alimosina*. If such a half-stress did not fall upon it, any vowel in a syllable unaccented in OE was developed as in an accented syllable, and then subjected to shortening and change similar to the processes to be observed in unaccented syllables of native words. Hence in OE unaccented syllables the Latin vowels develop as follows:

a > *æ* > *e*: *Sīġen* Seine, Lat. *Sēquana*.

e > *i* > *e*: *elehtre* lupin, Lat. *ēlectrum* (*e* < *ē* is not subject to mutation).

[1] It occurs in *clūdo* for *claudo* and derivatives, owing to the influence of *occlūdo* &c.

[2] This is assumed on the evidence of ME *P̨wel* Paul.

[3] Principal literature cited S–B, § 77.*a*.5.

[4] On *u* for Lat. *y* in Gr. words, cf. *murre* myrrh, beside *myrre*, Lat. *myrrha* *cruft* crypt, Lat. *crypta*.

i > *e* or remains as in native words, causing umlaut if possible: *ċemes* shirt, *cyrfet* gourd, *mæġester* master, *rǣdić* radish, Lat. *camisia, cucurbita, magister, *rādīca.*

o > *e*: *antefen* anthem, *cuneglæsse* dog's tongue, Lat. **antephŏna, cynoglōssum.*

u > *o* or remains: *eofole* danewort, *finugle* fennel, *trifolian, trifulian* grind, Lat. *ebulùs, fēnuculum, trībulāre.* Reduction to *e* in *ampelle* flask, beside *ampulle, ānpolle,* Lat. *ampulla.*

ā > *æ* > *e*: *alter* altar, *senep* mustard, *Embene* people of Amiens, Lat. *altāre, sināpi, Ambiāni.*[1]

ē > *i* (causing mutation) > *e*: *ċyren* sweet wine, *eċed* vinegar, *lempedu* lamprey, *mynet* coin, *mynster* monastery, Lat. *carēnum, acētum, lamprēda, monēta, monastērium.* There is syncopation of the vowel in *seġne* net, Lat. *sagēna.* In later borrowings there is no umlaut: *candel* candle, *polleie* penny-royal, Lat. *candēla, pūlēium.*

ī > *e*: *cylen* kiln, *Læden* Latin, *mylen* mill, Lat. *culīna, Latīna, molīna.*

ō > *u*: *capun* capon, Lat. *cāpōnem.*[2]

ū > *u* > *o*: *sicor* secure, **trifot* tribute, d.p. *trifetum* (cf. § 385), Lat. *sēcūrus, tribūtum.*

§ 512. Lat. *e* and *i* in hiatus were developed to *i̯* (*ii̯*), which caused consonant doubling after short syllables and then disappeared after both originally long and originally short syllables. After short syllables ending in *r*, however, *i̯* remains. These developments in loan-words are precisely parallel to those seen in native words (§§ 398.4, 407). Examples are *ċerfille* chervil, *mydd* bushel, *pytt* pit; *plȳme* plum, *spynġe* sponge, *strȳta* ostrich, *syrfe* service-tree, *ynne-* onion, *yntse* ounce; *pirġe* pear-tree, *sæþerie* savory; from Lat. *chaerefolium, modius, puteus, *prūnea, spongea, strūthio, *sorbea, *unnio* (§ 542, footnote), *uncia, *pirea, saturēia.*[3] But in later loan-words *i̯* remains, and causes no doubling,

[1] But by later borrowing or re-formation *ā* > *a* > *o*: *senap, senop, moraþ, morod, abbad, abbod* (cf. §§ 335–6 for similar developments of unaccented *a* to *o*).

[2] But perhaps the word was borrowed from French.

[3] Uninflected forms of *i̯a*-stems (Lat. *eo-, io*-stems) have *-e* (< vocalized *ii̯*), like native *ende, rīċe* (§ 355.3), e.g. *ċȳse* cheese, *cylle* bag, Lat. *cāseus, culleus.* Most such nouns, however, drop *-e* and pass into the *a*-declension: *belt* belt, *mynster* monastery, *pæll* pallium, *sċrīn* coffer, from Lat. *balteus, monastērium, pallium, scrīnium.*

e.g. *cuffie* hood, *feferfugie* feverfew, *oele* oil, *polleġie* pennyroyal, from Lat. **cuffia, febrifugia, oleum, pūlegium* (cf. § 542).

§ 513. Lat. *o* in hiatus is developed as *u̯* in OE loan-words, e.g. *alwe* aloe, *sideware* zedoary (§ 365), Lat. *aloe, zedoārium.*

§ 514. Final *-u* may be added to long syllable+short syllable, after the model of *hēafodu* (§ 353), e.g. *lempedu* lamprey, *tæppedu* n.p. carpets.

§ 515. Unaccented vowels are often lost in loan-words as in native words of similar pattern. Internal *i* and *u* are dropped after a long syllable in *pīsle* chamber, *tīgle* tile (beside *tīgele*), Lat. *pensilis, tēgula,* and the OE syncopation after short syllables (§ 388 ff.) is frequent, e.g. *antef(e)n* anthem, *cyl(e)n* kiln, *myl(e)n* mill, *seġne* net, *tæfl* gaming-board, from Lat. **antephŏna, culīna, molīna, sagēna, tabula.* But when no unsyncopated forms occur in OE, and when the vowel was post-tonic in Lat., Vulg. Lat. syncope is to be suspected, e.g. *ċæfl* halter, *finugle* fennel, *flȳtme* lancet, *prafost* officer, *sīġle* rye, are probably from Lat. **cap'lus,* **fēnuc'lum,* **flēt'ma,* **praepos'tus,* **sēc'le.* Similarly pre-tonic vowels were subject to loss in Vulg. Lat., hence OE *mynster* monastery, *miltestre* harlot, from Lat. **mon'stērium,* **mer'trīcem* (§ 541), and perhaps *ċerfille* chervil from **chaer'folium.*

§ 516. In a few words the stress was not retracted to the first syllable, but this was left unaccented and lost, e.g. *cyrfet* gourd, *stær* history, *rēnġe* spider, from Lat. *cucurbita, historia, arānea.* Vulg. Lat. prothetic *e* is never developed in OE loan-words, e.g. *spynġe, strȳta* quoted § 512.

§ 517. Parasiting takes place in loan-words as in native material. Instances in words already quoted are *ċeaster, clūster, copor, fefer, plaster, seġen, tempel*; cf. also § 509 on *cāwel, lāwer.* Note *Mæterne* Marne, < **Mætr̥ne* < Lat. **Matr'na* with post-tonic syncope.

§ 518. The phonological development of loan-words is often disturbed by the substitution of native suffixes for part of the Latin word. Some of these substitutions are already West Gmc. In particular, the suffix *-ere,* which sometimes reflects the cognate *-ārius, -āris* (e.g. *mynetere* moneyer, *sċolere* scholar, Lat. *monētārius, scholāris*) is freely extended to words which do not contain those Lat. suffixes, e.g. *fullere* fuller, *cantere* singer, *cāsere* emperor, Lat. *fullo, cantor, Caesar*; and so of things *cucelere* spoon,[1] *mortere*

[1] Here Lat. *o* was normally developed to *u* before *i̯* from *e* in hiatus (§§ 501,

mortar, *saltere* psalter from Lat. *cochlear*, *mortārium*, *psaltērium*. Other suffixes which appear in loan-words owing to substitution are:

-el, *-ol*:[1] these related suffixes often replace Lat. *-ell-*, *-ill-*, e.g. *ċytel* kettle, *ċeosol* hut, *eosol* ass, *mentel* cloak, *læfel* bowl, *sċamol* stool, *inseġel* seal, *teosol* die, cf. Lat. *catillus*, **casellum*, *asellus*, *mantellum*, *labellum*, *scamellum*, *sigillum*, *tessella*. Other instances of the transference of these suffixes are: *Eotol* Italy, *ċystel* chestnut-tree, cf. Lat. *Italia*, *castanea*.

-ele: *cugele* cowl, *fæcele* torch, *ferele* rod, *fifele* buckle, *-humele* hop-plant, cf. Lat. *cuculla*, *facula*, *ferula*, *fībula*, *humulus*.

-er, *-or*: *diner* coin, *pipor* pepper, *pundur* plumb-line, *sester* jar, *solor* chamber, cf. Lat. *dēnārius*, *piper*, *ponder-*, *sextārius*, *solārium*.

-en: this suffix corresponds etymologically to *-īn-*, e.g. *cypren* of copper, *Læden* Latin, Lat. *cuprīnus*, *Latīna*. It is extended in *byxen* of box, *piċen* of pitch, *Cristen* Christian, and in later formations without umlaut, e.g. *rosen* of roses; cf. Lat. *buxeus*, *piceus*, *Christiānus*, *roseus*.

-en, *-iċġe*, *-estre*: these fem. suffixes are extended to loan-words in *mynečenu* nun, *cāsern* empress,[2] *sealtiċġe* dancing-girl, *miltestre* harlot (cf. § 541.3).

-oc: *clīroc* clergyman, *munuc* monk, *persoc* peach, cf. Lat. *clēricus*, *monachus*, *persicum*.[3]

-isċ: this suffix often replaces *-ic-* in adjs. from names of races, e.g. *Arabisċ* Arabic; it is also extended to a few other words, e.g. *ġimmisċ* set with gems, *ċedrisċ* of cedar, *gramatisċ-* grammatical.

-iġ: *papiġ* poppy,[4] cf. Lat. *papāuer*.

Similar substitution of a native prefix occurs in *aspendan* spend, Lat. *expendere*.

§ 519. When a native suffix is extended to a loan-word it is naturally declined with its normal endings. Even if a native suffix

512); but the native suffix *-ǣri-* replaced the sounds developed from Lat. *-ear* before mutation took place.

[1] Earlier *-il*, *-ul*, and vocalic *l*, e.g. Cp. *lebil*, *tasul*, *lebl* for *læfel*, *teosol*.

[2] The suffix *-inni-* replaced *-anni̯-* from Lat. *-ane-* in **kastinni-* chestnut-tree, Lat. *castanea*, hence OE *ċistenbēam*, OHG *chestinna*.

[3] In later loan-words Lat. *-ic-* can be maintained without causing umlaut: *portiċ* porch, *tuniċe*, *-eċe* tunic, Lat. *porticus*, *tunica*.

[4] More frequently *popeġ* with unexplained *o*.

is not introduced, in early loan-words the Lat. declensional endings are replaced by native ones. Most m. and n. nouns of the Lat. second declension follow the *a*-declension in OE, e.g. *disċ* dish, *sealm* psalm, *clūster* bolt, *pund* pound, *teped* carpet, *wīn* wine, from Lat. *discus*, *psalmus*, *claustrum*, *pondo*, *tapētum*, *uīnum*. Some neuts. have become masc. in OE in whole or in part, e.g. *eċed* vinegar, *pīl* spike, *seġn* banner, from Lat. *acētum*, *pīlum*, *signum*. The fems. *laurus*, *synodus* become masc. in OE, *lāwer* laurel, *seonoþ* synod. Names of nations in *-i* are usually received into the *i*-declension in OE: *Ēgipte*, *Perse*, **Crēce* (once g.p. *-na*, beside *Crēcas*), &c. Many neut. pls. in *-a* are treated in OE as if fem. sg., and follow the *ō*-declension, e.g. *ċeaster* city, *peru* pear, or the *ōn*-declension, e.g. *butere* butter, *ċerfille* chervil, *earfe* tare, *flytme* lancet, *plūme* plum, *pise* pea, from Lat. *castrum*, *pirum*, *būtȳrum*, *chaerefolium*, *eruum*, **flētoma* (< *flebotomum*), *prūnum*, *pisum*.[1] The g.s. *sancti*, f. *sanctae* before names were retained in OE and both developed to *sancte* (§ 369).

§ 520. Nouns of the Lat. fourth declension become *a*-nouns in OE: *port* harbour, *portiċ* porch, *fers* verse (n.) from Lat. *portus*, *porticus*, *uersus*.

§ 521. Nouns of the Lat. first declension are mostly retained as fems. in OE, following either the *ō*-declension, e.g. *cylen* kiln, *earc* ark, *lempedu* lamprey, *strǣt* street, *tæfl* gaming-board, or the *ōn*-declension, e.g. *ælmesse* alms, *carte* document, *cugele* cowl, *mæsse* mass, *seġne* net, *sīde* silk, from Lat. *culīna*, *arca*, *lamprēda*, *strāta*, *tabula*, **alimosina*, *charta*, *cuculla*, *missa*, *sagēna*, *sēta*. Change to masc. gender is fairly frequent, e.g. *ancor* anchor, *ġimm* gem, *mylen* mill, *rǣdiċ* radish, *regol* rule, from Lat. *anchora*, *gemma*, *molīna*, **rādĭca*, **rĕgula*;[2] *mynet*, coin, becomes neut., Lat. *monēta*. Lat. *candēla* developed as a *i̯ō*-stem, OE *candel*, *-lle*.

§ 522. Lat. nouns in *-ea* and *-ia* mostly became OE *i̯ōn*- stems, e.g. *ċyrse* cherry, *pirġe* pear-tree, *plæce* place, *plȳme* plum, *spynġe* sponge, *syrfe* service-tree, from Lat. **cerasia*, **pirea*, *platea*, **prūnea*, *spongia*, **sorbea*. *Cemes*, shirt, is a *i̯ō*-stem, Lat. *camisia*. Lat. *ostrea*, oyster, was developed as an *ōn*-stem, and hence has no mutation, OE *ostre*. Lat. *uncia* develops as a *i̯ōn*-stem meaning 'ounce' (*yntse*), but as a masc. (? neut.) *i̯a*-stem meaning 'inch' (*ynċe*); on the difference of the consonants cf. §§ 532–3.

[1] Full list in Förster, *Flussname Themse*, p. 585.
[2] Full lists, ib., pp. 334–5.

§ 523. Lat. masc. nouns in *-ius*, *-eus*, and neuts. in *-ium*, *-eum*, can appear as *i̯o*-stems, with final *-e* after long syllables, consonant gemination after short ones, e.g. *ċȳse* cheese, *cylle* bag, *mydd* bushel, *pytt* pit, from Lat. *cāseus*, *culleus*, *modius*, *puteus*. Often, however, these nouns appear as *a*-stems, see § 512, footnote, although this change took place after mutation, as *belt* and *pæll* show. *Ele* oil, Lat. *oleum*, was borrowed too late for consonant gemination and hence retains *-i-* (> *-e*).

§ 524. Masc. and fem. *i*-stems and consonant stems of the Lat. third declension are mostly developed as *a*-nouns, based on the declined form of the Latin word; e.g.

i-stems: *fefer* fever, *post* post, *torr* tower, from Lat. *febris*, *postis*, *turris*.

cons.-stems: *font* font, *munt* mount, *part* part, *piċ* pitch, from Lat. *fontem*, *montem*, *partem*, *picem*.

Divergent developments appear in *bytt* cask (*i*-stem), *mertze* payment (? *i̯a*-stem), *stor* incense (*a*-stem, abnormal abbreviated form),[1] from Lat. *buttem*, *mercem*, *storacem*.

§ 525. Neut. nouns of the Lat. third declension mostly follow the OE *a*-declension, e.g. *alter* altar, *pipor* pepper, *pundur* plumb-line, from Lat. *altāre*, *piper*, *ponder-*. But *mīlia* is developed as a strong fem. sg., *mīl* mile; and **sīġle* rye, Lat. *sēcale*, passes into the weak declension (g.s. *sīġlan*).

§ 526. Lat. *n*-stems mostly appear in the OE weak declension, e.g. *draca* dragon, *pāwa* peacock, *strȳta* ostrich, from Lat. *dracōnem*, *pāuōnem*, *strūthiōnem*. But *punt*, punt, has passed to the *a*-declension, *ynne-*, onion, to the *i̯a*-declension, Lat. *pontōnem*, *ūniōnem*.

§ 527. The few OE adjs. borrowed from Lat. follow the *a*-declension, or when fem. the *ō*-declension, whether in adjectival or nominal use, e.g. *crisp* curly, *fals* falsehood, *Læden* Latin, *pīs* heavy, *sanct* saint, *sicor* secure, from Lat. *crispus*, *falsum*, *Latīna*, *pensus*, *sanctus*, *sēcūrus*.

§ 528. Verbs are taken into the weak conjugations, except the very early borrowing *sċrīfan* decree, Lat. *scrībere*. To the first weak

[1] There seems no reason for assuming that this word and the derived *steran*, burn incense, have *ō*, *ē*, as most dictionaries. Welsh *ystor* is perhaps from OE, not direct from Lat. (Förster, *ES* lxx. 49–54, would regard OE *stor* as from OIr. **stōr* < Vulg. Lat. *stōrax*, and *ystor* as from OE or direct from Irish).

conjugation belong *dihtan* direct, *glēsan* gloss,[1] *pynġan* prick, *aspendan* spend, *tyrnan* turn, from Lat. *dictāre*, *glōssāre*, *pungere*, *exspendere*, *tornāre*; and re-formed with a native element *salletan* sing, Lat. *psallere*. But most verbs pass into the second weak class, e.g. *þinsian* consider, *predician* preach, *trifolian* grind, *turnian* turn, from Lat. *pensāre*, *prædicāre*, *trībulāre*, *tornāre*, and re-formed with a native element *sċrūtnian* consider, Lat. *scrūtari*.

§ 529. In addition to the adjs. and verbs directly borrowed from Lat., others are very freely formed from borrowed nouns with native elements, e.g. *ġimmisċ* set with gems, *ġimbǣre* rich in gems, *beclȳsan* enclose, *cristnian* christen, *ġecyrtan* shorten (cf. Lat. *curtus*), *ġimmian* produce gems, *mæssian* say mass, *pīnian* torment, *sīman* load.

§ 530. **Consonants.** In Vulg. Lat. intervocalic *p*, *t*, *k* became first voiced and then open. Intervocalic *b*, *d*, *g* also became open. West Gmc. loan-words exhibit *v*, *d* or *ð* and *ʒ* for both series. Very early loan-words preserve the voiceless stops.[2] OE examples are:

p: *ċīpe* onion, *copor* copper, *nǣp* turnip, *pipor* pepper, *senop* mustard; *cæfester* halter, *prafost* officer, from Lat. *cēpa*, *cuprum*, *nāpus*, *piper*, *sināpi*, *capistrum*, *praepositus*.

t: *mynet* coin, *Sæterndæġ* Saturday, *strǣt* street, *trifetum* d.p. tributes; *abbod* abbot, *fiðele* fiddle, *Læden* Latin, *morað*, *morod* sweet wine, *sæþerie* savory, *tæpped* carpet, from *monēta*, *Sāturni-*, *strāta*, *tribūtum*, *abbātem*, *vītula*, *Latīna*, *mōrātum*, *saturēia*, *tapētum*.

k: *cyċene* kitchen, *draca* dragon; *cugele* cowl, *finugle* fennel, from *coquīna*, *draco*, *cuculla*, *fēnuculum*.

b: *fefer* fever, *tæfl* gaming-board, from *febris*, *tabula*.

d: *rǣdiċ* radish, *sinoð* synod, from **rādĭca*, *synodus*.[3]

g: *tīġle* tile, *regol* rule, from *tēgula*, **rĕgula*.

[1] Here and below the conventional view of the origin of *glēsan* is preferred to that of Ritter, *Vermischte Beiträge*, pp. 46–49.

[2] *Biscop* bishop, Lat. *episcopus* is of peculiar difficulty, for *p* is retained in the second syllable, but in the first becomes *b*. The intervocalic consonant of *epi-* probably became *b*, and this was retained in Gmc. with loss of the pretonic vowel (§ 516), for initial *b* was common in Gmc. The second *p* > *b*, but Gmc. substituted *p*, having no post-vocalic *b*. This suggests that Gmc. *p* replaced both Lat. *p* and *b*, and that Gmc. *v* indicates that the consonant had become open before the word was borrowed.

[3] Frequent *ð* (rarely *þ*) for *d* in classical, especially Gr., names, and occasionally in other classical words in the OE Orosius (both manuscripts) is unexplained, e.g. *Marðonius*, *Sarþinia*, *aðamans*; cf. Pogatscher, *Zur Lautlehre der . . . Lehnworte im Alteng.*, pp. 176–7; *Archiv* cxlvi. 132.

§ 531. Initially Lat. *p*, *t*, *k*, *b*, *d* were all represented by the corresponding native sounds (e.g. *peru*, *tæfl*, *copor*, *bytt*, *disċ*) but *ʒ* was used for *g*, and developed in OE as in native words, hence *ġimm* gem, but *glēsan* gloss, from *gemma*, *glōssāre*. In OE initial *k* was also fronted as in native words, e.g. *ċēast* strife, *ċӯse* cheese, *ċyst* box, from *causa*, *cāseus*, *cista*.

§ 532. Similarly in internal positions *k*, *ʒ*, and *g* were fronted (and in the case of *k*, *g* assibilated) in the same conditions as in native words. Fronted or assibilated sounds can be assumed in *eċed* vinegar, *ærċe-* archi-, *ynċe* inch, *pyleċe* robe, *polleġie* penny-royal, *spynġe* sponge, *pynġan* prick, from Lat. *acētum*, *archi-*, *uncia*, *pellicia*, *pūlegium*, *spongia*, *pungere*.

§ 533. In Vulg. Lat. *c* before *e* and *i*, and *t* before *i̯* (< *e*, *i* in hiatus) were developed to *ts*, and in some loan-words this stage is reflected, e.g. *mertze* payment, *yntse* ounce, *Profentse* Provence, *dracentse* dragon-wort, *plætse* place, *palendse* palace, from Lat. *mercem*, *uncia*, *Prouincia*, *dracontea*, *platea*, **palantium*. On various spellings for *ts* see § 53, and on *nts*, *ns* see § 477.1.

§ 534. In loan-words Lat. *ct*, *pt* > *ht*, *ft*, e.g. *cruft* crypt, *nefte* cat's mint, *dihtan* direct, *leahtriċ* lettuce, *traht* text, from Lat. *crypta*, *nepeta*, *dictāre*, *lactuca*, *tractus*. *ks* > *s* before a consonant in *sester* jar, Lat. *sextārius* (cf. § 417).[1] *ku̯* is preserved initially: *quatern* quaternion, Lat. *quaternio*; *cweartern* prison, if to Lat. *quartārium*; medially it becomes *k* or *g*; *cyċen* kitchen, *Sīgen* Seine, from Lat. *coquīna*, *Sēquana*. *Lēowe* league, Lat. *leuca* > *leuga*, shows a development of intervocalic *ʒ* (< *k*) as *u̯*.[2]

§ 535. The voiceless spirants *f* and *s* were preserved initially and in groups in Lat. loan-words, e.g. *fīċ* fig, *seġn* banner, *fals* falsehood, *disċ* dish, *clūster* bolt, from Lat. *fīcus*, *signum*, *falsum*, *discus*, *claustrum*. The group *sk* was subject to the same developments as in native words, hence assibilation is to be assumed initially (e.g. *sċolu*, *sċrin*), and in *disċ*, while metathesis occurs in *muxle* mussel (§ 440, footnote).[3]

§ 536. Intervocalic *f* and *s* were voiced in both the Vulg. Lat.

[1] Such consonant changes can be readily removed by influence of the Lat., hence e.g. *nepte*; note also *seoxter*, by influence of *seox* six.

[2] The development of *ʒ* here resembles that of *ʒu̯* before *u* in native words (§ 398.2), and hence the OE form should perhaps be derived from Vulg. Lat. **legua* (cf. *Arch. lat. lex.* iii. 510) > Prim. OE **leuu̯-*.

[3] On the abnormal assibilation in *biscop* cf. § 441, footnote.

and OE sound-systems, and so voicing can be assumed in loan-words, e.g. *scrofell* scrofula, *clūse*, *glēsan* (cf. § 543).

§ 537. *h* was silent in Vulg. Lat., and hence it is sometimes dropped in the spelling of loan-words, e.g. (*h*)*ymen* hymn, Lat. *hymnus*. In *sester* jar, Lat. *sextārius*, *ks*+cons. was developed like *χs*+cons. in native material (§ 417); so for *bises* intercalary day, read *bisest*, Lat. *bisextus*.

§ 538. The Gr. aspirated stops *ch*, *th* are developed as *c*, *t* in Lat. loan-words of ultimate Gr. origin, e.g. *carte* document, *Crist* Christ, *ærċe*- arch-, *tyriaca* antidote, from Lat. *charta*, *Christus*, *archi*-, *thēriaca*.[1] But divergent Lat. developments of *ph* to *p* and *f* are reflected, e.g. *ampelle* flask, but *antefen* anthem, *græf* style, from Lat. *ampulla*, **antephona*, *graphium*.

§ 539. *u̯* remains in the oldest loan-words, e.g. *weall* wall, *wīn* wine, *pāwa* peacock, *mealwe* mallow, from Lat. *uallum*, *uīnum*, *pāuo*, *malua*. In *cāwel* basket, from *cauellum*, Lat. -*auel*- is developed like -*aul*- (§ 509). But *u̯* > *v* in Vulg. Lat. and this is preserved medially in OE, e.g. *earfe* tare, *salfie* sage, from Lat. *eruum*, *saluia*, while initially *f* was substituted for it, in accordance with the OE sound-system, e.g. *fann* fan, *fers* verse, from Lat. *uannus*, *uersus*.[2]

§ 540. On the development of *i̯* from *e* or *i* in hiatus, see § 512.

§ 541. The following points may be noticed concerning the development of liquids and nasals in loan-words:

(1) *ns* > *s* with compensatory lengthening of the preceding vowel in Vulg. Lat., hence OE *Custantin* Constantine, *mīse* table, *pīs* heavy, from Lat. *Constantinus*, *mensa*, *pensus* (cf. § 506). *Pensāre*, consider, seems to have been at first a learned word, and hence was borrowed with *ns*, which remained in OE *pinsian* (and so French *penser*).

(2) Loss of final *n* after *ī* occurs in loan-words as in native material (§ 473), e.g. *pyle* pillow, *sæppe* fir, from Lat. *puluīnus*, *sappīnus*.

(3) In a number of words *r*–*r* > *l*–*r* or *r*–*l*: *miltestre* harlot < **mirtestre* from Lat. *meretrīcem* (§§ 501, 518); *turtle* turtle (beside *turtur*) from Lat. *turtur*; North. *purple* purple (infl. adj.; W-S

[1] Occasionally in loan-words and biblical names *þ* is written for *th*, e.g. *þeater*, *Þracia*, *biblioþece*. *tþ*, *tð* are also found, e.g. *Iūditþe*, *Bitðinia*.

[2] This spelling of initial *u̯* continues in purely literary loan-words (e.g. *Firgilius*, *Fulcania*), and Irish influence has been suggested (see *Archiv* cxlvi. 131).

purpure, noun), from Lat. *purpura*. But *cellendre*, coriander, is from Lat. *coliandrum* < *coriandrum*.

(4) Intrusion of *r* occurs in *leahtriċ* lettuce,[1] Lat. *lactūca*.

(5) Loss of *r* occurs in *lempedu* lamprey, Lat. *lamprēda*.

(6) Metathesis of *r* occurs in *cyrps* curly (beside *crisp*), Lat. *crispus* (cf. §§ 459.1, 460.4); and reciprocal metathesis of *r* and *s* in *ċisir-*, *ċiser-* cherry (beside *ċiris-*), Lat. **cerasia* (modified to **kirisịō* with Gmc. suffix).

(7) Isolated abnormalities in *plūme*, *plȳme* plum, Lat. *prūnum*, **prūnea*; *eolone* elecampane, Lat. *inula*.[2]

§ 542. Geminate consonants are normally preserved in loan-words, both when original and when due to gemination before *ị*, e.g. with original geminates *abbod* abbot, *mæsse* mass, *sacc* sack, from Lat. *abbātem*, *missa*, *saccus*; for examples of geminates before *ị* see § 512. A pre-tonic vowel (whether originally short, or shortened as described above, § 503) can develop a following double consonant in Vulg. Lat., and this can be preserved in OE, e.g. OE *tæpped* carpet, *polleġie* pennyroyal, *ynne-* onion,[3] Lat. *tapēte*, *pūlegium*, *ūniōnem*.[4]

§ 543. Latin geminates are sometimes shortened in OE when they stood before the vowel which bore the accent in Lat., e.g. *pileċe* robe, *teosol* die. Lat. *pellicia*, *tessella*. But *glēsan* is from Lat. *glōsa* < *glōssa*.

§ 544. **Abnormal developments.** A number of loan-words are not developed purely phonologically, but one of the following processes intervenes:

(1) An OE equivalent is substituted for an element of the Lat. word, e.g. *feferfugie* feverfew, *sōlsēċe* heliotrope, from Lat. *febrifugia*, *sōlsequium*.

(2) More frequently an OE word is substituted for an element

[1] On various forms of this word see § 544.2.

[2] OE *elene* is from Lat. *helenium*, and its existence seems to have promoted reciprocal metathesis in **eonole* < Lat. *inula* (unless Vulg. Lat. had already **iluna*), hence *eolone*; further mixture produces *eolene*, *elone*.

[3] Not to *ŭniōnem* as the composition form in *-e-* points to an original long first syllable, not to gemination after a short syllable (§ 359); in the latter case the composition form would be **yne-* or **yn-* (§ 348).

[4] *Cellendre* coriander (beside *celendre*), Lat. *coliandrum* (§ 541.3), seems to belong here, for the fluctuation between *ll* and *l* in OE suggests conflicting Lat. forms rather than the consistent native gemination before *ị*, and the latter process should not take place in company with the late mutation *o* > *oe*, *e* (as in *oele*, § 502).

of a borrowed word, with which, aided by a resemblance of sound, it had been falsely identified, as *Eofor*wiċ, *Ġeo*weorþ*a* are derived from *Eboracum*, *Iu*gurth*a* (§ 321). Examples are *ānpolle* (beside *ampulle*, § 511) flask, regarded as a measure and connected with *ān* one;[1] *biscopwyrt* betony, Lat. *hibiscum*; *carcern* prison, Lat. *carcer*, the ending being assimilated to *-ern* house (as in *bēodern*, § 372); *codæppel* quince, Lat. *malum cydonium*; *-lēctriċ* < **lēactriċ*, modified from *leahtriċ* (§§ 534, 541.4) by influence of *lēac*;[2] *lufestiċe* lovage, Lat. *lubestica*; *swiftlere* slipper < **suftlere*, Lat. *subtālāris*. Two elements of a borrowed word can fall under the influence of native words, e.g. *meregrot* pearl, Lat. *margarīta*, associated with *mere* sea, and *grot* particle;[3] *oflǣte* offering, Lat. *oblāta*, with association of the first element with OE *of-*, and of the second with *-lǣte* (as in *ǣlǣte* desert). The same process may be suspected elsewhere, e.g. *ælmesse*, alms, has in the first syllable confusion with the OE prefix *æl-*, as in OHG *alamuosan* (Lat. **alimōsina*); *lǣwede* lay, if from Lat. *laicus*, must be re-formed as if connected with *-lǣw* weakness, lack;[4] *amber* a measure, Lat. *amphora*, seems to undergo early West Gmc. modification due to assumed connexion with *beran* bear (OHG *einbar*, OS *embar*).

(3) Abnormal reductions of words sometimes occur, e.g. *ælmesse*, for **ælmōēsinæ* with *ss* of doubtful origin, *fille* (and hence *wudufille*) for *ċerfille*; *glæs*, *næglæs* for *cuneglæsse*; *stor* incense, from Lat. *storacem*.

c. Later Latin Loan-words

§ 545. Some distinction of early and late or popular and learned Latin loan-words in Old English is made by all authorities, and some distinguish from both a third group of 'foreign words' used without genuine assimilation into the language. In the present work a distinction is made between early loan-words which show modifications owing to native and Vulgar Latin sound-changes, and later ones, which are taken not from Vulgar Latin but from the learned Latin of the Middle Ages, in the pronunciation of which the phonological changes of Vulgar Latin were largely eliminated,

[1] Cf. OHG *einbar*, Lat. *amphora*; and OE *seoxter* for *sester* (§ 534).

[2] But *lēactrog*, *-troc* cluster, seems to be a different word.

[3] Cf. OS, OHG *merigriota*, *-grioz*, where the second element is 'gravel' (OE *grēot*).

[4] Cf. Lotspeich, *JEGP* xl. 3.

but in which the loan-words show considerable modifications of the classical quantities to have prevailed. In general, the first group will contain all sorts of words, the second mainly ones of a literary type. The second group will contain late re-borrowings of many words found in the first, e.g. *calic*, *dracontie*, *lactuce*, *palant*, *spongean* (a.s.), *istoriam*, beside older *ċelċ*, *dracentse*, *leahtriċ*, *palendse*, *spynġe*, *stær*. The distinction is, however, difficult to maintain. Some words probably came from monastic not Vulgar Latin, yet were borrowed early enough to undergo native sound-changes, e.g. *dracentse*, with umlaut in the medial syllable, yet without the Vulgar Latin change of intervocalic *c* > *g* (Lat. *dracontea*). Other words lack distinguishing criteria entirely, e.g. *salm* may be a late re-borrowing beside *sealm*, or merely an Anglian form. It has been emphasized in the preceding sections that there are many stages in the borrowing of loan-words (cf. §§ 496–8, 500, 502, 508–9, 512, 530). The sections below aim at describing the development of what appear to be the latest group of borrowings, but do not claim infallibility in the apportionment of words to it.

§ 546. Words of the latest group of borrowings generally reproduce the Latin vowels and consonants in writing without change, and it is uncertain how far their pronunciation was modified to conform with the normal sounds of OE, e.g. whether *ċ* and *ġ* developed as in native words.[1] It will appear below that *i* and *e* in hiatus become readily non-syllabic, so that e.g. *Gregorius*, *Bersabea* could be trisyllabic. Various other modifications are clearly due to OE native practice: an OE diphthong is introduced in *dēacon* beside *diacon*; the loss of unaccented initial syllables (§ 516) is repeated in *postol* apostle, *pistol* letter, Lat. *apostolus*, *epistola*, and in many names like *Commedia* Nicomedia, *Thrusci* Etruscans, *Spāneas* Spaniards, *Paminund* Epaminondas;[2] *g* is written for *i̯*, and *ig* for *i*, e.g. *Aquileġia*, *Uiġenna*, *Assyriġe*; some modifications like *f* for *ph* (*Fenix*, *Filistina*) and for initial *u̯* (*Firgilius*) occur. While the classical Lat. intervocalic stops are

[1] See on this question Pyles, *PMLA* lviii. 900–9. Alliteration shows that initial *ps*, *z* were pronounced *s* (see *Ps.* xci. 3; *Rid.* 41, 68), and that initial *sc* could be modified to the contemporary state of native *sċ* (see *Met.* 1, 2). The frequent spelling *sċrūdnian* beside *sċrūtnian* (Lat. *scrūtinare*) would seem to reflect native voicing of *t* before *n*.

[2] In later loan-words loss of internal syllables is unusual, e.g. *organe* marjoram, Lat. *orīganum*.

mostly written unchanged (e.g. *capitul*, *meter*, *diacon*, *Arabisċ*), it would seem that a spirantal pronunciation of *b* prevailed, and it can be written *f* or *u*, e.g. *safine*, *sauine* savine, Lat. *sabīna*, and names like *Galua* Galba, and hence inverted spellings like *Iōbes* g.s. Jove, Lat. *Iouis*.

§ 547. The earlier Lat. loan-words of OE show shortening of pre-tonic Lat. vowels (§ 503), but not shortening of accented vowels before two unaccented syllables, e.g. *clēricus*, *tēgula* are developed in OE as *clīroc*, *tīġle*;[1] similarly there is no evidence for lengthening accented vowels in open syllables when one unaccented syllable followed, e.g. *peru*, *sċolu*, Lat. *pirum*, *schola*. On the other hand, the later loan-words reflect a pronunciation of Lat. in which accented vowels had been shortened before two following syllables, e.g. *cleric*, *lilie*, Lat. *clēricus*, *līlium*; while they had been lengthened in open syllables when one unaccented syllable followed, e.g. *cōc* cook, *grād* degree, *scōl* school, *sōn* sound, *stōl* stole, Lat. **cocus* < *coquus*, *gradus*, *schola*, *sonus*, *stola*;[2] so OE *prōfian*, hold guilty, has *ō* from disyllabic forms of Lat. *probāre*.

§ 548. Late loan-words, like early ones, transferred the main stress to the first syllable, but a strong half-stress remained on the syllable which had borne the main stress in Lat., so that the accentuation *mágìster* arose. Now in the native system, a half-stress on a medial formative syllable only existed after long syllables, and hence, if the half-stress was maintained, the accented vowel had to be lengthened to give the normal native pattern *mā́gìster* like *ṓpèrne*. Accordingly we find verse evidence for long vowels in *māgister* master, and in *cālend* calend, *gīgant* giant, *sācerd* priest, following the inflected forms *cā́lèndas*, &c., and also in *Rōmane* Romans, Lat. *Rōmānī*, where the first syllable would be shortened pretonically and then re-lengthened in OE. We cannot tell how

[1] There is very little evidence in early OE loan-words for Lat. shortening of accented vowels in antepenultimate syllables. *Regol* rule, Class. Lat. *rēgula* is a certain instance as it can undergo back umlaut (§ 210.3), and the unsyncopated medial vowels in *fifele* buckle, *fiðele* fiddle, *tigele* tile (beside *tīgle* < *tēgula*) may point to short vowels in the first syllables. *Butere* butter, Lat. *būtȳrum*, has prevailingly no syncopation, so is perhaps from Lat. **bŭtĭrum*; less frequent *butre* would belong to § 388. The loan-word is latish, as no umlaut took place, and medial *t* points to a monastic rather than a popular origin (see § 545). The composition form is Cp. *buter-*, Ep., Erf. with suffix mixture *butur-*, lW-S *buttor-* (with *-tt-* from **buttre*, § 453).

[2] Of course the inflected form may determine the quantity of words imparisyllabic in Latin, e.g. *calic* < *calicem*. *Fenix* has a short first syllable irregularly, perhaps from mistaken declined forms *Phoenĭcem*, &c. (*AB* xxviii. 41–42).

far other words of similar pattern had lengthening, or if they abandoned the half-stress, e.g. *decan*, *safine*, Lat. *decānus*, *sabīna*. Conversely, a syllable short in Lat. receives a half-stress in OE because a long syllable precedes in *áspide* asp, Lat. *aspidem*.

§ 549. The Biblical and classical names in OE verse mainly follow the same principles of accent and quantity as the later loan-words. Hence disyllables have usually a long first syllable, e.g. *Ādam*, *Iūdith*, *Plāton*. This long syllable is maintained in inflected forms, and causes the middle syllable to acquire a light half-stress, like native *Bēowùlfes*, which is similarly neglectable in verse, e.g. *Ā́dàmes*, *Iā́còbes*.[1] There are no certain exceptions to the rule that the first syllable of a disyllabic name is long even in inflected forms, except *Tile*.

§ 550. Trisyllabic names which had a long penultimate, which accordingly had the accent in Lat., retain the Lat. accent as a half-stress, and hence (like *mā́gìster*) have a long first syllable, whatever the history of the vowel, e.g. *Ā́gùstus*, *Ṓmèrus*, *Nṓuèmbris*, *Dḗcèmbris*, and so with a closed first syllable *Albàno* d.s., *Septèmbris*. Trisyllabic names which had the Lat. accent on the first syllable, have in OE a short first syllable and no half-stress, e.g. *Babilon*, *Elene*, *Nineue*, *Lucifer*, *Salomon*. Lengthened inflected forms have a secondary stress on the penultimate, e.g. *Bábilònes*. But the two types are sometimes confused, e.g. *Lī́bànus*, *Stḗphànus* (Lat. *Libanus*, *Stephanus*) are developed in OE as if containing the formative element *-ān-* (as in *Rōmānus*). *Sodome* (and its derivatives *Sodome* Sodomites, *Sodomisċ*) would by rule have *ŏ*, but *Gomorre* would have *ō*: but these names already influence each other in Lat. verse, and in OE *Gomorre* shortens the first vowel and rejects half-stress on the second when linked by *ond* to *Sodome* in one half-line (*Gen.* 1926, 1966, 2008, 2505). Beside *Sodome* there occurs infl. *Sṓdòme* from disyllabic **Sōdom* (cf. *Sōdomware*). *Sḗràphin* (El. 755), beside normal *Seraphin*, *Cheruphin* is due to treating the word correctly as an inflexion of **Sēraph*.

§ 551. Names of four syllables usually take the form –́ × –̀ ×, e.g. *Ā́gamèmnon*, *Ā́gustìnus*, *Hṓlofèrnus*, and so with closed first syllable *Cónstantìnus*. Some, however, have a short first syllable, e.g. *Abimēlech*, *Benedictus*, and so *basilisca*. *Ā́pollìnus*, *Fīlistìna*, *Hiérusàlem* usually follow the latter type with short first syllables, more rarely the former.

§ 552. Of polysyllabic names, *Elamitare* is perhaps ⏑́⏑ × –̀ × like native *Ligoraċeaster*, while the handling of *Nabochodonossor* is uncertain.[2]

[1] e.g. *ne þæt Iā́cobes god*, Ps. xciii. 7, with which contrast *ond Iā́cóbes*, id. lxxxiii. 7; conversely, in disyllabic forms, as in native words of similar structure, the final syllable may be given half-stress, e.g. *Iābal noma* (Gen. 1078) like *Hrunting nama* (§ 90, footnote).

[2] See metrical appendix to K. R. Brooks's edition of *Andreas* (Oxford dissertation, unpublished).

§ 553. Trisyllabic names with *e* and *i* in hiatus usually follow the above rules, and hence long vowels appear in the first syllable and half-stress with metrical length on the vowel in hiatus in words like *Iū́dèas*, *Mắthèas*, *Mắrìa* following the type *Ắgùstus*.[1] Contrast words with the Lat. accent on the first syllable, which follow the type *Bắbilon*, e.g. *Iulius*, *Iunius*, *Libia*, *Siria*.[2] Synizesis is rarely demonstrable, e.g. *weo̯rcum Ebre̯a*, Cri. 67.

§ 554. Names of four syllables with hiatus *i* in the second conform to the type *Ắgamèmnon*, e.g. *Ắrriằnus*, *Cȳ́riằcus*, *Iū́liằna*. But those with hiatus *i* in the third syllable form ⊥́⊥́◡̀ ×, e.g. *Grḗgṓrìus*, *Ī́tā́lìa*. Synizesis occurs in both types, producing ⊥́⊥̀ ×, e.g. *Cȳ́ri̯ằcus*, *Grḗgṑri̯us*.

§ 555. Names of four syllables with hiatus *e* in the third syllable are treated as ◡̲́ × ⊥̀ × (types *Ắgamèmnon* or *Bénedìctus*), e.g. *Hḗlisḕus*, *Cánanḕa* (g.p.). Synizesis with shift of the secondary accent to the second syllable is allowed, e.g. *Ámmòrre̯a* (g.p.), *Bérsàbe̯a*, *Gắlìle̯am*.

§ 556. Names of five syllables containing *e* or *i* in hiatus are usually reduced to four syllables by synizesis, and then conform to the type *Ắgamèmnon*, e.g. *Bártholṑme̯us*, *Cámpotàne̯a*, *Máximi̯ằnes*, *Mérmedṑni̯a*.

§ 557. Vowels other than *e* and *i* in hiatus are often subject to synizesis. Disyllables are rarely so reduced to monosyllables (e.g. *Cāam*, *Cāin*, *Mōab*, *Nōe*, *Sīon*) but their inflected forms may be either ⊥́⊥̀ × or ⊥́ ×, e.g. contrast *Cā́ī́nes*, Gen. 1249, with *Cā̯́ines*, id. 1066. In names of three syllables, synizesis is freely allowed, changing the word to the disyllabic type (*Ắdam*), e.g. *Iṓ͜hannis* beside *Iṓhànnis*. It is sometimes indicated in spelling, e.g. (infl.) *Ā́rònes*, *Ī́sàce*, *Fā́rònes* beside *Ā́arònes*, *Ī́saàce*, *Fáraònes*. Here may be mentioned the scriptural doublets *Abra(ha)m*, *Bethle(he)m*, *Sarra(i)*, which are used for metrical convenience (sometimes against the manuscript spelling). Of four syllable names, synizesis can take place in *Malalēhel*, so that ◡́ × ⊥̀ × becomes ◡́◡̀ ×.

§ 558. In the quantitative patterning of foreign names, syllabic length seems to have been sometimes obtained by consonantal rather than by vocalic lengthening, and hence gemination often appears, e.g. *Commedia*, *Sarra*, and so *Sciððia* (Met. 1, 2), *Zefferus* (Rid. 41, 68), both incorrectly scanned as ⊥́⊥́ ×. Some of these geminates are, however, pure errors, e.g. *Annanias*, *Effessia*.

§ 559. The later loan-words, like the earlier ones, are freely assimilated into the OE declensional system. Hence masc. nouns of the Lat. second and fourth declensions are usually received into

[1] These half-stresses may be neglected in verse, e.g. contrast *wæs hira Mắtheus sum*, And. 11, with *þa wæs Mắthḗus*, id. 40.

[2] But poets sometimes confuse the two types, and, for example, scan *Sciððia*, *Þracia* as ⊥́ ⊥̀ ×.

the OE *a*-declension, e.g. *angel* angel, *cleric* ecclesiastic, *decan* dean; *accent* accent, *grād* degree.[1] Similarly neuts. of the second declension, e.g. *castel* village, *cantic* canticle (masc. in OE). A few become weak in OE, e.g. *basilisca* basilisk, *cristalla* crystal.

§ 560. Nouns of the first Lat. declension generally become fem. weak nouns in OE, e.g. *albe* alb, *murre* myrrh, *safine* savine; so Lat. nouns in *-ea*, *-ia*, e.g. *dracente* dragon-wort, *sponge* sponge. A large number of fem. nouns of the first declension become masc. strong nouns in OE, e.g. *cālend* calend, *epact* epact, *nōn* ninth hour, *pistol* letter, *reliquias* p. relics. But *glōria* hymn of praise, *crisma* (late Lat. f.) chrism, are masc. weak nouns in OE. Masc. nouns of the first declension become masc. weak nouns in OE, e.g. *baptista* baptist, *cometa* comet, *pāpa* pope.

§ 561. Lat. nouns in *-ium* mostly become weak fems. in OE, e.g. *centaurie* centaury, *marubie* horehound, and this ending is extended to *alexandrie* alexanders (Lat. *-īnum*). But *palant*, *palent* palace (cf. § 533) is masc.

§ 562. Third declension masc. and fem. nouns follow the OE masc. *a*-declension, e.g. *calic* cup, *centur* centurion, *dēmon* demon, *part* part, *trāmet* pąge (*Li.* path).

§ 563. Very often, however, late loan-words retain their Lat. declensional endings in whole or in part, e.g. *confessores*, *cristallum*, *istoriam*, *passio*, *-onem*, *paradisus*, *-um*, *-o*, *tigris*, *-es*; so with a Gr. ending *paralisin*. Neut. *-e* of the third declension is usually retained, e.g. *altare* altar, *scapulare* scapular. So many names, e.g. *Constantinus*, *-o*, but g. *-es*; *Holofernus*, all cases, but g. also *-es*; *Saducei*, beside *-eas*; to g. *Apollines* is formed n. *Apollinus*; *Siria*, *Þracia* serve as g.

§ 564. As in the earlier borrowings there are many instances of the addition of native suffixes to foreign words, especially *-ere*, *-isċ*, and verbs in *-ian*, e.g. *grammaticere* grammarian, *mechanisċ* mechanical, *tigrisċ* of tigers, *capitulian* divide into chapters, *declinian* decline.

D. Celtic Loan-words

§ 565. Place-names, especially river-names, were heavily borrowed from the language of the conquered British (Old British) by the English, and Celtic elements are also common in English

[1] In §§ 559–63 the Lat. forms of the examples are not given, as either they are very familiar words, or their forms are obvious from the loan-words.

place-names. Borrowings of this type are often difficult in form, and the attempt to deal with them in a general grammar of OE would make excessive demands on space.[1] The number of other words which may be reasonably regarded as borrowed from British into OE is small: Förster accepted[2] as such fourteen words, but of these others have queried the Celtic origin of *bannuc* bit, *becca* fork, *carr* rock, *dunn* dark (§ 404, footnote), *gafeluc* spear, *mattuc* mattock, and have doubted if *toroc*, bung, is an OE word. One certain addition has been made to Förster's list, *torr* rock. Förster also accepted six words as certain borrowings from OIr. into OE. Of these the most important are *drȳ*, magician, where *ui* is developed as *ȳ*, corresponding to the process in native words by which *ū* is mutated by, and then absorbs, immediately following *i* (§ 237; cf. BH *Lyc̈c̈idfelth* Lichfield < Brit. **Luitgęd*), and *cross* cross (in OE only in the place-name *Normannes Cross*), which clearly is from OIr. *cross*, though borrowing through ON is possible. Förster holds to the principle that borrowings from OIr. into OE would be of an exclusively monastic nature, but it is doubtful if this is the case: OE *bratt*, cloak, would be more readily derived from OIr. than OBrit. (Förster has to regard it as an OIr. loan-word in OBrit.), and OE *assa*, ass, is perhaps from OIr. **assan* (MIr. *assan*), rather than OBrit. **assin*. The *ss* in this word and in OE *assen*, she-ass, is in either event of Celtic origin. In Förster's list of Irish loan-words in OE *stær*, history, is uncertain (§ 507), but *ancora*, anchorite, may be added (to OIr. *anchara*, rather than direct to Lat. *anachoreta*).

E. Scandinavian Loan-words

§ 566. The great influx of Scandinavian words into OE caused by the Norse settlements in England is not fully reflected in OE texts, and the development of these words is mainly a branch of ME studies. The Scandinavian loan-words recorded in OE texts are mainly ones for ideas, persons, or things, which were either peculiarly Scandinavian, or of which the OE conception had been modified by contact with the Scandinavian civilization. Naturally,

[1] See Section N of the Bibliography for the principal works touching upon Celtic names in English.

[2] *Keltisches Wortgut im Englischen*, § 1. For the chief criticisms of and supplements to this work, see Bibliography, Section N.

they are found chiefly in late texts, especially in the *Chronicle* after 1000. Complete or partial assimilation to the native sound- and inflexional system is frequent. Examples are: ***brȳdlop*** bridal, ***butsecarl*** sailor, ***fēolaga*** partner, ***genge*** troop, ***grið*** truce, ***hamele*** rowlock, ***hāsæta*** oarsman, ***lagu*** law, ***lið*** fleet, ***liðsmen*** sailors, ***nīðing*** evil man, ***tīdung*** news, ***þēonestmen*** retainers, ***þrǣl*** thrall, ***unwine*** enemy, ***ūtlaga*** outlaw, ***wīcing*** pirate,[1] of which the ON forms in classical Icel. spelling[2] are ***brúðlaup***, ***buza*** boat+***karl*** man, ***félagi***, ***gengi***, ***grið***, ***hamla***, ***háseti***, ***lög***, ***lið***, ***liðsmenn***, ***níðingr***, ***tíðindi***, ***þjónostumenn***, ***þrǽll***, ***úvinr*** enemy, ***útlagi***, ***víkingr***. Interesting sound-substitutions occur in ***ċeallian*** call,[3] ***cnearr*** ship, ***seaht*** peace, ***wrāng*** wrong, OIcel. ***kalla***, ***knörr***, ***sátt*** (< ****saht-***), ***rangr*** (< ****wrang-***). The OE poetical word ***eorl***, man, was identified with Prim. ON ****earl***, OIcel. ***jarl*** earl, and was used for it. Loan-words may be combined with native formative elements, e.g. ***griþleas*** without protection, ***lahliċe*** lawfully. Partial translation of compounds also occurs, e.g. ***lahbryċe*** breach of law (cf. ON ***lögbrot***).

F. French Loan-words

§ 567. In OE no loan-words which can certainly be regarded as French occur in manuscripts older than 1066, except ***prūd***, ***prūt*** proud, whence are derived ***prȳte*** (f. wk.), ***prȳt*** (f. st.) pride.[4] There are, of course, a few words like ***capun***, ***castel***, which might be derived from Latin or French. Even after 1066 French words flow into the literary language more slowly than Norse ones, and they do not occur frequently till the last hand of the *OE Chron.* begins (1132, MS. E). Before that year *Chron.* has only ***serfis***, ***prisun***; Aldhelm Glosses (MS. Digby 146) add ***iugeleras*** n.p., ***-a*** g.p., glossing various words for 'magician'.

[1] The word is early (already *Ep.*, *Erf.*, *Cp.*), and may well be native, but its established use for the Scandinavian rovers is due to the fact that these called themselves *víkingar*.

[2] This reflects a later phonological state of ON than that reflected by the OE loan-words.

[3] Unless the word is native, cf. *hildecalla* herald, *Ex.* 252.

[4] On the phonological relationship of *prūd*, *prȳte* see *OED*, s.v. *pride* sb. Note *KG* 249 *prēde* (noun, cf. Williams, *Gramm. investigation of OKt. glosses*, p. 165), with substitution of typical Kt. *ē* for *ȳ*.

XI

NOUNS

§ 568. In Indo-European nouns were divided into (*a*) vowel stems, in which the case-endings were added to a stem ending in a characteristic vowel or diphthong, which might itself be subject to ablaut variation, and (*b*) consonant stems, in which the case-endings were added to a stem ending in a consonant. A sub-class of (*b*) were the *n*-stems, in which endings were added to a stem formed with *-ĕn-*, *-ŏn-*, or *-n-* (the variation was again due to ablaut), e.g. acc. sg. Lat. *sermōn-em*, Gr. *ποιμέν-α*. The *n*-stems are of great importance in Germanic, where they are known as the Weak Declension, while the vowel stems are known as the Strong Declensions. Consonant declensions other than the weak declension had only a limited survival in Germanic. In this book they are grouped together as Minor Declensions.

§ 569. In the Late Northumbrian dialect of OE there is considerable confusion in the declensional system in *Li.* and *Rit.*, while in *Ru.*[2] it is comparatively well preserved.[1] Other dialects show little decay of the declensional system except in the very late texts. In this *Grammar*, West Saxon paradigms are presented, and the forms of other dialects are mentioned when they diverge from them. No attempt is made to notice all the forms arising in Late Northumbrian and *Ru.*[1] from the confusion of unaccented vowels described in § 379, footnote, nor even all the forms which arise in other dialects for the same reason (e.g. neut. pl. in *-a* for *-u*, *-o*, gen. pl. in *-o* for *-a*, past pl. in *-an* for *-on*), and which are sufficiently covered by § 377.

[1] See U. Lindelöf, *Mémoires de la société néo-philologique à Helsingfors* i. 219 ff.; A. S. C. Ross, *JEGP* xxxv. 321 ff. Outstanding results of the decay of the declensional system in *Li.* and *Rit.* are: (1) gen. sg. *-es* is extended from the *a*-nouns, and is used beside the older forms in most other classes, e.g. *ō*-nouns and weak nouns; (2) similarly nom. acc. pl. *-as* is extended from masc. *a*-nouns to neuts., and to other declensions; (3) nom. acc. pl. neut. *-o*, *-a* (< *-u*) are extended from neut. *a*-nouns with short root syllables to those with long ones; (4) the distinction in nom. sg. of masc. and fem. weak nouns disappears, and both end prevailingly in *-a*, while the neuts. have *-o*, *-u* in all sg. cases and in nom. acc. pl.

A. Strong Declensions

I. *a*-NOUNS (MASC. AND NEUT.)

a. PURE *a*-NOUNS

§ 570.

	Masculine	Neuter	
Sg.			
Nom.	stān, *stone*	sċip, *ship*	word, *word*
Acc.	stān	sċip	word
Gen.	stānes	sċipes	wordes
Dat.	stāne	sċipe	worde
Pl.			
Nom.	stānas	sċipu	word
Acc.	stānas	sċipu	word
Gen.	stāna	sċipa	worda
Dat.	stānum	sċipum	wordum

§ 571. Origin of forms. The Prim. Gmc. forms of the above masc. case-endings were sg. *-az*, *-am*, *-as* (< *oso*, § 331.1), *-ai*, pl. *-ôs*, *-ôs* (extended from nom.), *-ôm*, *-umiz* (§ 331.6). These endings were developed in OE in accordance with the principles explained in Chapter VII. The gen. sg. and nom. pl. endings were those proper to nouns with the I-E accent on the endings, for in nouns with the accent elsewhere *s* would have become *z* and dropped in West Gmc. (§§ 398.2, 404).[1] The dat. sg. is generally used also in the functions of the instrumental and locative. In early texts, where the dat. sg. is still in *-æ*, forms in *-i* are found, and while they are mainly (so far as can be determined) instrumental, the form was probably originally locative in function, and derived from Gmc. *-ī*, I-E *-ei* (cf. Gr. *οἴκει*), developed according to § 355.1. This *-i* causes neither harmonization of *e* (§ 112) nor umlaut in the preceding syllable in extant forms, the vowel of the other cases having been extended through the paradigm.[2] Except in very early texts *-i* falls together with *-e* (< *æ*, § 369). There are also endingless forms in locative function of which the origin is obscure (discussion and references I. Dahl, *Substantival inflexion in early OE*, pp. 48 ff.). The

[1] The development of the I-E accented ending in the nom. pl., and its extension to acc. pl., was probably an Ingvaeonic peculiarity, for though it is traceable only in OE and OS, the recorded endings of OFris. are probably secondary; see Hammerich in *Acta Jutlandica* ix (*Mélanges . . . offerts à m. H. Pedersen*), p. 356.

[2] Note, however, mutation in the adverbial forms *ǣne* once, *hwōene* a little.

neuter nouns differed from masculines in Gmc. only in the nom. sg., which ended in *-om* like the acc., and in the nom. and acc. pl., which ended in *-ō*. The distinction was lost in OE in the nom. sg., but it persisted in the nom. and acc. pl., where *-ō* became *-ū* in West Gmc. (§ 331.5), which was retained as *-u* in OE after short syllables, but dropped after long ones.

§ 572. **Early, late, and dialectal forms.** The gen. and dat. sg. appear frequently as *-æs*, *-æ* in early texts. The original locative function of the case in *-i* appears in *on bergi*, Thornhill Cross II,[1] and in the temporal *thys ġēri*, Ep. 494.[2] Other instances of the form are Cp. *spelli*, *ðrēsi*, *werci*, and from disyllabic nouns *ċaefli*, *fācni*, *geabuli*, *hræġli*, most of which *Ep*. and *Erf*. confirm. The endingless locative is frequent with place-names in *-hām*, *-wīċ*, *-mynster*, and occurs less frequently with other elements, e.g. *-stān*, *-tūn*, *-þorp* (and so the *u*-stem *-feld*), and it is also frequent with the words *dæġ*, *hām*, *morgen*;[3] note also *sealtern*, twice Ct. 28, *ǣfen*, Ex. 16, 12. The dat. pl. ending appears as *-an*, *-on* in lW-S,[4] perhaps developed from *-um* through eW-S *-un* (§ 378). *Dæġ* has a weak gen. pl. in *-ena*, *-ana*, *-ona* in many texts, and in lNorth. and *Ru.*[1] this is found in other nouns also.

§ 573. Nouns declined like the above are numerous; examples are:

like *stān*: *āþ* oath, *beorn* warrior, *ċeorl* churl, *coss* kiss, *dōm* judgement, *hlāf* loaf, *hund* dog, *sċeatt* property, *þēof* thief, *weall* wall, *weġ* way, *wer* man;

like *sċip*: *ġeoc* yoke, *god* god, *hof* dwelling;

like *word*: *bearn* child, *dēor* animal, *ġēar* year, *sweord* sword, *weorc* work, *wīf* woman.

§ 574. Phonological variants. (1) Nouns with root vowel *æ* change this to *a* before *a* or *u* (*o*) of the following syllable (§ 157).

	Masculine	Neuter
Sg.		
Nom.	dæġ, *day*	fæt, *vessel*
Acc.	dæġ	fæt
Gen.	dæġes	fætes
Dat.	dæġe	fæte

[1] The preservation of *-i* is not necessarily early in North. (§ 369).

[2] *Erf*. 842 *uueġi* is not confirmed by *Ep*. and *Cp*.

[3] Also in the form *merġen*.

[4] This applies to dat. pl. of all declensions; so in contracted nouns, e.g. *Swēon*, *ġefān* for *Swēom*, *ġefām*.

Pl.		
Nom.	dagas	fatu
Acc.	dagas	fatu
Gen.	daga	fata
Dat.	dagum	fatum

Examples like *dæġ* are: *hwæl* whale, *pæþ* path, *stæf* staff; like *fæt*: *bæċ* back, *bæþ* bath, *dæl* dale, *wæd* water. In such words *VP* has in the root syllable *e*, *ea* for *æ*, *a*, except (1) before back consonants, where *e*, *æ* appear, and (2) before *l*, where *a* appears in the pl., the sg. is not recorded; e.g. *fet*, *featu*; *deġ*, *dægas*; *hwalas* (§§ 164–5). Kt. has *e* for *æ*, but retains *a* (§§ 288 ff.).

From *ġeat*, gate (§ 185), W-S has the phonological pl. *gatu* (VP *geatu*), but also *ġeatu* (§ 185, footnote).

W-S has a variation of *ǣ*, *ā* in *mǣġ* relative, pl. *māgas*, beside *mǣgas* (§ 162).

(2) Nouns in *-h* lost this between voiced sounds; if these sounds were both vowels contraction followed, if one was a consonant the root syllable underwent compensatory lengthening.

Sg.		
Nom.	mearh, *horse*	sċōh, *shoe*
Acc.	mearh	sċōh
Gen.	mēares	sċōs
Dat.	mēare	sċō
Pl.		
Nom.	mēaras	sċōs
Acc.	mēaras	sċōs
Gen.	mēara	[sċōna][1]
Dat.	mēarum	sċōm

In the type *mearh* short quantity can be transferred from nom. and acc. sg. to inflected forms (§ 240).

Like *mearh* are *ealh* temple, *eolh* elk, *fearh* pig, *healh* corner, *horh* rheum (also n.), *sealh* willow, *seolh* seal, *wealh* foreigner, and the neuters *feorh* life, person (n. and a.p. *feorh*), *holh* hollow.[2]

[1] So *fēona*, *þēona* (with ending from wk. declension) from *feoh*, *þēoh*; cf. re-formed *hōa*, Ps. xlviii. 5, from *hōh*.

[2] On inverted spellings like *feorg*, *mearg*, see § 447; *horh*, *horg*, *hōres*, *-as* is beside *horu* (El. 297, acc. after *mid*), *horwes*, *horwe*, *horwum*, and re-formed neut. nom. pl. *horwu*; and so *holh*, *holg* was beside **holw-*, see § 412.

Like *sc̄ōh* are *eoh* horse, *flēah* flea (or n.?; beside weak *flēa*), *hōh* heel, *lēah* (also f.) open country, *slōh* mire (also f. and n.), and the neuters *feoh* money, *flēah* albugo (beside weak *flēa*, *flēo*, *flīo*), *pleoh* danger, *þēoh* thigh (n. and a.p. *þēoh*).[1]

(3) Nouns with *l*, *r*, *m*, *n*, before the endings often develop a parasite vowel in the uninflected forms. Hence normal paradigms are:

	Masculine		Neuter	
Sg.				
Nom.	fugol, *bird*	finger, *finger*	tungol, *star*	wæter, *water*
Acc.	fugol	finger	tungol	wæter
Gen.	fugles	fingres	tungles	wætres
Dat.	fugle	fingre	tungle	wætre
Pl.				
Nom.	fuglas	fingras	tungol	wæter
Acc.	fuglas	fingras	tungol	wæter
Gen.	fugla	fingra	tungla	wætra
Dat.	fuglum	fingrum	tunglum	wætrum

There is, however, great fluctuation in these nouns, for forms without parasiting are frequent (e.g. *seġl*, sail), while, especially after short syllables before *r*, a parasite vowel is often transferred to inflected forms, where it is subject to vowel harmony (e.g. *wæteres*, *fugelas*, see §§ 363, 385). The nom. and acc. pl. of neut. nouns with parasiting should have no ending, as *-u* should drop after the long syllable before parasiting took place, e.g. **tunglu* > **tungl* > *tungol*, but *-u* is often restored, usually with rejection of the parasite vowel, e.g. *tācnu*, *tunglu*, *wǣpnu*, *wundru*, but also *wǣpeno*, *wolcenu*, and especially with short root syllables, *wæt(e)ru*.

Examples of nouns of this type are:

masculine: *æppel* apple, *cradol* cradle, *hæsel* hazel, *næġl* nail, *sadol* saddle, *seġel* sail (also n.); *æcer* field, *befer* beaver (cf. § 395, footnote), *hamor* hammer, *hleahtor* laughter, *ofor* shore, *þunor* thunder; *ǣþm* breath, *āþum* son-in-law, *blōstm* blossom, *bōsm* bosom, *botm* bottom, *fæþm* embrace, *māþm* treasure, *wæstm* fruit; *hræfn* raven, *ofen* oven, *reġn* rain, *þeġn* thane;

neuter: *botl* dwelling, *cnōsl* race, *cumbol* banner, *hræġl* garment,

[1] On re-formations like *sc̄ōes*, *sc̄ōas*, *sc̄ōum*, d.s. *slōe*, g.p. *hōa*, see § 239.

hūsl Eucharist, *setl* seat, *spātl* saliva, *sweġl* sky; *ātor* poison, *fōdor* fodder (or m.?), *fōdor* case (or m.?), *leġer* bed, *tūddor* progeny, *weder* weather, *wuldor* glory, *wundor* wonder;[1] *bēacen* beacon, *bræġen* brain, *fācn* crime, *tācn* token, *wǣpen* weapon, *wolcen* cloud.

(4) Originally trisyllabic nouns with a long root syllable syncopated an originally short middle syllable before inflexional endings, but often restored it analogically (§§ 341, 351). Those with a short root syllable did not normally syncopate (but cf. § 390).

	Masculine	Neuter	
Sg.			
Nom.	enġel, *angel*	hēafod, *head*	werod, *troop*
Acc.	enġel	hēafod	werod
Gen.	enġles	hēafdes	werodes
Dat.	enġle	hēafde	werode
Pl.			
Nom.	enġlas	hēafdu	werod
Acc.	enġlas	hēafdu	werod
Gen.	enġla	hēafda	weroda
Dat.	enġlum	hēafdum	werodum

The nom. and acc. pl. neut. should have *-u* after a long followed by a short syllable, but no ending after two shorts (§ 345); but analogy often occurs, hence, for example, eW-S *mæġenu*, lW-S *weredu*, and conversely eW-S *hēafod*.

When the medial syllable is not syncopated it is subject to vowel harmony (§ 385).

From *hēafod* a locatival dat. sg. *hēafdum* is frequent.[2]

Nouns of this type are readily distinguished from those of type (3) if the medial vowel was *-i-*, for umlaut then appears in the stem syllable; examples are: masculine: *brēmel* bramble, *bydel* beadle, *bȳtel* mallet (? or n.), *dryhten* lord, *ellen* courage (also n.), *ēþel* home, *sċyttel* bolt, *stȳpel* tower, *þȳmel* thimble (? or n.); neuter: *reċed* building, *þȳrel* hole. Other nouns of the type are distinguished

[1] *Sċuldor* shoulder, is masc., and its apparently neut. pl. *sċuldru* is to be regarded as dual in origin (cf. § 612, end).

[2] The form is perhaps instr. in origin: cf. *meolcum* which may be used as a sg. instr. as well as loc.

from those of type (3) by their etymology, e.g. masculine: *ǣled* fire, *awel* hook, *bismer* disgrace (also f. and n.), *daroþ* dart, *dēofol* devil (also n.), *eodor* enclosure, *eofor* boar, *falod* fold (? n.), *faroþ* sea near land (? n.), *heorot* hart, *metod* creator, *þēoden* prince, *waroþ* shore,[1] and nouns in *-uc*, *-oc* (of diverse origin),[2] as *bannuc* cake, *hafoc* hawk, *hassuc* hassock, *mattoc* mattock, *seoloc* silk, *weoloc* whelk; neuter: *gamen* game, *hǣmed* married state, *hrisel* shuttle, *mæġen* might (§ 334; Sievers, *Vokalismus*, pp. 23–24), *ofet* fruit, *waroþ* sea-weed, and diminutives in *-inċel* (see examples, § 204.6).[3] A few nouns remain which belong doubtfully here or to type (3), e.g. masc. *rodor* sky, *stapol* pillar.

(5) Forms with loss of medial χ occur beside forms with *-hh-* from masculine *hwēol* wheel, *tēar* tear, *þwēal* washing (also n.), and neuter *ēar* ear of corn. See §§ 242, 408 for the forms with *-hh-* (sometimes written *-h-*). *Fihl*, rag, does not occur with loss of χ.

(6) An originally long syllable is not usually syncopated when standing medially before inflexions. Here belong nouns with the masc. suffixes *-dom*, *-els*, *-had*, *-ing* (*-ling*), *-oþ* (*-noþ*), and the neut. suffixes *-lac* and *-en* (diminutive). Examples are *cynedom* royalty, *frēodom* freedom, *fǣtels* tub, *rǣdels* riddle, *camphad* warfare, *werhad* manhood, *cyning* king, *sċilling* shilling,[4] *fisċoþ* fishing, *huntoþ* hunting, *langoþ* longing, *oroþ* breath (with *-oþ* of different origin, § 374),[5] *wedlac* wedlock, *wītelac* punishment, *cliwen* clew, *lendenu* pl. loins, *mæġden* maiden, *nīten* animal, and with double suffix, *tynċen* tub, *þyrnċen* thorn-plant. A few isolated nouns also belong here, e.g. masc. *henġest* horse, *merisċ* marsh, neut. *īsern* iron; and obscured compounds, e.g. masc. *fæ̆reld* journey (also n.), *fultum* help, *hlāford* lord, neut. *fulwiht* baptism.

All such nouns decline like *stān* or *word*, except that neuters in *-en* form nom. and acc. pl. in *-u*, e.g. *mæġdenu*, *nītenu*. Vowel

[1] Here might be added with re-formed suffixes *eosol* ass, *heofon* heaven; cf. §§ 334, 381.

[2] Some of these may have an old long medial vowel and hence be under (6), cf. § 351, footnote.

[3] On the classing of *-inċel* as an *a*-stem, and the original nature of its second vowel, see Eckhardt, *ES* xxxii. 357, Dahl, *Substantival inflexion in early OE*, pp. 68 and 73.

[4] From words like *æþeling* prince, *lītling* little one, was extracted a new suffix *-ling*, e.g. *dēorling* darling, *rǣpling* prisoner.

[5] Another form of the suffix is *-noþ* (e.g. *fisċnoþ*); it is due to transference of *-n-* from verbs in *-nian* to related nouns, e.g. *drohtnoþ* way of life, for *drohtoþ* owing to *drohtnian*.

harmony (§ 385) can take place in nouns in *-oþ*, e.g. *longeþas*. On syncopation especially in the suffixes *-oþ* and *-en* see §§ 358, 390. On the quantity of formative elements consisting of words of reduced semantic force see § 90, footnote.

Here may also be mentioned the nouns in *-stafas*, although the vowel of that formative element is short, e.g. *fācenstafas* treachery, *wyrdstafas* fate.

b. *i̯a*-NOUNS

§ 575.	Masculine			Neuter	
Sg.					
Nom.	here, *army*	seċġ, *man*	ende, *end*	cynn, *race*	wīte, *punishment*
Acc.	here	seċġ	ende	cynn	wīte
Gen.	herġes	seċġes	endes	cynnes	wītes
Dat.	herġe	seċġe	ende	cynne	wīte
Pl.					
Nom.	herġas	seċġas	endas	cynn	wītu
Acc.	herġas	seċġas	endas	cynn	wītu
Gen.	herġa	seċġa	enda	cynna	wīta
Dat.	herġum	seċġum	endum	cynnum	wītum

§ 576. Origin of forms. The endings were in Gmc. the same as those of the *a*-nouns, preceded by *i̯* after short, *ii̯* after long syllables (§ 398.4). Before endings which remained in West Gmc. all consonants except *r* were doubled after a short syllable (§ 407). In OE *i̯* and *ii̯* were lost after both originally long syllables and ones lengthened by the West Gmc. doubling of consonants (§ 398.4). After *r* (< *r* or *z*, § 398.2) *i̯* caused no doubling and remained in OE. Hence, for example, Gmc. d.s. **χari̯ai*, **saʒi̯ai*, **andii̯ai* > West Gmc. **χari̯æ*, **saggi̯æ*, **andii̯æ* > OE *herġe*,[1] *seċġe*, *ende*, and similarly the g.s., g.p., d.p., and the n. and a.p. masc. Since Gmc. **saʒi̯az*, **saʒi̯am* would give **saʒi* by early vowel and consonant loss (§§ 331.1, 399, 404), the OE form should be **seġe*, and so **cyne*:[2] hence *seċġ* and *cynn* must be regarded as analogical forms from the other cases; for similar analogy in other West Gmc. languages see Dal, *Norsk tidsskrift for sprogvidenskap* vii. 243. On the development of *ende*, *wīte* from **andii̯az*, **u̯ītii̯am* see § 355.3; and on the development of nom. and acc. pl. neut. from **kuni̯ō*, *u̯ītii̯ō* see § 353 and footnote.

[1] Also *heriġe*, *herie*, § 365.

[2] Cf. § 579.3.

§ 577. **Early, late, and dialectal forms.** Early texts have n.s. *-i*, e.g. Ep., Cp. *durheri* folding door, *meeli* basin, *steeli* steel (Cp. *stēli*, *stǣli*), *-styċċi* piece, and names in *-heri* in many texts; g.s. *-æs*, e.g. CH *-cynnæs*, *-rīcaes*, inst. s. *-i*, Cp. *ġeddi* song. Names in *-here* always form g.s. and d.s. without *-i̯-*, e.g. *Ealdheres*, *-here* (d. also *-æ*, *-i* in early texts). So simplex *here* has in W-S very often (already eW-S) g. and d.s. *heres*, *here*, n. and a.p. *heras*.

§ 578. Like *here* is *durhere* folding door, pl. lW-S *durheras*. Examples of the other types are:

like *seċġ*: *bridd* young bird, *hyll* hill, *weċġ* wedge;
like *ende*: *esne* servant, *hierde* shepherd, *hwǣte* wheat, *lǣċe* physician, *mēċe* sword, *mēle* basin, *-sterri* coll. stars (cf. § 153.3), and nomina agentis in *-ere*, e.g. *bōcere* scribe, *leornere* learner;
like *cynn*: *bedd* bed, *webb* web, *wedd* pledge, *wiċġ* horse;
like *wīte*: *ǣrende* errand, *ierfe* inheritance, *rīċe* kingdom, *stȳle* steel, many in *ġe-*, e.g. *ġefylċe* troop, *ġetimbre* building, *ġeþēode* language, *ġewǣde* dress, and *fliċċe* flitch, *styċċe* piece, where *ċċ* is not due to West Gmc. gemination (pl. *fliċċu*, *styċċu*).

§ 579. **Phonological variants.** (1) Loss of χ and contraction occurred in W-S *ġesċȳ* neut. shoes (< **ġesċīe*, slightly corrupted *Letter of Alexander*, EETS, o.s. 161, p. 41); VP *ġesċōē*; Li. *ġ(e)sċeōē*, Ru.[2] *ġisċōē*, g.s. *ġisċōes*.

(2) West Gmc. gemination of consonants appears in the formative elements of the neut. nouns *ǣfenn* evening (also m.), *fæstenn* fortress, *fæstenn* fast, *wēstenn* desert (also m. and f.), and of nouns in *-ett*, e.g. masc. *þēowett* slavery, neut. *bærnett* arson, *þiċċett* thicket. In later texts they are increasingly liable to simplify the double consonant before inflexions (§ 457), e.g. lW-S d.s. *wēstene*, *þēowete*.[1] Nom. and acc. pl. is *-u*: lW-S *fæstenu*, *wēsten(n)u*, *þiċċet(t)u*. *Līġett*, lightning, makes pl. *līġet(t)u* (beside m. *līġetas*), and this may be treated as fem. sg. and declined fem. sg. and pl. (so already *VP*). The suffix *-ett* interchanges with *-ot*, which is without gemination, and hence liable to syncopation, e.g. *þēowot*, *þēowte*, &c.

(3) In a few nouns a formative element has retained the phonological nom. and acc. sg. in *-e* (< *-i*) without gemination, and the

[1] The interchange of *-n-* and *-nn-* in d.s. *ǣfen(n)e* caused frequent introduction of *-nn-* in the d.s. of *morgen*, *merġen* (already eW-S).

single consonant has been extended to the other cases. Here belong masc. *byrele* cup-bearer (also f. wk.), *mereċe* smallage, and doubtfully masc. or neut. *eowode* flock (also f.; on root vowel see § 211), *hemeþe* shirt, *sīþe* scythe (§ 267). On syncopated forms *byrle*, *merċe*, *eowde*, see §§ 388–9.

(4) A number of *-i̯a-* nouns had *-u̯-* before *-i̯-*. In OE *-i̯-* remained (written *ġ*), causing umlaut if possible in the root syllable. Examples are neut. *hīġ* hay, *trīġ* tray, with Gmc. *-au̯i̯-* > West Gmc. *-auu̯i̯-* (§ 120.2). But the OE development of West Gmc. *-iuu̯i̯-* is seen in *glīw*, *glīow* mirth, *hīew*, *hīw*, *hīow* hue, while *glīġ* is a re-formation (§ 411). Both types have nom. and acc. sg. under influence of the other cases: **hewi*, **gliwi* without gemination would be the undisturbed developments. In re-formed *glīow*, *hīow* final *-u̯-* should drop (§ 400); *glīo*, *glēo*, *hīo*, *hēo* are, however, rare, *-u̯-* being usually replaced from the inflected cases.[1]

(5) *Blēo* neut. colour, g.s. *blēos*, d.s. *blēo*, n.a.p. **blēo*, *blēoh*, g.p. *blēo*, *blēoa*, *blēona*, d.p. *blēom*, *blēoum*, has a diphthong due to early contraction (§ 120.3.c.), but is historically a *i̯a-* stem, Gmc. *blii̯a-*.[2] On forms with final inorganic *h* and internal *g* (*blēoh*, g.s. *blēoge*, g.p. *blēohga*) see §§ 447, 466. D.p. *blēowum* is analogical (as *cnēowum* to *cnēo*).

c. *u̯a*-NOUNS

§ 580.

	Masculine	Neuter
Sg.		
Nom.	bearu, *grove*	searu, *device*
Acc.	bearu	searu
Gen.	bearwes	searwes
Dat.	bearwe	searwe
Pl.		
Nom.	bearwas	searu
Acc.	bearwas	searu
Gen.	bearwa	searwa
Dat.	bearwum	searwum

§ 581. **Origin of forms.** The endings were in Gmc. the same as those of the *a*-nouns preceded by *u̯*. In the nom. and acc. sg. *u̯* became vocalic

[1] Ep., Cp. *glīu* is probably a spelling of *glīuw*, later *glīow* (§ 279).
[2] Distinguish Gmc. **bliu̯a-* lead, ON *blý*, OHG *blio*, *bli*.

after the loss of *-a-* in Gmc. (§ 331.4), so that **baru̯az*, **baru̯am*, **saru̯am* became **baruz*, &c. In OE breaking would not take place in these forms, but *ea*, *eo* were levelled out from the other cases, e.g. *bearu*, *teoru*. In the nom. and acc. pl. neut. Gmc. **saru̯ō* > West Gmc. **saru̯ū* > **sarū* (§ 405) > OE *searu* (with *ea* from other cases). In d.p. *-wum*, i.s. Ep., Erf. *smeruui*, the *u̯* is analogical, as it should disappear before *i* and *u* (§§ 405, 406).

§ 582. Early, late, and dialectal forms. Dat. sg. *-æ* is frequent in the place-name *Baruae* BH. The inst. (historically loc.) in *-i* occurs in *smeruui* Ep. Erf. On forms with parasite vowels (e.g. *bearewum*, *searuwa*, *meluwe*, *-owes*, *-ewes*) see § 365. Early forms without the levelling of *ea*, *eo* described in § 581 are Ep., Cp. *teru*, Erf. *smeruuuyrt*, Ep., Erf. *smeruui*. LG *smerum* is a pure phonological form, neither *eo* nor *u* being levelled into it. Cp. *sarwo* (88, apparently n.s.) shows abnormal levelling of *u̯* to the uninflected form.

§ 583. There is no other noun like *bearu*. Like *searu* (which is also f.) are *cudu* cud, *melu* meal (also *meolu*, § 210.1), *smeoru* grease, *teoru* tar.

§ 584. Phonological variants. (1) In some nouns a diphthong stood before *-u̯-*. These nouns are of two kinds:

(*a*) Nouns which have a diphthong of Gmc. origin before *-u̯-* in all cases. Final *u̯* should drop after the diphthong (§§ 272, 400), but it was practically always analogically retained or replaced. Here belong *bēow* barley, *dēaw* dew (m. and n.), *ġehrēow* lamentation, and probably *bēaw* gad-fly, *sēaw* juice (n.), with diphthongs of uncertain origin. Except as indicated the genders of these words are uncertain. These nouns inflect regularly so far as recorded, e.g. sg. *dēaw*, *dēawes*, *dēawe*, pl. *dēawas*, d. *sēawum*. No nom. acc. pl. neut. is recorded. Note Bd. Gl. *sēa*, without addition of *w* from inflected forms.

(*b*) Nouns which developed a diphthong phonologically only in the nom. and acc. sg. and the neut. nom. and acc. pl. (§ 120.3.a, b). To this diphthong *-u̯* might be added from inflected forms. Here belong masc. *þēow* servant (with its compounds *lāreow* teacher, *latteow* leader), *þēaw* custom, and neut. *cnēow* knee (after which *ancleow*, ankle, is perhaps re-formed), *hlēow* protection (? m.), *trēow* tree, *strēaw* straw. Words with internal *-eu̯-* subsequently developed this to *-eou̯-* (§ 146), while those with internal *-au̯-* could extend *-ēau̯-* from the uninflected form. Hence regular paradigms are:

	Masculine		Neuter	
Sg.				
Nom.	þēaw, *custom*	þēo(w), *servant*	strēaw, *straw*	cnēo(w), *knee*
Acc.	þēaw	þēo(w)	strēaw	cnēo(w)
Gen.	þēawes	þeowes	——	cneowes
Dat.	þēawe	þeowe	strēawe	cneowe
Pl.				
Nom.	þēawas	þeowas	——[1]	cnēo(w)[2]
Acc.	þēawas	þeowas	——	cnēo(w)
Gen.	þēawa	þeowa	——	cneowa
Dat.	þēawum	þeowum	——	cneowum

The uninflected form of *-ēaw-* words appears without *-w* only in the compound *strēa-beriġe*. Words in *-ēow* frequently have the uninflected form without *-w*. They can extend the long diphthong to the inflected forms: *cnēowes*, &c. *Hlēow* has as uninflected form prevailingly *hlēo*, which can also be used as d.s. (*Gen.* 102, *And.* 567). In this type and also in (*a*) d.p. in *-wum* has analogical *-u̯-* (cf. § 581). Fluctuation in forms of these words is often due to changes already discussed: lW-S *strēow*, *strēaw* (§ 274); North. *-ēuw-* (*-ēw-*, *-ēu-*) for *-ēow-* (§ 279); North. *ēa* for *ēo* as Li., Rit. *ðēa* for *þēo* (§ 280); *-ēow-* for *-ēaw-*, Ru.[2] *ðēow* for *þēaw* (§ 278); Ru.[1] *strēu* (§ 273, footnote). On the reduction of the second element in *lāreow*, *latteow* see §§ 356–7. North. has many readily understood analogical case-forms, e.g. *Li.* from *ðēa* (i.e. W-S *þēow*), g.s. *ðēas*, n.p. *ðēas*, g.p. *ðēana*; *Ru.*[2], *Rit.* g.p. *trēona*. From *trēow* VP has, beside regular forms, g.s. *-trēs*, g.p. *trēa*, and North. has n.a.s. *trē*, *strē*, g.s. *trees*, *strees*: see Ross in *Trans. Philological Soc.*, 1940, pp. 47–52.

(2) In the following words *-u̯-* was preceded by a long vowel: *snāw* snow (m.), *ġehlōw* lowing, *brīw* porridge (m.), *ġīw* vulture, *īw* yew (m.), *slīw* mullet, *Tīw* a god (m.). The genders are uncertain except as marked. *-u̯* should drop in uninflected forms, but it is usually restored, and hence the declension is regularly like *stān*, the d.p. in *-wum* being analogical. No nom. or acc. pl. neut. occurs. Except in nouns in *-īw-* uninflected forms without restoration of *u̯* are very unusual, e.g. Li. *snā*. In nouns in *-īw-*, however, an

[1] lW-S *strēwu* (? for *strēawu*, cf. note 2).
[2] W-S also *cnēowu*, *trēowu*; lW-S *andclēowa*.

uninflected form in -*ī* (often written -*īġ*) is frequent (see § 411) and gives rise to inflected forms of the type *Tīġes*. But more often *u̯* was added to the uninflected form, and *īu* > *īo*, *ēo* (e.g. *slēow*, i.e. **slēo* with re-addition of *u̯*), and *ēo* could be extended to inflected forms (e.g. *ġēowes*). See further § 411.

2. ō-NOUNS (FEM.)

a. PURE ō-NOUNS

§ 585.

Sg.		
Nom.	ġiefu, *gift*	lār, *learning*
Acc.	ġiefe	lāre
Gen.	ġiefe	lāre
Dat.	ġiefe	lāre
Pl.		
Nom.	ġiefa (-e nW-S)	lāra (-e nW-S)
Acc.	ġiefa, -e	lāra, -e
Gen.	ġiefa, -ena	lāra
Dat.	ġiefum	lārum

§ 586. **Origin of forms.** The Prim. Gmc. forms of the case-endings were sg. -*ō*, -*ōm*, -*ôz*, -*ai*, pl. -*ôz*, -*ōns*, -*ôm*, -*ūmiz* (§ 331.6). The OE development of these forms is regular except in the gen. sg., where the phonological development would be -*a*. Possibly the form has been influenced by the acc. pl., owing to the identity of acc. pl. and gen. sg. in the other main Gmc. fem. declension, the -*ōn*- stems (§ 616, footnote). On the survival of g.s. -*a* see § 589.6, 8. In the pl. -*a* is the phonological development of nom. -*ôz*, -*e* of acc. -*ōns* (§§ 331.5, 355.1). In W-S -*a* is extended to the acc., -*e* surviving rarely in eW-S, but always in its historical acc. function. *VP* has -*e* for both cases, *KG* use -*a* and -*e* indifferently. G.p.-*ena* is lW-S, and far more frequent with short than with long root syllables: eW-S and *VP* have already -*warena*. On this declension see particularly Flasdieck, *IF* xlviii. 53–66.

§ 587. **Early, late, and dialectal forms.** Besides the usual late change of -*u* to -*o* and -*a* in nom. sg. (§ 377), lW-S sometimes extends -*u* to other cases of sg. (e.g. acc. *talu*, Robertson, *A-S charters*, 152, 8; dat. *lufu*, Napier's Wulfstan, 302, 27). Acc., gen., dat. sg. all occur in early texts with -*æ*, e.g. acc. *aerigfaerae* LR, gen. *Humbrae* BH, *Aedilburgae* Ct. 5,[1]

[1] All examples of g.s. -*æ* are from fem. personal- or place-names in Lat. texts, hence the inflexion may be Lat.

dat. *nǣðlae*, *uuroctae* Ep., *wōdhae* Cp., *sāulæ* Urswick Cross. Very remarkable are two forms in *-i* used in a locative function, RC *rōdi*, FC *ċæstri*. *Ep.* 97 *ġitīungi* shows the same ending in instrumental function. The form is unexplained. Early Angl. texts have *-æ* for *-e* of nom. and acc. pl., e.g. LR *ueflæ*, Ep., Cp. *nabae*. The glossaries have *-a* also, e.g. Cp. *sċyfla*, Ep. *sċibla*, *fealga*.[1] *-a* is not found in *VP*, and it is doubtful if its occasional appearance in *Ru.*[1] and lNorth. is due to survival, or to the uncertain value of the vowel symbols in unaccented syllables in these texts. eKt. has *-a* for both nom. and acc.: *sāula* n. and a., Ct. 37; *ðearfa* a., Ct. 41. lNorth. sometimes has g.p. in *-ana*, *-ona*, e.g. Rit. *ġeafana*, *-ona*, Li. *reordana*.

§ 588. Short-syllable nouns declined like *ġiefu* are: *faru* journey, *lufu* love, *nafu* nave, *racu* narrative, *sċolu* troop, *-waru* people.[2]

Long-syllable nouns declined like *lār* are: *bōt* remedy, *gād* goad, *lād* way, *lāf* remainder, *meord* (*mēd*, § 404) reward, *reord* voice, *reord* food, *rōd* cross, *sorg* sorrow, *weard* protection, *wund* wound.

§ 589. Phonological variants. (1) While nouns with *a* in the root syllable usually retain it analogically before *-e* and *-ena* (e.g. *fare*, *-warena*), some forms with *æ* occur, e.g. LR *-faerae*, eW-S *wræce*; so with second fronting of *æ* to *e*, VP *sweðe*, *wrece*.

(2) In *brū* eyelash, eyebrow, a consonantal glide is sometimes indicated in forms with hiatus: n.p. *brūwa* or *brūa*, d.p. *brūwum* or *brūum* (Rit.), g.p. *brūna*.

(3) The fem. forms of *slōh* mire, drop *h* and contract: a., g., d.s. *slō* (Birch, no. 1176); those of *lēah* open country, have analogical *g* (§ 447), a., g., d.s. *lēage* (already Ct. 3), but also d.s. *-līeġ* (§ 627).

(4) Nouns with *l*, *r*, *m*, *n* before the inflexions drop *-u* in the nom. sg., and parasiting may then take place, e.g. *ċeaster* city, *ċeastre*, &c.[3] Parasiting may be analogically extended to inflected forms, e.g. d.p. *feðerum* Oros. 18, 17. Examples declined like *ċeaster* are:[4] *ādl* disease, *feþer* feather, *frōfor* comfort, *nǣdl* needle, *stefn* voice, *sweġer* mother-in-law, *wōcor* increase.

(5) Originally trisyllabic nouns reject *-u* in the nom. sg.,[5] and

[1] Perhaps 'harrows'; the root-syllable suggests that the gloss is W-S or Kt. in origin.

[2] On re-formations of compounds in *-waru* see § 610.7.

[3] *-ċeaster* as a place-name element usually has uninflected acc., but dat. in *-e*.

[4] The prevailing form of the nom. sg. is given.

[5] An exception is *eġenu* chaff. *-u* is also retained after short half-stressed syllables, e.g. BH *Wantsumu* a river, LV *Aebbino* fem. name. Names with *-u* after a long syllable are reductions of names of this type, arising later than the dropping of vowels after long syllables, e.g. LV *Beonnu*, *Bettu*, *Ēadu*.

generally retain the medial vowel in that case, but can syncopate it in other cases, e.g. *firen* crime, *firene* or *firne*, &c. Monosyllabic uninflected forms like *firn* also occur (§ 390). So are declined *bisen* example, *byden* barrel, *cylen* kiln, *eln* ell, *lyġen* lie; *feter* fetter; *netel* nettle, *spinel* spindle; the medial syllable is not syncopated in the inflected forms of *efes* eaves, *duguþ* warriors, *ġeoguþ* youth, but may have vowel harmony (e.g. *dugeþum*, and hence *dugeþe*, § 385). *Sāwol* soul (Gothic *saiwala*), and *lifer* liver (OHG *lebara*), had syncopation of medial *a* in all cases (§ 341), but parasiting subsequently arose in nom. sg., though *sāul*, *sāwl* also occur. W-S *æx*, axe, has syncope of a medial vowel in all forms: on Angl. trisyllabic forms see §§ 203, 341, footnotes.

(6) The medial syllable of nouns with the Gmc. fem. abstract suffix *-iþō* is syncopated in OE.[1] The final *-u* should then remain phonologically (§ 353), but it is often dropped on the analogy of the type *lār*. The other cases have the same endings as in *lār*. But already in early texts *-u* can be levelled out to all sg. cases, and to the nom. and acc. pl., e.g. VP *lǣððu*, *ēbylġðu* occur as acc., gen., and dat. sg., and eW-S *ġesǣlðo*, *iermðo* as nom. and acc. pl. In *VP* also occurs g.s. *ermða* (apparently the phonological development of Gmc. *-ôz*), and so eW-S *iermða*, CP 183, 3.

Examples of these nouns are: *ǣbylġþu* anger, *ierġþu* cowardice, *iermþu* poverty, *lǣþþu* hatred, *mǣrþu* glory, *myrġþ* mirth, *sǣlþ* happiness. After dentals consonant assimilation is frequent, e.g. *ġesċentu* shame, *ġesyntu* health, *ofermettu* pride (cf. *sċond*, *sund*, *mōd*); *weorþmynt* honour (< *-*mundiþō*, but cf. § 450); *-lēas*+*-iþō* > *-liest*:[2] *ġīemeliest* neglect.

(7) In OE fem. abstract nouns of the *īn*-declension (cf. Gothic *managei* multitude, acc. *managein*) would normally have *-e* < *i* < *īn* (§ 473) in the acc., gen., and dat. sg. and in the nom. and acc. pl. But their declension was early associated with that of nouns in *-iþō*, so that their nom. sg. received the ending *-u* (*-o*), and this was often extended to the whole sg. (so already *VP*), and to the nom. and acc. pl.[3] Examples are *bieldu* boldness, *brǣdu* breadth, *bysgu* trouble, *enġu* narrowness, *fyllu* fullness, *hǣlu* health, *hǣtu* heat (beside *hǣte* wk. fem.), *hyldu* homage, *ieldu* age, *lenġu* length,

[1] Most examples have a long root syllable: Ep. Erf. *siuida* is an error for *sifiðan* (so *Cp.* 940) but note *-brecþ* breaking, *frymþ* beginning, *gesihþ* vision, *trymþ* strength, all with analogical syncope.

[2] Also *-lest*, § 357; and by re-formation *-least*.

[3] Nom. and acc. pl. are rare, but note *snyttro*, v.l. *snyttra*, OE Bede 136, 29 (ed. Miller); *wlenċa*, CP 115, 1; *bisgu*, Boeth., preface.

meniġu multitude, ***ofermēdu*** pride, ***snyttru*** wisdom, ***strenġu*** strength, ***þēostru*** darkness (beside ***þēostre*** st. neut.), ***wæstmbǣru*** fertility, ***wlenċu*** pride, ***wyrþu*** honour; also ***ġebyrdu*** birth, ***ġecyndu*** race, &c., bye-forms to ***ġebyrd***, ***ġecynd*** (§ 609). Here also belong ***miċelu*** greatness, ***oferfyrru*** great distance, though forms in *-u* (*-o*) are not recorded, but only inflexions in *-e*. From several of these nouns nom. sg. occurs without ending, e.g. *fyll*, *hǣl*, *ield*, *lenġ*.

(8) Abstract nouns in *-ung*, *-ing* may be declined like *lār*, and in *VP* this is always the case, and also in the early glossaries so far as forms occur. In eW-S already there is considerable extension of *-a* (historically proper to gen. sg. and nom. pl.) not only to acc. pl. but also to acc. and dat. sg. It is doubtful if similar extension of *-a* in *Ru.*[1] and lNorth. is due to the same processes, or to the instability of the unaccented vowels in these texts. On d.s. *ġitīungi* Ep. see § 587; on the interchange of *-ung* and *-ing*, § 383. Examples are: ***costung*** temptation, ***langung*** longing, ***lēasung*** falsehood, ***niþerung*** humiliation, ***sċēawung*** contemplation, ***sċotung*** shooting.

b. *i̯ō*-NOUNS

§ 590.

Sg.		
Nom.	synn, *sin*	ġierd, *rod*
Acc.	synne	ġierde
Gen.	synne	ġierde
Dat.	synne	ġierde
Pl.		
Nom.	synna (-e nW-S)	ġierda (-e nW-S)
Acc.	synna, -e	ġierda, -e
Gen.	synna	ġierda
Dat.	synnum	ġierdum

§ 591. **Origin of forms.** n.s. *synn* is from Gmc. **suni̯ō* (cf. Goth. *sibja*), which developed in OE by the same processes that produced neut. pl. *cynn* (§ 576); *ġierd* is from Gmc. **ʒardī*[1] (cf. Goth. *bandi*), and the final vowel was shortened and lost regularly in OE (§§ 331.5, 345).[2] The other

[1] Or **ʒazdī* (cf. Goth. *gazds*), but cf. Cosijn in *Tijdschrift voor Ned. taal- en letterkunde* xiii. 19; S. Feist, *Vergleichendes Wörterbuch der got. Sprache*, s.v. *gazds*, for further references.

[2] Some regard Ep., Cp. *aetgǣru* as nom. sg. developed from Gmc. *-ii̯ō*, and Cp. *aetgǣre* as pl. of the same word. This agrees better with the numbers of the

cases have the same endings as the *ō*-stems, and the *-i̯-* (*-ii̯*) which preceded these caused consonant doubling after a short syllable, and was then lost after both old long syllables and new ones due to the gemination (§ 398.4), As in the *ō*-declension a dat. sg. in *-i* occurs in early texts: *Ep.*, *Erf.* 109 ***mēġsibbi***, and *Ld.* 179 ***tyndri*** (if this is not for ***tyndrin***, reading of *Cp.*, *Erf.* in the same gloss). When the root syllable is long, it is possible to distinguish *ō*-stems from *i̯ō*-stems only when the root vowel can show *i*-mutation, or when the final consonant of the root can be assibilated (e.g. *sprǣċ* speech).

§ 592. Examples of *i̯ō*-nouns are:

like *synn*: ***benn*** wound, ***bryċġ*** bridge, ***eċġ*** edge, ***hell*** hell, ***henn*** hen, ***sæċċ*** strife, ***seċġ*** sword, ***sibb*** relationship, ***syll*** base;

like *ġierd*: ***bend*** band (also masc. *i*-stem), ***rest*** rest, ***sprǣċ*** speech, ***wylf*** she-wolf, ***ȳþ*** wave.

Nouns with several fem. formative suffixes belong to the *i̯ō*-declension:

(*a*) Nouns in *-s* < *-si̯-*; ***blīþs*** bliss, ***līþs*** mercy (> *bliss*, *liss*, §§ 286, 481.2), ***milts*** mercy. Though the origin of the suffix is obscure (cf. § 445), OS *blidsea* indicates a *i̯ō*-stem.

(*b*) Abstract nouns in *-enn* < *-ini̯-*, e.g. ***byrþenn*** burden, ***byrġenn*** burial, ***hæftenn*** captivity, ***henġen*** hanging, ***rǣdenn*** state.[1] On simplification of *-nn-* in inflexion see § 457.

(*c*) Fem. derivatives in *-enn* from masc. nouns, e.g. ***gyden*** goddess, ***menen*** maid-servant, ***þēowenn*** the same, ***-wyrġenn*** female monster. These nouns also have very frequent simplification of *-nn-*, and double consonants are not recorded in nouns above spelled with *-n*. The *-u* of the *ġiefu* class is added to this suffix in ***myneċenu*** nun (§ 518).

(*d*) Fem. nouns in *-ess* < *-isi̯-*, e.g. ***ċiefes*** concubine, ***byres*** chisel, ***forleġess*** harlot, ***hæġtess*** witch, ***ides*** female. Similarly is inflected ***cnēoriss*** race, of uncertain formation. These nouns also have frequent simplification of the double consonants, and *ss* is not recorded in the ones above spelled with *-s*. Here originally belonged ***lynis*** linchpin, treated as a masc. *a*-stem in OE (n.p. *lynisas*).

(*e*) Nouns in *-ett* (< *-ati̯-*), e.g. ***ānett*** solitude, ***hyrnett*** hornet, ***lempet*** basin, ***ylfett*** swan. These nouns also have frequent simpli-

words glossed than the usual view that *aetgǣere* is sg., *aetgǣeru* pl. of a neut. *-i̯a* stem (§ 575).

[1] This is itself a fruitful suffix, e.g. *hīwrǣden* family, *manrǣden* fealty.

fication of the double consonants, and this is followed by addition of *-u* in *hyrnetu*, *ylfetu* (already early glossaries).[1] Treatment of the neut. pl. *līgetu* as a fem. sg. added a noun *līget(t)u* to this class (§ 579.2).

Fem. nouns of types (*c*), (*d*), and (*e*) often have alternative forms according to the weak declension, e.g. infl. *gydenan*, *hæġtesse*, *ylfete*.

(*f*) Abstract nouns in *-ness*, *-niss* (§ 384) are declined regularly like *synn*. But already in early texts *-nesse* is sometimes extended to the nom. sg. (*VP*, eW-S), and later this is frequent especially in *Ru.*[1] and North. (not *KG*). Examples of these nouns are: *clǣnness* purity, *mildheortness* mercy, *rihtwisness* justice, *wōdness* madness.

§ 593. Phonological variants. (1) A parasite vowel appears in *hlǣder*, *hlǣdder* ladder, infl. *hlǣdre*, &c.

(2) From Gmc. **au̯ī* sheep (transferred from the *i*-declension, cf. Lat. *ouis*) was regularly developed OE *ewe*, usually re-formed to *eowu* (§ 211), whence late *euwu* (§ 274). It declines both like *ġiefu* (acc. *eowe*, &c.) and as a weak noun, *eowe*, *-an*; there is also a masc. g.s. *eowes*.[2]

(3) On the development of *īeġ* island, see § 120.2. Here and probably in *cǣġ* key (beside wk. m. *cǣga*), the formative *-i̯-* followed directly on the root vowel, mutated it, and remained in OE (§ 398.4, footnote).

C. u̯ō-NOUNS

§ 594.

Sg.		
Nom.	sinu, *sinew*	lǣs, *pasture*
Acc.	sinwe	lǣswe
Gen.	sinwe	lǣswe
Dat.	sinwe	lǣswe
Pl.		
Nom.	sinwa (-e nW-S)	lǣswa (-e nW-S)
Acc.	sinwa, -e	lǣswa, -e
Gen.	sinwa	lǣswa
Dat.	sinwum	lǣswum

[1] Their forms are Ep., Cp. *aelbitu*, Erf. *hirnitu*, Cp. *hurnitu*, so OE *-ett* apparently represents a coalescence of *-itt* < *-iti̯-* and *-ett* < *-ati̯-*.

[2] **þeowu*, female servant, is a grammatical fiction to explain the *eo* of the existing weak fem. *þeowe*, *-an*, and *þeowen* beside *ðiwen*; the short diphthong is metrically well established in *þeowe* (Gen. 2747, &c.), but *þeowen* may have *ēo* from *þēow* (Jud. 74).

§ 595. **Origin of forms.** The only divergence from the *ō*-declension is in the nom. sg.: Gmc. *-u̯ō* > West Gmc. *-u̯ū* (§ 331.5) > OE *-ū* (§ 405), and this remains after a short, drops after a long syllable. The dat. pl. is analogical, the phonological development is seen in LR *ġeatum* (§ 405).

§ 596. **Early, late, and dialectal forms.** On forms with parasiting see § 365. Many words have alternative forms without *-w-*, following *ġiefu* and *lār* exactly; e.g. already before 900 n.p. *mēda*, Cts. 28 and 30; forms from later texts are a.s. *sċeade, sine, blōdlǣse, mǣde* (also *mǣd*, Oros. 92, 15, like *i*-stems); g.s. *mǣde*; d.s. *sċeade, lǣse*; n.a.p. *sċeada, sina, lǣsa, -e, mǣda, -e*; g.p. *sina*; d.p. *lǣsum*.

§ 597. Like *sinu* are declined *sċeadu* shade (beside neut. *sċead*), *searu* device (usually neut., § 580), and the plurals *frætwe* ornaments, *ġeatwe* armour; like *lǣs* are *blōdlǣs* blood-letting (beside re-formed *blōdlǣswu*), *mǣd* meadow, **rǣs* council (only d.p. *rǣswum*, Az. 126).

§ 598. **Phonological variants.** (1) When *w* follows a long vowel or diphthong, it should drop when final, but in n.s. of *u̯ō*-nouns it is restored analogically (§ 272), e.g. *hrēow* penitence, *stōw* place, *trēow* faith.

(2) On the development of n.s. **clēa* claw, *þrēa* affliction see § 120.3. *þrēa* extends that form to the whole sg., and nom., acc., gen. pl.; d.p. *þrēam, þrēaum*, but n.s. *thrauu* Ep., *thrauuo* Cp. is re-formed from inflected **þrawe*, &c.[1] Similarly developed *clawu* (already Ep., Erf., Cp. *clauuo*), inflected *clawe*, &c., has replaced **clēa*, which has, however, levelled out *ēa* to some surviving forms, *VP* a.p. *clēa*, lW-S n.p. *clēa*, d.p. *clēam*, and re-formed *clēum*, poetical n.p. *clēo*. On d.p. *clām* see § 236.2.

3. *i*-NOUNS

a. MASCULINE

§ 599.

Sg.		
Nom.	wine, *friend*	ġiest, *guest*
Acc.	wine	ġiest
Gen.	wines	ġiestes
Dat.	wine	ġieste

[1] *þrēa* can also follow the weak declension, inflected *þrēan*, and is then masc.

Pl.		
Nom.	wine, -as	ġiestas
Acc.	wine, -as	ġiestas
Gen.	wina (poetical -iġa)	ġiesta
Dat.	winum	ġiestum

§ 600. **Origin of forms.** The Gmc. forms were sg. *-iz*, *-im*, –, –, pl. *-îz*, *-ins*, *-iôn*, *-imiz*. The I-E gen. and dat. sg. were not developed in Gmc., where the endings are from the *a*-stems. In the sg. the OE nom. and acc. are regularly developed, *-i* being lost after long root syllables, retained as *-e* after short ones. In the pl., the OE nom. and acc. in *-as* and the dat. are from the *a*-declension. The nom. and acc. in *-e* < *-i* and the gen. in *-iġa* (only in poetical *Deniġa*, *winiġa*) of nouns with short root syllables represent the Gmc. forms. The gen. pl. in *-a* of the long root syllable type may represent the Gmc. form, but in the short root syllable type it is due to the combined influence of the long syllable type and of other declensions.

§ 601. **Early, late, and dialectal forms.** In early texts the nom. and acc. sg. are frequently recorded as *-i*, mostly in names in *-wini*, but also in BH *-stedi*, Ep., Erf. *meri*. Gen. sg. is not recorded in an early form.[1] Dat. sg. in *-i* occurs in early texts, e.g. Ep., Erf., Cp. *dǣli*, Wycliffe Stone, Thornhill I *-wini*; this case-form appears beside *-æ*, e.g. Ep. *faenġae*, *suiċae*. Survivals of n.p. in *-i* > *-e* are Cp. *stridi*, *dāele*, VP *ġehūsscipe*, poetical *byre*, *wine*; but early texts already have *-as*, e.g. Cp. *hegas*, LR *uyrmas*. In lNorth. an endingless form of the nom. and acc. sg. of nouns with short root syllables appears, e.g. *lyġ*, *styd*, *-wlit*; such forms are not found in *Ru*.[1]

§ 602. Examples of this large declension are: like *wine*: *byre* youth, *cyre* choice, *gryre* terror, *heġe* hedge, *lyġe* lie, *mere* lake, *mete* food (§ 610.5), *stede* place, *stride* stride, *swiċe* smell, *wlite* beauty; also compounds in *-sċipe*, e.g. *bēorsċipe* feast, *frēondsċipe* friendship, *wærsċipe* prudence; like *ġiest*: *ċierm* shouting, *ċierr* turn, *dǣl* part, *drenċ* drink, *ent* giant, *fenġ* grasp, *stenċ* smell, *wyrm* worm.

b. FEMININE

§ 603.		Singular	Plural
	Nom.	dǣd, *deed*	dǣda (-e nW-S)
	Acc.	dǣd, dǣde	dǣda, -e
	Gen.	dǣde	dǣda
	Dat.	dǣde	dǣdum

[1] Cts. 3, 5, 14 have already *-wines*. Frequent *-wini* in names is the Lat. gen., OE Bede *Ēadwinis* is too late to be of value, *BH*, MS. Cott. Tib. C ii, *Ēduine*

§ 604. **Origin of forms.** The case-endings in Gmc. were sg. *-iz*, *-im*, *-aiz*, *-ai*, pl. *-îz*,[1] *-ins*, *-iôn*, *-imiz*. In OE the nom. and acc. sg. without ending correspond to Gmc., the acc. in *-e* is from the ō-stems: it is already freq. in *VP* and eW-S. OE *-æ* > *-e* is a normal development in the gen. and dat. sg. In the pl. the nom. (used also as acc.) should give OE *-i* > *-e*; this is largely replaced by *-a* from the ō-stems in eW-S, where *-e* is rare, and confined to the acc. *KG* also have *-a* in the acc. pl. (nom. not recorded). The gen. is regularly developed, the dat. is from other declensions.

§ 605. **Early forms.** While g.s. *-æ* from female names in Lat. texts is merely the Lat. ending, *-æ* in ablatival function represents an early spelling of the OE dat., e.g. Ct. 35 *Cyneðryðae*, and similar forms in *BH*. G.s. *uyrdi* LR corresponds to OHG *geuurhti*. This gen. is usually regarded as representing I-E *-eis*, an ablaut variant of *-ois*, the source of normal Gmc. *-aiz* (Gothic *-ais*). But in view of the absence of other evidence for a reflex of I-E *-eis* in Gmc., it may be preferable to regard g.s. *-i* in West Gmc. as due to an identification of the gen. sg. and acc. pl. endings similar to that discussed above (§ 586), and due to the same cause.

N.p. *hȳfi* Cp., a.p. *maecti* CH, show early *i* < *ī*. N.p. *uuyrdae* Ep. suggests that *-æ* of the ō-stems began to replace *-i* before the two forms coalesced phonologically.

§ 606. There are very few short syllable fem. *i*-stems. They appear to have adopted early the endings of the ō-declension, and are now distinguishable only by the umlaut of the root vowel, e.g. *denu* valley, *fremu* benefit, and the compounds in *-legu*, *-neru*, though their nom. sg. does not occur, e.g. **ealdorlegu* death, **ealdorneru* safety.

Nouns declined like *dǣd* are *bēn* prayer, *brȳd* bride, *cwēn* queen, *fierd* army, *glēd* coal, *hȳd* hide, *hȳf* hive, *mieht* might, *nīed* need, *sċyld* guilt, *spēd* success, *tīd* time, *wēn* hope, *wyrd* fate, *ȳst* storm; abstract and collective nouns in *-t* < *-ti-* are mainly fem., so far as evidence is available, e.g. *cyst* choice, *ēst* favour, *hǣst* violence, *wist* sustenance; *lyft* air, is masc., fem., and neut.

(OET 136, 93) is an error, for the manuscript elsewhere has nom. *-wine* or *-i*, gen. *-i*. Ct. 8 *Folcuuinis* may, however, point to a contamination of a g.s. *-i* (as in the fem. nouns) with *-æs* of the *a*-declension.

[1] The retention of *-i* after long root syllables in the nom. and acc. pl. in OS and OHG and in OE at least in CH *maecti* (for OE *-e* could be regarded as from the ō-stems) indicates that it came from a sound with abnormal intonation (§ 330). The ending was I-E *-ei̯es*, and hence the development of abnormal intonation, which was possible only in long syllables, must have been in Gmc., after *-ei̯es* > *-ii̯iz* > *-īz*. The reason for the identification of the intonation of the new long vowel with that of the old abnormal vowels is obscure.

C. NEUTER

§ 607.

Sg.		
Nom.	spere, *spear*	ġeswinċ, *toil*
Acc.	spere	ġeswinċ
Gen.	speres	ġeswinċes
Dat.	spere	ġeswinċe
Pl.		
Nom.	speru	ġeswinċ
Acc.	speru	ġeswinċ
Gen.	spera	ġeswinca
Dat.	sperum	ġeswincum

§ 608. Origin of forms. Nom and acc. sg. had Gmc. *-i*, nom. and acc. pl. *-ō*, an early re-formation after the *a*-stems. The OE development of these cases is normal. The other cases have the same origin as in masc. nouns.

§ 609. Like *spere* were probably *clyne* lump, *ġedyre* door-post, *ġedyne* noise, *ġewife* fate,[1] *ġewile* wish, *ofdele* slope, *oferslege* lintel, *orleġe* strife, *sife* sieve; all have developments of the root vowel normal before *-i-* except *spere*, which has the vowel of early re-formed pl. **sperō*.

Like *ġeswinċ* are neuters with a long mutated root syllable and no ending in the uninflected form, e.g. *ǣcyrf* fragment, *flǣsċ* flesh,[2] *flīes* fleece, *hǣl* omen, and a considerable group of words in *ġe-*, e.g. *ġedwild* error, *ġegrynd* plot of ground, *ġehlȳd* noise, *ġeresp* conviction (of crime), *ġewēd* madness; also some nouns which fluctuate between neut. and fem., e.g. *wiht* creature, *fulwiht* baptism (also m.), *forwyrd* loss,[3] and many in *ġe-*, e.g. *ġebyrd* birth, *ġecynd* race, *ġehyġd* thought (and so *oferhyġd* pride), *ġemynd* memory, *ġenyht* sufficiency, *ġeþyld* patience, *ġewyrht* deed. These fem. and neut. nouns have neut. pl. in *-u*: *wihtu*, and so probably *ġiftu* marriage, *ġehyrstu* ornaments (beside fem. *ġifta*, *ġehyrste*), *ġedryhtu* fortunes, of which sg. is not recorded. In abstract nouns this form in *-u* is often treated as indeclinable fem. sg.,

[1] Also *a*-stem *ġewif*.

[2] Pl. lW-S *flǣsċu*.

[3] Here is usually classified *grīn*, snare, but this is rather an *ō*-noun (n.p. *grīne*, e.g. *Ps.* lvi. 7), beside a neut. *a*-noun *grin* (n.p. *grinu*).

e.g. *ġebyrdu*, *ġecyndu*,[1] *ġewyrhtu* both fem. sg. and neut. pl., *oferhyġdu* fem. sg.

§ 610. Phonological variants. (1) Obscuration of compounds produced a few apparently disyllabic *i*-stems, e.g. *æfest* malice (m. and f., § 356), *ǣrist* resurrection (m.f.n.), and with confusion of the apparent suffix vowel (§ 382) *weoruld* world (f., rare m.).[2]

(2) *Sǣ* sea (m. and f.) and *ǣ* law (f.) are developed from **saiu̯i-*, **aiu̯i-* (§ 406). The normal forms of *sǣ* are n. and a.s. *sǣ*, g.s.f. *sǣ*, g.s.m. *sǣs*, d.s. *sǣ*, n. and a.p.f. *sǣ*, m. *sǣs*, g.p. wanting, d.p. *sǣm*. Abnormal forms are *Blick. Hom.* and poetical g. and d.s. *sǣwe*, d.p. *sǣwum*. (lW-S d.s. *sēo* is an error.) *Ǣ* has indeclinable s. and n. and a.p.; g.p. analogical *ǣa*; also a., g., and d.s. *ǣwe*, d.p. *ǣwum*, hence n.s. *ǣw*, (on *ēaw-* see § 273); lNorth. has g.s. *ǣs*, lW-S once *ǣys*. *Mǣw* mew (m.) has only forms with *-w-*, *mǣwes*, &c.; for early forms see § 273.

(3) On the interchange of consonants in *brǣw*, *brēġ* eye-lid (m.) see § 412, on lW-S *brēaw* § 273.

(4) It has been pointed out (§ 204.5) that owing to substitution of endings of *a-* and *ō*-stems before umlaut took place, some *i*-declension nouns have forms without umlaut. Here belong n.p. *stapas*, d.p. *-um*, to *stepe* step, g.p. *gasta* to *ġiest* guest; similarly *meaht*, Angl. *mæht* beside *mieht*, Angl. *meht* might. Of the national names (type 7 below), *Seaxe* has no umlaut; so *ġesċeaft* creature, *ġeþeaht* counsel, nouns of the type of *ġecynd*, fluctuating between fem. and neut., and with pl. in *-u* (also fem. pl. *-a*, masc. *-as*).

(5) Some short syllable *i*-stems can be declined according to the *i̯a*-declension, and they then have double consonants (cf. *seċġ*, § 575). Hence the doublets *mete*, North. *mett* (lW-S frequent pl. *mettas*) food, *hyse*, **hyss* (g.s. *hysses*, d.s. *hysse*, n.p. *hyssas*) warrior, *ile*, **ill* (g.p. *illa*) sole of foot, *ġewile*, *gewill* will; so lNorth. *æfdæll* (Li., d.s.; *Ru.*[2] *æfdelle*) for *ofdele* slope.

(6) *Bere* barley, *eġe* terror, *hete* hate, *sele* hall,[3] *siġe* victory, are masc. nouns like *wine*, but are shown by cognate forms (Goth. **baris*, *agis*, *hatis*, *sigis*) to be *-es*, *-os*-stems in origin, which have passed into the masc. *i*-declension, because Gmc. *-iz* > OE *-i*.

[1] Neut. pl. *ġecyndu* gives rise to sg. *ġecynde*, since *wītu* is pl. of *wīte*. There is also a neut. pl. without ending.

[2] The typical endingless acc. sg. of the fem. *i*-stems is very frequent from *weorold*.

[3] Beside *a*-stem *sæl*, pl. *salu*; and *i̯a*-stem *sel*, i.e. **sell*; its *es-*, *os*-origin is shown by the variant *salor*, § 636.

Similarly, nouns of the type of *ġecynd*, which fluctuate between mutated and unmutated root vowels, are perhaps old *-es*, *-os*-stems, reflecting the interchange of mutating and non-mutating vowels in the formative element, e.g. *ġebann*, *ġebenn* proclamation, *ġefōg*, *ġefēġ* joint, *ġeheald*, *ġehyld* guard, *ġehnāst*, *ġehnǣst* clash, *ġewealc*, *ġewylċ* rolling. See also § 636 below.

(7) Many national names decline as follows:

Nom.	Mierċe, *Mercians*	Engle, *English*
Acc.	Mierċe	Engle
Gen.	Mierċna (-ena)	Engla
Dat.	Mierċum	Englum

Like *Mierċe* are declined (apart from absence of umlaut in the root syllable, cf. type 4 above): *Seaxe* Saxons,[1] and compounds with *-sǣte*,[2] e.g. *Sumorsǣte* men of Somerset;

like *Engle* are: *Beorniċe* Bernicians, *Dēre* Deirans, *Norþ(an)-hymbre*, *Sūþ(an)hymbre* men of Northumbria, Southumbria, and the words *ylde* men, *ylfe* elves, *lēode* people.[3]

To these declensions belong some names of ancient tribes imperfectly recorded, e.g. **Holmryċġe* (d.p. *-ryċum*), **Seċġe* (g.p. *-ena*).

**Ȳte*, **Īote*, **Ēote* Jutes, can follow either declension: g.p. *Īutna*, *Ēota*, d.p. *Īutum*, *Īotum*, *Ȳtum*. Here also belong probably g.p. *Ēotena*, d.p. *Ēotenum*, Beow.

Dene, Danes, has g.p. *Deniġa* or *Dena* (§ 599).

To territorial names in *-ġē* are formed names for the inhabitants in *-iġe*, which may follow either of the above declensions: *Sūþriġe* men of Surrey, g.p. *Sūþriġ(e)na*, *Sūþriġa*, d.p. *Sūþriġum*; cf. the quasi-Lat. g.p. *Sūderġēona* BH, and *Ēastrġena* Ct. 18, formed from **Sūþerġe*, **Ēastrġe*.[4]

See § 519 on foreign names which follow this declension.

Nouns in *-ware* (e.g. *burgware* citizens, *Rōmware* Romans) have nom. and acc. pl. in *-e* in eW-S, although this element is really a pl. of the *ō*-stem *waru*. The sg. *waru*, *-e* may also be used, e.g.

[1] Also weak *Seaxan*. [2] Also weak *-sǣtan*.

[3] Also *lēoda* owing to the fluctuation of *-e*, *-a* in pl. of fem. nouns.

[4] The locatival dat. of nouns in *-ġē* is seen in its original form in Ct. 35 *Ēosterġe*, but there is usually re-formation due to confusion with names in *-īeġ*, *-ēġ* 'island', e.g. Cts. 34–35 *Ēastoreġe*, *Ēastereġe*; BH *in regione Sūderiġe* (alteration in Cott. Tib. A xiv.) So *Ēlġe* Ely, was re-formed to *Ēliġe*, whence uninfl. *Ēliġ*.

Cantware (dat.), *OEC* 617. The element can also be declined as a weak pl.: this is already eW-S (*Wihtwaran*, OEC 661) and VP (*helwearan*), and is frequent later. Pl. in *-as* also occurs in later manuscripts, e.g. *Siġelwearas*. In g.p., eW-S has usually *-wara*, but also already *-warena*, VP *-wearena*, lW-S usually *-warena*. In lNorth. the element is confused with *waras* men (§ 210.2, footnote), e.g. Li. *burgwaras*.

The nom. and acc. pl. *-e* of these names of nations is clearly Prim. OE *-i*, the pl. of the *i*-declension. The re-formed dat. pl. in *-um* which accounts for forms without mutation (*Seaxe*), and the gen. pl. in *-a*, *-iġa* correspond to the *i*-declension forms. The adoption of g.p. *-ena*, *-na* is obscure; once adopted it caused further confusion with the weak nouns (*Seaxan*, *Englan*, &c.).

4. *u*-NOUNS (MASC. AND FEM.)

§ 611.	Masculine		Feminine	
Sg.				
Nom.	sunu, *son*	feld, *field*	duru, *door*	hand, *hand*
Acc.	sunu	feld	duru	hand
Gen.	suna	felda	dura	handa
Dat.	suna	felda	dura	handa
Pl.				
Nom.	suna	felda	dura	handa
Acc.	suna	felda	dura	handa
Gen.	suna	felda	dura	handa
Dat.	sunum	feldum	durum	handum

§ 612. **Origin of forms.** The Gmc. endings were sg. *-uz*, *-um*, *-auz*, *-au*, pl. *-iu̯iz*, *-uns*, *-ôm*, *-umiz*. From these, the OE forms are regularly developed except the nom. and acc. pl. It might be assumed to be from a Gmc. nom. *-au̯iz* > *-auz*, representing I-E *-ou̯es*, in ablaut with I-E *-eu̯es*, Gmc. *-iu̯iz* (Goth. *-jus*). No forms outside OE and OFris., however, suggest the existence of an IE nom. pl. *-ou̯es*.[1]

[1] C. E. Bazell (private communication) regards OE, OFris. n. and a.p. *-a* as the development of I-E n.p. *-eu̯es*. At least in the Ingvaeonic area he would limit the change *e* > *i* in unaccented final syllables (§ 331.2) to before *z* (e.g. n.p. **fōtiz*) and before a lost I-E *i* (e.g. 3rd sg. **biriþ*, I-E *-eti*). But *-eu̯es* > Ingvaeonic *-eus* > *-eu*, which shared the development of *-au* to OE, OFris. *-o* > *-a*.

The nom. sg. of *nosu* nose, and *duru* door, may be in origin a dual formation, I-E *-ōu*, Gmc. *-ō*: the root vowel of *nosu* supports this view, that of *duru* does not.

§ 613. **Early, late, and dialectal forms.** A number of erroneous forms are often quoted as belonging to *u*-stems: on FC *-flōdu* see § 346, footnote; Erf. *aetgāru* is an error for *ætgǣru*, §§ 346, 591, footnotes; OEC *Wihtgara-* is an error for *Wihtwara-*; certain names on the *Bewcastle Column* and an early coin have Lat. endings *-us*, *-um* (see Dahl, *Substantival inflexion in early OE*, pp. xii and 179). Forms from early texts illustrating the tendency of mascs. to take the endings of *a*-stems, and fems. those of *ō*-stems, are g.s.m. VP *feldes*, *flōdes*, eW-S *æples*, *eardes*, *hādes*, *wintres*, d.s.m. VP *-flōde*, eW-S *earde*, *flōde*, *hāde*, *sumere*, *wealde*, n. and a.p.m. VP *feldas*, *flōdas*, *hergas*, eW-S *æpplas*, *heargas*, d.s.f. eW-S *dure*, *nose*. Such forms become increasingly frequent later, e.g. *KG* g.s.f. *dure*, n.p.f. *borhhande*. The declension also shows the effects of the increasing OE confusion of back vowels (§ 377) from an early date. Already *BH*, MS. Cott. Tib. C ii, has d.s. *Derauudu*, and eW-S has a.s. *wuda*, d.s. *duru*, CP 167, 15; 104, 13. Such forms become frequent later, e.g. *KG* n.s. *suna*, and many forms in lNorth. and *Ru*.[1] In lOE an endingless loc. sg. like that of the *a*-stems appears, e.g. *Wynnefeld* (Kemble, no. 710, late copy).

§ 614. Like *sunu* are declined *medu* mead (also n., cf. *Trans. Philological Soc.*, 1954, pp. 96–99),[1] *sidu* custom, *wudu* wood, and several nouns with the inflexion of a *u*-stem only recorded in nom. and acc. sg., *bregu* prince, *heoru* sword, *lagu* lake, *magu* youth,[2] *spitu* spit (d.s. *spite*), and the composition forms *friþu-* peace, *leoþu-* limb.

Like *feld*: no noun of this type is entirely free from the encroachment of *a*-declension endings, but traces of *u*-declension forms are recorded from *eard* country, *flōd* flood (also n.), *ford* ford, *hād* person, *hearg* shrine, *weald* forest; also with parasiting, *æppel* apple, *sumor*[3] summer, *winter* winter (also n. pl. *winter* or *wintru*); disyllabic *færelt* journey (g.s. *-a*, CP 257, 9).

No fem. nouns are free from the influence of the *ō*-stems, but some *u*-stem forms occur from the following:

like *duru*:[4] *nosu* nose;

like *hand*: *cweorn* hand-mill, *flōr* floor (also m.).

[1] lW-S g.s. *medewes*, n.p. *medewa* (read *-as*), as if like *bearu*.

[2] Also weak *maga*.

[3] *u*-stem forms are due to analogy of *winter*.

[4] lW-S d.s. *dyre* (analogy of *hnutu*, *hnyte*), also mixed forms *dyru*, *dyran*, *duran*.

B. The Weak Declension

§ 615.

	Masculine	Feminine	Neuter
Sg.			
Nom.	guma, *man*	tunge, *tongue*	ēage, *eye*
Acc.	guman	tungan	ēage
Gen.	guman	tungan	ēagan
Dat.	guman	tungan	ēagan
Pl.			
Nom.	guman	tungan	ēagan
Acc.	guman	tungan	ēagan
Gen.	gumena	tungena	ēagena
Dat.	gumum	tungum	ēagum

§ 616. **Origin of forms.** The thematic element was I-E *-en-*, which was subject to ablaut variation to *-on-* (second full grade), *-ēn, -ōn-* (lengthened grades), and *-n-* (vanishing grade). These varieties existed still in Gmc., and are reflected in some languages, e.g. Goth. a.s.m. *hanan*, d.s.m. *hanin*, a.s.f. *tuggōn*, g.p.m. *auhsnē* reflect I-E *-onm̥, -eni, -ōnm̥, -nôm*. In OE *-an* < I-E *-on-* has been extended to the acc. sg. (except in neuters), the gen. and dat. sg., and the nom., acc., and gen. pl. The old variation is preserved only in the isolated g.p. *oxna* oxen. The case-ending of these six cases would be in Gmc. *-num, -niz, -ni, -niz* (neut. *-na*), *-nuns* (neut. *-na*), *-nôm*. Owing to normal loss of final consonants, and of the vowels of final syllables in trisyllabic forms (§§ 399, 331), the case-endings disappeared except in gen. pl.[1] Hence *-an* appears in OE as the final syllable in all these cases except the gen. pl., where *-anôm* developed to *-ena* (§ 385). The dat. pl. *-um* is of uncertain development, though paralleled in all Gmc. languages. It is usually assumed to be derived from I-E *-onmis*, which by assimilation (*-nm-* > *-mm-*) and simplification of the double consonants had in Gmc. the same development as I-E *-omis* of the *a*-declension, hence OE *-um*. I-E *-onmis* would itself be a re-formation, as the dat. pl. probably had originally vanishing grade of the thematic element, as seen in isolated Goth. *abnam, watnam*. These Goth. forms show partial assimilation to the *a*-declension, as *-num* would be the phonological development of I-E *-nmis*, so perhaps the prevailing Gmc. forms are due to total

[1] But it may be reasonably assumed that in West Gmc. the weak nouns, like other consonant stems, gave up the distinction of nom. and acc. in the pl., and that both these cases would have *-niz*.

assimilation of the dat. pl. to the *a*-stems in masc. and neut., to the *ō*-stems in fem.

In the nom. sg. and neut. acc. sg. Gmc. developed three forms, I-E *-ēn, -ōn, -ô*. In West Gmc. *-ô* was limited to the masc., *-ōn* to fem. and neut. nouns. These endings developed normally as OE *-a* and *-e* (older *-æ*).

§ 617. **Early, late, and dialectal forms.** In early texts *-æ* frequently appears for nom. sg. fem., e.g. BH *Earcongotæ,* Ep. *nectaegalae.* In eNorth. there are three forms reflecting the West Gmc. development of the thematic element before certain case-endings to *-un-* (§§ 331.6); a.s.m. *galgu* RC, a.s.f. *foldu*[1] CH, *eorðu* LR, North. Loss of final *-n* is shown by the three forms just quoted, and g.s.m. *sefa* FC, but *LR* still has g.s.f. *uullan.* On *-n* in *BH* see § 472. lNorth has loss of *-n* always, *Ru.*[1] usually; these texts have very great fluctuation in the vowels of the endings, but it is doubtful if these reflect the I-E ablaut, or are simply due to the fluctuation described in § 379, footnote.[2] Poetical texts have frequently syncope in the gen. pl. after long root syllables, e.g. *brōgna, ēagna, Francna, Frēsna, ūhtna, wilna, wræċna* (to *wræċċa*), and perhaps the first element of *Neorxnawang*; similarly, when the ending is transferred to *ō*-stems, *ārna, lārna, sorgna.* eW-S also has *wilna, tungna.* The ending appears early as *-ana* (Cp. 687 *-doccana*), and this remains frequent in lNorth. and *Ru.*[1]

§ 618. Masc. and fem. weak nouns are numerous; examples are: masculine: ***anda*** malice, ***bana*** slayer, ***bera*** bear, ***eafora*** son, ***flota*** sailor, ***ġealga*** gallows, ***lida*** sailor, ***mōna*** moon, ***naca*** boat, ***nama*** name, ***sċucca*** demon, ***steorra*** star, ***wita*** prophet, and compounds in *-bora*, e.g. ***mundbora*** protector, ***rǣdbora*** counsellor; feminine: ***burne*** stream, ***ċiriċe*** church, ***folde*** earth, ***hearpe*** harp, ***hrūse*** earth, ***sunne*** sun, ***wulle*** wool, and formations in *-iġe*, e.g. ***hlǣfdiġe*** lady, ***mōdriġe*** aunt,[3] and in *-ele*, e.g. *hacele* cloak, and many loan-words (§ 518). The only invariably weak neuters are ***ēage*** eye, ***ēare*** ear; ***wange***, cheek (also ***þunwange***), can be weak, but has also strong forms partly masc., partly fem.: g.s. *wonges*, d.s. *-wange*, n.p. *wangas*, *-wonge*, *-wonga*, g.p. *-wonga*; so (*þun*)*wenġe*, a strong form, has weak inflexion, d.s. *-wenġan.*

§ 619. **Phonological variants.** (1) (*a*) Traces of the I-E variations

[1] The reading of the Moore MS. was persistently attacked by Förster, most recently *Flussname Themse*, pp. 309–10; but the form is confirmed by the Leningrad MS.

[2] A few first elements of place-names may reflect a weak gen. sg. in Gmc. *-in-* (cf. Goth. *-ins*), e.g. Ct. 1 *Budinhaam.*

[3] The origin of *-iġe* is not identical in these words: cf. Holthausen, *Etym. Wb.*

in the thematic element appear in g.p. *oxna*, d.p. *oxnum*, from *oxa* ox: in these forms the thematic element was I-E *-n-*. With this grade of the thematic element extended, Gmc. had n.p. **oχsniz*; whence with parasiting after regular loss of the final syllable and mutation, VP *oexen*, North. *exen*, also used as acc. pl. But normal *oxan*, *oxena* also occur. (*b*) *Ēastre* Easter, usually forms inflected sg. cases and nom. and acc. pl. in *-on*, apparently from Gmc. *-ōn-*, a form of the thematic element frequent in fem. nouns in other languages; a strong nom. and acc. pl. *Ēastra*, *-o*, *-u* occurs in lW-S.

(2) Nouns with *-i̯-* before the thematic element have umlaut of the root vowel; if the root syllable is short, the West Gmc. consonant doubling appears except in the case of *r* (§ 407). Examples are, masculine: *āglǣċa* monster, *bēna* suppliant, *bylda* builder, *byrġa* surety, *fēþa* troop, *flīema* fugitive, *wyrhta* worker; feminine: *bēċe* beech, *bīeme* trumpet, *byrne* corslet, *mȳre* mare, *ȳċe* toad, and nouns in *-estre*, e.g. *hlēapestre* dancer, and *-iċġe*, e.g. *sealtiċġe* dancer.

Examples with the West Gmc. doubling are masc. *wræċċa* exile, fem. *smiþþe* smithy; and with *-i̯-* retained after *r*, fem. *beriġe* berry.

With *-i̯-* immediately after the root vowel: *frīġea* lord < **fraui̯ô* (Goth. *frauja*).[1]

(3) Nouns from roots ending in a vowel or diphthong are declined thus:

	Masculine	Feminine
Sg.		
Nom.	ġefēa, *joy*	bēo, *bee*
Acc.	ġefēan	bēon
Gen.	ġefēan	bēon
Dat.	ġefēan	bēon
Pl.		
Nom.	ġefēan	bēon
Acc.	ġefēan	bēon
Gen.	ġefēana	bēona
Dat.	ġefēam	bēom

[1] S–B, § 277.*a*.2, place here *twȳ* for *twēo* doubt, but the form does not occur before 1200 (Bodleian MS. of OE Boethius).

There is no difference in the declension of masc. and fem. nouns of this type. The phonology of most of the words has already been discussed. Here belong the masculines:

ġefēa joy (§ 235.2; 238.2.b), *ġefā* enemy, *rā* roe (§ 236.3), *frēa* lord (§ 120.3), and so *wēa* woe, *twēo* doubt (§ 235.2), Angl. *sċīa* shin (§ 238), *Swēon* Swedes, also the rare weak forms of *þrēa* affliction (§ 598.2);

feminines are: *dā* doe, *flā* arrow, *tā* toe, *þō* clay (§ 236), *sēo* pupil of eye (§ 235.2), *bēo* bee (§ 238.1), *cēo* crow, *rēo* blanket (§ 238.3), *pīe*, *pēo* sort of insect (origin unknown), *slahae* slay (§ 145);

of doubtful gender are: Ep., Cp. *ċīan* pl. gills, *flēa* flea, *flēa*, *flēo*, *flīo* albugo (§ 235.2), *mēo* shoe (origin unknown), *slā* sloe (§ 236). Beside *flā*, *slā*, *tā*, and *flēa* in both senses are strong forms: *flān* (m.f.), *slāg*, *slāh*, *tān* (f., rare), *flēah* (n.). Conversely lW-S has weak *tā* (f.) twig, beside strong *tān* (m.).

On *lēo*, lion, see § 510.

(4) Short syllable fem. weak nouns often have bye-forms declined according to the ō-declension. *VP* has only *lufe*, *lufan* love; W-S has always n.s. *lufu*, but often weak inflexions, *Ru.*[1] only once n.s. *lufu*; loss of *-n* and confusion of endings make the North. position obscure. Otherwise ō-declension forms are chiefly W-S, e.g. *ċinu* fissure, *faþu* aunt, *spadu* spade, *wucu* week, beside weak forms, and so the loan-word *peru*, *pere* pear.

(5) On the interchange of *g* and *w* in *hīgan*, *hīwan*, family, see § 412; g.p. *hīġna*, *hīna*, also *hīona* with vocalization, whence *īo* > *ēo* is extended to d.p. *hēowum* beside *hīgum*, *hīwum*.

C. Minor Declensions

I. ATHEMATIC NOUNS

§ 620. **a. MASCULINE**

Sg.		
Nom.	fōt, *foot*	mann, *man*
Acc.	fōt	mann
Gen.	fōtes	mannes
Dat.	fēt	menn

Pl.		
Nom.	fēt	menn
Acc.	fēt	menn
Gen.	fōta	manna
Dat.	fōtum	mannum

§ 621. **Origin of forms.** The Gmc. endings were sg. *-s*, *-um* (§ 331, footnote), *-iz*, *-i*, pl. *-iz*, *-uns*, *-ôm*, *-umiz*. In OE the gen. sg. is from the *a*-declension, the dat. sg. and nom. pl. (used also as acc.) are regularly developed from the Gmc. forms. The acc. sg. and gen. and dat. pl. may be equally from the Gmc. forms or from the *a*-declension. In nom. sg., consonant changes of various kinds would take place before *-s*, but in all Gmc. languages these are levelled away, so Gmc. may already have had, for example, **fōt* for **fōss* < **fōts*.

§ 622. Like *fōt* is *tōþ* tooth; *ōs* immortal being (recorded only in n.s. as a rune-name, and in g.p. *ēsa*, with extension of the mutated vowel from nom. pl.; cf. ON n.p. *ǣsir*). Compound names in *-mann* seem to have been declined according to the *a*-declension, g.s. *-mannes*, d.s. *-manne*.[1] There is no neut. athematic noun in OE.[2]

§ 623. **Early, late, and dialectal forms.** The mutated forms of *fōt*, *tōþ* often have *ōe* in early and Angl. texts. *VP* has already analogical pl. *tōðas* beside *tōeð*, and Martyrology *fōtas* (OET, p. 178), and later texts have other analogical forms after the *a*-declension from *fōt* and *tōþ*. *Mann* has a weak bye-form *manna*.

§ 624. b. FEMININE

Sg.		
Nom.	studu, *post*	bōc, *book*
Acc.	studu	bōc
Gen.	*stude	bēċ, bōce
Dat.	styde, stude	bēċ, bōc
Pl.		
Nom.	styde	bēċ
Acc.	styde	bēċ
Gen.	studa	bōca
Dat.	studum	bōcum (bōecum, Ct. 42)

[1] e.g. OE Bede *Ġearomonne*, Ct. 14 *Sulmonnesburg*. The element is sometimes not identical with OE *mann* but is Celtic, e.g. *Cædmon* < **Katumanos*.

[2] The d.s. **sċrȳd* often quoted as from *sċrūd*, garment, seems not to exist; the word is a neut. *a*-stem, pl. *sċrūd*.

§ 625. **Origin of forms.** The declension was originally identical with that of the masc. nouns, but many analogies intervened. Nom. sg. of short root syllable nouns in *-u* is from the *ō*-declension, or, since it is extended to the acc. (recorded for *studu*), perhaps rather from the *u*-declension. Other analogical forms are gen. and dat. sg. without umlaut, various gen. sg. forms in *-s* (*sūles, ēas, nihtes*) and in *-e* (*bōce, gǣte*), d.s. *āce, nihte* (VP already *nehte* beside *næht*), n.p. *burha*, gen. pl. forms in *-na* (*hnutena, gǣtena, cūna*), gen. and dat. pl. with umlaut (*brēċena, gǣtena, bōēcum*).

§ 626. Like *studu* are *hnutu* nut, *hnitu* nit. From *studu* forms with *ð* also occur, d.s. *styðe*, a.p. *styða*, KG *stoðe* (with *-a*, *-e* from *ō*-declension). From *hnutu* occur g.s. *hnute* or *hnyte*, d.s. and a.p. *hnyte*, g.p. *hnuta, hnutena*, d.p. *hnutum*. From *hnitu* only n.s., and a.p. *hnite*.

§ 627. Like *bōc* are declined a group of words, of which the recorded forms are given below, including those found only in composition. The acc. is not distinguished from the nom. in sg. or pl. in this declension, so it does not appear among the forms, though if the nom. is not recorded it is inferred from the acc. Forms due to the normal variety of spelling of mutated sounds (*ōē* for *ē*, *ĭ* for *y̆*, Kt. *ĕ* for *ǣ, y̆*) are not given.

āc oak:[1] g.s. *āce*, d.s. *ǣċ, āce, āc*, n.p. *ǣċ*, g.p. *ācana* (Birch, no. 219), d.p. *ācum*.

gāt goat: g.s. *gāte, gǣte*, d.s. *gǣt*, n.p. *gǣt*, g.p. *gāta, gǣtena*, d.p. *gātum*.

brōc, covering for the leg: n.p. *brēċ*, g.p. *brēċena*.

gōs goose: g.s. *gōse*, n.p. *gēs*, g.p. *gōsa*.

burg city:[2] g.s. *byrġ, burge*, d.s. *byrġ, burg*, n.p. *byrġ, burha*, g.p. *burga, burha*, d.p. *burgum, burhum* (§ 447).

**dung* prison: d.s. *diṅġ* (And. 1272).

turf, turf: g.s., d.s., n.p. *tyrf*,[3] g.p. *turfa*, d.p. *turfum*.

grūt, meal: d.s. *grȳt*,[4] *grūt*, g.p. *grūta*.

lūs, louse: n.p. *lȳs*, g.p. *lūsa*, d.p. *lūsum*.

mūs, mouse: g.s. *mūse*, n.p. *mȳs*.

On this class is modelled the late d.s. *-līeġ* (Birch, no. 1312) from *lēah*, open country (cf. § 589.3).

[1] But *āc* as a rune-name follows the *a*-declension, n.p. *ācas* (Rid. 43, 10).

[2] But fem. names in *-burg* follow the *ō*-declension, a.g.d. *-burge*. Variant forms of *burg* due to parasiting, and to the unvoicing of final *g*, are not given above.

[3] Apparent a.p. *turf* is probably collective sg.

[4] Spelled *gruiit*, Cp. 1619 (cf. § 199) as g.s.

§ 628. Phonological variants. (1) A number of nouns have final *-h* which is lost in inflected forms with endings:

furh, furrow: g.s. *fyrh, furh, fūre*, d.s. *fyrh, furh*, a.p. *fūra* (Birch, no. 945), g.p. *fūra, fūrena*, d.p. *fūrum*.
furh, fir: a.p. *fyrh*.
sulh, plough: g.s. *sūle, sūles*, d.s. *sylġ, sylh*, n.p. *sylh*, g.p. *sūla, sūlum*.
þrūh, trough: g.s. *þrȳh*, d.s. *þrȳh, þrūh, þrūge*, d.p. *þrūm*.
wlōh, fringe: a.p. *wlōēh* (Li.), g.p. *wglōana* (Li., sic).

Forms due to parasiting (e.g. *furuh*) are not given above. Early forms are Ep., Erf. *furhum, uulōhum* (§ 461); Cp. *uulōum* (uncontracted); Ep., Erf., Cp. *thuerhfyri* (for *-fyrih*). Extension of loss of *h* to final position occurs in lW-S a.s. *sul*, d.s. *syl*. On analogical *g, ġ* in *þrūge, sylġ* see § 447.

(2) In *ċū* cow, all inflexions (except g.p. *-a*, § 236) can be contracted with the root vowel, but they can be replaced by analogy, hence g.s. *cū, cūe, cūs*, d.s. *cȳ*, n.p. *cȳ*, g.p. *cūa, cūna*, d.p. *cūm, cūum*. *VP* has a.p. *cȳe* (with *-e* from *ō*-stems).

(3) *Neaht, nieht* night, differs from other athematic nouns in the completeness with which functional umlaut has disappeared. The mutated or the unmutated vowel can be levelled out to any case. In eW-S only forms with mutated vowel occur (*i* or *ie*), but *VP* has unmutated *æ* (i.e. *ea* smoothed) 32 times, mutated *e* twice, and *æ* is used nearly always in North. and *Ru.*[1] lW-S and poetry have occasional *ea* beside prevailing *i*. On Angl. forms with palatal umlaut see § 308. The usual declension is g.s. *nihte*, also *nihtes*,[1] d.s. *niht, nihte*, n.p. *niht*, g.p. *nihta*, d.p. *nihtum*.[2]

(4) *Ēa* water, river, can be used for all cases except d.p. *ēam*, also Ct. 44 *ēum*, W-S *ēaum*, lW-S *ēauum*. W-S has frequently also g. and d.s. *īe*. Analogical forms are eW-S g.s. *ēas*, lW-S n.p. *ēan*. But W-S has also mutated g.s. *ē* (nW-S form); cf. d.s. *ǣ*, Ps. 35, 8. Addition of analogical endings to this form gives Ct. 30 g.s. *ēe*, eW-S d.s. *ēæ, ēe*. Difficult forms in place-names are: Ct. 4 *Uuestanae*, probably dat. (loc.) for nom., with *ǣ* for *ē*; Ct. 6 *Liminaee* (for

[1] With this inflexion (mostly used adverbially) the noun can be masc., e.g. *ānes nihtes*, OEC 616.

[2] The first element of *nihtegale* nightingale, has in early texts the ending *-i* or *-æ*: while *-æ* may be an analogical ending from the *ō*-declension, *-i* (also found in OS and OHG) is not explicable as a case-ending of the athematic declension. It is perhaps identical with the *-i* of LR *uyrdi* (§ 605).

usual *Liminēa*) is acc., *-aee* is for *ēa* (cf. § 140) with analogical ending; later the form is used as loc. (syntactically nom., *fluvius qui dicitur L.*, Birch, nos. 148, 411, related texts).

(5) *Meoluc* milk, has d.s. *meoloc* or *meoloce* with levelling of the root and formative elements from nom. and acc. On syncopated forms see § 390. In Angl. *milc* (VP, Rit.) the form proper to gen. and dat. sg. (§ 331.3) is levelled to nom. and acc. So inst. loc. sg. (§ 574.4, footnote) *meolcum*, but Angl. *milcum* (BG).[1]

(6) Place-names of Celtic origin seem frequently to adopt the forms of the athematic nouns in OE, having gen. sg. in *-e*, otherwise no endings, e.g. a. and d.s. *Cent* Kent, a. and d.s. *Ī*, g.s. *Īe* Iona, a. and d.s. *Wiht*, g.s. *Wihte* Wight, d.s. *Tenet* Thanet. So native d.s. *Ċert*, Chart,[2] and other occasional forms.

2. NOUNS OF RELATIONSHIP

§ 629. The following are the W-S paradigms; starred forms do not occur in eW-S:

Sg.

Nom.	fæder, *father*	brōþor, *brother*	mōdor, *mother*	dohtor, *daughter*
Acc.	fæder	brōþor	mōdor	dohtor
Gen.	fæder	brōþor	mōdor	dohtor
Dat.	fæder	brēþer	mēder	dehter

Pl.

Nom.	fæd(e)ras	brōþor	*mōdra, *-ru	dohtor
Acc.	fæd(e)ras	brōþor	*mōdra, *-ru	dohtor
Gen.	fæd(e)ra	*brōþra	mōdra	dohtra
Dat.	fæderum	brōþrum	mōdrum	dohtrum

Normal variation between *-er*, *-or*, *-ur* is found in final syllables. In lW-S, words with mutation in the dat. sg. can extend it to the gen. (e.g. *mēder*, rare *brēþer*), or conversely remove it in the dat.

[1] If *io* of *mioloc* CP 459, 18 is not simply an inverted spelling for *eo*, it represents a crossing of **meluk* and **milik* to produce **miluk* whence **mioluk*.

[2] Foreign place-names are frequently indeclinable especially in the dat. (loc.), e.g. *Mailros*, *Gend*, *Paris*, *Rīn*. Names of English rivers are often indeclinable (about 40 per cent. of the ones recorded in OE, Förster, *Flussname Themse*, pp. 314 ff.). Other English place-names are sporadically indeclinable (especially those in *-ing*, examples *PBB* ix. 251–2).

(e.g. *dohter*). Collective *ġe-* may be added to the pl. forms of *brōþor* and *sweostor*. lW-S nom. and acc. pl. of all except *fæder* is normally in *-ru*, *-ra*; *fadero* is North. only. lW-S analogical forms are g.s. *fæderes*, d.s. *fædere*, g.p. *fæderena*.

Sweostor, sister, may be indeclinable except in gen. and dat. pl. *sweostra*, *-trum*. There is great variety of root vowel, *swostor*, *swustor*, &c. (§ 210.2, footnote). The nom. and acc. pl. is again lW-S *-tru*, *-tra*.

§ 630. **Early and dialectal forms.** *VP* g.s. *feadur*, CH *-fadur*, lNorth. *fador*, represent an I-E gen. form (cf. Sanskrit *pitur*),[1] different from that seen in *fædres* (cf. Lat. *patris*). In other cases *VP* has root vowel *e*, except d.p. *feadrum* beside *fedrum*. *VP* extends mutation to g.s. *mōēder*, *doehter*. Extension of mutation to pl. is rare, e.g. Ru.[1] *brōēþre*. Nom. and acc. pl. *-ra*, *-ro*, *-re* are frequent in lNorth.; *Ru.*[1] has only *-re*, *-ræ* (beside the endingless form). On FC *ġibrōþær* see § 369; on Kt. *-ar* for *-or* (e.g. Ct. 38) see § 377; on the root vowel of 'sister' in lNorth. and *Ru.*[1] see §§ 210.2, footnote, 319, 328. Collectives in *ġe-* are found in North. and *Ru.*[1] (not in *VP*). We appear to have in d.p. *soesternum* Rit. (*o* = *w*) a trace of a different collective formation (cf. OS *gisustruonion*). If correct, the OE form has metathesis, as in *westerne*, OS *uuestroni* (§ 459.4).

§ 631. **Origin of forms.** The I-E case-endings were added to *-r*, and the Gmc. paradigm would be sg. *-r*, *-rum*, *-raz*, *-ri*, pl. *-riz*, *-runs*, *-rôm*, *-rumiz*. In West Gmc. the nom. pl. was probably used for acc. pl. In OE the disappearance of all endings except those of gen. and dat. pl. was phonological, and endings appearing in recorded forms (e.g. *fædere*, *brōþru*) are analogical: their origin is obvious, except in the case of nom. and acc. pl. *-u*, which is of uncertain source. The formative element *-er-* was subject to ablaut variation. In the dat. sg. there was no vowel before *-r-*, and hence the root vowel was subject to umlaut in OE, but in the nom. pl. the full grade *-er-* appeared (cf. Gr. d.s. πατρί, n.p πατέρες), and hence the final syllable was lost in Gmc. (§ 331.3), and there was no umlaut in OE. D.s. *fæder* is analogical, cf. North. *feder* beside *fæder*. The vowels of the final syllables of the OE recorded forms in *-er*, *-or*, *-ur* are due to parasiting in the gen. and dat. sg. In the nom. and acc. sg. and pl. *-er* may be from I-E *-er-* (§ 331.2), and *-or*, *-ur* from I-E *-or-* in forms where *u* followed (acc. sg. and acc. pl.; see § 331.6). The gen. and dat. pl. had vanishing grade of the suffix (i.e. no vowel before *-r-*).

[1] Full discussion of this form by Lane, *JEGP* l. 522–8.

3. NOUNS IN *-nd-* (MASC.)

§ 632.

Sg.		
Nom.	frēond, *friend*	hettend, *enemy*
Acc.	frēond	hettend
Gen.	frēondes	hettendes
Dat.	frīend, frēonde	hettende
Pl.		
Nom.	frīend	hettend, -e, -as
Acc.	frīend	hettend, -e, -as
Gen.	frēonda	hettendra
Dat.	frēondum	hettendum

§ 633. The formative element *-nd-* is that found in the present participle, but this follows the *i̯a*-declension in OE, while the nomina agentis basically follow the athematic declension, as the mutation in the dat. sg. and nom. and acc. pl. shows. The gen. and dat. sg. in *-es*, *-e* are from the *a*-stems, while in the disyllables the nom. and acc. pl. in *-e*, gen. pl. in *-ra* are from the adjectival declension. The ending *-as* of the nom. and acc. pl. of disyllables appears already in eW-S, and is extended to *frēondas* and *fēondas* in lNorth., *Ru.*[1], and poetry. Some lW-S texts have forms from disyllables with *-r-* extended to other cases from the gen. pl., e.g. n.p. *wealdendras*, d.p. (less often) *wealdendrum*. The disyllables have levelled *-end* all through the paradigm from cases with mutation and from the pres. part. On VP *fīenda*, *-um*, see § 201.3, footnote.

§ 634. Like *frēond* are declined *fēond* enemy, *tēond* accuser (forms with mutation do not occur), and a.p. *gōddēnd* (El. 359) from *gōddōnd* benefactor.[1] *Frēond* and *fēond* may take the collective prefix *ġe-*, when the sense is usually 'reciprocal friends, enemies'. Further examples declined like *hettend* are *āgend* owner, *hǣlend* saviour, *wealdend* ruler, *wīġend* warrior.[2]

[1] But words of this type are usually re-formed as *-dōend* (disyllabic, sg. or pl.).

[2] *Swelgend* glutton is masc., but *swelgend* whirlpool is fem. (later also masc. and neut.).

4. STEMS IN INDO-EUROPEAN *-es*, *-os*

§ 635.

Sg.			
Nom.	ċealf, *calf*	lamb, *lamb*	ǣġ, *egg*
Acc.	ċealf	lamb	ǣġ
Gen.	ċealfes	lambes	ǣġes
Dat.	ċealfe	lambe	ǣġe
Pl.			
Nom.	ċealfru	lambru	ǣġru
Acc.	ċealfru	lambru	ǣġru
Gen.	ċealfra	lambra	ǣġra
Dat.	ċealfrum	lambrum	ǣġrum

The above are normal W-S paradigms for these neuters; in lW-S *ċealf*, *lamb* have also endingless nom. and acc. pl., and gen. and dat. pl. *-a*, *-um* (following *word*, § 570); lW-S has also n.p. *ċealfas*. The sg. forms are derived from the *a*-declension. Case-endings were originally added to a formative element, I-E *-es-*, with ablaut variant *-os-*, Gmc. *-iz*, *-az-*, West Gmc. *-ir-*, *-ar-*.[1] The Gmc. nom. sg. appears to have been **kalviz*, **lambiz*, whence OE n.a.s. *cælf* (Angl.: *VP.*, *Cp.*, *Erf.*), *lemb* (Rit.). From nom. sg. of this type is formed *Li.* g.s. *cælfes*, *celfes*. The original gen. sg., in which the case-ending would drop after the formative element, appears in *VP* g.s. *calfur*. Note also the composition form *ǣġer-*, beside *ǣġ*, in Ep. *ǣġerġelu* yolk. *VP* has nom. and acc. pl. *calfur*, *lombur*, beside *calferu*, *lomberu*; so North. *lombor*, beside *lomboro*, *calfero*; poetical *lomber* (Gu. 1015 = 1042), *lambru*.

§ 636. The following traces of *-es*, *-os* declension also occur:

ċild child, neut., is usually declined like *word*, but eW-S has also n.p. *ċilderu*, g.p. *ċildra*, lW-S also d.p. *ċildrum*, Rit., Ru.[1] g.p. *ċildra*; *lǣuw*, ham, has lW-S n.p. *lēower*, g.p. *lēwera*.

Isolated forms in glosses are *brēadru* crumbs, *hǣmedru* married relationships, *speldra* torches.

A considerable number of words have the formative element

[1] OE forms like VP *calfur*, North. *lombor* point to West Gmc. *-ur-* as a form of the suffix; this perhaps arose from *-ar-* in cases where *-u-* followed (§ 331.6). It is usually held to represent I-E *-ər-*, but such a form of the suffix, and the development I-E *ə* > Gmc. *u*, are alike doubtful.

always, and are to be recognized as old *-es*, *-os* stems only by etymological relationship to forms without it, and often by a dat. sg. without ending. Such are: *dōgor* day, *ēagor-*, *ēar-* sea, *hālor* salvation, *hrīþer* head of cattle, *hrōþor* solace, *salor* hall, *sigor* victory (changed to m.), North. *stǣner* stone, Ep., Cp. *sċērero*, Cp. *-sċēruru* n.p. shears, with which cf. *dōeġ* (North.), *ǣġ-*, *hāl*, *hrīþ-*, *hrēþ*, *sele*, *siġe*, *stān*, *sċēar*. Words originally *-es*, *-os*-stems in which the formative element appears in all surviving forms are *ċilfor-*, *ċeolfor-* (in *c.-lamb* she-lamb), *hæteru* pl. garments, *ēar*, North. *æhher* ear of corn. Here may also belong *grandor-* guile, *hōcor* mockery, *nicor* water-monster, *wildor-*, g.s. *wildres*, n.p. *wildru*, wild animal.[1] On nouns of the *i*-declension which appear to be old *-es*, *-os*-stems, see § 610.6. A number of others follow the masc. or neut. *a*-declension, but are shown to be old *es-*, *os*-nouns by alternative forms with umlaut or with *i* for *e*, e.g. *gāst*, *gǣst* spirit, *helt*, *hilt* hilt, *hlāw*, *hlǣw* mound, *hrāw*, *hrǣw* body, North. *breard*, *briord* point (cf. § 124, footnote 5).

5. DENTAL STEMS

§ 637. Nouns of the type of Lat. *nepos*, *nepotem* had in Gmc. short vowels *i*, *u*, or *a* before the dental consonant. The consonant was lost in the nom. sg., which was also used as the acc. In the gen. and dat. sg., and the nom. (used also as acc.) pl., the endings following the dental were lost in early OE (§ 345; cf. 331.3). The gen. and dat. pl. had the usual endings of consonant stems, and developed in OE normally. Hence a normal OE paradigm would be: n.s. *hæle* man, a.s. *hæle*, g.s., d.s., n.p. *hæleþ*, g.p. *hæleþa*, d.p. *hæleþum*. G.s. and d.s. *hæleþ* are not, however, recorded; analogical formations are d.s. *hæleþe*, n.p. *hæleþas*. A new nom. and acc. sg. *hæleþ* is also extracted from the other cases. On the root vowel *æ* (rarely *e*) see § 193.c. Further relics of this declension are:

ealu, *ealoþ*, n. ale; nom. and acc. sg. have normal variation of vowel *-u*, *-o*, *-a*; *ealoþ*, *-aþ* is recorded for gen. and dat. sg.;[2] in pl. only gen. *ealeþa* occurs. *Rit.* has analogical g.s. *alðes*. The root vowel is usually *ea* (§ 208), rarely *a* or *æ* (e.g. lW-S *alu*, *ælaþ*);

[1] *VP* already re-forms to *wild(d)ēor*; cf. § 458.

[2] The vowels of both syllables in gen. and dat. sg. are due to levelling: *ealuþ*, **ælep* (< **alupiz*, *-i*, §§331.3, 203) > *ealu*, *ealuþ*.

mōnaþ, m. month: this noun is fully adopted into the *a*-declension, except for n.p. ***mōnaþ*** beside ***mōnaþas***. On syncopated ***mōnþ*** see § 358. On lW-S ***mōnoþ***, ***-uþ***, lNorth. ***-oð***, ***-eð***, see §§ 377, 379.

mæġeþ, ***mæġþ***, f. maiden: the uninflected form is retained in gen. and dat. sg. and nom. and acc. pl.; *-þ* is always levelled to nom. and acc. sg.;[1] gen. and dat. pl. in *-a*, *-um*. On syncopation see § 341.

[1] The existence of **mæġ*, supposed to be the true nom. sg. of *mæġeþ*, is very doubtful; the instances rather belong to *mǣġ* (kins)woman.

XII

ADJECTIVES

§ 638. In the Germanic languages the adjective was declined mainly with nominal endings, but with an admixture of pronominal endings. Most adjectives could be declined according to a strong or vocalic declension, and also according to the weak declension. Broadly, the weak declension was used when the adjective followed a demonstrative (in OE *se*, *þes*, and possessives, *mīn*, &c.), the strong in other positions, e.g. *ælċ god treow byrð gode wæstmas* 'every good tree bears good fruits', but *þa godan menn* 'the good men'. OE verse admits a freer use of the weak adjective than prose, but the later the verse the less it diverges from the syntax of prose in this matter. Comparative adjectives and the superlatives in *-ma* (§ 675) are declined only weak. *Ōþer* 'second', 'other', is always declined strong, even after demonstratives, e.g. *þa oþre* 'the others'. From adjectives of indefinite quantity, *eall* all, *moniġ* many, *ġenōg* enough, &c., the weak forms are naturally rare, but are used when syntax demands, e.g. *þa monigan cyningas* 'the numerous kings'. *Fela* many, is indeclinable, and so generally are *ġewuna*, *bewuna* accustomed, and *wona* lacking, though some strong forms occur (n. and a.p. m. and f. *ġewune*; n.s.m. *wan*, f. *wonu*, n.p.m. *wone*).

Li. and *Rit.* show confusion in the adjectival, as in the nominal, declension, e.g. in the strong declension *-es* can be extended to gen. sg. fem.; inst. sg. masc. and neut. *-e* is often used in preference to dat. *-um*, and may be extended to the fem.; endingless forms are frequent in all cases, but more so in sg. than pl. The weak declension is much influenced by the strong, *-es* appearing in gen. sg., and forms without ending in the nom. and acc. sg. masc. and neut., while in the nom. and acc. pl. all distinction of strong and weak has disappeared, *-e*, *-o*, *-a* occurring in all syntactic positions.

In *Ru.*[1] the declension of the strong adj. is much disturbed by endingless forms.

A. Strong Declensions

I. *a*- AND *ō*-ADJECTIVES

§ 639.	Masculine	Feminine	Neuter
Sg.			
Nom.	blind, ***blind***	blind	blind
Acc.	blind*ne*	blinde	blind
Gen.	blindes	blind*re*	blindes
Dat.	blind*um*	blind*re*	blind*um*
Inst.	blinde		blinde
Pl.			
Nom.	blind*e*	blinde, -a	blind
Acc.	blind*e*	blinde, -a	blind
Gen.	blind*ra*	blind*ra*	blind*ra*
Dat.	blindum	blindum	blindum

Adjectives with a short root syllable differ from *blind* in the NOMINATIVE SINGULAR FEMININE and the NOMINATIVE AND ACCUSATIVE PLURAL NEUTER: in these cases they have final *-u* (*-o*), e.g. from *til* good, *tilu*.

§ 640. **Origin of forms.** The nominal inflexions require no comment as they are identical with the corresponding forms of the *a*- and *ō*-declensions. (The inst. sg. masc. and neut. is identical with the locative-inst. in *-i* of *a*-nouns, § 571; it is recorded as *-i* in early texts, e.g. Ep. *binumini*, *bisiuuidi*.) The pronominal endings are italicized in the above paradigm. The Gmc. forms of these were: a.s.m. *-anōn*, d.s.m. and n. *-ammō*, g.s.f. *-aizôz*, d.s.f. *-aizai*, n.p.m. *-ai*, g.p. *-aizôm*. In OE the Gmc. final syllables are regularly developed in a.s.m. *-ne*, g.d.s.f. *-re*, n.p.m. *-e*, g.p. *-ra*. On the syncope of medial vowels see §§ 341–2. In view of the absence in early OE of any trace of a vowel before the fem. ending *-re* and g.p. *-ra*, it is possible that the OE forms are derived from *-ezôz*, &c., and that these forms are due to assimilation of the endings to the pronominal declension seen in OHG *dera*, *deru*, *dero*: medial *-e-* would be syncopated earlier than the reflex of *-ai-*, cf. § 331.7. The forms of the dat. sg. masc. and neut. given above are inferred from the Goth. form *-amma*; in North and West Gmc. the medial vowel might be *-u-* (§ 331.6), though this is not certain, since the *-mm-* < *-zm-* (cf. Sanskrit *tasmai* d.s.). Even if this be assumed, it is difficult to derive ON, OE, OS *-um*, OS *-umu*, OHG *-emu* from the same form: the inflexion seems to have been inconsistent in Gmc. with regard both to the internal vowel and the internal consonant (*m* or *mm*). The reason why the final vowel is retained in some languages, while it is lost in others, is also obscure.

§ 641. **Early, late, and dialectal forms.** See § 640 for early forms of the inst. sg. masc. and neut. The pronominal endings *-ne*, *-re*, *-e* appear with *-æ* in early texts, e.g. RC *riičnæ*, *fūsæ*, Ep. *frōdrae*, *stǣġilrae*, from *rīċe* powerful, *fūs* eager, *frōd* wise, *stǣġel* steep. In lW-S and *KG* gen. and dat. sg. fem. and gen. pl. have very often parasiting to *-ere*, *-era*.[1] In *VP* compound adjs. in *-sum* have nom. sg. fem. and nom. acc. pl. neut. in *-sum* (not *-sumu*, e.g. *wynsum*, *wilsum*). In pass. parts. of both strong and weak verbs *-e* is extended to nom. acc. pl. neut. in VP, e.g. *agotene*, *tolēsde*. In eW-S this extension is found occasionally with other adjs., and in lW-S, lNorth., *Ru.*[1], and *KG* it is frequent. In W-S nom. acc. pl. fem. are frequently in *-e*, although in nouns *-e* is limited to the acc. But, as in the noun, W-S has prevailingly *-a*, and this also occurs in KG (*manega* 175, 476; but *ofermode* 249).

§ 642. Like **blind** are declined e.g. **beald** bold, **beorht** bright, *dēad* dead, *hāl* sound, *hwīt* white, *lang* long, *sēoc* sick, *wīs* wise, *wund* wounded; also adjs. with the formative elements *-cund*, e.g. *æþelcund* noble, *dēofolcund* devilish, *eorlcund* noble, *gǣstcund* spiritual, *weoroldcund* worldly; *-fæst*, e.g. *ārfæst* virtuous, *eorþfæst* fixed in the earth, *siġefæst* victorious, *trēowfæst* faithful; *-feald*, e.g. *ānfeald* single, *felafeald* manifold, and many compounds with numerals, *seofonfeald* sevenfold, &c.; *-full*, e.g. *bismerfull* disgraceful, *wunderfull* wonderful; *-iht*, e.g. *stǣniht* stony, *wudiht* woody (cf. § 204.6);[2] *-isċ*, e.g. *ċildisċ* childish, *Englisċ* English; *-leas*, e.g. *ārleas* merciless, *ġīmeleas* negligent, *hāmleas* homeless; *-līċ*, e.g. *dæġlīċ* daily, *heofonlīċ* heavenly, *tīdlīċ* temporary;[3] *-weard*, e.g. *andweard* present, *niþerweard* turned downward.

There are far fewer with short root syllables, e.g. *dol* foolish, *fram* active, *gram* angry, *til* good, *trum* firm, also *sum* some, and its compounds, e.g. *fremsum* beneficial, *langsum* lengthy, *wilsum* pleasant, *wynsum* delightful.

§ 643. **Phonological variants.** (1) Adjs. with the root vowel *æ*

[1] eW-S has already a few instances, mostly in g.d.s.f. *sumere*.

[2] There is also a form *-ihte* following the *i̯a-*, *i̯ō*-declension (§ 644); decisive inflexions are too rare to show which was the more frequent.

[3] The formative element *-līċ* underwent very early shortening, hence it has *-u* in the nom. sg. fem. and nom. acc. pl. neut. (§ 356, footnote 1); it is also subject to phonetic change (§§ 340, 371). Adjs. in *-isċ* can also take the ending *-u* (e.g. *mennisċu*, CP 71, 12, n.s.f.).

have in W-S *a* not only before back vowels in the inflexional syllables (like the corresponding nouns, § 574.1), but also as a rule before *-e* in the acc. sg. fem., in the gen. and inst. sg. masc. and neut., and in the nom. and acc. pl. masc. and fem. (and neut. if *-e* is extended to it). Hence normal forms are:

	Masculine	Feminine	Neuter
Sg.			
Nom.	hwæt, *active*	hwatu (hwæt)	hwæt
Acc.	hwætne	hwate	hwæt
Gen.	hwates	hwætre	hwates
Dat.	hwatum	hwætre	hwatum
Inst.	hwate		hwate
Pl.			
Nom.	hwate	hwate	hwatu
Acc.	hwate	hwate	hwæt
Gen.	hwætra	hwætra	hwætra
Dat.	hwatum	hwatum	hwatum

This restoration of Gmc. *a* before *-e* in adjs. appears to be a purely W-S development, cf. Li. *glæde*, Ru.[2] *glæde*, *læte*, VP *hreðe* (not **hræðe*), KG *unuuere*, all nom. or acc. pl. masc.

Like *hwæt* are declined *bær* bare, *blæċ* black, *glæd* glad, *hræd* swift, *læt* slow, *smæl* small, *sæd* sated, *stræċ* severe, *wær* cautious. Forms with *æ* levelled to positions before back vowels are not uncommon, especially from *hræd* and *stræċ*, e.g. d.s.m. *hrædum*, d.s.f. wk. *stræcan*.

(2) Adjs. with final *-h* lose it in inflexion between voiced sounds, and contraction follows if both sounds are vowels, compensatory lengthening if the first is a consonant. Between two consonants *h* is lost, e.g. a.s.m. *þweorne* from *þweorh+ne*, and so g.d.s.f. *þweorre*, g.p. *þweorra*. The system will be shown by the following paradigms:

	Masculine	Feminine	Neuter
Sg.			
Nom.	hēah, *high*	hēa	hēah
Acc.	hēane	hēa	hēah
Gen.	hēas	hēare	hēas
Dat.	hēam	hēare	hēam
Inst.	hēa		hēa

	Masculine	Feminine	Neuter
Pl.			
Nom.	hēa	hēa	hēa
Acc.	hēa	hēa	hēa
Gen.	hēara	hēara	hēara
Dat.	hēam	hēam	hēam
Sg.			
Nom.	þweorh, *crooked*	þwēoru	þweorh
Acc.	þweorne	þwēore	þweorh
Gen.	þwēores	þweorre	þwēores
Dat.	þwēorum	þweorre	þwēorum
Inst.	þwēore		þwēore
Pl.			
Nom.	þwēore	*þwēore, -a	þwēoru
Acc.	þwēore	*þwēore, -a	þwēoru
Gen.	þweorra	þweorra	þweorra
Dat.	þwēorum	þwēorum	þwēorum

On a.s.m. *hēanne* (lW-S; eW-S only in Junius' copy of *CP*), *wōnne* see § 484.[1] Nom. and acc. pl. neut. has both *hēa* and analogical *hēah*. Other analogical forms are frequent, e.g. *hēahne*, *hēaum*, *ġemāum*, *hrēoum*, *frīoum* (§ 239), *hēage*, *ġemāge*, *wōge*, *ðrōgum* (§ 447). On Angl. forms see § 238.2. On Angl. forms of *þweorh*, *sċeolh* see §§ 231–2; and on compensatory lengthening §§ 240–1.

Like *hēah* are declined: *fāh* hostile, *flāh* deceitful, *ġemāh* depraved, *hrēoh* rough, *sċēoh* shy, *tōh* tough, *þrōh* rancid, *anwlōh*, *ġewlōh* fruitful, *wōh* crooked.[2] The neuters of *flāh*, *ġemāh*, *þrōh*, *wōh* occur used as nouns.

Like *þweorh* are *ġefearh* pregnant (of the sow), *sċeolh* oblique. *Þweorh* forms nom. sg. fem., nom. acc. pl. neut. *þwēoru*, lW-S *þwēor*, but *ġefearh* is unchanged in nom. sg. fem. (only form recorded). Only weak inflexions of *sċeolh* occur.

(3) *Rūh* rough declines with intervocalic *-w-*, *rūwes*, &c.; or *-g-*, *rūge*, &c.; a.s.m. *rūhne*; cf. § 412.

(4) Adjs. with final syllabic consonants can develop a parasite vowel in forms without endings (§ 363), and before endings begin-

[1] But cf. Weyhe in *Germanica, Festschrift für Ed. Sievers*, p. 316.

[2] Here might be added *nēah* near, rare and late as adj.

ning with consonants (§ 364), hence, for example, from *fæġer* fair, a.s.m. *fæġerne*, g.d.s.f. *fæġerre*, g.s.m. *fæġres*, but also analogical *fæġeres* (§ 363). In later OE medial *rr* can be simplified, e.g. g.p. *fæġera* (§ 457). Adjs. of this type are *biter* bitter, *hlūtor* pure, *wacor* wakeful, *efen* even.

(5) Adjs. with syncopation of a medial vowel are of many kinds. Syncopation may be according to § 341, § 351, or § 388.

	Masculine	Feminine	Neuter
Sg.			
Nom.	hāliġ, *holy*	hāliġu	hāliġ
Acc.	hāliġne	hālġe	hāliġ
Gen.	hālġes	hāliġre	hālġes
Dat.	hālġum	hāliġre	hālġum
Inst.	hālġe		hālġe
Pl.			
Nom.	hālġe	hālġe, -a	hāliġu
Acc.	hālġe	hālġe, -a	hāliġu
Gen.	hāliġra	hāliġra	hāliġra
Dat.	hālġum	hālġum	hālġum

Restoration of the medial vowel is frequent, e.g. *moniġum*, *sāriġe*. Late syncopation after short syllables (§ 388) can be assumed not to have occurred when the vowel is written, e.g. *miċele*, *swutole*, *yfeles*. The nom. sg. fem. and nom. acc. pl. neut. should phonologically have *-u* only after long syllable+short syllable, and even then only if the medial syllable contained *i* or *u*, which was syncopated (type *hēafdu*, § 353). In practice *-u* is very frequently used in all types of disyllabic adjs., and the medial vowel is usually not syncopated (or is restored), e.g. eW-S *ǣniġu*, *āgenu*, *moneġu*; VP *ēadiġu*, *forċerredu*, *īdelu*, *miċelu*. The double consonant arising in acc. sg. masc. of adjs. in *-n*, gen. dat. sg. fem., and gen. pl. of adjs. in *-r* (e.g. *gyldenne*, *ōþerre*), seems to have been simplified early and then often restored, for sporadic simplification in spelling occurs before 900 (e.g. eW-S g.p. *ōþera*).

So are declined:

(*a*) Adjs. in *-iġ*, e.g. *hāliġ* holy, *moniġ* many, *ōmiġ* rusty. On the history of the suffix see §§ 358, 376. On *-eġ-*, *-i-*, *-e-* for *-iġ-* see § 371, 267.[1]

[1] It is doubtful if occasional spelling in eW-S of *-iġ* as *-ug*, *-og*, in endingless

(*b*) Adjs. in *-el, -ol*, e.g. *atol* terrible, *þancol* thankful, *lȳtel* little, *miċel* great, *yfel* evil; and in *-en* (< *-īna-*), e.g. *hǣþen* heathen, and the adjs. of material, *gylden* golden, &c., and later ones without umlaut, as *stānen* beside *stǣnen* of stone.

(*c*) The strong pass. part. in *-en*: here syncope is less usual in W-S, e.g. n.p. *ġebundene* bound, *forcorfene* cut, *afeallene* fallen, beside *ġehealdne* held, *-worpne* thrown. Syncope is frequent in *VP*, but less so in *Ru.*[1] and North.

(*d*) The weak pass. part. in *-ed*, in which syncope is usual in inflected forms after long syllables, but not after shorts, e.g. n.p. *ġedēmde* judged, *ġeflīemde* put to flight, *arǣrde* raised up, but *fremede* done, *ġetrymede* arranged, *aþenede* stretched out. But in W-S after long syllables syncope is frequently extended after dentals (rarely after other consonants) to the uninflected form, e.g. *afēd*(*d*) fed, *ġelǣd*(*d*) led. Cf. § 351, footnote.

(*e*) The weak pass. part. in *-od*, which is not subject to syncope, e.g. *lufod* loved, *ġemacod* made.

(*f*) Miscellaneous adjs. which also belong here are *āgen* own, *fæġen* glad, *open* open; also *arod* swift, *forod* broken, *fracoþ* bad, *nacod* naked, which are not found with syncope.

2. *i̯a-* AND *i̯ō-*ADJECTIVES

§ 644.

	Masculine	Feminine	Neuter
Sg.			
Nom.	midd, *middle*	midd	midd
Acc.	midne	midde	midd
Gen.	middes	midre	middes
Dat.	middum	midre	middum
Inst.	midde		midde
Pl.			
Nom.	midde	midde, -a	midd
Acc.	midde	midde, -a	midd
Gen.	midra	midra	midra
Dat.	middum	middum	middum

forms of nom. acc. pl. neut., shows influence of the apocopated *-u*: *monog*, *hefug* (and similarly *miċul*).

	Masculine	Feminine	Neuter
Sg.			
Nom.	wilde, *wild*	wildu	wilde
Acc.	wildne	wilde	wilde
Gen.	wildes	wildre	wildes
Dat.	wildum	wildre	wildum
Inst.	wilde		wilde
Pl.			
Nom.	wilde	wilde, -a	wildu
Acc.	wilde	wilde, -a	wildu
Gen.	wildra	wildra	wildra
Dat.	wildum	wildum	wildum

§ 645. **Origin of forms.** In adjs. with root syllables with West Gmc. gemination of consonants, the cases with nominal endings had the same Gmc. forms as the corresponding cases of *seċġ*, *synn*, *cynn*; adjs. with originally long root syllables agreed in these cases with *ende*, *ġierd*, *wīte* (see §§ 575, 590), except in the nom. sg. fem.: this was in *-iō*, an analogical form instead of *-ī*. The pronominal forms in the dat. sg. masc. and neut. and the nom. and acc. pl. masc. had the same inflexions as in *a*-stems with *-i̯-* (*-ii̯-*) before them and are regularly developed in OE. The acc. sg. masc. *-i̯anōn* or *-ii̯anōn* should give OE *-inæ* > *-ene*, and similarly the gen. dat. sg. fem. and gen. pl. should be *-iræ*, *-ira* > *-ere*, *-era* (cf. *-unæ*, *-uræ*, *-ura* > *-one*, &c., from *u̯a-*, *u̯ō*-stems); the absence of connecting vowel must be attributed to the influence of the *a-*, *ō*-stems.

§ 646. **Early, late, and dialectal forms.** In eW-S *-e* is found in use for both nom. and acc. pl. fem. In eW-S and *VP* *-e* is already frequently extended to the nom. sg. fem., nom. and acc. pl. neut., especially in present participles. Scribal retention of double consonants before inflexions beginning with consonants is frequent, e.g. *middre*, *nyttre*.

§ 647. Like *midd* are declined *nytt* useful, *ġesibb* related. Examples like *wilde* are *æþele* noble, *cēne* bold, *clǣne* clean, *ēċe* eternal, *fiþerfēte* four-footed,[1] *grēne* green, *līþe* gentle, *mǣre* famous, *rīċe* powerful, *ġesīene* visible, *wēste* waste, *wierþe* worthy;[2]

[1] This is an example of a frequent type of *i̯a-*, *i̯ō*-adj. meaning 'having a certain number of an object', e.g. *þrīsċӯte* triangular, *þrӯmylċe* having three milking hours, *sixeċġe* hexagonal, *sixnihte* six days old.

[2] *Īren*, iron, seems to be a *i̯a*-stem in OE as a noun, and a *i̯a-*, *i̯ō*-stem as an adj.; hence in *Beow.* g.p. *īrenna* (noun), a.s.n. *-īrenne* (adj.) have *-nn-* (sometimes graphically simplified), and so lW-S a.p.m. *ӯrenne* (adj.). But later poems have

also formations in *-bǣre*, e.g. *hālbǣre* wholesome, *wæstmbǣre* fruitful; in *-ede*, e.g. *hōcede* hooked, *hringede* ringed, *hoferede* humpbacked; in *-wende*, e.g. *hātwende* hot, *hwīlwende* temporary; and present participles in *-ende*.

§ 648. Phonological variants. (1) Prim. Gmc. **frīi̯a-* free, usually exhibits in W-S a declension from *frēo* (n.p. *frēo*, g.s.f. *frēore*, &c.); but a declension from *frīġ-* also occurs (n.s.m. *frīġ*, a.s.m. *frīġne*, g.s.m. *frīġes*, n.p. *frīġe*, &c.). On the origin of these alternatives see § 410; on forms with final *-h* § 466; on Angl. forms § 238.1.

(2) Prim. Gmc. *ni̯u̯i̯a-* new, West Gmc. *niuu̯i̯a-* (§ 120.2) develops as eW-S *nīewe*, *nīwe*, Angl. *nīowe*, *nēowe*, Li. *nīwe*; inflected *nīwne*, *nēowne*, &c. The retention of final *-i* > *-e* after an originally short root syllable is difficult (attempted explanation, Dahl, *Substantival inflexion in early OE*, p. 106).

(3) The formation of acc. sg. masc., gen. and dat. sg. fem., and gen. pl. of adjs. ending in consonant+liquid or nasal+*e* has been discussed, and a list of such adjs. given, in § 364. Recorded forms are a.s.m. *lȳðerne*, *fǣċne*, *frēċne*, d.s.f. *dīgolre*, g.p. *dȳġelra* (if these are to *dīeġle*, not to *dīegol*), *lȳðra*, *frēċenra*; divergent is lW-S d.s.f. *ġīferre*, greedy, beside *ġīfre*. *Dierne* secret, has no parasiting, g.p. *dyrnra*.[1] Similar words in double consonants simplify them (§ 476) in these cases, e.g. a.s.m. *þynne*, *ġinne*, d.s.f. *þynre*, to *þynne* thin, *ġinne* vast, a.s.m. *þicne*, d.s.f. *þicre* (also etymological spelling *þiccre*) to *þiċċe* thick.

(4) The neut. *i̯a*-stem *earfeþe* trouble, n.p. *earfeþu* was regarded as neut. of an adj. *earfeþe* difficult; *earfeþu* could also be treated as a fem. sg. and declined like *bieldu* (§ 589.7). *Earfeþe* both noun and adj. could also be transferred to the *a*-declension, when the development might be *earfoþ* or *earfeþ* (§§ 336, 356; both are frequent in inflected forms and in composition); hence with suffix mixture *earfoþe* is frequent beside *earfeþe* for the *i̯a*-, *i̯ō*-stem adj.

frequent forms with a short medial syllable or syncopation, pointing to inflexion as a nominal *a*-stem, adjectival *a*-, *ō*-stem (e.g. *Sol. Sat.* 28, 469, *Chr. Sat.* 518); note also *VP* d.p. *īrnum* (adj.), a.p.n. *īrenu* (adj.). Thus forms with *-n-* seem too early and numerous to belong to § 457, and it would appear that Gmc. **īsarna-* did not always change declension when OE **īsrana-* > **īrana-* developed from it (§ 459.4, footnote).

[1] From an OE point of view the adjs. of the points of the compass, *norþerne* northern, &c., are like *dierne* (cf. §§ 339, 459.4).

3. u̯a- AND u̯ō-ADJECTIVES

§ 649.	Masculine	Feminine	Neuter
Sg.			
Nom.	ġearu, *ready*	ġearu	ġearu
Acc.	ġearone	ġearwe	ġearu
Gen.	ġearwes	ġearore	ġearwes
Dat.	ġearwum	ġearore	ġearwum
Inst.	ġearwe		ġearwe
Pl.			
Nom.	ġearwe	ġearwe	ġearu
Acc.	ġearwe	ġearwe	ġearu
Gen.	ġearora	ġearora	ġearora
Dat.	ġearwum	ġearwum	ġearwum

§ 650. Origin of forms. The cases with nominal endings do not diverge from those of the corresponding nouns *bearu, sinu, searu* (§§ 580, 594). The pronominal cases are also developed regularly: see § 645 on the acc. sg. masc., gen. dat. sg. fem., and gen. pl.; the dat. sg. masc. and neut. have analogical -u̯- like the dat. pl. (§ 581).

§ 651. Early, late, and dialectal forms. On W-S parasiting, e.g. n.p. *ġearuwe, -owe, -ewe*, see § 365. Final *-u* can appear as *-o* and in later texts as *-a* (§ 377). Nom. acc. pl. fem. is not recorded with *-a* in eW-S. In lW-S both final and internal *uw* for *u* occurs, e.g. *ġearuw, -uwre.* Note g.p. *ġearra*, CP 433, 30 (twice).

§ 652. Adjs. declined like *ġearu* are *basu* purple, *calu* bald, *fealu* fallow, *ġeolu* yellow, *hasu* grey, *mearu* tender, *nearu* narrow.

§ 653. Phonological variants. (1) Here belong historically a group of adjs. with -u̯- after a long syllable: these all extend -u̯- through the entire paradigm (cf. § 272), e.g. *glēaw, glēawne, glēawe, glēawum.*[1] Early texts and North. have sometimes *-u-* for *-w-*, e.g. Cp. *glēu*, Li. *unglēu* (cf. § 273). Such adjs. are *slāw* slow, *ġedēaw* dewy, *glēaw* wise, *hnēaw* mean, *hrēaw* raw, *ġesēaw* juicy, *rēow* fierce, *rōw* mild, *þēow* servile.[2]

(2) The pl. *fēawe*, few (W-S also *fēawa*, influenced by *fela* many) has d.p. *fēam* < **faum* < **fau̯um* (§ 405), and analogical *fēawum*,

[1] Forms without *w* are rare, e.g. n.s.f. *glēa*, KG 693, a.s.m. *rēone*, Jul. 481.
[2] The uninflected form of *hlēow-* (*ġe-*, *un-*), warm, is uncertain.

fēaum. Frequent is n.a.p. *fēa* < **fau* < **fau̯u* < **fau̯ō* nom. acc. pl. neut. In lW-S an indeclinable *fēawa* (like *fela*) appears, e.g. *æfter feawa dagum*, *ofer feawa* (= super pauca), and often with gen. pl., *feawa fixa*.

4. *i*-ADJECTIVES

§ 654. Here belong the adjs. with short root syllables, *bryċe* brittle, *freme* excellent, *ġemyne* mindful, *swiċe* deceitful. Their declension is completely assimilated to that of *wilde* (§ 644), but they remain clearly distinguished by their short root syllables with no constant gemination.

Adjs. of this declension with long root syllables were also assimilated to *wilde*, and are only to be distinguished in OE by etymological means, e.g. *blīþe* joyful, *brȳċe* useful, *ġedēfe* becoming, *ġemǣne* common; traces of the original uninflected form without *-e* may be the adv. (*ġe*)*fyrn* formerly,[1] and *lȳt* little, used as noun and adv. and (rarely) as indeclinable adj.

5. *u*-ADJECTIVES

§ 655. Traces of the *u*-declension are preserved in W-S by the adj. *cwicu*, *cucu* alive, which has n.s. *cucu*, *-a* in all genders, a.s.m. *cucone*, *-une*, *-ene* (also with *-nn-*, § 457, footnote). Other cases follow the *a*-, *ō*-declension, *cuce*, *cucre*, *cucum*, &c., and a.s.m. also *cucne*. (The form *cwiċ* is the only one in Angl., and is frequent in W-S beside *cwicu*.)

Similar is *wlacu* tepid, nom. sg. for all genders, beside *wlæc*; the declension is *wlace*, *wlacre*, *wlacum*, &c.

Other *u*-adjs. have passed entirely into the *a*-, *ō*- or *i̯a*-, *i̯ō*-declensions. On etymological grounds the following may be regarded as old *u*-stems:[2] *eġle* troublesome, *enġe* narrow, *heard* hard, *myrġe* pleasant, *smolt*, *smylte* tranquil, *strang*, *strenġe* strong, *swǣr*, *swǣre* heavy (less certain), *swōt*, *swēte* sweet, *þyrre* dry, and compounds in *-wintre*.

[1] Very rarely *fyrn* is adjectival.

[2] Mere fluctuation between the *a*- and *i̯a*-declensions does not constitute evidence that an adj. is an old *u*-stem, e.g. *smōþ*, *smēþe* smooth, *gnēaþ*, *ungnȳþe* (un)stinting. See further Ross in *Trans. Philological Soc.*, 1952, pp. 131–42.

B. Weak Adjectives

§ 656.	Masculine	Feminine	Neuter
Sg.			
Nom.	blinda, *blind*	blinde	blinde
Acc.	blindan	blindan	blinde
Gen.	blindan	blindan	blindan
Dat.	blindan	blindan	blindan
Pl.			
Nom.	blindan	blindan	blindan
Acc.	blindan	blindan	blindan
Gen.	blindra, -ena	blindra, -ena	blindra, -ena
Dat.	blindum	blindum	blindum

The weak adj. differs from the weak noun in declension only in that the gen. pl. is usually in *-ra* (as in the strong adj.), and *-ana*, *-ena* is rare except in eW-S, where it is always used: VP has already *-ra* only, and this prevails in *Ru.*[1], lNorth., and lW-S. W-S develops d.p. *-an* earlier in the weak adj. than in the noun and the strong adj. (cf. § 378); it is already as frequent as *-um* in weak adjs. in eW-S. lW-S sporadically extends *-an* to gen. pl.

The adjectival declensions discussed above (1–5) have the same forms before the weak endings as before strong inflexions beginning with vowels, and hence in the nom. sg. masc. their forms are as follows: *hwata, hēa, þwēora, rūwa, fæġ(e)ra, hāl(i)ġa, midda, wilda, frīġea, nīwa, ġīfra, earfoþa, ġearwa, glēawa, swica, blīþa.* Before d.p. *-um* there is always analogical retention of *-w-*, e.g. *nīwum.*

Participles of all types can have the weak form, e.g. *foresprecena, ġelǣreda, ġehorsoda, lācniġenda.*

C. Comparison of Adjectives

§ 657. The compar. adj. ends in *-ra*, and is declined according to the weak declension. The gen. pl. may be in *-ra*, e.g. North. *ældra*, or *-rena*, e.g. VP *aeldrena*, eW-S *ġeongrena.*

The superlative normally ends in *-ost* < *-ust* (§ 355.4), more rarely in *-ast* (§ 331.6), and may be declined both strong and weak. The formative element is often changed to *-est-* by vowel harmony, especially in cases with *-osta-* (§ 385). In eW-S *-ost-*, *-ast-*, and the more archaic *-ust-* are used occasionally, but in all texts *-est-* prevails heavily. In lW-S and lNorth. *-ost-* prevails (lNorth. also *-ust-*). In *VP* and *Ru.*[1] it is not possible to determine if *-ost-* or *-ast-* originally prevailed in the dialects, in *VP* because all the forms have *-est-* by harmony, in *Ru.*[1] owing to entire absence of material. eKt. has *-ast*, *KG* has extended *-est-* to the uninflected form.

The compar. adj. is usually identical in the nom. sg. masc. with the gen. pl. of the positive. The superl. *-ost-* is added under the same conditions as the inflexions of the positive beginning with vowels. The following are examples of the comparison of the various declensions of adjectives discussed above:

blind, *blind*	blindra	blindost
hwæt, *active*	hwætra	hwatost
hāliġ, *holy*	hāliġra	hāl(i)ġost
nytt, *useful*	nyttra[1]	nyttost
blīþe, *joyful*	blīþra	blīþost
frēo, *free*	frēora, frīġra	
frēċne, *terrible*	frēċenra[2]	frēċnost
ġearu, *ready*	ġearora[3]	ġearwost
glēaw, *wise*	glēawra	glēawost
fēawe, *few*		fēawost, fēast

§ 658. A number of adjs. have mutation of the root vowel in the comparative and superlative. The common ones are:

eald, *old*	ieldra	ieldest[4]
ġeong, *young*	ġinġra, ġeongra, giongra	ġinġest[5]
hēah, *high*	hīer(r)a	hīehst[6]
lang, *long*	lenġra	lenġest
sċeort, *short*	sċyrtra	sċyrtest

[1] So usually with etymological *-tt-*.

[2] But from *tīdre* weak, both *tēderra* and *tēdra*.

[3] Also lW-S *ġearu(w)ra*; note also n.p. *ġearran*, g.p. *ġearra*, CP 401, 6; 433, 30 (cf. forms of positive, § 651).

[4] So Angl. *ald, ældra, ældest.*

[5] But VP, Ru.[1] *iung, ġung*, North. *ġiung* has comparison without umlaut, VP *iungra, ġungra*, North. *ġiungra*, VP *ġungest*; VP, North. *ġing* (§ 176) forms VP, North. *ġingra*, North. *ġingest*.

[6] But Angl. *hēra, hēst* may have smoothing without mutation. On *-h-* in W-S *hīehst*, Angl. *hēhst* see § 463; on *-rr-* in *hīerra* § 484. Analogical forms are frequent, e.g. compar. W-S *hēara, hēahra, hēarra*, superl. North. *hēist*, W-S *hēagost*, also *hēahst* whence *hēhst* (§ 312) and *hēxt* (§ 481.4).

Rarer examples of the same formation are *brǣdre* broader, W-S and poetry, *grȳttran* greater, E.E.T.S. o.s. 161, 20, 16, *ġehlīuran* warmer, id. 34, 12. *Strenġra*, *strengest* (also W-S *strenġst-*, § 352) are from *strenġe*, beside *strangra*, *strangost* from *strang* strong. The superl. elements *-ost-*, *-ust-* can be transferred to forms with mutation, e.g. *lenġust*, *sċyrtost*. On forms with syncopation of the medial vowel see § 352.

§ 659. Adjs. which derive their comparative and superlative from another root are:

gōd, *good*	betera, bet(t)ra	bet(e)st, best
	sēlra, sella	sēlest
yfel, *evil*	wiersa	wierrest, wyrst
miċel, *great*	māra	mǣst
lȳtel, *little*	lǣssa	lǣst

On syncope in *betra*, *betst* see §§ 388, 389; on *bettra* § 453; on *best* § 477.1; on *sella*, *wiersa*, *lǣssa* § 484.

Syncope in *wyrst*, *lǣst* is W-S; it is imitated in a few other lW-S superlatives, § 352. *KG* also have *werst* but Angl. *wyrrest*, *lǣsest* (Li. also *leasest* with *ea* from *leassa*, § 208).

Early texts have still *sōēlest*; North. has always superl. *māst* (often spelled with *aa*).

The endings *-ost*, *-ust* can be extended to superlatives of this group also.

§ 660. **Origin of forms.** The comparative and superlative suffixes which caused mutation were Gmc. *-izan-*, *-ista-*, and these were regularly developed in OE, apart from the W-S syncopation in superlatives. The non-mutating suffixes were Gmc. *-ōzan-*, *-ōsta-*. The latter develops regularly to OE *-ust*, *-ost*, *-ast* (§ 331.6). The development of *-ōzan-* in OE is very difficult, as the invariable syncope of an originally long medial syllable has no parallel. It is a peculiarly OE development, even OFris. having *-er-*, a normal development of *-ōz-*, corresponding to OS, OHG *-or-*, ON *-ar-*, Goth. *-ōz-*. The OE form is presumably due to the influence of the comparatives in *-iz-*, in which syncope is normal. This suffix *-iz-* may have been used in Prim. OE, as in OHG, not only with the few *a-*, *ō*-stems with mutated comparatives, but with most *i̯a-*, *i̯ō*-stems, e.g. OE *swētra* is not from **su̯ōtiōz-* but **su̯ōtiz-*, cf. OHG *suozziro*. It would also probably be used with *i*-stem adjs. so far as these survived. Hence *-r-* < *-iz-* would be a very frequent comparative suffix, and might replace the form derived from *-ōz-* in the other adjectival classes.

XIII

THE FORMATION OF ADVERBS

§ 661. The adjectival adverb is formed in OE by means of the suffix *-e* (< *-æ*,[1] Gmc. *-ǣ*), usually added to the same stem form as other inflexions beginning with vowels, e.g. *hearde*, *hraþe* (beside *hræþe*),[2] *fæġre*, *ġearwe*. In normal OE the adjs. in *-e* < *-i* and their advs. have the same form owing to the falling together of unaccented *-æ* and *-i*, e.g. *clǣne*, *nīwe*.

§ 662. The following advs. in *-e* have no corresponding adjs. in West Gmc.: *ǣdre* soon, *same* similarly, *snēome* quickly.

§ 663. The following advs. have unmutated vowels while those of the adj. are mutated: *ange* anxiously, *clāne* cleanly (beside *clǣne*), *ēaþe* easily, *murge* pleasantly (beside *myrġe*), *sōfte* softly, *swōte* sweetly, the advs. of *enġe*, *clǣne*, *īeþe*, *myrġe*, *sēfte*, *swēte*.[3] In the case of at least *enġe*, *myrġe*, *swēte* the reason for fluctuation between forms with and without mutation is that these adjs. were originally *u*-stems (cf. § 655).

§ 664. Since adjs. in *-liċ* normally formed advs. in *-liċe*,[4] this ending early became regarded as an adverbial suffix, which could be used beside or instead of *-e*, e.g. *heardliċe*, *holdliċe*, *hwætliċe*, *lætliċe* (beside *hearde*, *holde*, *late*), the advs. of *heard*, *hold*, *hwæt*, *læt*.

§ 665. The suffix *-unga*, *-inga* may be used to form advs. from adjs., e.g. *āninga* entirely, *dearnunga* secretly, *eallunga* entirely, *ierringa* angrily. It is also used with nouns, e.g. *fǣringa* suddenly, *nīedinga* of necessity, *wēnunga* by chance. In both uses it has an extended form *-lunga*, *-linga*, e.g. *brādlinga* on the broad side, *eċġlinga* on the edge, *grundlunga* to the ground. In origin *-unga*, *-inga* is a case form of the abstract noun in *-ung*, *-ing*, as is shown by e.g. *ēawunga* openly, *ednīwunga* anew. It can be used to modify or strengthen simple advs., e.g. *ġeġnunga* straight away, *samnunga* all at once, *symlinga* always (Rit.), cf. *ġeġnum*, *somen*, *symle*. The

[1] e.g. LR *uīdæ*.

[2] The adv. always has *þ* (also compar. and superl.), the adj. nearly always *d*.

[3] The advs. give rise to unmutated adjs. *ēaþe*, *sōfte*, *swōt*.

[4] e.g. *cræftliċe*, *lofliċe* from *cræftliċ* skilful, *lofliċ* honourable.

bye-form *-lung*, *-ling* is extracted from forms like *midlinga*, moderately, the adv. of *middel*.

§ 666. The suffix *-a* is used mainly in independent advs., and its origin is not always the same. In *fela* much, it is an indirect case-form of the *u*-declension, cf. Angl. *feolu* from nom. acc. sg. In *ġeāra* formerly, it is the ending of the gen. pl. Sometimes it is the element *ā*, ever, used in advs. of time, e.g. *sōna* soon, *āwa* ever, *ġēna*, *ġīeta* yet (cf. § 356). In *tela* well, from *til* good, its origin is uncertain.

§ 667. The adv. of *gōd* good, is *wĕl(l)* well (§ 100, footnote).

§ 668. The living case-forms of OE are often used adverbially. Adjs. which use the acc. sg. neut. adverbially are *efen* even, *full* full, *(ġe)fyrn* ancient, *ġehwǣde* little, *ġenōg* enough, *hēah* high (beside *hēa*), *lȳtel* little.[1] So the nominal acc. sg. is used in *āwiht* at all, *ealneġ* always (< *ealne weġ*), *hwōn*, *lȳthwon* a little; the pronominal in *hwæt* for what reason.

The gen. sg. neut. is used abverbially in *ealles* entirely (neg. *nealles*), *mićles* much, *singales* always, *samtenġes* together, *sumes* in some degree, *unġewisses* ignorantly, and in many compounds in *-langes*, e.g. *dæġlanges* for a day; so the gen. sg. of nouns, *dæġes* by day, *nihtes* by night, *nīedes* of necessity, *þonces* willingly, *wēas* by chance, *willes* willingly.[2] *Elles* otherwise, *endemes* together, are obscured genitival advs. Note also *lȳtes-* in *lȳtesna* nearly, and pronominal *ǣġhwæs* in every respect, *þæs* consequently, afterwards, so (also in *þæs ymb*, *þæs ofer* after, *to þæs* so).

The dat. sg. (including instances originally loc. or inst.) is used adverbially in *fācne* deceitfully, *hwēne* a little (i.s. of *hwōn*, small quantity, also used as acc. adv.), *nīede* of necessity (beside *nīedes*), *unġemete* without measure (beside *unġemetes*), *instæpe* at once (beside *instæpes*); so from adjs. *ǣne* alone, *ealle* entirely, *lȳtle* a little.

The dat. pl. is used adverbially in *ġifum* gratis, *firenum* criminally,[3] *hwīlum* at times, *unwearnum* irresistibly, *mićlum* much, *lȳtlum* little, and in compounds in *-mǣlum*, e.g. *nammǣlum* by names, *stæpmǣlum* gradually, *stundmǣlum* at intervals. Note also *furþum* even, apparently from the adv. seen in *forþ* with dat. pl. suffix.

[1] There are a few more examples in North., e.g. Li., Ru.[2] *long*, *sōð*, and *Li.* often *-lić* for *-liće*.

[2] Note that these are not always the normal gen. sg. of the related noun.

[3] But *firnum* very, in *Gen. B* is an Old Saxonism.

§ 669. In many compound advs. a gen. sg. depends on *to*, e.g. *tomiddes* in the middle, *toġifes* gratis; in others a gen. sg. or pl. is in vague dependence on some adverbial word, e.g. *hūmeta* how, *hūġerādes* why, *unfyrn faca* soon, *hūruþinga* especially, *ǣnġe þinga* for any reason, *ǣrest þinga* first of all. Other prepositional phrases used as adverbs are *ofdūne* down, *onefen* near by, *underbæċ* backwards, *æt nīehstan* finally, *onweġ* away. Many advs. are compounds of prep.+adv., and some receive a case-ending: *æt-*, *to-samne* together (cf. North. *somen* together), *æt-*, *to-gædere* together, *æt-*, *be-hindan* behind, *onuppan* above, *æt-*, *be-*, *to- foran* in front, *wiþinnan* within, *wiþūtan* without, *ymbūtan* around, *beġeondan* beyond, *be ēastan* in the east, *toġeġnes* in return, *onġēan* opposite;[1] and so with adv.+prep. *hider ofer* on this side, *ġeond ofer* on the other side.

§ 670. Comparison of adverbs. Adjectival advs. have normally compar. *-or*, superl. *-ost*, e.g.:

hearde, *severely*	heardor	heardost
ġearwe, *readily*	ġearwor[2]	ġearwost

-or also appears as *-ur* and *-ar*; *-ost* can appear as *-ust*, *-ast* (as in the superl. adj.). In origin *-ost* is merely the acc. sg. neut. of the superl. adjectival suffix. Compar. *-or*, *-ur*, *-ar* points to Gmc. *-ōz*, corresponding to Goth. *-os*. The final *r* (< *z*) should be lost in West Gmc., but is restored by analogy of the compar. adj.[3]

§ 671. The same suffixes are used with a few non-adjectival advs., e.g. *forþ* forth, *furþor*; *inne* within, *innor*; *oft* often, *oftor*, *oftost*; *ġelōme* often, *ġelōmor*; *seldan* seldom, *seld(n)or*, *seldost*; *sūþ*, southward, *sūþor*, and so *norþor*; so from *ġefyrn*, formerly (§ 654), *ġefyrnost*.

§ 672. From adjs. with umlaut in compar. and superl. only the following compared advs. occur:

hēa(h),[4] *high*	hēar, hēaor[5]	hȳhst
lange, *long*	lenġ[6]	lenġest[7]

[1] Many of these are themselves used as preps., e.g. *behindan* and most of those in *-an*, *toġeġnes*, *onġēan*.

[2] Beside *ġeare*, *ġearor*.

[3] The acc. sg. neut. of the compar. adj. is rarely used adverbially: a possible example is *wīdre*, Beow. 763, but cf. Klaeber in *Modern Philology* iii. 263; further examples are mainly North., e.g. Li., Ru.[2] *lenġre*, Li., Rit., Ru.[2] *māra*, Li. *rehtra*, Li., Ru.[2] *wyrse*.

[4] Late *hēage*.

[5] Late *hēgur*.

[6] Formed with suffix *-iz*, see § 673; also *lenġe*.

[7] Late *lenġst*, *lenġost*.

§ 673. From the following advs. the compar. was formed with the Gmc. suffix *-iz*, so that in OE mutation of the root vowel is the only indication of the degree (except in *nȳr*, *nēar* with analogical *r*). The superl. ending is either *-est* (with mutation of the root vowel) or *-ost*.

	ǣr, *before*	ǣrest
ēaþ(e), *easily*	īeþ[1]	ēaþost
feorr, *far*	fierr	firrest
nēah, *near*	nȳr[2]	nīehst, nēxt
	sīþ, *later*	sīþost
sōfte, *softly*	sēft[3]	sōftost
tulge, *firmly*	tylġ	tylġest

From *ǣr*, *sīþ* are formed double comparatives *ǣror*, *sīþor*.

§ 674. From a number of adverbs adjectival compar. and superl. are formed:

feorr, *far*	firra	
nēah, *near*	nēarra	nīehst[4]
ǣr, *before*	ǣrra	ǣrest
fore, *in front*		fyrest, fyrst

The neuters of *nīehst* and *ǣrest* are used as advs. and hence appear in § 673. The positives *feorr* and more rarely *ǣr*, *nēah* are also used as adjs., which inflect fully: *feorne*, *feorres*; *ǣrne*, *ǣran*, *ǣrum*; *nēahne*, *nēagum*; &c.

§ 675. When compared adjs. are derived from advs., however, the superl. has more frequently the ending *-mest*, a double superl. formed by adding *-est* to the superl. suffix seen in *forma* first, *hindema* last (cf. advs. *fore* in front, *hinder* behind).[5] The chief examples are:

inne, *inside*	innerra	innemest
ūte, *outside*	ūterra, ȳterra	ūtemest, ȳtemest

[1] Also *ēaþ*.

[2] But more often *nēar*.

[3] Also *sōftor*.

[4] *Nīehst* has a great variety of forms: Angl. *nēst*, Ru.[1] *nǣhsta*, *nēhst*, *nīhst*, §§ 463, 263, footnote, 310; *Li.* anal. *nēist*; without mutation W-S *nēahst*, whence *nēhst*, § 312, *nēxt*, § 481.4; *Ru.*[1] also *nēxt*.

[5] A similar double formation appears in Goth., e.g. *aftumists*, OE *æftemest*; but in West Gmc. the formation is peculiar to OE, for in the continental languages this group of words base the superl. on the compar., e.g. OFris. *ūtterst*, *innarost*, &c.

ufan, *from above*	uferra, yferra	ufemest, yfemest[1]
neoþan, *from below*	niþerra	niþemest
fore, *in front*		forma, fyrmest, formest
forþ, *forth*	furþra	forþmest (North., *Ru.*[1])
æfter, *after*	æfterra	æftemest
	elran, *other*[2]	
sīþ, *later*	sīþra	sīþemest, sīþest
norþ, *northward*	norþerra[3]	norþmest
sūþ, *southward*	sūþerra[4]	sūþmest
ēast, *eastward*	ēasterra	ēastemest
west, *westward*	westerra	westmest

Medial *-rr-* in compar. (*innerra*, &c.) is often simplified (§ 457). Syncopation is frequent in both compar. and superl., e.g. *ūtra*, *ūtmest* (§ 388, 392).

The suffix *-mest* was in lOE identified with *mǣst*, North. *māst* most, and was often spelled accordingly. On lW-S *-myst* see § 369, footnote.

The neut. of adjs. in *-mest* can be used adverbially. In lW-S *endemes* together, is assimilated to these words and can be spelled *-mest*.

The superl. in *-mest* also occurs from the adjs. *læt*, *lætra*, *lætemest* beside *lætest*; *midd* middle, *midemest*.

The superl. in *-m-* is developed as a positive following the *i̯a-*, *i̯ō*-declension in *medeme* moderate; compar. *medemra*, superl. *medemest*.

From *norþ*, *sūþ*, *ēast*, *west* are formed compounds *norþweard*, &c., with the same meaning. They may be used as fully declined adjs., and also as advs. in either acc. sg. neut. or gen. sg. neut. (*-weard* or *-weardes*).

§ 676. The advs. corresponding to the adjs. which form their positives and compared degrees from different roots (§ 659) are:

wĕl(l), *well*	bet, sēl	bet(e)st, best, sēlest
yfle, *evilly*	wiers	wyrrest, wyrst
miċle, *much*	mā[5]	mǣst
lȳtle, lȳt, (*a*) *little*	lǣs	lǣst, lǣsest

[1] Also *ȳmest*, not etymologically related to *ufan* (§ 203).

[2] *Beow.* 752, d.s.m.; cf. advs. *elles* otherwise, *ellor* elsewhere.

[3] Also *nyrþra*.

[4] Also *sȳþera*; and the adv. occurs as *sȳþ*. (Forms in this and previous note all from transcripts in Winchester Cartulary.)

[5] *VP*, *Ru.*[1] frequently *mǣ*; so *Li.* twice.

§ 677. Adverbs of place. The following are groups of related local adverbs:

Place where	Place to which	Place from which
þǣr, *there*	þider	þonan
hwǣr, *where?*	hwider	hwonan
hēr, *here*	hider	heonan
æfter, *after*		æftan
inne, *inside*	inn	innan
ūte, *outside*	ūt	ūtan
uppe, *above*	upp	uppan, ufan
	niþor, *to below*	neoþan
fore, *in front*		foran
	hinder, *to behind*	hindan
	feorr, *far*	feorran
nēah, *near*		nēan
norþ, *northward*		norþan
sūþ, *southward*		sūþan
ēast, *eastward*		ēastan
west, *westward*		westan

Generally the senses of rest and movement towards tend to be confused, and *hēr* is often used for *hider*, *þǣr* for *þider*, &c. Especially when there is only one form (e.g. *norþ*) it serves in both senses. *Nēah* is usually of position, *nēar* (compar.) of movement towards.

§ 678. lW-S has as variants of *þǣr*, *hwǣr*: *þār*, *hwār*, *þāra*; also *hwāra* in cpds. *hwæt-*, *æt-hwāra*, already Oros.

Variants of *þider*, *hwider* are *þæder*, *hwæder*, mostly in late manuscripts, but cf. *CP* 169, 13.

The advs. in *-an* have a bye-form in *-e*, e.g. *utane*; so some of those in *r*: *hidere*, *hwidere*. In North. the final *-n* is lost, *hwona*, &c.

Advs. in *-r* have occasionally genitival forms, e.g. *hidres þidres* hither and thither; and comparatives, e.g. *hideror* more this way.

See § 669 for phrases consisting of prep.+adv. in *-an*.

§ 679. *Hwǣr*, *hwider*, *hwonan*, may be made general advs. of place by the prefix *ġe-*: *ġehwǣr* everywhere, &c. So with or without *ġe-* they are generalized by *ā-* (*ō-*; neg. *nā-*, *nō-*) and *wĕl-*, e.g. *āhwǣr*, *ǣġhwǣr* (< **ā-ġi-hwǣr*), *wĕl(ġe)-hwǣr* (also *ġewĕlhwǣr*), *āhwider*, *ǣġhwider*, *āhwonan*.

§ 680. 'Somewhere' is *hwerġen*; this can also be generalized: *āhwærġen*, *āwyrn* everywhere (influenced by *hwǣr*), and so *ǣġwern*; negated *nāwern* nowhere.

§ 681. Note *nīwan*(*e*) recently, with extension of *-an*(*e*) to an adjectival adv. (already West Gmc., OHG *niuuanes*).

XIV

NUMERALS

1. Cardinal Numbers

§ 682. The following are the cardinals up to 'twelve' in W-S forms, with the most interesting dialectal forms:

1. *ān*.
2. *twēġen*; Angl. usually has *ōē* as root vowel; lNorth. always drops *-n*, *Ru.*[1] sometimes.
3. *þrīe*.
4. *fēower*; lNorth. also *fēwer*, *fēuor* (§ 279), *fēor*.
5. *fīf*.
6. *siex*, later *syx*, *six*, also *seox* (from **seoxa*, *-um*, § 305); eKt. *sex* (§ 307), Angl. *sex*.
7. *siofan*, *seofan*; lW-S also *syfon* (§ 299), *sufon* (§ 302); early texts have forms without back umlaut, Cp. *sibun-*, Ep. *sifun-*; lNorth. usually loses *-n*, *seofo*, *-a*, *siofu*, *-o* (§ 293); so eNorth. already *sifu* (Napier's *OE glosses*, p. 220).
8. *eahta*, later *ehta* (§ 312); lNorth. *æhtu*, *-o* (after *seofo*), rarely *-a*; also *æhtou*, *-uu*, *æhtowe* (influence of inflected form; cf. poetical *ehtuwe*); Merc., Kt. not recorded.
9. *nigon*; North. only inflected forms, *ni(g)one*, *-a*.
10. *tīen*; nW-S *tēn*, lNorth. also *tēo*, *tēa*.
11. *en(d)lefan*, *endleofan*; Ru.[1] *enlefan*; *Li.* once *ællef*, otherwise no uninflected North. forms.
12. *twelf*, lNorth. also *twoelf*, Ru.[1] and Kt. also *twǣlf* (§ 197).

§ 683. These cardinal numbers inflect as follows: *ān* is fully declined like *blind* (§ 639), but it has irregular a.s.m. *ǣnne* (beside *ānne*); beside this nW-S (already *VP*) has *enne* (§ 193); *ān* may be used in pl. before collective expressions, e.g. *ane nigon naman* 'a batch of nine names'; meaning 'alone' it can be declined weak (but generally only in n.s.m. *āna*, which may be extended to fem. and pl., e.g. *ond heo ana læġ swa*; *ġe hlyston þa word ana*; *þæt hi ana wæron ġecorene*).

	Masculine	Feminine	Neuter
Nom. Acc.	twēġen[1]	twā	twā, tū
Gen.	twēġ(e)a, twēġ(e)ra		
Dat.	twǣm[2]		

This paradigm applies to W-S and Merc., except that *VP* has g. *twōēġa*, and *Ru.*[1] n.a.m. *twēġe(n)*, *twǣġen*. Kt. has only *twǣġen*, *twā*, eNorth. only FC *twōēġen*. In lNorth. n.a.m. is usually *twōēġe*, other forms are erroneous or uncertain,[3] and *Li.* occasionally disregards limitation of the form to masc.; *twā* (usually fem.), *tuū* (i.e. **twū*; usually neut.)[4] appear; g. *twōēġ(e)ra* (Li. also *twōēġe*); d. *twǣm* (Li. once *tuōēm*).

Similarly declined is *bēġen*, both:

	Masculine	Feminine	Neuter
Nom. Acc.	bēġen	bā	bā, bū
Gen.	bēġra, bēġ(e)a		
Dat.	bǣm[5]		

For *bā* and *bū* W-S has frequently the compound *bātwā*, *būtū* (*būta*); *būtū*, *-a* is especially frequent (it is the only nom. acc. in eW-S) and may be used for fem. and masc. Dat. *bām twām* is also frequent. eKt. has g. *b(o)ēga*, d. *bǣm*, *bōēm*. *VP* has no forms, *Ru.*[1] only *bēġen*, *bū*. eNorth. has *bā* (acc. neut.), *RC*; lNorth. has n.a. *bōēġe*, *-o* (m.), *bā* (f.), g. *bōēġera*, d. *bǣm*.

	Masculine	Feminine	Neuter
Nom. Acc.	þrīe	þrēo	þrēo
Gen.	þrēora		
Dat.	þrim		

eW-S has frequently *-īo-* for *-ēo-*; lW-S has *þrȳ*, *þrī* for *þrīe*. eKt. uses both *þrīe* and *þrēo* as neut. (Cts. 34, 41). In Angl. there

[1] The length of the root vowel is proved metrically.

[2] W-S also *twām* (with vowel of *twā*).

[3] But *tuoge* (Li. 9 times), *twoge* (Ru.[2] once) seem to reflect a genuine form without umlaut: see Ross, *Studies in the accidence of the Lindisfarne Gospels*, p. 109

[4] Cf. Li. *twū-*, *tuū-* beside *tuī-* in composition.

lW-S also *bām*.

is no distinction of gender: Merc. *þrēo*, *þrim* (gen. not recorded). lNorth. has a great variety of diphthongs: *ðrēo*, *ðrēa*, *ðrīo*, *ðrīa*, also *ðrīu* (Li. once); g. *ðrēa*, *ðrēana*;[1] d. *ðrim*.[2]

When not immediately before the qualified noun the numerals 4–12 may be declined,[3] e.g. *niceras nigene*, *syxa sum*, *mid nigonum ðara niwena scipa*. The forms in W-S and *Ru.*[1] are nom. acc. *-e* (neut. also *-u*, *-o*), gen. *-a*, dat. *-um*, e.g.

Nom. Acc.	fēow(e)re	fīfe, -u, -o
Gen.	fēow(e)ra	fīfa
Dat.	fēow(e)rum	fīfum

lNorth. has nom. acc. in *-a*, *-o*, *-u* as well as *-e*. Note *Ru.*[2] d. *æhtowum*. In North. and *Ru.*[1] the inflected numerals are often used without regard to the syntactic distinction defined above.

§ 684. The following are the composition forms of the numerals so far as they differ from the cardinals given above: 2. *twī-* (rarely *twā-*); 3. *þrī-* (but also *þrīe-*, *þrēo-*);[4] 4. lW-S *fyþer-*, Angl. *feoþor-*, *feoþur-* (but also *fēower-*), Li. *fēar-*.

§ 685. The numerals 13–19 are formed with *-tīene*, nW-S *-tēne* (North. also *-tēno*), suffixed to *þrēo-*, *fēower-*, *fīf-*, *six-*, *seofon-*, *eahta-*, *nigon-*, with variety of form according to date and dialect, as in the simple numerals. *-tīene* can have gen. *-a*, dat. *-um*.

§ 686. The decades 20–120 are formed with *-tiġ* (North. also *-tih*, § 452) from forms of the numerals 2–12; those from 70 to 120 have usually the unaccented prefix *hund-*, but this is already sometimes dropped in eW-S, and it can be reduced to *un-* in Li. Apart from the fluctuations due to these causes and regular dialectal sound-changes, the forms are:

20. *twēntiġ*; lNorth. also Li. *tuōentiġ*, Ru.[2] *twōēġentiġ*.
30. *þrītiġ*; later with *-tt-*, W-S, *Ru.*[1], North. (§ 287).
40. *fēowertiġ*; North. also *fēortiġ*.
50. *fīftiġ*.
60. *siextiġ*, nW-S *sextiġ*.
70. *hundseofontiġ*.

[1] *Li.* once, perhaps for **ðrēara*.
[2] Length is sometimes indicated by spelling *ðriim* Li.
[3] Also when divided from the noun by a metrical pause, e.g. *feowere fet*, Rid. 37, 3.
[4] Cf. § 282.

80. *hundeahtatiġ*.
90. *hundnigontiġ*; but *Li*. a phonological variant (< **niχ*-), *hundnēontiġ*, *-nēantiġ*.[1]
100. *hundtēontiġ*; *Ru*.[1] and North. also *-tēantiġ*.
110. *hundændlæftiġ*, Birch, no. 619, very late copy.
120. *hundtwelftiġ*, *hundtwēntiġ*.

These numerals can form gen. both in *-es* and in *-a*, *-ra*; dat. only in *-um*; in late texts indeclinable use appears. They can be treated syntactically both as adjs. and nouns.

§ 687. 'Hundred' can also be expressed by the neut. nouns *hund* and *hundred*.[2] These may be indeclinable. *Hund* also uses *hunde* as dat. sg., acc. pl., dat. pl., e.g. *mid þriddan healf-hunde sċipa*,[3] *ymb feower hunde wintra*, *mid twam hunde sċipa*; the dat. pl. may also be *hundum*. *Hundred* has nom. acc. pl. *-u* (*-o*, *-a*), dat. pl. *-um*, which may be used when it does not stand immediately before a noun.

§ 688. Multiples of 100 are formed with *hund* (inflected according to § 687), and the cardinals *tū*, *þrēo*, &c. In these compounds cardinals above *þrēo* are not declined, e.g. *siex hunde wintrum*. *Hundred* is rarer in these multiples, *hundtēontiġ* is unusual.[4]

§ 689. *Þūsend* thousand, is a neut. noun, g.s. *-es*, d.s. *-e*, n.a.p. unchanged or *-u* (*-o*, *-a*), g.p. *-a* (rarely *-ra*), d.p. *-um*. It may also be used as an uninflected adj., e.g. *on six þusend wintrum*.

§ 690. The use of *healf* with ordinals in forming virtual cardinals should be noticed, e.g. *eahtoþe healf hid* means '(seven hides and) half the eighth,' hence 'seven hides and a half'; very often a multiple of 100+50 is so expressed, e.g. § 687; the system is also used with *þūsend*, e.g. *fifte healf þusend*, 4500.

§ 691. In compound numerals the units usually precede the tens, e.g. *seofon and twentiġ ġeara*. The hundreds usually come first, e.g. *feower hund and twa and eahtatiġ*, *mid feower hunde sċipa and þritiġum*. In compound numerals the units are not usually declined, and for 2 and 3 *twā* and *þrēo* are used for all genders, e.g. *þreo and twentiġ manna*, *þara twa and twentiġra manna*.

[1] But Ru.[2] *hundnīontiġ*, with *i* for *iġ* (§ 267).
[2] lNorth. also *hundrað*, *-ræð*, *-reð* owing to Norse influence.
[3] 'With 250 ships', *PC* 893; MS. *mid ccl hunde scipa*.
[4] It is indeclinable when so used: examples *PBB* ix. 266.

2. Ordinal Numbers

§ 692. The ordinals up to 'twelfth' are:

1. *forma*, *fyrmest*; also *fyrest* (*fyrst*, § 389) in sense foremost;[1] *ǣrest*, also *ǣrra* usually of the first of two.
2. *ōþer*, *æfterra*.
3. *þridda*, North. usually *ðirda* (§ 459.2).
4. *fēorþa*, North. usually *fēarða*.
5. *fīfta*.
6. *siexta*; nW-S *sexta*, Ru.[1] also *syxta* (§ 308), North. also *sesta* (§ 417), *seista* (*ei* = *e*, § 42, footnote).
7. *seofoþa*, later *-eþa* (§ 385); but Ru.[1], North. *seofunda*, *siofunda*.
8. *eahtoþa*, *-eþa*; lW-S also *eahteoþa*.
9. *nigoþa*, *-eþa*.
10. *tēoþa*; but texts of Mercian colour also *teogeða*; Li. *tēi*(*ġ*)*ða*.
11. eW-S *enlefta*, later *endlefta*, *-leofta*, *-lyfta*; *Ru.*[1], North. *ællefta*, Ru.[1] also *ellefta*.
12. *twelfta*.

§ 693. The ordinals 13–19 are formed with W-S *-tēoþa* added to the cardinal units, *þrēotēoþa* (lW-S *þreottēoþa*, § 287), *fēowertēoþa*, &c. Merc. coloured texts have also *-teg*(*e*)*ða*, *-teog*(*e*)*ða*; North. *-tegeða*, *-teiða*.

§ 694. The ordinals of the tens 20–120 are formed by changing *-tiġ* of the cardinals to *-tigoþa*, of which *-tegoþa*, *-tiogoþa*, *-teogoþa*, and with syncopation *-tigþa*, &c., are normally developed variants. Occasionally a form in *-tiga*, *-tega* is used, e.g. *PC* 763, *on þone feowertegan dæġ*.[2]

§ 695. The ordinals in *-a* are declined as weak adjs.; *ōþer* is always declined strong. The forms in *-st* for 'first' are superl. adjs., and may be declined strong and weak. Compound ordinals are usually formed by placing an uninflected cardinal before the ordinal ten, which can then be inflected, e.g. *on þæm an and ðritigoþan psalme*.

[1] Rarer variants with this root are Ru.[1], Li. *forðmest*, Ru.[2] *foer*(*ð*)*mest*, Rit. *ruma*.

[2] In lW-S there appears to be some confusion of *-tigoþa* with *-tēoþa*; already Oros. 252, 31 *fēowertēoþan* quadragesimo.

3. Miscellaneous Numerals

§ 696. **Fractions.** On the expression of cardinals $+\frac{1}{2}$ see § 690. Other fractions are expressed by phrases with *dǣl*, e.g. *tweġen dælas weres* 'two-thirds of the wergild'. But $\frac{2}{3}$ is also expressed by *twǣde* (noun or adj.), *twīdǣl* (noun).

§ 697. **Multiplicatives.** These are expressed by compounds of the cardinals with *-feald*, *-fald*: *ānfeald*, *twīfeald*, *þrēo-*, *þrīfeald*,[1] *fēowerfeald*,[2] &c. *Li.* has once a different formation, *hunduelle*.

§ 698. **Distributives.** 'One each' is expressed by *ānlīepiġ*, e.g. *þa underfengon hi ǣnlipiġe penegas* 'then they received a penny each'. 'Two each' is *ġetwinne*; for the rest Ælfric equates the Lat. distributives with *twām and twām*, *þrim and þrim*, &c.

§ 699. **Collectives.** The declension of *bēġen* both, has been given with that of *twēġen* (§ 683). Another collective is preserved as the second element of *betwēoh* between.

§ 700. **Adverbs.** The questions 'How often?' and 'Which time?' are mainly answered by phrases with *sīþ* time, occasion, e.g. *fēower sīþum* 'four times', *forman sīþe* 'on the first occasion'.[3] Separate forms are:

1. *ǣne* (also *ǣne sīþa*), *ǣnes*.[4]
2. *twuwa*, *tuwa*, *tweowa*, *twiwa*, *twiġ(e)a*.
3. *þreowa* (< *þriowa*, § 148), *þriwa*, *þriġa*.

The forms for 2 and 3 with *-ġ-* are exclusively used in North., where there is characteristic fluctuation of the final vowel, *-a*, *-e*, *-o* (Li. *ðria* has *i* for *iġ*, § 267), but occur rarely in W-S. Merc. has only Ru.[1] *þriowa*, *þriuwa*. The form *twuwa* < **twiw-* shows a retraction of Prim. OE *i* similar to that seen between *w* and *r* (§ 149); on *tuwa* see § 470. *Twiwa*, *þriwa* shows the influence of forms with *-ġ-*, *tweowa* that of *þreowa*.

The neuter cardinals *tū*, *twā*, *þrēo*, and uninflected forms of other cardinals may be used adverbially, 'twice', &c., in multiplicative expressions with *swa* and *swylċ*, e.g. *tu(twa) swa lange* 'twice as long' (pl.), *twa swylċ swylċe* 'twice as much as', *feower swa fela* 'four times as much'.

Note the adverbial phrase *on emtwā* 'into two equal parts'.

[1] lW-S has some doubly declined dat. forms: *twāmfealdum* (Oros. 248, 2, Cott. MS.), *þrimfealdum*, *-re*, *-an* (legal texts, Ælfric); note also adv. *twǣmfaldum* doubly, *Ru.*[1]

[2] Ru.[2] also *feoðorfald*.

[3] *Cierr* and less often *sǣl* may be similarly used.

[4] Note *on ænne sið*, once, *Beow.* 1579.

XV

PRONOUNS

§ 701. In this chapter no sections are included on 'origin of forms', as the pronominal paradigms could be adequately discussed only on a basis of the forms of all the early Germanic languages.

§ 702.

1. Personal Pronouns

Nom.	iċ, *I*	þu, *thou*	we, *we*	ġe, *ye*
Acc.	me	þe	ūs	ēow
Gen.	mīn	þīn	ūre	ēower
Dat.	me	þe	ūs	ēow

On the quantity of final open vowels see § 125.

VP has acc. *meċ*, *ðeċ*, *ūsiċ*, *ēowiċ* beside the shorter forms. In lNorth. and Ru.[1] the forms with *-ċ* are frequent. In *Ru.*[1] they invade the dat. only in the case of *ēowiċ*, which is acc. 16 times, dat. 3 times. In North. the forms with *-ċ* are generally limited to acc. except in the 2nd pl., where confusion is complete in *Ru.*[2], while *iuih* is generalized for acc. and dat. in *Rit.*, and this seems to have been the original state of the dialect of *Li.* (see Ross in *JEGP* xxxii. 481–2). The *-ċ*-forms are frequent in verse, and note Ælfred Jewel *meċ*. On lNorth. *-h*, *-ġ* for *-ċ* in *iċ* and the acc. forms see § 452. On North. *ġi(e)* beside *ġe* see § 186, on Li. *woe* beside *we* § 319.

For g. *ūre* VP has *ūr* (also found in *RG*), Ru.[1] *ūre*, but North. *ūser*, *ūsra*; verse frequently *ūser*.

In *ēow*, *ēower* eW-S has frequently, North. always *īow-*, with normal spelling variants *īu-*, *īw-* in North. (§ 279).

§ 703.

Nom.	wit, *we two*	ġit, *ye two*
Acc.	unc	inċ
Gen.	uncer	inċer
Dat.	unc	inċ

Acc. forms with final *-et*, *-it*[1] occur. *RC* and late prose *unket* us

[1] *-et* appears not to be for older *-it*, because there is no mutation in *uncet*; it is perhaps transferred from an accented nom. **wet*, beside unaccented *wit*.

two, poetic *inċit* you two. Of the Angl. glosses only *Ru.*[1] has dual pronouns, but they are frequent in eW-S, lW-S, and verse.

Nom.	he, *he*	hēo, *she*	hit, *it*	hīe, hī, hēo, *they*
Acc.	hine	hīe, hī	hit	hīe, hī, hēo
Gen.	his	hire	his	hira, heora
Dat.	him	hire	him	him

eW-S has often *ie* for *i* in *hiene*, *hiere*, *-a*; and *ĭo* for *ĕo* in *hīo*, *hiora*.

lW-S has frequently *ȳ̆* for *i*, *īe* in all forms. A peculiar n.p. *he* occurs *Reg. Psalt.* (e.g. 17, 18; 21, 16). lW-S especially after 1000 has frequent d.p. *heom*.

VP has n.s.f., n.a.p. *hie*, g.p. *heara*[1] (rarely *heora*, *hiera*), otherwise the same forms as the first alternatives in the above paradigm.

Ru.[1] has mainly the same forms as W-S, but also n.s.f. *hīu*, a.s.f. *hiæ*, *hēo*, *hīo*, d.s.m., d.p. *heom*.

North. forms also resemble W-S, but note also n.s.f. *hīu* (only *Li.* where it prevails), a.s.f., n.a.p. *hīa* (and Li. *hēa*, Ru.[2] *hiæ* for all three), g.p. usually *hiora*, but forms with *-ia-*, and in *Li.* also with *-eo-*, *-ea-*, occur.[2]

KG have *hī* beside *hīo* in n.s.f. (a.s.f. not recorded), and in n.p.; beside g.s.f. *hire* also *hiore*, *hiora*. Interesting forms in early texts are a.s.m. *hinæ* RC; n.s.f. *hīa* frequent eKt.; a.s.f. *hīo* Martyrology fragment; n.a.p. *hiæ* RC, FC; d.p. *heom* Ct. 45 (Surrey).

§ 704. It is a peculiarity of the Ingvaeonic languages, distinguishing them from OHG, that the pronoun of the third person is also used as the reflexive and reciprocal pronoun of the third person, e.g. OE *ða beþohte he hine* 'then he bethought himself', *hie . . . hie ġemetton* 'they met one another'.

2. Possessive Adjectives

§ 705. The possessive adjs. are *mīn*, *þīn*, *ūre*, *ēower*, *uncer*, *inċer*; there is also a mainly reflexive possessive *sīn* his, her, their, but it is largely superseded by the gen. forms of *he*. Possessive use of the other pronominal genitives is rarer, e.g. *ūser yldran* 'our ancestors', *ēower hundas* 'your dogs', *ūre sāula* 'of our souls', *hyġeþoncum mīn* 'in my thoughts'; it occurs most frequently in groups like *uncer*, (*inċer*) *twēga* 'of us (you) two', *ūre selfra* 'of ourselves'.[3]

[1] Also *RG*; the form is perhaps influenced by *þeara*.

[2] On apocopated North. *hir*, d.s.f., rarely g.s.f. see § 708, footnote 1, p. 291.

[3] The sg. of this construction requires the poss. adj. agreeing with *selfes*, *-re*,

§ 706. For W-S, Ru.[1] *ūre*, VP *ūr*, poetry has **ūser*,[1] a.s.m. *ūserne*.[2] With syncope *sr* > *ss*, e.g. *ūsses*, *ūssa*, *ūssum* < **ūsres*, &c., and *-ss-* can then be levelled to other forms like *ūsserne*, *ūssera* (with *r* < *rr*, § 457).[3] In North. *ūser* appears to be the basic form, and inflected forms with and without syncope appear, *ūserne*, *ūsra*, &c.; but inflexions from a simplified stem *ūs-* also occur, *ūses*, *-um*, &c. In North. *ēower* is subject to spelling variation like *ēow* (§ 701).

§ 707. The declension of the possessives is as strong adjs. like *blind* and *fæger* (§§ 639, 643.4); *ūre* is like *wilde* (§ 644), although absence of umlaut shows that its *-e* is not from *-i*. Simplification of *-rr-* often takes place (§ 457), e.g. g.s.f. *ūre*, g.p. *ūra*, *ūssera*, *uncera*; and syncope can then follow (§ 392), e.g. g.s.m. *uncres*, g.p. *ūsra*, *īowra*.

3. Demonstrative Pronouns

§ 708.

	Masculine	Feminine	Neuter	Plural
Nom.	se, *that*, *the*	sēo	þæt	þā
Acc.	þone	þā	þæt	þā
Gen.	þæs	þǣre	þæs	þāra, þǣra
Dat.	þǣm, þām	þǣre	þǣm, þām	þǣm, þām
Inst.[4]	þon, þȳ		þon, þȳ	

On less frequent a.s.m. *þane*, i.s.m.n. *þan* (all dialects) see § 333; on a.s.m. *þæne* (all dialects) see § 380.

eW-S has *sīo* beside *sēo*; *þām* for *þǣm* is W-S and rare Kt., not Angl.; *þāre* for *þǣre* is frequent lW-S. eKt. (including Surrey) has forms reflecting the change of *ǣ̆* to *ē̆* beside others with *ǣ̆*: *þet*, *þes*, *þēre*, *þēm*; also n.s.f. *sīa*, d.s.f. *þāre*, g.p. *þeara*. *KG* have d.s.f. *ðāra* (cf. *hiora*, § 703), d.s.m., &c., *ðām*.

VP owing to second fronting has *ðet*, *ðes* beside *ðæt*, *ðæs* (§ 166) and g.p. *ðeara*.[5] It has also n.s.f. *sie* (once *sēo*), g.d.s.f. *ðēre* (? *ðere*).

or with the noun possessed, e.g. *mines selfes sunu*, *on minne selfes dom*; but pl. poss. adjs. are unusual with *self*, e.g. *iowra selfra anwaldes*.

[1] Marked as a theoretical form because in the uninflected form it is indistinguishable from the gen. of *we*.

[2] *Ru.*[1] once.

[3] *CP* has *ūssum* once, and *-ss-* forms occur in many lW-S texts.

[4] The classification of these forms as instrumental is traditional, but reflects neither their origin nor their prevailing use.

[5] *ðeara* also occurs in *LP*; in the Kt. charters it is a Mercianism. The origin of the form would be unaccented *þara* (with short *a*) becoming re-accented, to undergo second fronting and back mutation.

Ru.[1] has forms similar to those of W-S, but also n.s.m. *þe* (beside *se*), a.s.m. *þene* (beside *þone, þane, þæne*), n.s.f. *sīu, sie* (beside *sēo, sīo*). North. forms also resemble those of W-S, but new forms n.s.m. *ðe*, n.s.f. *ðīo, ðīu, ðȳ*, are developed, beside *se, sīo.*[1]

§ 709. The i.s.n. *þon* and d.s.n. *þǣm* are freely used in forming phrases, which are used as advs., and (with or without the particle *þe*) as conjunctions, e.g. *æfter þǣm (þe)* after, *for þon (þe)* because. Note also *siþþan* after, i.e. *sīþ+þon*, and the comparative uses of *þon* (1) as 'than' (usually *þonne*), and (2) in phrases like *þon mā* the more, where it interchanges with *þȳ* and *þē.*[2]

§ 710. The lack of a relative pronoun in OE is largely made up for by the use of *se* either alone or followed by the particle *þe* (which shows it to be relatival, not demonstrative, in function), e.g. *se mon-dryhten se eow ða maðmas ġeaf* 'the lord who gave you the treasures', *his feoh þæt to lafe biþ* 'his money which shall remain', *se ellen-gæst se þe in þystrum bad* 'the mighty spirit who lingered in darkness', *ond ðætte* (= *þæt þe*, § 481.3) *tælwyrðes sie, ðæt hie ðæt tælen* 'and that they may blame what is blameworthy'.[3]

§ 711.

	Masculine	Feminine	Neuter	Plural
Nom.	þes, *this*	þēos	þis	þās
Acc.	þisne	þās	þis	þās
Gen.	þisses	þisse	þisses	þissa
Dat.	þissum	þisse	þissum	þissum
Inst.	þȳs		þȳs	

eW-S already has considerable variety owing to fluctuation of *y* and *i* (hence e.g. i.s.n. *ðis*, g.s.m. *ðysses*) and to the simplification

[1] North. has sometimes apocopated a.s.m. *ðon*, g.d.s.f. *ðǣr*. The latter was mainly used as dat., *ðǣre* is more frequent as gen. So *hire* is distinguished from *hir*, and *ðisser* is rare as gen., frequent as dat. This limitation of forms in *-r* to the dat. is seen in *Li., Rit., Ru.*[2], and many crosses have d.s.f. *þǣr, þēr*.

[2] Strictly *þon mā* is comparative 'more than some other already indicated', and is rarely used with resultative force 'more for a reason already indicated', *þē (þȳ) mā* is both comparative and resultative. Examples B–T, s.v. *mā*.

[3] *þe* also functions as a relative alone or after a personal pronoun, e.g. *iċ hit eom þe wiþ þe sprece* 'it is I who speak with thee'; *þæt se mon ne wat þe him on foldan fæġrost limpeð* 'that the man knows not to whom the fairest (fortune) falls on earth'. Relatival 'such as' is *swilċ* with or without correlatival demonstrative *swilċ*, e.g. *swylċ sċolde eorl wesan swylċ Æsċhere wæs*, 'Æ. was such as a warrior should be'; *hæfde his ende ġebidenne swylċne he ær æfter worhte* 'he had met his end, such a one as he worked for previously'. On the expression of the generalizing relatives, 'whoever', &c., see § 720.

of *-ss-* (§ 457), hence g.s.m.n. *ðises*, d.s.m.n. and d.p. *ðisum*, *ðysum*. These dative forms also appear as *þios(s)um*, *þeosum*. n.s.f. is *þīos* beside *þēos*.

lW-S has g.d.s.f. *þissere*, g.p. *þissera* developed by parasiting from *þisre*, *þisra*, which also occur; also occasionally a.s.m. *þeosne*, d.s.m.n. and d.p. *þeossum*, g.p. *þeossa*.

eKt. has g.p. *ðeassa* (Ct. 24), Surrey g.d.s.f. *ðeosse*.[1]

VP forms largely agree with the above paradigm, but a.s.m. always *ðeosne*, d.p. once *ðeossum* (beside *ðissum*).

Ru.[1] agrees with the above paradigm, but also a.s.m. *þeosne*, n.s.f. *þīos*, d.s.f. *þissere*.

North. frequently develops *a* as root vowel, e.g. d.s.f. *ðasse*, d.p. *ðassum*; n.s.f. *ðius*, *ðys* (Li.) beside usual *ðios*; analogical forms with *r* appear in g.d.s.f. (cf. § 708, footnote 1, p. 291), g.p. *ðisra*: a.s.m. *ðiosne* (Li. also *ðionne*, § 484); i.s.m.n. *ðisse*. Other forms as in the above paradigm.[2]

§ 712. A third demonstrative pronoun is preserved only in eW-S in d.s.f. in the phrase *to ġeonre byrġ* 'to that city', *CP* 443, 25.

§ 713. In lW-S (Gospels and Exeter diplomata), ON *þei-r* they, is borrowed as *þæġe*, showing *-æġ-* for ON *-ei-*,[3] and addition of the pronominal nom. pl. *-e*. It is used as a demonstrative (nom. and acc.), less often as a relative (nom.); since it is equivalent to OE *þā*, it is also used as a.s.f. Cf. Förster in *AB* lii. 274–80; liii. 86–87.

§ 714. *Self* self, declines strong and weak; on phonology see §§ 146, 302, 325.

§ 715. *Ilca* same, is declined weak; strong forms are late and rare.

4. Interrogative Pronouns

§ 716.

	Masculine, Feminine	Neuter
Nom.	hwa, *who?*	hwæt
Acc.	hwone	hwæt
Gen.	hwæs[4]	
Dat.	hwǣm, hwām	
Inst.[5]	hwȳ	

[1] On eKt. d.s.m.n. *ðis(s)em* see § 378, footnote.

[2] *Li.* and *Rit.* (not *Ru.*[2]) have occasional simplification of intervocalic *-ss-*, e.g. *ðises*, *ðisum*, *ðasum*.

[3] Cf. *scæġþ* beside *sceġþ* from ON *skeið*, ship.

[4] In lW-S the compound *ġehwa* (§ 719) has a special fem. gen. and dat. *ġehwǣre*, *ġehwāre*, often introduced by scribes into verse against metre, e.g. *Beow.* 25.

[5] Cf. footnote to § 708 (on inst. of *se*).

On a.s.m. *hwane* see § 333; on *hwæne* § 380; on early unrounding in i.s. § 316.

There is an alternative i.s. *hwon*, *hwan* used only in phrases, *for hwon* why?, &c.

The only dialectal variations are those caused by normal sound-changes, e.g. *VP*, Kt. *hwet*; but *hwām* is W-S only.

§ 717. Other interrogative pronouns are *hwæþer*, *hweþer* which of two?, *hwelċ*, *hwilċ* which? They are declined as strong adjs.[1] The interchange *hwæþer*, *hweþer* is found in all dialects.[2] eW-S has *hwelċ*, which gives way later to *hwylċ*, *hwilċ*; *Ru.*[1], Kt. have both, VP *hwelċ*, North. *hwelċ*, *hwoelċ* (§ 319); *Ru.*[1], North. also *hwǣlċ* (§ 197).

Hūlic, of what sort?, declines like adjs. in *-lic* (§ 642); on North. *hūliġ* see § 452; on eW-S *hūlucu*, North. *hūluco* § 340 (but cf. § 643.5, footnote).

5. Indefinite Pronouns

§ 718. The interrogative pronouns in *hw-* may be used as indefinite pronouns: *hwa* anyone, someone, *hwæþer* either of two, one or other, *hwelċ*, *hwilċ* anyone (but often adjectival, any . . .); e.g. *ġif hwa to hwæðrum ðissa ġenied sie* 'if anyone be forced to one or other of these things'; *sona swa sacerda hwylċ hwone . . . ġesyhþ* 'as soon as anyone of the priests observes anyone'. *Āhwā*, *āhwæþer*[3] have the same sense as the simple forms.

§ 719. A general inclusive sense is given to the same words by the prefix *ġe-*: *ġehwa* everyone; *ġehwæþer* each of two, *ġehwilċ* each (often adjectival); e.g. *forði sċeal ġehwa . . .* 'therefore everyone must . . .', *wæs ġehwæþer oðrum laþ* 'each of the two was hateful to the other'. The same senses are more frequently expressed by *ǣġhwa* (< **ā-ġi-hwa*), *ǣġhwæþer*, *ǣġhwilċ*.[4] Other modifications of the interrogative pronouns to obtain generalizing pronouns are *æthwa*, *welhwylċ*, *ġewelhwylċ* everyone.[5]

[1] Variety of root vowel is of Gmc. origin; cf. Goth. *ƕaþar*, OHG *uuedar*; OS *huilik*, OHG *huelih*.

[2] Not recorded as pron. in *VP*, where it occurs as a conjunction, always in the form *hweðer* (§ 164).

[3] Contracted *āwþer*, *ōwþer*, *āþer*; negated *nāhwæþer*, &c.

[4] Interrogative advs. may be modified by *ā-*, *ġe-*, *ǣġ-* like prons., e.g. *hwǣr* where?, *āhwǣr* (*āwer*, *ōwer*) anywhere, *ġehwǣr*, *ǣġhwǣr* everywhere. So similar compounds of *hwanon*, *hwider*, *hū*.

[5] So with advs., (*ġe*)*welhwǣr* everywhere, &c., see § 679.

§ 720. Generalizing relative pronouns can be made from interrogatives in *hw-* by adding *swa . . . swa*, e.g. *swa hwa swa* whoever, *swa hwæþer swa*, *swa hwilċ swa* whoever. Single *swa* is less usual; *swa hwa* is very rare, *swa hwæþer* (contracted *swǣþer*) fairly common, and *swilċ* may be sometimes for *swa hwilċ*, not *swilċ* such (e.g. *Beow.* 72). The same meaning is expressed by *lōc(a) hwa*, *lōc hwæþer*, *lōc hwilċ*;[1] and also by *swelċ*, *swilċ* with a normal relative clause, e.g. *swælċ monn se ðe to minum ærfe foe* 'whichever man succeeds to my estate'.

§ 721. 'In case anyone' is *weald hwa*, e.g. *weald hwæt heom tide* 'in case anything befall them'.[2]

§ 722. *Hwæthwugu* something; *hwilċhwugu* someone (also adjectival 'some').[3] The second element also appears as *-hwugu*, *-hwegu*, *-hwigu* (also with *-a*); Cp. *-huegu* but Ep. *-huuoegu*, and forms with *oe* prevail in North., where inflexion of this element is also found, e.g. *huoelċhuoeges* alicuius.

§ 723. 'Someone', 'anyone' can be expressed not only as described in § 718, but by *nāthwa*, *nāthwelċ*, *samhwelċ*; 'something', 'anything' not only by the neuters of these, but also by *āwiht*, *āwuht*[4] (neg. *nāwiht*, *nānwiht*). Note also the use of nom. sg. *man* as 'someone', frequently giving a periphrasis for the passive voice, e.g. *hine man heng* 'someone hanged him', 'he was hanged'.

§ 724. 'A certain' is *sum*, declined strong;[5] it may be used as pron. 'a certain person'.

§ 725. Other common indefinite pronouns (adjs.) are: *eall* all, *ǣlċ* each (VP *ylċ*),[6] *ǣniġ* any, *nǣniġ*, *nān* none,[7] *se ilca*, *se sylfa* the same, *nānþing* nothing, *swelċ*, *swilċ*,[8] *þyslic*, *þuslic* (also *þyllic*, *þullic* § 484) such.

[1] So with advs., *lōca hwonne* whenever, *lōc hwǣr* wherever.

[2] So with advs., *weald hwænne*, in case at any time, *weald hū* in case in any way (*And.* 1355).

[3] So with advs., *hwonanhwugu* from somewhere, *hūhwugu* about (before numbers, to show approximation); note also the adv. *æthwega* a little.

[4] On the phonology see § 338, footnote; on reduction in the adverb *āteshwōn*, at all, § 393.

[5] n.s.f. eW-S *sumu*, lW-S and poetry usually *sum*.

[6] *Ǣfre ǣlċ*, whence modern 'every', appears about 1000.

[7] a.s.m. *nǣnne* and *nānne*.

[8] The root vowels of *swelċ*, and its adv. *swelċe*, are distributed in the texts very much like those of *hwelċ*, *hwilċ* (§ 717).

XVI

VERBS

§ 726. In the Germanic languages there are two main classes of verbs: strong verbs, which form their past tense with vowel variation, e.g. OE *beran* bear, *bær* bore, and weak verbs, which form their past tense with a dental element, e.g. OE *hīeran* hear, *hīerde* heard. Strong verbs practically all have a present tense with *e*, interchanging with *o*, as thematic vowel. Weak verbs all have present tenses in which the thematic *e/o* is preceded by -*i̯*-: there are three main classes, the -*i̯e*-, -*ōi̯e*-, and -*ǣi̯e*- classes. There is also a class of verbs known as the preterite-present[1] verbs: they are not numerous, but most of them are very common. Originally strong past tenses of present meaning (like Lat. *novi*, Gr. *οἶδα*) they developed a past tense with a dental formative element in Gmc., e.g. OE *sċeal* shall, *sċolde* should. There are very few verbs in OE outside these three groups, and they will be classed together below as anomalous verbs.

§ 727. Most of the independent forms of the OE verb belong to the active voice. This has two moods, indicative and subjunctive, which have each two independently formed tenses, present and past. It has also an imperative mood, which has a present tense only; an infinitive mood, which consists of the verbal noun of the present; and a verbal adjective, the present participle. The passive voice has only a verbal adjective, the passive participle: it expresses pure passivity, not necessarily passivity in past time.[2] Apart from this form, the only trace of an independent passive in OE is *hātte* is or was called, pl. *hātton* (cf. Goth. *haitada*, § 341).

§ 728. In addition to the above, the OE verb has many periphrastic forms. While the present can normally be used with future meaning, the future can also be formed with *willan*+inf., when there is a sense of desire, and with *sċulan*+inf., when

[1] The term 'strong-weak' is to be avoided, for it implies commitment to the view that the dental element in the preterite of these verbs is identical in origin with that of the Gmc. weak preterite. Cf. Prokosch in *PMLA* xlii. 334–5.

[2] Note that therefore Lat. *amatus est* is OE *he wæs ġelufod*; but from intransitive verbs the part. is past: *ða wæs ġeworden* 'then it had come to pass'.

there is a sense of obligation. There is a periphrastic past imperfect, e.g. *wǣron feohtende* 'they were fighting', and a periphrastic perfect, e.g. *ðu hæfst ġehǣled* 'thou hast healed'.[1] The passive voice is formed by combinations of *weorþan* and *wesan* with the passive participle.[2]

§ 729. The independent tenses of the indicative and the subjunctive have three persons in the singular, but it is a peculiarity of the Ingvaeonic languages that there is only one form for the three persons of the plural.[3] There are no dual forms, and dual pronouns are followed by plural verbs. The imperative has only two forms, the 2nd pers. sg. and pl. The infinitive has an inflected form used after *to*. The participles are fully inflected adjectives (§§ 643.5.c, d, e; 647).

1. Strong Verbs

a. INFLEXIONS

§ 730.	Indicative	Subjunctive	Imperative
Present			
Sg. 1.	rīde, *I ride*	rīde	
2.	rītst	rīde	rīd
3.	rītt	rīde	
Pl.	rīdaþ	rīden	rīdaþ
Past			
Sg. 1.	rād	ride	
2.	ride	ride	
3.	rād	ride	
Pl.	ridon	riden	
	Inf.	rīdan, to rīdenne	
	Pres. part.	rīdende	
	Pass. part.	riden	

When a pronoun of the 1st or 2nd pers. follows, the pl. endings *-aþ*, *-on*, *-en* can be reduced to *-e*, e.g. *rīde we, ġe*. The final consonant of monosyllabic forms can be dropped under the same

[1] The part. may be uninflected, or inflected to agree with the object.

[2] See further C. Pessels, *The present and past periphrastic tenses in A-S* (Strassburg, 1896); J. Klingebiel, *Die Passivumschreibungen im Altenglischen* (Berlin diss., 1937); F. Mossé, *La périphrase verbale* être+*participe présent en ancien germanique* (Paris, 1938).

[3] In OE the three sg. persons of the subj. tenses have also fallen together. Li. *wutum* let us, for normal OE *wuton, uton,* may preserve an old 1st pl. ending.

circumstances, e.g. *fō we* 'let us take'. Such forms are mainly W-S: *VP* has no instances in strong verbs, but cf. *wynsumie we* 'let us rejoice'; *Ru.*[1] has instances only from pret.-pres. verbs, *sċule ġe*, *ðurfe wæ*. In North. such forms are distinguished only in the indic., as final *-n* is lost normally in the subj. In the indic. both normal and reduced forms occur, e.g. *Ru.*[2] pres. *forstonde we*, past *ġisēge we*.

The conjugation of the present system of contracted verbs should be carefully observed:

	Indicative	Subjunctive	Imperative
Sg. 1.	sēo, *I see*	sēo	
2.	siehst	sēo	seoh
3.	siehþ	sēo	
Pl.	sēoþ	sēon	sēoþ
	Inf.	sēon, to sēonne	
	Pres. part.	sēonde	

Like *sēon* (Class V) are *ġefēon* rejoice, *plēon* risk. The contracted verbs of Classes I and II, *lēon* grant, *sēon* sieve, *þēon* thrive, *wrēon* cover, *flēon* flee, *tēon* draw, differ only in that they have long diphthongs in the forms with preserved *h*, e.g. imper. *tēoh*, 2nd and 3rd sg. pres. indic. *tīehst*, *tīehþ*. The contracted verbs of Class VI, *flēan* flay, *lēan* blame, *slēan* slay, *þwēan* wash, have *ĕa* where *sēon* has *ĕo*, hence pres. indic. *slēa*, *sliehst*, *sliehþ*, *slēaþ*, imper. *sleah*, etc. The contracted verbs of Class VII, *fōn* take, *hōn* hang, have *ō* where *sēon* has *ĕo*, and *ē* (< *ōe*) where *sēon* has *ie*, hence pres. indic. *fō*, *fēhst*, *fēhþ*, *fōþ*, imper. *fōh*, &c.

These contracted present systems show great diversity of form in the dialects: see the discussions of the various classes below, and the excellent conspectus of forms S–B, § 374.

§ 731. **Origin of forms.** (*a*) The OE endings of the present indicative were developed from Gmc. *-ō*, *-isi*, *-iþi*, *-anþi*.[1] On the loss of final *-i* see § 331.3; on syncopation and consonant changes in 2nd and 3rd sg. pres. indic. see below; on the development of *-anþi* in Ingvaeonic see § 332. The final *-t* in 2nd sg. pres. indic. arose in inverted forms, e.g. *rītstu* < *rīdes þu* dost thou ride (§ 481.1). The 1st sg. pres. indic.

[1] The 2nd and 3rd sg. and the pl. are assumed to be derived from forms accented on the thematic vowel, otherwise the voiceless spirants following that vowel would have been voiced in Gmc. (§ 398.2), and would have become West Gmc. *r*, *d* (§§ 404, 409).

in *-u* (*-o*), found in nW-S, corresponds to Gmc. *-ō*,[1] the mainly W-S ending *-e* must be from Prim. OE *-æ*, and this would correspond to Gmc. *-ōm*, with *-m* added from the tenses with secondary endings (see (*b*) below).[2]

(*b*) The Gmc. subj. mood is from an I-E viewpoint optative. The present optative of verbs with thematic *e/o* was formed with *-oi-* to which endings similar to those of the indic. but lacking final *-i* (secondary endings) were added. In Gmc. the sg. and 3rd pl. would be *-aim*, *-aiz* (*-ais*), *-aiþ*, *-ainþ*, to which, with the loss of the final consonants (§§ 399, 404), OE sg. *-e*, pl. *-en* correspond.[3]

(*c*) On the root vowels of OE strong past tenses see § 736.c, d. The endings of the 1st and 3rd sg. strong perfect in I-E were *-a*, *-e* (cf. Gr. οἶδα, -ε), and these vowels dropped in Gmc. (§ 331.1). The 2nd pers. ended in I-E in *-tha*, and the reflex of this is seen in the pret.-pres. verbs (§ 767). But in Gmc. the pl. of the strong past tense, and in West Gmc. the 2nd sg. also, were derived not from the I-E perfect, but from the I-E thematic aorist (Gr. ἔλιπον to pres. λείπω). The ending of the 2nd sg. of this tense was in I-E *-es*, which developed in Gmc. as *-iz* > OE *-e*.[4] The West Gmc. strong past sg. is accordingly a mixture of two I-E sg. tenses. The 3rd pl., levelled to all persons in Ingvaeonic, was in Gmc. *-unþ*. This form will be discussed further below (§ 736.d).

(*d*) In Gmc. the past subj. extended a formative element *-ī-* (proper historically to the pl. opt. of athematic tenses) to all forms; hence the OE forms are to be derived from Gmc. *-īm*, *-īz* (*-īs*), *-ī*, *-īnþ*. The development in OE is normal.[5] On umlaut of the root vowel in this tense see § 736.m.

(*e*) The imper. sg. had in I-E final *-e* which was lost early in Gmc. (§ 331.1). In the pl. the I-E ending *-ete* coincided with the ending of the 2nd pl. pres. indic., and in Ingvaeonic it was replaced in both indic. and imper. by the ending of the 3rd pl. pres. indic.[6] In OE *-aþ* is extended to the imper. pl. of pret.-pres. verbs, though pres. indic. pl. has *-on*.

[1] Final *-u* (*-o*) should remain only after short root syllables (§ 345), but it appears analogically after long ones also, e.g. VP *ġeldu*, *singu*, *ġefallu*, Li. *drīfo*, *delfo*, *drinco*.

[2] See Bazell in *Neophilologus* xxiv. 64; but cf. Cowgill in *Symbolae linguistical in honorem Georgii Kurylowicz*, pp. 44-50.

[3] The unaccented ending *-aiz* was developed in the 2nd sg.; in other persons the accented and unaccented endings would develop identically in Gmc.

[4] The aorist had the I-E accent on the thematic vowel, and hence the Gmc. development of the 2nd sg. should be *-is*; but *-iz* arose also owing to the fluctuation of *s* and *z* in the pres. indic. and subj., and was developed in all the languages. (Another view, Bazell, l.c.)

[5] As in the pres. subj., the unaccented ending is developed in 2nd sg., while in the other persons accented and unaccented endings would have the same development in OE. See, however, Bazell in *Neophilologus* xxiv. 64–66, on various theories of the development of the subj. endings.

[6] Lancaster Cross has imper. pl. *ġibidæþ*, Falstone Hogback *ġebidæd*, Urswick

(*f*) The infinitive is derived from the acc. sg. of a verbal noun, Gmc. *-anam* < I-E *-onom*. This verbal noun is not developed as an infinitive outside Gmc., nor has it been certainly shown to exist elsewhere in any function (cf. Hirt, *Urgermanisch* ii, § 158). In West Gmc. other cases (gen., dat., inst.) can be formed from the inf. according to the *-i̯a*-declension: of these OE has only the dat. in *-enne*, used after *to*.

(*g*) The pres. part. ending is derived from the I-E element *-nt-*, found elsewhere in the same function (Lat. *ferent-*, Gr. *φέροντ-*). Gmc. has *a* (< I-E *o*) as the thematic vowel, and after an unaccented vowel *þ* (< I-E *t*) > *ð* (Verner's law) > West Gmc. *d*. In West Gmc. the formation follows the *i̯a-* and *i̯ō-* declensions (§ 647), and *-and-* therefore becomes *-end-* in OE owing to umlaut.

(*h*) The passive participle is a verbal adj. in I-E *-en-* or *-on-*. In OE, Gmc. *-an-* from *-on-* was usually developed (§ 334). On traces of Gmc. *-in-* (< I-E *-en-*) see § 735.k, and on umlaut of the root vowel § 736.m. The part. is declined in Gmc. as an *a-*, *ō*-adj. (§ 643.5.c), and this was already the case in I-E.[1] In OE it usually has the prefix *ġe-* if the verb has not some other unaccented prefix.

§ 732. The 2nd and 3rd sg. pres. indic. The endings of these are derived from Gmc. *-isi*, *-iþi* (see above), and hence there is by normal development in OE umlaut of the root vowel, and change of *e* to *i* (§ 112), e.g. 3rd sg. *bīett*, *lȳċþ*, *cymþ*, *briċþ*, *stent*, *fieht*, *hǣtt*, *fielþ* from *bēodan*, *lūcan*, *cuman*, *brecan*, *standan*, *feohtan*, *hātan*, *feallan*. In W-S there is generally syncope of *-i-* (§ 347), and consequent assimilation of consonants and simplification of double consonants within groups according to the principles discussed in §§ 476, 480. For clarity the rules which there emerge are repeated here in so far as they affect the 2nd and 3rd sg. pres. indic. and are reflected in OE spelling.

In the 2nd pers.:

dst > *tst*: *rǣtst*, inf. *rǣdan*; later *t* can be dropped (§ 477.1): *finst*, inf. *findan*, and so with original *t*, *hǣst*, inf. *hātan*.

þst > *sst* > *st*: *cwist*, inf. *cweþan*; but analogically restored *þs* > *ts*: *snīþst*, *snītst*, inf. *snīþan*.

ngst > *nċst*: rare, *brinċst*, inf. *bringan*; also *brinst* (§ 477.4).

Cross *ġebidæs*. This is not to be regarded as a survival of the I-E imper. pl. (Bazell, *Litera* ii. 31) or as a subj. (Ross, *MLN* xlvii. 377), but as a lNorth. form for normal *ġebiddaþ*, with extension of *-d-* from the 2nd and 3rd sg. (cf. Li. *bidas*, Matt. 20, 22, and fairly frequent pres. indic. pls. in *-æþ*, *-æs*).

[1] The I-E verbal adj. in *-eno*, *-ono* was developed as a pass. part. in Slavonic also.

ġst > *hst*: *stīhst*, inf. *stīgan* (cf. 480.3, footnote 1).
hst > *xt*: rare, see § 481.4.

In the 3rd pers.:

tþ, *dþ* > *tt*: *lǣtt*, *bīett*, *bint* (< **bintt*), infs. *lǣtan*, *bēodan*, *bindan*.
sþ > *st*: *ċīest*, inf. *ċēosan*.
ġþ > *hþ*: *līehþ*, *abelhð*, *byrhð*, infs. *lēogan*, *belgan*, *beorgan* (§ 481.4).
nġþ > *nċþ*: rare, see § 482.

Note the simplification of geminates in groups of three consonants: *cwist*, *bint*, *wierþ* < **cwisst*, **bintt*, **wierþþ* (inf. *weorþan*). Analogical replacement of consonants is frequent, e.g. *findst*, *cweþst*, and usual with *-ng-*, e.g. *singþ* (§ 482). Final double consonants are often graphically simplified, e.g. 3rd sg. *rīt*, *snīþ*, i.e. *rītt*, *snīþþ* (§ 66). For some rare changes of final *-þ* to *-t* see § 481.4, footnote, 5, 8; S–B, § 359.9.

§ 733. (*a*) The 2nd and 3rd sg. pres. indic. are rarely syncopated in Angl. texts: e.g. *VP* has from strong verbs syncopation only in *ġefihð*, *ġefiht* beside *ġefīð*, *-fōeht* beside *-fōeð*,[1] and always *cwið*, inf. *ġefēon*, *fōn*, *cweþan*. *VP* normally has no syncope, and levels away umlaut, e.g. *falleð*, *ċeorfeð*, *-weorðeð*, *-ċēoseð*, *-lūceð*, *-sċādeð*, *-cnāweð*, *flōweð*.[2] But *VP* retains *i* in the root syllable, e.g. *trides*, *-eð*, *ites*, *ætfīleð*, *bireð*, *ġildeð*, *swilteð*, inf. *tredan*, *etan*, &c. The position is similar in *Ru.*[1], but there *e* is as a rule also restored,[3] e.g. *eteþ*, *-ġefeþ*, *-ġeteþ*, *bereþ*, *swælteþ* (§ 328). In North. there is practically never syncope, and the mutation of the root vowel is levelled away, e.g. *falleð*, *worðes*, *eteð*, *bereð*.

(*b*) The 3rd sg. forms occurring in eKt. are uncontracted, e.g. Ct. 41 *bibēadeð*, *forġifeð*; but in *KG* there is prevailing syncope, umlaut, and consonant assimilation, e.g. *ġebēġð*, *toġīot*, *helt*, inf. *būgan*, *ġēotan*, *healdan*. But root vowel *e* is often restored, e.g. *ġelpð*, *tret*, inf. *ġelpan*, *tredan*; and so in 2nd sg. *byrst* (*y* = *e* in

[1] When there is no syncope, loss of intervocalic χ and contraction naturally take place in forms of this type.

[2] *VP.*, *Ru.*[1], North. 3rd sg. pres. indic. *cymeð*, he comes, will be separately considered in § 742.

[3] But *Ru.*[1], while having *cwiðst*, *cwið* once each only, beside unsyncopated forms, has a few more syncopated forms from other verbs than *VP*, e.g. *cymþ*, *ġewyrð*, to *cuman*, *weorþan*; note also *ġewyrfeþ* demolitur, with mutation but no syncope (unless it is to weak *hwierfan*, not *hweorfan*); on syncopated forms in contracted verbs in *Ru.*[1] see §§ 743–5.

Kt. spelling), *aġelts*, inf. *beran*, *ġeldan*. The vowel of the 3rd sg. in *-et* (§ 735.b) is not syncopated: *forberet*, *aweġet*, inf. *beran*, *wegan*.

§ 734. Even in W-S occasional forms of Angl. type occur; they are especially common in *CP*, e.g. *hāteð*, *bēodeð*, *drīfeð*, *hilpeð*, and there are also mixed forms, with syncope but no umlaut, or umlaut but no syncope, e.g. *weaxð*, *-hǣtest*, inf. *weaxan*, *hātan*.

§ 735. **Early, late, and dialectal forms.** (*a*) the 1st sg. pres. indic. appears in two forms, *-e*/*-æ* and *-o*/*-u*. *-e* is practically universal in W-S, the only eW-S exception being *CP* once *cweðo*. eKt. varies between *-e* and *-o*, *KG* have only 1871 *stele*. The early Angl. texts have prevailingly *-o*/*-u*, but there are a few cases of *-e* in *VP*, some of them probably due to misunderstanding of Lat. future in *-am* as subj. *Ru.*[1], however, has *-e* about 20 times, *-u* once. In lNorth. *-o* prevails, *-a* is frequent, *-u* less so, and *-e* appears fairly often: this agrees well with the state of unaccented vowels in these texts (§ 379, footnote). In Angl. monosyllabic forms occasionally add *-m* on the analogy of *eam*, &c., e.g. VP *flēom*, Li. *-sēom*.

(*b*) The 2nd and 3rd sg. pres. indic. often have *-i-* as the vowel of the endings in early texts, e.g. LR *hlimmith*, Cp. *mīðið*, but also already *ġehēres thu*, *onhrīoseð*, &c. Forms with *-i-* occur sporadically later, especially *Ru.*[1] and North.

Early the 2nd sg. ends in *-s*, but later *-st* replaces this widely. *VP* has *-st* only in monosyllabic forms, e.g. *-sīst*, *-fōest*. eW-S has already always *-st* (or *sð*, § 481.1, footnote). *Ru.*[1] has both *-st* and *-s*. North. has *-st* rarely, chiefly in monosyllabic forms, e.g. *ġesīst*, *KG* have *byrst*, but *aġelts ðu*.

The 3rd sg. has in some texts *-it*, *-et* beside *-iþ*, *-eþ*. While in *Ep.*, *Cp.* this might be regarded as graphic (§ 57.7, footnote), the appearance of the form in later texts suggests a genuine phonetic variant. In eW-S and *Ru.*[1] examples are all from weak verbs, but *Ru.*[2] has *ġiscīnet*, *fallet*, KG *forberet*, *aweġet*.

The inflexions of the 2nd and 3rd sg. are confused in *Ru.*[1] and North. owing to the increasing weakening of distinction between unaccented vowels and perhaps also because of confusion with the endings of weak verbs of Class II. *Ru.*[1] has historically correct forms (contracted or uncontracted) in the 2nd sg., but in the 3rd *-aþ*, *-æþ* appear beside *-eþ*. In North. *-að* is frequent in 3rd sg., *-æð* occasional, and 2nd sg. also has *-as*, *-æs*. A further confusion in North. (perhaps aggravated by Scandinavian influence) is for 2nd and 3rd sg. to fall together under the 2nd, hence 3rd sg. appears as *-es*, *-as*, *-æs*[1] (see Bazell in *Litera* ii. 28–31).

(*c*) The pl. of the pres. indic. shows little variation outside North.;

[1] North. has in verbs of all kinds occasionally 2nd sg. in *-ð* because in 3rd sg. *-ð* = *-s*; so *Ru.*[1] once *hæfeþ* habes.

Ru.[1] has occasionally *-eþ*. In North. *-as* is rather more frequent than *-að*, and in both forms reduction of the vowel is frequent, giving *-eð*, *-es*.

(*d*) The 2nd sg. of the past indic. sometimes adds *-s*(*t*) in *Ru.*[1] and North. owing to analogy of the weak verbs. Instances seem limited to verbs of Class VII with root syllables ending in *-t*, e.g. Ru.[1] *forlētes*, Li. *hehtes*, Rit. *ġihehtest*.

(*e*) The pl. of the past indic. has *-un* in the earliest texts, and this remains in *Cp.* and *VP* beside *-on*, rarely *-an*. eKt. and *KG* have both *-on* and *-an*. Although in eNorth. there are cases of the past pl. in *-u* (RC *bismæradu*, *cwōmu*), *-n* is rarely lost in lNorth.,[1] which usually has *-on* beside *-un* (especially Ru.[2]). *Ru.*[1] has usually *-un*, beside frequent *-on*, *-an*, and occasional *-en*.

(*f*) The pres. subj. exhibits no variety of form in early texts. In lW-S *-an*, *-on* generally replace pl. *-en*, and so always *KG*. In lNorth. the loss of *-n* destroys the distinction of sg. and pl., and while *-e* remains the prevailing vowel, *-a*, *-æ*, *-o* are also found. *Ru.*[1] also has sg. in *-e*, beside more rarely *-a* and *-æ*, but in pl. *-en* like eW-S, *-an*, *-on* like lW-S, and *-e*, *-æ* like North.

(*g*) The past subj. has little variety of form in early texts, except eW-S pl. without *-n* (§ 473). In eW-S, however, *-on* (*-an*) from the indic. begins to appear in the pl., and these endings are usual in lW-S; so KG *beswican*. In lNorth., owing to loss of *-n*, *-e* prevails in sg. and pl. with some fluctuation of vowel (*-a*, *-o*, *-æ*); but *-en* also appears, beside *-on*, *-un* from the indic. *Ru.*[1] has sg. *-e*, pl. *-e*, beside *-en*, *-an*, *-un*.

(*h*) The pl. of the imper. has variants in *Ru.*[1] and North. like those of the pres. indic.

(*i*) The inf. appears in all early Merc. and southern texts in *-an*, later *-on* also appears in lW-S and *KG*. In eNorth. the inf. already occurs with loss of *-n* (§ 472); lNorth. has always loss of *-n*, and while the vowel is usually *-a*, *-e* is frequent, and *-æ*, *-o* are found. In Ru.[1] *-an* is usual, *-a*, *-en*, *-e* rare.

Of the major monuments only *VP* has always *-enne* in the inflected inf. In eW-S *a* is introduced from the uninflected inf., and *-anne* prevails beside rare *-onne* and forms with *-n-* (§ 457); but *-enne*, *-ene* also occur. The position is similar in North., *Ru.*[1], eKt., but *KG* have only *-en*(*n*)*e*.

(*j*) The ending of the pres. part. is *-ende* in all texts, and *Ru.*[1], North. occasional *-ænde* can be regarded as a spelling variant (*æn* = *en*, § 193.d). In *Ru.*[1] there are scattered instances of *-ande*, mostly in *gangande* going. In *Rit.* and *Li.* (not in Ru.[2]) *-ande* is frequent in weak verbs of Class II, *Li.* has it sporadically with other verbs.

[1] A few cases of *-o* in Li. are mere scribal omission of the consonant; on *-e* before pronouns see § 730. But in *Li.* (not in *Rit.*, *Ru.*[2]) loss of *-n* is fairly frequent in the pres. indic. pl. of pret.-pres. verbs, e.g. *wuto*, *cunno*, *ðurfu*, *sċiolo*, *mago*.

(*k*) The pass. part. appears in early texts with both *-in-* and *-æn-* (cf. §§ 204.8, 334), e.g. Ep. *forsleġinum*, *ġibaen*. The development proper to the uninflected form (*-an*, *-on*) is not found in OE.[1]

§ 736. **Formation of tenses.** (*a*) The first five classes of strong verbs had in the present as root vowel *e*, and were distinguished by the sound which followed it: this was in I-E *i* in Class I, *u* in Class II, liquid or nasal+consonant in Class III, liquid or nasal alone in Class IV, some other single consonant in Class V. Since I-E *ei* > *ī* in Gmc., and since Gmc. *eu* > *ēo* in OE, the first two classes have in OE *ī* and *ēo*, e.g. *rīdan*, *ċēosan*. In Classes III and IV *i* appears before nasal+consonant and before single *m*, before liquids *e* remains, subject to the usual sound-changes, e.g. *bindan*, *niman*, *helpan*, *weorþan*, W-S *ġieldan*, *beran*, VP *beoran*, W-S *sċieran*. In Class V *e* remains except when subject to dialectal modification, e.g. *metan*, VP *meotan*, W-S *ġiefan*. The modification of these sounds in 2nd and 3rd sg. pres. indic. has been fully described in § 732.

(*b*) A few verbs are placed in Classes I–V because of the form of their past tenses and passive participles, but their presents diverge from those of most verbs of the classes in which they are placed. A large group of verbs in Class II have *ū* (not *ēo*) in the present system, e.g. OE *brūcan* enjoy, *lūcan* close. The reason for the intrusion of *ū* into the present of this class is uncertain, but may be no more than analogy with Class I in Gmc.: after *ei* > *ī*, since verbs with *ai* in the past had *ī* in the present system, those with *au* in the past might develop *ū* in the present system. In Classes I, III, and IV there are some aorist presents (e.g. *ripan*, *murnan*, *cuman*), i.e. presents with the reduced grade of ablaut proper to many aorist tenses (see below). A group of verbs usually included in Class III are in origin verbs of Class V (i.e. they have presents with *e*+a single consonant not a liquid or nasal), but their presents were extended by the addition of a dental element, e.g. OE *streġ-d-an* strew, *feoh-t-an* fight, *friġ-n-an* ask. In Gmc. this element was levelled from the pres. to all forms, and the past pl. and pass. part. adopted the vocalism of Class III (e.g. OE *fuhton*, *fohten*). Lastly, a group of verbs which had *-i̯-* before the endings in the present system, and hence might be expected to be conjugated as weak verbs, have nevertheless their past tense and pass. part. according to Class V: they are known as 'weak presents', e.g. OE *biddan* < **bidi̯an-*.

(*c*) The singular of the past tense has as root vowel Gmc. *a*, I-E *o*. In Classes I and II *ai* and *au* give OE *ā*, *ēa*, e.g. *rād*, *ċēas*. In Classes III–V *a* is subject to the usual OE changes, e.g. W-S *band*, *healp*, *wearp*, *feaht*, *stæl*, *mæt*, *ġeaf*, *seah*. This Gmc. past tense represents a very

[1] Occasional forms like Cp. *ġeborone* are scribal; in *Ru.*[1] and North. occasional *-an*, *-on* is due to the failing distinction of unaccented vowels.

common type of I-E perfect, which had *o* while the present system had *e* (cf. Gr. λείπω, λέλοιπα).

(*d*) The plural of the past tense of Classes I–III had loss of the vowel *o* which characterized the singular, and hence, corresponding to sg. I-E *oi*, *ou*, *or*, *ol*, *on*, the pl. had *i*, *u*, *r̥*, *l̥*, *n̥*. These gave Gmc. *i*, *u*, *ur*, *ul*, *un*, hence OE *ridon*, *curon*, *wurdon*, *hulpon*, *bundon*. This reduction of vocalism was clearly due to absence of accent from the root syllable, for if that syllable ended in Gmc. in a voiceless spirant in the past sg., in the pl. the spirant was voiced, e.g. OE *snāþ*, *snidon* (*d* < *ð*); *ċēas*, *curon* (*r* < *z*); *tēah*, *tugon*. It is not entirely certain whether these past pls. were in I-E a perfect or an aorist formation. Clearly there were in I-E perfects with *o* in the sg., in which this *o* vanished in the pl. because the chief accent of the word was now not on the root syllable (cf. Gr. οἶδα, ἴσμεν). Yet in the aorist also I-E verbs often exhibit loss of the vowel of the root (cf. Gr. ἔλιπον, present λείπω), and it has been noted in § 731.c that the 2nd sg. of the past is in West Gmc. aorist in origin, so perhaps the pl. is from the same I-E tense. The ending Gmc. *-unþ* does not help this matter to be decided for it is not original: the thematic aorist 3rd pl. was I-E *-ont*, which would have given Gmc. *-anþ*, and the perfect 3rd pl. seems to have contained *-r-* (cf. Lat. *fuere*, &c.). The Gmc. subj. is based on the same form of the root syllable as the indic. pl.

(*e*) The pass. part. of Classes I–III had the same I-E root vowel as the pl. of the past tense, and the same consonant changes in Gmc. But in Gmc. a root vowel *u* became *o*, unless a nasal consonant followed (§ 115), while *i* remained (§ 114). Hence corresponding to the past tense pls. just quoted the OE pass. parts. are *riden*, *coren*, *worden*, *holpen*, *togen*, but *bunden*.

(*f*) Classes IV and V form the pass. part. with a reduction of the root vowel seen in the present. But in I-E before a single consonant this reduction did not cause complete loss (as in Classes I–III), but change to *ъ* (§ 101), and this developed in Gmc. as *u* (subject to change to *o*, § 115), before liquids and nasals, as *e* before other consonants. Hence OE pass. parts. *stolen*, *numen*, *meten*.

(*g*) While resembling verbs of Classes I–III in the present system, the past sg., and the pass. part., those of Classes IV and V have an entirely different formation in the pl. of the past, where the root vowel is I-E *ē*, Gmc. *ǣ*, West Gmc. *ā*, OE *ǣ* (nW-S *ē*), but *ō* before nasals (§ 127–8), e.g. OE *stǣlon*, *mǣton*, *nōmon*.[1] While there is some evidence for I-E perfects with lengthening of the root vowel (see Hirt, *Urgermanisch* ii. 148), it is more likely that the source of the Gmc. past with long root vowel is an I-E aorist of the type of Gr. ἔβην. Such formations contribute to the Lat. perfect with lengthening of the root vowel, e.g. *ēdi*, *sēdi*,

[1] The same vowel appears in the past sg. in *ǣt*, *nōm*, *cwōm*.

vēni, lēgi. Here clearly a formation with a fully accented root vowel was involved, and so far as we find Verner's law operating in these verbs, the voiced spirant must have been levelled to the past pl. from the pass. part.[1] The usual Gmc. past pl. with reduction of the root vowel appears in pret.-pres. verbs of Class IV, OE *sċulon, munon.*

(*h*) The verbs of Classes VI and VII are of a different type. They had in the past sg. an accented vowel, and the present system had an unaccented vowel (thus resembling the aorist presents referred to above, under (*b*)). The pass. part. had as usual an unaccented vowel, and hence the same root syllable as the present. The form of the past pl. in Gmc. is doubtful,[2] but in West Gmc. the vowel of the sg. was extended to it. A long vowel or diphthong stood in the forms with accented root vowel (i.e. the past sg.), and the present system and the pass. part. had in Gmc. *a* either alone or as first element of a diphthong. Hence the main types are:

Gmc. *a, ō*; OE the same, e.g. *faran, fōr, faren.*
Gmc. *ai, ē* (< *ēi*, § 100.3); OE *ā, ē*, e.g. *hātan, hēt, hāten.*
Gmc. *au, ēu*; OE *ēa, ēo*, e.g. *bēatan, bēot, bēaten.*
Gmc. *al, ēl*; OE the same, e.g. *fallan, fēll, fallen.*[3]
Gmc. *an, ēn*; OE the same, e.g. **fanχan,*[4] *fēng, fangen.*

In OE, however, there is considerable analogical disturbance of the distribution of *ē* and *ēo* in the past tense, *ēo* having almost completely replaced *ē* in the *l* verbs (*fēoll*, &c.), and in all *n* verbs except *fōn* and *hōn* (*bēonn*, &c.).

(*i*) Although the past tense pl. had an accented vowel in Classes VI and VII, and this would normally be followed by voiceless spirants, the voiced spirant proper to the pass. part. was transferred to the past in Gmc., e.g. OE *slōg, fēng* < Gmc. **slōȝ-, fēŋg-* (infs. **slaχan-, *faŋχan-*).

(*j*) In I-E the perfect tense was usually marked by reduplication, and this remains in Sanskrit, Gr., and often in Lat. (e.g. Gr. λέλοιπα, Lat. *pepigi*). It is doubtful if all past tenses had in Gmc. reduplication

[1] What is known as the 'Michels–Streitberg theory' of the origin of Gmc. *ǣ* in the past pl. of Classes IV and V seeks to explain the formation as similar to the past pls. of Classes I–III, having loss of the root vowel. This in Classes IV and V involved loss of a syllable; and so the preceding reduplicating syllable suffered compensatory lengthening, and was preserved in Gmc. Thus from the root *sed*, sit, the I-E perf. pl. would be **sesed-* > **sēsd-* > **sēzd-* > Gmc. **sǣt-*. This theory involves many difficulties (especially with regard to the simplification of the consonant groups) and is better abandoned.

[2] If it had reduced grade, the root syllable would be the same as in the present and in the pass. part. Then it would be the source of the Goth. past tense of Class VII, with the same vowel as present and pass. part. (e.g. *haihait*, inf. *haitan*), and of a small group of OE pasts with the same vowel as their presents, *sċeād, gang, -bland, -ban.*

[3] W-S *feallan, feallen.*

[4] OE *fōn* (§ 119).

inherited from the I-E perfect, but in Goth. reduplication is developed as the main distinguishing feature of the past of Class VII. In OE also a small group of verbs of Class VII are developed from reduplicated tenses with the accent on the reduplicating syllable and consequent loss of the root syllable, e.g. *heht* < **χeχēit-* (or **χeχait-*, with reduced vowel in the root syllable) beside *hēt* as the pret. of *hātan*. The ME development suggests that *heht* in OE acquired the long *ē* of *hēt*, but other reduplicated pasts had short vowels capable of breaking (*reord*, &c., § 746).[1]

(*k*) Like Class V, Classes VI and VII have a number of weak presents, e.g. OE *hebban*, *wēpan* < **χavi̯an-*, **u̯ōpii̯an*. In Class VI two verbs have infixed *-n-* in the present, OE *sta-n-dan*, *wæċ-n-an*, past *stōd*, *wōc* (cf. Lat. *vinco*, *vīci*, *sterno*, *strēvi*). This *-n-* is extended in OE to the past part. *standen*.

(*l*) A considerable number of verbs is included in Class VII of which the forms are not to be explained according to (*h*) above. One group had I-E *ē* or *ō* in the present, *ō* in the past, all accented vowels, e.g. Goth. *lētan*, *lailōt*, *flōkan*, *faiflōk*. In OE they developed *ē* or *ēo* as the vowel of the past, e.g. *lǣtan*, *lēt*, *hrōpan*, *hrēop*. This was perhaps due to the continuance of reduplication in these verbs,[2] which might cause them to be associated with the reduplicated verbs of Class VII with *ē* and *ēo* in the past tense. OE *wēpan* < **u̯ōpii̯an* is a weak present of this class. Another group of verbs had open root syllables, and sometimes formed their past tenses with the element *-u̯-* seen in Lat. perfects (e.g. *sē-v-i*), but in OE this element was extended to all forms, e.g. *blāwan* < **blǣu̯an* (§ 151), *flōwan*, past *blēow*, *flēow*.[3] The past should have final *ēo* (< *eu*) in OE, but *u̯* was added from inflected forms, and then *ēou̯* was taken as the base to which inflexions were added. The pass. part. has the vowel of the present system in these verbs on the analogy of other types with *ē* and *ēo* in the past.

(*m*) From what has been said in § 731.d, h of the endings of the past subj. and pass. part., it is clear that the root vowel of the former should always have umlaut while that of the latter might be expected to have

[1] It will be seen that the 'Brugmann–Wood theory' of the origin of the past tenses of Classes VI and VII, as defended by E. Prokosch (*A comparative Germanic grammar*, pp. 176 ff.), has been regarded above as offering the most reasonable solution to the problem. It is, however, at present inadvisable to attempt to reconstruct the I-E form of the ablaut which appears in Gmc. as variation between *a* and a long vowel (cf. §§ 106–7).

[2] In OE reduplicated past tenses survive from *lǣtan*, *-drǣdan*, and *rǣdan* (see below, § 746).

[3] This explanation of the *-u̯-* of these verbs is the most probable of several. The objection to it is the uncertain antiquity of the Lat. *u̯*-perfect, and consequent doubt if it is evidence for an I-E formation which could reappear in Gmc. Cf. Flasdieck in *A* lx. 305–6.

umlaut sometimes, as the formative element was Gmc. *-in-* beside *-an-*. In the past subj. umlaut is frequent in pret.-pres. verbs (e.g. *sċyle*, see § 767), but otherwise instances are few and uncertain (see S–B, § 377.a). In the pass. part. there are, however, a number of forms with umlaut: *CP*, Hatton MS., *-cymen*, *-ðrǣwen*, Cott. MS. also *-sleġen*; lW-S *cymen*, *ġedefen*, *-tiġen* (Gn. Ex. 41, for *togen*), *-þweġen*, *bȳn* cultivated, *ġerǣwen*; Ep. *forsleġinum*; Li. has often umlaut of *o* in the pass. part. (§ 196) and also *-hefen*, *-ðueġen* (*-ðuēn*, § 244), *-sċyfen* (for *sċofen*, shoved);[1] Rit. *-hefen*, Ru.[2] *ġibroeċen* broken, Ru.[1] *-ðweġen*. The North. analogical pass. parts. *-fōen*, *-hōen* for *fangen*, *hangen* are probably disyllabic,[2] with *ō+e*, not *ōe*, but a similar but older re-formation with umlaut is preserved in poetical *-fēn* (§ 237). A similar formation is the participial adj. *ǣġen* own, beside *āgen*.

§ 737. The origins of the verbal classes suggested above should not be assumed to be true of every strong verb occurring in the historic Gmc. languages separately considered. The types of conjugation had the origins suggested, and they drew to themselves all verbs which did not form weak past tenses. Class I could even draw a loan-word, OE *sċrīfan*, Lat. *scrībere*. Especially in Classes VI and VII, although the prevailing origin of the conjugation is, as suggested above, verbs with an accented root vowel in the past and an unaccented one in the present, such a conjugation was very liable to confusion with one with I-E *a* or *o* in the present and having a past tense with lengthening: here may belong e.g. *faran*, *fōr* (cf. Gr. πόρος ford, Sanskrit *piparmi* I conduct).[3]

b. THE CLASSES OF STRONG VERBS

§ 738. From the paradigm in § 730 it appears that an OE strong verb can be conjugated if the infinitive (or some other part of the present system), the singular and plural of the past, and the passive participle are known. These parts of typical verbs of the various classes will now be recorded, and divergent forms noted.

§ 739. CLASS I

rīdan, *ride*	rād	ridon	riden

Similarly a large number of verbs, e.g. *ætwītan* reproach, *belīfan* remain, *drīfan* drive, *glīdan* glide, *hrīnan* touch, *sċrīfan* decree, *wrītan* write.

[1] But *ġesċryncan* shrunken, is beside *-sċriuncen*, and hence seems due to the usual North. change *u* > *iu/y* after *sċ* (§ 181), despite the intervening *r*.

[2] So *-dōen* done, beside poetical *-dēn*.

[3] On the composite origin of Class VI cf. Mezger in *Language* xviii. 223–5.

The operation of Verner's law (§ 398.2) is seen in

snīþan, *cut* snāþ snidon sniden

and similarly *līþan* go, *sċrīþan* go;[1] but *þ*, *s* are extended to all forms of *mīþan* conceal, *rīsan* rise, *wrīþan* twist; *ætclīþan* adhere, occurs only in pres.

Verbs with internal *g* frequently have *-h* in the past sg., e.g. *stīgan* ascend, *stāh* (§ 446).

Verbs of this class are liable to back umlaut in the past pl., but in W-S this was analogically removed, while in Angl. it commonly remains, especially in *VP*[2] (details and examples §§ 214–15).

There is evidence in a few verbs for aorist presents with *i* (§ 736.b, h), especially VP *reopan*, Ru.[1] *hriopan*, North. *riopa*, (*h*)*rioppa* reap,[3] Li. *grioppa* grip.

A few verbs of the class pass partially into the weak class in lNorth. Weak past forms occur from *grīpan* grip, *fordwīnan* vanish, *hrīnan* touch, *stīgan* ascend, e.g. *Li. ġegrĭ̄pp*(*e*)*de*, *forduĭ̄nde*, *ġehrĭ̄n*(*a*)*don*, *stĭ̄g*(*a*)*de*, formed from the present (or the past pl.), Ru.[2] *astǣgdon* formed from past sg.

VP has from *ætwītan*: pres. part. *edwītende*, past. pl. *edwiton*, but also past *edwitte*, *-un*, *edwetede*, whence pres. part. *edwetende*.

Contracted verbs.

wrēon, *cover* wrāh wrigon wrigen

So with consonantal change *h–g* owing to Verner's law *lēon* grant, *þēon* thrive; with change *h–w*, *sēon* sieve, *sāh*, *asiwen*. In W-S these verbs preserve *h* in the imper. sg. and 2nd and 3rd sg. pres. indic., e.g. *sēoh* sieve, *onlīhþ* grants.

Already in eW-S these verbs are affected by the analogy of Class II, so that *tēon*, accuse (< **tīχan*), has past *tēah*, *tugon*. In lW-S occur from *tēon* frequently *tēah*, *tugon*, *togen*, and similar forms from *þēon*, *wrēon*; from *þēon* occur also *þungon*, *þungen* according to Class III.[4]

In Angl. VP has inf. *-wrēan* (§ 238.2), 3rd sg. pres. indic. *-wrīð* (§ 237.2), imper. *-wrīh*, past *-wrāh*, pass. part. *-wrigen*; but beside

[1] But pass. part. *sċrīþen*, Gu. 1039.

[2] In Kt. material is practically lacking.

[3] The quantity in W-S *ripan* is uncertain. *OEC* 1089 *rǣpon*, past. pl., suggests a bye-form *repan* (Class V).

[4] These forms are historically correct, as *þēon* < **þiŋχan*- (§ 119).

similar forms, *Ru.*[1] and *Li.* have also present system from *wrīga*(*n*) with analogical extension of *g* from past system. Other Angl. forms are regular except *Rit.* pres. subj. *ġiðii*, pres. part. *ðiiende* (cf. Cp. *ðīendi*, § 237.3).

Ct. 45 (Surrey) has 3rd sg. pres. indic. *ġelīð* grants, but KG *-wrīhð*, imper. *-wrīh* (§ 310).

§ 740. CLASS II

bēodan, *command*	bēad	budon	boden

Similarly a large number of verbs, e.g. *brēotan* destroy, *ġēotan* pour, *nēotan* use, *rēocan* smoke, *sċēotan* shoot, *smēocan* smoke.

The operation of Verner's law is seen in:

ċēosan, *choose*	ċēas	curon	coren
sēoþan, *boil*	sēaþ	sudon	soden

Like *ċēosan* are *drēosan* fall, *forlēosan* lose, *frēosan* freeze, *hrēosan* fall; but *abrēoþan*, fail, extends *þ* to all forms.

Verbs with internal *-g-* often have *-h* in past sg., e.g. *flēogan* fly, *flēah*, and so *drēogan* endure, *lēogan* tell lies.

Occasional forms in Merc. with *ī* instead of *ē* (< *ēo*) by smoothing before back consonants in the present system of these verbs are to be attributed to the analogy of 2nd and 3rd sg. pres. indic., e.g. VP, Ru.[1] *līgende*, VP *flīgu*, Ru.[1] *smīkende*.[1]

A considerable group of verbs have *ū* instead of *ēo* in the present system (§ 736.b), and hence *ȳ* in the 2nd and 3rd sg. pres. indic. Examples are *brūcan* use, *būgan* bend, *lūcan* lock, *strūdan* rob, *sūcan* suck.

In North. both *ēo*- and *ū*-presents tend to extend the vowel of the 1st and 3rd sg. past to the pl., the 2nd sg., and the subj., e.g. *Li.* pl. *ġeċēason*, *ġebrēcon*, *Rit.* 2nd sg. *onlēce*, *Li.* subj. *ġeċēase*, beside frequent forms with *u*. *Li.* has frequently past sg. with *æ* (? analogy of Class V) instead of *ē* (smoothing of *ēa*), e.g. *ġebræc*, *ataeh*, *flaeh*.

In North. *sċūfan*, shove, has in present system *sċȳf-*, past pl. Rit. *-sċyufon* (§ 181), pass. part. Li. *ġesċyfen* (§ 736.m); lW-S inf. *sċeōfan* (§ 180).

Weak forms develop from a few verbs; Li. *ġesŭpedon*, they tasted (but sg. *ġesēap*); lW-S *rēohte* smoked.

The verbs *cnēodan*, attribute to, *snēowan*, hasten, stand beside

[1] Cf. § 227. Another view, Bülbring, *Altengl. Elementarbuch*, § 513.

the Class VII forms *cnōdan, snōwan. Lēoran*, go, probably had past part. **loren* (cf. *Ruin* 7 *ġeleorene*, sic) beside weak forms. The past tenses *ahnēop* plucked, *ġenēop* overcame (*Guth.* 847, *Ex.* 475) may belong to this class, with archaic or dialectal *ēo* for *ēa* (§§ 275, 278).

Contracted verbs.

fleon, *flee* fleah flugon flogen

Similar is *tēon* draw. In W-S these verbs preserve *h* in 2nd and 3rd sg. pres. indic. and imper. sg., e.g. *flīehþ, flēoh.* In VP *flēon* extends *ēo* to all forms where the root vowel contracted with a back vowel of the ending, e.g. 1st sg. pres. indic. *flēom* (§ 735.a), pl. *flēoð*, and by further extension pres. part. *flēonde*, but subj. pl. *flēn*, 3rd sg. pres. indic. *-tīð* (§ 237.2), imper. *-tēh*. Ru.[1] has *ēo* in all pres. forms of both verbs, even imper. *flēoh, tēoh*, except occasionally *ēa* when the ending had *-a-*, e.g. *flēaþ*, beside *flēoþ* (§ 238.2.b); 2nd and 3rd sg. pres. indic. are not recorded. North. has *ēa* in all forms where there is contraction with a back vowel, e.g. inf. *flēa, tēa*, pres. indic. pl. *flēas*; but imper. Li. *flēh*, 3rd sg. pres. indic. Li. *fliið*, Rit. *fleeð*, Ru.[2] *flēs*, Rit. *tēð*, subj. Rit. *flee, flii*; pres. part. Rit. *fleende*.

eKt. has inf. *-tēon, -tīon*; pres. subj. *atee*, Ct. 38, is perhaps an error, cf. KG *flīo, atīo. KG* have 3rd sg. pres. indic. *atīohð* but *aflīhð* (§ 310), past sg. *tēah*, pass. part. *togen*.

§ 741. CLASS III

bindan, *bind* band, bond bundon bunden

Similarly many verbs, e.g. *drincan* drink, *ġelimpan* happen, *grindan* grind, *springan* spring, *climban* climb, *hlimman* resound, *swimman* swim. On the distribution of *a, o* in the past sg. see § 130, footnote.

Findan find, has in W-S 1st and 3rd past sg. *funde* (replacing *fand*). *Swingan* flog, has pass. part. *sungen* (Martyrology fragment)[1] beside *swungen*. On North. forms of *sċrincan* shrink, see § 181, footnote.

In the verbs *brinnan* burn, *rinnan* run, forms with metathesis are usual:[2]

birnan barn, born burnon burnen

[1] If correct, the form may be Gmc., and comparable to *sund* swimming, *sulh* plough (cf. *OED* s.v. *sullow*), with early loss of *u̯* before *u* in West Gmc. (§ 405) or Prim. OE (§ 470).

[2] Unmetathesized forms of *rinnan* are fairly frequent, and are usual in the compound *ġerinnan* congeal; note also *onbran*, Ex. 398.

On the root vowels of the present system, W-S *birnan*, *biernan*, *byrnan* VP, Ru.[1] *beornan*, North. *biorna*, and similar forms of *irnan*, see §§ 155, 299.a, 459. In past sg. *VP*, eW-S have *orn*, North, *Ru.*[1], lW-S *arn*, lW-S also *earn* (analogy of *wearþ*); similarly *born*, *barn* (but *Ru.*[1] lacks the form).

North. has scattered weak forms, e.g. Li., Ru.[2] *ġibinde* (past sg.), Li. *ġeðringdon*, *ġeðringed*; also levelling of vowel of past sg. to pl., e.g. Li. *ongannon*; and levelling of vowel of pres. to past and passive part., e.g. Ru.[2] *drincon*, Li. *besuingene* (a.s.m.).

helpan, *help* healp, halp hulpon holpen

Similar are, for example, *beteldan* cover, *delfan* dig, *meltan* melt, *swelgan* swallow, *swellan* swell, *sweltan* die. On the distribution of *healp*, *halp* see § 143. Verbs with initial *ġ* have *ie* (*i*, *y*) in the present system in W-S, e.g. *ġieldan* pay, *ġiellan* yell, *ġielpan* boast.

Breaking in the present system occurs in *aseolcan*, become languid, past part. *be-*, *asolcen* (§ 146). *Fēolan* press on (< **felχan*) has breaking in the present system, but smoothing intervenes in Angl. before inflexions beginning with front vowels (§ 231), hence VP *-fēalan*, subj. *fēle*, Rit. subj. *-fēla*; on *VP* 3rd sg. pres. indic. *-fīleð* see § 148; past *fealh*, *falh*, *fulgon*, showing the action of Verner's law, but also analogical past pl. VP *-fēlun*.

Li. has weak past *-suelte*, *suoelte*.

weorpan, *throw* wearp wurpon worpen

Similar verbs are, for example, *beorgan* protect, *ċeorfan* cut, *hweorfan* go, *steorfan* die, *sweorcan* grow dark.

Verner's law is effective in

weorþan, *become* wearþ wurdon worden

On dialect variety in the root syllable of *weorpan* and *weorþan* see §§ 147, 149, 320, 323; also § 156 on past part. *ġewarden*. North. has past pl. *-worpon* (with vowel of pass. part.), and *Ru.*[2] also weak *worpadun*.

Aorist presents are *murnan* mourn (pass. part. wanting), *spurnan* spurn (also *spornan*, § 115; pass. part. *-spornen*[1]), and perhaps the isolated inf. *forcwolstan* swallow; from *murnan* a weak past pl. *murndan* occurs (*And.* 37, cf. 154), from *spurnan* a weak pass. part. *-spurned* (Gregory's *Dialogues* 60, 28).

[1] Rare *-spurnen* (cf. *Lambeth Psalter* 94, 10).

feohtan, *fight*	feaht	fuhton	fohten
breġdan, *brandish*	bræġd	brugdon	brogden
streġdan, *strew*	stræġd	strugdon	strogden
berstan, *burst*	bærst	burston	borsten
þerscan, *thresh*	*þærsċ	þurscon	þorsċen
friġnan, *ask*	fræġn	frugnon	frugnen

On the formation of these verbs see § 736.b. In every instance the element originally infixed in the present was extended in Gmc. to all forms. Metathesis intervened in *berstan*, *þerscan* < **bres-t-*, **þre-sk-*. On absence of breaking before metathesized *r* see § 155 and footnote; sporadic forms with breaking are Li. *ġeðearsca*, *-nne*, beside *ðærsċende* (§ 327). A few forms without metathesis occur: *Ru.*[1] past pl. *brustæn*, lW-S infl. inf. *presċenne*.

On loss of *ġ* and *g* in *breġdan*, *streġdan* see § 243 and footnote.

In W-S *streġdan* is treated as a weak verb, hence contracted 3rd sg. pres. indic. always *strētt* (while *breġdan* forms *brētt* or *brītt*), past *strēdde*, pass. part. (*ġe*)*strēd*(*ed*); *Ru.*[1] and North. have also many forms of a weak past *stræġde*, *strugde*, *strogde*.

In eW-S *friġnan* often loses *ġ* in the present system, and in lW-S *ġ*, *g* disappear in all forms (§ 243 and footnote); lW-S has also past sg. *frān* (analogy of Class I); this analogy is not usually extended to past pl. and pass. part., though *frinon*, *-en* occur. On spellings *fræng*, *frungon* see §§ 62, 400, footnotes.

The reason for *i* of W-S *friġnan* beside North. *freġna* (also *fræġna*, § 327), Ru.[1] *fræġnan* (cf. *þæġn*, § 328) is unknown. *Li.*, *Rit.* also have *fraiġna*,[1] Ru.[1], North. past sg. *fræġn*, but various analogical formations in past pl. (Ru.[2] *-fræġnun*) and pass. part (Li., Ru.[2] *-frognen*). *Li.* has also weak forms *-freġnde*, *-fræġn*(*a*)*de*, etc.

§ 742. CLASS IV

beran, *bear* bær bǣron boren

Similarly *cwelan* die, *helan* hide, **hwelan* roar (3rd sg. pres. indic. *hwileþ*), *stelan* steal, *teran* tear, *-þweran* stir, and the participial adj. *ġedwolen* perverse; also *brecan* break, *hlecan* unite, though not formally of the class (pass. part. *brocen*, *-hlocen*); and nW-S *sċeran*, cut, beside W-S *sċieran*, past *sċear*, *sċēaron*.

Divergence of forms is often due to normal dialect developments,

[1] The phonological development is not clear; cf. Li., Rit. *cnaiht* beside *cnæht* (§§ 227, footnote, 327), Li. past *fraiġn* (beside *fræġn*).

e.g. *VP* and Kt. *e* in past sg., nW-S *ē* in past pl. Back umlaut in the present system generally appears in North. and *Ru.*[1] when phonologically justified (e.g. *beora, beorað,*) while *VP* even extends the diphthong analogically, e.g. *beorende, ġebreocu. Li.*, *Rit.* often have *ea* for *eo*, e.g. *beara.* Similar forms with back umlaut are a feature of many dialectically coloured W-S texts. Cf. § 210.2.

North. has a few forms with *æ* from the past sg. in pres. system, e.g. *Li.* imper. *-bær* (§ 327).

niman, *take*	nam, nōm	nōmon, nāmon	numen
cuman, *come*	c(w)ōm	c(w)ōmon	cumen

The variants given above are found already in eW-S except past sg. *nam.*[1] In Angl. *niman* has always pret. *nōm(on)*, except *Ep.* 113 *naamun.* Angl. texts have prevailingly *-w-* in past of *cuman*, except *Ru.*[2], which always has *cōm(on)*.

Cuman has in eW-S alternative pres. subj. and past part. *cyme, cymen.* In Angl. the pres. subj. with *y* appears in all texts, and 2nd and 3rd sg. pres. indic. usually preserve mutation, e.g. VP *cymes, -eð*; *y* is frequently levelled into other forms of the pres. system, e.g. *VP*, *Ru.*[1], North. imper. *cym*, Ru.[1], North. pres. indic. pl. *cymað*, part. *cymende.*

§ 743. CLASS V

metan, *measure*	mæt	mǣton	meten

Similar verbs are *cnedan* knead, *drepan* slay, *sċrepan* scrape, *sprecan* speak, *swefan* sleep, *tredan* tread, *wefan* weave, *wegan* carry, *wrecan* avenge. So also *plegan*, play, used only in pres. system, and pass. part *forrepen* caught (*Li.*).

Drepan has pass. part. both *drepen* and *dropen* (Beow. 2981), so *cnedan* both *cneden* and *-cnoeden* (Li., cf. §§ 196, 736.m).

Verner's law operates in:

cweþan, *say*	cwæþ	cwǣdon	cweden
wesan, *be*	wæs	wǣron	

But it is not operative in *lesan* gather, *ġenesan* escape.

Palatal influence has effect in the W-S forms of:

ġiefan, *give*	ġeaf	ġēafon	ġiefen

[1] *Nam* is due to analogy of nasal verbs of Class III, *nāmon* is due to early analogical processes (Flasdieck in *AB* xli. 288).

and so -*ġietan* get (only in compounds). *Li.* also has past sg. -*ġeaf*, -*ġeat* beside forms with *æ*.

Etan, eat, *fretan*, devour, have *ǣ* (nW-S *ē*) in past sg. *ǣt*, *frǣt*. Forms of the present system of *etan* often have an accent on the vowel in *Li.*, and this may indicate spread of *ē* from the past.

Dialectal variants are largely as in Class IV: *e* for *æ* in past sg.; *ē* for *ǣ* in past pl.; *eo* (North. also *ea*) in pres. system; North. *æ* for *e* in pres. system (from pret. sg., e.g. Li. *spræcende*, -*ætta*).

North. and *Ru.*[1] have sometimes *ē* in past sg. (from pl., e.g. *sprēc*, *cwēð*, *sēh*); North. has conversely occasionally *æ* in past pl., especially in *wæron*.

On North. *e* > *oe* after *u̯* see § 319; on North. *wosa*, be, see § 210.2.

Contracted verbs.

sēon, *see*	seah	sāwon	sewen
ġefēon, *rejoice*	ġefeah	ġefǣgon	
plēon, *risk*	pleah		

In Angl., where contraction is with *e* and a back vowel of the inflexion, *VP* and North. have mostly *ēa* but Ru.[1] *ēo*,[1] e.g. VP, North. inf. *sēa*(*n*),[2] Ru.[1] *sēon* (§ 238.2.b). With a front vowel contraction is to *ē*, but *ee* may be restored, and analogical *ēo*, *ēa*, *īo*, *ie*, *ii*[3] can appear; e.g. pres. part. Ru.[1], Li. -*seende*, Ru.[1] -*sēonde*, VP -*sīonde*, -*siende*; pres. subj. pl. VP -*sēn*, Li. -*see* (-*sēa*, -*sēæ*), Ru.[2] -*sie*, -*sii*, -*sēa*. *VP* 1st sg. pres. indic. -*sie*, *ġefie* beside -*sīo*, *ġefīo* are difficult (§ 237.3); North. -*sīom*, -*sīum*.

In W-S these verbs retain *h* in 2nd and 3rd sg. pres. indic. and imper., e.g. *siehþ*, *seoh*. Angl. forms have -*h* in the imper., but not in the indic. forms, e.g. VP -*sīst*, -*sīð*, *ġefīð*, Ru.[1] *sīs*,[4] -*sīð*, North. -*sīs*(*t*), -*sīð*.[5] *KG* have 3rd sg. both -*siohð* and -*sīoð* (§ 306).

For past pl. *sāwon*, Angl. has *sēgon*, and this is sometimes West Saxonized as *sǣgon*. *Ru.*[1] has -*sēgon*, -*sǣgon*, -*sāgun* (§ 257, footnote). Pass. part. Angl. *ġeseġen*.[6]

[1] Of these verbs VP has *ġefēon* and -*sēon*, Ru.[1] and North. have many forms of -*sēon*, but *ġefēon* is not certainly used there in the present system, being replaced by weak *ġifēaġ*(*i*)*a*, see § 761.6.

[2] *VP* also -*sīan*.

[3] Forms with -*ie*- are based on a stem -*i*- inferred from 2nd and 3rd sg. pres. indic. (cf. Rit. *ðiiende*, § 739). The pres. subj. *ġesii* (found *Li.*, *Rit.*, *Ru.*[2] as sg., *Ru.*[2] also as pl.) seems to be modelled on the indic.: as *fōeð* is to *fōe*, so is *ġesiið* to *ġesii*. So also *Rit.* subj. -*ðii*, -*flii* (§§ 739–40).

[4] Also -*sees*, -*sihst*.

[5] North. forms often spelled with -*ii*-.

[6] Cf. § 398.2, and Lane in *JEGP* xxxv. 20.

Another verb of this type is possibly (*ġe*)*sċēon* happen, pass, 1st sg. pres. indic. *sċīo*, Gen. 1103, 3rd sg. *sċeet*, *sċeot* (corrupt forms in transcripts, Whitelock *OE wills*, no. xxxiv); but in OE weak past and past part. *ġesċēode*, *-sċēod*, And. 18, Dan. 619,[1] Ex. 507; cf. OHG *geskehan*, *-skah*.

Weak presents.

biddan, *ask*	bæd	bǣdon	beden
sittan, *sit*	sæt	sǣton	seten
liċġan, *lie*	læġ	lǣgon	leġen
þiċġan, *partake*	þeah, þāh	þǣgon	þeġen[2]
friċġan, *ask*[3]			ġefræġen, -freġen, -friġen

On the present system of these verbs see § 749 below. North. and *Ru.*[1] have a few instances of *ē* from past pl. in the sg., e.g. *bēd*, *sēt*. W-S has past pl. *lāgon* beside *lǣgon* (§ 162), nW-S *lēgon*.

§ 744. CLASS VI

faran, *go* fōr fōron faren

Similarly many verbs, e.g. *dragan* draw, *galan* sing, *grafan* dig, *hladan* load, *wadan* go; also the participial adjs. *ġedafen*, *-dæfen* fitting, *ġeþracen* enduring.

Owing to palatal influence *sċafan* shave, *sċacan* shake, have forms with *sċea-* in pres. system in W-S and North., past *sċeōc* in lW-S (§§ 179, 181).

Spanan entice, has already eW-S past *spēon* beside *spōn*; hence in some manuscripts confused with *spannan* span, e.g. past pl. *spēonnan*, OE Bede.

Verbs with a nasal infix are *wæċnan* awake, past *wōc*,[4] and *standan* stand, past *stōd*, past part. *standen*.

Formed with infix *-sk-* is *waxan*[5] wash (*x* < *sk*, § 440), past *wōx*, pass. part. *wæsċen*, *waxen*, *wōxen*; also past *wēox* (analogy of Class VII, OE Bede); but also apparently weak present system, inf. *wæsċan*, &c.

In W-S these verbs have usually *æ* in 2nd and 3rd sg. pres. indic.

[1] But *Dan.* 266 read *sċynde* for *sċyde*.
[2] In lW-S *aþeġen* surfeited.
[3] Only certainly recorded in verse.
[4] But past part. weak *wæcned*.
[5] From **ǥat-sk-*.

(§ 160), but they generally level *a* from inf. and pres. indic. pl. to 1st sg. pres. indic., imper., pres. subj., pres. part. and inflected inf., e.g. *fare*, *far*, *fare*, *-en*, *farende*, *-enne*. The pass. part. fluctuates between *æ* and *a*, e.g. *færen*, *faren*,*slæġen*, *slagen*, no doubt because the ending fluctuated in Prim. OE between *-an* and *-æn-* (§ 334).

VP has 3rd sg. pres. indic. *-fereð*, imper. *fer* (i.e. *æ* undergoes second fronting); but *ea* appears before back vowels, e.g. *fearu*, *-að*, *-hleadað*, and by analogy in pres. part. *fearende* (but *galende*, *-sċaecende*, §§ 164–5). The subj. does not occur.

In *Ru.*[1] and North. the phonological distinction of *a* and *æ* generally prevails, e.g. *fara*, *fære*, *færende*, &c.; levelling is usually in favour of *æ*, e.g. Ru.[1] *færan*, Li. *færo*, &c.

In the pass. part. *VP* has *e* (second fronting), but *Ru.*[1] and North. have *æ* apart from the few mutated forms quoted § 736.m.

KG suggest that the dialect had *e* in 2nd and 3rd sg. pres. indic. (*hlet* from *hladan*), *a* in the rest of the present system (*farað*, *faran* subj. pl., *farende*), *a* in pass. part. (*ahafene*).

Contracted verbs.

flēan, *flay*	flōg	flōgon	flagen
lēan, *blame*	lōg	lōgon	lagen
slēan, *slay*	slōg	slōgon	slagen
þwēan, *wash*	þwōg	þwōgon	þwagen[1]

These verbs all exhibit the operation of Verner's law, but *g* is extended into the past sg., and spellings with *-h* are to be explained by § 446. The 2nd and 3rd sg. pres. indic. and imper. preserve *h* in W-S, e.g. *sliehþ*, *sleah*.

In *VP* the present system has *ēa* by contraction when the inflexion contained a back vowel (§ 238.2.a), otherwise *ē* (§ 237.2), e.g. indic. *slēa*, *slēs*, *slēð*, *-slēað*, subj. sg. *-slē*, and similar forms from *þwēan*; imper. *slæh*, *-ðuaeh*.

In other Angl. texts *ǣ* is the prevailing vowel in the present system, so already *Cp.* 3rd sg. pres. indic. *slāet* (§ 237.d, footnote). Examples from North. are *Li.* inf. *slǣ*, pres. indic. sg. *slǣ*, *slǣs*, *slǣð*, pl. *-slǣð*, pres. part. *slǣnde*. But North. has also inf. *slā*, *-ðoā* (*o* = *w*), and many corresponding forms, e.g. ind. pres. pl. Li. *-slās*, *ðwās*, Ru.[2] *-slāð*, pres. subj. sg. Li. *slāæ*, and even imper. Li., Ru.[2] *-slāh*, *ðwāh*.

[1] Also lW-S *ġeþwogen*.

Ru.[1] has both the Northumbrian *ǣ* and *ā* types, and some *ēa* forms of W-S type: pres. indic. sg. *slǣ*, *slægst*, *slǣþ*, *slæhþ*, pl. *-slǣþ* (*slæhþ*, *-gþ*), *thuāð*; pres. subj. *slǣ*; imper. *slāg*, *þwāh*, inf. *slā*(*n*), *-slēan*, *-slǣan*.

On various forms of the pass. part. of *þwēan* in *Li.* see §§ 244, 736.m[1]; on mutated *sleġen*, *þweġen* see also § 736.m.

KG have only inf. *slēan*, pres. part. *slēande*, pres. indic. 2nd and 3rd sg. *slehst*, *slæhð*, pl. *-slēað*, but inflected inf. *-slānne* (§ 145).

Weak presents.

hebban, *raise*	hōf	hōfon	hafen
swerian, *swear*	swōr	swōron	sworen[2]
sċeþþan, *injure*	sċōd	sċōdon	sċeaðen (*Gen.* 869)
hliehhan, *laugh*	hlōg	hlōgon	
sċieppan, *create*	sċōp	sċōpon	sċapen
stæppan,[3] *step*	stōp	stōpon	

On the present system of these verbs see § 749. In the past the consonant proper to the pl. is levelled to the sg. in *sċōd*, *hlōg*. The dialectal forms vary mainly owing to the normal operation of sound-changes. The present system of *hliehhan* has root vowel *æ* in Angl. texts, but *e* in poetry (§ 200.3, footnote).

In poetry a strong present *sċeaþan* occurs; poetry and lW-S have weak past *sċeþede*; lW-S also weak past *hefde*, pass. part. *-hefed*.

Li. has re-formed pass. part. *-hofen* (or *ō* from past?), beside *-hæfen*, and mutated *-hefen* (cf. § 736.m).

§ 745. CLASS VII

The past tense of verbs of this class has the same root vowel and consonants in singular and plural, so it will not be necessary to quote past plural forms. The class is divided into subclasses by the forms of the present system.

(*a*) hātan, *command* hēt hāten

and so *lācan* play; *sċ*(*e*)*ādan* divide, has eW-S past *sċeād* and *sċēd* (§ 185, footnote). But *swāpan* sweep, has past *swēop*, pass. part. *swāpen*

[1] Add *unðweanum*, error for *-ðwǣn-*, re-formed from inf. *ðwā* (cf. *-fōen*, *-hōen*, § 736.m).

[2] Rare *-swaren* (Laws of Ine 35).

[3] Beside *steppan*, cf. § 194.

(but Ru.[1] *aswopen*); *spātan* spit (*Li.* only, pres. part.) has no unreduplicated past (cf. § 746).[1]

(*b*) bēatan, *beat*	bēot	bēaten

and so *hēawan* hew, *hlēapan* leap; the past *hēof*[2] lamented; and the participial adjs. *ēacen* increased, *ēaden* granted. Also probably past *dēog*, concealed himself (*Beow.* 850), confirmed by OHG pass. part. *tougan* concealed.

(*c*) feallan, *fall*	fēoll	feallen

and so *fealdan* fold, *healdan* hold, *wealcan* roll, *wealdan* rule, *weallan* boil, and the past *stēold* possessed; *weaxan* grow, has been assimilated to this type.[3]

North. can have *ēa* for *ēo* in the past, as in all types with *ēo*. *Ru.*[1] has once *fēllun*, beside normal *-ēo-*.

(*d*) (1) blandan, *mix*	blēnd[4]	blanden
spannan, *span*	spēonn[5]	spannen
gangan, *go*	ġēong, ġīong	gangen
bannan, *summon*	bēonn	bannen

and the pass. part. n.p.m. *abloncgne* angered (*Li.*).

(2) fōn, *take*	fēng	fangen
hōn, *hang*	hēng	hangen

Sometimes these verbs have *a* in the past, e.g. *gang* (verse), *ġeban* (OE Bede, v. 1), *ġebland* (And. 33; glossary in MS. Cott. Cleop. A iii). But *gieng* (Gen. B 626, MS. *gien*), subj. *genge* (id. 834) are OS forms.

North. *ġeonga* (frequent *Li.*, rare *Ru.*[2], cf. Ru.[1] *iongaþ*) shows transference of *ġ* from the past (cf. *BDS* d.s. *hiniongae* departure). *Li.* 1st sg. pres. indic. *ġiungo* may reflect the root vowel seen in OEFris. *gunga*, with initial consonant from past.

In W-S *fōn* and *hōn* preserved *h* in 2nd and 3rd sg. pres. indic. and imper., e.g. *fēhþ*, *fōh*.

[1] Perhaps to be added is past *ahwēt* drove away, *Gen.* 406 (see Smithers, *English and Germanic studies* iv. 80 ff.).

[2] Beside weak W-S *hēofan*, *hēofde* (*ēo*, *īo* for *īe*, § 202), VP *hīofende*; past *hōf*, Gen. B, is not an OE form but to OS *hiofan*, Class II.

[3] On *Ru.*[1], North. *wex-*, beside *wæx-*, in the pres. system of *weaxan* see §§ 223–4.

[4] Not certain, as the recorded forms might be from a weak past (*ġe*)*blende*.

[5] Gen. B *spēnn* is not an OE form, and is corrected in the manuscript.

VP has pres. indic. *-fō* (also *-fōu*, with *-u* from uncontracted verbs), *-fōest*, *-fōeð* (also *-fōeht*, § 732), *-fōð*, imper. *-fōh*, pres. part. *-fōnde*, but pres. subj. analogical *-fōe* disyllabic). *Ru.*[1] has inf. *-fō*, inflected inf. *fōne*, but mostly analogical disyllabic forms, e.g. pres. indic. pl. *-fōað*, *hōaþ*, pres. subj. *fōe*, inf. *-fōa*, infl. inf. *hōanne*; but 3rd sg. pres. indic. syncopated *-fōehþ* (beside *fōeþ*) and imper. *-fōh*. In North. the present system of both verbs is re-formed into disyllables with the endings of uncontracted verbs, e.g. inf. *fōa*, pres. indic. 3rd sg. *-fōeð*, *-fōas*, &c.; but imper. *fōh*, *-hōh*.

On abnormal pass. parts. of *fōn*, *hōn* see § 736.m.

(*e*) (1) lǣtan *let* lēt lǣten

and so *ondrǣdan* dread, *rǣdan* advise, *slǣpan* sleep.

(2) cnāwan, *know* cnēow cnāwen

and so *blāwan* blow, *crāwan* crow, *māwan* mow, *ġerāwan* divide, *sāwan* sow, *þrāwan* twist, *wāwan* blow.

(*f*) (1) blōtan, *sacrifice* blēot blōten

and so *flōcan* clap, *hrōpan* shout, *hwōpan* threaten, *swōgan* sound, *wrōtan* root up; also *cnōdan* (beside Class II forms), and possibly past tenses *ahnēop*, *ġenēop* (§ 740).

(2) grōwan, *grow* grēow grōwen

and so *blōwan* bloom, *flōwan* flow, *hlōwan* low, *rōwan* row, *snōwan* hasten (beside Class II forms), *spōwan* succeed; and probably *hwōsan* cough (pres. indic. 3rd sg. *hwēst*, pl. *hwōsað*, past *hwēos*).

(3) wēpan, *weep* wēop wōpen

This verb has a weak present system: the root vowel *ē* is a mutation of *ō*, and Angl. usually preserves *ōe*.

In types (*e*) (2) and (*f*) (2) North. often has past in *-ēw* (graphic for *-ēow*, § 279), and so sometimes *VP*, *Ru.*[1]; but in eW-S occasional *cnēw* seems to indicate levelling of *ē* from other types. On rare North. past in *-ǣw* (Li. *-cnǣw*, Ru.[2] *sǣwe*, Rit. *-flǣue*) see § 279, footnote.

(*g*) Here belong a group of defective verbs with *ū* in the pres. system and pass. part.: *būan* cultivate, pass. part. *būn*, *bȳn*;

ġeþrūen compacted (*Met.* 20, 134; probably to be read for *ġeþuren* Beow. 1285, *Rid.* 89, 1); *aþrūten* swollen.

§ 746. The following are the certain instances of reduplicated preterites occuring in OE. The verbs belong to Class VII, types (*a*) and (*e*) (1).

hātan	hē̆ht:	poetry, all major Angl. glosses, OE Bede, Ælfred Jewel, *PC* 688, *Martyrology*, *Blick. Hom.*, *St. Chad*, Birch, nos. 574, 579 (late transcripts of Merc. charters)
lācan	leolc:	poetry, Boeth.
ondrǣdan	ondreord:	*VP*, *Ru.*[1], *Ru.*[2], *Li.*
lǣtan	leort:	poetry, all major Angl. glosses, OE Bede
rǣdan	reord:	poetry, *Ru.*[1], OE Bede

eo in *ondreord*, *leort*, *reord* is due to breaking, and *leolc* appears to have *eo* on the analogy of these. *Leort* < **lert* for **lelt*, and *-dreord* < **drerd* for **dredrd* both show dissimilation of consonants. On *ē̆* of *hē̆ht* see § 736.j. The North. glosses (*Li.*, *Ru.*[2], *Rit.*) and *VP* have only reduplicated pasts from these verbs,[1] but *Ru.*[1] has also *lēt* frequently.

Possible further reduplicated past forms are North. *speoft*, *speaft*, and *beoftun*, *beaftun* (Li., Ru.[2]), if to *spātan* and *bēatan*. **Speft*, **beft* might have developed from I-E **spept-*, **bhebht-*: the diphthongs in OE would be analogical. Cf. Jordan in *ES* xxxviii. 28–34; Schulze in *Archiv* cxli. 176–80.

§ 747. A number of verbs of Class VII have also weak forms, e.g. *genġan* go, *spǣtan* spit, *rǣdan* advise (the prevailing W-S form, with *ǣ* < *ai*+*i*), *sǣwan* sow (eW-S), *bȳa* cultivate (North.). It has been pointed out above that the past forms of *blandan* may be from a weak verb **blendan*.

North. has a number of new weak forms from Class VII verbs: Li. *-sċeād(a)de*, *-sċeāde*, *rēdde* (pass. part. *ġerēded*), *ġesaudes*, *wǣpde*,[2] pass. part. *ġespeoftad* (formed from past *speoft*). More general is *slēpte* (VP, Ru.[1], OE Bede), *slēpde* (Li., Rit.), *-slēpedon* (Li.), *slēpade* (Ru.[1]),[3] *slǣpte* (eW-S). Note also lW-S *iċ eom ondrǣd* timeor.

[1] *Li.* also once *hǣt* (dubious, cf. Lea, *A* xvi. 136).
[2] The root vowel is probably an error, cf. *ġewǣp* for *ġewēap*.
[3] Strong past *slēp* seems not Angl. at all.

2. Weak Verbs

§ 748. CLASS I

	Indicative			Subjunctive		
			Present			
Sg. 1.	fremme, *I do*	herie, *I praise*	hīere, *I hear*	fremme	herie	hīere
2.	fremst, -est	herest	hīerst	"	"	"
3.	fremþ, -eþ	hereþ	hīerþ	"	"	"
Pl.	fremmaþ	heriaþ	hīeraþ	fremmen	herien	hīeren

	Imperative		
Sg. 2	freme	here	hīer
Pl.	fremmaþ	heriaþ	hīeraþ

	Indicative			Subjunctive		
			Past			
Sg. 1.	fremede	herede	hīerde	fremede	herede	hīerde
2.	fremedest	heredest	hīerdest	"	"	"
3.	fremede	herede	hīerde	"	"	"
Pl.	fremedon	heredon	hīerdon	fremeden	hereden	hīerden

Inf. fremman, to fremmenne; herian, to herienne; hīeran, to hīerenne.

Pres. part.	fremmende	heriende	hīerende
Pass. part.	fremed	hered	hīered

§ 749. Examples of verbs similarly conjugated are, like *fremman*: *cnyssan* knock, *hrissan* shake, *swebban* kill,[1] *trymman* strengthen, *þennan* stretch, *weċġan*[2] move, *wennan* accustom, *wreþþan* support; the weak present tenses of strong verbs *biddan*, *sittan*, *liċġan*, *þiċġan* (also weak past and pass. part. *þiġde*, *-ede*, *-ed*), *friċġan*, *hebban* (also weak past and pass. part. *hefde*, *-hefed*, *-hefod*),[3] *sċeþþan* (also weak past and pass. part. *sċeþede*, *-ed*), *hliehhan*, *sċieppan*, *stæppan*; like *herian*: *derian* hurt, *nerian* save, *onhyrian* emulate, *werian* defend, *werian* clothe, and the weak present of strong *swerian*; like *hīeran* (with due regard to consonant changes in the past tense): *bīeġan* bend, *cȳþan* make known, *dēman* judge, *drēfan* disturb, *drenċan* make to drink, *fēdan* feed, *īeċan* increase, *lǣdan* lead, *lǣran* teach, *alīefan* allow, *mētan* meet, *senġan* singe, *tȳnan* close, *þryċċan*[4] oppress, *wendan* turn, and the weak present *wēpan*; also verbs in *-lǣċan*, as *efenlǣċan* imitate, *nēalǣċan* approach.

[1] 'Put to sleep', causative of *swefan*; *-bb-* < *-vį-* (§ 407), hence *f* in forms with single consonant, *aswefede*, &c.

[2] *ċġ* = *ġġ*, hence *ġ* in forms with single consonant, *weġe*, *weġede*, &c.

[3] In these weak presents with originally short root syllable, *ċġ* and *bb* again simplify to *ġ*, *f*; hence imper. *liġe*, *þiġe*, *friġe*, *hefe*, 2nd and 3rd sg. pres. indic. *līst* (*ī* < *iġ*), *liġeþ*, *liġþ*, *līþ*, *hefst*, *hefþ*.

[4] Here *ċċ* is not due to West Gmc. gemination, and appears in all parts if a vowel follows, 3rd sg. pres. ind. *þryċċeþ*, pass. part. *þryċċed*.

§ 750. **Origin of forms.** From a Gmc. point of view the present system of these verbs is distinguished from that of the strong verbs by the presence of an element *-i̯-* before the endings: cf. Lat. *capio* compared with *rego*. This element was vocalic after long syllables ending in a consonant (Sievers' law, § 398.4). After short syllables it was consonantal, and by the usual West Gmc. processes (§ 407) it caused doubling of all preceding consonants except *r* (< *r* and *z*). In OE it disappeared after both old long closed syllables and old short ones made long by the West Gmc. doubling, but remained after short syllables.[1] This explains the divergence of *fremman*, *herian*, *hīeran* in the 1st sġ. and pl. of the indic., the subj., imper. pl., inf., and pres. part.

In the 2nd and 3rd sg. indic., *i̯* was lost before *i* in West Gmc. before causing consonant doubling, and hence e.g. **frami̯iþi* > **framiþ* > OE* *fremiþ* > *fremeþ* (see § 405). The imper. sg. is regularly developed from Gmc. **χazi̯e*, **χauzii̯e* (§§ 331.1, 5, 345, 398.4).

The past of all Gmc. weak verbs was formed with an element *ð*, the origin of which is the most disputed problem of Gmc. philology.[2] From a West Gmc. point of view, in the weak verb of Class I, *ð* (West Gmc. *d*) was added to the *-i-* which appears before the endings of the present system, e.g. **framið-*, **χauzið-*. In OE *i* is syncopated after long syllables (§ 351). The endings adopted for the weak past were probably simply those of the strong past in the indic. pl. and the subj., while the indic. sg. had the endings *-ōm*, *-ǣs*,[3] *-ǣþ*. These developed regularly to OE *-æ*, *-æs*, *-æ*, later *-e*, *-est*,[4] *-e* (§§ 331.5, 399). The pass. part. of all weak verbs was formed with the dental element seen in Lat. *rectus*, *auditus*, &c., and in the verbs of Class I this was added to the stem in *-i-*, e.g. Gmc. **framið-*, **χauzið-*. In West Gmc. *ð* (< I-E *t* when the accent of the word did not fall on the preceding vowel, § 398.2) became *d* (§ 409).

§ 751. **Primitive Old English development of the forms.** (1) The 2nd and 3rd sg. pres. indic. are subject to syncopation, like those of the strong verb, and similar consonant changes arise (cf. § 732):

dst > *tst*: *lǣtst*, *fētst*, infs. *lǣdan*, *fēdan*; later *t* can be dropped, *fēst*, and so with original *t*, *lȳhst*, inf. *līhtan*.

þst > *st*: but usually *þ* is restored, e.g. *cȳðst*, inf. *cȳðan*, and then *þst* > *tst* later, *cȳtst* (miswritten *cȳstð*, John viii. 13).

ġst > *hst*: *bīhst*, inf. *bīeġan* (§ 447).

nġst > *nċst* > *nst*: *sprenst*, inf. *sprenġan*.

[1] It remained also after long open syllables, e.g. *ċīeġan* < **kaui̯an-*, cf. § 398.4, footnote.

[2] Cf. Prokosch, *Comparative Germanic grammar*, pp. 194 ff.

[3] Final *-s*, not *-z*, because the tense-forming element had at first the stress of an independent word.

[4] Final *-t* of the same origin as in 2nd sg. pres. indic. (§ 731.a).

tþ, dþ > tt: *mētt, fētt*, infs. *mētan, fēdan.*
sþ > st: *alȳst*, inf. *alīesan* release.
ġþ > hþ: *bīhð*, inf. *bīeġan* (cf. § 447).
nġþ > nċþ: *glenċð*, inf. *glenġan.*

Analogical modification of these processes is frequent, e.g. *bidst, bidt* to *biddan, hȳd* to *hȳdan, cnysð* to *cnyssan*, and especially with *nġ, sprænġst, glenġð* (cf. § 482).

On further lW-S changes in these persons see § 483.

There are in W-S more unsyncopated forms of 2nd and 3rd sg. pres. indic. in the weak than in the strong verb. These are especially frequent after liquids and nasals, e.g. *seleþ, dereþ, þeneþ, fremeþ, trymeþ*, beside *selþ, trymþ*. The type *nerian* seems never to have syncope, but *fremst, fremþ* is put in the paradigm above on the model of *wiðtremð*, CP 441, 27 (Hatton MS.).

Angl. texts rarely have syncope in these persons: VP *aċersðu, selð*, Ru.[1] *bit, selð*. The eKt. charters have only uncontracted forms, *KG* fluctuate like W-S.

(2) Consonant changes followed also upon the syncopation of *-i-* after long root syllables in the past tense:

p, t, ċ + d > pt, tt, ċt: *slǣpte, mētte, īeċte*, infs. *slǣpan, mētan, īeċan.*
ff, ss + d > ft, st: *pyfte, cyste*, infs. *pyffan* puff, *cyssan.*
x + d > xt: *līxte*, inf. *līxan* shine.

Etymological spellings are in general rare, e.g. Cp. *ræfsde*, lW-S *hyspdun*, infs. *ræpsan* (§ 418), *hyspan*. Such spellings are more frequent in *Li.*, e.g. *-ēċde, slēpde.*

Less frequent changes in the past tense are:

sċt > st: VP *ġehnistun*, lW-S *wīste*, infs. *hnisċan* soften (cf. *hnescian*), *wȳsċan.*
þd > dd: *cȳdde* for *cȳþde* (lOE, § 481.7, 482).
mbd > md: *cemde* (lW-S, § 477.6).
nġd > nd: KG *ġemende*, inf. *menġan.*

When in forming the past tense a double consonant came to be in a triple group, it was simplified, e.g. *cende, cyste, sende*, infs. *cennan, cyssan, sendan*. Etymological spellings occur, e.g. Li. *ġefyllde*, eW-S forms quoted § 476, footnote.

In North. double *-dd-, -tt-* are sometimes simplified in the weak past even between vowels, e.g. past indic. 1 sg. Ru.[2] *ġimōete*, 2 sg. Rit. *ġilǣdest*, pl. Li. *ġelǣdon.*

A frequent change in W-S in the weak past is *ċt > ht*. This is due to the analogy of verbs of the type of *rǣċan, rǣhte* (§ 753.9.b.2). eW-S has already *nēalǣhte* (beside *-lǣċte*), *ōlehte* (beside *ōleċte*), from *nēalǣċan,* *ōleċċan*; lW-S examples are *īhte*, *bepǣhte*, *ġesīhte*, from *īeċan* increase, *bepǣċan* deceive, *sȳċan* suckle, and frequent *-lǣhte* from verbs in *-lǣċan*; so with *ċ* < *ċċ*, *ġeþryhte* from *þryċċan* oppress. Such verbs can have the pass. part. either regularly formed or with *-ht*; e.g. *ġeīċed*, *ġeīht*, *bepǣht*, *ġesīċed*, *ġeþryċċed*, and so *ġewǣċed*, *ġewǣht* from *wǣċan* weaken. *Wleċċan* warm, although having a short root syllable has pass. part. *ġewleht*, *ġewlæht*, beside *ġewleċed*.

Similar forms are sporadic in nW-S, e.g. VP *-nīoleāhtun*, Ru.[1] *nēa-lehċtun*,[1] Li. *ġeðryhton*, KG pass. parts. *ġefērlēhte*, *ġeaht* (296, read *ġeēht* increased).[2]

(3) The pass. part. should have syncope of *-i-* in open syllables after long root syllables in trisyllabic forms (§ 351, footnote). *VP* reflects this, e.g. *ġetrymed*, pl. *ġetrymede*, but *ġelǣded*, pl. *ġelǣdde*. In W-S, however, there is a tendency for parts. in dentals to extend syncopation to uninflected forms, e.g. *ġelǣdd*, *ġehȳd*, *send* beside *ġelǣded*, *ġehȳded*, *sended*;[3] and to closed medial syllables in inflected forms, e.g. a.s.m. *ġesċendne*, *ġewildne*, infs. *sċendan*, *ġewieldan*. On the other hand, parts. not in dentals frequently level out the unsyncopated form to inflected cases, e.g. *ġehǣlede*, *ġelǣreda*, *ġelīefede*.

Ru.[1] usually follows the phonological rule, distinguishing, for example, *ġehēred*, pl. *ġehērde*, and so even after dentals, e.g. *lǣded*, *ġelǣdde*, *sended*, *sende*. Syncope is extended to the uninflected form in *befest*, and occasionally fails, e.g. *abælġede*, *ġeċerrede*, *awærġede*.

In North., so far as new formations do not arise (§ 752), the uninflected form is always in *-ed*, but syncope is often eliminated in inflected forms, especially in *Li.*, e.g. *ġeċerredo*, *ġefylledo*.

KG, like W-S, have frequent syncope in the uninflected form of parts. in dentals, e.g. *fēd*, *ġesċend*, *aheld*.

Syncopated forms of pass. parts. show the same consonant changes as the past tense, e.g. *besenċte*, *ġeþryċte*, pl. of *besenċed*, *ġeþryċċed*.

§ 752. **Early, late, and dialectal forms.** What has been said above of the endings of the present system of strong verbs is also true of those of weak verbs of Class I. Hence we find in the 1st sg. pres. indic. *-e* in W-S and *Ru.*[1], *-u* (*-o*) practically always in *VP*, while eKt. has *-o* and *-e*, KG *-e*, North. *-o* (less often *-a*, *-u*, *-e*). In the 2nd pers. the same variation of *-s* and *st* is found as in the strong verb: W-S and *Ru.*[1] have *-st*, *VP* has *-s*, with a few exceptions (*uphēst*, inf. *-hēġan*, and four in uncontracted verbs). North. has *-st* seldom. KG *alēst*, *ġeorwēnst*, but *asets*, infs. W-S *-līesan*, *-wēnan*, *-settan*. In the 3rd sg. *-iþ* is often

[1] With assimilation to verbs in *-eċċan*, *-ehte*; note also the compromise spelling.

[2] Note also North. past *ġicnyhte* beside *tocnuiċte* bound, pass. part. *ġecnyht*, presumed from inf. **cnyċċan*.

[3] The syncopated form is always used from the participial adj. *fǣtt* fat.

recorded in early texts, e.g. Cp. *ġehnǣġith* subdues; as in the strong verb, forms in *-t* occur in early texts, and recur in eW-S, *Ru.*[1], *Ru.*[2], *KG*. As in the strong verb, *Ru.*[1] and North. have many innovations beside historical forms: *Ru.*[1] 3rd sg. in *-aþ*, *-æþ*, pl. *-eþ*; North. 2nd sg. *-as*, *-æs*, 3rd sg. *-að*, *-æð*, also *-es*, *-as*, *æs*; pl. *-eð*, also *-es*, *-as*.

What has been said of the pres. subj., inf., inflected inf., and pres. part. of the strong verb (§ 735.f, i, j) applies closely to the weak verb of Class I.

On the variation between *-ġ-*, *-iġ-*, *-iġe-*, *-i-* in the type *herian* in W-S and *Ru*[1] see § 365; and in North. § 361. *VP* has only *-ġ-*.

The middle vowel of the past and pass. part. often appears as *-i-* in early texts, e.g. past CH *astelidæ* (but RC *ġeredæ*), part. BDS, *dōemid*, Cp. *helbid*, *ġesmirwid*.

On pass. parts. in final *-t* for *-d* (e.g. Cp. *ġerǣdit*) see § 450.

What has been said of the endings of the past indic. pl. and past subj. in strong verbs (§ 735.e, g) is also true of weak verbs of Class I. In the 3rd sg. *æ* is recorded in early texts, e.g. RC *ġeredæ*, FC *afōeddæ*.[1] The 2nd sg. has *-st* beside *-s*; W-S, *Ru.*[1] have usually *-st*, VP always *-s*,[2] North. *-es* more frequently than *-est*. In lW-S *-st* is frequently extended to the 2nd sg. past. subj., so that past indic. and subj. are no longer distinguished (since in pl. of subj. *-en* > *-on*).[3]

In W-S verbs with an originally short root syllable have a strong tendency to join the second weak class. This could occur early enough for back umlaut to be caused by the new endings (§ 211), and in eW-S texts the new conjugation is well evidenced, e.g. pl. pres. indic. *lemiað*, pres. subj. *ġetrymiġe*, *-en* (beside *ġetrymme*, *-en*), inf. *aðenian*. In the *herian* type all forms of the present system are ambiguous except 2nd and 3rd sg. pres. indic. and imper. sg., and these forms are not yet affected in eW-S. In lW-S the analogy spreads to them, and to the past, e.g. *neraþ* (sg.), *nerode*; so *KG -wreoðað* (sg., 645).

Occasional analogical extension of the double consonant is found, e.g. lW-S, Rit. pass. part. *ġetrymmed*, lW-S imper. *telle*, and Ru.[1] unsyncopated 3rd sg. pres. indic., *biddeþ*, *selleþ*, and so North., Li. *biddes*, *selles*, *settes*. Extension of the single consonant is less common: it occurs *Li.*, *Rit.*, *Ru.*[2] in 1st sg. pres. indic. of *sellan* (*selo*, *silo*), but otherwise it is sporadic.

Syncopation is rarely found in the past of verbs with a short root syllable, e.g. *CP* 451, 29 *ðiġden*, Ps. cviii. 25 *weġdan*, Li. *sceðde*.

In *Ru.*[1] and North. (especially *Li.*) the influence of Class II upon Class I is strong in the past and in the pass. part., so that past *-ade* and

[1] 1st sg. does not occur, but cf. RC *dorstæ* (pret.-pres.).

[2] But in verbs of other classes *-st* occurs: *acunnadest*, *dydest* (5 times, beside *dydes* 16 times).

[3] See F. J. Mather, *The conditional sentence in Anglo-Saxon*, pp. 16–18.

especially pass. part. *-ad* occur, e.g. past Li. *ġeōehtadon*, Ru.[1] *fylġadun*, pass. part. Li. *ġedrōefad*, Ru.[2] *ġiwendad*, Ru.[1] *ġefyllad*.

Li. and *Rit.* have frequent extension of *-en* from the strong to the weak pass. part.; nearly all examples are inflected forms, e.g. Li. *ġeseteno*, *ġesendeno*, *ġewaehten*, Rit. *ġilēseno*, *ġilēfeno*; more rarely in Ru.[2]: *onsetnum*, *ġilēfenne*.

In lW-S, North., *Ru.*[1] there is considerable fluctuation in the form of the imper. sg., *-e* being sometimes added to long root syllables (e.g. Li. *bilēore* go), while from verbs with originally short root syllables the types *tel* and *telle* appear beside regular *tele* (inf. *tellan*).

§ 753. **Phonological variants.** (1) Verbs with originally short root syllables ending in *t* or *d* syncopated the medial vowel in the past tense, e.g. *hredde* (not **hredede* like *fremede*), inf. *hreddan* save. In the pass. part. they have in W-S similar syncope, e.g. *ahredd*; it is usually held that they had no syncope in the pass. part. in Angl., but there is no direct evidence.[1] Verbs of this type are *cnyttan* bind, *hreddan* save, *hwettan* urge, *lettan* hinder, *spryttan* sprout, *treddan* investigate, and verbs in *-ettan*, e.g. *līċettan* pretend, *sārettan* lament, and so with suffix of different origin (§ 455) *ōnettan* hasten, &c.

(2) Verbs with a long closed syllable before liquid or nasal have in W-S no syncope in the past tense, e.g. *frēfrede*, *hynġrede*, *timbrede*, *dīġlede*, *wrixlede*, *symblede*,[2] infs. *frēfran* comfort, *hynġran* hunger, *timbran* build, *dīġlan* conceal, *wrixlan* exchange, *symblan* feast. This *-ede* is often replaced by *-ode*, and the verbs tend to pass into Class II, e.g. inf. *frēfrian*, *hynġrian*, *timbrian*.

VP forms the past of such verbs according to Class II, e.g. *-dēġlade*, *timbrade*; but pass. part. has *-ed* beside *-ad*: *frōefred*, *timbred*, *ġedēġlad*. Ru.[1] has *hynġrade* beside *-ede*, and pass. part. *-ed*: *afrōefred*, *wēpned*.

North. has great variety, having past (*a*) with syncope and parasiting, e.g. *hynġerde*, see § 364; (*b*) *-ede*, e.g. Li. *frōefredon*, Ru.[2] *-bēċnede*; (*c*) *-ade*, e.g. Ru.[2] *bēċnade*, *frōefradun*. Pass. part. has usually *-ed*, but Li. *ġedēġlad*.

(3) Verbs with a short closed syllable before liquid or nasal have syncope in the past in W-S, e.g. *efnde*, *eġlde*, *seġlde*, *þrysmde*,[3] infs. *efnan* perform, *eġlan* trouble, *seġlan* sail, *þrysman* suffocate. Yet

[1] The assumption is based on the forms of the pass. part. of *settan*, the history of which is different, see (9) (*b*) (7) below (p. 331).

[2] But *wyrsmde*, *wyrmsde* to *wyrsman*, *wyrmsan* suppurate.

[3] So *oferfæðmde*, Dan. 501.

forms in *-ede* appear also, eW-S *bytlede* (inf. *bytlan* build), *siġelede*, lW-S *efnede*, *eġlede*, *acwylmede* (inf. *cwielman* kill). The few Anglian forms are inconsistent: VP *arefnde*, Li. *ġenæġlede*; transference to Class II also occurs, e.g. Li. *ġeefnade*.

(4) On reduction of heavy consonant groups in past *nem(n)de*, *cem(b)de* see § 477.5, 6.

(5) Owing to the loss of *u̯* before *i* (§ 406) verbs like *ġierwan*, prepare, should have no *w* in the forms in which *fremman* has single *m* (2nd and 3rd sg. pres. indic., imper., past system and pass. part.), and regular forms for these would be *ġierest*, *-eþ*, *ġiere*, *ġierede*, *ġiered*. But such verbs are prone to re-formation. Sometimes they follow the analogy of forms without *w*, and conjugate like *herian*, e.g. *wylian*, roll, for *wielwan*, past *wylede*, later *-ode*. But they can also follow the analogy of forms with *w*, e.g. *hierwan*, despise, 3rd sg. pres. indic. **hierwð* (cf. *nyrwð* from *nierwan*), past *hyrwde*, pass. part. *ġehyrwed*. In W-S phonologically correct variation of forms with and without *w* is frequent with *ġierwan* prepare, *sierwan* devise, *smierwan* anoint; retention of *w* in all forms is usual with *hierwan* despise, *nierwan* constrain;[1] loss of *w* in all forms is usual with *wylian* roll. Divergences from these general rules are frequent, e.g. eW-S pl. pres. indic. *-sieriað*, *smiriað*, pass. part. *ġehiered*, lW-S pass. part. *ġewylwed*.

In the early glossaries these verbs are no longer conjugated phonologically, e.g. *Cp.* pass. part. *ġeġeruuid*, *ġesmirwid*; but cf. RC *ġerede*. *VP* has regular forms from *ġerwan*, *smirwan*, but *w* is levelled through in *herwan*, *nerwan*; past pl. *herwdun*, pass. part. *ġenerwed*, pl. *-wde*.

*Ru.*¹ and North. have mostly phonological forms of *ġerwan*,[2] though *Ru.*² has pass. part. *ġiġerwed*. From *smirwan* there is levelling away of *w* in *Ru.*² *smiranne*, Li. *smiriane*; extension of *w* in *Rit.* pass. part. *ġesmiruad* (with *-ad* from Class II); otherwise only forms phonologically without *w* occur, e.g. *Ru.*¹ imper. *smere*, Li., Ru.² past *smiride*.

Frætwan, adorn, has *w* in all recorded forms, e.g. 3rd sg. pres. indic. *frætweþ*, pass. part. *frætwed*. **Agǣlwan* has pass. part. *agǣled* and *agǣlwed*. *Rǣswan*, think, shows many processes of analogy: 3rd sg. pres. indic. *rǣsweþ*, past *rǣswede* lead to re-formation

[1] These verbs may also follow Class II with retention of *w*, inf. *hyrwian*, *nyrwian*, pres. indic. pl. *hyrwiaþ*, imp. *nyrwa*, &c.

[2] *Ru.*¹ also pres. part. *-ġærwende* (§ 193.*a*).

according to Class II: *rǣswian*, past *rǣswode*; but forms like past *rǣsede* lead to re-formation as *rǣsian*, *rǣsode*.[1]

(6) Verbs with root syllables ending in a vowel followed by *u̯* retain *w* in all forms in W-S, although it should drop where *i* originally followed (§ 406), e.g. *lǣweþ*, *lǣwþ*, *lǣwde*, *lǣwed*, inf. *lǣwan* betray, and similar forms from *þȳwan*, *þēwan* press, *-slǣwan* make slow. North. has the phonological past Ru.[2] *bilēde*, Li. *beleede*, Cp. pass. part. *ġeðēdum*.

From an OE point of view here belong also *īewan*[2] show, *trīewan* trust, *hlȳwan* warm (see § 120.1, 2). These have *-w-* in most recorded forms in all dialects: sporadic exceptions are eW-S past *ætīede*, lW-S pass. part. pl. *ġehlȳde*[3] (Job iv=xxxi. 20).

The infs. **spīowan* spit, **sīowan* sow, are assumed to account for a few forms mentioned in § 120.2, footnote. The past system of these verbs was at first of the type **spiu̯id-*, with analogical retention of *u̯*;[4] then transference to Class II and back umlaut gave *spiowode*,[5] *siowode*, hence inf. *siowian*, &c.

(7) Verbs in which *-i̯-* followed upon a diphthong are *ċīeġan* call, *hnǣġan* neigh, nW-S *strēġan* strew, *hēġan* exalt.[6] In W-S *ġ* is extended to all forms, e.g. *ċīġþ*, *ċīġde*, *hnǣġþ*, and so in most dialect forms of *ċēġan*: for sporadic occurrences without *ġ* see § 237.1.b. The other verbs have recorded only infs. as quoted (poetical), forms of *strēġan*[7] with phonological loss of *u̯* before *i* and contraction, quoted § 237.1.b, and similarly *VP* 2nd and 3rd sg. pres. indic. *-hēst*, *-hēð*, poetical past *ġehēde*; but with extension of *ġ*, lW-S pass part. infl. *ġehīġde*, *ġehȳd* (§ 243).

[1] So the verbal noun is *rǣswung* or *rǣsung*.

[2] Past and pass. part. would be phonologically **eid-* (< **eu̯id-*) before vowel contraction, and from this **eu̯id-* was produced by analogical restoration of *u̯*; with transference to Class II and back umlaut this gave *eowode*, whence inf. *eowian*, &c. The phonological relationship *īewan*, *eowian* appears also in *bȳwan* polish, pass. part. *abȳwed* and *ġebeowed*.

[3] The corresponding Angl. form would be **hlīode*, **hlēode*: hence analogical pres. indic. pl. *hlēoð* (Az. 85).

[4] Recorded forms are frequent pass. part. *ġesiwed* (§ 154.2), and many which have adopted Class II endings: *siwode*, *ġesiwud*, and hence pres. *siwiġe*, &c.

[5] Recorded *Jul.* 476 as *spiowedan* (cf. § 385).

[6] See § 120.1, 2 on the formation of these verbs. Phonologically they should lose *i̯* before *i* in 2nd and 3rd sg. pres. indic., and imper.; then (except in *hnǣġan*) there should be loss of *u̯* before *i* (§§ 405–6) in these forms and also in the past and pass. part., e.g. **kau̯i̯iþ* > **kau̯iþ* > **kaiþ* > OE *ċēþ*, **kau̯id-* > **kaid-* > OE *ċēd*.

[7] Normal *strewian*, *streowian* (also *strēawian* influenced by the noun) arises by the same processes as *siowian* from past **streu̯id-* for **streid-* from **strau̯id-*.

Here may belong VP *milcdēondra*, Ru.[1], Li. *dīendra* g.p. sucklings, Li. *ġediides* thou didst suck, pointing to a verb **dīon*, < **dīi̯an-* with generalization of loss of *i̯* to all forms from 2nd and 3rd sg. pres. indic., imper., past and pass. part.

(8) Contracted verbs. Verbs with a long root syllable ending in *χ* would lose this between vowels in the 2nd and 3rd sg. pres. indic., imper., past and pass. part., and the mutated vowel of the root would absorb a following front vowel, e.g. **þūχiþ > þȳþ*[1] (§ 237.1.d), and so past *þȳde*, pass. part. *þȳd*, whence inf. *þȳn*, press, and the entire paradigm may be derived analogically.[2] So also *tȳn*, instruct, and rarer verbs quoted § 237.1.d, footnote. In forms where a back vowel followed *χ*, contraction was to *īo > ēo*, and here would belong *þēon*, *tēon*, badly evidenced[3] alternative forms of *þȳn*, *tȳn* (§ 238.3).

Early uncontracted forms are Ep., Cp. *fāēhit* he paints (but past pl. *fāēdun*), Ep. *sċȳhend*, Cp. *sċȳend* persuader.

lW-S has curious forms from *þȳn*, 1st sg. pres. indic. *-þȳġe*, past *þȳġde*, with analogical *ġ* from verbs like *ċīeġan*.

(9) A considerable group of verbs formed the past and pass. part. in Gmc. without using as a connexion between root and dental element the formative *-i-* of the present system.[4] There are two main groups of these: (*a*) those with root syllables ending in *l*, and (*b*) those with root syllables ending in a velar consonant and having *ht* in the past and pass. part., for every velar+*t* became *ht* in Gmc. These verbs are often distinguished by the absence of mutation in the root syllable in the past and pass. part., although it is present in the pres. system: this follows from the absence of the connecting vowel *-i-* in past and pass. part. In

[1] These verbs have no forms with *h* in 2nd and 3rd sg. pres. indic. of type of W-S *siehþ*. The occurrence of such forms from strong verbs (and the weak present *hliehhan*) suggests that in the weak verbs the past *þȳde*, &c. influenced the pres. indic. On various theories see M. T. Löfvenberg in *Studia Neophilologica* xxi. 231–76.

[2] It is necessary to assume Gmc. **þūwii̯an-* (under (6) above), beside *þūxii̯an-*, to explain the OE forms.

[3] It is doubtful if *tēon* instruct, is not always the strong verb of Class II in its frequent transferred use; *þēon* press, is inferred from *ġeþēon*, Rid. 40, 91, *forþēode*, Dream of the Rood 54 (which may be *forþ-ēode*). Yet the existence of *þēon* beside *þȳwan* would explain by mixture past *þēowde*; also Class II pres. part. *þēowiġende*.

[4] The absence of the connecting vowel probably went back to I-E in some of the roots, but was due to Gmc. phonological or analogical syncope in others: see Prokosch in *PMLA* xlii. 331–8.

the tables below the inf., past, and pass. part. of these verbs will be given.

(*a*) cwellan, *kill* cwealde cweald

and so *dwellan* mislead, *sellan* give, *stellan* place, *tellan* tell. These verbs are exactly like *fremman* in the present system. In the past and pass. part. they have *a* or *ea* according to dialect.

A number of forms occur with the connecting vowel; past *astelidæ* CH, *ġetelede* lNorth., lW-S; pass. part. *onsteled* eW-S, *ġeteled* eW-S, lNorth., poetry. But lW-S past *dwelode*, *dwelede* is due rather to transference to Class II.

Li. has past *sealde* beside *salde* with the vowel of *sealla* (§ 211).

(*b*) (1) reċċan, *narrate* reahte, rehte reaht, reht

and so *ċweċċan* shake, *dreċċan* afflict, *leċċan* moisten, *streċċan* stretch, *þeċċan* cover, *w(r)eċċan* awaken. These verbs also show mutation of Gmc. *a* and consonant doubling in the present system. In the past and pass. part. they have phonologically *ea* or its smoothing *æ*; but in *VP* and eW-S *e* from the pres. often appears in the past and pass. part., and this is general in lW-S. In Angl. the early glossaries have already *e*: Ep. *arectae*, Cp. *arecte*, *arehtun*. So *Ru.*[1] and North. vary between *e* and *æ*, and the strong influence of the pres. is shown in North. by the levelling of *oe* from the present system of verbs in *w*-, e.g. Rit. *-woehte*. So KG *areahtum*, but *rehton*, *awehte*.

(2) tǣċan, *teach* tāhte, tǣhte tāht, tǣht

and so *rǣċan* reach. These verbs have in the present system *ǣ* (mutation of *ā* < *ai*), in the past and pass. part. *ā*, but *ǣ* is often levelled to all forms in W-S (already eW-S), while Angl. retains *ā*: Ru[1] *ġetāhtæ*, lNorth. *rāhte*, *betāht*.

(3) sēċan, *seek* sōhte sōht

Angl. and eKt. preserve *ōē* in the present system.

(4) læċċan, *seize* lāhte, lǣhte lāht, lǣht
reċċan, *care* rōhte rōht

On the shortening in the present system of *reċċan* see § 287, footnote. Similar shortening seems present in *læċċan*, for the variation in the past W-S *ǣ* or *ā*, Angl. *ā* (North. *ġelāhte*), suggests that the verb was originally of the class of *tǣċan*, lW-S 3rd sg. pres. indic. *lǣhð* beside *læċð* (§ 483).

(5)	brenġan, *bring*	brōhte	brōht
	þenċan, *think*	þōhte	þōht
	þynċan, *seem*	þūhte	þūht

In these verbs the past and pass. part. had in Gmc. *-aŋχt-*, *-uŋχt-*, which became regularly *-āχt-* (OE *-ōχt-*), *-ūχt-* (§ 119). The present system of *brenġan* occurs occasionally W-S, Kt., *Ru.*[1], but it is in regular use only in North., being elsewhere replaced by that of the strong verb *bringan*, which has in OE no strong past, but occasionally pass. part. *brungen* (poetry).

(6)	byċġan, *buy*	bohte	boht
	wyrċan, *work*	worhte	worht

The present system has mutation of Gmc. *u*, the past and pass. part. Gmc. *o* < *u* (§ 115); *byċġan* has consonant doubling (*ċġ*) in the usual forms; 2nd and 3rd sg. pres. indic. W-S *byġst*, *byġð*.

For *wyrċan* VP has in the pres. system *wirċan*, with a different vowel, for *y* does not unround in the text; past and pass. part. do not occur.[1] Occasional *i* for *y* in the pres. elsewhere (e.g. *Ru.*[1]) is insignificant.

On past *warhte*, pass. part. *ġewarht* see § 156; on *wrohte*, *ġewroht* § 459.3.

(7)	leċġan, *lay*	leġde	leġd
	settan, *set*	sette	sett

These verbs are special West Gmc. additions to the type, cf. OS *leggian*, *settian*, past *lagda*, *satta*, beside *legda*, *setta*. Although *e* is the prevailing vowel in OE in all forms owing to the influence of the present system, a few traces of past and pass. part. without mutation occur: *Ru.*[1] past *ġesætte*, *læġdun* (but pass. part. *aleġd*), Li. past *ġesætte*, pass. part. *ġesattedo* (a.p.n.). In W-S pass. part. of *settan* never has a connecting vowel, but in Angl. the form without connecting vowel appears only in inflected forms, e.g. VP, Ru.[2] *ġeseted*, pl. *gesette*. North. can also retain the connecting vowel in inflexion, level out *tt* from the present, and also form quasi-strong forms (§ 752), e.g. Li. *ġeset(t)et*, infl. *ġesettedo*, *ġeseteno*.

[1] *VP*, Hy. 1, 3 *wyrctun* in Sweet's text is an error; manuscript *wȳsċtun* wished.

§ 754. CLASS II

		Indicative		Subjunctive	Imperative
Present					
Sg.	1	lufiġe,	*I love*	lufiġe	
	2	lufast		lufiġe	lufa
	3	lufaþ		lufiġe	
Pl.		lufiaþ		lufiġen	lufiaþ
Past					
Sg.	1	lufode		lufode	
	2	lufodest		lufode	
	3	lufode		lufode	
Pl.		lufodon		lufoden	

Inf.	lufian, to lufienne
Pres. part.	lufiende
Pass. part.	lufod

§ 755. Examples of the very large number of verbs so conjugated are *āscian* ask, *bodian* announce, *endian* end, *fandian* try, *hālgian* hallow, *langian* long, *lōcian* look, *lofian* praise, *macian* make, *rēafian* plunder, *þancian* thank, *þolian* suffer, *wunian* dwell; also various formative elements: *-ecian*, as *aswefecian* eradicate, *bedecian* beg; *-sian*,[1] as *blissian* rejoice, *clǣnsian* cleanse, *mǣrsian* make famous. Verbs with root vowel *i* often have alternative forms with back umlaut, owing to the many forms in which a back vowel follows, e.g. eW-S *clipian*, *cliopian*, *cleopian*, VP *cleopian*, North. *cliopiġa* call; such verbs are *bifian* tremble, *clifian* adhere, *ġinian* yawn, *hlinian* lean, *hnipian* droop, *tilian* strive for. In W-S extension of *i* to forms where a back vowel follows is frequent, e.g. past *clipode*, *hnipode*, *tilode*. *Stician* stick, can have back umlaut only in Kt., hence Bd. Gl. *stiocode* (but KG *-sticoð*). On *swugian*, *swigian*, be silent, see § 218.

§ 756. Origin of forms. This conjugation is a mixture of one in which endings were added to Gmc. *-ō-* < I-E *-ā-* (2nd and 3rd sg. pres. indic. and imper.) and of one in which they were preceded by *-i̯-* as in Class I,

[1] Extracted from verbs like *eġesian* terrify (cf. *eġesa* terror).

but this *-i̯-* followed *-ō-*. Hence the Gmc. endings of the pres. would be: *-ōi̯ō*, *-ōsi*, *-ōþi*, *-ōi̯anþi*. In OE the medial *-ōi̯-* became *-i-*, *-iġ-* (§§ 339, 355.5, 376, 267). The imper. was the stem *-ō* without ending. The pres. subj. had the same endings as strong verbs preceded by *-ōi̯-*. In the past system and the pass. part. the dental formative elements were the same as in Class I, but were added to *-ō-*.

§ 757. **Dialectal variants.** On the variation of medial *-i-* and *-iġ-* see § 267. The above paradigm, with *-iġ-* before *e*, *-i-* before *a*, represents the prevailing spelling of eW-S and lW-S (but note usually pres. part. *-iende*, inflected inf. *-ienne*). VP has nearly always *-i-* before all vowels, but *Ru.*[1] has *-iġ-* prevailingly. All North. texts have mainly *-iġ-*, though they also have *-i-* frequently before *a*. *KG* have *-iġe-*, but *-ia-*, like W-S; here also the pres. part. is an exception with *-ie-*.

In the past *-ode* (older *-ud-*, Ep. *aslacudae*, and occasionally in eW-S) heavily predominates in W-S, *-ade*[1] in Kt. and Angl. Pl. *-edon*, and hence sg. *-ede*, occurs in all dialects (§ 385).

The pass. part. generally has *-od* or *-ad* corresponding to the prevailing form of the past in the text. *KG*, however, have part. *-ad* beside *-od*, but past only *-ade*, *-ede*. All dialects have examples of *-ed*, inflected *-ede*, &c., originating by vowel harmony in forms where a back vowel followed, e.g. eW-S *ġehorsedan*.

1st sg. pres. indic. is in *-iu* (*-io*) in *VP*; *Ru.*[1] has *-iġe*, *-io*; North. *-iġo* prevails, beside *-iġa*, rarely *-iġe*; eKt. *-ie*, *KG* not recorded.

2nd and 3rd sg. pres. indic. sometimes has *-o-* in lW-S and *KG*; *Ru.*[1] has frequent *-e-*. In North. reduction to *-e-*, *-æ-* can be accompanied by replacement of *-ð* by *-s* in the 3rd pers., so the endings are, 2nd pers.: *-as*, *-es*; 3rd. pers.: *-að*, *-as*, *-eð*, *-es*, *-æð*, *-æs*.

As in strong verbs and weak verbs of Class I there is interchange of *-s* and *-st* in the 2nd pers., and occasional *-t* in the 3rd (eW-S, *KG*, not *Ru.*[1]).

The pres. indic. pl. varies only in North., where the final consonant may be *-s* and the vowel *-e-*, hence *-iġað*, *-iġas*, *-iġeð*, *-iġes*.

The vowel of the imper. may be reduced to *-e*, *-æ* in *Ru.*[1], North.

There was originally a special development of *-iġ-* in the pres. part. and inflected inf. Between a main and a secondary stress the vowel was syncopated, and the resulting *-i̯-* was lost after long syllables (and after two syllables), but remained after short syllables, and was usually replaced by *-i-*, *-ii̯-* from other forms. The early glossaries show this distinction, e.g. Cp. *tācnendi* but *dobġendi* (inf. **dofian*, cf. *dofung*, stupidity).[2] Metrical tests often show that the distinction obtained in

[1] On the origin of this distinction see § 331.6.
[2] So Cp. *tuiġendi* doubting < **tu̯iχi̯endi-* < **tu̯iχēi̯endi-*.

the language of verse though obliterated in the spelling of the surviving transcripts (cf. *PBB* x. 482). In W-S the distinction did not survive, *-iende*, *-ienne* (*-ianne*) being levelled to all verbs, and this is also true of *VP*, although there *-ende*, *-enne* occasionally appear after long syllables, e.g. *ġelōcende*, *mildsende*, *nīosenne*. But *Ru.*[1] generally extends the forms without *-i-* to all verbs of Class II, e.g. *lōkende*, *wagende*, *sċēawenne*. In North. forms without *-i-* are found practically always after long syllables, and in nearly half the instances also after short.

Ru.[1] and North. have very many forms in the present system in which *-i-*, *-iġ-* has been extended to the forms in which historically it should not appear, and others in which it is removed although historically justified, e.g. *Ru.*[1] pres. indic. 1 sg. *ðrōwa*, 3 sg. *þrōwiaþ*, pl. *-somnaþ* beside *somniaþ*; Li. 1 sg. *lufo*, 3 sg. *uunias*, pl. *ġewunas*. Omission of *-i-* is less frequent in the pres. subj., e.g. Ru.[1] *folge*, Li. *fultume*.

Particularly in *Li.* and *Rit.* occurs contamination of *-a-* and *-iġ-*, e.g. imper. in *-iġ*, *-iġa* (*-iġe*), Li. *āriġ*, *ġeclǣnsiġa*, *-e*; pres. subj. *-aġe*, *-aiġe*, Li. *ġerīxaġe*, *losaiġe*.

What has been said above of the endings of the present subjunctive, infinitive, inflected infinitive, and present participle of the strong verb (§ 735.f, i, j) applies also to those of weak verbs of Class II. The inflexions of the past and the pass. part. are the same as in Class I.

§ 758. Contracted verbs.

		Indicative	Subjunctive	Imperative
Present				
Sg.	1	smēaġe, *I think*	smēaġe	
	2	smēast	smēaġe	smēa
	3	smēaþ	smēaġe	
Pl.		smēaġaþ	smēaġen	smēaġaþ
Past				
Sg.	1	smēade	smēade	
	2	smēadest	smēade	
	3	smēade	smēade	
Pl.		smēadon	smēaden	
		Inf.	smēaġan, to smēaġenne	
		Pres. part.	smēaġende	
		Pass. part.	smēad	

§ 759. Origin of forms. The above paradigm may be inferred for eW-S from the recorded forms of *smēan* think, *þrēan* afflict. The stems from which these were conjugated in Gmc. were *_smauχōi̯-_, *_smauχō-_, and the development of these in the southern dialects is explained in § 235.2. In Angl., owing to smoothing, contraction would be of e.g. *_smǣχii̯-_, *_smǣχa-_, hence _VP_ pres. indic. sg. _ðrēġu_ (see § 238.2.a, footnote), _ðrēas(t)_, _ðrēað_, pl. _smēġað_, past _ðrēade_, pres. subj. _ðrēġe_, imper. _ðrēa_, pres. part. _ðrēġende_, pass. part. _smēad_.

§ 760. All dialects have some confusion of the two stems, e.g. lW-S, _Ru._^{1} pres. part. _smēande_. But in lNorth. the stem _smēġ-_ is eliminated, and all forms have _smēa-_, _þrēa-_ (also with _ēo_), except for a few mixtures (mostly in _Ru._^{2}) of _smēġ-_ with _smēa-_, producing _smēaġ-_, _smēoġ-_, e.g. _Rit._ inf. _-smēaġa_, _Ru._^{2} pres. indic. pl. _smēoġas_, imper. _smēoġe_.

On KG _smȳaġenne_ see § 298; on eW-S _smēġeanne_, KG _smēġan_ § 314, footnote.

§ 761. Similarly formed verbs are:

(1) _Twēoġan_, doubt, past _twēode_, is conjugated from the stems _twēoġ-_ (Angl. _twīġ-_), _twēo-_ (Angl. also _twīo-_, _twīa-_, § 238) < *_tu̯iχōi̯-_, *_tu̯iχō-_ (§ 235). W-S and _Ru._^{1} have regular forms, _VP_ has no occurrences; most reliable forms are regular in North., e.g. _Ru._^{2} pres. indic. 3rd sg. _twīas_, past _twīade_, pl. _twīodun_; but pres. opt. _twīoġe_ shows a mixture of stems (Li. _ġetuīġa_). On pres. part. Cp. _tuiġendi_ see § 757 footnote.

(2) A similar verb *_tiχōi̯-_, *_tiχō-_, arrange, is indicated by past _tēode_, _tīode_, CH _tīadæ_, pass. part. _ġetēod_, OE Bede _ġetēad_, inflected inf. _tēaġenne_, _tēġenne_ (OE Bede, Miller, p. 366, variants), perhaps faultily transmitted for *_tiġenne_ (developed like Cp. _tuiġendi_).[1]

(3) _Hēan_, exalt (beside _hēġan_, § 753.7), has forms from the second stem only, pres. indic. pl. _hēaþ_, pass. part. _ġehēad_.

(4) _Frēoġan_ set free, love, past _frēode_, is developed from *_frīōi̯-_, *_frīō-_. These would give OE *_frīeġ-_ > *_frīiġ-_ (§ 376) > _frīġ-_, and _frīo-_, _frēo-_. Accordingly _VP_ has pres. indic. sg. _ġefrīġu_, _-frēos_, _-frīoð_, _-frēoð_, _-frēað_, pl. _-frīġað_, imper. _-frīa_, _-frēa_, past. _-frīode_, _-frēode_, _-frēade_, and so pass. part.[2] In view of this clear distinction of two stems _frīġ-_, _frīo-_ in _VP_, the W-S stem _frēoġ-_ is to be regarded as a contamination of _frīġ-_ by _frēo-_; so also _Ru._^{1} pres. subj. _ġefrēoġe_.

North. has many forms with the second stem _frīo-_, _frīa-_ (which

[1] An entirely different view, Flasdieck in _A_ lix. 50–51.

[2] On the fluctuations of the diphthong in _VP_ see § 238.1.

are much confused, cf. § 238.1), e.g. *Ru.*[2] pres. indic. 3rd sg. *ġifrīaδ*, *-frīoδ*, pass. part. *ġifrīad*, pl. *ġifrīode*. But some forms are analogically formed with *frī-* and common endings, e.g. *Rit.* pres. indic. 1st sg. *frīa*, subj. *-frīe*, Li. pres. part. *frīende*. The second stem seems not to invade the field of the first; but the first stem *frīġ-* can be used not only where historically proper, e.g. *Li.* inf. *ġefrīeġa*,[1] but in many forms belonging historically to the second stem, e.g. *Li.* pres. indic. 3rd sg. *gefrīgeδ*, imper. *-frīġ*, past *-frīgade*.

(5) Similar is **fēoġan* hate (not recorded in W-S). *VP* has regular forms from stems *fīġ-*, *fīo-* (e.g. pres. indic. pl. *fīġaδ*, pres. part. *fīgende*, past *fīode*), but also analogical pres. indic. pl. *fīaδ*, past *fīede* (with *-ede* for *-ade* as in uncontracted verbs, § 757). So *Ru.*[1] distinguishes the two stems: pres. indic. 3rd sg. *fīaþ*, pl. *fīeġaþ*, subj. (?) *fīeġæ*. North. mainly distinguishes the two stems, but contaminates *fīġ-* to *fīoġ-*, *fīaġ-* (from the second stem *fīo-*, *fīa-*), hence *Ru.*[2] 3rd sg. pres. indic. *fīaδ*, inf. *-fīoġe*, past pl. *-fīadun*; *Li.* for same forms *-fīaδ*, *-fīaġe*, *-fīadon*. But some forms are simply *fī-* and normal endings, e.g. *Li.* 3rd sg. pres. indic. *ġefīeδ*, *-iδ*.

(6) In North. the strong verb *ġefēon*, rejoice, is not certainly recorded, having been replaced by *ġefēaġa*. This has stems *fēaġ-*, *fēoġ-* (contamination of *fēġ-*), and *fēa-*, *fēo-*. There is much confusion of the two stems. *Ru.*[2] has inf. *ġifēaġa*, but all other forms from the second stem; pres. indic. 1st sg. *ġifēo*, pres. part. *-fēande*, *-fēonde*, past *-fēode*, *-fēade*. *Li.* and *Rit.* have similar forms, but have also pres. subj. from first stem *-fēaġe*. Some forms from the second stem could be regarded as from the strong verb, e.g. indic. 1st sg., and pl.; also inf. Li., Rit. *-fēa*, imper. Li. *-fæg* (for **feh*). The weak verb is found outside North. only in *Ru.*[1] pres. indic. 3rd sg. *ġefēaþ*, and in lW-S transcripts of the gloss on the *Psalter* (e.g. Royal, Arundel, Lambeth), where it is a survival from ultimate Angl. originals.

(7) Defectively preserved verbs of the same type are:

Poetical pres. indic. 3rd sg. *bōþ* boasts, lW-S subj. *bōġie*, past *bōde*, and hence analogical 3rd sg. *bōġaþ*.

OE Bede pres. part. *gōiende* lamenting, 3rd sg. pres. indic. *gōaδ* (analogical for **gōδ*).[2]

[1] On the spelling with *ie* see § 765.

[2] There are also corrupt forms in the Bede MSS., see B–T, Supp., s.v. *gōian*.

W-S pres. indic. 1st sg. *sċōġe* shoe, pl. *sċeōġeað*, subj. pl. *-sċōġen*, imper. *sceō*, pass. part. *-sċōd*, North. analogical disyllable *-sċōed*.

CLASS III

§ 762. The following are W-S paradigms of the four verbs which preserve the clearest signs of belonging to Class III, *habban* have, *seċġan* say, *libban* live, *hyċġan* think. For clarity, the first person singular only will be given in the past indicative, and in the subjunctive tenses, as these all have the same endings as in Classes I and II. The imperative plural is omitted, being identical with the plural of the present indicative.

		Present			
Indic.					
Sg.	1	hæbbe	libbe	seċġe	hyċġe
	2	hæfst	leofast	sæġst	hyġst
	3	hæfþ	leofaþ	sæġþ	hyġþ
Pl.		habbaþ	libbaþ	seċġaþ	hyċġaþ
Subj.		hæbbe	libbe	seċġe	hyċġe
Imper.		hafa	leofa	sæġe	hyġe
		Past			
Indic.		hæfde	lifde	sæġde	hogde
Subj.		hæfde	lifde	sæġde	hogde
Inf.		habban	libban	seċġan	hyċġan
Pres. part.		hæbbende	libbende	seċġende	hyċġende
Pass. part.		hæfd	lifd	sæġd	hogod

As in other types, uncontracted forms of the 2nd and 3rd sg. pres. indic. sometimes occur in W-S, e.g. *sæġeþ*, *hyġeþ*.

In W-S prose 2nd and 3rd sg. pres. indic. *hafast*, *hafaþ* occur occasionally. In the pl. W-S has occasionally root vowel *æ*, especially in inverted forms: *hæbbe we*. On negated forms see § 469.[1] lW-S has frequently pres. subj. *habbe*, pass. part. (OE Bede) *hæfed*.

The forms of *libban* with *eo* have back umlaut of *i*, and forms with *io* occur in eW-S; forms with *i* before a back vowel do not occur in eW-S, except once *lifað* in Junius' transcript of *CP*, 282, 21, but *lifiende*, *lifġende* occur once each. lW-S has a re-formed verb following Class II, *leofian*, *lifian*.

[1] Note the curious negated pass. part. *ġenæfd*, Boeth. 30, 26 (late manuscript only).

The present system of *seċġan* is re-formed in lW-S to indic. *seċġe*, *seġ(e)st*, *seġ(e)þ*, *seċġaþ*, imper. *seġe*, subj. and part. unchanged. On past *sǣde* see § 243.

In eW-S *hyċġan* has already 3rd sg. pres. indic. *-hogað*; past *-hogode*, pass. part. *-hogod* appear, and are normal lW-S.

Various re-formed past tenses occur in late texts, e.g. *sagode*, *hyġde*, *hyġede*.

eKt. has 1st sg. pres. indic. *hebbe*, subj. *hebbe*, *hæbbe*, *habbe*, KG 3rd sg. pres. indic. *hefð*, *-heġeð* (to *hyċġan*), pl. *habbað*, imper. *seġe*, all forms agreeing with W-S with regular *æ*, *y* > *e*; but eKt. subj. *lifiġe*, pres. part. *libġende*, forms of a type frequent in Angl.

The chief forms of the Anglian texts are:

VP Pres. indic. 2nd sg. *hafast*, 3rd *hafað*, pl. *habbað*, past *hefde*, pres. part. **habbende*,[1] pass. part. *hefd*.
Pres. indic. 1st sg. *lifġu*, 3rd *leofað*, pl. *lifġað*, subj. *lifġe*, pres. part. *lifġende*, pass. part. *lifd*.
Pres. indic. 1st sg. *seċġu*, *-o*, 2nd *-sagas*, 3rd *seġeð*, pl. *seċġað*, past *seġde*, inflected inf. *seġġenne*, pres. part. *seċġende*, pass. part. *seġd*.
Pres. indic. 3rd sg. *-hogað*, pl. *-hyċġað*, past *-hogde*.

Ru.[1] Pres. indic. 2nd sg. *hæfest*, 3rd *hæfeþ*, *hæfþ*, pl. *habbaþ*, subj. *hæbbe*, imper. *hæfe*, past *hæfde*, inflected inf. *habbanne*, pres. part. *hæbbende*.
Pres. indic. 3rd sg. *leofaþ*, pl. *lifġaþ*, pres. part. *lifġende*, past *lifde*.
Pres. indic. 1st sg. *sæċġe*, *seċġe*, 2nd *sæġest*, 3rd *sæġeþ*, pl. *sæċġaþ*, *seċġaþ*, subj. *sæċġe*, imper. *sæċġe*, *sæġ(e)*, past *sæġde*, inf. *seċġan*, pass. part. *sæġd*.

North.[2]
Li. 1st sg. pres. indic. *hafo*, 2nd *hæfes*, 3rd *hæfeð*, pl. *habbað*, subj. *hæbbe*, imper. *hæfe*, past *hæfde*, inf. *habba*, pres. part. *hæbbende*.
Rit. and *Ru.*[2] do not differ significantly from *Li.*
Li. 1st sg. pres. indic. *liofo*, 3rd *liofað*, *lifeð*, pl. *lifiað*, subj. *lifiġe*, past *lifde*, inf. *lifiġa*, pres. part. *lifiġiende*.
Rit. does not differ from *Li.* significantly.
Ru.[2] 1st sg. pres. indic. *lifo*, 3rd *lifeð*, pl. *lifġas*, subj. *lifġe*, past *lifde*, inf. *lifġa*, pres. part. *lifġende*.

[1] Cf. negated *nabbende*.

[2] North. variants will not be given which depend merely on features of the dialect already discussed, e.g. the interchange of *-as*, *-að* in the pres. indic. pl.; the confusion of *-s* and *-ð* in the endings of the 2nd and 3rd sg. pres. indic. In the forms of *habban*, simple analogical disturbance of the root vowel is disregarded, e.g. *Li.* pres. indic. sg. *hæfo*, *hafis*, *hafeð*.

Li. 1st sg. pres. indic. *sæġo*, 2nd *sæġes*, 3rd *sæġeð*, pl. *sæċġað*,[1] subj. *sæġe*, imper. *sæġ(e)*, past *sæġde*, inf. *sæċġa*, pres. part. *sæċġende*, pass. part. *-sæġ(e)d*.

Rit. and *Ru.*[2] do not differ significantly from *Li.*

Li. 3rd sg. pres. indic. *-hogas*,[2] pl. *hogað*, past pl. *-hogdon*, inf. *-hyċġa*, pres. part. *-hyċġende*.

Rit. has in present system only imper. pl. *hogað*; past *hogade*, pl. *-hogdon*, pass. part. pl. *-hogodo*.

Ru.[2] does not differ significantly from *Li.*

§ 763. On the basis of the characteristic features of these four verbs, a list of peculiarities may be compiled which are often displayed by verbs originally belonging to the class in Anglian texts, even though they have passed in the main into Class II.

(1) A sign of Class III inflexion is syncopation of the medial vowel in the past tense, for this is shared by all four fundamental verbs.[3]

(2) Forms with non-syllabic medial *-i̯-* (symbol *g*) instead of the syllabic *-iġ-*, *-i-* of Class II are generally a sign of Class III, as in the *VP* and *Ru.*[2] paradigms of *libban*. But this will not apply to all present participles and inflected infinitives, where in Anglian Class II verbs have regularly *-i̯-* after short root syllables (§ 757).

(3) A mark of Class III is the appearance side by side of forms with and without (*a*) *i*-umlaut of the root vowel; (*b*) consonant gemination.[4]

§ 764. The verbs which show traces of these characteristics, and may reasonably be regarded as having been originally Class III verbs in OE, are the following; the forms characteristic of Class III are given for each:

bifian tremble: *Ru.*[1] pres. part. *bifġende* is not decisive, but cognates (OHG *biben*, &c.) point to Class III.

bismerian disgrace: *Li.* past pl. *bismerdon*.

fetian fetch: Angl., poetry (with late exceptions), and sometimes W-S have Class II *fetian*, *fetode*; but W-S has also *feċċ-* as

[1] There are also contaminations of 3rd sg. by pl. and the reverse: 3rd sg. Ru.[2] *sæċġað*, pl. Li. *saeġas*.

[2] Also *-hyċġað* (contamination with pl.).

[3] It is rare for verbs of Class II to have syncopation in the past owing to the analogy of Classes I and III: on possible instances in *Li.* see S–B, § 413.*a*.7; Ross, *Studies in the accidence of the Lindisfarne Gospels*, pp. 151–2.

[4] But characteristics (3) (*a*) and (*b*) by themselves may point only to the existence of Class I and Class II conjugation side by side, e.g. *fylġan*, *folgian*; *tellan*, *talian*.

the first stem, pointing to Prim. OE *feti̯-* (§ 434), and past *fette*, pass. part. *ġefett*, thus showing characteristics 1 and 2 above.

ġiowiġe desire (North.): *Rit.* pres. indic. pl. *ġīuġað*; *Li.* inf. *ġīuġe*, past *ġīude*.

hlinian lean: *Cp.* 1st sg. pres. indic. *onhlinġo*.

īewan show: Angl. *ēawan*, when compared with the W-S verb, shows characteristic (3) (*a*), and its past. *ēawde* characteristic (1).

lēoran go: see § 293 on the interchange of forms with and without umlaut.

leornian learn: see similarly § 154.3, footnote.

losian perish: *Rit.* inf. *loesia*; *Ru.*[2] pres. indic. pl. *loesiġað*, inf. *loesġa*, &c. (So *Ru.*[2] has forms with umlaut and medial *-ġ-* from trans. *losian*, destroy.)

murnan mourn: past pl. *murndan* (And. 37).

plagian play: *Li.* past *plæġde*, and hence root vowel of *plægade*.

onsċunian dread: *VP* past pl. *onsċynedun* shows characteristic (3) (*a*), and is supported by North. *y* forms which might in themselves be due to palatal influence.

sorgian sorrow: *Ep.* pres. part. *soærġændi* shows characteristic (3) (*a*), and is confirmed by ME *serrghenn* (Orrm). The Goth. and OHG cognates are of Class III.

sparian spare: this verb does not show any of the characteristics listed above, but *Rit.* inf. *spæria*, imper. *spær*, past *-spærede* beside *VP* forms with back mutation (pres. indic. 3rd sg. *spearað*, &c.) suggest Prim. OE forms both with and without back vowels in the syllables after the root syllable, hence conjugation according to Class II or Class III.

swiġian be silent: *Li.*, *Ru.*[2], *Martyrology* past *swiġde*. (On W-S pres. part. *swīgende* see Flasdieck, *A* lix. 49).

tilian strive for: *CP* pres. subj. pl. *tilġen*, PC pres. part. *tilġende*.[1]

ġetrēwa trust (North.): beside *ġitrīowa*, this form (*Li.* only) would seem open to the same explanation as *ġelēora* beside *ġelīora*. (So Sievers, *Vokalismus*, p. 35; Flasdieck is unconvinced, *A* lix. 75–76.)

truwian, *trugian* trust: eW-S past *-truwdes*; Ru.[2] *ġitrygade*.

[1] The medial *-ġ-* in W-S is probably decisive as it is there a very rare spelling for the medial element of Class II (in eW-S only once, *lufġe*, CP 145, 16); *Ep.*, *Cp.* pres. part. *tilġendum* is indecisive.

þeowian serve: *VP* pres. subj. pl. *ðiwġen* (§ 279), past *ðeawde*, pl. *ðeowdun*; OE Bede pres. part. *þēoġende*, past *þĕo(w)de*; lW-S past *þeowde*.

þolian suffer: *Rit.* pres. subj. *-ðoeliġa*; Ru.[2] pres. indic. pl. (used as 3rd sg. by contamination) *-ðoelġas*; inf. *-ðoelġe*.

wacian be awake: *Ru.*[1], North. *wæċċa*, poetical pres. part. *wæċċende* show characteristics (3) (*a*) and (*b*).[1]

wunian dwell: *Ru.*[1] imper. pl. *wyniġaþ*.

§ 765. **Contracted verbs.** Here may belong *frēoġan* and **fēoġan*, of which the formation is described in § 761.4, 5. It will be seen there that while the first stem is in Angl. generally *frīġ-*, *fīġ-*, the spellings *frīeġ-*, *fīeġ-* also occur. It has been suggested above that *frīeġ-* would in OE develop to *frīġ-*, and in that case the spellings with *īe* would be archaic. It may well be, however, that in OE *frīoġ-* > *frīeġ-* and did not develop further, and that *frīġ-* < *frīį-*, and that *frīeġ-* and *frīġ-* accordingly represent Class II and Class III conjugation, parallel to *lufie* and *lifġu*.

§ 766. **Origin of forms.** In the pres. system of the weak verb of Class III, reflexes of three Gmc. formative elements are traceable in OE: (1) *-ǣį-*, (2) *-ǣ-*, (3) *-į-*. (1) and (2) stand in the same relationship as *-ōį-* and *-ō-* in Class II, (3) is an ablaut variant of (1) with vanishing grade of the vowel.

Forms with (1) have in OE *-į-* (written *-ġ-*), the preceding vowel having been syncopated too late for consonant gemination to take place, but sufficiently early for *-į-* to cause umlaut. Such forms are VP *lifġu*, *lifġað*, *lifġe*; Ru.[2] *lifġas*, *lifġa*, *lifġe*, and a number of forms from other verbs quoted § 764. Forms with umlaut are Ru.[2] *loesġa*, *-ðoelġe* (inf.); and with substitution of formative element of Class II, Rit. *loesia*, Ru.[2] *loesiġað*, Rit. *-ðoeliġa*.[2] On W-S *feċċan* with *-tį-* > *-ċċ-* see § 486, footnote.

(2) is found in OE in 2nd and 3rd sg. indic. and imper. sg.[3] The 2nd and 3rd sg. indic. are subject to W-S syncope, but are distinguished

[1] *Ru.*[2] differentiated this verb from causative *weċċa*; it uses *-wehte* as past of *weċċa*, *-wæhte* of *wæċċa* (both forms are historically past of *weċċan*, § 753.9.b.1). *Li.* and *Rit.* are in confusion. *Ru.*[1] generalizes *wæċċan* (the past occurs once only, *wehton*, causative).

[2] Or perhaps by phonological development, § 361.

[3] Phonologically the OE forms could correspond to Goth. *habaiþ*, &c., but I assume Ingvaeonic *-ǣ-* parallel to *-ō-* of Class II. In OHG the present systems of Classes II and III are made perfectly parallel, all forms being derived from the stem *-ō-* in Class II, from *-ē-* (< *-ǣ-*) in Class III.

from those of strong verbs and weak verbs of Class I by absence of umlaut: *hæfst*, *hæfþ*, *sæġst*, *sæġþ*. Here may be placed imper. *sæġe*, but *hafa*, *leofa*, and lW-S and poetical *saga* follow Class II. In Angl., imper. in *-e*, 2nd and 3rd sg. indic. in *-est*, *-eþ* from the basic verbs may be regarded as Class III forms: VP *seġeð*, *hefeð* (with second fronting); Ru.[1] *sæġe*, *sæġest*, *sæġeþ*, *hæfest*, *hæfeþ*, and similar forms in North.; North. *lifeð*. But in verbs which largely follow Class II *-e*, *-est*, *-eþ* are to be regarded as weakened from Class II *-a*, &c. Even in the basic verbs many forms follow Class II: VP *hafast*, *-að* (§ 166), *sagas*, *leofað*, *-hogað*, Ru.[1] *leofaþ*, Li. *liofað*, *-hogas*.

Forms with (3) have consonant doubling and mutation and hence resemble forms from weak verbs of Class I. Here belong all forms of the type of *seċġan*, *libban* in 1st sg. and pl. indic., subj., part. and inf. In *seċġan* North. has root vowel *-æ-*, and so *Ru.*[1] usually, lW-S occasionally in impure and poetical texts (*Blick. Hom.*, *Ps.*). This may be explained by § 193.e or regarded as transferred from *sæġeþ*, *sæġde*, &c. Similarly, forms of *habban* with *-bb-* may have root vowel a^1 or *æ*, and **hebban* does not occur.

In verbs other than the basic four the analogy of Class II has eliminated practically all Class III forms. Other analogies produce 1st sg. indic. North. *hafo*, *liofo*, *sæġo*, based on the 2nd and 3rd sg., and so LR *hafæ*.

Hyċġan has in W-S the pres. system according to Class I, Angl. forms are from Class I *hyċġan*, Class II *hogian*.[2] Only the past is Class III.

The past and pass. part. have no medial vowel and no umlaut. *VP* has second fronting in *hefde*, *hefd*, *seġde*, *seġd*. Analogy of Class II appears only in pass. part. *hogod* (W-S, *Rit.*).

The chief problems concerning these verbs are (*a*) the formation of the past and pass. part., and (*b*) the cause of the syncopation of the long medial vowel in forms of type (1).

(*a*) The past and pass. part. are formed in Goth. and OHG by the addition of the normal dental elements to a stem in *-ǣ-* (written *ai* in Goth., *e* in OHG). In Ingvaeonic there is no connecting vowel before the dental elements.[3] Since syncopation of a long medial vowel is unlikely, it is probable that the Goth., OHG forms have *-ǣ-* analogically introduced from the present system, and that the Ingvaeonic forms are older. This view is supported by relict forms without connecting vowel in OHG.[4] The medial consonant groups, however, show forms of this

[1] Transferred from *hafaþ*, &c. The elimination of **hebban* was perhaps due to a desire to differentiate 'have' and 'raise' (*hebban*).

[2] North. indic. and imper. pl. *hogað* is a normal analogy in the dialect (§ 757).

[3] ON agrees with Ingvaeonic, but its greater tendency to syncopation of medial vowels makes it possible that its forms are based on ones resembling those of OHG.

[4] e.g. *hapta* for *habeta*.

type to have been late in origin in Gmc., otherwise the OE forms would be **hæfte*, **sæhte*, &c. (cf. *brōhte*).

(*b*) Present forms of type (1) are found with certainty in OE only. In them *-ǣi̯-* seems to have undergone very early shortening to *-æi̯-*, and in this position before *-i̯-* the vowel *æ* was syncopated early enough for *-i̯-* to cause umlaut of the root syllable in forms like Ru.[2] *-ðoelġe*.[1]

3. Preterite-Present Verbs

§ 767. The nature of these verbs has been indicated above, § 726. They can be classified under the classes of strong verbs according to the form of their present (in form a strong past) as follows:

CLASS I

wāt, *know*.

Pres. indic. 1st, 3rd sg. *wāt*, 2nd *wāst*, pl. *witon*, subj. *wite*, imper. pl. *witaþ*,[2] past *wiste*, *wisse*, inf. *witan*, pres. part. *witende*, pass. part. *witen*.

On negated forms see §§ 265, 469. Dialectal variety is mainly due to the regular operation of sound-changes, e.g. eW-S *wioton*, *wieton* (§§ 218, 299.b), *Ru.*[1], North. *wutan*, *-on* (§ 218). In North. the normal endings of the pres. indic. *-að*, *-as*, *-eð* may be extended to this verb, *wutað*, *-as*, &c. *Li.* imper. sg. *ġewit*.

āh, *possess*.

Pres. indic. 1st, 3rd sg. *āh*, *āg*, pl. *āgon*, subj. *āge*, past *āhte*, inf. *āgan*.

On negated forms see § 354. 2nd sg. pres. indic. is *āhst* lW-S, *āht* Li., and does not elsewhere occur. Pres. part. *-āgende* is frequent in compounds, the pass. part. *āgen*, *ǣġen* own (§ 736.m) occurs in adjectival use.

Li., *Ru.*[2] have pres. indic. sg. *āh*, and hence in view of the rarity of final *-g* > *-h* in North. (§ 446) it would seem that Verner's law was operative in the Prim. OE forms, as in the cognate languages,[3] and that lW-S *āg* is an inverted spelling (§ 447). The pres. indic. sg. is not recorded eW-S, *Ru.*[1], the verb is wanting entirely *VP*, *Rit*.

[1] Flasdieck, *A* lix. 36–38 regards this early syncopation as general, not limited to before *-i̯-*, and challenges the chronology of the loss of medial *æ* suggested above, § 353.

[2] These verbs generally employ subj. forms for imper., e.g. *wite*, *āge* (but note eW-S *ġemun*). But the development of *witaþ* as imper. pl. is found in all dialects, in North. *-að* interchanging with *-eð*, *-as* as in the pres. indic. pl.

[3] Goth. *aih*, *aigum*; ON *á*, *eigum*.

CLASS II

dēag, *avail.*

Pres. indic. 1st, 3rd sg. *dēag*, *dēah* (§ 446), pl. *dugon*, subj. *dyge* (§ 736.m), *duge*, past *dohte*, pres. part. *dugende*.

Angl. has only *Li.* pres. indic. 3rd sg. *dēg*; eKt. pres. part. *dugunde*, Ct. 37 (*-u-* from scribal influence of preceding *-u-*).

CLASS III

ann, *grant.*

Pres. indic. 1st, 3rd sg. *ann*,[1] pl. *unnon*, subj. *unne*, past *ūþe*, inf. *unnan*, pres. part. *unnende*, pass. part. *ġeunnen*.

Beside the subjunctival imper. *unne*, an endingless form appears, lW-S *ġeunn*, Rit. *ġionn*.

cann *can*, *know.*

Pres. indic. 1st, 3rd sg. *cann*,[1] 2nd *canst*, pl. *cunnon*, subj. *cunne*, past *cūþe*, inf. *cunnan*, pass. part. *-cunnen*, and adjectival *cūþ*.

The pass. part. exists only from *oncunnan* accuse; *Ru.*[1] has *-að*, *-eþ* beside *-un*, *-on* in pres. indic. pl.

þearf, *need.*

Pres. indic. 1st, 3rd sg. *þearf*, 2nd *þearft*, pl. *þurfon*, subj. *þurfe*, *þyrfe* (§ 736.m), past *þorfte*, inf. *þurfan*, pres. part. *þearfende*.

Ru.[1], North. pres. part. *ðorfende*, Ru.[1] also *þurfende*; North. has re-formed pres. *ðorfeð*, used as 3rd sg. and pl. (*Li.* also *ðurfu*).

dearr, *dare.*

Pres. indic. 1st, 3rd sg. *dearr*, 2nd *dearst*, pl. *durron*, subj. *durre*, *dyrre* (§ 736.m), past *dorste*.

RC past *dorstæ*, but later Anglian has many re-formations, *Ru.*[1] past *durste*, *dy(r)ste*, Li., Ru.[2] *darste*; Li. also 1st sg. pres. indic. *darr* (cf. § 144). *VP* lacks the verb.

CLASS IV

sċeal, *shall.*

Pres. indic. 1st, 3rd sg. *sċeal*, 2nd *sċealt*, pl. *sċulon*, subj. *sċyle* (§ 736.m), *sċule*, past *sċeolde*.

[1] With the normal variation of *a*, *o*, and of final *-n*, *-nn*.

2nd sg. pres. indic. should be Angl. *sċalt*, which occurs *Ru.*[1], and *a* is extended to 3rd sg. *sċal*, Ru.[1] and a southern rubric in *Rit.*; but usually *ea* (from *æ* by palatal diphthongization) is extended from 1st and 3rd persons, hence Ru.[1], Li. *sċealt*. Ru.[1] has past subj. *sċylde* (analogy of pres. subj.).

Much variety of form is due to the operation of sound-changes: on W-S variation between *sċu-*, *sċeo-* in pres., *sċo-*, *sċeo-* in past see §§ 179–80; on North. pres. pl. *sċylun*, *sċilun*, *sċiulun*, *sċiolun* § 176; on past Ru.[1] *sċalde* (beside *sċulde*), North. *sċealde*, § 156. *VP* lacks the verb.

ġeman, ***remember***.

Pres. indic. 1st, 3rd sg. ***ġeman***, 2nd ***-manst***, pl. ***-munon***, subj. ***-mune***, ***-myne*** (§ 736.m), imper. sg. ***-mun***, pl. ***-munaþ***,[1] past ***-munde***, inf. ***-munan***, pres. part. ***-munende***, pass. part. ***-munen***. The simplex ***man*** occurs occasionally.

The verb is very prone to re-formation in lW-S, e.g. pres. indic. *ġemune*, *-munst*, *-manð*.

This verb appears not to be pret.-pres. in Angl. *VP* has pres. indic. 1st sg. *ġemunu*, 2nd *ġemynes*, subj. pl. *ġemynen*, imper. sg. *ġemyne*, pl. *ġemunað*, past *ġemunde*, inf. *ġemunan*. *Ru.*[1] has pres. indic. 2nd sg. *ġemynest*, past *ġemunde*. Thus the Merc. forms with their variation between *u* and *y* suggest a weak verb of Class III. North. has similar forms, but *y* is extended to all,[2] imper. sg. Li., Rit., Ru.[2] *ġemyne*, pl. Li., Ru.[2] *-as*, pres. indic. 3rd sg. Li. *-es*, pl. *-as*, subj. *-a*, past *ġemy(n)ste*.

be-, ġeneah ***be enough***.

Pres. indic. 3rd sg. ***-neah***, pl. ***-nugon***, subj. ***-nuge***, past ***-nohte***.

CLASS VI

mōt, ***must***.

Pres. indic. 1st, 3rd sg. ***mōt***, 2nd ***mōst***, pl. ***mōton***, subj. ***mōte***, past ***mōste***.

UNCERTAIN CLASS

mæġ, ***may***.

Pres. indic. 1st, 3rd sg. ***mæġ***, 2nd ***meaht***, pl. ***magon***, ***mægon***, subj. ***mæġe***, past ***meahte***.

lW-S phonological modifications and additional forms are pres. indic.

[1] Later the subjunctival imper. *ġemune*, *-en* is used.

[2] Except *Li.* once imper. sg. or inf. *ġemona* (Luke 16, 25) and once pres. indic. pl. *ġemonas* (John 15, 20, *o* corrected to *y*).

2nd sg. *miht*,[1] past *mehte* (already eW-S, § 312), *mihte*,[1] subj. *mage*, *muge*, inf. *magan*, pres. part. *magende*.

The nW-S forms vary only owing to the sound-changes of the dialects, e.g. *VP* pres. indic. 3rd sg. *meġ*, Li. 2nd *mæht*; Merc., North. past *mæhte*; KG pres. indic. 2nd sg. *meht* (§ 314), subj. *meiġe*, part. pres. *meġende*.

This verb cannot be classified under any of Classes I–V, for the root appears to have had I-E *a* (not *o*), nor under Classes VI and VII, as these have past tenses in *ō*, *ē*, or *ēo*.

4. Anomalous Verbs

§ 768. This small group of verbs presents many difficulties of formation, and it would not be possible to discuss their origin briefly. They have all been subjected to thorough study by H. M. Flasdieck in a recent series of articles in *A* and *ES* (see Bibliography, Section C).

(*a*) Willan *will*

		Indicative	Subjunctive
Present			
Sg.	1	wille	wille
	2	wilt	wille
	3	wile	wille
Pl.		willaþ	willen
Past		wolde	
		Inf.	willan
		Pres. part.	willende

In W-S and Kt. *-ll-* is seldom extended to 3rd sg. pres. indic. (alleged instances are mostly subj.).

eKt. has 1 sg. pres. indic. *willa* (< *willu*) beside *wille*; Surrey also *willio*.

The Angl. forms are:

VP: pres. indic. 3rd sg. *wile*, pl. *willað*, pres. part. *wellende*, past *walde*.

Ru.[1]: pres. indic. 1st sg. *wille*, 2nd *wilt*, 3rd *wile*,[2] pl. *willaþ*, subj. *wille*, imper. pl. *wellaþ*, past *wolde*, *walde*.

[1] These forms seem influenced by the noun *miht*; in the past subj. there may be umlaut, eW-S **miehte*.

[2] Alleged exceptions are subj.

Li.: pres. indic. 1st sg. *willo*,[1] 2nd *wilt*, 3rd *wil(l)*,[2] pl. *wallað*,[3] *-as* (once *-on*), subj. *wælle, welle*, past indic. *walde*, subj. *wælde*.[4]

Rit.: pres. indic. 3rd sg. *uil*, pl. *uallað*, subj. *uælle*, past *ualde*.

Ru.[2]: pres. indic. 1st sg. *willo*, 2nd *wilt*, 3rd *wil(l)*, pl. *wallað*, *-as* (and inverted *wallon we*), subj. *welle*, past *walde*.

The W-S negated forms *nyllan, nellan, nolde*, are discussed in §§ 265, 469. In lW-S imper. *nelle, nellaþ* occurs.

The only Kt. negated forms are pres. subj. *nylle* (Ct. 41), past pl. *noldan* (CA, Surrey).

The Anglian forms are:[5]

VP: imper. sg. *nyl*, pl. *nyllað*, past *nalde*.

Ru.[1]: pres. indic. 1st sg. *nyllic̓*, 3rd *nyle*, pl. *nylleþ*, imper. pl. *nellaþ*, past pl. *naldun, noldan*.

Li.: pres. indic. pl. *nallað*, *-as*, *-es* (inverted *nallo we*), imper. sg. *nælle, nelle*, pl. *nallað*, &c. (see footnote 3), past *nalde*.

Rit.: pres. indic. 2nd sg. *nylt*, imper. sg. *nælle*, pl. *nællað*, past pl. *naldon*.

Ru.[2]: pres. indic. pl. inverted *nallan we*, imper. sg. *nelle*, pl. *nallað*, *-as*, *nallon ġe*.

(*b*) Don *do*

	Indicative	Subjunctive	Imperative
Present			
Sg. 1	dō	dō	
2	dēst	dō	dō
3	dēþ	dō	
Pl.	dōþ	dōn	dōþ
Past	dyde		

Inf.	dōn
Pres. part.	dōnde
Pass. part.	ġedōn

In W-S and Kt. there is little deviation from the above paradigm, except for occasional analogical re-formations such as eW-S subj. *dōe*, pres. part. *-dōende* (with disyllabic *o*+*e*). Accordingly *KG* past *dede* can be regarded as having *e* < *y*.

[1] Rarely *will(e)*, *wællo*, *-e*; inverted *nuillic̓*.

[2] So all three lNorth. glosses; already LR *uil*.

[3] As imper. may have vowel of subj. *wællas*, *-að*, beside *wallað*. And so negated *nællað*, *-as*, *-eð*, *-es*, *nellað*, &c. beside *nallað*, &c.

[4] Both instances are subj. (Matt. 14, 7; Luke 1, 62).

[5] Angl. texts have also uncontracted forms, e.g. Ru.[1] *newylle*, Li. *nuillic̓*.

VP and *Ru.*[1] have pres. indic. 1 sg. *dōm* (§ 735.a), 2nd *dōest*, 3rd *dōeð*; pass. part. *ġedōen* (§ 736.m), *Ru.*[1] also *ġedōan*. Otherwise they differ from W-S mainly in having more frequent analogical re-formation, e.g. inf. *dōan*, pres. indic. pl. *dōaþ* (Ru.[1] only), imper. *dōa* (after weak Class II, *VP* only), subj. *dōe* (VP only; Ru.[1] *dō*, *dōa*, pl. *dōan*).

The North. texts also have pres. indic. sg. *dōm*, *dōēs(t)*, *dōēð*, but re-form pl. to *dōað* (also *dōas*, *-es*, *-eð*, forms which can invade 3rd sg.). Re-formation is frequent in the present system, e.g. infin. *dōa* (beside *dō*), subj. *dōe*, part. *dōende*.

Beside past *dyde*, Li. and Ru.[2] have *dede*.[1] The form occurs in CA *deodan*, where the vowel is shown to be short by back umlaut. *Dæde* in transcripts of poetry is due to the assumption that *dede* had Angl. *ē*, W-S *ǣ*;[2] there is no evidence for an OE form equivalent to OHG *tātun*, OS *dādun* they did.

(*c*) Gān *go*

		Indicative	Subjunctive	Imperative
Present				
Sg.	1	gā	gā	
	2	gǣst	gā	gā
	3	gǣþ	gā	
Pl.		gāþ	gān	gāþ
Past		ēode		

Inf.	gān
Past part.	ġegān

For the past *ēode*, North. and Ru.[1] have also *ēade*. Instead of past part. *ġegān*, North. has *ġeēad*; there are no Mercian instances. The present system is as follows in the Mercian texts:

VP: indic. as above, but also 1st sg. often *-gaa*, once *-gān* (? for **gāu*), subj. *-gāe*, imper. sg. *-gāa* (cf. *dōa*); there is a pres. part. *-gānde*.

Ru.[1]: indic. as above, but 3rd sg. largely replaces pl. (but conversely *gāð* is once 3rd sg.), imper. sg. *gā(e)*, pl. *gāþ* (but more frequently *gǣþ*), subj. *gā*, pl. *gǣn* (once *-gān*), inf. *gǣ*, *-gā*.

Like *Ru.*[1], the North. texts show extension of *gǣ-* to pres. indic. pl., inf., and subj.,[3] and there is free formation of analogical disyllabic

[1] The instances are all pl., and many are subj.

[2] And the paraphrast of the *Psalms* appears to have given the first syllable metrical length. (*Dan.* 101 length is indifferent; *Gen.* 722 *dǣdun* transliterates OS *dādun*.)

[3] In North. *gǣ-* is extended to 1st sg. pres. indic. also; and to imper. sg. in Li. *gǣa* (once).

forms, with use of the characteristic North. endings. The chief forms are:

Li.: pres. indic. 1st sg. *gǣ, gāe, gāæ*, 2nd *-gǣstu, gāst, -gāas, gāes, gāæs, -ġāð*, 3rd *gǣð, gǣs, gāð, gāað, -as, -es*, &c., pl. *gāað, -as, -es, -eð, gǣð, gǣs*, subj. *gāe, gǣ*, imper. sg. *gā, gāa, gāe*, &c., inf. *gāa, gāe, gǣ*.

Rit.: pres. indic. 1st sg. *-gǣ* (uncertain), 2nd *gǣst*, 3rd *gǣð*, pl. *-gāð, -gās, -gāað, -as*, subj. *-gǣ* (sg. and pl.), *-gāe* (pl. only), inf. *-gāa*.

Ru.[2]: pres. indic. 1st sg. *gǣ, gāa*, 2nd *gǣst*, 3rd *gǣð, gǣs, gāð, gās, -gāað*, pl. *gāð, gās, gāas*, also as imper. *gāað*, subj. sg. and pl. *gǣ, gāa*, pl. also *gāe, gā*, imper. sg. *gāa*, inf. *gāa*.

Kt. differs from W-S only phonologically (e.g. pres. indic. 3rd sg. KG *gēð*).

(*d*) Bēon *be*

Indicative

Present			
Sg.	1	eom, *I am*	bēo,[1] *I shall be*
	2	eart	bist
	3	is	biþ
Pl.		sindon, sint	bēoþ

Subjunctive

Present		
Sg.	sīe	bēo
Pl.	sīen	bēon

Imperative

Sg.	bēo
Pl.	bēoþ

Infinitive

bēon

Variations from the above paradigms in W-S are occasioned only by normal developments, e.g. eW-S still frequently *io* in the forms of *bēon*; lW-S *sī, sȳ* for *sīe*. In eleventh-century texts the participles *bēonde, ġebēon* appear. On negated forms see § 354.

Kt. has mostly similar forms to W-S, but note *KG* pres. indic. 1st sg. *eam*, pl. *sin*(*t*), *sīon*(*t*), subj. *sīo, sī*; Cts. 37 (Kt.), 45 (Surrey) pl. *seondan, siondan* (§ 217); Cts. 34, 58 *earan* (apparently use of Merc. form in a summarizing formula); Ct. 45 subj. *sēo, sīo*.

[1] Not recorded eW-S.

The chief Mercian forms are:

VP: pres. indic. 1st sg. *eam*, 2nd *earð*, 3rd *is*, pl. *sind*(*un*), *earun*, subj. *sīe*.

pres. indic. 1st sg. *bīom*, 2nd *bist*, 3rd *bið*, pl. *bīoð* (once *bīað*, § 238), imper. sg. *bīo*, pl. *bīoð*.

Ru.[1]: pres. indic. 1st sg. *eam* (negated *nam*, *næm*), 2nd *eart*, *earþ*, *arþu*, 3rd *is*, pl. *sindun*, *sint*, *arun*, subj. *sīe*, *sȳ*, *sē*, *sēo*.

Pres. indic. 1st sg. *bēom*, 2nd *bist*, 3rd *biþ*, *bēoþ*, pl. *bēoþ*, *bīoþ*, *biþon*, *beoþan*, subj. *bēo*, imper. sg. *bēo*, pl. *bēoþ*, *bīoþ*, inf. *bēon*.

The North. glosses *Li.*, *Rit.*, *Ru.*[2] all have: pres. indic. 1st sg. *am*, 2nd *arð*, 3rd *is*, pl. *sint*, *sindon*, *aron*, subj. *sīe*, *sē*;

Pres. indic. 1st sg. *bīom* (Li. also *bēom*, *bīum*), 2nd *bist*, 3rd *bið*, pl. *biðon* (or *bioðon*), Li., Ru.[2] also *bīað*.[1]

Li. has also subj. *bīe*, *bīa*, inf. *bīan*.

As in *gān* there is some mutual influence of pres. indic. 3rd sg. and pl.: *bið* is pl. twice *VP*, twice *Li.*; *bēoþ* is 3rd sg. once Ru.[1], *bīað* once *Ru.*[2]

There are no imperatives from these roots in North., all the glosses using *wes*, *wæs*, *woes*, which is also found in *VP* and *Ru.*[1]; pl. *wesaþ* Ru.[1], *wosað*, *-as* North.

The past is supplied by *wesan*, defective strong verb of Class V, subject to Verner's law: indic. sg. 1st and 3rd *wæs*, 2nd *wǣre*, pl. *wǣron*, subj. *wǣre*. The present system supplies in lW-S imper. sg. *wes*, pl. *wesaþ*, inf. *wesan*, pres. part. *wesende*. Less usual are a pres. indic. and subj. *weseþ*, *-aþ*, *-e* (poetry, *Blick. Hom.*). In Angl. the present system is represented by the imper. discussed above, *Cp.* inf. *wesan*, pres. part. *aetweosendne*, North. inf. *wosa*, Ru.[1] *wesa*.

The various forms of *wesan* in the dialects are due to normal changes: nW-S has *-ē-* in past 2nd sg., pl., and subj. *wēre*, *-on*; *VP* and Kt. have past *wes*; on North. *wosa* see § 210.2; on imper. *woes* § 319, *wæs* §§ 327–8; on *was* for *wæs* § 335; on negated forms § 354.

The distinction of the pres. indic. tenses *eom* and *bēo* is fairly well preserved in OE: *bēo* expresses what is (*a*) an invariable fact, e.g. *ne bið swylċ cwenliċ þeaw* 'such is not a queenly custom',[2] or (*b*) the future, e.g. *ne bið þe wilna gad* 'you will have no lack of pleasures',[3] or (*c*) iterative extension into the future, e.g. *biþ storma ġehwylċ aswefed* 'every storm is always allayed' (i.e. on all occasions of the flight of the Phoenix, past and to come);[4] *eom*

[1] This form is also found *LR* and *Cp.*

[2] *Beow.* 1940.

[3] id. 660.

[4] *Phoen.* 185–6.

expresses a present state provided its continuance is not especially regarded, e.g. *wlitiġ is se wong* 'the plain is beautiful'.[1]

The distinction of the imperatives *bēo* and *wes* is one of dialect, not of meaning. Broadly *bēo* is W-S and Merc., *wes* (*woes*, *wæs*) North.; but while *bēo* is never North., *wes* is found in W-S and Merc. (details above).

Similarly inf. *bēon* (*bīon*, *bīan*) is W-S and Merc., *wosa* North.; but *Ru.*[1] has once *wesa*, Li. once *bīan*.

The subj. forms *bēo* and *sīe* (*sēo*) are also dialectally distinguished: *sīe* is eW-S, Kt., *VP*, North., *bēo* is *Ru.*[1] But already in eW-S *bēo* appears, and in lW-S it is the prevailing form (it does not appear, however, in *KG*). In North. it only appears in *Li.* (twice).

[1] id. 7.

SELECT BIBLIOGRAPHY

TREATMENTS of individual problems of phonology and accidence are referred to in the present work at the relevant places. The Select Bibliography indicates editions of the texts upon which this *Grammar* is founded, and general aids to their linguistic study.

A. *Bibliography*

In the absence of a complete bibliography for Old English studies, the sections devoted to Old English in the following annual publications are invaluable:

Jahresbericht über die Erscheinungen auf dem Gebiete der germanischen Philologie. Berlin, 1880–2, Leipzig, 1883– (published by the Gesellschaft für deutsche Philologie).

Bibliography of English language and literature. Modern Humanities Research Association. Cambridge, 1921–

The year's work in English studies. English Association. Oxford, 1921–

Selective bibliographies are included in the grammars of Luick, Girvan, and Sievers–Brunner (see § C below), and the following are also useful:

KENNEDY, A. G. *A bibliography of writings on the English language from the beginning of printing to the end of 1922*. Cambridge (Mass.) and New Haven, 1927.

HEUSINKVELD, A. H., BASHE, E. J. *A bibliographical guide to Old English*. University of Iowa Humanistic Studies, 1931.

The Cambridge bibliography of English literature, I. Cambridge, 1940, Supplement, 1957.

FUNKE, O. *Englische Sprachkunde: ein Überblick ab 1935*. Bern, 1950.

Bibliographical information concerning individual texts is given in the various literary histories; especially useful are:

BRANDL, A. *Geschichte der altenglischen Literatur. Paul's Grundriss der germanischen Philologie ii*, 2nd ed.; also separately, Strassburg, 1908.

ANDERSON, G. K. *The literature of the Anglo-Saxons*. Princeton, 1949.

The early work on Old English is well recorded by:

WÜLKER, R. *Grundriss zur Geschichte der angelsächsischen Litteratur*. Leipzig, 1885.

B. *Dictionaries*

A fairly complete lexicographical record of Old English is offered by:

BOSWORTH, J., TOLLER, T. N. *An Anglo-Saxon dictionary*. Oxford, 1898. Supplement (by Toller alone), Oxford, 1921.

The poetical vocabulary is separately treated in:

GREIN, C. W. M. *Sprachschatz der angelsächsischen Dichter*. Revised ed. by J. J. Köhler, assisted by F. Holthausen, Heidelberg, 1912.

Hand dictionaries are:

SWEET, H. *The student's dictionary of Anglo-Saxon*. Oxford, 1897. (Uses spelling normalized on West-Saxon basis.)

HALL, J. R. CLARK. *A concise Anglo-Saxon dictionary*. Cambridge, 1894, revised and enlarged, 1916 and 1931.

On the origin and meaning of Old English words note also:

HOLTHAUSEN, F. *Altenglisches etymologisches Wörterbuch*. Heidelberg, 1934.

SCHÜCKING, L. L. *Untersuchungen zur Bedeutungslehre der angelsächsischen Dichtersprache*. Heidelberg, 1915.

An extensive record of Old English personal names is offered by the following, which is supplemented by the works of Björkman, Boehler, Von Feilitzen, Forssner, Redin, and Tengvik (§ c):

SEARLE, W. G. *Onomasticon Anglo-Saxonicum*. Cambridge, 1897.

There is no record of geographical names of comparable fullness, but parts of the field are covered by:

MEZGER, F. *Angelsächsische Völker- und Ländernamen*. Berlin, 1921. (Cf. review, *Archiv* cxlvi. 131.)

MIDDENDORFF, H. *Altenglisches Flurnamenbuch*. Halle, 1902.

TENGSTRAND, E. H. R. *A contribution to the study of genitival composition in Old English place-names*. Uppsala, 1940.

FORSBERG, R. *A contribution to a dictionary of Old English place-names*. Uppsala, 1950.

C. *Grammars*

The most complete grammar is:

BRUNNER, K. *Altenglische Grammatik nach der angelsächsischen Grammatik von Eduard Sievers neubearbeitet*. Halle, 1942, slightly revised re-issue, 1951.

The most orderly presentment of the phonological history of Old English is:

LUICK, K. *Historische Grammatik der englischen Sprache*. Leipzig, 1914–Wortweiser zu § 63–§ 614, Stockholm, 1949 (by E. Wiessner, revised by Th. Katz).

The following works occasionally supplement the above:

BÜLBRING, K. D. *Altenglisches Elementarbuch. I. Teil: Lautlehre*. Heidelberg, 1902.

WRIGHT, J., WRIGHT, E. M. *Old English grammar*. Third ed., Oxford University Press, 1925.

GIRVAN, R. *Angelsaksisch handboek*. Haarlem, 1931.

The above standard works are regarded in this *Grammar* as offering a satisfactory codification of earlier work, and so the books and articles by their own authors and others upon which they were largely based are not included in the bibliography. Other works dealing with important questions of Old English phonology and accidence are:

ÅNGSTRÖM, M. *Studies in Old English MSS. with special reference to the delabialisation of* ȳ̆ (< ŭ+i) *to* ī̆. Uppsala, 1937.

BAZELL, C. E. 'Kasusgruppierungen in der germ. Deklination.' *IF* liv (1936), 265–8.

—— 'IE final unaccented *ē* in Germanic.' *JEGP* xxxvi (1937), 1–9.

—— 'Four West Germanic verbal endings.' *Neophilologus* xxiv (1939), 62–66.

—— 'Case-forms in *-i* in the oldest English texts.' *MLN* lv (1940), 136–9.

BJÖRKMAN, E. *Nordische Personennamen in England*. Halle, 1910.

BLOOMFIELD, L. 'Old English plural subjunctives in *-e*.' *JEGP* xxix (1930), 100–13.

BOEHLER, M. *Die altenglischen Frauennamen*. Berlin, 1930.

BOROWSKI, B. *Zum Nebenakzent beim altenglischen Nominalkompositum*. Halle, 1921.

—— *Lautdubletten im Altenglischen*. Halle, 1924.

(Both works have invaluable material, but uncertain conclusions.)

BROSNAHAN, L. F. *Some Old English sound changes*. Cambridge, 1953.

BRUNNER, K. 'The Old English vowel phonemes.' *English Studies* xxxiv (1953), 247–51.

DAHL, I. *Substantival inflexion in early Old English*. Lund, 1938.

ECKHARDT, E. *Die vokalische Dissimilation im Altenglischen*. *ES* lxxiii (1938), 161–79.

ELIASON, N. E. 'Old English vowel lengthening and vowel shortening before consonant groups.' *Studies in philology* xlv (1948), 1–20. (A phonetic consideration.)

VON FEILITZEN, O. *The pre-conquest personal names of Domesday Book*. Uppsala, 1937.

FLASDIECK, H. M. 'Ae. *ēow*.' *A* lvii (1933), 208–15.

—— 'Die zweite Person des Singulars im ae. Verbalsystem.' *A* lviii (1934), 113–21.

—— 'Untersuchungen über die germanischen schwachen Verben III. Klasse unter besonderer Berücksichtigung des Altenglischen.' *A* lix (1935), 1–192.

—— 'Die reduplizierenden Verben des Germanischen (unter besonderer Berücksichtigung des Altenglischen).' *A* lx (1936), 241–365.

—— 'Das Verbum *wollen* im Altgermanischen (unter besonderer Berücksichtigung des Altenglischen).' *A* lxi (1937), 1–42.

—— 'Ae. *dōn* und *gān*.' Ibid., 43–64.

—— 'Das altgermanische Verbum substantivum unter besonderer Berücksichtigung des Altenglischen.' *ES* lxxi. 321–49; lxxii. 158–60 (1936–8).

—— 'Miszellen zur ae. Grammatik.' *AB* xli (1930), 37–39, 283–8.

FLASDIECK, H. M. 'Zur Geschichte der fem. ō-Flexion im Westgermanischen.' *IF* xlviii (1930), 53–66.

—— 'Old English *nefne*: a revaluation.' *A* lxix (1950), 135–71. (Full study of the assimilation *fn* > *mn*, cf. § 484.)

—— 'The phonetic aspect of Old Germanic alliteration.' *A* lxix (1950), 266–87.

FÖRSTER, M. 'Zur *i*-Epenthese im Altenglischen.' *A* lix (1935), 287–98.

FORSSNER, TH. *Continental-Germanic personal names in England*. Uppsala, 1916.

GABRIELSON, A. 'On the late Old Northumbrian (*w*)*æ* for regular (*w*)*e*.' *AB* xxi (1910), 208–19.

—— *The influence of* w- *in Old English as seen in the Middle English dialects*. Göteborg–Leipzig, 1912.

GERICKE, B., GREUL, W. *Das Personal-pronomen der 3. Person in spätags. und frühmittelenglischen Texten*. Leipzig, 1934. (Palaestra cxciii.)

GEVENICH, O. *Die englische Palatalisierung von* k > č *im Lichte der englischen Ortsnamen*. Halle, 1918. (Cf. Ekwall, *AB* xxx. 221–8.)

HEDBERG, J. *The syncope of the Old English present endings*. Lund, 1945. (Cf. Löfvenberg, *Studia Neophilologica* xxii. 225–9.)

HEIDEMANN, G. 'Die Flexion des Verbum substantivum im Ags.' *Archiv* cxlvii (1924), 30–46.

JIRICZEK, O. L. 'Tenuis für Media im Altenglischen.' *IF* xxxviii (1917–20), 196–9. (Regards spellings discussed in § 450 as graphic; unlikely.)

VAN LANGENHOVE, G. *The assibilation of palatal stops in Old English*. A grammatical miscellany offered to Otto Jespersen, Copenhagen–London, 1930, pp. 69–75.

LINKE, G. '*standeð* und *stent* und dergleichen in ags. sicher fixierten HSS.' *ES* lxxiii (1939), 321–30.

LOCKWOOD, W. B. 'Welsh *ystwyrian* and *i*-epenthesis in Old English.' *English and Germanic studies* v (1952–3), 90–98.

LÖFVENBERG, M. T. 'On the syncope of the Old English present endings.' *Studia Neophilologica* xxi (1948–9), 231–76.

LOEWE, K. 'Der germanische Pluraldativ.' *Zeitschrift für vergleichende Sprachforschung* xlviii (1918), 76–99. (On *þǣm, þām, twǣm, twām*, &c.)

MALONE, K. *When did Middle English begin?* Curme volume of linguistic studies, Baltimore, 1930, pp. 110–17.

MARCKWARDT, A. H. *Verb inflections in late Old English*. Philologica: the Malone anniversary studies, Baltimore, 1949, pp. 79–88.

PROKOSCH, E. 'The Old English weak preterites without medial vowel.' *PMLA* xlii (1927), 331–8.

REDIN, M. *Studies on uncompounded personal names in Old English*. Uppsala, 1919.

RITTER, O. *Vermischte Beiträge zur englischen Sprachgeschichte*. Halle, 1922.

ROSS, A. S. C. 'The 1st sg. pres. ind. *-e* in Old English.' *Neuphilologische Mitteilungen* xxxiv (1933), 232–9.

ROSS, A. S. C. 'Old English *æ* ∞ *a*.' *English Studies* xxxii (1951), 49–56. (Attempts an explanation of the greater frequence in adjectives than nouns of *æ* for *a* in the root syllable, cf. § 643.)

SALMEN, H. w + *westgerm.* ĕ *und* ĭ *im Angelsächsischen*. Berlin, 1936. (Valuable material.)

SCHLEMILCH, W. *Beiträge zur Sprache und Orthographie spätae. Sprachdenkmäler der Übergangszeit (1000–1150)*. Halle, 1914.

SCHUBEL, F. 'Die Aussprache des anlautenden ae. *sc*.' *Studia Neophilologica* xiv (1942), 255–76. (Summary *AB* liii. 219–20.)

SEELIG, F. *Die Komparation der Adjektiva und Adverbien im Altenglischen*. Heidelberg, 1930.

SLETTENGREN, E. 'On the development of Old English initial *sc*.' *Studier i modern språkvetenskap* xv (1943), 45–50.

STANLEY, E. G. 'The chronology of *r*-metathesis in Old English.' *English and Germanic studies* v (1952–3), 103–15.

TENGVIK, G. *Old English bynames*. Uppsala, 1938.

WATSON, J. W. 'Northumbrian Old English *ēo* and *ēa*.' *Language* xxii (1946), 19–26.

—— *Smoothing and palatal umlaut in Northumbrian*. English studies in honor of J. S. Wilson (University of Virginia Studies iv), 1951, pp. 167–74.

WEBER, G. *Suffixvokal nach kurzer Tonsilbe vor* r, n, m *im Angelsächsischen*. Leipzig, 1927. (Valuable material.)

WOKATSCH, W. *Unhistorisches* ea *in angelsächsischen und frühmittelenglischen Handschriften*. Berlin, 1932. (Valuable material.)

WRENN, C. L. 'Standard Old English.' *Trans. Philological Soc.*, 1933, pp. 65–88.

ZESSIN, W. *Über die in- und auslautende Spirans* g *im Spätwestsächsischen*. Halle, 1922.

D. *Metre*

Metre is not directly treated in the present *Grammar*, but the evidence for the accentuation of native and foreign words described in Chapters II and X (§§ 549–58) is largely metrical. For the determination of accent, the metrical system of Sievers is sufficient, as described in:

SIEVERS, E. *Altgermanische Metrik*. Halle, 1893.

SCHIPPER, J. *Grundriss der englischen Metrik*. Vienna and Leipzig, 1895. English ed., *A history of English versification*. Oxford, 1910.

Works in which the lines of various Old English poems are classified according to the system of Sievers are listed in § C of the *List of works used* in *The battle of Brunanburh*, ed. by A. Campbell (London, 1938). The following works go more deeply than that of Sievers into the nature of Old English verse rhythm, but diverge greatly from each other:

BOER, R. C. *Studiën over de metriek van het alliteratievers*. Amsterdam, 1916.

HEUSLER, A. *Deutsche Versgeschichte, I*. Berlin and Leipzig, 1925.

POPE, J. C. *The rhythm of Beowulf*. Yale University Press, 1942.

E. *Collections of texts*

Practically all Old English texts preserved in manuscripts older than 900, except the *Parker Chronicle*, and the translations of the *Cura Pastoralis* and Orosius (see § L), are edited with a full glossary in:

SWEET, H. *The oldest English texts*. London, 1885.

The poetical texts are conveniently edited with concise notes and extensive bibliographical references by G. P. KRAPP and E. VAN K. DOBBIE in *The Anglo-Saxon poetic records*, 6 vols., Columbia University Press,[1] as follows:

I. *The Junius Manuscript*. 1931.
II. *The Vercelli Book*. 1932.
III. *The Exeter Book*. 1936.
IV. *Beowulf and Judith*. 1954.
V. *The Paris Psalter and the Metres of Boethius*. 1933.
VI. *The Anglo-Saxon minor poems*. 1942.

Vol. IV supplements but does not supersede:

KLAEBER, F. *Beowulf and the Fight at Finnsburg*. D. C. Heath & Co., 1941 (3rd ed.).

The following are comprehensive collections of texts of particular kinds:

THORPE, B. *The Anglo-Saxon Chronicle*. 2 vols. Rolls series, 1861. (Complete texts of all versions.)

COCKAYNE, O. *Leechdoms, wortcunning, and starcraft of early England*. 3 vols. Rolls series, 1864–6.

SKEAT, W. W. *The four gospels in Anglo-Saxon, Northumbrian, and Old Mercian versions*. 4 vols. Cambridge, 1871–87.

WRIGHT, T., WÜLCKER, R. P. *Anglo-Saxon and Old English vocabularies*. 2 vols. London, 1884.

LIEBERMANN, F. *Die Gesetze der Angelsachsen*. 3 vols. Halle, 1903–16.

F. *Inscriptions*

The most important runic inscriptions are those of the Ruthwell Cross and the Franks Casket (see § 6). These are edited in *Anglo-Saxon poetic records* vi. The best linguistic commentaries are given in:

DICKINS, B., ROSS, A. S. C. *The Dream of the Rood*. London, 1934 and 1945.

NAPIER, A. S. *The Franks Casket*. An English miscellany presented to Dr. Furnivall, Oxford, 1901, pp. 362–81.

[1] This collection supersedes C. W. M. Grein and R. P. Wülcker, *Bibliothek der angelsächsischen Poesie*, 3 vols., Cassel and Leipzig, 1883–98, but this work is frequently the basis of references.

The most important of the remaining runic inscriptions are:[1]

NORTHUMBRIAN: Bewcastle Column (ed. A. B. Webster, in G. B. Brown, *The arts in early England* v); Thornhill, Urswick, Lancaster Crosses, Kirkheaton Stone (all ed. by Bruce Dickins, *Leeds studies in English* i. 18–19); Falstone Hogback (W. Viëtor, *Die northumbrischen Runensteine*, Marburg, 1895, pp. 17–18; Collingham Cross (ibid., pp. 19–20);[2] Monkwearmouth Panel (British Museum, *A guide to the Anglo-Saxon and foreign Teutonic antiquities*, 1923, p. 123); Æthred's ring (ibid., p. 115); Coquet Island Ring (*OET*, p. 128); Lindisfarne Slabs (ed. A. S. C. Ross, *ES* lxx. 36–39); Hartlepool Slabs (A. Hübner, *Inscriptiones Britanniae Christianae*, Berlin, 1876, nos. 188–96).

MERCIAN: Overchurch Stone (ed. Bruce Dickins, loc. cit.); Mortain Casket (M. Cahen, M. Olsen, *L'Inscription runique du coffret de Mortain*, Paris, 1930);[3] Derbyshire Bone Plate (*BM guide*, p. 118).[4]

SOUTHERN: Thames Knife (ed. Bruce Dickins, loc. cit.); Dover Slab (ibid.); Sittingbourne Knife (*BM guide*, p. 95); Brussels Cross (S. T. R. O. d'Ardenne, *English Studies* xxi. 145–64; *Anglo-Saxon poetic records* vi. 115).

Interesting inscriptions in Latin letters are Falstone Hogback (see above), Dewsbury Cross (*BM guide*, p. 125), Carlisle Cross (W. G. Collingwood, *Trans. Cumb. and West. Antiq. and Arch. Soc.*, N.S. xv. 125), Yarm Cross (W. G. Collingwood, *Victoria History of the County of York* ii. 128), Ælfred Jewel (frequently quoted), Breamore Arch, and the long Kirkdale Sundial 1055–65 (both ed. by M. Förster, *ES* xxxvi. 446–9).

A very large number of Old English coins inscribed with names of kings and moneyers survive. On these, however, abnormal and bad spelling is so frequent that only recurrent forms are of any linguistic value. Forms abound which diverge from the dialect which might be expected in the relevant kingdom, e.g. on Anglian coins, *Ealraed*, *Beagstan*, and many names in *-heah*, beside *Alred*, *Baeghelm*; on West-Saxon coins *-bearht* beside *-beorht* (§ 338, footnote), *Biorn-*, *Liof-*, beside *Beorn-*, *Leof-* (though these peculiarities are mainly on coins from south-eastern mints), *Berht-*, *Biorht-*, beside *Beorht-*. But the coins are mainly of value for their occasional help in dating sound-changes (see, for example, §§ 329.2; 369). The most comprehensive collection of coin-inscriptions is:

KEARY, C. F., GRUEBER, H. A. *A catalogue of English coins in the British Museum*. Anglo-Saxon Series. 2 vols. London, 1887–93.

For the late Old English period the following are especially valuable:

HILDEBRAND, B. E. *Anglosachsiska mynt i Svenska kongliga myntkabinettet*. Second ed., Stockholm, 1881.

[1] Unintelligible inscriptions are not included in this list.

[2] A form *Onswini* alleged by S–B, § 186.*a*.2, to occur on this cross is a misreading of early editors.

[3] To be regarded as probably Merc. owing to the form *ġewarahtæ*, rare except in Merc. texts (cf. § 156).

[4] Perhaps North. in origin, as final *-n* is dropped in *Hadda* (a.s.), but it is wiser not to remove it definitely from the area of discovery, since *Ru.*[1] frequently rejects *-n*.

HOLM, S. *Studier öfver Uppsala universitets Anglosaxiska myntsamling.* Uppsala, 1917. (Adds useful linguistic notes.)

SCHNITTGER, B. 'Silverskatten från Stora Sojdeby.' *Fornvännen* x (1915), 53–116, 189–246.

G. *Glossaries*

The *Epinal, Erfurt, Corpus,* and *Leiden Glossaries* (cf. § 12) are all edited in Sweet's *Oldest English texts,*[1] the *Corpus Glossary* also in Wright–Wülcker (see § E). Other editions are:

SCHLUTTER, O. B. *Das Epinaler und Erfurter Glossar. I. Teil: Faksimile und Transliteration des Epinaler Glossars.* Hamburg, 1912. (Bibl. d. ags. Prosa viii. 1.)

LINDSAY, W. M. *The Corpus Glossary.* With an Anglo-Saxon index by H. McM. Buckhurst. Cambridge, 1921.

HESSELS, J. H. *A late eighth-century Latin–Anglo-Saxon glossary preserved in the library of the Leiden University.* Cambridge, 1906. (Review by Holthausen, *AB* xix. 160–9.)

GLOGGER, P. *Das Leidener Glossar.* 3 vols. Augsburg, 1901–8.

HOLTHAUSEN, F. 'Die Leidener Glossen.' *ES* l. 327. (The most convenient edition, with annotations, of the English glosses.)

On the language of the early glossaries:

DIETER, F. *Ueber Sprache und Mundart der ältesten englischen Denkmäler. I. Der Vocalismus.* Göttingen, 1885.

KUHN, S. M. 'The dialect of the Corpus Glossary.' *PMLA* liv (1939), 1–19.

SAUER, R. *Zur Sprache des Leidener Glossars.* München and Augsburg, 1917.

For later glossaries the collection of Wright–Wülcker remains invaluable, but is supplemented by:

BOUTERWEK, K. 'Die angelsächsischen Glossen in dem Brüsseler Codex von Aldhelms Schrift *De Virginitate.*' *ZfdA* ix (1853), 401–530. (Collation by E. Hausknecht, *A* vi (1883), 96–103.)

FÖRSTER, M. 'Die altenglische Glossenhandschrift Plantinus 32 (Antwerpen) und Additional 32246 (London).' *A* xli (1917), 94–161.

HOLDER, A. 'Die Bouloneser angelsächsischen Glossen zu Prudentius.' *Germania* xxiii (1878), 385–403.

MERITT, H. D. *Old English glosses.* New York, 1945.

NAPIER, A. S. *Old English glosses chiefly unpublished.* Oxford, 1900.

ZUPITZA, J. 'Englisches aus Prudentiushandschriften.' *ZfdA* xx (1876), 36–45.

—— 'Altenglische Glossen zu Abbos *Clericorum Decus.*' *ZfdA* xxxi (1887), 1–27.

[1] Only the vernacular glosses are given. Sweet's edition of the *Leiden Glossary* is not satisfactory, see Steinmeyer, *ZfdA* xxxiii. 248–9.

On the language of later glossaries:

BOLL, P. *Die Sprache der altenglischen Glossen im MS. Harl. 3376.* Bonn, 1904. (Bonner Beiträge zur Anglistik xv.)

SCHIEBEL, K. *Die Sprache der altenglischen Glossen zu Aldhelms Schrift 'De laude virginitatis'.* Göttingen, 1907.

On the Kentish glosses on Bede and *Proverbs* see § K.

H. *Charters*

The English charters and English words in Latin charters preserved in manuscripts older than 900 are given in Sweet's *Oldest English texts.* A useful selection of documents from the period 900–1066 is added in the same editor's *Second Anglo-Saxon reader* (Oxford, 1887). The fundamental collection of charters of all types remains:

KEMBLE, J. M. *Codex diplomaticus aevi Saxonici.* 6 vols. London, 1839–48.

Rather more complete for the period down to 975 is:

BIRCH, W. DE G. *Cartularium Saxonicum.* 3 vols. London, 1885–93. *Index Saxonicus: an index to all the names of persons in Cartularium Saxonicum.* London, 1899.

Selections are edited in:

THORPE, B. *Diplomatarium Anglicum aevi Saxonici.* London, 1865.

EARLE, J. *A hand-book to the land-charters, and other Saxonic documents.* Oxford, 1888.

Facsimiles of charters preserved on approximately contemporary single sheets are given in:

BOND, E. A. (THOMPSON, E. M.). *Facsimiles of ancient charters in the British Museum.* 4 vols. London, 1873–8.

SANDERS, W. B. (chief editor). *Facsimiles of Anglo-Saxon manuscripts.* 3 vols. Ordnance Survey Office, Southampton, 1878–84.

Practically all charters which are written entirely in Old English are edited with excellent commentaries in the following collections:

NAPIER, A. S., STEVENSON, W. H. *The Crawford collection of early charters and documents.* Oxford, 1895.

HARMER, F. E. *Select English historical documents of the ninth and tenth centuries.* Cambridge, 1914.

WHITELOCK, D. *Anglo-Saxon wills.* Cambridge, 1930.

ROBERTSON, A. J. *Anglo-Saxon charters.* Cambridge, 1939.

HARMER, F. E. *Anglo-Saxon writs.* Manchester, 1952.

I. *Northumbrian*

The early non-runic texts (see § 6) are edited in *The Anglo-Saxon poetic records* vi, and also in:

SMITH, A. H. *Three Northumbrian poems: Cædmon's Hymn, Bede's Death-Song and The Leiden Riddle.* London, 1933.[1]

[1] Smith's text of the *Leiden Riddle* is slightly corrected by R. W. Zandvoort, *English and Germanic studies* iii. 42–56.

The names in early manuscripts of Bede's *Historia Ecclesiastica* and in the *Liber Vitae Dunelmensis* are given in Sweet's *Oldest English texts*. Anderson provides the material of a further Bede MS. (see below). The chief aids to study are:

PLUMMER, C. *Venerabilis Baedae Historia ecclesiastica gentis Anglorum, etc.* 2 vols. Oxford, 1896.

KÖHLER, TH. *Die altenglischen Namen in Baedas Historia ecclesiastica und auf den altnordh. Münzen*. Berlin, 1908.

STRÖM, H. *Old English personal names in Bede's History*. Lund, 1939.

ANDERSON, O. S. *Old English material in the Leningrad manuscript of Bede's Ecclesiastical History*. Lund, 1941.

BJÖRKMAN, E. 'Zum nordhumbrischen Liber Vitae.' *AB* xxix (1918), 243–7. (A collation.)

THOMPSON, A. H. *Liber Vitae Dunelmensis*. A collotype facsimile. Surtees Society (Publications vol. cxxxvi), 1923.

HELLWIG, H. *Untersuchungen über die Namen des nordh. Liber Vitae* i, Berlin, 1888.

MÜLLER, R. *Untersuchungen über die Namen des nordh. Liber Vitae*. Berlin, 1901. (Palaestra ix.)

For the late Northumbrian gospel glosses on the Lindisfarne and Rushworth manuscripts (§ 6) we are still dependent upon Skeat's *Gospels in Anglo-Saxon*. A facsimile of *The Lindisfarne Gospels* edited by R. Bruce-Mitford, J. J. Brown, A. S. C. Ross, and others, has appeared (*Urs Graf Verlag*, Lausanne, 1956). The chief aids to study are:

COOK, A. S. *A glossary of the Old Northumbrian Gospels* (*Lindisfarne Gospels or Durham Book*). Halle, 1894.

LEA, E. M. 'The language of the Northumbrian gloss to the Gospel of St. Mark.' *A* xvi (1894), 62–206.

FÜCHSEL, H. 'Die Sprache der northumbrischen Interlinearversion zum Johannes-Evangelium.' *A* xxiv (1901), 1–99.

FOLEY, E. H. *The language of the Northumbrian gloss to the Gospel of St. Matthew. Part I, Phonology*. New York, 1903. (Yale Studies in English xiv.)

KELLUM, M. D. *The language of the Northumbrian gloss to the Gospel of St. Luke*. New York, 1906. (Yale Studies in English xxx.)

STOLZ, W. *Der Vokalismus der betonten Silben in der altnordhumbrischen Interlinearversion der Lindisfarner Evangelien*. Bonn, 1908.

CARPENTER, H. C. A. *Die Deklination in der nordhumbrischen Evangelienübersetzung der Lindisfarner Handschrift*. Bonn, 1910.

KOLBE, TH. *Die Konjugation der Lindisfarner Evangelien*. Bonn, 1912.

ROSS, A. S. C. *Studies in the accidence of the Lindisfarne Gospels*. Leeds, 1937.

BLAKELEY, L. 'The Lindisfarne s/ð problem.' *Studia Neophilologica* xxii (1949–50), 15–47.

LINDELÖF, U. *Glossar zur altnorthumbrischen Evangelienübersetzung in der Rushworth-handschrift*. Helsingfors, 1897. (Acta Societatis Scientiarum Fennicae xxii. 5.)

LINDELÖF, U. *Die südnorthumbrische Mundart des 10. Jahrhunderts: die Sprache der sog. Glosse Rushworth*[2]. Bonn, 1901. (Bonner Beiträge zur Anglistik x.)

The gloss on the Durham Ritual is re-edited in:

LINDELÖF, U. *Rituale Ecclesiae Dunelmensis.* Surtees Society (Publications vol. cxl), 1927.

Aids to study are:

LINDELÖF, U. *Die Sprache des Rituals von Durham.* Helsingfors, 1890.

—— *Wörterbuch zur Interlinearglosse des Rituale Ecclesiae Dunelmensis.* Bonn, 1901. (Bonner Beiträge zur Anglistik ix. 105–220.)

More general works on Old Northumbrian are:

HILMER, H. *Zur altnordhumbrischen Laut- und Flexionslehre. I. Lautlehre.* Goslar, 1880.

LINDELÖF, U. 'Beiträge zur Kenntnis des Altnordhumbrischen.' *Mémoires de la société néo-phil. à Helsingfors* i (1893), 219–302.

J. *Mercian*

The gloss on the *Vespasian Psalter* is edited in Sweet's *Oldest English texts.* Collations in *Leeds studies in English and kindred languages* i (R. Roberts), *JEGP* xl (S. M. Kuhn). Aids to study are:

ZEUNER, R. *Die Sprache des kentischen Psalters.* Halle, 1881.

GRIMM, C. *Glossar zum Vespasian-Psalter und den Hymnen.* Heidelberg, 1906.

D'ARDENNE, S. T. R. O. *An edition of þe liflade ant te passiun of Seinte Iuliene.* Liège, 1936. (Fundamental on the relationship of the dialect of *VP* to that of certain Middle English texts.)

The gloss on St. Matthew and the other small Mercian portions of the *Rushworth Gospels* (§ 11) is available in Skeat's *Gospels in Anglo-Saxon.* Aids to study are:

SCHULTE, E. *Glossar zu Farmans Anteil an der Rushworth-Glosse.* Bonn, 1904.

SVENSSON, J. V. *Om språket i den förra (merciska) delen af Rushworth-handskriften. I. Ljudlära.* Göteborg, 1883.

OTTEN, G. *The language of the Rushworth gloss to the Gospel of St. Matthew.* Leipzig and Nordhausen, 1890–1.

BROWN, E. M. *Die Sprache der Rushworth Glossen zum Evangelium Matthäus und der mercische Dialect.* Göttingen, 1891–2.

MENNER, R. J. 'Farman vindicatus.' *A* lviii (1934), 1–27.

KUHN, S. M. '*e* and *æ* in Farman's Mercian glosses.' *PMLA* lx (1945), 631–69.

The minor Mercian texts mentioned in § 12 are all in Sweet's *Oldest English texts.* The following works touch upon them:

LEONHARDI, G. *Die Lorica des Gildas.* Hamburg, 1905. (Also in *Kleinere ags. Denkmäler,* Bibl. d. ags. Prosa vi.)

RÖSEMEIER, E. *Über Sprache und Mundart einiger kleinerer altenglischer Denkmäler aus Sweet's Oldest English Texts*. Münster, 1913.

For the later Mercian texts mentioned in § 13 see:

ZUPITZA, J. 'Mercisches aus der HS. Royal 2 A 20 im Britischen Museum.' *ZfdA* xxxiii (1889), 47–66.

NAPIER, A. S. 'Ein altenglisches Leben des hl. Chad.' *A* x (1888), 131–56.

BRUNNER, K. 'Die Sprache der Handschrift Junius 24.' *AB* li (1940), 207–13.

VLEESKRUYER, R. *The life of St. Chad*. Amsterdam, 1953.

The Lichfield genealogies (see § 7, footnote), are printed in Sweet's *Oldest English texts*, and discussed by:

WILLIAMS, O. T. 'The dialect of the text of the Northumbrian genealogies.' *MLR* iv (1908–9), 323–8.

K. *Dialects of Kent and Surrey*

The early charters, the Codex Aureus inscription, and the Bede glosses are all in Sweet's *Oldest English texts*. The Bede glosses are better edited by:

HOLTHAUSEN, F. 'Die altenglischen Beda-Glossen.' *Archiv* cxxxvi (1917), 290–2.

The chiefs aids to the study of the early texts are:

WOLFF, R. *Untersuchung der Laute in den kentischen Urkunden*. Heidelberg, 1893.

TAXWEILER, R. *Angelsächsische Urkundenbücher von kentischen Lokalcharakter*. Berlin, 1906.

BRYAN, W. F. *Studies in the dialects of the Kentish charters of the Old English period*. University of Chicago, 1915. (Valuable, stressing the partly Mercian spellings of the Kentish charters.)

CAMPBELL, A. 'An Old English will.' *JEGP* xxxvii (1938), 133–52.

Of the later Kentish texts (§ 15), the *Kentish Psalm* and the *Kentish Hymn* are both in *The Anglo-Saxon poetic records* vi; of the glosses to *Proverbs* the following are the standard edition and study:

ZUPITZA, J. 'Kentische Glossen des neunten (*sic*) Jahrhunderts.' *ZfdA* xxi. 1–59, xxii. 223–6 (1877–8).

WILLIAMS, I. *A grammatical investigation of the Old Kentish Glosses*. Bonn, 1905. (Bonner Beiträge zur Anglistik xix. 92–166.)

L. *Early West-Saxon*

The following are the editions of the major texts regarded as Early West-Saxon (§ 16).

PLUMMER, C. *Two of the Saxon Chronicles parallel*. 2 vols. Oxford, 1892–9. (Includes complete text of the *Parker Chronicle*.)[1]

[1] To be preferred to the edition in Thorpe (§ E), for additions in later hands are more clearly distinguished.

SWEET, H. *King Alfred's West-Saxon version of Gregory's Pastoral Care.* Early English Text Society, 1871.
—— *King Alfred's Orosius.* Early English Text Society, 1883.

The linguistic features of these texts are described with considerable fullness by:

COSIJN, P. J. *Altwestsächsische Grammatik.* 2 vols. Den Haag, 1883–6.

The following are additional aids to the linguistic study of these texts; works dealing with their relationship to the Latin originals are not given here:

GIESCHEN, L. *Die charakteristischen Unterschiede der einzelnen Schreiber im Hatton MS. der Cura Pastoralis.* Greifswald, 1887.
JOST, K. 'Zu den Handschriften der Cura Pastoralis.' *A* xxxvii (1913), 63–68.
KÜGLER, H. ie *und seine Parallelformen im Angelsächsischen.* Berlin, 1916. (Cf. reviews *AB* xxvii. 246; *ES* liv. 399.)
OLBRICH, R. *Laut- und Flexionslehre der fremden Eigennamen in den Werken König Alfreds.* Strassburg, 1908.

Of the minor fragments of Early West-Saxon (see § 16), the genealogies are printed in Sweet's *Oldest English texts*, p. 179, while one fragment of the *Martyrology* is printed ibid., pp. 177–8; another (by C. Sisam), *RES* xxix (1953), 209–20. A fragment of a further early manuscript of the *Cura Pastoralis* is edited and discussed by H. M. Flasdieck *A* lxii (1938), 193–233, lxvi (1942), 56–58.

M. *Late West-Saxon*

Of the extensive monuments extant in Late West-Saxon of various degrees of purity, the works mentioned in §§ 16–17 are merely an introductory selection. The following are the best editions of these works:

BRENNER, E. *Der altenglische Junius-Psalter.* Heidelberg, 1908.
LEONHARDI, G. *Lǣċebōc* in *Kleineré ags. Denkmäler.* Hamburg, 1906.
ROSITZKE, H. A. *The C-text of the Old English chronicles.* Bochum-Langendreer, 1940.
BRIGHT, J. W. *The gospels in West-Saxon.* 4 vols. Belles-Lettres Series, Boston, 1904–6.
BOSWORTH, J. *King Alfred's Anglo-Saxon version of the compendious history of the world by Orosius.* London, 1859. (The text is from the late West-Saxon Cottonian MS.)
LOGEMAN, H. *The Rule of S. Benet.* Early English Text Society, 1888.
SCHRÖER, A. *Die angelsächsischen Prosabearbeitungen der Benediktinerregel.* Cassel, 1885–8. (Bibl. d. ags. Prosa ii.)
MILLER, T. *The Old English version of Bede's Ecclesiastical history of the English people.* 2 vols. Early English Text Society, 1890–8.
SCHIPPER, J. *König Alfreds Übersetzung von Bedas Kirchengeschichte.* Cassel, 1899. (Bibl. d. ags. Prosa iv.)
HECHT, H. *Bischof Wærferths von Worcester Übersetzung der Dialoge Gregors des Grossen.* Cassel, 1900–7. (Bibl. d. ags. Prosa v.)

SEDGEFIELD, W. J. *King Alfred's Old English version of Boethius*. Oxford, 1899.

MORRIS, R. *The Blickling Homilies*. Early English Text Society, 1880.

HARMER, F. E., CLASSEN, E. *An Anglo-Saxon chronicle*. Manchester, 1926. (Text of MS. D.)

For editions of the works of Ælfric, see M.-M. Dubois, *Ælfric, sermonnaire, docteur, et grammarien*, Paris, 1943, pp. 375–8, and add:

HENEL, H. *Aelfric's De temporibus anni*. Early English Text Society, 1942.

The following aids to the linguistic study of the above works may be mentioned, in addition to the studies included in some of the editions:

ANDERSON, G. K. 'Notes on the language of Aelfric's English Pastoral Letters.' *JEGP* xl (1941), 5–13.

ASSMANN, B. *Abt Ælfric's ags. Bearbeitung des Buches Esther*. Halle, 1885 (supplemented *A* ix (1886), 25–42).

BRÜHL, C. *Die Flexion des Verbums in Aelfrics Heptateuch und Buch Hiob*. Marburg, 1892.

BRÜLL, H. *Die altenglische Latein-Grammatik des Aelfric*. Berlin, 1904.

FISCHER, F. 'The stressed vowels in Ælfric's homilies.' *PMLA* iv (1888–9), 194–213.

GLAESER, K. *Lautlehre der Ælfricschen Homilien in der HS. Cotton Vesp. D. XIV*. Leipzig, 1916.

SCHÜLLER, O. *Lautlehre von Aelfric's 'Lives of Saints'*. Bonn, 1908.

SCHWERDTFEGER, G. *Das schwache Verbum in Aelfrics Homilien*. Marburg, 1893.

TESSMANN, A. *Aelfrics altenglische Bearbeitung der Interrogationes Sigewulfi*. Berlin, 1891.

WELLS, B. J. 'Strong verbs in Aelfric's Judith and Saints.' *MLN* iii (1888), 13–15, 178–85, 256–62.

WILKES, J. *Lautlehre zu Aelfrics Heptateuch und Buch Hiob*. Bonn, 1905. (Bonner Beiträge zur Anglistik xxi.)

HARRIS, M. A. *A glossary of the West-Saxon gospels*. Boston, 1899.

TRILSBACH, G. *Die Lautlehre der spätwestsächsischen Evangelien*. Bonn, 1905.

HERMANNS, W. *Lautlehre und dialektische Untersuchung der altengl. Interlinearversion der Benediktinerregel*. Bonn, 1906.

ROHR, G. W. *Die Sprache der altengl. Prosabearbeitungen der Benediktinerregel*. Bonn, 1912.

SCHMITT, L. *Lautliche Untersuchung der Sprache der Læċebōc*. Bonn, 1908.

CAMPBELL, J. J. 'The dialect vocabulary of the Old English Bede.' *JEGP* l (1951), 349–72.

DEUTSCHBEIN, M. 'Dialektisches in der ags. Übersetzung von Bedas Kirchengeschichte.' *PBB* xxvi (1901), 169–244, 266.

EGER, O. *Dialektisches in den Flexionsverhältnissen der ags. Beda-Übersetzung*. Leipzig, 1910.

KLAEBER, F. 'Zur altenglischen Bedaübersetzung.' *A* xxv. 257–315; xxvii. 399–435 (1902–4).

KUHN, S. M. 'Synonyms in the OE Bede.' *JEGP* xlvi (1947), 168–76.

LINKE, G. 'Zum Velarumlaut in der starken Verbalflexion der Hs. T des ags. Beda.' *Archiv* clxxiii (1938), 210–12.

—— 'Zur Präposition "betweoh" und zum Zahlwort "tuwa" im ags. Beda.' Ibid. 71–72.

—— 'Grammatische und phraseologische Tautologie im altengl. Beda.' Ibid. clxxv (1939), 98–101.

MILLER, T. *Place-names in the English Bede and the localisation of the MSS.* Strassburg, 1896. (Quellen und Forschungen lxxviii.) (Cf. review by G. Binz, *ZfdPh* xxix. 414–17.)

HECHT, H. *Die Sprache der altengl. Dialoge Gregors des Grossen. I* (*Die Vokale der Stammsilben in den HSS. C und O*). Berlin, 1900.

KRAWUTSCHKE, A. *Die Sprache der Boëthius-Übersetzung des Königs Alfred.* Berlin, 1902.

HARDY, A. K. *Die Sprache der Blickling Homilien.* Leipzig, 1899.

FLORSCHÜTZ, A. *Die Sprache der Hs. D der angelsächsischen Annalen.* Jena, 1910.

A valuable general discussion of linguistic conditions in the late West-Saxon period is:

FLASDIECK, H. M. 'Zur Charakteristik der sprachlichen Verhältnisse in altengl. Zeit.' *PBB* xlviii (1924), 376–413.

N. *Development of Loan-words*

The fundamental studies of Latin loan-words in Old English are:

POGATSCHER, A. *Zur Lautlehre der griechischen, lateinischen und romanischen Lehnworte im Altenglischen.* Strassburg, 1888. (Quellen und Forschungen lxiv.)

FUNKE, O. *Die gelehrten lateinischen Lehn- und Fremdwörter in der altenglischen Literatur von der Mitte des x. Jahrhunderts bis um das Jahr 1066.* Halle, 1914.

Valuable additions to and criticisms of these works are made by L. Morsbach, *Literaturbl. f. germ. und rom. Phil.*, 1889, 96–101 (review of Pogatscher); E. Sievers, *Vokalismus*, pp. 3–14; K. Luick, *Archiv* cxxvi. 35–39; J. H. Kern, *A* xxxvii. 54–61; F. Hüttenbrenner, *AB* xxviii. 33–61 (review of Funke and thorough study of the use of foreign names in verse); Th. Pyles, *PMLA* lviii. 891–910. Luick gives a clear summary of the subject, *Historische Grammatik*, §§ 208–19, 330–3, 661–6.

The development of Celtic place-names in Old English is not treated in this *Grammar*, as the subject is full of problems which would demand disproportionate space. The most useful works on the subject are:

EKWALL, E. *English river-names.* Oxford, 1928.

FÖRSTER, M. *Der Flussname Themse und seine Sippe.* Munich, 1941. (Bayer. Akad., Sitzungsber., phil-hist. Abt., 1941, I.)

JACKSON, K. *Language and history in early Britain.* Edinburgh, 1953.

On other Celtic loan-words the standard study is:

FÖRSTER, M. *Keltisches Wortgut im Englischen*. Halle, 1921 (reprinted from *Texte und Forschungen zur englischen Kulturgeschichte, Festgabe für Felix Liebermann*).

Important additions and criticisms are made by J. Pokorny, *Z. für kelt. Phil.* xiv. 298–9; E. Ekwall, *AB* xxxiii. 73–82, *ES* liv. 102–10; M. Förster, *ES* lvi. 204–39, lxx. 49–54.

The most extensive list of the Scandinavian loan-words recorded in Old English texts (although containing some questionable material) remains:

KLUGE, F. *Geschichte der englischen Sprache* (Grundriss der germ. Phil., 2nd ed., i. 5, 7, Strassburg, 1901), pp. 932–5.

Additions to Kluge's material mostly concern the form of words, rather than additional borrowings (e.g. A. S. C. Ross, 'Four examples of Norse influence in the Old English gloss to the Lindisfarne Gospels', *Trans. Philological Soc.*, 1940, pp. 39–52). The Old English loan-words are fully discussed by:

HOFMANN, D. *Nordisch-englische Lehnbeziehungen der Wikingerzeit*. Copenhagen, 1955. (Bibliotheca Arnamagnæana xiv.)

The very few certain French loan-words in Old English texts are listed by:

METTIG, R. 'Die französischen Elemente im Alt- und Mittelenglischen (800–1258).' *ES* xli. 177–252 (also separately, Marburg, 1910).

O. *Vocabulary*

Distinctions between Old English dialects in vocabulary and attempts to decide the dialectal colour of the vocabulary of various texts are the subjects of:

JORDAN, R. *Eigentümlichkeiten des anglischen Wortschatzes*. Heidelberg, 1906.

MEISSNER, P. 'Studien zum Wortschatz Aelfrics.' *Archiv* clxv. 11–19, clxvi. 30–39, 205–15 (1934).

MENNER, R. J. 'Anglian and Saxon elements in Wulfstan's vocabulary.' *MLN* lxiii (1948), 1–9.

—— 'The vocabulary of the Old English poems on Judgment Day.' *PMLA* lxii (1947), 583–97.

—— *The Anglian vocabulary of the Blickling Homilies*. Philologica: the Malone anniversary studies, Baltimore, 1949, 56–64.

RAUH, H. *Der Wortschatz der altengl. Übersetzungen des Matthäus-Evangeliums untersucht auf seine dialektische und zeitliche Gebundenheit*. Berlin, 1936.

SCHERER, G. *Zur Geographie und Chronologie des angelsächsischen Wortschatzes, im Anschluss an Bischof Wærferth's Übersetzung der 'Dialoge' Gregors*. Berlin, 1928. (See, however, P. N. U. Harting in *Neophilologus* xxii. 284–5.)

See also the editions and studies of the Old English version of Bede quoted in § M; Vleeskruyer's *St. Chad* (§ J above), pp. 23–37; K. Sisam, *Studies in the history of Old English literature* (Oxford, 1953), pp. 126–31.

A number of studies deal with semantic sections of the vocabulary. Holthausen gives an excellent list of these, *Altenglisches etym. Wörterbuch*, Bibliography, § C. *c*, to which the following may be added:

BÄCK, H. *The synonyms for 'child', 'boy', 'girl' in Old English*. Lund, 1934.

BEER, H. *Führen und Folgen, Herrschen und Beherrschtwerden im Sprachgut der Angelsachsen*. Breslau, 1939.

BONSER, W. 'Anglo-Saxon medical nomenclature.' *English and Germanic studies* iv (1951–2), 13–19.

GNEUSS, H. *Lehnbildungen und Lehnbedeutungen im Altenglischen*. Berlin, 1955.

GRAMM, W. *Die Körperpflege der Angelsachsen*. Heidelberg, 1938.

GRANDINGER, M. M. *Die Bedeutung des Adjectivs 'good' in der religiösen Literatur der Angelsachsen*. Landshut, 1933.

HALVORSON, N. O. *Doctrinal terms in Aelfric's homilies*. University of Iowa Humanistic Studies, 1932.

HENDRICKSON, J. R. *Old English prepositional compounds in relationship to their Latin originals*. 1948 (supplement to *Language* xxiv).

JUZI, G. *Die Ausdrücke des Schönen in der altengl. Dichtung*. Zürich, 1939.

LAMBERT, C. 'The Old English medical vocabulary.' *Proceedings of the Royal Society of Medicine* xxxiii (1940), 137–45.

MARTZ, O. *Die Wiedergabe biblischer Personenbezeichnungen in der altengl. Missionssprache*. Bochum-Langendreer, 1939.

SCHUBEL, F. 'Zur Bedeutungskunde altenglischer Wörter mit christlichem Sinngehalt.' *Archiv* clxxxix (1953), 289–303.

STIBBE, H. *'Herr' und 'Frau' und verwandte Begriffe in ihren altengl. Äquivalenten*. Heidelberg, 1935.

WEMAN, B. *Old English semantic analysis and theory with special reference to verbs denoting locomotion*. Lund, 1933.

Numerous articles deal with the meaning and etymology of individual difficult words, or treat groups of such words, and many problems concerning Old English words are dealt with in notes and articles on difficult glosses. This extensive literature is not dealt with here, but a useful selection of it is mentioned in the bibliographies listed in § A.

P. *Word-formation*

The following are useful works on strictly Old English (as distinct from Germanic or West Germanic) word-formation:

BERGSTEN, N. *A study on compound substantives in English*. Uppsala, 1911. (Deals with Old English only incidentally.)

BEST, K. *Die persönlichen Konkreta des Altenglischen nach ihren Suffixen geordnet*. Strassburg, 1905.

BOTH, M. *Die konsonantischen Suffixe altenglischer Konkreta und Kollektiva*. Kiel, 1909.

ECKHARDT, E. 'Die angelsächsischen Deminutivbildungen.' *ES* xxxii (1903), 325–66.

JENSEN, J. *Die I. und II. Ablautsreihe in der altenglischen Wortbildung.* Kiel, 1913.

KÄRRE, K. *Nomina agentis in Old English,* i. Uppsala, 1915.

MARCKWARDT, A. H. 'The verbal suffix *-ettan* in Old English.' *Language* xviii (1942), 275–81.

NICOLAI, O. *Die Bildung des Adverbs im Altenglischen.* Kiel, 1907.

PALMGREN, C. *English gradation-nouns in their relation to strong verbs.* Uppsala, 1904.

RAITH, J. *Die englischen Nasalverben.* Leipzig, 1931.

ROSS, A. S. C. 'Aldrediana I: three suffixes.' *Bilag* to *Moderna Språk,* forthcoming. (On *-ness, -ung, -ere,* mainly in North.)

SCHÖN, E. *Die Bildung des Adjektivs im Altenglischen.* Kiel, 1905.

SCHULDT, CL. *Die Bildung der schwachen Verba im Altenglischen.* Kiel, 1905.

STORCH, TH. *Angelsächsische Nominalcomposita.* Strassburg, 1886.

THIELE, O. *Die konsonantischen Suffixe der Abstrakta des Altenglischen.* Darmstadt, 1902.

UHLER, K. *Die Bedeutungsgleichheit der altenglischen Adjektiva und Adverbia mit und ohne* -lic (-lice). Heidelberg, 1926.

WEYHE, H. *Zu den altenglischen Verbalabstrakten auf* -nes *und* -ing, -ung. Borna-Leipzig, 1910.

A considerable group of Kiel studies deal with prefixes commonly used in Old English word-formation:

LEHMANN, W. *Das Präfix* uz- *besonders im Altenglischen.* Kiel, 1906.

And with similar titles J. Lenze on *bi-*, 1909; O. Siemerling on *for(e)-*, 1909; W. Lüngen on *on(d)-* and *oð-(ūð-)*, 1911; C. Hohenstein on *wið(er)-*, 1912.

Other works in the same field are:

BECHLER, K. *Das Präfix* to *im Verlaufe der englischen Sprachgeschichte.* Königsberg, 1909.

LENZ, PH. *Der syntactische Gebrauch der Partikel* ge *in den Werken Alfred des Grossen.* Darmstadt, 1886.

LINDNER, F. *Über das Präfix* a *im Englischen.* Jena, 1873.

PILCH, H. 'Das ae. Präverb *ge.*' *A* lxxi (1952), 129–39.

SAMUELS, M. L. 'The *ge*-prefix in the Old English gloss to the Lindisfarne Gospels.' *Trans. Philological Soc.*, 1949, pp. 62–116.

INDEX

References are to sections; f. = footnote.

In alphabetization no distinction is made between *ae* and *æ*, *c* (*k*) and *ċ*, *g* and *ġ*, *u* (*uu*) in consonantal function and *w*, *þ* and *ð*; *th* is distinguished from *þ*, *ð* only when it equals *t*+*h* (e.g. *æthwa*), and it then precedes them. Forms with prefixed *ġi*- are indexed under *ġe*-.

When a word is discussed in only one phonological form, this is usually used as head-word (e.g. *hǣlsent*, *hebild*), otherwise the forms discussed are collected under a West-Saxon head-word. Cross-references are not given for regular variants (e.g. *mann—monn*, *hīeran—hȳran*) and inflexions (e.g. *fōt—fēt*, *bindan—band*, *se—þǣm*).

The phonological variants and inflected forms given in the chapters on accidence are not indexed, but only the n.s.(m.), or in the case of verbs the inf. (or the pres. indic. of pret.-pres. verbs with no inf. in use). All forms discussed in the chapters on phonology are indexed under the relevant head-words. Occasionally, when the only form of a word discussed is an inflected one, this form is used as a head-word (e.g. *ǣmptiġe*).

Variation of root-vowel is often indicated in round brackets, e.g. *nīewe* (*ī*, *ēo*, *īo*) implies that the forms *nīewe*, *nīwe*, *nēowe*, and *nīowe* are discussed in the sections cited.

Words occurring only in sentences and phrases quoted to illustrate points of grammar are not indexed.